Readings in
Ethnic Psychology

Readings in
Ethnic Psychology

Edited by
Pamela Balls Organista
Kevin M. Chun
Gerardo Marín

ROUTLEDGE
New York and London

Published in 1998 by
Routledge
29 West 35th Street
New York, NY 10001

Published in Great Britain by
Routledge
11 New Fetter Lane
London EC4P 4EE

Printed in the United States of America on acid-free paper.
Design and Typography: Jack Donner

Library of Congress Cataloging-in-Publication Data

Readings in ethnic pyschology / edited by Pamela Balls Organista, Kevin M. Chun, and Gerardo
   Marín.
       p.   cm.
   Includes bibliographical references and index.
   ISBN 0–415–91962–2 (hardcover). — ISBN 0–415–91963–0 (pbk.)
   1. Minorities—Mental Health—United States. 2. Minorities—United States—Psychology.
I. Balls Organista, Pamela. II. Chun, Kevin M. III. Marín, Gerardo.
RC451.5.A2R42   1998
616.89'0089'00973—dc21   97–44675
                                                                       CIP

Contents

Acknowledgments

As is true with any book, the final product has benefited from a large number of individuals. First, are the authors of the original articles and chapters who have struggled to provide significant information about the members of the four ethnic groups addressed in this book. Present among the selected authors are individuals who have dedicated most of their professional lives to the advancement of ethnic psychology in the United States. We have learned from their wisdom and, in some cases, benefited from their mentoring and example. The book also was enriched by the contributions of Heidi Freund, our editor at Routledge, whose enthusiasm from the beginning made it possible for us to finish the manuscript almost on time. Heidi was always a perceptive reviewer of our ideas and a supportive editor. We owe a special debt of gratitude to Stanley Nel, Dean of the College of Arts and Sciences at the University of San Francisco, whose vision and dedication made it possible for us to have a supportive environment where the idea for this book could develop and grow. Special thanks also are due to Julian Lute who served as a creative and caring research assistant for the project; Sharon Li who showed once again her dependability and attention to detail by obtaining the copyright clearances; and Liz Michael, our secretary, who was always helpful despite requests that may fray anyone else's nerves.

Other individuals have supported us throughout our professional and personal lives and during the process of developing this book. Pamela Balls Organista would like to mention the constant caring and loving support of her husband, best friend, and closest collaborator in ethnic research, Kurt Organista. Her greatest inspiration, their daughter, Zena Laura Organista, gives joy and hope for the future and all that is good in our multicultural world. In addition, Pamela would like to acknowledge the guidance and love given to her throughout her life by her parents, Zevonzell Balls and Cynthia Balls, and the warmth and support of her sisters, Zoneice Balls and Tunderleauh Griffin and nephews, Demerrio and Tory. Pamela dedicates this book to her family. Kevin Chun wishes to thank his parents, family and friends for their constant love and guidance. He dedicates this book to his grandparents, Alfred and Alice Chun, and Peter and Muriel Toy, who embodied compassion and strength in the face of tremendous odds, and his nephews, Garrett and Harrison, who represent bright beacons for the future. Gerardo Marín recognizes the continued support and love of his children (Melisa Ann Marín and Andrew Daniel Marín) and the loving care of Lois Ann Lorentzen who gently prodded him to finish the book. In particular, Gerardo wishes to recognize the love and support provided by Gerardo Marín Sr. and Noemí Marín. The sacrifices they endured as immigrants contributed to this book in ways that cannot be retold or repaid. Gerardo dedicates this book to them.

—San Francisco, September 1997

Permissions Acknowledgments

Introduction

Almost since the beginning of its history, the United States has been blessed by the cultural and ethnic diversity of its people. American Indians trace their early roots to massive population moves from other continents. Later, the country was peopled by immigrants from Europe searching for economic advancement or religious and philosophical freedoms; Africans brought against their will to labor the land; Mexicans whose land was annexed to the United States; Asians who worked the land and built railroads; and, the groups of Europeans, Asians, and Latin Americans who in the past few decades have contributed with their labor to the economic advancement of the country. The resulting tapestry of cultures and ethnicities created a multicultural society that continually tries to define itself, probably because of its uniqueness and the extent of its diversity.

Unfortunately, this multicultural process while enriching people's lives also has created interpersonal difficulties and societal problems that are still unresolved. At the end of the twentieth century, residents of the United States are grappling with issues such as prejudice, racism, unequal distribution of resources, moves to declare English as the official language, limited nature of services to immigrants, lack of culturally appropriate research and services, and challenges to affirmative action policies to redress past injustices. Social and behavioral scientists have made important, although at times limited, contributions to our understanding of these problems.

Psychologists also have been slow to recognize the benefits of ethnic diversity and to apply psychological principles to the solution of social problems. For example, researchers and practitioners alike have typically ignored the role of culture and ethnicity on human behavior. Our research has seldom looked at the beliefs, attitudes, norms, and behaviors of members of our various ethnic groups. Our practitioners have seldom incorporated ethnic and cultural characteristics in the design or implementation of their interventions. Our training of professionals often ignored the variations brought about by ethnicity and culture in our theories and related research findings. Fortunately, this sad state of affairs has begun to change. Training programs, including undergraduate departments, have begun to include cultural and ethnic components in their curricula. Researchers are being asked by governmental and private funding sources to include members of ethnic groups in their samples and to use culturally appropriate method-ologies. Likewise, practitioners have become more responsive to the needs and characteristics of members of ethnic groups.

Demographic realities, and the extent of society's problems, are producing an awareness of the need for culturally appropriate and culturally responsive research, training, and professional practice. This book was designed to further this process. By providing undergraduate and graduate students with significant and heuristically important readings, we hope to make students aware of the need for considering ethnicity as a significant determinant of human behavior. While the readings included in this book do not cover all relevant issues, the selections serve as guideposts for future research in the area.

AFRICAN AMERICANS, AMERICAN INDIANS, ASIAN AMERICANS, AND HISPANICS/LATINOS

We chose to target four ethnic groups (African Americans, American Indians, Asian Americans, and Hispanics/Latinos) because of their demographic significance and due to the importance and similarities of their special needs. This does not mean that we do not recognize the existence of other ethnic groups in the United States (e.g., Jews, Irish Americans, Italian Americans, Haitians, Russians, Polish Americans). Rather, the four ethnic groups covered in this book account for a significant proportion of the population of the country and historically, they have shared experiences of discrimination and lack of attention on the part of psychologists.

Table 1 shows how the members of these four groups (African Americans, American Indians, Asian Americans, and Hispanics/Latinos) compare with the rest of the population of the country. Approximately, 25% of the population of the United States is a member of one of those four groups. Projections by the Bureau of the Census suggest that by the year 2050 more than half of the population of the United States will be made up of individuals belonging to the four major ethnic groups. Furthermore, Bureau of the Census projections indicate that by the year 2025 members of the four ethnic groups will overshadow the number of non-Hispanic whites in a number of states including California, Texas, and New York. Table 1 also shows a number of important differences among members of the ethnic groups when compared with non-Hispanic whites. For example, the members of the four groups tend to be younger than non-Hispanic whites with fewer adults attaining a high school education. While the employment status of members of the four ethnic groups does not differ from that of non-Hispanic whites, their per capita income tends to be lower. Members of at least three of the ethnic groups (African Americans, Asian Americans, and Hispanics/Latinos) tend to reside in urban environments in proportions that are higher than those of non-Hispanic whites.

Despite these demographic figures attesting to their importance in the country, there is a dearth of information about the psychological characteristics of members of the four ethnic groups and of multiethnic individuals (those who trace their background to two or more ethnic groups or cultures). A few journals (e.g., *Hispanic Journal of Behavioral Sciences, Journal of Black Psychology, Ethnic Studies*) have been publishing research on members of these ethnic groups for more than a decade and they serve an important and pioneering role in disseminating research reports. Unfortunately, it is difficult for most professors and students to easily identify appropriate readings to be used as primary texts in ethnic

Table 1. Selected Demographic Characteristics for the U.S. Population, by Ethnicity, 1990

Characteristic	African Americans	American Indians/ Alaska Natives	Asian Americans/ Pacific Islanders	Hispanics	Whites*
Population	29,930,524	2,015,143	7,226,986	21,900,089	188,424,773
Women (percentage)	52.8	50.4	51.2	49.2	51.3
Median age (years)	28.2	26.9	30.1	25.6	34.9
Foreign born (percentage)	4.9	2.3	63.1	35.8	3.3
Education (percentage) of persons aged ≥ 25 years)					
High school education	63.1	65.5	77.5	49.8	79.1
Bachelor's degree or higher	11.4	9.3	36.6	9.2	22.1
English-language ability (% of persons aged ≥ 5 years)					
Speak a language other than English	6.3	23.8	73.3	77.8	5.7
Do not speak English "very well"	2.4	9.2	38.4	39.4	1.8
Number of persons per family	3.5	3.6	3.7	3.8	3.0
Percentage of families with own children aged < 18 years	56.5	60.7	59.5	64.5	45.2
Employment status† (percentage of persons aged ≥ 16 years)					
Employed	62.7	62.1	67.5	67.5	65.3
Unemployed	12.9	14.4	5.3	10.4	5.0
Percentage of employed persons aged ≥ 16 years in a managerial/professional occupation	18.1	18.3	30.6	14.1	28.5
Household income in 1989 ($)					
Median	19,758	20,025	36,784	24,156	31,672
Mean	25,872	26,602	46,695	30,301	40,646
Per capita income in 1989 ($)	8,859	8,328	13,638	8,400	16,074
Poverty rate (percentage)					
Families	26.3	27.0	11.6	22.3	7.0
Persons	29.5	30.9	14.1	25.3	9.2
Urban residents (percentage)	87.2	56.0	95.4	91.4	70.9

* Excludes persons of Hispanic origin.
† These figures do not include several categories of people who were not in the civilian labor force for various reasons, such as students, housewives, retired workers, seasonal workers in an off season who were not looking for work, institutionalized persons, and persons doing only incidental unpaid family work (less than 15 hours during the reference week).
   Source: U.S. Department of Health and Human Services. *Tobacco Use Among U.S. Racial Groups: A Report of the Surgeon General.* Atlanta, Georgia: U.S. Department of Health and Human Services, Public Health Service, Centers for Disease Control and Prevention, National Center for Chronic Disease Prevention and Health Promotion, Office on Smoking and Health, 1988.

psychology courses or as adjunct readings for courses where an ethnic diversity component is desired. This book presents some of the best articles in the field published in the last decade. The selections included here will fill gaps in knowledge currently found in undergraduate textbooks, and will guide advanced undergraduate and graduate students toward future research in a given area.

A NOTE TO OUR READERS

The process of carefully selecting the readings included in this book was a difficult one. We reviewed databases going back for over a decade and read approximately 7,000 abstracts. The second step included the reading of possible selections. This process lasted for well over seven months and it afforded us the opportunity of reading exciting articles while also frustrating us for the large number of poorly designed research efforts. Particularly disappointing were the large number of publications that used culturally inappropriate instruments, or those that lacked an understanding of the culture, or publications that failed to disaggregate their data by ethnicity. While a large number of articles, chapters, and books have included in their samples members of one or more of the four ethnic groups, many of those publications add little to our understanding of their behavior given the serious methodological limitations.

In selecting the articles included in these pages we followed a number of criteria. First, the publication would need to show attention to current principles for conducting culturally appropriate research. In addition, we looked for articles that were clear, well organized, and easily read by individuals who had little if any knowledge of sophisticated statistical procedures. Also important in our selection of possible articles were the currency of the concepts and theoretical models, the representativeness and usefulness of samples (we tended to exclude studies with small samples or with college students), the cultural appropriateness of measures, the methodology's parsimony, and the cogency of the discussion. Finally, we tried to include selections that could serve as catalysts for classroom discussion, and that would present opportunities for further expansion and written analysis on the part of students.

These criteria made it difficult to properly cover all ethnic groups or even all areas of interest in psychology. For example, we found few if any publications that properly covered American Indians, Hawaiians, and Alaska Natives. Also difficult was to identify selections that disaggregated across ethnic groups (often lumping all groups together) or within Asian Americans or Hispanics/Latinos. Of particular concern were the difficulties we faced in identifying publications that took into consideration the role of social class and social stratification in the problems we study as psychologists. We hope that, soon, these shortcomings in the literature will be resolved so that future editions of this book can expand its coverage.

In deciding on a title for the book we chose to use "ethnic psychology" rather than "racial" or "minority psychology" for a number of reasons. Primarily, we decided not to use "racial" because of the conceptual problems associated with the construct of race in the social and behavioral sciences (as made explicit by the readings in Section II). We also avoided the term "minority" because of its negative and pejoric implications while fully recognizing that "ethnic" may not properly fit the issues under analysis in the book.

We are sure that we did not include selections that in the view of some of our readers may better represent the field or a specific topical area. We hope that you will communicate those options to us as well as your general impressions of the book. You can reach us by E-mail as follows:

Pamela Balls Organista   organistap@usfca.edu
Kevin Chun   chunk@usfca.edu
Gerardo Marín   marin@usfca.edu

A NOTE TO INSTRUCTORS

We realize that you may wish to use this book as a reader for classes as varied as ethnic psychology, abnormal psychology, social psychology, and even general psychology. We have organized the readings beginning with methodological considerations about theory and research in psychology with ethnic groups and ending with selections that cover more specific issues such as substance use, psychopathology, and treatment. Each section of the book and each selection stands on its own and can be assigned in an order that is different from the one used in the book. Each section includes a number of suggested readings that can be used for class presentations and discussions or to encourage students' personal interests.

FURTHER READING

Despite the need for ethnic psychology sources, few publications have properly addressed the topic. Below are some recent books that may provide additional sources of information:

Overviews of the Role of Culture on Behavior

Brislin, R. (1993). *Understanding culture's influence on behavior.* Fort Worth, TX: Harcourt Brace College Publishers.

Goldberger, N. R., and Veroff, J. B. (Eds.). (1995). *The culture and psychology reader.* New York: New York University Press.

Lonner, W. J., and Malpass, R. (Eds.). (1994). *Psychology and culture.* Boston: Allyn and Bacon.

Matsumoto, D. (1996). *Culture and psychology.* Pacific Grove, CA: Brooks/Cole.

Monteiro, K. P. (Ed.). (1995). *Ethnicity and psychology.* Dubuque, Iowa: Kendall/Hunt Publishing Company.

Triandis, H. C. (1994). *Culture and social behavior.* New York: McGraw-Hill.

Books Specifically Targeting One Ethnic Group

Burlew, A.K.H., Banks, W. C., McAdoo, H. P., and Azibo, D. A. (Eds.). (1992). *African American psychology: Theory, research and practice.* Newbury Park, CA: Sage.

Duran, E., and Duran, B. (1995). *Native American postcolonial psychology.* Albany, NY: State University of New York Press.

Jones, R. L. (Ed.). (1995). *Advances in Black psychology.* Los Angeles: Cobb and Henry.

Neighbors, H. W., and Jackson, J. S. (Eds.). (1996). *Mental health in Black America.* Thousand Oaks, CA: Sage.

Padilla, A. M. (Ed.). (1995). *Hispanic psychology: Critical issues in theory and research.* Thousand Oaks, CA: Sage.

Root, M.P.P. (Ed.). (1997). *Filipino Americans: Transformation and identity.* Thousand Oaks, CA: Sage.

Uba, L. (1994). *Asian Americans: Personality patterns, identity, and mental health.* New York: Penguin Books.

Sources of Methodological Guidelines

Blea, I. I. (1995). *Researching Chicano communities.* Westport, CT: Praeger.

Marín, G., and VanOss Marín, B. (1991). *Research with Hispanic populations.* Newbury Park, CA: Sage.

Stanfield, J. H., II, and Dennis, R. M. (Eds.). (1993). *Race and ethnicity in research methods.* Newbury Park, CA: Sage Publications.

van de Vijver, F., and Leung, K. (1997). *Methods and data analysis for cross-cultural research.* Thousand Oaks, CA: Sage.

PART I

Psychology and Ethnicity

Theoretical and Methodological Considerations

In its relatively short history, psychology has paid significant attention to the development and evaluation of methodological approaches to study human behavior. Whether developing an interview schedule or a test, or planning an experiment or the evaluation of an intervention, psychologists have been trained to pay close attention to the validity and reliability of measurements, to the proper definition of variables and operationalization of hypotheses, to the internal and external validity of research designs, to the inherent limitations in generalizing research findings, and to other important considerations. Surprisingly, little attention has been given to the analysis of the role on behavior of such social characteristics as gender, ethnicity, culture, and social class. Nevertheless, the last few decades have seen an increase in the awareness of researchers and theoreticians of the need to consider these variables. For example, few studies are currently published that do not address the gender of the respondents and its possible effects on the results. Psychologists also have become more attentive to the role of culture and ethnicity in shaping a person's behavior. Unfortunately, not enough has happened. Indeed, there are journals dedicated to publishing research where ethnicity or culture plays a major role as a variable. But it is still unusual to find culture or ethnicity addressed in psychology textbooks or for ethnicity to be included in research published by the major journals.

As Lee Anna Clark mentions in the first article in this section, there has been what seems to be a general disinterest on the part of "mainstream" psychology for what is going on in cross-cultural psychology. As Clark suggests, this process of mutual ignorance could be due to factors such as the value given to some specific variables and problems with the unfortunate result that important explanatory elements are being ignored in the psychology we teach and apply. Other authors have suggested that the lack of attention to culture and ethnicity in psychology is the result of myopic postures on the part of psychologists who favor the dismissal of such social variables as gender, poverty, ethnicity, and social structure as important predictors or mediators of behavior. A possible third group of critics argue that psychology has been intensely sexist and racist, making it difficult for established individuals to accept the role of gender and culture on human behavior or even to consider that culture, ethnicity, social class, and gender can produce attitudes, norms, expectancies, and behaviors that differ from those found among male, middle class, non-Hispanic whites. Whatever the explanation, and probably there is a kernel of truth in all of them, the fact is that psychology must acknowledge the role of ethnicity in shaping human behavior if it is to remain vital and relevant.

But crucial in this process is not only the recognition that culture plays an important role in explaining and predicting human behavior. Also important is the need to conduct research that properly reflects the experiences and perceptions of the individuals in question. This concern for proper methodologies is close to psychologists' traditions and some of the central issues are presented in the article by Sumie Okazaki and Stanley Sue. Researchers often have argued that culturally appropriate research must go beyond translating instruments or even adapting them for use with individuals of different cultures. As argued by Okazaki and Sue, the development of appropriate methods must address the careful selection of samples, the development of equivalent measures, and the culturally sensitive interpretation of the results. The use of appropriate methodologies can, of course, enhance the validity and usefulness of the results.

The two selections in this section of the book serve to set the stage against which to judge the value and generalizability of the scientific literature you will read as part of your psychology classes. The issues discussed in both readings are central as students and researchers come in contact with an increasing number of published research that involve members of ethnic groups.

FURTHER READINGS

Betancourt, H., and López, S. R. (1993). The study of culture, ethnicity, and race in American psychology. *American Psychologist, 48,* 629–37.

Hall, C. C. I. (1997). Cultural malpractice: The growing obsolescence of Psychology with the changing U.S. population. *American Psychologist, 52,* 642–51.

Helms, J. E. (1992). Why is there no study of cultural equivalence in standardized cognitive ability testing? *American Psychologist, 47,* 1083–1101.

Howitt, D., and Owusu-Bempah, J. (1994). *The racism of psychology: Time for change.* New York: Harvester/Wheatsheaf.

Landrine, H., Klonoff, E. A., and Brown-Collins, A. (1992). Cultural diversity and methodology in feminist psychology. *Psychology of Women Quarterly, 16,* 145–63.

Marín, G., and VanOss Marín, B. (1991). Research with Hispanic populations. Newbury Park, CA: Sage.

Root, M. P. P. (1992). Back to the drawing board: Methodological issues in research on multiracial people. In M. P. P. Root (Ed.), *Racially mixed people in America* (pp. 181–89). Newbury Park CA: Sage.

Stanfield, J. H., II, and Dennis, R. M. (eds.). (1993). *Race and ethnicity in research methods.* Newbury Park, CA: Sage.

Triandis, H. C. (1996). The psychological measurement of cultural syndromes. *American Psychologist, 51,* 407–415

van de Vijver, F., and Leung, K. (1997). *Methods and data analysis for cross-cultural research.* Thousand Oaks, CA: Sage.

1.

Mutual Relevance of Mainstream and Cross-Cultural Psychology

Lee Anna Clark

Mainstream and cross-cultural psychologists have shared one salient characteristic: a general disinterest in each other's work. However, despite this mutual neglect, the two subdisciplines actually address many of the same basic issues. If culture is seen as a complex, multidimensional structure rather than as a simple categorical variable, cross-cultural studies can be viewed as a direct and logical extension of our search for the causes of variation in human psychology and psychopathology. More important, the search for culturally correlated factors is necessary for any comprehensive psychological theory. Differences in theoretical orientation and methodological approach that serve to divide the field are seen as complementary when such a framework is adopted. Barriers to communication, such as stereotyping and the use of specialized terminology, are also discussed.

Many psychologists do not read beyond the titles of articles bearing the cross-cultural label, even if the substantive content of such articles appears to be related to their field of interest. Originally touted as an important source for theoretical ideas and a powerful methodology, (e.g., Strodtbeck, 1964; J. Whiting, 1968), the very words *cross-cultural* have become alienating to mainstream psychologists, whereas some cross-cultural researchers read little else. They have become so focused on cross-cultural comparisons, universal generalizations, and methodological refinements that they have lost touch with advances in their field within their home countries.

Of course, this split is not absolute, and even the importance of the distinction has been challenged. Many important research problems have relied on cross-cultural data for verification.[1] Some analysts believe that a split once existed but that great strides toward integration have been made, perhaps rendering the distinction unimportant (Brislin, 1983). Others assert that the boundaries between the fields continue to impede understanding (Kleinman and Good, 1985). Certainly, we may agree that it is the rare investigator who integrates cross-cultural findings into research hypothesis or who uses a cross-cultural approach as one of many tools in a broad program of research (Segall, 1986).

Why has the promise of cross-cultural research been only partially fulfilled? What factors have contributed to the relative lack of integration between mainstream and cross-cultural psychology? How might we begin to bridge such a gap? The goal of this article is to examine these issues. The approach will be twofold. First, the bases for the division between these two groups and barriers to communication, including negative mutual stereotypes and cross-cultural terminology, will be examined. Second, alternative ways of viewing the field of psychology that can encompass both traditions will be proposed. The purpose is to heighten awareness that the distinction between mainstream and cross-cultural psychology is artificial and unnecessary, that the issues that plague one area are concerns of the other as well, and that the variables comprising what we call "culture" are not qualitatively different from other commonly studied psychological variables.

GAP BETWEEN MAINSTREAM AND CROSS-CULTURAL PSYCHOLOGISTS

Distinctions of this sort arise and are maintained for many reasons. There are often fundamental differences in the philosophical or theoretical underpinnings of the two points of view, in what investigators in each group find interesting or important; and in their definitions of, or their goals for, studying the field. There may also be a sense of uniqueness or specialness in each subgroup. In the case of mainstream versus cross-cultural psychology, several of these explanations are likely, and two basic reasons for alignment with one camp or the other can be isolated.

Two Underlying Bases of Division

The first divergence is primarily theoretical and depends on the importance placed on culture as a causal variable in human psychology. Brislin, Lonner, and Thorndike (1973) formulated a widely accepted definition of cross-cultural psychology as based on the belief that members of various cultural groups have "different experiences that lead to predictable and significant differences in behavior" (p. 5). Although few readers would dispute the truth of this assertion, cultural variables do not play a central role in the theories or research of most mainstream psychologists; indeed, they are often viewed as nuisance variables if they are considered at all (Segall, 1986). Cross-cultural articles are happily given a passing citation if they support one's hypotheses but are usually ignored if they do not. Contradictory results may be dismissed as uninterpretable due to the cultural factors, and the issues raised by contradictory findings may be judged irrelevant. I am not suggesting that such arguments are ordinarily made in print. On the contrary, researchers make these decisions (often with little serious consideration of the issues) as they review the relevant literature. Likewise, mainstream practitioners of psychology tend to emphasize either the importance of general intrapsychic processes or the importance of specific factors unique to each individual's history. In either case, cultural variables rarely play a major role.

In contrast, cross-cultural psychologists maintain that cultural factors must not be dismissed so lightly. They view cultural factors as essential to a psychological understanding of all human beings, not as nuisance variables to be controlled or ignored. Cross-cultural psychologists emphasize that the study of diverse cultures not only tests the generality of a theory developed in one culture but, if carried out systematically, sheds light on which of many cultural variables are related to the phenomena of interest and, ultimately, may lead to theories of how cultures exert their psychological effects. (Admittedly, few psychologists have carried out a systematic investigation of this sort, and we are far from understanding what the psychologically relevant cultural variables are or how they operate.) Similarly, practitioners with a cross-cultural orientation view culture, and especially cultural differences (either between therapists and client or between the client's home culture and adopted culture), as a primary cause of difficulty, both in the client's life and in therapy. Cultural differences are also a good source of hypotheses for understanding causal factors in client distress, test scores, and so on (Pedersen, Draguns, Lonner and Trimble, 1981).

The second divergence is related to the first but is basically methodological. It involves differing beliefs about the most appropriate, and effective, and efficient way to study psychology, that is, it involves a difference in approach to the field. Discussions of cross-cultural psychology as a field inevitably include, and often emphasize, the importance and uniqueness of its methodologies (e.g., Brislin et al., 1973: Draguns, 1981; Price-Williams, 1975). Triandis (1980b) noted that, whereas cross-cultural psychology borrows theories from mainstream psychology, "it does have a unique set of methods. Thus, cross-cultural psychology is defined by its methodology rather than by its theory" (pp. 6–7). This is meant not to imply that all cross-cultural psychologists use a single, common methodology but that they are committed to a set of "guidelines for not imposing one's own cultural standards when gathering data in another" (Brislin, 1983, p. 365). In contrast, the imposition of the researcher's standards, assumptions, and theoretical constructs is the norm in mainstream research: The assumption is made that the subject's standard and structures will be the same.

An analogy to the idiographic-nomothetic distinction has been made in which within-culture study (i.e., most mainstream research) corresponds to the idiographic approach and cross-cultural study corresponds to the nomothetic approach (Butcher and Pancheri, 1976). In this view, mainstream and cross-cultural research each possess the strengths and liabilities of their counterpart. For example, mainstream research, like idiographic research, may provide a rich characterization but has limited generalizability because interpretation of the data depends too exclusively on the meanings attached to stimuli by one subject (whether that be a single person or a single culture). Cross-cultural, nomothetic research ideally promotes the development of general laws but may produce unfruitful or even misleading results depending on the extent to which the investigated concepts are not basic psychological variables but are poorly conceived hypothetical constructs that have been imposed on subjects by the experimenter. Thus, when constructs are interpreted without subjects' views of what the stimuli meant to them, the actual contribution of the hypothesized constructs to the overall variance observed may be very slight. As with proponents on each side of the idiographic-nomothetic distinction, both mainstream and cross-cultural researchers tend to focus on and elevate the strengths of their approach while minimizing the seriousness of its limitations. Furthermore, the disadvantages of the opposition are usually noted, and issues that are central to the opposition are downplayed.

Thus, mainstream psychologists tend to ignore the methods developed by cross-cultural psychologists for dealing with cultural variables, and they are largely unconcerned about the issues that cross-cultural psychologists raise. They deal with cultural variables simply by holding them constant and by working within a single culture. Even when these issues cannot (or should not) be ignored, as in the psychological assessment of a person of non-majority status, they are often minimized or given superficial treatment.

Cross-cultural psychologists, in contrast, emphasize how the increased range of variables available for study in different cultures allows for better tests of hypotheses. They are very concerned with finding commonalities between variables that are clearly related but have different manifestations across cultures, and they stress the importance of this activity for generalization (e.g., Brislin, 1983). This is especially true in the psychological assessment of nonmajority clients, where questions are continually raised concerning the appropriateness of test usage outside the specific culture or subculture of development or concerning the equivalence of translation (e.g., Brislin, 1980; Irvine and Carroll, 1980). On the other hand, the commitment of cross-cultural psychologists to the search for universals (nomothetics) may lead to such a level of abstraction that the resulting generalizations are "vague tautologies and forceless banalities" (Geertz, 1965, p. 103; see also Berry, 1980; Lonner; 1980).

Two Major Barriers to Communication

In addition to underlying differences in theoretical orientation and preferred methodological approach, there are at least two other factors that influence each group's judgment of the other and that inhibit the fruitful interplay between groups. These factors are in one sense more superficial, but they are also thereby more concrete and may contribute more strongly to each group's consciously stated disinterest in the other.

Negative stereotypes: truths, half-truths, and falsehoods. Cross-cultural psychology has acquired a reputation for sloppily designed studies in which there are so many uncontrolled relevant variables that no reasonable conclusions can be drawn. This negative stereotype may hold more than a grain of truth. The unhappy fact is that there have been many theoretically empty and methodologically weak cross-cultural studies (Triandis, 1980b). For a time, it was fashionable to take one's sabbatical abroad, gather data with a favorite test or procedure in the visited culture (using a popular cross-cultural sampling method, the catch-as-catch-can approach; Butcher and Pancheri, 1976, p.12), and compare the results in an us-versus-them fashion (Brislin et al., 1973). Although the heyday of this strategy may have, at last, passed on, many lingering examples remain. Such sabbatical opportunism has added little systematic knowledge to the field and has understandably contributed to its poor reputation. Many mainstream psychologists have rejected cross-cultural studies categorically after reading one or two of these poorly conceived articles.

However, if we ask if this reputation is deserved for the field as a whole, we must conclude that it is not. There is an abundance of well-designed cross-cultural studies with a reasonable theoretical base. A recent review (Brislin, 1983) and the six-volume *Handbook of Cross-Cultural Psychology* (Triandis, 1980a) attest to their existence, yet the stereotype remains. Why are these studies overlooked when the field is evaluated as a whole?

The answer may be found in the literature on stereotyping. It has been found that if two comparison groups are of unequal size and if the proportion of two behaviors is identical in each group, then the percentage of the less common behavior is overestimated for the smaller group and underestimated for the larger group (Hamilton, 1979). In this case, it is true that the mainstream psychological literature is much larger than the cross-cultural literature; furthermore, let us assume both that the ratio of good-to-bad publications is the same in each literature (few would deny that mainstream psychology has its share of duds) and that bad publications are less common. If psychologists fall prey to the stereotyping error, they will overestimate the percentage of poor cross-culture studies and underestimate the percentage of poor mainstream studies. Although we cannot be sure that the conditions described exist in the two literatures compared here, the explanation seems reasonable for the persistence of the negative view of cross-cultural psychology despite evidence that there is much of worth in the field. In support of this interpretation, Brislin (1983) asserted that the wider the scope of one's reading (i.e., the more equal the two comparison groups), the more favorable is one's view of cross-cultural psychology.

Conversely, once exposed to the cross-cultural way of thinking, it is easy to view within-culture research, especially laboratory studies, as narrow and ecologically invalid or uninteresting. This contrast between well-controlled (but sterile and artificial) research versus interesting and relevant (but imprecise and unclear) research is familiar within mainstream psychology as well, and the issues are simply more exaggerated when the cross-cultural element is introduced. However the solution, in both cases, is not to abandon one approach or the other or to persist in mutual mud-slinging but to improve the methodologies of each approach to lessen the impact of their appropriately criticized limitations.

As for understanding the gap between mainstream and cross-cultural practitioners, we need only examine the widely cited preferred client of most practitioners, who is young, attractive, verbal, intelligent, and successful (the YAVIS phenomenon: Schofield, 1964). Similarly, many widely used psychological tests have been developed by researchers in mainstream American culture and have been normed on groups that share many dominant-culture characteristics. The attributes of the typical nonmajority client may be, of course, quite different. As a result, practitioners with a cross-cultural orientation may view mainstreamists as ethnocentric, prejudicial, self-serving, and least likely to help those who need it most; whereas mainstream practitioners may either defend the limited use of traditional tests and modes of therapy because they are less appropriate for other groups (allocating other clients to social workers, for example) or may instead use the same tests and procedures for everyone, maintaining that their commonalities are more important than their differences. It is difficult to discuss these issues straightforwardly and non-emotionally. Subtly disguised, scorned attributes and guilt-generating accusations inevitably activate defenses and produce little fruitful communication. It is my hope that we can transcend these barriers and discuss the issues from a higher perspective in which cultural variables take their place along with other, more traditionally studied variables.

Cross-cultural terminology: No doubt one stumbling block for mainstream researchers is the extensive use of specialized terminology in cross-cultural psychology. Every field initially develops its own terms to clarify new and apparently unique issues. Often, however, an undesirable (although perhaps not undesired) side-effect is the formation of a closed subdiscipline, with knowledge of the special terminology a prerequisite to membership. In cross-cultural psychology, some of the forbidding terms are *emic* and *etic* (not to mention *imposed etic, derived etic,* and *pseudoetic*); *functional, conceptual, metric* (and several other kinds of) *equivalence; subjective culture; compound bilinguals* versus *coordinate bilinguals; backtranslation; cultunit;* and *centricultural* (to list but a few). It is the purpose of this article not to initiate readers into the club but to argue that such terminological barriers are counterproductive because they interfere with the free and open communication that is essential for a healthy science. Some specialized terms are indeed unique to subcultural and cross-cultural psychology, for example, distinctions among different types of bilinguals or terms relating to translation issues. As such, these may need to be preserved, but because they can be easily explained, their divisive force should be minimal. For example, back-translation simply refers to an independent translation of a measure from a new (target) language back into its original (source) language for comparison with the original measure; it is used to identify basic errors in translation. Mainstream researchers who expand their thinking to include cultural variables can easily learn and apply these terms and concepts.

Other terms express concepts that are relevant in within-culture research but that are unfamiliar and underutilized due to the greater similarity of subjects within cultures than across cultures, for example, equivalence, and the emic–etic distinction. These terms may create more problems by alienating mainstream researchers than they solve by providing cross-cultural psychologists with a convenient shorthand, so here the burden should be placed on cross-cultural researchers to translate their terminology into mainstream language, that is, to use mainstream language whenever possible or to otherwise demonstrate the value of their terminology for mainstream researchers. An examination of how these concepts apply to within-culture research may help to reduce the barriers between groups.

One cannot read anything in cross-cultural psychology without encountering the terms *emic* and *etic*. They are usually explained as meaning culture-specific or culturally unique versus culture-general or humanly universal, but these definitions are biased, and their more basic distinction is analogous to idiographic versus nomothetic.[2] Whenever psychologists ponder questions of whether their measures are tapping different constructs for some of their subjects (e.g., because of important differences in the way individuals categorize or interpret their experience), of whether a test is applicable to a particular client, or of whether a therapeutic or experimental procedure may have quite different meanings across individuals, they are asking themselves whether their measures or procedures are etic (generally applicable/nomothetic) or emic (only specifically applicable/idiographic). Because within-culture subjects share the same language, it is tempting to conclude (usually without actually testing the hypothesis) that a measure of procedure is equally applicable to all subjects. However, clinicians have known for years that it is important to determine the specific ways in which a client uses language (what is meant by "disappointed" or "hostile," for example), and sophisticated investigations using idiographic analyses have shown that nomothetically derived structures are not universally applicable. In each of several independent studies (only one of which was cross-cultural) using different stimuli to investigate relations among subjective experiences or among the objective properties of objects, the data of roughly 10 percent of the subjects did not conform well to the modal structure (Forsythe, 1987; Watson, Clark, and Tellegen, 1984; Zevon and Tellegen, 1982). In cross-cultural terminology, the variations found were emic differences: to the extent that a single structure could be used to explain the data, a true etic had been found, whereas interpreting the nonconforming subjects' data in terms of the modal structure would be an imposed etic, and so on, but this terminology is both unnecessary and unimportant. The authors cited previously were able to discuss their results quite adequately using the more familiar nomothetic-idiographic distinction. What matters is that notable individual differences in the structural relations among variables were found and that applying one interpretation to all the results will involve some distortion. This point is relevant to both mainstream and cross-cultural research.

This by no means minimizes either the greater difficulty or the absolute necessity of resolving these issues when one's subjects are individuals from more than one culture or subjects who speak different languages. The distortion is so severe in these cases that many data simply become uninterpretable if these issues are not considered because of the large number of plausible alternative hypotheses (Campbell, 1968). Precisely because they are so critical in cross-cultural research, these issues have generated much thought and many new methodologies. However, cross-cultural researchers have made little attempt to bring their techniques and insights home. Having sharpened their thinking and refined their methods in the crucible of cross-cultural research, researchers must now carry the message back and demonstrate how their insights are also applicable in within-culture studies.

Mainstream researchers have generally not concerned themselves with these issues, perhaps because the consequences of ignoring structural variations or differences in the meaning of the stimuli across subjects are not as readily apparent. However, this certainly does not make the problem nonexistent: That the data of 10 percent of subjects did not conform to the modal structure may surprise some psychologists. The trends and inconsistent data of many studies, or even the statistically significant but unexciting results, may result from idiographic (i.e., emic) variation, even though all the subjects speak English and come from apparently similar cultural backgrounds. In ignoring this potential variation and assuming that a single structure (i.e., imposed etic) applies to the data of all subjects, these studies commit an error that cross-cultural psychologists identified and labeled some time ago. Thus, if investigators take a cue from cross-cultural psychology and increase their attention to idiographic differences in subjects' interpretations of measures and procedures as an important source of variance, both research design and data analysis might be greatly improved and might eventually lead to theoretical advances.

A related set of concepts concerning types of equivalence was developed in conjunction with the emic–etic distinction. Whereas the emic-etic distinction concerns meaning or structural similarity across subjects, equivalence concerns the question of whether different forms of a measure or procedure are tapping the same construct. Mainstream psychologists concerned with parallel-forms reliability, with the comparability of two different measures of a construct (e.g., the Taylor Manifest Anxiety Scale [Taylor, 1953] and Welsh's Anxiety Scale [Welsh, 1956], or with sex differences on the Minnesota Multiphasic Personality Inventory (MMPI; Hathaway and McKinley, 1943) Depression (D) scale are all concerned with issues of equivalence. Thus, the term has wide applicability, and recognition that these superficially diverse problems all share the common issue of equivalence can serve as a point of unification. For example, test comparability is basically concerned with conceptual equivalence, that is, with whether the tests are measuring the same construct. The study of sex differences is concerned with metric equivalence: Given that the same construct (e.g., depression) is being measured, are the properties of the scale the same in both sexes (i.e., are men and women with MMPI T scores of 70 on Scale D equally depressed).[3] Parallel-forms reliability is concerned with scalar equivalence, that is, with whether identical scores are truly identical. The close correspondence between requirements for the types of equivalence, and the types of scales (nominal, ordinal, interval and ratio) is not coincidental but is due to the commonality of the problems studied (van de Vijver and Poortinga, 1982). It is also not coincidental that cross-cultural psychologists have discussed these issues extensively (e.g., Brislin et al., 1973; Hui and Triandis, 1985; Irvine and Carroll, 1980; Lonner, 1979; Poortinga, 1982; Price-Williams, 1975; Przeworski and Teune, 1970) because inappropriate conclusions may be drawn if metric equivalence is assumed (a common assumption in mainstream research) when conceptual equivalence has not yet been determined. It is unfortunate that the impact of these writings has been largely limited to cross-cultural psychologists because mainstream psychologists could benefit from their analyses. Again, the burden must be placed on those who have thought about these issues deeply to share their views more widely.

TOWARD INTEGRATION

Although cross-cultural psychology has developed specialized terminology for dealing with the particular difficulties of its research and claims to have a unique set of methods for handling these research issues (by which it defines itself as a subfield; Triandis, 1980b), we have seen that only some of these problems and methods are in fact peculiar to cross-cultural investigation (e.g., translation issues and techniques). In principle, the problems that cross-cultural psychologists confront are (or ought to be) faced by mainstream psychologists as well. Similarly, many of the concepts and methods developed in cross-cultural psychology are quite relevant to mainstream research; we might even say they are actually extensions of concepts and methods already used by mainstream psychologists in a more limited way. Thus, an important first step toward rapprochement is to increase awareness (on both sides) of the relevance of cross-cultural methods for addressing issues equally important in mainstream research until there emerges both a broader utilization and extension of these methodologies and a conceptual collaboration regarding further ways of addressing common concerns. Cross-cultural psychology is further advanced in dealing with these problems, of course, simply because it must pay a heavier price for ignoring them. This difference in contingencies is quantitative rather than qualitative, however, and I hope I have convinced the reader that the gap between the two research traditions has not only outlived any usefulness it might have had but may actively be hindering productive collaboration across subdisciplines.

We are still faced with the problem of how to integrate the positive aspects of each domain with the other. Conceptual progress in psychology requires a unified base for investigating psychological phenomena, with culture-relevant variables included as part of the matrix. To date, those researchers interested in developing such a base have proceeded largely by taking an already existing paradigm and using it as a starting point for cross-cultural exploration or hypothesis testing. For example, a researcher may compare the incidence or prevalence of depression (often as defined by a Western-based nosological system) in two countries or may compare samples from two countries on the scales of a translated psychological test (e.g., the MMPI).

The worst of these studies suffer from ethnocentric bias, but even the best have made little progress toward a theory that includes cultural variables that can account for both intracultural and cross-cultural variation; that is, that begins to answer questions of why incidence or prevalence rates differ across cultures or subcultures or why any two groups (either within or across cultures) score differently on a specific test. Given that both subdisciplines are concerned with qualitatively similar issues, it follows that the fundamental problems inherent in developing a theoretical paradigm to explain variations in psychopathology are the same whether or not cross-cultural variables are included. It is therefore more efficient to include culture-relevant variables from the beginning rather than to start with a strictly within-culture paradigm and to build from there. Furthermore, even a purely within-culture paradigm cannot be completely developed without a broader frame of reference. That is, culture-relevant variables are operating even within a culture (whether or not we choose to acknowledge them), but they can only be partially understood in that restricted context. Within-culture effects can only be fully clarified when the entire range of cultural variation is available for study. In familiar terms, focus on the restricted range of variation within a culture leads to a distorted view of overall relations among cultural variables.

Even given the perspective that cross-cultural and mainstream psychology are complementary, indeed are mutually dependent fields, we are far from articulating a unified theory, and it is not the goal of this article to do so. Although several writers have set forth broad outlines for a substantive theory (e.g., Berry, 1980; Jahoda, 1980; Lonner, 1980; Segall, 1983; Triandis, Malpass, and Davidson, 1972), several more basic issues must be worked through before we can truly begin the task of building an integrated paradigm. I shall discuss two of these issues.

Common Approach—A Psychological View of Cultural and Social Factors

A distinguishing feature of cross-cultural psychology is the prominence it gives to culture as a causal variable. In standard terminology, culture is the independent variable, so it would seem important to define it precisely and to specify the unit of analysis. Accordingly, a section defining culture is often found in general treatises on cross-cultural psychology (e.g., Brislin, 1983; Brislin et al., 1973; Jahoda, 1980; Price-Williams, 1975, 1980; Triandis, 1980b). Careful study of these works reveals that they can be placed along a continuum characterized by the degree to which culture is treated as a simple categorical variable versus a complex multidimensional structure. For simplicity's sake, we can divide these studies into two types. It is not my intent to create divisions where they do not exist or to describe straw figures so that I may then knock them down. Rather, I hope to highlight some subtle differences in points of view within the field in order to focus more sharply on their implications (see Price-Williams, 1980, for a discussion of a related distinction).

The dominant approach is more categorical and typically offers definitions of culture from anthropology, either directly (e.g., Geertz, 1973; Kroeber and Kluckhohn, 1952) or as modified by psychologists (e.g., Brislin et al., 1973; Triandis et al., 1972). These definitions are usually followed by a discussion regarding the importance of delineating the specific variables that actually produce cross-cultural differences; nonetheless, writers in this tradition see culture as an important overarching concept and tend to agree with Jahoda (1980) that "advances in cross-cultural psychology will probably depend to a considerable extent on a more rigorous operationalization of the concept of 'culture'" (p. 131).

The second approach focuses more directly on specification of the cultural variable(s) involved when two or more cultures are compared; abstract definitions of culture are seen as tangential to this process. Segall (1983) stated that "an effort to enhance its [culture's] conceptual clarity is not needed; indeed it would be fruitless" (p. 127). In this view, the independent variable is not culture but rather is a set of culture-related variables that must be identified. These writers stress that, even if all the appropriate modifications of measures and procedures have been made, it is not enough to compare members of a variety of cultures on a dimension; what is important is investigating the specific variables mediating the pattern of similarities and differences. "We need to know precisely what cultural element in these two cultures is being tapped.... To connect psychological variables with 'culture' at large tells us nothing" (Price-Williams, 1975, pp. 8–9). This view also emphasizes the importance of process variables (how culture-related variables influence people) in addition to static characteristics (which variables account for differences between members of separate cultures) (B. Whiting, 1976).

Given that the former, anthropological tradition dominates cross-cultural psychological theory, it comes as no surprise that most empirical cross-cultural research is also in this tradition. This is, in some respects, unfortunate, because when culture is considered the basic independent variable, all else becomes elaboration that may be jettisoned for compelling practical reasons. That is, in the anthropological tradition, one can justify basing research on a fairly simplistic view of culture, although one must ignore those portions of theoretical discussion dealing with the importance of issues such as confounding, plausible rival hypotheses, and so on to do so. Studies that have followed this approach (and they are numerous) reflect a more simple categorical view than would be approved of even by those who espouse the first type. Research of this sort may result in part from unavoidable compromises made in implementing theoretically important considerations, but it also results in part from investigators who are "innocent of theory" (Jahoda, 1980, p. 71), that is, less sophisticated regarding the complex issues involved. Not surprisingly, such studies have generally not produced theoretically significant results and are criticized by theoreticians of all approaches (e.g., Brislin et al., 1973; Jahoda, 1980.) For example, even if the appropriate steps have been taken to ensure equivalence in translation, our understanding of depression is advanced little if we are told only that Japanese score higher than Americans on the MMPI D scale. We need to have some notion of what in the two cultures produces this difference before we can interpret these data. Differences in the social acceptability of symptom expression (either in general or with regard to specific problems, such as somatic complaints), in social norms regarding the expression of positive emotions, or in social expectations of perfectionism are all plausible hypotheses that could operate within each culture as well.

There is a danger, then, that the anthropological tradition unwittingly provides less scrupulous researchers with a rationale for simplistic thinking. As an antidote, those who are seriously committed to the cross-cultural enterprise can lean in the opposite direction and emphasize that we are interested not in some abstract notion of culture but rather in the psychological factors generated by culture-related variables. This should not be seen as a call for rapprochement within the field of cross-cultural psychology because the distinction between the two approaches reflects historical or training differences rather than an important theoretical schism. And in reality, fully elaborated versions of the two approaches converge. Given this communality, let us choose a framework that does not contain a seed from which poor research can draw nourishment and grow.

If this argument is not convincing, there is another reason for choosing an approach that aims to identify and clarify precisely which culture-related factors are responsible for observed cross-cultural differences: Such an approach is more compatible with that of mainstream researchers. If culture is viewed as a complex multidimensional structure, cross-cultural psychology becomes a direct and logical extension of the search for the psychological causes of variation in human behavior (including affect, cognition, and so forth). Conversely, when viewed in this light we see that insights from cross-cultural psychology may illuminate parallel mainstream problems.

For example, many of the factors we ordinarily treat as independent variables, or at least as relevant factors that need to be controlled, are not psychological variables at all (Sechrest, 1976, 1977). Education level, sex, socioeconomic status, and all our other favorite demographic variables are themselves no more psychological than is culture, but we have become so accustomed to using such variables as stand-ins for the correlated psychological factors that progress toward understanding the underlying concepts has virtually stopped in many areas. For example, many mainstream researchers routinely match subjects for education level, but merely having the same number of years of schooling does not automatically render two subjects equivalent on any psychological dimension. "If the researcher ... is unable to specify in advance the psychological variables for which [demographic variables] are surrogates, then the research promises to be little more than a fishing expedition" (Sechrest, 1977, p. 77). This point is applicable to both within-culture and cross-cultural research, but the consequences of ignoring it are more severe cross-culturally. As a result, the importance of specifying the relevant underlying psychological variables has been more widely recognized (although not perhaps more widely practiced) in cross-cultural psychology. Thus, adopting a psychological view of cultural variables may also facilitate exploration for related variables in mainstream research.

Moreover, variables identified as cultural in cross-cultural studies may be identified as social in within-culture research, so clarification of relations at a psychological rather than a demographic or sociocultural level in either subdiscipline will have positive ramifications for the other. For example, sex differences have been noted for a number of diagnostic categories in this country: Antisocial personality disorder and alcohol abuse and dependence are found predominantly in men, whereas agoraphobia and major depression are found predominantly in women (Robins et al., 1984). Biological sex may play some role in these differences, and to the extent that similar sex differences are found in widely diverse societies around the world, the role of biological factors must be seriously considered (cf. the relatively constant proportion of men and women with schizophrenia worldwide). However, it is also likely that psychological or sociocultural factors account for a large portion of the variance. Research in countries where different ratios of men to women are obtained for these disorders may illuminate the factors underlying the sex differences seen in this country.

Common Methodological Framework–Construct Validity and the Nomological Net

If we accept this common model for understanding psychological phenomena, we can agree that the final form of a unified psychological theory will consist primarily of psychological variables, with the hodge-podge of cultural, socioeconomic, and biological variables now included in our paradigms forming systematic supporting networks. Even so, we still need a methodological framework to interpret findings, one that is sufficiently flexible to incorporate the tremendous complexity of psychological phenomena. The construct-validation approach outlined by Cronbach and Meehl (1955) provides such a framework.[4] It may be disappointing to some that I do not propose a new and exciting methodological framework but instead turn to a preexisting model. However, this is in keeping with a recurrent theme in this article: that the methods and concepts we have already developed, both in cross-cultural and in mainstream psychology, will, if appropriately, flexibly, and innovatively applied, provide a solid foundation for the integration of these subdisciplines.

As described by Cronbach and Meehl (1955), the construct-validation approach is concerned with understanding the meaning of our measurements and with clarifying the nature of the causal network underlying our observations. It is ideally suited for studying covariation when (a) there is no definite criterion measure of the attributes of interest,

(b) indirect measures must be used, (c) generalized attributes rather than specific operations are being investigated, and (d) the "construct is defined implicitly by a network of associations or propositions in which it occurs" (pp. 299–300). All of these conditions apply to the psychological effect of culture-related variables. Such variables have no definite criterion; indeed, the criteria vary from setting to setting. Indirect measures, highly abstracted from the construct, are the norm. The variables studied are necessarily generalized if cross-culturally meaningful statements are to be made, and they are certainly highly contextual, embedded in complex association networks. Thus, such an approach frees us from the limitation of trying to predict specific behaviors—a problem even intraculturally (Epstein and O'Brien, 1985; Mischel and Peake, 1982) and an impossible nightmare cross-culturally—but does not thereby open the door to unrestricted speculation.

Due to the greater complexity of, and the special difficulties inherent in, cross-cultural research (e.g., language differences), constructing a nomological net that includes a wide range of cultural variables is inherently more problematic than if such factors are held constant, but the logic of the approach and the basic procedures to be followed are essentially the same in either case. In developing a measure of a construct, culturally relevant variables are unavoidably included, whether or not the scale is intended for cross-cultural use. If it is not for cross-cultural use, these variables go virtually unnoticed; if it is to be used cross-culturally, such variables must be specified as clearly as the main construct under investigation, which obviously complicates understanding the relevant correlations.

Let us take, for example, the MMPI Social Introversion scale, which contains a number of items that refer to social situations such as dances, parties, group discussions, social gatherings, and so on. In the original American English version, it was assumed that such situations were relatively common and that individual behavior and preference with regard to such situations could be interpreted as an expression of internal trait variables. Whether or not a person endorsed being "more likely to sit by myself . . . than join in with the crowd" in such a situation reflected something about the person relevant to his or her social introversion. These assumptions, however, must be specified as hypotheses (i.e., they are also part of the nomological net) when such items are to be used cross-culturally. In another culture, sitting by oneself at a social gathering may not be an option, or it may reflect social status rather than social introversion; alternatively, there may be specific types of gatherings in which these assumptions hold and others in which they do not. For a social introversion scale to be conceptually equivalent across cultures (i.e., to assess the same general psychological attribute, to occupy the same place in the nomological net) these underlying assumptions must be examined and made equivalent. Obviously, this is no small task, and it is just these problems that cross-cultural researchers must confront rather immediately, even with circumscribed projects.

However, we must remember that to understand fully the trait of social introversion or any other construct, even within American culture, these assumptions must eventually be specified and tested. That is, to the extent that a construct validated on dominant-culture college sophomores requires alteration for use with working adults, older people, ethnic minorities, and so on, specification of the nomological net in which the construct is embedded is incomplete. Research concerned with such generalization, including cross-cultural research, forces us to clarify variables and relations that we might otherwise leave unspecified. Thus, although it appears to require several steps backwards, cross-cultural research may actually hasten progress toward the ultimate goal of identifying the important causal factors underlying behavior.

An even more difficult issue is encountered when a construct developed in one culture appears to have no counterpart in the other, that is, when the structural relations (the nomological nets themselves) do not seem readily comparable. (In cross-cultural terminology, this describes an emic construct, one with no obvious conceptual equivalent; some so-called culture-bound syndromes may fall in this category.) However, this situation may prove to be only a very complex version of the more familiar situation in which relations observed in one population (e.g., normal adults) are not found in another (e.g., schizophrenic patients), and thus we must look at another level of abstraction to find congruence. As Cronbach and Meehl (1955) stated, when a predicted relation fails to occur, the fault may lie in any of a number of areas: theoretical network, measures, or experimental design. Any part of these three components may be altered in response to a set of disconfirming observations, so this case may not really be qualitatively different from the previous one. However, we are far from developing a comprehensive theory of human psychopathology and currently have no solutions to this frequently occurring problem. As we progress in our field and underlying causal (genotypic) relations are clarified, even extreme surface (phenotypic) variation may be more easily understood.

CONCLUSION

Much of this article has proceeded at a rather abstract level of discourse. To make my observations more concrete, I would like to illustrate them by using the research study of Watson et al. (1984). The basis for this research was a longitudinal, English-language study conducted in the United States that used daily ratings of mood adjectives to study the structure of mood change both idiographically and nomothetically (Zevon and Tellegen, 1982). Despite some individual variation, Zevon and Tellegen found a highly convergent structure that characterized changes in daily mood. Two broad, independent mood dimensions (positive affect [PA] and negative affect [NA]) were identified and were shown to have distinctive distributions; they also have been found to have differential correlates with psychopathology (Watson and Clark, 1984), personality variables (Costa and McCrae, 1980), and daily events (Stone and Neale, 1984) and to show differential patterns of cortical regulation (Sackeim and Weber, 1982). Thus, these two basic mood dimensions appear to be embedded in a rather extensive nomological net. We were interested in further testing the construct validity of these basic mood dimensions: Were they peculiar to the English language or American culture (i.e., emic dimensions); would they be unaffected by language and cultural difference (etic dimensions); or would certain aspects be constant and others variable? We chose to answer these questions using the Japanese culture and language partly because we thought that such a different culture would provide a stringent test of the null hypothesis.

Our first task was to construct a parallel set of mood adjectives that would adequately represent the Japanese (emic) emotional space while retaining enough overlap with the English terms to establish comparability (conceptual equivalence). A simple translation of the English list would have invalidated the findings to the extent that the English and Japanese mood adjective vocabularies were divergent, and a finding of no comparable terms would have rendered the Japanese data uninterpretable in English. Neither of these situations occurred (the details of this process are set forth in Watson et al., 1984). Japanese subjects were used to construct the mood list and bilingual raters provided the comparability data. Approximately one-half the terms overlapped rather exactly between the two lists, and both the positive and negative affect dimensions were replicated in the Japanese language, again with some individual variation in that country. The distributions found were quite similar to those found in the United States (one indication of metric equivalence), and one significant cross-cultural difference was illuminated: Sleepiness was found to covary (negatively) with energy and alertness in English but was unrelated to these attributes in Japanese. That this is probably not a chance finding was supported by an anthropological description of the role of sleep in Japan (Benedict, 1946). This finding may have implications for the study of depression in Japan, particularly if the study is replicated with related words such as *tired* and *fatigued* that are considered important symptoms of depression in this country. Finally, analyses of our subjects' diaries (kept in conjunction with their mood ratings) indicated that several of the differential correlates found for the two affective dimensions are also cross-culturally constant in their broad outlines, although a number of types of events had unstable effects across individuals or across cultures (Clark and Watson, 1987).

These results considerably strengthened our confidence in the construct validity of these dimensions, although it remains to be seen whether the remaining points in the nomological net (e.g., the discriminant correlations with psychopathological and personality variables and the brain correlates) will also be validated in the Japanese context. We have not identified the culture-relevant psychological factors that affect the role of sleepiness in the United States and Japan, nor have we explicated the intracultural or cross-cultural factors involved in those mood-event relations that did not replicate cleanly. Finally, the broader (e.g., ecological) implications of finding essentially identical cross-cultural mood structures have not been explored. Thus, although the study produced as many questions as answers, it did illustrate that, with careful attention to both individual and cultural variables and with the use of appropriate procedures for assuring comparability, solid findings with implications for both mainstream and cross-cultural research are possible.

NOTES

Author note: The author wishes to thank David Watson for his thoughtful suggestions regarding many previous versions of this article.

1. The author wishes to credit an anonymous reviewer for this point.
2. The terms are borrowed from phonemic versus phonetic analysis in linguistics, and as Brislin (1983) noted, they have been freely adapted for use in psychology. The original distinction is perhaps most clearly explained as subjective versus objective. If we follow the original paradigm exactly, an etic analysis of behavior is one that involves no inference about the meaning of the behavior but describes only the observable properties (e.g., holds right arm in air with open palm and swings it from side to side or holds right arm in air with open palm and bends hand back and forth from wrist). In an emic analysis, conversely, a judgment of whether these actions are the same or different would be required. In the United States, most would agree that both actions signal "good-bye," whereas in Japan, only the former means good-bye and the latter signals "come here." As the terms are commonly used in cross-cultural psychology, however, this restricted meaning is not maintained and the terms are used broadly to refer to any culturally unique versus general contrast. My discussion considers this latter, more common usage.

3. Means need not be the same for metric equivalence as long as the relations within and among variables remain constant.

4. This is not meant to imply that criterion-based research should not be conducted. First, construct and criterion validity are not mutually exclusive. Second, the strength of the criterion approach is its ability to address practical problems, and there are certainly many such problems that require immediate solutions, both intraculturally and cross-culturally. One reason for the popularity of cross-cultural MMPI research (Butcher and Pancheri, 1976; Butcher and Spielberger, 1985; Greene, 1987) is that the test has proven useful for tackling real problems in the assessment of psychopathology, even in countries where psychological science is still in its infancy. Provided they pay careful attention to equivalency issues, psychologists in such countries have a reliable diagnostic aid available in a much shorter time than if they were to construct an instrument from scratch. However, the criterion approach becomes more limited as the problems grow more abstract, making it unlikely that studies using this approach can lead directly to the development of a comprehensive theory concerning the role of cultural variables in human psychology.

BIBLIOGRAPHY

Benedict, R. (1946). *The chrysanthemum and the sword*. Boston: Houghton Mifflin.

Berry, J. W. (1980). Introduction. In H. C. Triandis and J. W. Berry (Eds.), *Handbook of cross-cultural psychology: Vol. 2. Methodology* (pp. 1–28). Boston: Allyn and Bacon.

Brislin, R. W. (1980). Translation and content analysis of oral and written material. In H. C. Triandis and J. W. Berry (Eds.). *Handbook of cross-cultural psychology: Vol. 2. Methodology* (pp. 389–444). Boston: Allyn and Bacon.

Brislin, R. W. (1983). Cross-cultural research in psychology. *Annual Review of Psychology*: 34, 363–400.

Brislin, R. W., Lonner, W. J., and Thorndike, R. M. (1973). *Cross-cultural research methods*. New York: Wiley.

Butcher, J. N., and Pancheri, P. (1976). *A handbook of cross-national MMPI research*. Minneapolis: University of Minnesota Press.

Butcher, J. N., and Spielberger, C. (1985). *Advances in personality assessment*. Hillsdale, NJ: Erlbaum.

Campbell, D. T. (1968). A cooperative multination opinion sample exchange. *Journal of Social Issues*, 24, 245–255.

Clark, L. A., and Watson, D. (1987). *Mood and the mundane: Relations between daily life events and self-reported mood*. Manuscript submitted for publication.

Costa, P. T., and McCrae, R. R. (1980). Influence of extraversion and neuroticism on subjective well-being: Happy and unhappy people. *Journal of Personality and Social Psychology*, 38, 668–678.

Cronbach, L. J., and Meehl, P. E. (1955). Construct validity in psychological tests. *Psychological Bulletin*, 52, 281–302.

Draguns, J. G. (1981). Counseling across cultures: Common themes and distinct approaches. In P. B. Pedersen, J. G. Draguns, W. J. Lonner, and J. E. Trimble (Eds.), *Counseling across cultures* (pp. 3–21). Honolulu: University of Hawaii Press.

Epstein, S., and O'Brien, E. J. (1985). The person-situation debate in historical and current perspective. *Psychological Bulletin*, 98, 513–537.

Forsythe, B. (1987). The subjective attributes of natural categories: An application of a constrained generalized Euclidean model. In F. W. Young and R. M. Harner (Eds.), *Multidimensional scaling: History, theory, and applications* (pp. 281–306). Hillsdale, NJ: Eribaum.

Geertz, C. (1965). The impact of the concept of culture on the concept of man. In J. R. Platt (Ed.), *New views on the nature of man* (pp. 93–118). Chicago: University of Chicago Press.

Geertz, C. (1973). *The interpretation of cultures*. New York: Basic Books.

Greene, R. L. (1987). Ethnicity and MMPI performance: A review. *Journal of Counseling and Clinical Psychology*: 55, 497–512.

Hamilton, D. L. (1979). A cognitive-attributional analysis of stereotyping. In L. Berkowiz (Ed)., *Advances in experimental social psychology* (Vol. 12, pp. 53–84). New York: Academic Press.

Hathaway, S. R., and McKinley, J. C. (1943). *The Minnesota Multiphasic Personality Inventory*. Minneapolis, MN: University of Minnesota Press.

Hui, C. H., and Triandis, H. C. (1985). Measurement in cross-cultural psychology: A review and comparison of strategies. *Journal of Cross-Cultural Psychology*, 16, 131–152.

Irvine, S. H., and Carroll, W. K. (1980). Testing and assessment across cultures: Issues in methodology and theory. In H. C. Triandis and J. W. Berry (Eds.), *Handbook of cross-cultural psychology: Vol. 2. Methodology* (pp. 181–244). Boston: Allyn and Bacon.

Jahoda, G. (1980). Theoretical and systematic approaches. In H. C. Triandis and W. W. Lambert (Eds.), *Handbook of cross-cultural psychology: Vol. 1. Perspectives* (pp. 69–141). Boston: Allyn and Bacon.

Kleinman, A., and Good, B. (1985). Introduction: Culture and depression. In A. Kleinman and B. Good (Eds.), *Culture and depression: Studies in the anthropology and cross-cultural psychiatry of affect and disorder* (pp. 3–29). Berkeley: University of California Press.

Kroeber, A. L., and Kluckhohn, C. (1952). *Culture: A critical review of concepts and definitions* (Papers of the Peabody Museum, Vol. 57, No. 1). Cambridge, MA: Harvard University.

Lonner, W. J. (1979). Issues in cross-cultural psychology. In A. J. Marsella, R. G. Tharp, and T. J. Ciborowski (Eds.), *Perspectives on cross-cultural psychology* (pp. 17–45). New York: Academic Press.

Lonner, W. J. (1980). The search for psychological universals. In H. C. Triandis and W. W. Lambert (Eds.), *Handbook of cross-cultural psychology: Vol. 1. Perspectives* (pp. 143–204). Boston: Allyn and Bacon.

Mischel, W., and Peake, P. K. (1982). Some facets of consistency: Replies to Epstein, Funder, and Bem. *Psychological Review*, 90, 394–402.

Pedersen, P. B., Draguns, J. G., Lonner, W. J., and Trimble, J. E. (Eds.), (1981). *Counseling across cultures*. Honolulu: University of Hawaii Press.

Poortinga, Y. H. (1982). Psychometric approaches to intergroup comparison: The problem of equivalence. In S. H. Irvine and J. W. Berry (Eds.), *Human assessment and cultural factors* (pp. 237–257). London: Academic Press.

Price-Williams, D. R. (1975). *Explorations in cross-cultural psychology*. San Francisco: Chandler and Sharp.

Price-Williams, D. R. (1980). Toward the idea of a cultural psychology: A superordinate theme for study. *Journal of Cross-Cultural Psychology*, 11, 75–88.

Przeworski, A., and Teune, H. (1970). *The logic of social inquiry*. New York: Wiley.

Robins, L. N., Helzer, J. E., Weissman, M. M., Orvaschel, H., Gruenberg, E., Burke, J. D., and Regier, D. A. (1984). Lifetime prevalence of specific psychiatric disorders in three sites. *Archives of General Psychiatry*, 41, 949–958.

Sackeim, H. A., and Weber, S. L. (1982). Functional brain asymmetry in the regulation of emotion: Implication for bodily manifestations of stress. In L. Goldberger and S. Brenitz (Eds.), *Handbook of stress: Theoretical and clinical aspects* (pp. 183–199). New York: Free Press.

Schofield, W. (1964). *Psychotherapy: The purchase of friendship*. Englewood Cliffs, NJ: Prentice-Hall.

Sechrest, L. (1976). Personality. *Annual Review of Psychology*, 27, 1–27.

Sechrest, L. (1977). On the dearth of theory in cross-cultural psychology: There is madness in our methods. In Y. H. Poortinga (Ed.), *Basic problems in cross-cultural psychology* (pp. 73–82). Amsterdam: Swets and Zeitlinger.

Segall, M. S. (1983). On the search for the independent variable in cross-cultural psychology. In S. H. Irvine and J. W. Berry (Eds.), *Human assessment and cultural factors* (pp. 127–137). London: Academic Press.

Segall, M. S. (1986). Culture and behavior: Psychology in global perspective. *Annual Review of Psychology*, 37, 523–564.

Stone, A. A., and Neale, J. M. (1984). Effects of severe daily events on mood. *Journal of Personality and Social Psychology*, 46, 137–144.

Strodtbeck, F. (1964). Considerations of meta-method in cross-cultural studies. *American Anthropologist*. 66, 223–229.

Taylor, J. A. (1953). A personality scale of manifest anxiety. *Journal of Abnormal and Social Psychology*, 48, 285–290.

Triandis, H. C. (Ed.), (1980a). *Handbook of cross-cultural psychology* (Vol. 1–6). Boston: Allyn and Bacon.

Triandis, H. C. (1980b). Introduction. In H. C. Triandis and W. W. Lambert (Eds.), *Handbook of cross-cultural psychology: Vol. 1. Perspectives* (pp. 1–14). Boston: Allyn and Bacon.

Triandis, H. C., Malpass, R. S., and Davidson, A. (1972). Cross-cultural psychology. *Biennial Review of Anthropology, 1971*, 1–84.

Van de Vijver, F. J. R., and Poortinga, Y. H. (1982). Cross-cultural generalization and universality. *Journal of Cross-Cultural Psychology*, 13, 387–408.

Watson, D., and Clark, L. A. (1984). Negative affectivity: The disposition to experience aversive emotional states. *Journal of Personality and Social Psychology*, 96, 465–490.

Watson, D., Clark, L. A., and Tellegen, A. (1984). Cross-cultural convergence in the structure of mood: A Japanese replication and a comparison with U.S. findings. *Journal of Personality and Social Psychology*, 47, 127–144.

Welsh, G. S. (1956). Factor dimensions A and R. In G. S. Welsh and W. G. Dahlstrom (Eds.), *Basic readings on the MMPI in psychology and medicine*. Minneapolis, MN: University of Minnesota Press.

Whiting, B. (1976). The problem of the packaged variable. In K. F. Riegel and J. A. Meacham (Eds.), *The developing individual in a changing world* (pp. 303–309). The Hague, The Netherlands: Mouton.

Whiting, J. (1968). Methods and problems in cross-cultural research (2nd ed.). In G. Lindzey (Ed.), *Handbook of social psychology* (pp. 693–728). Reading, MA: Addison-Wesley.

Zevon, M. A., and Tellegen, A. (1982). The structure of mood change: An idiographic/nomothetic analysis. *Journal of Personality and Social Psychology*, 43, 111–122.

2.
Methodological Issues in Assessment Research with Ethnic Minorities

Sumie Okazaki and Stanley Sue

Assessment research on ethnic minorities presents multiple methodological and conceptual challenges. This article addresses the difficulties in defining and examining ethnicity as a variable in psychological research. The authors assert that many of the problems stem from not making explicit the assumptions underlying the use of ethnicity as an explanatory variable and from inadequately describing cultural and contextual characteristics of ethnic minority samples. Also raised are common methodological problems encountered in examining race, ethnicity, and culture in assessment research, such as decisions regarding which populations to study, sampling methodologies, measure selection, method of assessment, and interpretation of results. Finally, some guidelines are offered for tackling some of the methodological dilemmas in assessment research with ethnic minorities.

Assessment research on ethnic minority groups has had a controversial history. For example, comparisons of intellectual abilities and cognitive skills, of self-esteem and self-hatred, of personality patterns, and of prevalence rates and degrees of psychopathology among different ethnic and racial groups have generated considerable controversy regarding the validity of findings. It is our belief that conducting valid assessment research with ethnic minority groups is particularly problematic because of methodological, conceptual, and practical difficulties that arise in such research. This article addresses common methodological problems that have plagued assessment research on ethnic minorities. Our intent here is not to provide definitive solutions to methodological problems but rather to raise issues that many researchers may not have otherwise considered, so that informed decisions can be made about how to handle variables related to ethnicity. We also pose some guidelines for future assessment research with ethnic minorities to improve the knowledge base not only for ethnic minorities but also for the field of psychological assessment. In doing so, we will closely examine fundamental problems such as sample heterogeneity, measurement of culture and underlying assumptions about ethnicity, all of which make assessment research with ethnic minorities inherently challenging. Because our work involves Asian Americans, many of the cited examples deal with this population, although the point behind the examples may apply to other ethnic groups.

We refer to assessment research in a broad sense and use examples from extant literature on cognitive, personality, and clinical psychodiagnostic assessment with various ethnic minority groups. The focus is not on particular assessment instruments but on underlying conceptual and methodological issues with respect to ethnicity.

ETHNICITY AND RACE

Use of Terms

From the outset let us address some definitional issues. It must be noted that the notions of race and ethnic minority status are highly charged with potential political ramifications. A prevailing example of a classification system with vast political consequences is the use of the terms race and Hispanic origin by the U.S. Bureau of Census, whose population count influences each region's allotment of federal funds as well as possible district realignment for voting purposes. The U.S. Bureau of the Census uses the following categories: White; Black; American Indian, Eskimo, or Aleut; Asian or Pacific Islanders; Hispanic origin (of any race); and Other. The use of the term "race" appears to imply biological factors, as races are typically defined by observable physiognomic features such as skin color, hair type and color, eye color, stature, facial features, and so forth. However, some researchers have argued that designation of race is often arbitrary and that within-race differences in even the physiognomic features are greater than between-race differences (Zuckerman, 1990), and this topic continues to be hotly debated (e.g., Yee, Fairchild, Weizmann, and Wyatt, 1993).

There is no one definition of ethnicity, race, and culture that is agreed on by all. Indeed, it is common for both researchers and others to refer to ethnicity, culture, and race interchangeably when identifying and categorizing people by background (Betancourt and Lopez, 1993). Granted, these terms are closely related, as illustrated by a definition of ethnic status provided by Eaton (1980, p. 160):

> Ethnic status is defined as an easily identifiable characteristic that implies a common cultural history with others possessing the same characteristic. The most common ethnic "identifiers" are race, religion, country of origin, language, and/or cultural background.

It is quite obvious that various characteristics serving as ethnic identifiers do not usually occur as independent features but appear in interrelated patterns and configurations (Dahlstrom, 1986), thus the common practice of interchanging the terms is understandable to a degree. However, confusion or a lack of differentiation among race, ethnicity, and culture at the terminology level likely reflects confusion at the conceptual level. That is, is the research concerned with race as a biological variable, ethnicity as a demographic variable, or some aspect of subjective cultural experience as a psychological variable?

Often, the implicit rationale behind grouping together individuals of the same racial or ethnic background and conducting assessment research using ethnicity as an independent or predictor variable is based on the assumptions that (a) these individuals share some common psychological characteristics associated with culture and (b) such shared cultural-psychological characteristics are related to personality or psychopathology. However, ethnicity is a demographic variable that is relatively distal to the variable of psychological or clinical interest. In many research studies, the participants' ethnicity may be serving as a proxy for psychological variables such as cultural values, self-concept, minority status, and so forth. Nonetheless, communications of findings (in the form of journal reports) often fail to clarify what assumptions were made about psychological characteristics of the particular sample in research studies. We believe that imprecisely using race and ethnicity to categorize individuals and then conducting studies on such population groups have contributed to the problems in assessment research with ethnic minorities. In the absence of each research study explicating the assumptions underlying the use of such categorical variables, we cannot assume that researchers are studying and communicating about the same constructs. Therefore, we echo the assertions made by Clark (1987) and by Betancourt and Lopez (1993) that research involving individuals from different ethnic and cultural backgrounds must specify and directly measure the underlying psychological variables associated with culture that are hypothesized to produce cultural or ethnic group differences.

Individual Differences Versus Group Characteristics

Some have argued that grouping together individuals based on ethnicity or race perpetuates unnecessary stereotyping or useless categorizations. Although we will, in the next section, point to the pitfalls of underestimating within-group heterogeneity, we still uphold the value of conducting research on broad groups of individuals classified into ethnic minority groups to the extent that, as previously discussed, certain sets of characteristics covary with racial, ethnic, or cultural groups. After all, what is culture, if not a set of values and attitudes, a world view, and so forth that are shared by a large number of people who also share, to a greater or lesser extent, other demographic and physical characteristics? One caveat in examining characteristics of a broad group rests on a basic principle, namely, the greater the heterogeneity, the less precise the prediction is apt to be. Thus, although we may conclude that in general, White Americans are more individualistic than are Mexican Americans, we cannot predict with any certainty the level of individualism of a particular person. It is obvious that the confounding of an individual with the individual's culture results in stereotyping. Furthermore, an awkwardness exists when terms such as *Asian Americans* or *African Americans* are used because within-group heterogeneity cannot be conveyed by such terms. By making explicit the meaning of the terms and the context in which they are used, one can reduce some of the awkwardness.

COMMON METHODOLOGICAL PROBLEMS

Methodological problems with respect to ethnic minorities can occur at all stages of assessment research. We will examine salient issues in the stages of design (with respect to the population focus), sampling, measure selection and establishing equivalence of measures, method of assessment, and interpretation of data.

Population Focus

Selecting participants. In the initial design of assessment research a salient dilemma confronting researchers may be which ethnic groups to include in the design and for what purpose. Let us examine two scenarios, one case in which the primary research question does not involve ethnicity or culture and another case in which the research question does concern ethnic minorities. In the scenario in which the main investigation does not involve ethnicity, a researcher must decide which ethnic minority group(s), if any, to include in the design. If ethnic minority individuals comprise a subsample that is too small with which to run separate or comparative analyses with the majority ethnic group, a researcher may choose to exclude them from analyses altogether. This certainly simplifies the problem, but it does not contribute to the much needed knowledge of whether the findings may be generalized to ethnic minorities. If a subsample of ethnic minorities is too small for meaningful analyses but large enough not to be discarded, a researcher must contend with the knowledge that observed variance in the variables of interest may contain some unmeasured or unanalyzed factors related to ethnicity. On the other hand a well-intentioned researcher may collect data from sizable ethnic minority groups but without a sound conceptual basis or a planned course of analyses for handling the ethnicity variable. A common outcome in such a case may be that ethnicity is relegated to the status of an extraneous variable, to be dealt with as an afterthought in the analysis.

In the second scenario, where the primary research question is concerned with ethnic minorities (e.g., establishing psychometric properties of an established assessment measure for an ethnic minority group), a frequent dilemma involves deciding whether to collect data solely from the target ethnic minority group or to compare the ethnic minorities with a control group. It is a common practice to compare one or more ethnic minority groups with Whites on a psychological characteristic of empirical interest. A part of this practice is rooted in the existing research paradigm that emphasizes differences (with "statistical significance") across groups. And because many assessment measures and methods have been developed and normed on largely, if not exclusively, White populations (e.g., the original Minnesota Multiphasic Personality Inventory; MMPI), researchers are taken to task to assess whether these measures and methods are psychometrically and practically valid with ethnic minorities. However, the race comparison paradigm should not go unquestioned. The comparative approach has been criticized for potentially reinforcing racial stereotypes or the interpretation of non-White behavior as deviant as well as underestimating or overlooking within-ethnic group variations (Azibo, 1988; Campbell, 1967; Graham, 1992). The question often posed is, Are within-group differences as important or as valid as between-group differences? An example of the dilemma was presented by Korchin (1980). Korchin wanted to assess the determinants of personality competence among two groups of African American men—those demonstrating exceptional and average competence. Results of the study were analyzed and a paper on the study was submitted to a major journal. One of the paper's reviewers criticized the study as being "grievously flawed," because no White control group was employed. Korchin raised several questions. Why should a White control group have been employed when the purpose of the study was to analyze within-group differences? What would happen if someone submitted a study identical in all respects except that all participants were White? Would it be criticized because it lacked an African American control group? There are no easy answers to these questions. As suggested by Korchin, assumptions concerning the appropriateness of comparisons should be guided by the purpose of a particular study.

Ethnic comparisons. Once the question of population focus (i.e., inclusion or exclusion of specific ethnic minority groups) has been resolved, the next issue to consider is "matching" two or more ethnic groups for comparison purposes. Group comparisons are commonly achieved through two methods: (a) matching the participants a priori on the relevant but secondary variables or (b) controlling for those variables post hoc in analyses. With respect to matching, ethnic groups are typically matched on demographic characteristics such as age, sex, and possibly socioeconomic status, as well as defining characteristics such as psychiatric diagnoses. However, it may be difficult to match two or more ethnic groups on all relevant characteristics, as it has been well documented that various sectors of ethnic minority populations differ in the nature and distribution of characteristics. For example, American Indians have a much higher rate of unemployment, a larger number of individuals living under the poverty level, a higher school-dropout rate, and a shorter life expectancy than other ethnic groups (LaFromboise, 1988). Graham (1992) noted the paramount importance of controlling for group differences in socio-economic status when comparing African Americans and Whites, given overrepresentation of African Americans in economically disadvantaged segments of the population.

In deciding which variables need to be controlled for in the ethnic group comparisons, again, there is no agreed list of variables that are considered as essential control variables for each ethnic group. It is advised that variability in social and demographic characteristics (e.g., educational attainment income level, language fluency, etc.) be statistically controlled in the analysis when ethnic differences exist on such variables and when the researcher has a reason to believe such differences may moderate the relationship between the variables of interest. A potential problem that remains in matching participants or controlling for differences in social characteristics is that a researcher may assume, given similar demographics of two ethnic groups, that individuals constituting the study are similar on a number of other unmeasured variables. Some have argued that similar demographics may have different effects for ethnic minorities, such as the interactive effect of ethnicity and social class on stress and distress (Cervantes and Castro, 1985; Kessler and Neighbors, 1986). A more sophisticated understanding of psychological correlates of demographic characteristics, including ethnicity, is needed.

Sampling

The design problem over inclusion or exclusion of ethnic minorities in assessment research is closely tied to problems in sampling. In this section we review specific sampling techniques used to identify and solicit participation of ethnic minority participants. Some of the examples for obtaining ethnic minority samples are not from personality assessment research but from epidemiological and community studies targeting subclinical or nonclinical ethnic minority populations. They are used here as illustrations of methods for obtaining difficult-to-reach samples.

Identifying participants. Foremost in the sampling problem is identifying the ethnicity of participants. Self-identification of ethnicity by participants' self-report is the most common method, and this is most often accomplished by a limited categorical listing of ethnic groups, as defined by the investigator. Ethnicity may be defined at a broad level (e.g., Latino or Hispanic) or at a more specific level (e.g., Puerto Rican, Mexican American, etc.). Researchers are also faced with the decision of how to classify persons of mixed racial or ethnic backgrounds (see Hall, 1992; Root, 1992). Another method for identifying potential participants' ethnicity is through the surname identification method. Some ethnic groups such as Asians and Hispanics have unequivocally ethnic surnames (e.g., "Kim" for Koreans, "Nguyen" for Vietnamese, and "Gutierrez" for Latino), which enables surname-based community sampling methodology. Indeed some studies have used surnames or other key characteristics as the sole basis for determining participants' ethnicity (e.g., Dion and Giordano, 1990; Dion and Toner, 1988). This method for ascertaining the ethnicity of participants (i.e., without cross-validation from the participants) is sometimes the only option, particularly when working with archival data, but this obviously limits the certainty with which the results may be interpreted. There are further issues with respect to identification of ethnicity. Sasao and Sue (1993) pointed to the faulty but commonly made assumption that once individuals are identified as belonging to a certain ethnic-cultural group, they share a common understanding of their own ethnicity or culture and identify with the ethnic-cultural group. To illustrate, in a high school drug abuse survey conducted in multicultural communities in Southern California (Sasao, 1992), approximately 20% of the Chinese American students indicated their primary cultural identification was Mexican, though the self-perceived ethnicity of these Chinese students was Chinese.

Small sample size. Collecting data from a large enough sample of ethnic minorities has long posed a challenge, partly because of the small overall population size. Let us take the example of American Indians (technically categorized as American Indians, Eskimo, or Aleut by the U.S. Bureau of the Census), who comprised only 0.8% of the total U.S. population according to the 1990 U.S. Census (U.S. Bureau of the Census, 1991). American Indian populations tend to be geographically much more concentrated than does the general U.S. population, as the majority of American Indians lived in just six states in 1990. The American Indian population was highest in Alaska, where it comprised about 16% of that state's total population, but there were 35 states in which American Indians represented less than 1% of the total population of each state in 1990 (U.S. Bureau of the Census, 1991). About half of the American Indian population lives in urban areas and about half lives in rural areas or areas on or adjacent to reservations that are located in the Plains States (Bureau of Indian Affairs, 1991). Thus, locating an adequate sample size of American Indian participants is difficult, if not impractical, in many states and regions.

The problem of small sample size often results in researchers combining the data from a number of ethnic-cultural groups with some common origin (e.g., combining Chinese Americans, Japanese Americans, and Korean Americans into one group), or in the case of American Indians, across tribal groups (e.g., combining Hopis, Lakotas, and Navahos into one group). However, broadening the ethnic grouping increases heterogeneity. Again, taking the case of American Indians, there are over 510 federally recognized tribes, including more than 200 Alaskan Native villages (Bureau of Indian Affairs, 1991). American Indian tribes vary enormously in customs, language, and type of family structure, so much so that Tefft (1967) argued that differences between certain tribal groups are greater than those between Indians and Whites on some variables. American Indian individuals also vary in their degree of acculturation and exposure to tribal or White American cultures, whether they live on or off a reservation, ethnic or tribal identification, experience with racism, and so forth. Given such a list of even the most basic sources of sample heterogeneity, a researcher is inevitably faced with the decision of which sources of variability can or cannot be overlooked in aggregating individuals into an ethnic group classification. This discussion is not to underestimate the cultural diversity within the White American population; in fact it is intended to stimulate a more refined treatment of ethnicity and culture in psychological research.

Recruiting participants. In efforts to recruit ethnic minority participants, researchers must consider possible ethnic and cultural differences in participants' likelihood to participate in psychological assessment research. Are ethnic minorities less likely to cooperate with research? Are the rates of attrition from research studies equal across ethnic groups?

For some ethnic groups, cultural values may influence their participation or response patterns in research. Ying (1989) analyzed the cases of nonresponse to Center for Epidemiological Studies-Depression scale (CES-D) items in a community sample of Chinese Americans. The original study was conducted as a telephone interview study with randomly selected Chinese-surnamed households listed in the San Francisco public telephone directory. Ying found that demographic factors such as age, sex, and education as well as item content were related to the rates of nonresponse to CES-D items. Ying explained that older Chinese women were less likely to be familiar with telephone surveys, the methodology which, in and of itself, may reflect a middle-class American life-style and set of values. Older Chinese women may experience being questioned by a stranger about mood and somatic symptoms as foreign and intrusive yet refrain from directly refusing to participate because such behavior would be too assertive and impolite. For other Chinese community cohorts such as middle-aged Chinese men, endorsement of positive feelings (e.g., feeling good about self or feeling happy and enjoying life) may be regarded as indicative of immodesty and frivolousness in Chinese culture, thus such values may also contribute to nonresponse. This type of in-depth analysis of nonresponse illustrates the importance of considering the potential influence of cultural and social norms in responding to and participating in psychological research.

Use of college samples. For ethnic minority groups for which it is extremely difficult to obtain a large community sample of participants, sampling from college populations is a particularly attractive and viable option because of the ease of access to a relatively large captive pool of potential participants. For example, a significant portion of Asian American personality and psychopathology literature has been conducted with college students (Leong, 1986; Uba, 1994). This sampling strategy clearly impacts the question of representativeness of the sample. Sears (1985) argued that a significant portion of psychological research is conducted with college sophomores, and he pointed to the hazards of basing much of what we know about human processes on a sample not representative of the larger population. Sears named a number of differences between American college undergraduates and the general population, such as education, test-taking experience, and restricted age range, which in turn are associated with intrapsychic characteristics such as a less than fully formulated sense of self, less crystallized social and political attitudes, highly unstable peer relationships, and so forth. The same criticisms apply to assessment research with ethnic minorities, and the representativeness of ethnic minority college students must be carefully assessed, not only with respect to socioeconomic and educational attainment of student participants in relation to their age cohorts who do not attend college but also with respect to a correspondent set of values and attitudes, a limited range of political awareness of self-identification, and an American education. For language minority groups such as some American Indians, immigrant Asian Americans, and immigrant Latinos (and some would argue African Americans; see Helms, 1992), good or adequate English language skills are necessary to gain entrance into colleges and universities. However, those with university-level English skills may not be representative of a significant portion of immigrant ethnic minorities. Ethnic minority college samples tend to underestimate both the demographic and the psychosocial diversity of the larger ethnic minority populations. Consequently, sample heterogeneity, as high as it may be in college samples, may still be an underestimate of true population heterogeneity.

Use of community samples. Given the questionable generalizability of resear with ethnic minority college students to the ethnic community population at often desirable, although also extremely challenging, to sample from ethnic ......y communities. Many research studies conducted with ethnic minorities in the community rely on systematic or captive sampling or snowball sampling (a method in which one starts with a known group of participants and recruits more participants through contacts) in intact ethnic groups or organizations such as churches, temples, professional associations, political organizations, social clubs, kinship associations, and so forth. It is clear that each of these organizations attracts a subsample of the target ethnic community, and the results cannot be easily generalized to the entire group. Sasao and Sue (1993) criticized psychological research with ethnic minorities for its lack of ecological and contextual considerations. Specifically, Sasao and Sue argued that too often, research ignores the societal context in relation to other relevant ethnic-cultural community groups. Many psychological characteristics of clinical interest may be greatly influenced by the target community group's geographical and political context in which ethnic minority individuals function, such that psychological research on African Americans in South Central Los Angeles must take into account the community's relation to Korean Americans and the contemporary political climate. When the research question involves the assessment of psychopathology, studies may be conducted with those ethnic minority participants who utilize clinical services. There is some evidence to indicate differential patterns of mental health services utilization among different ethnic minority groups (Sue, Fujino, Hu, Takeuchi, and Zane, 1991), thereby making it difficult to assess the generalizability of the findings. Clearly, the procurement of representative and adequately sized samples of ethnic minorities poses a considerable methodological challenge.

Establishing Equivalence of Measures

One goal of assessment research with ethnic minorities is to conduct reliable and valid assessment while minimizing cultural or ethnic bias. Use of assessment measures in research with ethnic minorities presents several problems, primarily with respect to equivalence. Brislin (1993) discussed three types of equivalence (translation, conceptual, and metric) as being of foremost concern in cross-cultural research methodology. To the extent that assessment research is concerned with effects of culture on assessed psychological characteristics among ethnic minorities, the cross-cultural principles apply to research with ethnic minorities.

Although some of the frequently used assessment instruments such as the Wechsler scales, the SCL-90-R, the Zung Self-Rating Depression Scale, and the MMPI have been translated into languages such as Spanish, Japanese, and Chinese, researchers and clinicians are often faced with the sheer lack of relevant assessment measures in the language of the target ethnic minority populations that also have established translation equivalence. Importantly, linguistic equivalence issues also cannot be ignored for ethnic minority participants who are functionally English-speaking. For example, Helms (1992) argued that most African Americans in the United Stated are probably exposed to some versions of both Black and White English, yet commonly used standardized tests are in White standard English. A recent study examining Spanish-English bilingualism among Hispanic immigrants (Bahrick, Hall, Goggin, Bahrick, and Berger, 1994) indicated a complex interaction among language dominance, the assessment task (e.g., oral comprehension, vocabulary recognition, category generation, etc.), age at immigration, and other factors. Such findings suggest that the type of language skills used to assess bilingual participants in either English or their first language may influence some results.

In the absence of appropriate assessment measures for which the translated versions' psychometric properties have been established, a researcher may choose to translate and adopt the instrument to the ethnic minority group of research interest. In order to ensure that a newly translated measure has achieved translation equivalence, a multistep method has been recommended, in which translation (e.g., from English to Spanish) is followed by back translation (from Spanish to English), comparison of the two versions (e.g., English and English), revisions in the translation and so forth (Brislin, 1993). Geisinger (1994) has outlined a set of rigorous methodological steps for translating an assessment instrument and adopting it to a new culture. However it must be acknowledged that carefully following the methodological steps suggested by Geisinger and performing psychometric analyses would require multiple, adequately sized samples of ethnic minorities, leaving the researcher once again with dilemmas in obtaining large sample sizes.

Conceptual equivalence is concerned with whether the psychological construct under investigation (e.g., depression, intelligence, or assertiveness) holds the same meanings in two or more cultural groups. Conceptual equivalence of a construct may be highly dependent on the context in which the assessment takes place. Although this may be true for any participant population, researchers must be aware that for ethnic minorities, variability of and sensitivity to contextual factors may be increased as they move between a traditional cultural setting (e.g., family and ethnic communities) and a more mainstream American cultural setting (e.g., work, school, etc.). For example, in assessing the meaning of aggressiveness in youths, an assessment may be conducted in a school setting, in which Latinos, Asians, and Whites share the same environmental space, and to a large extent, the same ecological context. If the construct is found to be equivalent in this setting, it may not necessarily translate into conceptual equivalence in other settings, such as the family or the street culture.

Metric equivalence refers to the assumption that the same metric can be used to measure the same concept in two or more cultures. For example, the test score of 100 for a White participant is assumed to be interpretable in the same manner as the test score of 100 for a Mexican American participant. Metric equivalence is often overlooked or assumed without empirical validation in research with ethnic minorities, particularly if the measure does not involve translation. The danger of assuming equivalence of translated measures was illustrated by an analysis comparing the Wechsler Adult Intelligence Scale (WAIS) and its Spanish adaptation, Escala de Inteligencia Wechsler para Adultos (EIWA; Lopez and Romero, 1988), in which major differences between the two instruments were found with respect to the conversion of raw scores to scale scores, administration, and content. Lopez and Romero pointed to the importance of noting the rural, less educated characteristics of the Puerto Rican sample on which the EIWA was normed, and concluded that "psychologists should not expect the scores of the EIWA to be comparable with those of the WAIS, and perhaps even with the scores of the WAIS-R" (Lopez and Romero,

1988 p. 269). It is also critical to note here the heterogeneity within an ethnic minority group (e.g., rural Puerto Rican vs. urban Mexican American), which may be underestimated or overlooked because of a common language (in this case, Spanish) when a translated version is available.

In research, psychometric statistical analyses are often performed in order to address equivalence problems of a measure across ethnic groups. For example, Ben-Porath (1990) advocated the use of replicatory factor analysis (i.e., using the same factor analytic method to examine the factor structure of a newly translated or adopted instrument that was used in the original measure) to establish cross-cultural validity of the instrument. Ben-Porath also suggested that prior to conducting factor analyses, it is important to examine the distribution of the scale items across ethnic and cultural groups in order to detect possible range restrictions and outliers. This is particularly vital to the assessment studies involving ethnic minorities, as Helms (1992) cautioned that cultural and inter-ethnic factors may compromise the basic assumptions underlying statistics, such as independence of ethnic groups with respect to culture or equal range and variance between ethnic groups. Regression analyses have also been used to study instrument or test bias, specifically to examine whether tests make predictions that are similar, and similarly accurate, to those of a criterion measure. If, for example, regression slopes for a test or evaluation procedure and a criterion differ for different groups, tests bias exists. Such studies require that fairly clear-cut criteria can be found on which to judge the adequacy of predictors. An example of this approach was provided by Timbrook and Graham (1994), who examined ethnic differences between African Americans and Whites in the restandardization sample of the MMPI-2. The researchers used ratings of interpersonal behavior and personality characteristics of the participants made by their partners as external criteria against which the accuracy of predictions of five MMPI-2 clinical scales could be examined. Regression equations were developed to predict the partner rating scale scores, and no ethnic differences were found on the accuracy of the MMPI-2 scale predictions.

Methods of Assessment

Thus far our discussion of methodological issues in measure selection for use with ethnic minorities has been primarily focused on standardized objective personality assessment measures (with the exception of the Wechsler scales), most often of the self-report variety. However, it is debatable whether some methods of assessment may be more likely to result in cultural or ethnic bias than others. There are at least three approaches to assessment that have been understudied with respect to ethnic minorities: (a) behavioral observations, (b) qualitative assessment, and (c) projective tests. One may question for ethnic minorities whether behavioral observation methods are more prone to bias than self-report instruments, whether qualitative assessment is more prone to bias than quantitative data, or whether projective tests are more prone to bias than objective tests.

Surveying the assessment research on ethnic minorities, there is a shortage of assessment methodology using observational data. Behavioral observation methodologies often involve in-depth, microlevel analysis of behavior. Although largescale surveys are necessary in order to obtain some normative information on ethnic minorities, the field is ripe for a contribution in microlevel analysis as well. The behavioral observation methods also have the advantage of requiring relatively small sample sizes that are necessary to conduct analyses, although generalizability to the larger population is likely to be compromised with potential self-selection of ethnic or cultural minority participants who are willing to participate in such indepth assessment research.

Psychological assessment research, which is heavily rooted in psychometric tradition has favored quantitative research. Although the limitations of qualitative methodologies must be acknowledged, little empirical work has examined the relative advantages and disadvantages of collecting qualitative data from ethnic minorities. Brink (1994) argued that purely quantitative measurement methodologies used to assess ethnic minority populations (e.g., elderly Hispanics) are insufficiently sensitive to cultural factors and recommended integrating psychometric data with qualitative methodologies (e.g., in-depth interviews and life histories).

Finally, some have argued that cross-cultural (and by extension, ethnic minority) research may have prematurely dismissed the usefulness of projective measures of assessment because of the assumption that such instruments are too rooted in Western culture (Draguns, 1990). The problem here is the lack of empirical evidence to argue for or against the notion that ambiguous stimuli used in projective tests are less culturally bound but that clinical interpretations are more prone to bias by the interpreter's cultural background. Research on the use of projective tests with Asian Americans is notably absent (Okazaki and Sue, 1995), but a body of research exists on the use of the Rorschach and picture-story tests (e.g., the Thematic Apperception Test) with African Americans, Latinos, and several American Indian tribes (see Gray-Little, 1995; Rogler, Malgady, and Rodriguez, 1989; Velasquez, 1995). Increased attention in ethnic minority assessment research to various methods of assessment is consistent with recommendations made by cross-cultural methodologists to use multiple assessment measures to establish convergent validity of cultural constructs.

Interpretation of Data

A common problem in conducting ethnic comparison research is that differences tend to be evaluated in disfavor of ethnic minorities. For example, Rogler, Malgady, and Rodriguez (1989) argued that ethnic differences on personality measures are often interpreted negatively from the Western perspective. In the case of Latinos, their scores on personality measures are often interpreted as indicating low verbal fluency, less emotional responsiveness, and more pathology, all of which are considered as undesirable characteristics in American society. However, the same scores may be interpreted as reflecting appropriate restraint and respect for authority. In a study comparing clinical evaluations by Chinese American and White therapists of the same clients (either Chinese American or White), therapists' ratings of client functioning have been found to vary as a function of the interaction of therapist and client ethnicity (Li-Repac, 1980), which suggests interpretive bias. At the same time, one must also be aware of the danger of underestimating pathology for culturally different clients through overattribution of bizarre behavior or thought patterns to that person's culture (Lopez, 1989). It is essential to be aware of possible cultural bias, either in overpathologizing or underpathologizing ethnic minorities when interpreting ethnic differences on assessment measures.

GUIDELINES

Based on the various methodological issues we have raised with respect to assessment research with ethnic minorities, we summarize several guidelines for considering ethnicity and related variables below:

1. Assumptions underlying the use of ethnicity should be made explicit. A researcher must ask, Is the research concerned with ethnicity as a demographic variable, or is it being used as a proxy for a psychological construct hypothesized to covary with ethnicity?
2. Research reports should contain more elaborated, fuller discussions of the sample and the sampling methodology used. That is, rather than merely indicating the number of African Americans, Asian Americans, Latinos, and American Indians included in the sample, details should be made explicit on variables such as generational status, acculturation, self-identification, ethnic and cultural composition of the neighborhoods or communities, and so forth. Such discussions will help promote better communication among researchers and focus future research efforts by identifying what we know about whom.
3. Given inherent problems with small sample size in ethnic minority research, we suggest the following strategies to maximize the significance of each study: (a) For studies examining ethnic differences on various assessment instruments, enough details regarding the sampling methodology, data analyses, and statistical findings should be reported to allow meta-analyses and cross-study comparisons and (b) individual studies with small samples of ethnic minorities should test specific cultural hypotheses that may contribute to ethnic variance on assessment processes or instruments, with increased attention on whether statistically significant ethnic differences are also clinically significant (see Timbrook and Graham, 1994, for an example of this approach).
4. Individual studies should consider using multiple measures and multiple methods of assessments. Given that many assessment tools and instruments have not been widely used or cross-culturally validated with ethnic minority groups, it is advisable to use several different measures in order to test convergent validity. To the extent that results converge, there is incremental validity.
5. Expert cultural or ethnic consultants should be involved in evaluating the translation and conceptual equivalence of the measures prior to data collection or in interpreting the results of studies. These consultants can often provide the cultural context for anticipating and interpreting the responses of ethnic minorities.
6. Findings from assessment tools pertinent to ethnic and cultural variables should generate hypotheses for further testing or confirmation rather than routine assumptions that the findings are valid.

CONCLUSION

Little attention in the past has been paid to the relevance of ethnicity and cultural issues in psychological research. Graham (1992) recently conducted a content analysis of empirical articles concerned with African Americans that were published in six top psychology journals between 1970 and 1989. The results, which indicated a decline in the amount of African American research over the years and a relative lack of methodological rigor of existing research, were a sobering indictment of the scientific psychological community's level of sophistication in examining ethnic and cultural factors. Lack of research, training, or both in cross-cultural assessment often leads to misdiagnosis, overestimation, underestimation, or neglect of psychopathology, which in turn has grave consequences, such as treatment failure, at individual levels (Westermeyer, 1987).

However, assessment research with ethnic minorities should not be encouraged merely because of a potential for negative consequences in neglecting ethnic minorities. As noted by proponents of cross-cultural psychology and science (Triandis and Brislin, 1984). For one, the inclusion of ethnicity and culture-related variables increases the range of human behavior variables to explore and understand. For instance, an examination of the collectivism-individualism dimension of interpersonal orientation within the middle-class White American college student population will yield a fairly narrow and skewed range. By including ethnic minorities and individuals from other cultures, the full range of this construct as well as its relationship to other personality and clinical variables can be fruitfully examined. Another advantage to including ethnic and cultural variables in research is that it provides a better test of theories. Establishing the generalizability or limitations of personality theories and of assessment tools through systematic testing with a broad range of individuals benefits the field (Ben-Porath, 1990). And lastly, the American Psychological Association (APA) Board of Ethnic Minority Affairs in 1991 developed a set of guidelines for providers of psychological services to ethnically, linguistically, and culturally diverse populations (APA, 1993), which parallels the APA Ethical Standards guidelines. It is clearly stated in this guideline (APA, 1993, p. 46) that:

> Psychologists consider the validity of a given instrument or procedure and interpret resulting data, keeping in mind the cultural and linguistic characteristics of the person being assessed. Psychologists are aware of the test's reference population and possible limitations of such instruments with other populations.

Hence, it is crucial that research on the validity of various assessment tools and procedures for ethnic minority population continue to add to the necessary database in order for the psychological community to responsibly carry out these guidelines.

There are many methodological challenges to conducting assessment research with ethnic minorities, but this is not a cause for throwing out the baby with the bath water. By making explicit the assumptions underlying the use of ethnicity as a predictor variable, the collective scientific community will begin to differentiate between racial stereotypes and legitimate uses of ethnic or cultural generalizations.

BIBLIOGRAPHY

Author note: This article is supported by National Institute of Mental Health Grant RO1 MH44331.

American Psychological Association. (1993). Guidelines for providers of psychological services to ethnic, linguistic, and culturally diverse populations. *American Psychologist*, 48, 45–48.

Azibo, D. A. (1988). Understanding the proper and improper usage of the comparative research framework. *Journal of Black Psychology*, 15, 81–91.

Bahrick, H. P., Hall, L. K., Goggin, J. P., Bahrick, L. E., and Berger, S. A. (1994). Fifty years of language maintenance and language dominance in bilingual Hispanic immigrants. *Journal of Experimental Psychology: General*, 123, 264–283.

Ben-Porath, Y. S (1990). Cross-cultural assessment of personality: The case for replicatory factor analysis. In J. N. Butcher and C. D. Spielberger (Eds.), *Advances in Personality Assessment* (Vol. 8, pp. 27–48). Hillsdale, NJ: Erlbaum.

Betancourt, H., and Lopez, S. R. (1993). The study of culture, ethnicity, and race in American psychology. *American Psychologist*, 48, 629–637.

Brink, T. L. (1994). The need for qualitative research on mental health elderly Hispanics. *International Journal of Aging and Human Development*, 88, 38, 279–291.

Brislin, R. W. (1993). *Understanding culture's influence on behavior*. New York: Harcourt Brace Jovanovich.

Bureau of Indian Affairs. (1991). *American Indians today* (3rd ed.). Washington, DC: U.S. Department of the Interior.

Campbell, D. T. (1967). Stereotypes and the perception of group differences. *American Psychologist*, 22, 817–829.

Cervantes, R. C., and Castro, F. G. (1985). Stress, coping, and Mexican American mental health: A systematic review. *Hispanic Journal of Behavioral Sciences*, 7, 1–73.

Clark, L. A. (1987). Mutual relevance of mainstream and cross-cultural psychology. *Journal of Consulting and Clinical Psychology*, 55, 461–470.

Dahlstrom, W. G. (1986). Ethnic status and personality measurement. In W. G. Dahlstrom, D. Lacher, and L. E. Dahlstrom, *MMPI patterns of American minorities* (pp. 3–23). Minneapolis: University of Minnesota Press.

Dion, K. L., and Giordano, C. (1990). Ethnicity and sex as correlates of depression symptoms in a Canadian university sample. *International Journal of Social Psychiatry*, 36, 30–41.

Dion, K. L., and Toner, B. B. (1988). Ethnic differences in test anxiety. *Journal of Social Psychology*, 128, 165–172.

Draguns, J. G. (1990). Applications of cross-cultural psychology in the field of mental health. In R. W. Brislin (Ed.), *Applied cross-cultural psychology*. (pp. 302–324). Newbury Park, CA: Sage.

Eaton, W. W. (1980). *The sociology of mental illness*. New York: Praeger.

Geisinger, K. F. (1994). Cross-cultural normative assessment: Translation and adaptation issues influencing the normative interpretation of assessment instruments. *Psychological Assessment*, 6, 304–312.

Graham, S. (1992). "Most of the subjects were White and middle class": Trends in published research on African Americans in selected APA journals, 1970–1989. *American Psychologist*, 47, 629–639.

Gray-Little, B. (1995). The assessment of psychopathology in racial and ethnic minorities. In J. N. Butcher (Ed.), *Clinical personality assessment: Practical approaches* (pp. 40–157). New York: Oxford Press.

Hall, C. C. I. (1992). Please choose one: Ethnic identity choices for biracial individuals. In M. P. P. Root (Ed.), *Racially mixed people in America* (pp. 250–264). Newbury Park, CA: Sage.

Helms, J. E. (1992). Why is there no study of cultural equivalence in standardized cognitive ability testing? *American Psychologist*, 47, 1083–1101.

Kessler, R. C., and Neighbors, H. W. (1986). A new perspective on the relationships among race, social class and psychological distress. *Journal of Health and Social Behavior*, 27, 107–115.

Korchin, S. J. (1980). Clinical psychology and minority problems. *American Psychologist*, 35, 262–269.

LaFromboise, T. D. (1988). American Indian mental health policy. *American Psychologist*, 43, 388–397.

Leong, F.T.L. (1986). Counseling and psychotherapy with Asian-Americans: Review of the literature. *Journal of Counseling Psychology*, 33, 196–206.

Li-Repac, D. (1980). Cultural influences on clinical perception: A comparison between Caucasian and Chinese-American therapists. *Journal of Cross-Cultural Psychology*, 11, 327–342.

Lopez, S. R. (1989). Patient variable biases in clinical judgment: Conceptual overview and methodological considerations. *Psychological Bulletin*, 106, 184–204.

Lopez, S., and Romero, A. (1988). Assessing the intellectual functioning of Spanish-speaking adults: Comparison of the EIWA and the WAIS. *Professional Psychology: Research and Practice*, 19, 263–270.

Okazaki, S., and Sue, S. (1995). Cultural considerations in psychological assessment of Asian Americans. In J. N. Butcher (Ed.), *Clinical personality assessment: Practical approaches* (pp. 107–119). New York: Oxford Press.

Rogler, L. H., Malgady, R. G., and Rodriguez, O. (1989). *Hispanics and mental health: A framework for research*. Malabalar, FL: Krieger.

Root, M.P.P. (1992). Back to the drawing board: Methodological issues in research on multiracial people. In M. P. P. Root (Ed.), *Racially mixed people in America* (pp. 181–189). Newbury Park, CA: Sage.

Sasao, T. (1992). *Correlates of substance use and problem behaviors in multiethnic high school settings*. Unpublished manuscript, University of California, Los Angeles.

Sasao, T., and Sue, S. (1993). Toward a culturally anchored ecological framework of research in ethnic-cultural communities. *American Journal of Community Psychology*, 21, 705–727.

Sears, D. O. (1985). College sophomores in the laboratory: Influences of a narrow data base on psychology's view of human nature. *Journal of Personality and Social Psychology*, 51, 515–530.

Sue, S., Fujino, D. C., Hu, L., Takeuchi, D., and Zane, N.W.S. (1991). Community mental health services for ethnic minority groups: A test of cultural responsive hypothesis. *Journal of Consulting and Clinical Psychology*, 59, 533–540.

Tefft, S. K. (1967). Anomie, values, and culture change among teen-age Indians: An exploratory study. *Sociology of Education*, 40, 145–157.

Timbrook, R. E., and Graham, J. R. (1994). Ethnic differences on the MMPI-2? *Psychological Assessment*, 6, 212–217.

Triandis, H. C., and Brislin, R. W. (1984). Cross-cultural psychology. *American Psychologist*, 39, 1006–1016.

Uba, L. (1994). *Asian Americans: Personality patterns, identity, and mental health*. New York: Guilford.

U.S. Bureau of the Census. (1991). Race and Hispanic origin. *1990 Census Profile (No. 2)*. Washington, DC: U.S. Department of Commerce.

Velasquez, R. J. (1995). Personality assessment of Hispanic clients. In J. N. Butcher (Ed.), *Clinical personality assessment: Practical approaches* (pp. 120–139). New York: Oxford Press.

Westermeyer, J. (1987). Cultural factors in clinical assessment. *Journal of Consulting and Clinical Psychology*, 55, 471–478.

Yee, A. H., Fairchild, H. H., Weizmann, F., and Wyatt, G. E. (1993). Addressing psychology's problems with race. *American Psychologist*, 48, 1132–1140.

Ying, Y. (1989). Nonresponse on the Center for Epidemiological Studies-Depression scale in Chinese Americans. *International Journal of Social Psychiatry*, 35, 156–163.

Zuckerman, M. (1990). Some dubious premises in research and theory on racial differences: Scientific, social, and ethical issues. *American Psychologist*, 45, 1297–1303.

PART II.

Psychology and Ethnicity

Basic Questions

As psychologists struggle to meet the challenge of constructing methodologically sound studies, so must we begin the quest to define pertinent constructs and respond to critical questions that clarify the nature and extent of influence of culture on behavior. The next two selections concern basic yet essential issues that set the foundation of ethnic psychology. In the first selection, The National Advisory Mental Heath Council surveys the literature on the influence of culture on a broad number of constructs such as motivation, emotion, and coping as well as reviews the role that culture plays within social environments.

Understanding the significance of the impact of ethnicity requires that we address related yet poorly understood concepts. Hotly debated questions in ethnic research have often centered on the issues of race. For example, "What is race?" and "Does race matter?" Marvin Zuckerman questions the scientific accuracy and premises that surround the definition of race as a biological construct and, particularly, the interpretation of research findings that indicate so-called racial differences. Indeed, he offers intriguing data that suggest that among several psychological dimensions intergroup racial differences are minimal compared to intragroup variation.

FURTHER READINGS

Burnett, M. N., and Sisson, K. (1995). Doll studies revisited: A question of validity. *Journal of Black Psychology, 21,* 19–29.

Marger, M. N. (1997). *Race and ethnic relations: American and global perspectives* (4th ed.). Belmont, CA: Wadsworth Publishing Company.

Markus, H. R., and Kitayama, S. (1991). Culture and the self: Implications for cognition, emotion, and motivation. *Psychological Review, 98,* 224–253.

Triandis, H. (1989). The self and social behavior in differing cultural contexts. *Psychological Review, 96,* 506–520.

UNESCO International Scholars. (1993). III. Proposals on the biological aspects of race. In D. Gioseffi (Ed.), *On Prejudice* (pp. 621–626). New York: Anchor Books. (Original work published 1964).

3.
Basic Behavioral Science Research for Mental Health
Sociocultural and Environmental Processes
Basic Behavioral Science Task Force of the National Advisory Mental Health Council

Social, cultural, and environmental forces shape who we are and how well we function in the everyday world. The culture we belong to, the neighborhood we live in, the demographic composition of our community, and the opportunities and frustrations of our work environment all profoundly affect our mental health. Other powerful factors include whether we are rich or poor, native born Americans or immigrants or refugees, and residents of a city or a rural area. Together, these contextual factors, interacting with our individual biological and psychological characteristics, color our experience, limit or enhance our options, and even affect our conceptions of mental illness and mental health.

Does poverty cause mental disorders or do those disorders cause some people to drift into poverty? What allows some neighborhoods to band together against drug pushers and violence while others do not? How do immigrant children adapt to public schools? What kinds of school and work environments encourage good relations among various ethnic populations? What community resources promote positive mental health in workers who recently lost their jobs? Answering these questions requires understanding our sociocultural world and the social trends and issues that reflect its complex dynamics. These issues include the growing disparity between the resources of the rich and the poor, the effects of the changing racial and ethnic composition of the United States on such social institutions as schools, and the increasing diversity of family structures related to such factors as the increase of women in the workforce and patterns of immigration.

Basic sociocultural research can help us solve many pressing public health and social welfare problems. Knowing how social processes influence attitudes and behaviors in different cultural groups can strengthen efforts to prevent AIDS and substance abuse. Discovering whether existing research findings on the parent-child-school relationship are relevant to homeless parents and children can help us respond better to their social and educational needs. Understanding the family dynamics of child rearing under varied nontraditional circumstances may aid in designing intervention programs for teenage mothers and their children.

The increasing multiculturalism of our nation represents both a challenge and an opportunity for behavioral science to expand its knowledge base. Such knowledge will be enhanced if researchers embrace a wide range of methods, including ethnographic approaches as well as the more typically used quantitative methods.

This chapter provides a selective overview of accomplishments in this research area as well as promising directions for the future. We begin with a fundamental issue: how culture influences the course of mental illness.

THE COURSE OF MENTAL ILLNESSES: THE ROLE OF CULTURE

In 1979, the World Health Organization (WHO) published the results of its nine-country study indicating that people with a diagnosis of schizophrenia fare far better in developing countries than they do in North America and Europe. For example, 58% of the patients in Nigeria and 51% of those in India were reported as being in full remission two years after their first treated episode of schizophrenia. In Denmark, by contrast, only 6% were reportedly in full remission at two-year follow-up. Recently, a more rigorous study by WHO has supported the earlier finding of a better outcome among patients in developing countries.

It has long been thought that major mental illness is almost inevitably chronic and incurable. Research now shows that schizophrenia and many other severe forms of mental illness (such as manic depressive illness and depression) have extremely diverse courses, ranging from complete recovery through patterns of waxing and waning, to nearly complete disability. Basic research is now exploring how social and cultural factors amplify or attenuate symptoms and disability. Several lines of study provide important clues.

Anthropological and cross-cultural studies show that cultural beliefs about the nature of mental illness influence the community's view of its course and treatment. These views may affect, in turn, the actual duration of the illness. Mexican Americans in the Los Angeles area tend to view people with symptoms of schizophrenia as vulnerable and ill, but they explain those symptoms as resulting from "nerves" and from being "sensitive" and assume that recovery is possible. In contrast, Anglo Americans in the same area are more likely to categorize the same people as "crazy," with little or no hope of recovery.

Another line of study shows that diagnoses of mental illness differ across cultures and subcultures. For example, among psychiatric inpatients in the United States, African Americans are more likely than White Americans to be diagnosed with schizophrenia and less likely to be diagnosed with affective disorder. Research has yet to disentangle the myriad possible factors, such as socioeconomic status (SES) and hospitalization, that may help to explain such differences, but several studies provide evidence of the role of culture in the accuracy of psychiatric diagnosis and assessment.

Research has revealed differences in how individuals in different cultures experience and express symptoms of mental illness. Since most psychiatric diagnosis is based on symptoms, those symptoms that are unique to certain cultures or subcultures (e.g., believing in devils, hearing voices of the dead, or describing physical sensations in vivid metaphors not used in English) may lead clinicians to misunderstand and misdiagnose individuals from cultures different from their own.

Culturally based variations in diagnosis also occur because current diagnostic categories are derived largely from research among majority populations, particularly those in hospitals or specialty psychiatric clinics. Such studies tend to support the impression that the observed expressions of illness are universal. Cross-cultural research seriously challenges this assumption. Several generations of research make it quite clear that however universal broad categories of mental illness may be, the patterns of onset and duration—and even the nature and clustering of specific symptoms—vary widely across cultures.

These findings have many practical as well as theoretical implications. For example, at present, the vast majority of medically trained clinicians in our health care system come from the White majority, while a sizable proportion of their clients—especially in public facilities—are members of ethnic minorities. In addition to attempting to increase ethnic minority participation in the health professions, we also need to use the insights of research on cultural differences to aid today's health care workers in recognizing and responding to the special perspectives of ethnic minorities.

SOCIOCULTURAL VARIATION IN BASIC PSYCHOLOGICAL PROCESSES

Members of subcultures, cultures, and societies often share particular historical traditions, challenges, opportunities, and stresses that provide a common core of experience. These experiences create a distinctive context that influences how basic psychological processes are expressed within a given culture. By comparing attitudes and behavior across cultural and subcultural groups, researchers can clarify how diverse social experiences and conditions influence individual functioning and wellbeing. Such "natural experiments" are uniquely able to demonstrate the power of the social context to affect psychological strength and vulnerability.

Culture and the Self

The sense of self is fundamental to individual identity. Increasing numbers of research studies are demonstrating that cultural experience plays a vital role in shaping this sense. One group of studies has shown that many cultures, especially Asian, stress the fundamental connectedness or interdependence of members; the self is defined in relation to others, especially one's family. This interdependent view also is characteristic of many cultures in Africa, Latin America, and southern Europe. By contrast, in North American middle-class cultures, the self is defined primarily by internal attributes, reflecting a view of the self as independent.

These diverse ways of grounding individual identity are influenced by social and cultural differences in such areas as child rearing, family life, and the organization of schools. For example, studies show that in Japan and China, people tend to describe themselves in relation to their group affiliations (e.g., families, companies), while Americans usually describe themselves in abstract individual characteristics, such as hard-working or self-confident.

These distinctions operate not only for geographically and traditionally segregated groups (e.g., nations, East versus West), but also for subgroups defined by gender and ethnicity who have developed their own patterns of social beliefs and practices. For example, even within the independent culture of the United States, researchers find that ethnic minorities and women are more likely to define themselves in interdependent terms than are men or members of the White majority.

Cultural Influences on Psychological Experience

The false uniqueness effect. Cultural influences have been found to affect aspects of psychological experience in unexpected ways. For example, many years ago a research program focused on a presumably basic phenomenon, the *false uniqueness effect*—a tendency to underestimate the extent to which others also possess one's desirable traits. As early as four years of age, American children think they are better than most others, while American adults typically believe they are more intelligent and attractive than average. In addition, a national survey of American students showed that 70% thought they were above average in their ability to lead; none thought they were below average in their ability to get along with others, and 60% thought they were in the top 10%.

Cross-cultural research has revealed significant gender and cultural variation in the strength of this effect. It is stronger, for example, in men than in women in North America and is very low for both men and women in Japan, Korea, and Thailand. In our culture, the effect appears to be one way of enhancing self-esteem, a quality closely related to mental health. Among cultures that stress interdependent concepts of self, self-esteem (and, therefore, mental health) is based much more strongly on satisfactory relationships with others. These findings suggest that our theories of self-esteem and ways to enhance it need to be approached from a sociocultural perspective, especially with regard to women and people from different cultures.

The fundamental attribution error. Culture plays a role in how we view other people and explain their actions. Research has shown that in cultures that stress an independent concept of self, people often infer that other people's behavior stemmed from their internal attributes (such as personality, attitudes, and abilities) even when obvious situational factors may have played a role in their actions.

This tendency is called the *fundamental attribution error.* However, it may not be as fundamental as once thought. Cross-cultural research has shown that in cultures that stress interdependence, people tend to explain others' actions in terms of situational factors rather than internal or personal factors. Hindu Indians, for example, explain social events primarily in terms of a person's social roles and obligations rather than in terms of that individual's personality. Similarly, Japanese people are less willing than Americans to draw inferences about people's attitudes from their behavior. Furthermore, Asians tend to be unwilling to infer people's emotional states from their facial expressions, although Americans readily do so.

Culture and Emotion

In 1872, Charles Darwin published "The Expression of Emotion in Man and Animals," in which he proposed that some emotional expressions, such as smiles, frowns, and looks of disgust, are innate and universal. He saw these facial expressions of emotion in every culture studied and concluded that such emotions, and the way they are expressed, must be part of our biological heritage.

Subsequent research has shown that there are, indeed, many similarities across cultures in facial expressions of emotion. However, cross-cultural psychologists are finding that how we experience emotions may vary from culture to culture. When researchers asked people in North America to pose several positive and negative emotional expressions, such as smiles and frowns, they found that such expressions caused changes in people's feelings and in the responses of their autonomic nervous systems. Smiles resulted in positive feelings, and frowns or expressions mimicking negative emotions caused negative feelings.

When people in a non-Western culture (the Minangkabau of Sumatra) posed various emotional expressions, their autonomic responses were very similar to the North Americans'. This finding suggests that the physiological and neurochemical networks connecting sensory signals from the face to the autonomic nervous system are largely unaffected by cultural differences. However, at the subjective level, a striking cross-cultural difference was observed. Unlike the Americans, the Minangkabau who posed various expressions did not report any corresponding changes in their subjective feelings.

This difference may reflect the fact that people from many cultures tend to interpret certain bodily changes with somatic explanations, such as fatigue, muscle tension, and headache, whereas Westerners tend to focus more on psychological states. These different explanatory styles predispose people to perceive and communicate certain classes of bodily sensations while ignoring or deemphasizing others. This interpretation is consistent with well-documented cross-cultural differences in the experience and communication of symptoms of depression.

Culture and Motivation

Classic research on achievement motivation has shown that, in Western cultures, the desire for excellence is linked closely with seeking and actively striving for individual success. However, this finding has subsequently been shown to be more applicable to men than to women, whose concerns also involve connectedness with others.

Excellence may also be defined in terms of broad social goals and group success, as often occurs among Asians. Research in China, for example, has shown that those individuals who are most motivated to excel take most seriously their duties and obligations to family members, especially parents.

Because achievement motivation is important to mental well-being as well as success in school and other life endeavors, researchers are now studying sociocultural factors that influence such motivation. Recent cross-cultural studies on school achievement, for example, have raised important questions about the effect of cultural factors. In a comparison of the mathematics achievement of students in the United States, Japan, and Taiwan, the U.S. students consistently performed least well. This "achievement gap" appeared as early as first grade, increased dramatically by fifth grade, and was maintained at eleventh grade.

Other studies have shown that this effect, which cannot be attributed to differences in intelligence, reflects the impact of diverse factors, including how parents and students in U.S. and Asian families explain success and failure. Chinese and Japanese fifth graders and their mothers stress the importance of hard work as the route to success: American mothers, however, give greater emphasis to the importance of a child's "natural" ability. This study suggests that Asian parents and children view working hard and persisting in mathematics as simply a requirement for achievement, while Americans regard the need to try harder as evidence of low innate ability and are less likely to value or encourage such effort.

Findings such as these emphasize the importance of understanding the role of cultural factors in other aspects of motivation as well. For example, models of rational choice and decision making have been highly influential in social and behavioral science in the

United States. However, their relevance, nature, and operation need to be validated in other sociocultural settings.

RACE AND ETHNICITY IN A MULTICULTURAL SOCIETY

Recent projections indicate that people of color—African Americans, Hispanic or Latino Americans, Asian Americans, and Native Americans—who constitute 18% of the U.S. population now, will account for 47% by the year 2050. Our country's racial and ethnic diversity is being increased yearly by immigrants and refugees from many parts of the world. These demographic changes raise many basic research questions with mental health implications: What are the dynamics of conflict between indigenous and immigrant populations? What are the mechanisms that affect immigrant children's acculturation? How does the workplace influence and respond to cultural and ethnic diversity?

As cultural diversity steadily increases in the United States, our scientific understanding of social and psychological functioning and mental health must be based on knowledge of these varied populations and their relations with each other. It is especially important to understand how belonging to an economically disadvantaged racial, ethnic, or cultural group can harm or help mental health and psychological functioning.

During the 1970s and 1980s, some observers suggested that race and ethnicity were of declining significance and hence worthy of "benign neglect." Changes in demographics as well as recent research findings strongly challenge that attitude. Race and ethnicity continue to be major risk factors for mental and physical illness and for psychosocial dysfunctions. For example, in 1988, the death rate among African Americans between ages 25 and 44 was more than double that of White Americans. African Americans and Hispanic Americans are at higher risk for many mental disorders. Some of this increased risk is due to the lower average SES of most racial and ethnic minorities and their concentration in more hazardous urban environments. However, race and ethnicity have health consequences not simply accounted for by SES and place of residence.

Discrimination and Mental Health

Many people assume that changing attitudes, laws, and policies in the public and private sectors have largely eliminated racism and discrimination (and even created reverse discrimination). Recent research indicates, however, that racial and ethnic discrimination continues to be a daily fact of life for many people, leading to increased stress and its psychological consequences.

Discrimination is found, for example, in employment and housing practices, as revealed by a study conducted in Washington, DC, and Chicago. In this research, both Black and White applicants were sent to seek employment after having been matched as carefully as possible on all attributes that could affect a hiring decision (e.g., age, physical size, education, experience, and other "human capital" characteristics as well as intangibles such as openness, apparent energy level, and articulateness). Differential treatment in job offers occurred 20% of the time, with the White applicant three times more likely to be favored. A similar study conducted with Hispanic and Anglo applicants in Chicago and San Diego found differential treatment 30% of the time, with the Anglo applicant 2.7 times more likely to be favored.

Other studies document continuing discrimination in housing and suggest that almost all racial and ethnic minorities, including middle-class suburban residents, experience discrimination. Its forms include avoidance and rejection by strangers, suspicion and poor service in public accommodations, verbal epithets, and police harassment.

Coping with such discrimination can result in chronic levels of stress that have physical and mental health consequences. This discrimination-related stress is exacerbated, researchers have discovered, by empathizing with the discriminatory acts experienced by other members of their group. In one study, for example, researchers found elevations in blood pressure among Black subjects when viewing videotaped vignettes of discriminatory acts toward Blacks, such as poor service, verbal abuse, and police threats.

In addition to increasing stress, the experience and anticipation of discrimination may also disrupt social interaction and behavior in ways that can undermine mental health treatment. For example, a distrust of Whites may lead some racial and ethnic minority group members to have diminished confidence in White therapists' ability to address their needs in counseling.

Pervasive direct and indirect experiences of discrimination and stigmatization place an individual's sense of identity under constant attack. One new line of research indicates that, in anticipation of academic stigmatization in college, some African American students devalue and "disidentify" with academic activities. This reaction has both negative and positive effects: It harms school grades, but it preserves self-esteem.

An intervention to address disidentification has shown that a program of academic support and intergroup relationships can improve academic performance while maintaining a strong sense of self. Understanding the psychological processes that mediate and sustain such self-protective behaviors among people victimized by prejudice and discrimination in our society needs to be a high research priority.

Acculturation, Diversity, and Adaptive Coping

As the United States becomes more culturally diverse, many members of racial, cultural, and ethnic minority groups are attempting to cope with the conflicts created by their *marginality*—the experience of living simultaneously within more than one cultural context. The concept of acculturation has historically been applied only to immigrant groups, but it is also relevant in understanding the experience of indigenous minority groups coping with a mainstream majority culture that has different values and practices discrimination and stigmatization.

Researchers studying this bicultural adaptation process describe several alternative strategies used by members of the nondominant culture in coming to terms with marginalization and stigmatization. These strategies include *assimilation* (being absorbed into the dominant cultural group), *acculturation* (acquiring the salient elements of the dominant culture), *alternation* or *biculturalism* (becoming proficient in two cultural systems and switching between them as the situation requires), and *multiculturalism* (maintaining a separate cultural identity while working in collaboration with other groups to achieve mutual goals).

The processes involved in working out these varied accommodations have important implications for mental health and well-being. For example, these coping strategies often put the individual's own culture in a subordinate position. This dilemma presents challenges and conflicts that can increase stress and mental discomfort. A key research task is to understand better how these conflicts are formed, which strategies are most effective in coping with them, and what possibilities exist for reducing their negative health and mental health consequences.

Some research has shown positive effects of biculturalism on the adjustment of Hispanic youth. One study showed that having the ability to develop social skills characteristic of both Hispanic and Anglo cultural contexts lessened youths' chances of experiencing family or school conflict or of becoming involved in illegal drug use. This finding was especially true for youths whose parents were also bicultural.

While on practical grounds, immigrants need to acquire skills in their new cultural context, on psychological grounds they often need to remain rooted in their own culture. A study of Southeast Asian refugees assessed the mental health of immigrants who came to the United States with other family members, or who came to cities with a sizable population of individuals from the home culture. After one year in the United States, these refugees were less depressed than were others who had emigrated alone or who lacked ties with people from the home culture.

Studies have shown that variations in age, gender, family structure, SES, and country of origin are but a few of the factors influencing how and how well people cope with the task of belonging and adapting to a multicultural environment. Within any population of individuals experiencing similar stressful circumstances, some will be more "environment resistant" than others.

Recent studies on racial and ethnic minorities and refugees have begun to illuminate the environmental sources of strength, resilience, and hardiness that some people show in the face of adversity. As an example, analyses of the NIMH-funded National Survey of Black Americans indicated that diverse supportive influences aid the general coping, adaptation, and mental health of many African Americans. These sources of support range from informal social networks and extended families to such community resources as ministers and religious groups.

Ethnic Relations

The intensification of interracial conflict between minority and majority groups born in the United States, as well as additional tensions between native-born Americans and immigrant groups, has once again placed issues of ethnic conflict in the forefront of our national consciousness. Do such conflicts stem from competition for scarce resources or differences in cultural values and beliefs? Do they reflect genuinely different cultural perspectives brought by divergent groups to the same interaction? Answering these questions requires understanding the ethnic identities involved and the stereotypical thinking that influences the groups' interpretations of one another's intentions and behavior. We also need to understand how social institutions set the conditions for intergroup conflict or cooperation.

A consistent finding from social psychology research is that biases operating between groups are more strongly influenced by preferences toward their own members (in-group bias) than by negative feelings toward members of other groups. But when—as a response to bias, discrimination, and stigmatization—members of ethnic groups increasingly interact only with members of their own group, that interaction ultimately heightens their negative feelings toward out-group members. How can the tension be resolved between

the feeling of belonging and protection provided by in-group identification and the resulting estrangement with out-group members?

One promising line of research suggests that it may be possible to capitalize on in-group
bias by creating a new, superordinate group with which members of different groups can
identify. Merging two groups reduces favoritism toward former in-group members,
increases liking for former out-group members, and heightens feelings of oneness in the
new group situation. Field experiments reveal that these positive effects occur whether
dealing with ethnic differences in high school or with newly merged corporate employ-
ees from diverse parts of the country.

SOCIOECONOMIC STATUS AND MENTAL HEALTH

"The pauper class furnishes, in ratio of its number, sixty-four times as many cases of insanity
as the independent class." That was the finding of one of the first epidemiologic studies in
the United States, which was carried out in mid-nineteenth-century Massachusetts. Despite dramatic changes in our notions of mental disorder and social stratification, the fundamental relationship between mental illness and SES in the United States was reaffirmed
in 1990 in an epidemiological survey based on a standardized psychiatric diagnostic system.

For the American population, the highest rates of diagnosable mental disorder were
found among the groups with the lowest SES—usually defined in terms of education,
income, or occupation. For example, people with less than a high school education or
$20,000 annual income experienced three or more psychiatric disorders in the past year at
almost four times the rate found among those with a college education or annual income
of $70,000 or more.

Mental health differences related to age, race, or sex appear modest in comparison with
these socioeconomic differences. To some extent, these differences may reflect the fact that
having a mental disorder can cause people to drift into poverty. However, recently
improved methods of research design and data analysis have shown that these differences
also reflect a reverse effect—the powerful influence of poverty on mental disorder.

For example, recent research on schizophrenia suggests that while poverty does not
cause the disorder, it is powerfully related to the experience of those suffering from it, their
resources for coping with it, and perhaps their likelihood of recovery. However socioeconomic or other psychosocial deprivations and stresses do seem to play a causal role in
both the onset and course of depressive, substance abuse, and antisocial disorders. Further,
researchers now know that virtually all major psychosocial risk factors for mental illness
(including chronic and acute stress, lack of social relationships and supports, and lack of
control and mastery) are more prevalent at lower socioeconomic levels. Alleviating acute
socioeconomic deprivation can often lessen the more serious long-term psychological
consequences of these disorders.

SES and Mental Health Across the Life Span

The long-term behavioral and emotional effects of socioeconomic disadvantage during
childhood can be particularly severe. Recent research shows that, during childhood, low
SES is one of many environmental factors, including poor parental mental health and
deprived family and community environments, that can contribute to later delinquency,
school dropout, premarital childbearing, and poor parenting. Studies in the United

Kingdom and the United States indicate, however, that positive family relationships and child rearing practices, or preschool support programs for children and families, can markedly reduce or eliminate these later adverse effects.

Other factors have been shown to lessen the negative impact of socioeconomic disadvantage on adults. Recent research on the long-term mental health impact of the Great Depression has shown that economic hardship during the 1930s was, on average, more deleterious for men's later mental health than for women's, especially if the hardship was sustained or if the men showed signs of emotional instability prior to the Depression or lacked supportive spouses.

Interestingly, the Depression actually enhanced the later resilience and competence of some women—those who entered the 1930s in good health, were gainfully employed during that decade, and had supportive marriages. Such a finding supports the need for more in-depth research on factors related to hardship experiences that can actually provide mental health *benefits* to some individuals in some circumstances.

Taken together, these studies indicate that many social and personal characteristics and resources may exacerbate or buffer the impacts of stress and other health hazards related to SES. Most prominent among these are social relationships and supports as well as personal control, mastery, or self-efficacy in life and work. Understanding these processes in a larger sociocultural context may suggest important new ways to weaken the link between low SES and psychological distress and disorder.

SES, the Family, and Work

Low SES often affects mental health through its impact on the family. Economic problems can severely disrupt skillful parenting and family interactions, with adverse long-term mental health implications for children. A striking finding from recent research is that mothers faced with chronic financial problems interact with their children in a more rejecting and inconsistent way (either harshly punitive or indifferent about the same behavior) than do mothers not faced with these problems. The caregiving behavior of the financially strained mothers resembles that of mothers with clinical depression. Discovering how these findings apply to both single- and two-parent families across varied cultural, ethnic, and racial groups represents an important future research direction.

Insecurity about job stability, increases in overtime, and disruptions in child-care arrangements can also have negative effects on family life. Parents' efforts to increase income by working longer hours detract from the time, energy, and attention they have for each other and their children.

Reduced earning power is not the only economic stressor that affects family life. The nature of jobs and work environments varies with SES, and more than three decades of research suggests that the nature of one's work is critical to one's attitudes, intellectual flexibility, emotional well-being, and approaches to child rearing. People whose work is substantively complex and offers opportunities for self-direction (generally characteristic of higher SES jobs) place greater value on independence and are less concerned with conformity than are those in less demanding and less autonomous jobs. As parents, people with more complex occupations display more warmth and involvement and report using less physical punishment with their children than those in occupations offering less complexity and self-direction.

Alternatively, research has shown that work that is routine, heavily supervised, and low in complexity—generally characteristic of lower SES jobs—tends to produce a sense of hopelessness and alienation that undermines beliefs about the possibility of control in other aspects of life and causes psychological distress. When work experiences leave parents feeling devalued and emotionally distressed, they are less able to be emotionally supportive of children and to provide them with responsive stimulating environments.

These SES-related occupational conditions affect adults' mental and physical health as well as their child-rearing practices. However, this only partially accounts for the substantial differences in psychological distress and disorder across SES levels. Because many people do not work, or work only part time or part year, an equally strong research focus is needed on how and why education and economic well-being affect behavior, psychological functioning, and social conditions of life in ways that either promote or damage mental health.

CHANGING WORK ROLES AND MENTAL HEALTH

Few social changes have so altered the sociocultural landscape in recent years as the increasing number of women who have entered the workforce. Social science research over the past decade has begun to describe the impact of this major social transformation. The findings have sometimes confirmed and sometimes challenged conventional wisdom and previous scientific theories.

Many people expected that women's growing participation in the labor force would adversely affect their own well-being and that of their spouses and their children. However, research during the past decade consistently indicates that female employment per se has few negative effects—and even some beneficial ones—on women, their spouses, and their children.

One of the most consistent, and perhaps least expected, findings is that even among married women with children, employment generally has positive effects on women's psychological well-being. Married women who are employed have less depression, anxiety, and other forms of psychological distress than do married women who do not work outside the home. Although a married woman's employment has less clear benefits for her husband's well-being than for her own, it generally does not increase his distress.

Paid work benefits women and their families by decreasing economic hardship and by promoting husbands' involvement in the division of household labor, which in turn improves the women's mental health. Employed wives provide about 31% of all family income. While only about 20% of the husbands of employed women share the housework and child care equally, this figure is almost triple the proportion of husbands (7%) that do so if their wives are not employed. The more a wife earns compared to her husband, the greater is his share of the housework and child care: the more a husband shares the household work, the lower is his wife's level of depression.

Early studies had suggested that married women's employment decreased both partners' marital satisfaction. It now appears that wives' employment reduces marital satisfaction only in those traditional families in which, despite the belief by both spouses that the wife's place is in the home, she needs to work for economic reasons while retaining full responsibility for the home. The increasing diversity of family arrangements in our society needs to be taken into account as this important line of research continues.

It is now clear that the emotional well-being of working mothers depends not only on the division of labor in the home but also on the availability of child care. One study has shown that when women are primarily responsible for the care of children, have major responsibility for making day-care arrangements, but live in a community where quality care is scarce and expensive, they are likely to obtain less benefit from paid employment than would men. Another study revealed that when women and men share household labor and child care equitably, and when satisfactory, affordable child care is available, mothers who work have greater emotional well-being than mothers who do not.

The nature of women's employment affects their behavior toward their children. One study, for example, has shown that among working mothers matched for education, income, and family size, mothers whose occupations give them greater opportunity to solve problems and to address varied tasks provide more support to their children at home than do the other mothers. Such women also offer their children a greater range of stimulating materials, restrict their exploration less, and are warmer in their interactions. Conversely, mothers whose work is repetitive and routine seem less available emotionally to their children and less able to assist their development.

The increased employment of women is likely to challenge old marital roles, family commitments, and family satisfaction. When husbands had clear responsibility for providing for the family, wives usually subordinated their own job interests to those of their husbands, with little room for bargaining. As beliefs about gender roles change, husbands and wives may face greater conflict as they struggle to work out jointly satisfying occupational and family arrangements.

Ironically, women's increased access to better jobs—defined in terms of wages and occupational complexity—may increase marital conflict. Wives with good jobs may be less willing to subordinate their own preferences and forego job opportunities. Husbands with good jobs may feel entitled to claim breadwinner privileges and be less willing to jeopardize their own careers by accommodating to their wives.

One intriguing hypothesis is that, at least in the short term, occupational conditions that enhance individual well-being will challenge those aspects of the marriage involving previously established gender roles. Whether such a potential conflict will emerge and under what conditions it might become a long-range asset or liability to the marriage are important research questions.

COMMUNITIES, ORGANIZATIONS, AND MENTAL HEALTH

Just as the family provides a critical context for individual mental health and functioning, communities and organizations such as churches, schools, and neighborhood development associations strongly influence the functioning of both families and individuals. Research on communities was central to the early development of social science in the 1950s. As methods of collecting and analyzing data on populations of individuals were developed in the 1960s and 1970s, many findings suggested that characteristics of families and individuals were the primary determinant of individual functioning and mental health; community and organizational factors appeared to be less important.

Further advances in theory, methods, and research over the past decade have indicated, however, that the characteristics of neighborhoods and of educational, community, and work organizations are more influential than previously believed. Indeed, they are often significantly related to depression, infant mortality, child abuse, criminality, school performance, and the ability to find employment.

Risk and Protective Factors in Communities

Research documenting an increase in concentrated poverty and a decrease in jobs in urban areas, particularly among African Americans, has stimulated interest in how living in a high-poverty community contributes to joblessness, family disruptions, out-of-wedlock births, crime and delinquency, substance abuse, and mental disorders. Current findings suggest that as neighborhood composition changes from a working-class or middle-class environment to one of increasing poverty, residents are more likely to face severely reduced access to jobs. They also have fewer social networks and role models of stable, jobholding, intact families.

The structure of such communities has been found to limit the opportunities for children and adolescents to have access to parental and nonparental supervision. Community disorganization is also associated with increased numbers of births to single mothers. However, in terms of impact on children, mothers' marital status is not as important as household composition. Research has shown that when single mothers are the only adults in the household, children are at greater risk for maladaptive outcomes than when other adults are present as well. Further study is now needed to assess the extent and intensity of neighborhood effects. Even more important, research needs to specify which aspects of communities, through which kinds of mechanisms, contribute to positive or negative outcomes for children and adolescents.

Effective community support systems can improve parenting or even overcome the effects of poor parenting. One study of two demographically similar neighborhoods, one with far more cases of abuse and neglect than the other, suggested that the neighborhood with less child maltreatment had more highly developed social networks and organizational supports for child rearing. Another study showed that close social and organizational networks in a community fostered child supervision and held afloat marginal families with poor parenting skills.

Both attachment to schools and participation in community organizations such as churches and religious youth groups, school-based groups, and scouts have been shown to protect youths from delinquency and antisocial behavior. In addition, adults' participation in community organizations has been related to lower rates of child maltreatment and decreased crime rates in those communities. More research is needed to explain how these beneficial effects take place and to what extent other features of individuals or communities may protect residents from maladaptive outcomes.

Instability in Community and Organizational Contexts

A growing body of evidence indicates that instability in people's relationships to communities and organizations is often linked to poor physical and mental health. For example, residential mobility, which typically entails breaking and reestablishing connections with most settings of daily life, is often associated with considerable distress, described by one author as "grieving for a lost home."

Research suggests that the mental health impact of residential moves depends in part on their psychological meaning. More adverse effects occur when moves are forced, when the new setting does not meet residents' needs, and when few attractive alternatives are available. Even desirable moves, such as those associated with a job transfer or promotion, can have negative mental health effects on workers and their families.

Homelessness, an extreme form of residential instability, is strongly associated with mental illness: an estimated one-third of homeless people in the United States have severe mental disorders. Yet recent research suggests that most homelessness results from factors such as adverse economic conditions and the unavailability of affordable housing rather than from the disabilities associated with mental illness.

Further, although people who suffer from severe mental illness are more likely than others to become homeless, recent studies show that in some cases, homelessness precedes and may precipitate depression and alcoholism. It was once believed that impoverished social networks are a cause of homelessness, but one recent study showed that homeless families receive more support from families and friends prior to entering a shelter than do poor families with homes. Eventually, however, they wear out their welcome in others' homes.

Most of our knowledge about the relationship between homelessness and mental illness still comes from studies of groups of homeless people at one point in time. To understand the sources and impact of homelessness, more longitudinal studies are needed that follow homeless people over many months, and even years, ideally beginning with high-risk groups before they become homeless.

Recent research has shown that residential instability may be especially problematic for children. In homeless families, children suffer an excess of health problems, developmental delays, psychological problems, and educational underachievement compared with children in other low-SES families. Migrant and refugee children have been shown to have elevated rates of anxiety, depression, somatic complaints, and difficulties in establishing relationships with peers.

More research is needed to determine the factors affecting children's vulnerability or resilience in the face of these environmental stressors. By understanding the processes involved, we may be able to protect homeless children, migrants, and others who experience high rates of residential mobility. Another important research task is to determine whether emotional damage to children is permanent or reversible once the family has obtained stable housing.

RESEARCH DIRECTIONS

Important directions for future research on sociocultural and environmental processes include the following:

- The exploration of the role of cultural factors in basic processes of cognition, motivation, and emotion has only begun. Research is needed that explores how ethnicity influences social cognition and achievement motivation as well as how cultural differences affect the expression and labeling of emotion. More generally, cross-cultural research is needed to distinguish what is universal in human behavior from its more culturally specific aspects.

- Research shows striking cultural differences in the diagnosis and course of major mental disorders. However, the processes that vary across cultures and underlie these differences have yet to be clarified. Research is needed on such issues as the role of culture in the expression of psychiatric symptoms, the factors that place poor and minority persons at elevated risk for misdiagnosis and involuntary hospitalization, the influence of social and cultural processes on the course of mental illness and the prognosis for recovery, the differences among subcultures in patterns of caring for people with mental illness and how families cope with the burden of a mentally ill member, and the differences among cultural and subcultural views of mental illness and its treatment.

■ Sociocultural markers, such as race, ethnicity, and immigrant status, continue to play an important role in the social fabric and social life of our society. Research is needed on how and in what settings ethnic discrimination continues to be expressed and how it affects various groups.

■ Increasing cultural diversity makes clear the importance of research on interracial and interethnic dynamics. Increased research is needed on three issues: (a) explicating more clearly the mechanisms through which discrimination in school and work settings takes its toll on mental health, (b) discovering how both individuals and social and community settings develop successful strategies for dealing with disempowering situations, and (c) clarifying how the mental health of immigrants is influenced by such factors as acculturation, SES, the presence or absence of an accessible ethnic community, the ethnic composition of schools, and support systems available in the work environment.

■ The consistent and pervasive implications of low SES for the mental health of children and adults has been well described. Basic research is now needed to identify and study those processes that mediate the effects of SES on the mental health of children and adults. It is critical to understand how SES is expressed in the lives of individuals, including its implications for children's school performance, the effects of low-paying and routine jobs on family life, and SES differences in the availability of health care and counseling. It is also important to examine the variations among groups of similar SES but of differing cultures, races, and geographical regions.

■ A critical social change in the United States has been the enormous increase of women in the work force. Recent studies have revealed important and unexpected effects of this change on marital relationship, parenting practices, and children's adjustment. Future research should emphasize how the interdependence of the work environment, the husband's supportiveness for the wife's work, and the varying kinds of family constellations found in today's society affect the well-being of both parents and children. Specific attention should be given to discovering the kinds of arrangements that succeed and the kinds of school or work environments that prevent the potential negative effects of this changing pattern on children and their parents.

■ New theories and methods indicate that community contexts can have substantial effects, both positive and negative, on mental health and psychological functioning. Earlier studies focused heavily on documenting such effects. Research now should focus on identifying key aspects of communities that may threaten or protect mental health and well-being. Promising research directions include the contributions of community structure to violence, the effects of poverty on community life and opportunities, the contributions of communities to access to health care, the supportive role of social networks in buffering stress and promoting coping, and the coping processes necessitated by instability in educational, occupational, and residential environments. An important methodological issue concerns developing improved ways to measure the microsystems that constitute the community environment.

FURTHER READING

Berry, J. W., Poortinga, Y. H., Segall, M. H., and Dasen, P. R. (1992). *Cross-cultural psychology: Research and applications*. Cambridge, England: Cambridge University Press.

Cross, W. (1991). *Shades of Black*. Philadelphia: Temple University Press.

Eckenrode, J., and Gore, S. (Eds.). (1991). *Stress between work and family*. New York: Plenum.

Kleinman, A. (1988). *The illness narratives*. New York: Basic Books.

Robertson, M. J., and Greenblatt, M. (1992). *Homelessness: A national perspective*. New York: Plenum.

Stokols, D., and Altman, I. (1987). *Handbook of environmental psychology*. New York: Wiley.

Terkel, S. (1992). *Race*. New York: The New Press.

Wilson, W. J. (1993). *Sociology and the public agenda*. Newbury Park, CA: Sage.

4.

Some Dubious Premises in Research and Theory on Racial Differences

Scientific, Social, and Ethical Issues

Marvin Zuckerman

The scientific premises for looking for statistical differences between groups designated as *races* (on somewhat arbitrary grounds) are questionable. The explanation of such differences in strictly biological-evolutionary terms is even more dubious. Studies of temperament, basic personality traits, disorders (such as antisocial personality), and specific genetic markers show that there is much more variation within groups designated as races than between such groups. Investigators and theoreticians interpreting such differences on the basis of limited sampling within the three broad racial groups should be careful to avoid selectivity and misrepresentation of data that serve racist ideology, and should be cautious about presenting their theories to the public through inappropriate media forums.

The belief in the innate superiority of one's own tribe to neighboring tribes, or one's own nation or "race" to other nations or races, is probably as old as our species. Those who offer evolutionary racial-genetic explanations for behaviors or values of groups that can change radically within a generation seem to ignore all history between the Pleistocene era and the last 20 years. As scientists, we are not obliged to publish theories based on dubious premises, reasoning, or data. But once such theories are published, we must critically examine the thesis rather than reject it out of hand. I will raise some questions about contemporary racial theory and research and illustrate my points with data on temperament and its diversity within races.

WHAT IS RACE?

The answer to the question "What is race?" seems simple to the layperson who makes judgments from prototypical images derived from caricatures found in art, literature, and the media. Stereotyping varies inversely with the extent of personal experience with individual members of other groups. Although the distinctions between the races may be clear to some psychologists operating from the best anthropological thinking of the nineteenth century, they are not so simple to the modern anthropologist. Nearly everyone agrees that there is only one species of humans living in the world today: *Homo sapiens*. To the biologist, a race, or subspecies, is an inbreeding, geographically isolated population that differs in distinguishable physical traits from other members of the species. Members of such a population are capable of breeding with members of other populations in their species, but they usually do not do so for some period of time during which the specific physical characteristics of the group emerge from the limited but adaptive gene pool. Geographical isolation may have been a significant factor producing inbreeding in the distant evolutionary past, but now the barriers that separate populations are political, cultural, and religious rather than geographic. The Amish group living in the United States represents such an inbreeding group, maintained not by geographical isolation but by religion and culture. One could speculate on whether "natural selection" has eliminated "aggressive genes" from the group, or whether their nonviolent nature is maintained by culture.

Most modern anthropologists believe that *Homo sapiens* evolved only once. The variations that are used to distinguish populations are relatively recent and represent climatic adaptations or mere peculiarities of relatively isolated breeding populations. The problem of race is one of taxonomy of current populations (Barnicott, 1964). Although there is considerable speculation on the origin of races, little can be proved other than that a species, *Homo sapiens,* gradually evolved from its predecessor *Homo erectus* about 200,000 years ago in East Africa and spread through Africa and Eurasia (Cann, Stoneking, and Wilson, 1987). All extant human races are members of that species. We do not know what the skin color of the original population was or when the races began to differentiate. Some have proposed that certain races may have evolved to a "higher level" than others because of a historical sequence (i.e., Negroids to Caucasoids to Mongoloids) and the need for social organization to survive in more difficult climate conditions (Rushton, 1989; Rushton and Bogaert, 1987). All of this reconstruction of evolutionary history is totally speculative, unverifiable, and post hoc. Actually, Rushton's theory is contrary to the evolutionary theory on which he bases his conclusions because, as Lynn (1989) has pointed out, a high reproductive and low parental investment strategy has been theorized as more likely to occur in unstable arctic environments than in stable tropical environments such as those in Africa.

Races have been defined in terms of observable physical features, such as skin color, hair type and color, eye color, stature, head shape and size, and facial features (with special attention to noses). The problem is that many of the features are not correlated and none by themselves could furnish an indisputable guide to the anthropologists' definitions of racial groups. For features like skin color, which can be ranged on a metric, there is great variation within, as well as between, so-called races. In Africa, skin color of groups called *Negroid* ranges from black or dark brown to yellowish tan. There are groups classified as *Caucasoid* who are darker than certain African groups classified as Negroid. The same diversity in various physical features exists in European groups (Barnicott, 1964). Many groups, such as the black population in America, represent unknown admixtures of White and Black populations. At what point is White Black or Black White? It is not a "Black and White" question, but depends on legal-cultural definitions. In America prior to the Civil War, anyone with any Black ancestry was defined by the law of southern states as Black. In South Carolina anyone with 1/32nd degree of Black "blood" (one ancestor five generations back) was called Black regardless of his or her physical appearance. In Brazil, however, anyone with any degree of Caucasian appearance is regarded as White. In Britain much of the populace regards immigrants with any degree of skin darkness as "Blacks" including those from the Near East or Asia and those of African descent from the West

Indies. Prejudice makes for poor discrimination between peoples of other racial groups. Unfortunately, some psychologists seem equally blind to intraracial diversity.

The differential distribution of blood types or antigens has been used extensively by the new science of population genetics to classify groups. Because all of the A, B, and O blood types are found in all groups, it is only the relative population statistics that can be used to distinguish among groups. Knowing that someone had blood type B, for instance, would not enable one to decide if he were of African or European Caucasian descent, even though the type is more common in the former (29%) than in the latter (7%–12%; Mourant, 1983). Studying distributions of blood types shows that some groups with common blood type frequencies do not resemble each other in classical racial features, whereas others, like Africans and Oceanic Negroids, who have common features of color and hair form, differ in blood types. Australoid aborigines resemble American Indians far more than they do Africans, Asians, or Europeans in their low frequencies of the type B gene even though they are markedly different in physical type. The modern anthropology of population genetics raises serious questions about the old concepts of race based on phenotypes.

RACE AND TEMPERAMENT

Because *race* is defined as an inbreeding group of individuals with a specific geographic locus, smaller tribal units fit this definition better than do the huge superraces with their tremendous range of genetic and cultural diversity. Africa contains hundreds of groups with extreme differences in physical phenotypes, such as the difference in stature between the Pygmy and the Watusi. But the range in physical traits is minor compared with the range of temperaments in this or in any other continent. Groups with very similar genetic constitutions, as judged from physical appearance or even blood types, may be worlds apart in cultural patterns and temperament. A vast literature in cultural anthropology testifies that superficial physical similarity can coexist with drastic differences in cultural-behavioral patterns.

De Vries and Sameroff (1984) compared infants from three African tribes—the Kikuyu, Digo, and Masai—on infant rating scales. Significant differences between the tribal groups were found on every dimension except threshold. If such variation exists between groups within the "Negroid race," what kind of generalizations can be made from limited samplings of American or British Blacks with their admixtures of unknown African and Caucasian genes? In order to make such a generalization, one would need a stratified sample with proportional representation from all of the hundreds of African groups.

It is true that almost all psychological data depend on sampling assumptions. However, when we deal with social behavior we are usually careful not to generalize too far beyond the population from which we have drawn our samples. If I obtained data on sexual behavior from University of Delaware undergraduates, I certainly would not generalize beyond the American college student, and even this would not be done unless the Delaware data seemed to be in line with data from other American universities. Yet typically we see studies comparing American Blacks and Whites from a particular region of the country and a particular socioeconomic level, with no criteria for race other than a self-report. The African tribal ancestry of these Blacks is unknown, and their ancestry may consist of various admixtures with Whites of equally unknown ancestry.

When we make generalizations about the social behavior of selected populations (such as extraverts and introverts) from limited samples, there is also some tendency to ignore the limitations of the samples used in the research. However, in the case of extraversion and introversion, the selection criteria are well-defined (e.g., scores on a trait test or behavioral observations) and there is usually a sound theoretical basis for the hypothesis generating the research (e.g., predicting that extraverts will socialize more than will introverts). In the case of race, the criteria for group selection are not well-defined and consist of external physical features rather than behavioral traits. The assumptions about behavioral correlates of these physical traits owe more to popular stereotypes than to biopsychological theory.

A Cross-National and Racial Study of Personality

I would like to illustrate the problem of ignoring the diversity within the classically defined racial groups by using the data from a cross-cultural study by Paul Barrett and Sybil Eysenck (1984). Some of the data from this study were described in a recent review (Rushton, 1988) purporting to show racial differences in temperament related to differences in socialization, sexual behavior, impulsivity, and criminality (see the critique by Zuckerman and Brody, 1988). The study by Barrett and Eysenck is a masterpiece of cross-cultural research. The authors made great efforts to develop modified forms of the Eysenck Personality Questionnaire (EPQ: Eysenck and Eysenck, 1975) that were comparable across nations and cultural groups. I chose to look at the Psychoticism (P) scale because this scale was, for some unknown reason, totally ignored in Rushton's review, despite its obvious relevance to the behavioral variables on which the three major races were hypothesized to differ. Except for successful German artists, English male art students, and Indian writers, the highest scoring groups on the scale are English delinquents and prisoners (Eysenck and Eysenck, 1975). I have suggested that this scale should more appropriately be called *Psychopathy* or *Social Nonconformity* rather than *Psychoticism* (Zuckerman, 1989). In a general factor analysis the scale provides one of the best markers for a dimension that includes impulsivity, lack of socialization, sensation seeking, and aggression (Zuckerman, Kuhlman, and Camac, 1988). These are some of the traits that have been hypothesized to be highest in the Negroid and lowest in the Mongoloid race, with Caucasians intermediate (Rushton, 1988).

Table 1 shows the transformed means on the P scale of the 3 highest and 3 lowest countries among the 25 countries in the Barrett and Eysenck (1984) study. India, representing the White race, was highest on P for both sexes. For the men, India was closely followed by Australia, another predominantly White sample, and Hong Kong, a representative of the supposedly restrained Mongoloid race. At the low end of P, among the male samples, we find 2 White samples, 1 from Israel and the other from Spain, and 1 of the 2 Black countries, Nigeria. The other group of Black men, Ugandans, fell in the middle range of this scale with a mean of 6. Ugandan women did score among the top 3 female groups on P, along with Caucasoid Indians and Yugoslavians. Hungarian, British, and Icelandic women were lowest on P, but the next lowest were Nigerian and Israeli women, consistent with the male data. Apparently Blacks, as well as Whites, can be found at both extremes on this scale. Race seems to be irrelevant to the dimension.

In order to compare countries in terms of their total pattern of personality on the basis

**Table 1. Transformed Means on the P Scale for the 3 Highest
and 3 Lowest of 25 Countries**

Scale/country	n	P-scale mean
	Men	
High P		
India	509	8.41
Australia	336	8.41
Hong Kong	270	8.36
Low P		
Israel	688	3.74
Nigeria	329	3.59
Spain	435	3.14
	Women	
High P		
India	555	7.92
Yugoslavia	491	6.91
Uganda	921	6.12
Low P		
Hungary	414	3.01
United Kingdom	598	2.89
Iceland	567	2.70

Note: Adapted from "The Assessment of Personality Factors Across 25 Countries"
by P. Barrett and S. B. G. Eysenck, *Personality and Individual Differences,* 5, p. 618.
Copyright © 1984 by Pergamon Press. Adapted by permission.

of four EPQ scales (Extraversion, Neuroticism, Psychoticism, and Lie), matrices containing Euclidian distance measures were computed. Similar methods are being used by modern anthropologists to group populations on the basis of genetic similarity. If there is any validity to the idea of differential temperaments among the three superraces, we would expect to see the 2 African nations, Uganda and Nigeria, grouped closely on the unidimensional scales of distance. Similarly, the 4 Asian representatives of the Mongoloid race, China, Japan, Hong Kong, and Singapore, should be close in pattern, and the White populations should constitute a third grouping. Figure 1 shows the placements of the samples of men and women from the 25 countries along the unidimensional scale of similarity. Male samples show no grouping of samples by race. China and Japan, for instance, lie at two ends of the scale, almost as different as possible. Different races lie close together on the scale. Israelis and Nigerians are quite similar in personality patterns and have scores that are very close on all four EPQ scales. Ugandan men resemble those from Hong Kong and the United Kingdom more than they resemble those from Nigeria. Ugandan women are more like Australian women than like Nigerian women. There is nothing here to support the hypothesis that overall similarities in personality are based on racial similarities.

Genetic Diversity

The data on personality suggest that the variation within broad populations, such as those defining the three major races, is large, relative to the variations between these populations. New methods enable us to examine genotypical as well as phenotypical variation. Protein variation between human populations is small relative to the variation among individuals

**Figure 1. Distances Between Country Samples on Patterns of Eysenck Personality
Questionnaire Scores, Based on Euclidian Distance Matrices
for Male and Female Samples, One Dimensional Model**

	MALES	FEMALES
100–	China	China
90–		
80–		
		Sri Lanka
70–		
	Israel	Israel
60–	Nigeria	Nigeria
50–		Bangladesh
	Sri Lanka, Iran	
40–	Bangladesh, Egypt	Yugoslavia, Egypt
	Yugoslavia	Iran
30–	Brazil, France	Brazil
	Singapore	Singapore, Puerto Rico
20–	Hungary	
	Spain, Sicily	Hungary
10–	India	Hong Kong, India
	Puerto Rico	Bulgaria
0–	Bulgaria	Spain, Sicily
	Greece	Greece
10–	Hong Kong, Uganda	
		United Kingdom
20–		
	United Kingdom	
30–		France, Iceland
	Iceland	
40–	Germany	Germany
50–		Japan
60–		
70–	Japan	
80–		Australia
90–		
100–	Australia	Uganda

Note. Distances are portrayed on an arbitrary scale ranging from −100 to +100.
From "The Assessment of Personality Factors Across 25 Countries" by P.
Barrett and S. B. G. Eysenck: *Personality and Individual Differences, 5*, p. 629.
Copyright 1984 by Pergamon Press. Reprinted by permission.

within populations. Latter (1980) analyzed 18 genetic systems (blood groups, serum proteins, and enzymes) in 40 populations within 16 regional subgroups around the world. Using a multivariate measure of individual differences, he calculated the variability within and between populations, breaking down the population variance into geographic regions and racial groups. *The major component of genetic diversity is between individuals in the same tribe or nation:* it accounts for 84% of the variance. Of the remaining variance, 10% is accounted for by racial groupings and 6% by geographical regions. Similar conclusions were reached for sequencing of mitochondrial and nuclear DNA for human populations (Cann et al., 1987; Wainscoat et al., 1986). When interpopulation distances are corrected for intrapopulation variation, they become quite small, amounting to 14% of the mean within population variation. The genetic analyses support the phenotypical analyses of personality. Racial groups are much more alike than they are different.

CRIME AND ANTISOCIAL PERSONALITY

Racial differences in American crime rates and patterns of sexual behavior have also been cited as evidence of inherited racial patterns of socialization or antisocial tendencies (Ellis, 1988a, 1988b). Most of these high rates of crime for Blacks represent young adolescent and adult males living in inner-city ghettoes. Twin studies indicate that although adult criminality shows evidence of heritability in the concordance ratio of identical to fraternal twins, juvenile delinquency shows little evidence of heritability, with fraternal twin concordance rates nearly as high as those for identical twins (Christiansen, 1977). Although most chronic adult criminals have a record of teenage and earlier delinquency, most teenage delinquents do not show a pattern of prepubertal delinquency and most do not go on to become adult criminals (Wolfgang, Figlis, and Sellin, 1972). The twin concordance rates in studies conducted between 1931 and 1961 indicated a somewhat stronger genetic pattern for adult criminality, with concordance rates of about 69% for identical and 33% for fraternal twins. However, the results from later Scandinavian studies (Christiansen, 1977; Dalgaard and Kringlen, 1976) have shown much lower rates for identical twins (about 33%) and fraternal twins (about 16%). Stronger evidence for genetic rather than shared-environment influence on criminality comes from a study by Mednick, Gabrielli, and Hutchings (1986). Using data from adoption studies in Denmark, these investigators found that criminality in the biological parents of adoptees was related to criminality in the adoptees, whereas the criminal records of the adoptive parents were not predictive of crime in their adoptive children. But they also found that the socioeconomic class of the adoptive family was a significant influence on crime in adoptees even after controlling for the class of the biological parents. If this is true within the narrower range of social class difference in Denmark, it is likely to be even truer for the wider ranges within the United States and the United Kingdom. The results from Swedish adoptees also showed a strong influence of postnatal environment on crime (Cloninger and Gottesman, 1987). Risk of criminality in their sample was not increased unless both the congenital and postnatal factors were predisposing. The recent tendency to account for racial differences in arrests and convictions by biological factors alone ignores the demonstrated influence of drugs and general family disruption in lower-class Black communities.

If we turn to studies of diagnosed antisocial personality rather than crime statistics, there is no evidence of racial differences. A major study of the prevalence of psychiatric disorders in the general community was undertaken by the National Institute of Mental Health in the United States. Robins et al. (1984) interviewed about 2,700 Blacks and 6,900 Whites randomly sampled from census tracts in three U.S. cities. There were no significant racial differences in diagnoses of antisocial personality in any of the cities, and in two of the cities the rates were slightly higher for Whites than for Blacks. Thus when random sampling is used there is no evidence supporting the idea that Blacks as a group in the larger American community have a greater disposition to antisocial personality disorders than do Whites. The contrast with the crime rate statistics is illuminated by the high rates of environmentally produced delinquency in poverty-stricken environments. Robins (1978) found that adult criminality is more related to socioeconomic class of origin in Blacks than in Whites. Cloninger, Reich, and Guze (1975) reported that their data showed no genetic differences in sociopathy between Blacks and Whites. One would expect behavior geneticist psychologists interested in racial differences to use the data from their own disciplines, particularly those data derived from proper sampling methods, rather than the crude population statistics (uncorrected for social class and other variables) from the World Almanac.

REFLECTIONS ON RACIST SCIENCE AND RESPONSIBILITIES OF SCIENTISTS

The word *racism* is often used in a pejorative sense. According to *Webster's Third New International Dictionary of the English Language, Unabridged* (1981), racism is

> The assumption that psychocultural traits and capacities are determined by biological race and that races differ decisively from one another which is usually coupled with a belief in the inherent superiority of a particular race and its right to domination over others. (p. 1870)

Note that the definition consists of two parts: The first is the ideology, and the second is the application of the ideology. Some researches on race seem dedicated to establishing the racist ideology on a scientific basis while denying the political beliefs that are associated with it. Non-scientists are not likely to make the distinction between scientific theory and what seems to be its political implications, or between generalizations based on population statistics and their applications to individual members of a given group. In terms of the possibilities for social change, most would equate *inherited* with *unchangeable*.

I have been accused by colleagues of bringing moral values to bear on "purely scientific" questions. These colleagues describe themselves as liberal in belief and absolutely opposed to racism as a political doctrine. I share with them the belief that all questions should be open to scientific investigation if they are answerable by current scientific methods. I have raised questions about the likelihood of finding the role of genetic mechanisms in racial differences, using prevalent definitions of race. For the sake of argument, let us suppose that these questions are answerable. Is this an important scientific question, worth the harm it might do in fostering and reinforcing stereotypes that are applied to individuals in the broader society? Harrington (in press) has challenged the assumption of a value-free science that is above criticism related to topic. Is anything studied by the methods of science beyond challenge on moral grounds? Everyone agrees that the scientific studies of survival time in freezing water conducted by the Nazis on concentration camp inmates were immoral, regardless of the quality of the methodology and data. But we do not agree on the reprehensibility of theories that reinforce negative stereotypes of large segments of the human population and thereby foster racism in all of its more malignant aspects.

Of course one should not criticize the study of nuclear physics because of possible extrapolations to hydrogen bombs. However, a scientist who decides to work on the interesting problem of developing a small portable hydrogen bomb is not above criticism. Similarly, research on the genetic and biological bases of intelligence should not be criticized because some might make unwarranted racist extrapolations from the findings. Generalizations about the innate intelligence or social responsibility of large and genetically diverse segments of the species are open to criticism on the grounds that they serve no important scientific purpose, given the present ambiguities in definition of the independent variable and immense sampling problems. A more important task is to discover the biological and social bases of individual differences in personality and intelligence within populations. Questions of population differences could be better addressed after we understand the proximate biological bases of the phenomena and can provide a better biological definition of the populations now called *races*.

I would not argue with the right of investigators to study these problems now and to attempt to form some hypotheses. Misguided attempts at censorship tend to elicit protective reactions from the academic community and lead some academics to suspend critical judgment of the work and reasoning of the person under public censure. However, there is a general responsibility of scientists to strive for objectivity, to avoid selectivity of data in reviews, to consider the sampling and controls required for tests of hypotheses, to evaluate the adequacy of data sources and methods, and to give more than perfunctory consideration to other hypotheses. These are responsibilities of scientists in any area of science, but in socially sensitive areas they are of even greater importance.

How a scientist behaves after a discovery is also a matter of social concern. The expected course of behavior is to publish in scientific journals and consider the reactions of peers before appearing on talk shows to present one's viewpoint to the general public. There are proper forums for scientists to present findings to the public, and there is nothing wrong with this as long as investigators are cautious and qualifying in their conclusions. However, television does not like complicated and qualified ideas. Most popular programs in this medium serve an audience that seems to want simplicity and sensation. They are not good vehicles for informing the public of complicated scientific issues that lend themselves to distortion by those with political axes to grind. Eysenck (in press) has acknowledged the danger of misinterpretations of research to serve racist purposes, but he suggests that these dangers are less than those of censorship in science. This assumes of course that the basic research is unbiased and nonselective. Critical peer review is not censorship.

Scientists also have a social responsibility to be extracritical on research or theory that serves racism. Rushton (in press) has claimed that standards of evidence for research on evolutionary and genetic hypotheses concerning race are held to "ludicrously high levels." One must read the critiques of his work to decide whether his critics are unreasonable in their demands for standards of proof and deduction (Lynn, 1989; Zuckerman and Brody, 1988). However, as Rushton's work on race has been published in respectable journals, there is obviously some disagreement about the standards or the work. But why shouldn't one impose high standards for those interpretations that have such large potential for abuse and social or physical harm? When the tobacco companies or their paid investigators report that cigarettes are really safe, one should scrutinize their evidence with great care, not only because of the questionable objectivity of the findings, but also because of the harm to smokers if they really believe the findings, and the findings are false. The question of whether ideas are based on good or bad science, scholarship, and logic is *not* an irrelevant question. The question of whether racial studies are racist largely depends on the quality of the research and the reasonableness of the deductions. The lay public is often unable to make these distinctions and is prone to accept anything coming from a person in a white lab coat as fact. While defending the academic freedom of promoters of racist science, we should make our disagreements and the reasons for the disagreement quite clear. Emotional reactions unsupported by reasons are useless because they undermine our credibility as scientists. If we fail to express our disagreement with practitioners of racist science, their pronouncements will be accepted by the public as the final word of scientific truth.

All questions should be open to scientific investigation for those who choose to study them and offer reasonable hypotheses based on sound data. This is a tenet of scientific values that most of us would endorse. However, certain topics are regarded with justified skepticism because the premises on which they are based are either not scientifically justified or are basically untestable using the scientific approach. If an investigator claims to have irrefutable scientific evidence for astrology, conscious life after death, the existence of God, or the content of the mental life of preverbal infants, it is quite natural for scientists to regard such claims with skepticism and disbelief. When the evidence is not due to deliberate fraud, the fault is usually the lack of proper controls in the research, lack of attention to alternate, more parsimonious interpretations, and unwarranted generalizations from the data. In medical science, the consequences of bad research can be a matter of life or death. In psychology, the harm done by bad science is usually of little consequence. However, when the fallacious ideas generated are used to support pernicious political doctrines like racism, the results are a disservice to our science and, more important, to the larger human community.

BIBLIOGRAPHY

Barnicott, N. A. (1964). Taxonomy and variation in modern man. In A. Montagu (Ed.), *The concept of race* (pp. 180–227). Westport, CT: Greenwood Press.

Barrett, P., and Eysenck, S. B. G. (1984). The assessment of personality factors across 25 countries. *Personality and Individual Differences*, 5, 615–632.

Cann, R. L., Stoneking, M., and Wilson, A. C. (1987). Mitochondrial DNA and human evolution. *Nature*, 325, 31–36.

Christiansen, K. O. (1977). A preliminary study of criminality among twins. In S. A. Mednick and K. O. Christiansen (Eds.), *Biosocial bases of criminal behavior* (pp. 89–108), New York: Gardner Press.

Cloninger, C. R., and Gottesman, I. I. (1987). Genetic and environmental factors in antisocial behavior disorders. In S. A. Mednick, T. E. Moffitt, and S. A. Stack (Eds.), *The causes of crime: New biological approaches* (pp. 74–91). Cambridge, England: Cambridge University Press.

Cloninger, C. R., Reich, T., and Guze, S. B. (1975). The multifactorial model of disease transmission: II. Sex differences in the familial transmission of sociopathy (antisocial personality). *British Journal of Psychiatry*, 127, 11–22.

Dalgaard, O. S., and Kringlen, E. (1976). A Norwegian twin study of criminality. *British Journal of Criminality*, 16, 213–232.

DeVries, M. W., and Sameroff, A. J. (1984). Culture and temperament: Influences on human temperament in three East African societies. *American Journal of Orthopsychiatry*, 54, 83–96.

Ellis, L. (1988a). Criminal behavior and r/K selection: An extension of gene-based evolutionary theory. *Personality and Individual Differences*, 9, 697–708.

Ellis, L. (1988b). The victimful-victimless crime distinction, and seven universal demographic correlates of victimful criminal behavior. *Personality and Individual Differences*, 9, 525–548.

Eysenck, H. J. (in press). The study of racial differences. *Psychologische Beitrage*.

Eysenck, H. J., and Eysenck, S.B.G. (1975). *Manual of the Eysenck Personality Questionnaire*. London: Hodder and Stoughton.

Harrington, A. (in press). Studying race differences, or the problem of "value free" science. *Psychologische Beitrage*.

Latter, B.D.H. (1980). Genetic differences within and between populations of the major human subgroups. *The American Naturalist*, 116, 220–237.

Lynn, M. (1989). Criticisms of an evolutionary hypothesis about race differences: A rebuttal to Rushton's reply. *Journal of Research in Personality*, 23, 21–34.

Mednick, S. A., Gabrielli, W. F. Jr., and Hutchings, B. (1987). Genetic factors in the etiology of criminal behavior. In S. A. Mednick, T. E. Moffitt, and S. A. Stack (Eds.), *The cause of crime: New biological approaches* (pp. 74–91). Cambridge, England: Cambridge University Press.

Mourant, A. E. (1983). *Blood relations: Blood groups and anthropology*. Oxford, England: Oxford University Press.

Robins, L. N. (1978). Aetiological implications in studies of childhood histories relating to antisocial personality. In R. D. Hare and D. Schailing (Eds.), *Psychopathic behavior: Approaches to research* (pp. 255–272). Chichester, England: Wiley.

Robins, L. N., Helzer, J. E., Weissman. M. M., Orvarechel, H., Gruenberg, E., Burke, J. D., and Regier, D. A. (1984). Lifetime prevalence of specific psychiatric disorders in three sites. *Archives of General Psychiatry*, 41, 949–958.

Rushton, J. P. (1988). Race differences in behaviour. A review and evolutionary analysis. *Personality and Individual Differences*, 9, 1009–1024.

Rushton, J. P. (1989). The evolution of racial differences: A reply to M. Lynn. *Journal of Research in Personality*, 23, 7–20.

Rushton, J. P. (in press). Race differences are real and should be studied. *Psychologische Beitrage*.

Rushton, J. P., and Bogaert, A. F. (1987). Race differences in sexual behavior: Testing an evolutionary hypothesis. *Journal of Research in Personality*, 21, 529–551.

Wainscoat, J. S., Hill, A.V.S., Boyce, A. L., Flint, J., Hernandez, M., Thein, S. L., Old, J. M., Lynch, J. R., Falusi, A. G., Weatherall, D. J., and Clegg, J. B. (1986). Evolutionary relationships of human populations from an analysis of nuclear DNA polymorphisms. *Nature*, 319, 491–493.

Webster's Third New International Dictionary of the English Language, unabridged. (1981). Springfield, MA: Merriam-Webster.

Wolfgang, M. E., Figlis, R. M., and Sellin, T. (1972). *Delinquency in a birth cohort*. Chicago: University of Chicago Press.

Zuckerman, M. (1989). Personality in the third dimension: A psychobiological approach. *Personality and Individual Differences*, 10, 391–418.

Zuckerman, M., and Brody, N. (1988). Oysters, rabbits and people: A critique of "Race differences in behaviour" by J. P. Rushton. *Personality and Individual Differences*, 9, 1025–1033.

Zuckerman, M., Kuhlman, M., and Camac, C. (1988). What lies beyond E and N? Factor analyses of scales believed to measure basic dimensions of personality. *Journal of Personality and Social Psychology*, 54, 96–107.

PART III.

Ethnic Identity

Psychologists are beginning to discover the importance of ethnic identity in shaping our behaviors, thoughts, and emotions. However, in the past, divergent research strategies and inconsistent definitions of this concept have made this quite a formidable task. The two articles selected for this section represent landmark attempts to clarify the meaning of ethnic identity and the developmental processes underlying ethnic identity formation. Furthermore, they highlight the significance of ethnic identity in relation to various indices of psychological functioning.

As you read Jean Phinney's definitive research review, particular attention should be given to the multifaceted nature of ethnic identity and how it affects numerous aspects of our lives. As noted in her article, greater appreciation for the different components comprising ethnic identity will bring about greater conceptual and methodological clarity in this promising area of research.

Maria Root offers a unique perspective on ethnic identity by outlining the psychosocial issues faced by multiethnic individuals. As detailed in her article, social marginalization is a common experience for many biracial individuals as evidenced by their "other" status. Root also challenges us to address a basic question: Do current models of ethnic identity development overlook the unique experiences of multiethnic individuals? As you will discover in this article, Root answers this question quite directly in her conceptualization of identity resolution for this growing population.

MEASUREMENT OF ETHNIC IDENTITY

Ethnic identity measures have traditionally focused on the cultural behaviors and attitudes of individual ethnic groups. This includes measuring one's sense of belonging to a particular ethnic community, ethnic pride, political beliefs, and religious and cultural practices. Some researchers believe that measures created for specific groups prevent interethnic comparisons on universal aspects of ethnic identity. Still, others believe that global measures of ethnic identity overlook important culture-specific issues. Regardless of these differing views, there is a growing consensus that ethnic identity is intimately tied to our psychological functioning. The articles listed below provide an opportunity to further your understanding of the different approaches to ethnic identity measurement.

Baldwin, J. A., and Bell, Y. (1985). The African self-consciousness scale: An Africentric personality questionnaire. *The Western Journal of Black Studies, 9,* 61–68.

Helms, J. E. (1990). The measurement of Black racial identity attitudes. In J. E. Helms (Ed.), *Black and White racial identity: Theory, research, and practice* (pp. 31–47). Westport, CT: Greenwood Press.

Moran, J. R., Fleming, C. M., Somervell, P., and Manson, S. M. (In press). Measuring ethnic identity among American Indian adolescents. *Journal of Research on Adolescence.*

Oetting, E., and Beauvais, F. (1990–91). Orthogonal cultural identification theory: The cultural identification of minority adolescents. *International Journal of the Addictions, 25,* 655–685.

Phinney, J. S. (1992). The Multigroup Ethnic Identity Measure: A new scale for diverse groups. *Journal of Adolescent Research, 7,* 156–176.

Thompson Sanders, V. L. (1991). A multidimensional approach to the assessment of African American racial identification. *The Western Journal of Black Studies, 15,* 154–158.

FURTHER READINGS

Bernal, M. E., and Knight, G. P. (Eds.). (1993). *Ethnic identity: Formation and transmission among Hispanics and other minorities.* Albany, NY: State University of New York Press.

Cross, W. E., Jr. (1995). The psychology of Nigrescence: Revising the Cross model. In J. G. Ponterotto, J. M. Casas, L. A. Suzuki, and C. M. Alexander (Eds.), *Handbook of multicultural counseling* (pp. 93–122). Thousand Oaks, CA: Sage Publications, Inc.

Harris, H. W., Blue, H. C., and Griffith, E. E. H. (Eds.) (1995). *Racial and ethnic identity.* New York: Routledge.

Kerwin, C., and Ponterotto, J. G. (1995). Biracial identity development: Theory and research. In J. G. Ponterotto, J. M. Casas, L. A. Suzuki, and C. M. Alexander (Eds.), *Handbook of multicultural counseling* (pp. 199–217). Thousand Oaks, CA: Sage Publications, Inc.

Phinney, J. S., and Chavira, V. (1995). Parental ethnic socialization and adolescent coping with problems related to ethnicity. *Journal of Research on Adolescence, 5,* 31–53.

Thompson Sanders, V. L. (1995). The multidimensional structure of racial identification. *Journal of Research in Personality, 29,* 208–222.

5.
Ethnic Identity in Adolescents and Adults
Review of Research
Jean S. Phinney

Ethnic identity is central to the psychological functioning of members of ethnic and racial minority groups, but research on the topic is fragmentary and inconclusive. This article is a review of 70 studies of ethnic identity published in refereed journals since 1972. The author discusses the ways in which ethnic identity has been defined and conceptualized, the components that have been measured, and empirical findings. The task of understanding ethnic identity is complicated because the uniqueness that distinguishes each group makes it difficult to draw general conclusions. A focus on the common elements that apply across groups could lead to a better understanding of ethnic identity.

The growing proportion of minority group members in the United States and other Western countries has resulted in an increasing concern with issues of pluralism, discrimination, and racism in the media. However, psychological research on the impact of these issues on the individual is uneven. Most of the research dealing with psychological aspects of contact between racial or ethnic groups has focused on attitudes toward racial or ethnic groups other than one's own and particularly on stereotyping, prejudice, and discrimination. The emphasis has been on attitudes of members of the majority or dominant group toward minority group members; this is a research area of great importance in face of the daily evidence of ethnic tensions and racial violence.

A far less studied aspect of diversity has been the psychological relationship of ethnic and racial minority group members with their own group, a topic dealt with under the broad term *ethnic identity*. The study of attitudes about one's own ethnicity has been of little interest to members of the dominant group, and little attention has been paid by mainstream, generally White researchers to the psychological aspects of being a minority group member in a diverse society.

Recent concern with ethnic identity has derived in part from the ethnic revitalization movements in the 1960s. Growing awareness in society of differences associated with ethnic group membership (e.g., lower educational and occupational attainment) has been accompanied by social movements leading to increased ethnic consciousness and pride (Laosa, 1984). Attitudes toward one's ethnicity are central to the psychological functioning of those who live in societies where their group and its culture are at best poorly represented (politically, economically, and in the media) and are at worst discriminated against or even attacked verbally and physically; the concept of ethnic identity provides a way of understanding the need to assert oneself in the face of threats to one's identity (Weinreich,

1983). The psychological importance of ethnic identity is attested to by numerous literary writings of ethnic group members about the struggle to understand their ethnicity (e.g., Du Bois, 1983; Kingston, 1976; Malcolm X, 1970; Rodriguez, 1982).

The issue of ethnic identity has also been brought to the fore by changing demographics, including differential birthrates and increasing numbers of immigrants and refugees throughout the world. Projections suggest that by the mid-1990s, minority youth will constitute more than 30% of the 15- to 25-year-olds in the United States (Wetzel, 1987). The topic not only has important implications within psychology (e.g., Ekstrand,1986) but also has broad political significance. In response, Canada has developed an explicit policy of multiculturalism and supports continuing study of the issue (Berry, Kalin, and Taylor, 1977). Many European countries will be dealing for years to come with struggles of ethnic minorities to maintain or assert their identities (Kaplan, 1989).

Within the social sciences, many writers have asserted that ethnic identity is crucial to the self-concept and psychological functioning of ethnic group members (e.g., Gurin and Epps, 1975; Maldonado, 1975). Critical issues include the degree and quality of involvement that is maintained with one's own culture and heritage; ways of responding to and dealing with the dominant group's often disparaging views of their group; and the impact of these factors on psychological well-being. These issues have been addressed conceptually from a variety of perspectives (e.g., Alba, 1985; Arce, 1981; Atkinson, Morten, and Sue, 1983; Dashefsky, 1976; DeVos and Romanucci-Ross, 1982; Frideres and Goldenberg, 1982; Mendelberg, 1986; Ostrow, 1977; Parham, 1989; Staiano, 1980; Tajfel, 1978, 1981; Weinreich, 1988; Yancey, Ericksen, and Juliani, 1976; Zinn, 1980).

However, the theoretical writing far outweighs empirical research. Most of the empirical work on ethnic identity has concentrated on young children, with a focus on minority children's racial misidentification or preference for White stimulus figures. This work has been widely discussed and reviewed (e.g., Aboud, 1987; Banks, 1976; Brand, Ruiz, and Padilla, 1974) and is not addressed here. Far less work has been done on ethnic identity beyond childhood and particularly the transition from childhood to adulthood; this gap has been recently noted (Kagitcibasi and Berry, 1989). In published studies on ethnic identity in adolescents and adults, researchers have generally focused on single groups and have used widely discrepant definitions and measures of ethnic identity, which makes generalizations and comparisons across studies difficult and ambiguous. The findings are often inconclusive or contradictory.

The topic is of sufficient importance to warrant serious research attention, but in order for the research to yield useful and meaningful results, greater conceptual and methodological clarity is needed. The primary goal of this article is to provide such clarity through a review of the empirical literature on ethnic identity in adolescents and adults. I describe the definitions and conceptual frameworks that have guided empirical research, the way in which the construct has been defined and measured, and the empirical findings. The article concludes with recommendations for future research.

In order to review the literature, an extensive search was carried out to locate journal articles from psychology, sociology, and allied social sciences, published since 1972, that dealt empirically with ethnic or racial identity in adolescents (12 years or older) or adults. The material reviewed was limited in several ways. In order to focus on research that had been subject to peer review and that was accessible to readers, only published journal articles were included. Books, chapters, dissertations, and unpublished papers were excluded, with some noted exceptions. Also excluded were (a) articles that dealt only with social identity (social class, political affiliation, national and religious identity) and did not include ethnicity and (b) articles in which the term *ethnic identity* was used to mean simply the ethnic group membership of the subjects (e.g., Furnham and Kirris, 1983). Only English-language articles were examined. Conceptual articles that included no empirical data were reviewed and are referred to but are not included in the analyses.

Seventy empirical articles dealt substantively with ethnic identity beyond childhood. The authors of those articles examined many ethnic groups and presented widely differing approaches to the meaning, the measurement, and the study of ethnic identity in adolescents and adults. The articles varied widely both in conceptualization and in the terminology applied to ethnic identity and its components. They differed in whether ethnic identity was simply described or was considered a variable whose antecedents, correlates, or outcomes were studied. However, all dealt with ethnic identity in minority or nondominant group members, including White ethnics. Ethnic identity among members of a dominant group in society, although it can be conceptualized (Helms, 1985), has apparently not been studied empirically. The next section is an overview of the studies.

OVERVIEW: STUDIES OF ETHNIC IDENTITY

The articles reviewed focused on a variety of ethnic groups. The largest group of studies, nearly half the total, dealt with White ethnic groups, such as Greek and Italian Americans or French Canadians. These articles included (in order of frequency) studies from the United States, Canada, the United Kingdom, Israel, and Australia. Within White ethnic groups, Jews have been the subgroup most studied. In a few studies, White subjects were included primarily as a group in contrast to an ethnic minority group (Hispanic, Black, or Asian); in these cases the White subjects were undifferentiated as to ethnic origin.

The second largest group of studies involved Black subjects; these studies were mostly from the United States. A smaller group of studies, entirely from the United States, dealt with Hispanic subjects. A few studies focusing on Asians were primarily from the United States, but some were from Canada and Great Britain; the studies from Great Britain dealt with East Indians, mostly Pakistanis. The distribution of studies has been very uneven; many studies focused on White ethnic groups and Black Americans, but few on Asian Americans, Hispanics, or American Indians.

The articles represented research from a diversity of fields, published in 36 different journals; the majority were from psychology but some were from sociology, anthropology, social work, and education. Researchers often appeared unaware of previous work; that is, they did not cite relevant prior work. Therefore, there was much duplication of effort as researchers developed new measures independently.

The research overall presented a picture of fragmented efforts by many researchers working individually with particular ethnic groups and developing measures of limited generality. Rarely have researchers conducted follow-up studies to develop or extend a measure or to elaborate on concepts developed in a study. Nevertheless, the studies provided a starting point for understanding how different researchers have sought to understand and study ethnic identity.

DEFINITIONS OF ETHNIC IDENTITY

Ethnic identity was defined in many ways in the research reviewed. The fact that there is no widely agreed-on definition of ethnic identity is indicative of confusion about the topic. A surprising number of the articles reviewed (about two-thirds) provided no explicit definition of the construct. The definitions that were given reflected quite different understandings or emphases regarding what is meant by *ethnic identity*.

In a number of articles, ethnic identity was defined as the ethnic component of social identity, as defined by Tajfel (1981): "that part of an individual's self-concept which derives from his knowledge of his membership of a social group (or groups) together with the value and emotional significance attached to that membership" (p. 255). Some writers considered self-identification the key aspect; others emphasized feelings of belonging and commitment (Singh, 1977; Ting-Toomey, 1981; Tzuriel and Klein, 1977), the sense of shared values and attitudes (White and Burke, 1987, p. 311), or attitudes toward one's group (e.g., Parham and Helms, 1981; Teske and Nelson, 1973). In contrast to the focus by these writers on attitudes and feelings, some definitions emphasized the cultural aspects of ethnic identity: for example, language, behavior, values, and knowledge of ethnic group history (e.g., Rogler, Cooney and Ortiz, 1980). The active role of the individual in developing an ethnic identity was suggested by several writers who saw it as a dynamic product that is achieved rather than simply given (Caltabiano, 1984; Hogg, Abrams, and Patel, 1987; Simic, 1987).

In summary, researchers appeared to share a broad general understanding of ethnic identity, but the specific aspects that they emphasized differed widely. These differences are related to the diversity in how researchers have conceptualized ethnic identity and in the questions they have sought to answer; these issues are reviewed in the next section.

CONCEPTUAL FRAMEWORKS FOR THE STUDY OF ETHNIC IDENTITY

About a quarter of the studies suggested no theoretical framework, but most of the studies were based on one of three broad perspectives: social identity theory, as presented by social psychologists; acculturation and culture conflict, as studied by social psychologists, sociologists, or anthropologists; and identity formation, drawn from psychoanalytic views and from developmental and counseling psychology. There is considerable overlap among the frameworks on which the studies were based, as well as great variation in the extent to which the relevant framework or theory was discussed and applied to the research. However, these three approaches provide a background for understanding the empirical research.

Ethnic Identity and Social Identity Theory

Much of the research on ethnic identity has been conducted within the framework of social identity as conceptualized by social psychologists. One of the earliest statements of the importance of social identity was made by Lewin (1948), who asserted that individuals need a firm sense of group identification in order to maintain a sense of well-being. This idea was developed in considerable detail in the social identity theory of Tajfel and Turner (1979). According to the theory, simply being a member of a group provides individuals with a sense of belonging that contributes to a positive self-concept.

However, ethnic groups present a special case of group identity (Tajfel, 1978). If the dominant group in a society holds the traits or characteristics of an ethnic group in low esteem, then ethnic group members are potentially faced with a negative social identity. Identifying with a low-status group may result in low self-regard (Hogg, Abrams, and Patel, 1987; Ullah, 1985). An extensive literature deals explicitly with the notion of "self-hatred" among disparaged ethnic groups, generally with reference to Black Americans (Banks, 1976; V. Gordon, 1980). Much of the research reviewed was concerned with this issue; that is, whether or to what extent membership in, or identification with, an ethnic group with lower status in society is related to a poorer self-concept. A number of studies addressed these issues (Grossman, Wirt, and David, 1985; Houston, 1984; Paul and Fischer, 1980; Tzuriel and Klein, 1977; White and Burke, 1987); the specific findings are discussed later in the article.

Tajfel (1978) asserted that members of low-status groups seek to improve their status in various ways. Individuals may seek to leave the group by "passing" as members of the dominant group, but this solution may have negative psychological consequences. Furthermore, this solution is not available to individuals who are racially distinct and are categorized by others as ethnic group members. Alternative solutions are to develop pride in one's group (Cross, 1978), to reinterpret characteristics deemed "inferior" so that they do not appear inferior (Bourhis, Giles, and Tajfel, 1973), and to stress the distinctiveness of one's own group (Christian, Gadfield, Giles, and Taylor, 1976; Hutnik, 1985).

Social identity theory also addresses the issue of potential problems resulting from participation in two cultures. Both Lewin (1948) and Tajfel (1978) discussed the likelihood that identification with two different groups can be problematic for identity formation in ethnic group members because of the conflicts in attitudes, values, and behaviors between their own and the majority group (Der-Karabetian, 1980; Rosenthal and Cichello, 1986; Salgado de Snyder, Lopez, and Padilla, 1982; Zak, 1973). The issue in this case is whether individuals must choose between two conflicting identities or can establish a bicultural ethnic identity and, if so, whether that is adaptive.

A distinct but related approach to ethnic identity is based on symbolic interactionism and identity theory (Stryker, 1980). Research in this framework emphasizes the importance of shared understandings about the meaning of one's ethnic identity, which derive both from one's own group and from a "countergroup" (White and Burke, 1987).

Acculturation as a Framework for Studying Ethnic Identity

Ethnic identity is meaningful only in situations in which two or more ethnic groups are in contact over a period of time. In an ethnically or racially homogeneous society, ethnic identity is a virtually meaningless concept. The broad area of research that has dealt with groups in contact is the acculturation literature.

The term *ethnic identity* has sometimes been used virtually synonymously with *acculturation,* but the two terms should be distinguished. The concept of acculturation deals broadly with changes in cultural attitudes, values, and behaviors that result from contact between two distinct cultures (Berry, Trimble, and Olmedo, 1986). The level of concern is generally the group rather than the individual, and the focus is on how minority or immigrant groups relate to the dominant or host society. Ethnic identity may be thought of as an aspect of acculturation, in which the concern is with individuals and the focus is on how they relate to their own group as a subgroup of the larger society.

Two distinct models have guided thinking about these questions: a linear, bipolar model and a two-dimensional model. In the linear model, ethnic identity is conceptualized along a continuum from strong ethnic ties at one extreme to strong mainstream ties at the other (Andujo, 1988; Makabe, 1979; Simic, 1987; Ullah, 1985). The assumption underlying this model is that a strengthening of one requires a weakening of the other; that is, a strong ethnic identity is not possible among those who become involved in the mainstream society, and acculturation is inevitably accompanied by a weakening of ethnic identity.

In contrast to the linear model, an alternative model emphasizes that acculturation is a two-dimensional process, in which both the relationship with the traditional or ethnic culture and the relationship with the new or dominant culture must be considered, and these two relationships may be independent. According to this view, minority group members can have either strong or weak identifications with both their own and the mainstream cultures, and a strong ethnic identity does not necessarily imply a weak relationship or low involvement with the dominant culture.

This model suggests that there are not only the two acculturative extremes of assimilation or pluralism but at least four possible ways of dealing with ethnic group membership in a diverse society (Berry et al., 1986). Strong identification with both groups is indicative of integration or biculturalism: identification with neither group suggests marginality. An exclusive identification with the majority culture indicates assimilation, whereas identification with only the ethnic group indicates separation. Table 1 is an illustration of this model and some of the terms that have been used for each of the four possibilities in empirical research. A number of the studies reviewed were based on this model (e.g., M. Clark, Kaufman, and Pierce, 1976; Hutnik, 1986; Ting-Toomey, 1981; Zak, 1973), and in some the authors explored empirical evidence for the bipolar versus the two-dimensional models (e.g., Elias and Blanton. 1987; Zak, 1976). Research on this issue is summarized later.

An important empirical issue in this area has been the question of the extent to which ethnic identity is maintained over time when a minority ethnic group comes in contact with a dominant majority group (DeVos and Romanucci-Ross, 1982; Glazer and Moynihan, 1970; M. Gordon, 1964) and the impact of the process on psychological adjustment (e.g., Berry, Kim, Minde, and Mok, 1987). Underlying both these issues is the theme of culture conflict between two distinct groups and the psychological consequences of such conflicts for individuals. How such conflicts are dealt with at the individual level is part of the process of ethnic identity formation.

Table 1. Terms Used for Four Organizations, Based on Degree of Identification with Both One's Own Ethnic Group and the Majority Group

Identification with majority group	Identification with ethnic group	
	Strong	Weak
Strong	Acculturated Integrated Bicultural	Assimilated
Weak	Ethnically identified Ethnically embedded Separated Dissociated	Marginal

Ethnic Identity Formation

Both the social identity and the acculturation frameworks acknowledge that ethnic identity is dynamic, changing over time and context. In a similar vein, several of the definitions cited earlier include the idea that ethnic identity is achieved through an active process of decision making and self-evaluation (Caltabiano, 1984; Hogg et al., 1987; Simic, 1987). In a conceptual chapter, Weinreich (1988) asserted that ethnic identity is not an entity but a complex of processes by which people construct their ethnicity. However, in research based on the social identity or acculturation frameworks, investigators in general have not examined ethnic identity at the level of individual change—that is, developmentally.

A developmental framework was provided by Erikson's (1968) theory of ego identity formation. According to Erikson, an achieved identity is the result of a period of exploration and experimentation that typically takes place during adolescence and that leads to a decision or a commitment in various areas, such as occupation, religion, and political orientation. The ego identity model, as operationalized by Marcia (1966, 1980), suggests four ego identity statuses based on whether people have explored identity options and whether they have made a decision. A person who has neither engaged in exploration nor made a commitment is said to be *diffuse;* a commitment made without exploration, usually on the basis of parental values, represents a *foreclosed* status. A person in the process of exploration without having made a commitment is in *moratorium;* a firm commitment following a period of exploration is indicative of an *achieved identity* (see Table 2). Although Erikson alluded to the importance of culture in identity formation, this model has not been widely applied to the study of ethnic identity.

The formation of ethnic identity may be thought of as a process similar to ego identity formation that takes place over time, as people explore and make decisions about the role of ethnicity in their lives. A number of conceptual models have described ethnic identity development in minority adolescents or adults. Cross (1978) described a model of the development of Black consciousness in college students during the Civil Rights era. In a dissertation, Kim (1981) described Asian-American identity development in a group of young adult Asian-American women. A model of ethnic identity formation based on clin-

Table 2. Marcia's Ego Identity Statuses (Top) and Proposed Stages of Ethnic Identity (Bottom)

Marcia (1966, 1980)	Identity diffusion	Identity foreclosure	Identity crisis*	Moratorium	Identity achievement
Cross (1978)		Pre-encounter	Encounter	Immersion/emersion	Internalization
Kim (1981)		White identified	Awakening to social political awareness	Redirection to Asian American consciousness	Incorporation
Atkinson et al. (1983)		Conformity: Preference for values dominant culture	Dissonance: Questioning and challenging old attitudes	Resistance and immersion: Rejection of dominant culture	Synergetic articulation and awareness
Phinney (1989)	Unexamined ethnic identity		Ethnic identity search (Moratorium):		Achieved ethnic identity
	Lack of exploration of ethnicity Possible subtypes: Diffusion: Lack of interest in or concern with ethnicity — Foreclosure: Views of ethnicity based on opinions of others		Involvement in exploring and seeking to understand meaning of ethnicity for oneself		Clear, confident sense of own ethnicity

* Identity crisis is not one of Marcia's original four statuses.

ical experience was proposed by Atkinson et al. (1983), and Arce (1981) conceptualized the issues with regard to Chicanos.

In a recent article, Phinney (1989) examined commonalities across various models and proposed a three-stage progression from an unexamined ethnic identity through a period of exploration to an achieved or committed ethnic identity (see Table 2). According to this model, early adolescents and perhaps adults who have not been exposed to ethnic identity issues are in the first stage, an unexamined ethnic identity. According to Cross (1978) and others (e.g., Atkinson et al., 1983; Kim, 1981), this early stage is character-ized for minorities by a preference for the dominant culture. However, such a preference is not a necessary characteristic of this stage. Young people may simply not be interested in ethnicity and may have given it little thought (their ethnic identity is diffuse). Alternatively, they may have absorbed positive ethnic attitudes from parents or other adults and therefore may not show a preference fot the majority group, although they have not thought through the issues for themselves—that is, are foreclosed (Phinney, 1989).

A second stage is characterized by an exploration of one's own ethnicity, which is simi-lar to the moratorium status described by Marcia (1980). This may take place as the result of a significant experience that forces awareness of one's ethnicity ("encounter," accord-ing to Cross, 1978, or "awakening," according to Kim, 1981). It involves an often intense process of immersion in one's own culture through activities such as reading, talking to people, going to ethnic museums, and participating actively in cultural events. For some people it may involve rejecting the values of the dominant culture.

The stage model suggests that as a result of this process, people come to a deeper under-standing and appreciation of their ethnicity—that is, ethnic identity achievement or inter-nalization. This culmination may require resolution or coming to terms with two fundamental problems for ethnic minorities: (a) cultural differences between their own group and the dominant group and (b) the lower or disparaged status of their group in society (Phinney, Lochner, and Murphy, 1990). The meaning of ethnic identity achieve-ment is undoubtedly different for different individuals and groups because of their differ-ent historical and personal experiences. However, achievement does not necessarily imply a high degree of ethnic involvement: one could presumably be clear about and confident of one's ethnicity without wanting to maintain one's ethnic language or customs. A recent conceptual article suggested that the process does not necessarily end with ethnic iden-tity achievement but may continue in cycles that involve further exploration or rethink-ing of the role or meaning of one's ethnicity (Parham, 1989). A similar idea has been suggested with regard to ego identity (Grotevant, 1987).

Empirical research based on these models has involved describing changes over time in a person's attitudes and understanding about his or her ethnicity. In addition, researchers have looked at factors related to ethnic identity formation, such as parental attitudes and social class, and at correlates, including self-esteem or adjustment and attitudes toward counselors. Results of research on these questions are discussed later.

COMPONENTS OF ETHNIC IDENTITY

In order to examine questions that derive from theory or to address research questions of current interest, it is necessary to begin with a measure of ethnic identity. In this section, the various aspects of ethnic identity that were selected for study are reviewed. The majority of the studies focused on components related to what might be called the *state* of ethnic identity—that is, a person's identification at a given time. In studies of this type, the components most widely studied were self-identification as a group member, a sense of belonging to the group, attitudes about one's group membership, and ethnic involvement (social participation, cultural practices and attitudes). A much smaller group of studies emphasized *stages* of ethnic identity, or changes over time in a person's identification. In the following section, I examine these components and the ways in which they have been assessed.

Ethnicity and Ethnic Self-Identification

Self-identification (also called *self-definition* or *self-labeling*) refers to the ethnic label that one uses for oneself. Research with children has been concerned largely with the extent to which children "correctly" label themselves—that is, whether the label they choose corresponds to the ethnicity of their parents (Aboud, 1987). A related issue has been whether "incorrect" labeling is associated with a poor self-concept (Cross, 1978). Beyond childhood, the concerns are different. Adolescents and adults can be assumed to know their ethnicity; the issue is thus one of choosing what label to use for oneself. Although this appears to be a simple issue, it is in fact quite complex, inasmuch as one's ethnicity, as determined by descent (parental background), may differ from how one sees oneself ethnically.

In countries settled by Europeans (where much of the research under review was conducted), the use of an ethnic label, for example, Polish American, is for the most part optional for people of European descent. Many Whites under these circumstances use no ethnic label and may in fact be unable to identify their country of origin (Singh, 1977).

However, among those who are racially distinct, by features or skin color, or whose culture (language, dress, customs, etc.) clearly distinguishes them from the dominant group, self-identification is at least partly imposed. Calling oneself Black or Asian American is less self-categorization than recognition of imposed distinctions, and the issue is less *whether* to use an ethnic label than *which* ethnic label to adopt. For example, people whose parents or grandparents came from Mexico can call themselves Mexican American, Hispanic, Latino, or Chicano (among others) each of which has a different connotation (Buriel, 1987).

Regardless of whether an ethnic label is chosen or imposed, people may feel that a single label is inaccurate, inasmuch as they are part of two or more groups. Ethnic groups members may identify themselves as only partly ethnic and partly mainstream. For example, among a group of second-generation Irish adolescents in England, about half considered themselves part English and part Irish; the remainder called themselves either English or Irish (Ullah, 1985, 1987). Selection of a label is particularly problematic for those whose parents are from two or more distinct groups; they may, for example, call themselves mixed, such as half Hispanic and half White, or they may ignore part of their heritage and call themselves either White or Hispanic (Alipuria and Phinney, 1988).

Although ethnic self-identification is clearly an essential starting point in examining ethnic identity, it was not specifically assessed in about half the studies reviewed. In some cases, subjects were recruited from groups whose ethnicity was known to the researchers (e.g., Jewish student groups were recruited by Davids, 1982, and by Lax and Richards, 1981; students at Armenian schools were recruited by Der-Karabetian, 1980). In other studies, the subjects were simply defined as group members without explanation of how this was determined. None of the studies with Black subjects included self-identification.

The failure to assess self-definition with any group raises the possibility that the studies included subjects who did not consider themselves members of the group in question.

When self-identification was assessed, items were presented in a variety of ways. If the participants were assumed to be from a given group or groups, it was possible to provide multiple-choice items appropriate for the particular group (e.g., Ullah, 1985, 1987) or to have subjects rate themselves or match labels of themselves in terms of similarity to individuals with particular labels (Christian et al., 1976; Giles, Llado, McKirnan, and Taylor, 1979; Giles, Taylor, and Bourhis, 1977; Giles, Taylor, Lambert, and Albert, 1976; Rosenthal and Hrynevich, 1985).

However, to use these sorts of questions, the researcher must preselect participants of known ethnicity. Determining ethnicity for research purposes is in itself a methodological problem that has often been ignored. An alternative is to use an unselected sample and determine ethnicity by asking participants about their parents' ethnicity. Ethnic self-identification can then be assessed with open-ended questions or multiple-choice items with a wide range of possible alternative labels, or both. However, the responses of some subjects will vary, depending on whether they are forced to choose from a list of labels provided or are simply given a blank to fill in.

In summary, ethnic self-identification is an important but complex aspect of ethnic identity, and the way in which it is assessed needs to be considered when the results obtained are interpreted.

Sense of Belonging

People may use an ethnic label when specifically asked for one and yet may not have a strong sense of belonging to the group chosen. Therefore, it is important to assess the feeling of belonging. However, a sense of belonging was evaluated in only about a quarter of the studies reviewed, perhaps because of the difficulty of accurately tapping this subtle feeling. Researchers have devised a number of approaches to this problem; some examples are the following: "I am a person who (never, seldom, sometimes, often, very often) feels strong bonds toward [my own group]" (Driedger, 1976); "My fate and future are bound up with that of [my own group]" (Der-Karabetian, 1980; Zak, 1973, 1976): "I feel an overwhelming attachment to [my own group]" (Krate, Leventhal, and Silverstein, 1974; Parham and Helms, 1981, 1985a, 1985b). The subject may express a sense of "peoplehood" (Lax and Richards, 1981) or present self with an ethnic label (M. Clark et al., 1976; Elizur, 1984). A variation of this attitude is the importance attributed to one's ethnicity (Davids, 1982; Zak, 1973, 1976) or a feeling of concern for one's culture (Christian et al., 1976).

A sense of belonging to one's own group can also be defined in contrast to another group—that is, the experience of exclusion, contrast, or separateness from other group members (Lax and Richards, 1981): for example, "How much difference do you feel between yourself and [members of another group]?" (Ullah, 1987) or "[How similar are you to] kids from other countries who don't fit in well?" (Rosenthal and Hrynevich, 1985).

Positive and Negative Attitudes Toward One's Ethnic Group

In addition to their self-identification and a sense of a belonging, people can have both positive and negative attitudes toward their own ethnic group. These attitudes were examined in more than half the studies reviewed. Positive attitudes include pride in and pleasure, satisfaction, and contentment with one's own group. They are assessed by items such as "[I am] proud to identify with [my own group]" and "[I] consider [my own] culture rich and precious" (Driedger, 1976) and "[I am similar to] people who feel good about their cultural background" (Rosenthal and Hrynevich, 1985) or by questions such as "How much pride do you feel toward [your own group]?" (Phinney, 1989; Ullah, 1987).

The term *acceptance* is frequently used for positive attitudes, particularly in studies involving Black subjects (Paul and Fischer, 1980). Typical items include "I believe that being Black is a positive experience" and "I believe that because I am Black I have many strengths" (Parham and Helms, 1981, 1985a, 1985b) and "I feel excitement and joy in Black surroundings" (Krate et al., 1974; Parham and Helms, 1981, 1985a, 1985b). Acceptance of being Black is often phrased in contrast to White culture: "When I think of myself as a Black person, I feel I am more attractive and smarter than any White person" (Morten and Atkinson, 1983). Acceptance of being Black has also been assessed indirectly, through having subjects draw figures and determining whether they include Black characteristics. Although this method has been used commonly with children, it has also been employed in studies with adults (Bolling, 1974; Kuhlman, 1979).

Two indirect ways of measuring positive (and negative) attitudes are to have subjects rate themselves and their group in relation to adjectives with good and bad connotations (Grossman et al., 1985) or to rate a speech that had been tape-recorded in different languages and accents (Bourhis et al., 1973). The latter case included adjectives such as "arrogant," "friendly," "self-confident," and "snobbish."

The absence of positive attitudes, or the presence of actual negative attitudes, can be seen as a denial of one's ethnic identity. They include "displeasure, dissatisfaction, discontentment" with one's ethnicity (Lax and Richards, 1981); feelings of inferiority; or a desire to hide one's cultural identity (Driedger, 1976; Ullah, 1985). An item used to tap negative feelings is "[I am like/unlike] kids from other countries who try to hide their background" (Rosenthal and Hrynevich, 1985). Negative feelings may be a normal aspect of ethnic identity for some groups; Lax and Richards (1981) stated that "Jewish identity by itself does not imply acceptance of one's Jewishness. . . . Being Jewish stirs up many ambivalent feelings" (pp. 306–307). An indirect but presumably powerful way of assessing negative attitudes is to determine whether the subject would remain a group member if given the choice. Several researchers asked whether the subject, if given a chance to be born again, would wish to be born a member of their ethnic group (Der-Karabetian, 1980; Tzuriel and Klein, 1977; Zak, 1973).

In studies with Black subjects, the negative attitudes are phrased both as denial of Blackness and as preference for White culture (Morten and Atkinson, 1983; Paul and Fischer, 1980; Phinney, 1989): "Most Black people I know are failures" (Parham and Helms, 1981, 1985a, 1985b); "I believe that large numbers of Blacks are untrustworthy" (Krate et al., 1974); "Sometimes I wish I belonged to the White race"; and "I believe that White people are intellectually superior to Blacks" (Krate et al., 1974; Parham and Helms, 1981, 1985a, 1985b).

In summary, the terms and phrasing vary with the groups under study, particularly in assessments of negative attitudes. Items for most White ethnic groups are more likely to make reference to hiding or denying one's group; for Blacks and Jews, lack of acceptance or wishing to change groups suggest negative attitudes.

Ethnic Involvement (Social Participation and Cultural Practices)

Involvement in the social life and cultural practices of one's ethnic group is the most widely used indicator of ethnic identity but also the most problematic. As long as measures are based on specific practices that distinguish an ethnic group, it is impossible to generalize across groups; this issue is explored in detail later. The indicators of ethnic involvement that are most commonly assessed are language, friendship, social organizations, religion, cultural traditions, and politics.

Language. Language is the most widely assessed cultural practice associated with ethnic identity, but it was included in less than half of the studies. Language was most intensively assessed in studies of White subjects. Most of these studies dealt with subjects who had emigrated from Continental Europe to an English-speaking country (the United States, Canada, England, or Australia) and had the option of retaining their language; some were living in their country of origin (Wales) where English is dominant. Language was also assessed in a study involving American Jews in Israel, and of the nine studies of Hispanics in the United States, seven included assessment of the use of Spanish. In addition, several researchers examined the desire of adults to have their children learn their ethnic language (Caltabiano, 1984; Leclezio, Louw-Potgieter, and Souchon, 1986; Teske and Nelson, 1973).

Although language has been considered by some as the single most important component of ethnic identity, its importance clearly varies with the particular situation, and it is inappropriate for some groups. None of the studies of Black identity have included language, even though familiarity with Black English is considered an important marker of Black identity (Kochman, 1987).

Friendship. In roughly a fourth of the studies, the researchers assessed friendship, using items such as ratings of "importance of ingroup friends" and "ingroup dating" (Driedger, 1975), "ethnic background of friends" (Garcia, 1982), or other measures of ethnic friendships. Friendship was included as an aspect of ethnic identity in studies with most groups; however, only a few studies with Black subjects include this component.

Religious affiliation and practice. This component was assessed in less than a fourth of the studies; the researchers used items related to church membership, attendance of religious ceremonies, parochial education, and religious preference. The subjects of those studies came largely from White ethnic groups, from some Hispanic groups, and from one Jewish group; no studies of Blacks included religion as an aspect of ethnic identity.

Structured ethnic social groups. Participation in ethnic clubs, societies, or organizations was included as a component of ethnic identity in studies involving primarily White subjects; Asians and Hispanics were also represented, but no Black groups were.

Political ideology and activity. Involvement in political activities on behalf of one's ethnic group was included in a few studies; a disproportionately large number of those studies focused on Blacks. Typical items were "I frequently confront the system and the man" (Krate et al., 1974; Parham and Helms, 1981, 1985a, 1985b); "A commitment to the development of Black power dominates my behavior" (Krate et al., 1974); and "I constantly involve myself in Black political and social activities" (Parham and Helms, 1981, 1985a, 1985b). One measure of Black identity focused primarily on political ideology (Terrell and Taylor, 1978).

A study of Mexican-Americans included the question "Are you active in any political organization which is specifically Mexican-American oriented?" (Teske and Nelson, 1973). Some studies with White ethnics mentioned involvement with the politics of one's country of origin as an indicator of ethnic identity (Constantinou and Harvey, 1985).

Area of residence. In a few studies, the subject's area of residence was included. In some cases, the geographical region was assessed (Giles et al., 1977, 1976; Taylor, Bassili, and Aboud, 1973). In others, items tapped the number or proportion of in-group members in one's neighborhood (Der-Karabetian, 1980)—for example, "[Subject] chooses to live in an area where others [ingroup members] have settled" (Caltabiano, 1984)—or were worded to assess "[subject's] readiness to live in an integrated neighborhood" (Tzuriel and Klein, 1977). This component has not been included in studies of Blacks.

Miscellaneous ethnic/cultural activities and attitudes. In addition to those elements already mentioned, a wide variety of specific cultural activities and attitudes were assessed. Half the studies, distributed across all the groups studied, included one or more of the following miscellaneous cultural items: ethnic music, songs, dances, and dress; newspapers, periodicals, books, and literature; food or cooking; entertainment (movies, radio, TV, plays, sports, etc.); traditional celebrations; traditional family roles, values, and names; visits to and continued interest in the homeland; the practice of endogamy or opposition to mixed marriages; and knowledge about ethnic culture or history. These items were most often assessed by direct questions. However, in one study (of Chinese Americans), subjects were asked to rate themselves on attitudes or values that were presumed to be characteristic of a group; for example, agreement with the statement that "A good child is an obedient child" (Ting-Toomey, 1981).

Reliability of Measures

Specific measures of ethnic identity as a state have included various combinations of the aforementioned elements: differing numbers of items have been used to assess each one. The reliability of measures is often not reported or is low enough to raise questions about conclusions based on the measure. Of the studies analyzed, less than a fifth furnished reliability information on the measures used. The reliability coefficients cited (usually Cronbach's alpha) ranged widely (from .35 to .90), and many were quite low. Rarely was the same measure used in more than one study in order to establish reliability with different samples, and in no studies was there evidence for test-retest reliability with the same subjects. A reliable measure of ethnic identity is clearly essential to the further study of this topic.

Ethnic Identity Development

Measuring stages of ethnic identity development presents quite different problems. In only a small number of the studies reviewed did researchers attempt to deal with individual changes in ethnic identity over time; they used one of two basic approaches.

One group of studies was based on the model of Black identity formation described by Cross (1978). The researchers used variations of the Racial Identity Attitude Scale (RIAS), developed by Parham and Helms (1981) on the basis of Cross's earlier work. This scale is essentially an attitude scale, aimed at tapping negative, positive, or mixed attitudes of Blacks toward their own group and toward the White majority, attitudes that are assumed to change as the person moves through the stages. Items tap each of the four proposed stages—pre-encounter, encounter, immersion, and internalization—with reliabilities of .67, .72, .66 and .71, respectively (Parham and Helms, 1981). Issues related to the reliability of the scale were addressed in two articles (Helms, 1989; Ponterotto and Wise, 1987). Ponterotto and Wise found support for the existence of all the stages except the second, the encounter stage. However, Akbar (1989) questioned whether ethnic or racial identity, as a core personality trait, could be assessed by an attitudinal measure such as the RIAS.

A second group of studies were aimed at developing measures of stages of ethnic identity that can be applied across ethnic groups. This approach, which was based on the ego identity measures of Marcia (1966) and Adams, Bennion, and Huh (1987), focused on the two components of the process of identity formation: (a) a search for the meaning of one's ethnicity and (b) a commitment or a decision about its place in one's life. A questionnaire used with college students from four groups (Asian American, Black, Mexican American, and White) yielded reliabilities of .69 for ethnic identity search and .59 for ethnic identity commitment (Phinney and Alipuria, 1990). In a subsequent study, interviews were used to assess ethnic identity among high school students from three minority groups (Asian American, Black, and Mexican American); raters then judged each subject as being in one of three stages of ethnic identity (Phinney, 1989). Absolute agreement between raters on stage assignment was .80 (Cohen's kappa = .65).

The variety of components of ethnic identity in the research reviewed makes it difficult to summarize or draw conclusions about exactly what ethnic identity consists of. Most researchers have acknowledged its complex, multidimensional nature and have tried to understand this complexity in some way, as is examined in the next section.

INTERRELATIONSHIPS, SALIENCE, AND GENERALITY OF COMPONENTS

Researchers have approached the complexity of ethnic identity by attempting to identify its essential components, their interrelationships, and their relative salience. One common approach has been factor analysis. However, because of the variety of types and the numbers of items used, factor analysis has yielded widely discrepant results in different studies. Researchers have found a single factor for ethnic identity (Garcia and Lega, 1979); two factors, differing widely among the studies (Constantinou and Harvey, 1985; Driedger, 1976; Leclezio et al., 1986); three factors (Hogg et al., 1987); or four or more factors, again different in each study (Caltabiano, 1984; Driedger, 1975; Garcia, 1982; Makabe, 1979; Rosenthal and Hrynevich, 1985). When several groups were studied, the factors varied, depending on the group (Driedger, 1975; Rosenthal and Hrynevich, 1985).

Interrelationships of Components

A specific question that has concerned researchers is the relationship between what people say they are (ethnic self-identification) and what they actually do (ethnic involvement) or how they feel (ethnic pride). In a study of Irish adolescents in England, Ullah (1987) found a close relationship between ethnic self-definition and indices of ethnic group behavior, as did Der-Karabetian (1980) in a study with Armenian Americans. In contrast, a study of East Indian adolescents in England (Hutnik, 1986) revealed little relation between ethnic identification and behavior. In a comprehensive study in which a variety of components of ethnicity for Chicanos were measured separately, Garcia (1982) found a complex set of relationships, including a negative relationship between ethnic self-identification and preference for various ethnic practices. Pride in their Irish background, among second-generation Irish adolescents in England, was related to self-identification as Irish; those who called themselves English were more likely to hide the fact of their Irish background (Ullah, 1985).

Salience of Components

Assumptions regarding salience were implicit in the components of ethnic identity selected for study with particular groups, and these components differed widely among groups. For White ethnic groups, language and a variety of miscellaneous cultural activities were most widely used as indicators of ethnic identity, and attitudes were considered somewhat less important. In the assessment of Jewish identity, ethnic affirmation and denial were included far more than with other White groups, whereas language was less frequently included. In studies with Hispanics, language was treated as a dominant component. A distinctive pattern emerges from the studies of American Blacks: Attitudes were the most widely used element, and the measures generally included both pro-Black and anti-White attitudes. Also, political activity was more evident as a criterion for Black identity than for the other groups, but assessment of language, friends, social groups, and neighborhood were almost completely absent.

A number of studies have suggested that language is one of the most important elements of ethnic identity (Giles et al., 1976, 1977; Leclezio et al., 1986; Taylor et al., 1973). However, a study carried out in a different setting showed that language was not salient (Giles et al., 1979). Language was seldom included in studies involving particular groups, such as Blacks.

Furthermore, salience can be manipulated. When salience of ethnicity was increased through an experimental manipulation, Welsh subjects expressed closer affiliation with their group (Christian et al., 1976).

General Versus Specific Aspects of Ethnic Identity

The widely differing results from attempts to define the components and structure of ethnic identity raise a fundamental conceptual question: Is it possible to study ethnic identity in general terms, or, because each group and setting is unique, must each be studied separately? It is interesting that in the theories and definitions presented by researchers, ethnic identity was treated as a general phenomenon that is relevant across groups. Yet researchers have attempted to answer theoretical and definitional questions almost exclusively in terms of one group or, sometimes, a few specific groups.

A starting point in resolving this dilemma is to recognize that there are elements that are both common across groups and unique to ethnic identity for any group. On the basis of the research reviewed, it appears that self-identification, a sense of belonging, and pride in one's group may be key aspects of ethnic identity that are present in varying degrees, regardless of the group. Furthermore, the developmental model postulates that all ethnic group members have the option to explore and resolve issues related to their ethnicity, although they may vary in the extent to which they engage in this process, at both the individual and the group levels. A focus on these common elements would allow for comparisons across groups and permit one to determine whether general conclusions can in fact be drawn. A measure aimed at assessing common aspects of ethnic identity requires both selection of common components and wording of items in general rather than specific terms. Such a measure has recently been proposed as a start toward studying ethnic identity as a general phenomenon (Phinney, 1990).

On the other hand, the specific cultural practices, customs, and attitudes that distinguish one group from another are essential for understanding individual groups and the experience of members of those groups in particular settings and time frames (e.g., Keefe and Padilla, 1987). The study of ethnic identity at this more specific level may be of particular value for education, counseling, and therapeutic applications.

EMPIRICAL FINDINGS

Because of the different conceptualizations, definitions, and measures that have been used in the study of ethnic identity, empirical findings are difficult or impossible to compare across studies. Not surprisingly, the findings are often inconsistent.

Self-Esteem, Self-Concept, and Psychological Adjustment

A key issue in conceptual writing about ethnic identity has been the role of group identity in the self-concept: Specifically, does a strong identification with one's ethnic group promote a positive self-concept or self-esteem? Or, conversely, is identification with an ethnic group that is held in low regard by the dominant group likely to lower one's self-esteem? Furthermore, is it possible to hold negative views about one's own group and yet feel good about oneself?

Early interest in these questions stemmed from the work of K. Clark and Clark (1947), which showed that young Black children tended to prefer White dolls to Black dolls. The meaning of such findings continues to be debated, and a number of reviewers have discussed the findings (Aboud, 1987; Banks, 1976; Brand et al., 1974; V. Gordon, 1980). However, this controversy has been dealt with almost entirely in studies with children, and there has been little extension of the work into adolescence and adulthood, the topic of the current review. Given the theoretical importance of this issue, it is surprising that in only 11 of the studies reviewed, the researchers assessed self-esteem or a related construct and examined its relationship to some measure of ethnic identity. The researchers who did address this question presented conflicting results.

Three of the studies suggested positive effects of ethnic identity, although the measures used were different in each case. Among Black early adolescents (ages 13–14) of low socioeconomic status (SES), "acceptance of racial identity," as measured by six items (no reliability given), was found to be significantly related to self-concept as measured by the Tennessee Self Concept Scale (Paul and Fischer, 1980). A study with Anglo-American and Mexican-American junior high school students revealed a positive relationship between self-esteem, assessed by Rosenberg's (1979) Self-Esteem Scale, and ethnic esteem, as measured by adjective ratings of one's own group (Grossman et al., 1985). Among Israeli high school students, ego identity, which is suggestive of good adjustment, was higher among those with high ethnic group identification than among those with low identification (on a scale with reliability of alpha equal to .60), especially among the Oriental Jews, a minority group in Israel (Tzuriel and Klein, 1977).

Four studies revealed no relationship between ethnic identity and various measures of adjustment. A study of Black and White college students revealed no relationship between self-esteem (Rosenberg scale) and ethnic identity, measured in terms of similarity-to-group scores on semantic differential ratings of Blacks and Whites—that is, similarity to a stereotype of one's own group (White and Burke, 1987). Also, for Black college students, "Black consciousness," measured by attitudes toward Blacks and Whites, was unrelated to two measures of self-esteem (Houston, 1984). Among Arab-Israeli college students, self-esteem (Rosenberg scale) was not related to measures of Arab identity (scale reliability= .81) or Israeli identity (scale reliability = .83; Zak, 1976). Finally, a study of Italian Australians revealed "Italian identity" (scale reliability = .89) to be unrelated to psychosocial adjustment, according to the Offer Self-Image Questionnaire and the Erikson Psychosocial Stage Inventory (Rosenthal and Cichello, 1986). In summary, these studies of ethnic identity, in which a variety of measures of ethnic identity as a state were used, permit no definitive conclusion about its role in self-esteem.

In contrast to the preceding studies, researchers in four studies examined self-esteem in relation to the stage model of ethnic identity. By analogy with the ego-identity literature, in which positive psychological outcomes have been associated with an achieved identity (Marcia, 1980), the developmental model predicts higher self-esteem in subjects with an achieved ethnic identity. This prediction was supported in a study with 10th-grade Black, Asian-American, and Mexican-American adolescents, in which subjects at higher stages of ethnic identity, as assessed by interviews, were found to have significantly higher scores on all four subscales of a measure of psychological adjustment (self-evaluation, sense of mastery, family relations, and social relations), as well as on an independent measure of ego development (Phinney, 1989). A similar relationship between ethnic identity search and commitment (scale reliabilities = .69 and .59, respectively) and self-esteem was found among college students from four ethnic groups (Asian American, Black, Mexican American, and White); the relationship was stronger among minority group students than among their White peers (Phinney and Alipuria, 1990). A study with Black college students, which was based on Cross's (1978) process model, revealed that low self-esteem was related to the earliest (pre-encounter) stage and to the immersion (moratorium) stage, whereas high self-esteem was associated with the encounter stage, which involves events that precipitate a search or immersion (Parham and Helms, 1985a). In a related study, the pre-encounter and immersion stages were found to be related to feelings of inferiority and anxiety (Parham and Helms, 1985b). These studies suggest that a positive self-concept may be related to the process of identity formation—that is, to the extent to which people have come to an understanding and acceptance of their ethnicity.

Ethnic Identity in Relation to the Majority Culture

The acculturation framework for studying ethnic identity suggests that for understanding ethnic identity, it is necessary to consider also the individual's relationship to the dominant or majority group. Whereas a number of the studies reviewed focused on a single ethnic group, without reference to the dominant group (e.g., Asbury, Adderly-Kelly, and Knuckle, 1987; Constantinou and Harvey, 1985; Garcia and Lega, 1979; Keefe, 1986; Masuda, Hasegawa, and Matsumoto, 1973), many researchers took into consideration the relationship to the dominant group.

A central question, as discussed earlier, is whether ethnic identity is directly related to degree of acculturation or whether, conversely, it is independent, so that, for example, one could have a strong ethnic identification and also have strong ties to the dominant culture (see Table 1). Several studies suggest that the two are independent. In a study with adolescent girls of East Indian extraction who were living in England, Hutnik (1986) assessed separately self-identification (as Indian or British) and Indian and British cultural behaviors; the results showed the two dimensions to be unrelated. A similar picture emerged from a study of seven White ethnic groups in Canada (Driedger, 1976). Group scores demonstrated varying degrees of ethnic affirmation and denial for each group, which resulted in three types of ethnic identity, depending on degree of ethnic identification or denial: majority assimilator, ethnic identifiers, and ethnic marginals. Similarly, studies of Armenian Americans (Der-Karabetian, 1980), Jewish Americans (Zak, 1973), and Chinese Americans (Ting-Toomey, 1981) revealed ethnic identity and American identity to be independent dimensions.

However, other studies gave different results. A comparison of bipolar and orthogonal models of ethnic identity among Israelis living in the United States suggested that attitudes and behaviors relative to being Israeli, Jewish, or American were not independent (Elias and Blanton, 1987). Affective measures of the three aspects of identity were positively intercorrelated, whereas behavioral measures were negatively related; subjects who engaged in many typical American behaviors showed fewer Israeli behaviors. In another study of Israelis residing in the United States (Elizur, 1984), Jewish and American identity tended to be negatively related.

More complex results emerged from two studies in which qualitative data were used. An extensive study of Mexican-American and Asian-American adults (M. Clark et al., 1976) revealed six profiles representing different combinations of attitudes, behaviors, and knowledge relative to one's own culture and American culture. A qualitative study of Mexican-American high school students (Matute-Bianchi, 1986) demonstrated five types of ethnic identity, depending on the students' degree of involvement in their own ethnic culture and in the mainstream culture of the high school. Moreover, the types of identity were related to school achievement. Those students who were more embedded in the barrio culture were the least successful academically.

The value of studies such as these, in which mainstream as well ethnic orientation is assessed, has been in emphasizing that ethnic identity is not necessarily a linear construct; it can be conceptualized in terms of qualitatively different ways of relating to one's own and other groups. A problem in using this more complex conceptualization is in assessing the attributes of the contrast group. The characteristics of mainstream culture are far more difficult to define than those of a particular subculture. The issue of measurement of mainstream attitudes belongs property to the topic of acculturation; these measurement issues were thoroughly discussed by Berry et al. (1986).

The two-dimensional model provides some clarification of the importance of ethnic identity to the self-concept. Some of the contradictions and inconsistencies noted in this review may be a function of differences in the degree to which researchers have considered identification with both the ethnic group and the mainstream culture. For example, although ethnic identity, in the sense of identification with one's ethnic group, can range from strong to weak, an understanding of how ethnic identity is related to self-concept may require also determining an individual's relationship to the majority group. There is some evidence that the acculturated or integrated option may be the most satisfactory and the marginal, the least (Berry et al., 1987). However, the other two possibilities, assimilation and separation, may also provide the basis for a good self-concept, if the person is comfortable with these alternatives and is in an environment that supports them (Phinney et al., 1990).

Changes in Ethnic Identity Related to Generation of Immigration

A second focus of research within the acculturation framework is the way in which ethnic identity changes with contact with another group. Writers generally have agreed that ethnic identity is a dynamic concept, but relatively few have studied it over time. However, a number of researchers have examined changes related to generational status among immigrant groups.

Studies of generational differences in ethnic identity have shown a fairly consistent decline in ethnic group identification in later generations descended from immigrants (Constantinou and Harvey, 1985; Fathi, 1972). Ethnic identity was found to be similarly weaker among those who arrived at a younger age and had lived longer in the new country (Garcia and Lega, 1979; Rogler et al., 1980) and among those with more education (Rogler et al., 1980). However, a study of third- and fourth-generation Japanese-American youth revealed virtually no generational difference (Wooden, Leon, and Toshima, 1988), and a study of Chinese Americans suggests a cyclical process whereby ethnic identity became more important in third- and fourth-generation descendents of immigrants (Ting-Toomey, 1981). A recent study (Rosenthal and Feldman, in press) found that among adolescent Chinese immigrants, ethnic knowledge and behavior decreased between the first and second generations, but that there was no change in the importance or positive valuation of ethnicity. The authors suggest that although some behavioral and cognitive elements of ethnic identity decline, immigrants retain a commitment to their culture. Furthermore, specific programs can foster ethnic identity (Zisenwine and Walters, 1982).

A study of three age groups in Japan (Masuda et al., 1973) illustrates the possible confounding of generation with age and cultural change. Older Japanese scored higher than did younger people in a measure of Japanese identification, in results similar to the generational differences among Japanese immigrants. Comparisons between younger (second-generation) and older (first-generation) subjects may thus tap age as well as cohort differences. In a retrospective interview study with elderly Croatians, Simic (1987) noted an intensification of ethnic sentiments during later life.

Ethnic Identity and Gender

Gender may be a variable in acculturation in those cultures in which men are more likely to get jobs in the mainstream culture while the women remain at home. There may also be different cultural expectations for men and women, such as the assumption that women are the carriers of ethnic traditions. The very little research that addresses this issue suggests a greater involvement in ethnicity by women than by men. Research with Chinese-American college students revealed women to be more oriented to their ancestral culture than were men (Ting-Toomey, 1981), and a drawing study showed higher Black identification in women (Bolling, 1974). Among Irish adolescents in England, girls were significantly more likely than boys to adopt an Irish identity (Ullah, 1985). Japanese girls and women tended to score higher than boys and men on Japanese ethnic identity (Masuda et al., 1973).

In contrast, Jewish boys in Canada were found to show greater preference for Jewish norms than did girls (Fathi, 1972), a fact that the author suggested may be related to the Jewish emphasis on male dominance. Among East Indian and Anglo-Saxon adolescents in England, girls were more inclined than boys to mix with their own group, but they were also more willing to invite home someone from a different group (Hogg et al., 1987). Gender was found to interact with ethnic identity on attitudes toward counseling (Ponterotto, Anderson, and Grieger, 1986) and on a measure of visual retention (Knuckle and Asbury, 1986).

In the sparse literature on identity formation, Parham and Helms (1985b) found that Black men were more likely than Black women to endorse attitudes from the earliest stages and less likely to show evidence of the highest stage. A similar trend among Black adolescents was noted by Phinney (1989). These fragmentary results clearly allow no conclusions about sex differences in ethnic identity.

Contextual Factors in Ethnic Identity

Ethnic identity is to a large extent defined by context; it is not an issue except in terms of a contrast group, usually the majority culture. The particular context seems to be an essential factor to consider, yet relatively few researchers have examined it in any detail. There is some evidence that ethnic identity varies according to the context (e.g., Vermeulen and Pels, 1984) and the characteristics of the group (Rosenthal and Hrynevich, 1985). Adolescents report that their feelings of being ethnic vary according to the situation they are in and the people they are with (Rosenthal and Hrynevich, 1985). Ethnic identity is positively related to the ethnic density of the neighborhood (Garcia and Lega, 1979) and negatively to the occupational and residential mobility of subjects (Makabe, 1979); it varies among communities within the same state (Teske and Nelson, 1973).

Some writers have suggested that ethnic identity is less likely to be maintained among middle-SES than among lower-SES ethnic group members. Among second-generation Irish adolescents in England, those from lower socioeconomic backgrounds were significantly more likely to identify themselves as Irish than were middle-SES youth, perhaps because they lived in areas with a higher concentration of Irish immigrants. However, research based on the developmental model has revealed no relationship between stages of ethnic identity and social class among high school students (Phinney, 1989) or college students (Phinney and Alipuria, 1990), and racial identity attitudes were not predictive of socioeconomic status among Black college students (Carter and Helms, 1988).

The impact of the context on Black identity has been investigated through studies of transracial adoption. Racial identity was more of a problem for Black children and adolescents adopted into White homes than for those adopted by Black parents, although the self-esteem of the two groups did not differ (McRoy, Zurcher, Lauderdale, and Anderson, 1982). Transracially adopted Hispanic adolescents were similarly likely to identify themselves as Americans, whereas those adopted by Mexican-American couples overwhelmingly called themselves Mexican American (Andujo, 1988). Furthermore, the parental attitudes and perceptions had an important impact on the racial identity of transracial adoptees (McRoy, Zurcher, and Lauderdale, 1984).

There has been little research on such presumably important factors as the relative size of the ethnic group (at the local or the national level) or its status in the community.

Ethnic Identity Formation

The developmental model assumes that with increasing age, subjects are more likely to have an achieved ethnic identity. Although there is little empirical support for this assumption, some results suggest that there is a developmental progression. In an interview study with Black and White 8th graders, about a third of the subjects showed evidence of ethnic identity search (Phinney and Tarver, 1988); among 10th graders in a related study, the comparable figure was about half (Phinney, 1989). Thus it appeared that the older students had done more searching. In a study based on Cross's (1978) model, Black college students reported their perceptions of themselves over the past, present, and future as shifting from lower to higher levels of Black identity (Krate et al., 1974). Both longitudinal and cross-sectional studies are needed to examine changes toward higher levels of ethnic identity formation.

Although the process model of ethnic identity has not been validated, it provides an alternative way of thinking about ethnic identity. Both attitudes and behaviors with respect to one's own and other groups are conceptualized as changing as one develops and resolves issues and feelings about one's own and other groups. Differing ethnic attitudes and behaviors may therefore reflect different stages of development, rather than permanent characteristics of the group or the individuals studied. Some discrepancies in the findings regarding relationships among components of ethnic identity, reported earlier in this review, may result from studying subjects at different stages of development.

Another topic of interest in this area has been the impact of ethnic identity stages on attitudes regarding the ethnicity of counselors. Black college students in the early stages preferred White counselors (Parham and Helms, 1981), whereas those in the intermediate stages showed a preference for Black counselors (Morten and Atkinson, 1983; Parham and Helms, 1981). Results for subjects at the highest stage are mixed; they may show Black preference (Parham and Helms, 1981) or no preference (Morten and Atkinson, 1983). Stages of ethnic identity development in Blacks are also related to perceptions of White Counselors (Pomales, Claiborn, and LaFromboise, 1986).

In examining the relationship of stages of Black identity to Black value orientations, Carter and Helms (1987) found that certain values could be predicted from the stages; for example, the highest stage, internalization, was associated with a belief in harmony with nature.

The study of stages of ethnic identity is at present rudimentary; however, a developmental perspective may be able eventually to provide a more complete understanding of this phenomenon across age.

RECOMMENDATIONS FOR FUTURE RESEARCH

The most serious need in ethnic identity research is to devise reliable and valid measures of ethnic identity. To accomplish this, it is important to distinguish between general aspects of ethnic identity that apply across groups and specific aspects that distinguish groups. General measures would be valuable in addressing the important questions about ethnic identity that are raised by theory.

A key question is the implication of ethnic identity for psychological adjustment. The relationship is complex, and a clarification requires consideration not only of the strength of ethnic identity but also of the relationship to the majority culture, as outlined in Table 1, and of the stages of ethnic identity development suggested in Table 2. A specific question to be answered is whether self-esteem can be equally high in people who are acculturated, ethnically embedded (or dissociated), or even assimilated. The extent to which these alternatives are equally healthy forms of ethnic identity may depend on whether a person has an achieved ethnic identity—that is, has explored the issues and made a conscious decision.

Another critical issue is the impact of ethnic identity on attitudes toward both the dominant group and other minority groups. Is it the case that feeling good about one's own group is associated with positive attitudes toward other groups? The answer to this question could have important policy implications, as is seen in the case of Canada (Berry et al., 1977).

The role of the context—family, community, and social structure—needs further study. In particular, past researchers have generally neglected socioeconomic status as a variable and, like most psychological researchers, have mostly used middle-SES samples. Because some ethnic minority groups are substantially underrepresented in the middle class, findings based on college students or other middle-class samples may lack generality. Even data from high school surveys may be distorted because lower-class students are more likely not to obtain parental permission to participate, to be absent from school, or to have reading problems (Phinney and Tarver, 1988). The confounding of socioeconomic status and ethnicity as a personal identity issue was eloquently stated by Steele (1988).

The vast majority of the research on ethnic identity is descriptive or correlational; only a very few investigators have used experimental manipulations (e.g., Rosenthal, Whittle, and Bell, 1988). As long as purely descriptive approaches are used, ethnic identity may be confounded with other personality characteristics, and it will be impossible to identify the effect of ethnic identity on behavior and attitudes.

A significant problem that has been virtually ignored in research is that of people from mixed backgrounds. There has been little documentation of this growing phenomenon, and it has been difficult to study, as many subjects identify themselves as members of one group even though they in fact have a mixed background (Alba and Chamlin, 1983; Salgado de Snyder et al., 1982; Singh, 1977). Anecdotal evidence indicates that in some cases women who have married Hispanics are considered to be Hispanic because of their surnames, as are children whose father is Hispanic, regardless of their mothers' ethnicity. In general, persons with one minority-group parent are considered to belong to that group. The responses of all such persons to items assessing aspects of ethnic identity may well distort the findings. Collecting data on the ethnicity of both parents and distinguishing subjects who are from mixed backgrounds is an essential step in dealing with this problem.

SUMMARY

In a world where the populations of most countries are increasingly diverse, both ethnically and racially, it is essential to understand the psychological impact of such diversity (Albert, 1988). Although attitudes of the majority toward minority ethnic groups have received most attention, it is equally important to understand how ethnic group members deal with being part of a group that may be disparaged or discriminated against, that must struggle to maintain its own customs and traditions, and that is not well represented in the media, among other problems. The task of understanding ethnic identity is complicated by the fact that the uniqueness that distinguishes each group and setting makes it difficult to draw general conclusions across groups.

There are important research questions to be addressed, such as the role of ethnic identity in self-esteem, its relationship to acculturation, and its place in the development of personal identity. Currently, researchers can offer few answers to these questions because of widely differing approaches to the study of ethnic identity, including lack of agreement on what constitutes its essential components, varying theoretical orientations that have guided the research, and measures that are unique to each group. It is hoped that this article brings some conceptual clarity to this important area and stimulates further research on ethnic identity.

BIBLIOGRAPHY

Author note: Preparation of this article was supported in part by Public Health Service Grant RR-08101 from the Minority Biomedical Research Support Program Division of the National Institutes of Health.

Aboud, F. (1987). The development of ethnic self-identification and attitudes. In J. Phinney and M. Rotheram (Eds.), *Children's ethnic socialization: Pluralism and development* (pp. 32–55). Newbury Park, CA: Sage Publications.

Adams, G., Bennion, L., and Huh. K. (1987). *Objective measure of ego identity status: A reference manual.* Logan: Utah State University Laboratory for Research on Adolescence.

Akbar, N. (1989). Nigrescence and identity: Some limitations. *The Counseling Psychologist*, 17, 258–263.

Alba, R. (1985). *Ethnicity and race in the U.S.A.* London: Routledge and Kegan Paul.

Alba, R., and Chamlin, M. B. (1983). A preliminary examination of ethnic identification among Whites. *American Sociological Review*, 48, 240–242.

Albert, R. (1988). The place of culture in modern psychology. In P. Bronstein and K. Quina (Eds.), *Teaching a psychology of people: Resources for gender and sociocultural awareness* (pp. 12–18). Washington, DC: American Psychological Association.

Alipuria, L., and Phinney, J. (1988, April). *Ethnic identity in mixed-ethnic college students in two settings.* Paper presented at the meeting of the Western Psychological Association, Burlingame, CA.

Andujo, E. (1988). Ethnic identity of transethnically adopted Hispanic adolescents. *Social Work*, 33, 531–535.

Arce, C. (1981). A reconsideration of Chicano culture and identity. *Daedalus*, 110(2), 177–192.

Asbury, C., Adderly-Kelly, B., and Knuckle, E. (1987). Relationship among WISC-R performance categories and measured ethnic identity in Black adolescents. *Journal of Negro Education*, 56, 172–183.

Atkinson, D., Morten, G., and Sue, D. (1983). *Counseling American minorities.* Dubuque, IA: Wm. C. Brown.

Banks, W. (1976). White preference in Blacks: A paradigm in search of a phenomenon. *Psychological Bulletin*, 83, 1179–1186.

Berry, J., Kalin, R., and Taylor, D. (1977). *Multiculturalism and ethnic attitudes in Canada.* Ottawa, Canada: Minister of Supply and Services.

Berry, J., Kim, U., Minde, T., and Mok, D. (1987). Comparative studies of acculturative stress. *International Migration Review*, 21, 491–511.

Berry, J., Trimble, J., and Olmedo, E. (1986). Assessment of acculturation. In W. Lonner and J. Berry (Eds.), *Field methods in cross-cultural research* (pp. 291–324). Newbury Park, CA: Sage.

Bolling, J. (1974). The changing self-concept of Black children. *Journal of the National Medical Association*, 66, 28–31, 34.

Bourhis, R., Giles, H., and Tajfel, H. (1973). Language as a determinant of Welsh identity. *European Journal of Social Psychology*, 3, 447–460.

Brand, E., Ruiz, R., and Padilla, A. (1974). Ethnic identification and preference: A review. *Psychological Bulletin*, 86, 860–890.

Buriel, R. (1987). Ethnic labeling and identity among Mexican Americans. In J. Phinney and M. Rotheram (Eds.), *Children's ethnic socialization: Pluralism and development* (pp. 134–152). Newbury Park, CA: Sage.

Caltabiano, N. (1984). Perceived differences in ethnic behavior: A pilot study of Italo-Australian Canberra residents. *Psychological Reports*, 55, 867–873.

Carter, R., and Helms, J. (1987). The relationship of Black value-orientations to racial identity attitudes. *Measurement and Evaluation in Counseling and Development*, 19, 185–195.

Carter, R., and Helms, J. (1988). The relationship between racial identity attitudes and social class. *Journal of Negro Education*, 57, 22–30.

Christian, J., Gadfield, N., Giles, H., and Taylor, D. (1976). The multidimensional and dynamic nature of ethnic identity. *International Journal of Psychology*, 11, 281–291.

Clark, K., and Clark, M. (1947). Racial identification and preference in Negro children. In T. Newcomb and E. Hartley (Eds.), *Readings in social psychology* (pp. 551–560). New York: Holt.

Clark, M., Kaufman, S., and Pierce, R. (1976). Explorations of acculturation: Toward a model of ethnic identity. *Human Organization*, 35, 231–238.

Constantinou, S., and Harvey, M. (1985). Dimensional structure and intergenerational differences in ethnicity: The Greek Americans. *Sociology and Social Research*, 69, 234–254.

Cross, W. (1978). The Thomas and Cross models of psychological nigrescence: A literature review. *Journal of Black Psychology*, 4, 13–31.

Dasheksky, A. (Ed.). (1976). *Ethnic identity in society*. Chicago: Rand McNally.

Davids, L. (1982). Ethnic identity, religiosity, and youthful deviance: The Toronto computer dating project. *Adolescence*, 17, 673–684.

Der-Karabetian, A. (1980). Relation of two cultural identities of Armenian-Americans. *Psychological Reports*, 47, 123–128.

DeVos, G., and Romanucci-Ross, L. (1982). *Ethnic identity: Cultural continuities and change*. Chicago: University of Chicago Press.

Driedger, L. (1975). In search of cultural identity factors: A comparison of ethnic students. *Canadian Review of Sociology and Anthropology*, 12, 150–161.

Driedger, L. (1976). Ethnic self-identity: A comparison of ingroup evaluations. *Sociometry*, 39, 131–141.

Du Bois, W.E.B. (1983). *Autobiography of W. E. B. Du Bois*. New York: International Publishing.

Ekstrand, L. (1986). *Ethnic minorities and immigrants in a cross-cultural perspective*. Lisse, Netherlands: Swets and Zeitlinger.

Elias, N., and Blanton, J. (1987). Dimensions of ethnic identity in Israeli Jewish families living in the United States. *Psychological Reports*, 60, 367–375.

Elizur, D. (1984). Facet analysis of ethnic identity: The case of Israelis residing in the United States. *Journal of General Psychology*, III, 259–269.

Erikson, E. (1968). *Identity: Youth and crisis*. New York: Norton.

Fathi, A. (1972). Some aspects of changing ethnic identity of Canadian Jewish youth. *Jewish Social Studies*, 34, 23–30.

Frideres, J., and Goldenberg, S. (1982). Myth and reality in Western Canada. *International Journal of Intercultural Relations*, 6, 137–151.

Furnham, A., and Kirris, R. (1983). Self-image disparity, ethnic identity and sex-role stereotypes in British and Cypriot adolescents. *Journal of Adolescence*, 6, 275–292.

Garcia, J. (1982). Ethnicity and Chicanos: Measurement of ethnic identification, identity, and consciousness. *Hispanic Journal of Behavioral Sciences*, 4, 295–314.

Garcia, M., and Lega, L. (1979). Development of a Cuban ethnic identity questionnaire. *Hispanic Journal of Behavioral Sciences*, 1, 247–261.

Giles, H., Llado, N., McKirnan, D., and Taylor, D. (1979). Social identity in Puerto Rico. *International Journal of Psychology*, 14, 185–201.

Giles, H., Taylor, D., and Bourhis, R. (1977). Dimensions of Welsh identity. *European Journal of Social Psychology*, 7, 165–174.

Giles, H., Taylor, D., Lambert, W. E., and Albert, G. (1976). Dimensions of ethnic identity: An example from northern Maine. *Journal of Social Psychology*, 100, 11–19.

Glazer, N., and Moynihan, D. (1970). *Beyond the melting pot*. Cambridge, MA: Harvard University Press.

Gordon, M. (1964). *Assimilation in American life*. London: Oxford University Press.

Gordon, V. (1980). *The self-concept of Black Americans*. Lanham, MD: University Press America.

Grossman, B., Wirt, R., and Davids, A. (1985). Self-esteem, ethnic identity, and behavioral adjustment among Anglo and Chicano adolescents in West Texas. *Journal of Adolescence*, 8, 57–68.

Grotevant, H. (1987). Toward a process model of identity formation. *Journal of Adolescent Research*, 2, 203–222.

Gurin, P., and Epps, E. (1975). *Black consciousness, identity, and achievement*. New York: Wiley.

Helms, J. (1985). Toward a theoretical explanation of the effects of race on counseling: A Black and White model. *The Counseling Psychologist*, 12, 153–165.

Helms, J. (1989). Considering some methodological issues in racial identity counseling research. *The Counseling Psychologist*, 17, 227–252.

Hogg, M., Abrams, D., and Patel, Y. (1987). Ethnic identity, self-esteem, and occupational aspirations of Indian and Anglo-Saxon British adolescents. *Genetic, Social, and General Psychology Monographs*, 113, 487–508.

Houston, L. (1984). Black consciousness and self-esteem. *Journal of Black Psychology*, 11, 1–7.

Hutnik, N. (1985). Aspects of identity in a multi-ethnic society. *New Community*, 12, 298–309.

Hutnik, N. (1986). Patterns of ethnic minority identification and modes of social adaptation. *Ethnic and Racial Studies*, 9, 150–167.

Kagitcibasi, C., and Berry, J. (1989). Cross-cultural psychology: Current research and trends. In M. Rosenzweig and L. Porter (Eds.), *Annual review of psychology* (Vol. 40. pp. 493–531). Palo Alto, CA: Annual Reviews.

Kaplan, R. (1989, July). The Balkans: Europe's third world. *The Atlantic*, 263, 16–22.

Keefe, S. (1986). Southern Appalachia: Analytical models, social services, and native support systems. *American Journal of Community Psychology*, 14, 479–498.

Keefe, S., and Padilla, A. (1987). *Chicano ethnicity*. Albuquerque: University of New Mexico Press.

Kim, J. (1981). *The process of Asian-American identity development: A study of Japanese American women's perceptions of their struggle to achieve Positive identities*. Unpublished doctoral dissertation, University of Massachusetts.

Kingston, M. H. (1976). *The woman warrior*. New York: Vintage Books.

Knuckle, E., and Asbury, C. (1986). Benton revised visual retention test: Performance of Black adolescents according to age, sex, and ethnic identity. *Perceptual and Motor Skills*, 63, 319–327.

Kochman, T. (1987). The ethnic component in Black language and culture. In J. Phinney and M. Rotheram (Eds.), *Children's ethnic socialization: Pluralism and development* (pp. 219–238). Newbury Park, CA: Sage.

Krate, R., Leventhal, G., and Silverstein, B. (1974). Self-perceived transformation of Negro-to-Black identity. *Psychological Reports*, 35, 1071–1075.

Kuhlman, T. (1979). A validation study of the Draw-a-Person as a measure of racial identity acceptance. *Journal of Personality Assessment*, 43, 457–458.

Laosa, L. (1984). Social policies toward children of diverse ethnic, racial and language groups in the United States. In H. Stevenson and A. Siegel. (Eds.), *Child development research and social policy* (pp. 1–109). Chicago: University of Chicago Press.

Lax, R., and Richards, A. (1981). Observations on the formation of Jewish identity in adolescents: Research report. *Israel Journal of Psychiatry and Related Sciences*, 18, 299–310.

Leclezio, M. K., Louw-Potgieter, J., and Souchon, M.B.S. (1986). The social identity of Mauritian immigrants in South Africa. *Journal of Social Psychology*, 126, 61–69.

Lewin, K. (1948). *Resolving social conflicts*. New York: Harper.

Makabe, T. (1979). Ethnic identity scale and social mobility: The case of Nisei in Toronto. *The Canadian Review of Sociology and Anthropology*, 16, 136–145.

Malcolm X. (1965). *Autobiography of Malcolm X*. New York: Golden Press.

Maldonado, D., Jr. (1975). Ethnic self-identity and self-understanding. *Social Casework*, 56, 618–622.

Marcia, J. (1966). Development and validation of ego-identity status. *Journal of Personality and Social Psychology*, 3, 551–558.

Marcia, J. (1980). Identity in adolescence. In J. Adelson (Ed.), *Handbook of adolescent psychology* (pp. 159–187). New York: Wiley.

Masuda, M., Hasegawa, R., and Matsumoto, G. (1973). The ethnic identity questionnaire: A comparison of three Japanese age groups in Tachikawa, Japan, Honolulu, and Seattle. *Journal of Cross-Cultural Psychology*, 4, 229–244.

Matute-Bianchi, M. (1986). Ethnic identities and pattern of school success and failure among Mexican-descent and Japanese-American students in a California high school: An ethnographic analysis. *American Journal of Education*, 95, 233–255.

McRoy, R., Zurcher, L., and Lauderdale, M. (1984). The identity of transracial adoptees. *Social Casework*, 65, 34–39.

McRoy, R., Zurcher, L., Lauderdale, M., and Anderson, R. (1982). Self-esteem and racial identity in transracial and inracial adoptees. *Social Work*, 27, 522–526.

Mendelberg, H. (1986). Identity conflict in Mexican-American adolescents. *Adolescence*, 21, 215–222.

Morten, G., and Atkinson, D. (1983). Minority identity development and preference for counselor race. *Journal of Negro Education*, 52, 156–161.

Ostrow, M. (1977). The psychological determinants of Jewish identity. *Israel Annals of Psychiatry and Related Disciplines*, 15, 313–335.

Parham, T. (1989). Cycles of psychological nigrescence. *The Counseling Psychologist*, 17, 187–226.

Parham, T., and Helms, J. (1981). The influence of Black student's racial identity attitudes on preferences for counselor's race. *Journal of Counseling Psychology*, 28, 250–257.

Parham, T., and Helms, J. (1985a). Attitudes of racial identity and self-esteem of Black students: An exploratory investigation. *Journal of College Student Personnel*, 26, 143–147.

Parham, T., and Helms, J. (1985b). Relation of racial identity attitudes to self-actualization and affective states of Black students. *Journal of Counseling Psychology*, 32, 431–440.

Paul, M., and Fischer, J. (1980). Correlates of self-concept among Black early adolescents. *Journal of Youth and Adolescence*, 9, 163–173.

Phinney, J. (1989). Stages of ethnic identity in minority group adolescents. *Journal of Early Adolescence*, 9, 34–49.

Phinney, J. (1990). *The Multigroup Ethnic Identity Measure: A new scale for use with adolescents and adults from diverse groups*. Manuscript submitted for publication.

Phinney, J., and Alipuria, L. (1990). Ethnic identity in older adolescents from four ethnic groups. *Journal of Adolescence*, 13.

Phinney, J., Lochner. B., and Murphy, R. (1990). Ethnic identity development and psychological adjustment in adolescence. In A. Stiffman and L. Davis (Eds.), *Ethnic issues in adolescent mental health*. Newbury Park, CA: Sage.

Phinney, J., and Tarver, S. (1988). Ethnic identity search and commitment in Black and White eighth graders. *Journal of Early Adolescence*, 8, 265–277.

Pomales, J., Claiborn, C., and LaFromboise, T. (1986). Effect of Black students racial identity on perceptions of White counselors varying in cultural sensitivity. *Journal of Counseling Psychology*, 33, 57–61.

Ponterotto, J., Anderson, W., and Grieger, I. (1986). Black students' attitudes toward counseling as a function of racial identity. *Journal of Multicultural Counseling and Development*, 14, 50–59.

Ponterotto, J., and Wise, S. (1987). Construct validity study of the Racial Identity Attitude Scale. *Journal of Counseling Psychology*, 34, 218–223.

Rodriguez, R. (1982). *Hunger of memory*. Boston: Godine.

Rogler, L., Cooney, R., and Ortiz, V. (1980). Intergenerational change in ethnic identity in the Puerto Rican family. *International Migration Review*, 14, 193–214.

Rosenberg, M. (1979). *Conceiving the self*. New York: Basic Books.

Rosenthal, D., and Cichello, A. (1986). The meeting of two cultures: Ethnic identity and psychosocial adjustment of Italian-Australian adolescents. *International Journal of Psychology*, 21, 487–501.

Rosenthal, D., and Feldman, S. (in press). The nature and stability of ethnic identity in Chinese youth: Effects of length of residence in two cultural contexts. *Journal of Cross-Cultural Psychology*.

Rosenthal, D., and Hrynevich, C. (1985). Ethnicity and ethnic identity. A comparative study of Greek, Italian, and Anglo-Australian adolescents. *International Journal of Psychology*, 20, 723–742.

Rosenthal, D., Whittle, J., and Bell, R. (1988). The dynamic nature of ethnic identity among Greek-Australian adolescents. *Journal of Social Psychology*, 129, 249–258.

Salgado de Snyder, N., Lopez, C. M., and Padilla, A. M. (1982). Ethnic identity and cultural awareness among the offspring of Mexican interethnic marriages. *Journal of Early Adolescence*, 2, 277–282.

Simic, A. (1987). Ethnicity as a career for the elderly: The Serbian-American case. *Journal of Applied Gerontology*, 6, 113–126.

Singh, V. (1977). Some theoretical and methodological problems in the study of ethnic identity: A cross-cultural perspective. *New York Academy of Sciences: Annals*, 285, 32–42.

Sommerlad, E., and Berry, J. (1970). The role of ethnic identification in distinguishing between attitudes towards assimilation and integration of a minority racial group. *Human Relations*, 13, 23–29.

Staiano, K. (1980). Ethnicity as process: The creation of an Afro-American identity. *Ethnicity*, 7, 27–33.

Steele, S. (1988). On being Black and middle class. *Commentary*, 85, 42–47.

Stryker, S. (1980). *Symbolic interactionism: A social structural version*. Menlo Park, CA: Benjamin Cummings.

Tajfel, H. (1978). *The social psychology of minorities*. New York: Minority Rights Group.

Tajfel, H. (1981). *Human groups and social categories*. Cambridge, England: Cambridge University Press.

Tajfel, H., and Turner, J. (1979). An integrative theory of intergroup conflict. In W. Austin and S. Worchel (Eds.), *The social psychology of intergroup relations* (pp. 33–47). Monterey, CA: Brooks/Cole.

Taylor, D. M., and Bassili, J. N., and Aboud, F. E. (1973). Dimensions of ethnic identity: An example from Quebec. *Journal of Social Psychology*, 89, 185–192.

Terrell, F., and Taylor, J. (1978). The development of an inventory to measure certain aspects of Black nationalist ideology. *Psychology*, 15, 31–33.

Teske, R., and Nelson, B. (1973). Two scales for the measurement of Mexican-American identity. *International Review of Modern Sociology*, 3, 192–203.

Ting-Toomey, S. (1981). Ethnic identity and close friendship in Chinese-American college students. *International Journal of Intercultural Relations*, 5, 383–406.

Tzuriel, D., and Klein, M. M. (1977). Ego identity: Effects of ethnocentrism, ethnic identification, and cognitive complexity in Israeli, Oriental, and Western ethnic groups. *Psychological Reports*, 40, 1099–1110.

Ullah, P. (1985). Second generation Irish youth: Identity and ethnicity. *New Community*, 12, 310–320.

Ullah, P. (1987). Self-definition and psychological group formation in an ethnic minority. *British Journal of Social Psychology*, 26, 17–23.

Vermeulen, H., and Pels, T. (1984). Ethnic identity and young migrants in The Netherlands. *Prospects*, 14, 277–282.

Weinreich, P. (1983). Emerging from threatened identities. In G. Breakwell (Ed.), *Threatened identities* (pp. 149–185). New York: Wiley.

Weinreich, P. (1988). The operationalization of ethnic identity. In J. Berry and R. Annis (Eds.), *Ethnic psychology: Research and practice with immigrants, refugees, native peoples, ethnic groups and sojourners* (pp. 149–168). Amsterdam: Swets and Zeitlinger.

Wetzel, J. (1987). *American youth: A statistical snapshot*. Washington, DC: William T. Grant Foundation.

White, C., and Burke, P. (1987). Ethnic role identity among Black and White college students: An interactionist approach. *Sociological Perspectives*, 30, 310–331.

Wooden, W., Leon, J., and Toshima, M. (1988). Ethnic identity among Sansei and Yonsei church-affiliated youth in Los Angeles and Honolulu. *Psychological Reports*, 62, 268–270.

Yancey, W., Ericksen, E., and Juliani, R. (1976). Emergent ethnicity: A review and reformulation. *American Sociological Review*, 41, 391–403.

Zak, I. (1973). Dimensions of Jewish-American identity. *Psychological Reports*, 33, 891–900.

Zak, I. (1976). Structure of ethnic identity of Arab-Israeli students. *Psychological Reports*, 38, 239–246.

Zinn, M. (1980). Gender and ethnic identity among Chicanos. *Frontiers*, 5, 18–24.

Zisenwine, D., and Walters, J. (1982). Jewish identity: Israel and the American adolescent. *Forum on the Jewish People, Zionism, and Israel*, 45, 79–84.

6.

Resolving "Other" Status

Identity Development of Biracial Individuals

Maria P. P. Root

The current paper describes the phenomenological experience of marginal socio-ethnic status for biracial individuals. A metamodel for identity resolution for individuals who struggle with other status is proposed. Subsequently, multiple strategies in the resolution of ethnic identity development are proposed among which the individual may move and maintain a positive, stable self-image.

Half-breed, mulatto, mixed, eurasian, mestizo, amerasian. These are the "others," biracial individuals, who do not have a clear racial reference group (Henriques, 1975; Moritsugu, Foerster, and Morishima, 1978) and have had little control over how they are viewed by society. Because of their ambiguous ethnic identity and society's refusal to view the races as equal, mixed race people begin life as *marginal people.* Freire (1970) observes that *marginality is not a matter of choice, but rather a result of oppression of dominant over subordinate groups.*

The challenge for a nonoppressive theory and therapy, as feminist perspectives attempt, is twofold. First, racism must be recognized and challenged within the therapist's and theorist's world. Without meeting this challenge, it is unlikely that nonpathological models of mental health for mixed race persons can be developed. Second, theoretical conceptualization and application to therapy must become multiracial and multicultural to accurately reflect the process of more than a single racial group. New templates and models for identity development are needed which reflect respect for difference. Necessarily, these theories will need to deviate from traditional linear or systemic models which both have singular endpoints to define mental health. These models are based upon male mental health or, more recently, alternative models define White women's mental health. Current models of mental health do not accommodate the process by which individuals who have "other" identities, such as biracial and or gay/lesbian, arrive at a positive sense of self-identity or maintain a positive identity in the face of oppressive attitudes.

In this paper, the phenomenological experience of "otherness" in a biracial context is described and its socio-political origins explored. The integration of biracial heritage into a positive self-concept is complicated and lengthy. An alternative model for resolution of ethnic identity is offered which takes into account the forces of sociocultural, political, and familial influences on shaping the individual's experience of their biracial identity. The uniqueness of this paper's approach is that several strategies of biracial identity resolution are offered with no inherent judgment that one resolution is better than another. Instead, the problems and advantages inherent with each type of resolution are discussed. It is proposed that the individual may shift their resolution strategies throughout their lifetime in order to nurture a positive identity.

While early sociological theory might suggest that such a model as proposed here describes a "marginal personality" (Stonequist, 1937), or in DSM-III-R nosology (American Psychiatric Association, 1987) inadequate personality or borderline personality, recent research suggests that biracial young adults are generally well adjusted (Hall, 1980; Pouissant, 1987). Thus, the resolution of major conflicts inherent in the process of racial identity development may result in a flexibility to move between strategies which may reflect positive coping and adaptive abilities and be independent of the integrity of the individual's personality style.

ASSUMPTIONS ABOUT THE HIERARCHY OF COLOR IN THE UNITED STATES

Several general assumptions are made throughout this paper which are important for understanding the origins and dynamics of conflict surrounding the biracial individual. These dynamics further influence the developmental process of identity resolution.

First, in the United States, despite our polychromatic culture, we are divided into White and non-White. The positive imagery created by the "melting-pot" philosophy of the United States is relevant to White ethnic groups of immigrants such as the Irish, French, and Scandinavian people and not Africans, Asians, Hispanics, or even on home territory, American Indians. Cultural pluralism is neither appreciated nor encouraged by the larger culture.

Second, White is considered superior to non-White: The privileges and power assumed by Whites are desired by non-Whites. It is from this assumption attempts are made to prevent racial mixing because free interaction assumes equality. A corollary of this assumption is that mixed race persons who are part White and can pass as such will be very likely to strive for this racial identity in order to have maximum social power and to escape the oppression directed towards people of color.

The third assumption is that there is a hierarchy of racial/cultural groups based upon their similarity to middle-class White social structure and values. Thus, in general, Asian Americans have a higher social status than Black Americans in White America.

The hierarchical social status system based upon color has oppressed biracial people in two major ways. Both reasons stem from American society's fear of "racial pollution" (Henriques, 1975) (an attitude that was acutely reflected in Hitler's Germany). First, biracial persons have been given little choice in how they are identified. Any person with non-White ethnic features or traceable non-White blood is considered non-White (cf. Henriques, 1975). As a result, Poussaint (1984) notes that any individual with one Black and one non-Black parent is considered Black. Because Asian ethnic groups can be equally oppressive in their fear of "racial pollution" (cf. Murphey-Shigematsu, 1986; Wagatsuma, 1973), a child that is half Asian and half anything else, particularly Black, is identified by the blood of the non-Asian parent. Mixed race persons from two minority groups are likely to experience oppression from the racial group of heritage which has higher social status. This method of "irrational," incomplete racial classification has made identity resolution for the biracial individual very difficult and oppressive.

The second source of oppression stems from society's silence on biracialism as though if it is ignored, the issue will go away. It was only as recently as 1967 that the Supreme Court ruled in the *Lovings* case of Virginia that anti-miscegenation laws were unconstitutional, a ruling based on an interpretation of the 14th amendment (1868) to the Constitution that could have been made any time in the previous 100 years (Sickels, 1972). Subsequently, the last 12 states with anti-miscegenation laws were forced to overturn them. However, this ruling does not change attitudes. Society still prohibits interracial unions (Petroni, 1973).

The last assumption about the hierarchy of color is necessary for understanding the marginality of biracial persons who are part White. Because Whites have been the oppressors in the United States, there is a mistrust by people of color of those accepted by or identified as White. Subsequently, those biracial individuals who are part White (and look White) will at times find it harder to gain acceptance by people of color by virtue of the attitudes and feelings that are projected onto them because of their White heritage and the oppression it symbolizes to people of color (Louise, 1988).

Being mixed race, like interracial marriages has meant different things at different times (e.g., whether it reflects sexual oppression of a minority group, or equity and similarity of racial groups). Nevertheless, mixed race persons have always had an ambiguous ethnic identity to resolve. *It is the marginal status imposed by society rather than the objective mixed race of biracial individuals which poses a severe stress to positive identity development.* There are few if any role models due to the lack of a clear racial reference group. Friends, parents, and other people of color usually do not comprehend the unique situation and intrapersonal conflict inherent in the resolution of an ambiguous ethnic identity for mixed race persons.

THE BEGINNING OF "OTHERNESS"

The themes described in the development of awareness of otherness in biracial persons have been highlighted in several recent research reports, e.g., Asian-White (Murphy-Shigematsu, 1986), Black-Asian (Hall, 1980), and Black-White mixes (Pouissant, 1984). The themes of the early years are around race, family, acceptance, difference, and isolation. It is suggested that the intrapersonal and interpersonal conflicts which emerge out of these themes are circular and transitory. They reemerge at different points in development with a chance for a greater depth of resolution and understanding with each cycle.

The awareness of "otherness," or ambiguous ethnicity begins early when a child starts to be aware of color around age three (Goodman, 1968) but before a sense of racial identity is formed. An ethnic name or non-ethnic name, which may not be congruent with how a child is perceived, can intensify this awareness. Initially this awareness develops from being identified as different from within any ethnic community. Questions and comments such as, "Where are you from?" "Mixed children are so attractive," and "You are so interesting looking," heighten the feeling of otherness. This acknowledgment of a child's ethnic mix or differentness is natural and not in and of itself harmful or particularly stressful. In fact, the special attention initially may feel good. It is the combination of inquisitive looks, longer than passing glances to comprehend unfamiliar racial-ethnic features (an "unusual or exotic look"), and comments of surprise to find out that the child is one or the other parent's biological child *along with* disapproving comments and non-verbal communication that begin to convey to the child that this otherness is "undesirable or wrong." Suddenly, previously neutral acknowledgment or special attention is interpreted as negative attention. It is with these reactions that the child in her or his dichotomous way of knowing and sorting the world may label her or his otherness as bad. The child's egocentrism can result in assuming blame or responsibility for having done something wrong related to their color; subsequently, one may notice in young children peculiar behaviors to change racial characteristics such as attempts to wash off their dark color (Benson, 1981). Because the child is not equipped to resolve this conflict at such an early age, the conflict in its complexity is suppressed. It emerges only when negative experiences force the conflict to the surface.

During the early grade school years, children start comprehending racial differences consciously (Goodman, 1968). Self-concept is in part internalized by the reflection of self in others' reactions (Cooley, 1902). Subsequently, a significant part of identification of self in reference to either racial group is influenced by how siblings look, their racial identification, and people's reactions to them. Racial features can vary greatly among the children of the same parents; for example in a Black-White family, one child may look white, one may look black, and one may look mixed.

They are teased by their schoolmates, called names, and or isolated—all the result of the prejudice that is transmitted by relatives, the media, and jokes. For those children who are products of interracial unions during foreign wars (i.e., WW II, Korean War, Vietnam War), fear of the "enemy," translated into national hatred towards the "enemy," may be projected onto interracial families and their children.

Once the child comprehends that there is a concept of superiority by color, she or he may attempt to achieve acceptance by embracing membership in the "hierarchically superior" racial group of their heritage, and rejecting the other half of their heritage. For example, Black-White children may want their hair straightened if it is kinky; Asian-White children may want blue eyes.

A teacher's oppressive assumptions and projections can also contribute to the marginality of the biracial child. This child may be singled out in ways that set her or him apart from peers. Unrealistic expectations of the child may be assumed, and misperceptions of the child's environment perpetuated. For example, in assuming that the child identifies with a culture unfamiliar to the teacher, she or he may be asked to "teach" the class about their racial/cultural group (while other children are not asked to do the same). By her or his action, the teacher is likely to project stereotypes onto the child with which they may not identify.

During the process of ethnic identity development, the biracial child from mid-grade school through high school may be embarrassed to be seen with one or both parents. This embarrassment reflects internalized oppression of societal attitudes towards miscegenation, possible internalized family oppression, as well as more typical American adolescent needs to appear independently functioning of their parents.

The Role of Family

The family environment is critical in helping the child and teenager to understand their heritage and value both races. A positive self-concept and view of people is promoted in interracial partnerships and extended families in which a person's value is independent of race though race is not ignored. This environment, whether it be as a single or two parent household, gives the individual a security that will help them weather the stress of adolescence. It is this unusual objectivity about people which determines the options the biracial person has for resolving their identity.

Unfortunately, the stress that has been experienced by interracial families, particularly those that have developed during wartime (e.g., Vietnam and the Korean War), has often resulted in a lack of discussion of race, discrimination, and coping strategies for dealing with discriminatory treatment. This silence has perhaps reflected these families' needs for a sanctuary from the painful issue of racial differences. Similar to issues of sexuality, the silence may also reflect the difficulty most people appear to have in discussing race issues.

Being identified with a minority group that is oppressed can generate feelings of inferiority within the biracial person, particularly if this parent is treated as such in the extended family. If the extended family is primarily composed of the socially dominant racial group, overt or covert prejudicial remarks against the parent with less racial social status will increase the child's insecurity about their acceptance. He or she may subsequently also devalue cultural and racial features associated with this parent in an attempt to be accepted.

Outright rejection of the parent with less racial social status, in the aspiration of being conditionally accepted by the dominant cultural group, reflects internalization and projection of discriminatory, oppressive attitudes towards one's own racial heritage (Sue, 1981) and creates tremendous intrapersonal conflict in resolving racial identity. Rejection at this age stems from the awareness that one is judged by those with whom they affiliate; color is a social issue that regulates acceptance and power.

In general, the intensity of the child's reaction is mediated by the racial diversity present in the community, the amount of contact the individual has with other biracial individuals, and the presence of equity among racial groups in their community (Allport, 1958). A child is much less likely to be embarrassed or to reject that part of their heritage that is judged negatively by society if there are ethnic communities which live side by side, if the parent with less racial social status has pride in themselves, and if parents have equal social status within the family. (It is important to be aware that persons of different races in relationships are not exempt from acting prejudicially or in an oppressive manner towards each other.) Based upon the pervasiveness of racism and the widespread oppression of women in American culture, it is hard to imagine equity in an interracial, heterosexual marriage.

Some families have a difficult start when an interracial relationship results in the severing of emotional and physical ties by the extended family such as in refusals to visit or accept a marriage or the children. It is a type of abandonment which contributes to mixed race children feeling more different and insecure from other children. Emotional cutoffs are more subtle than physical ones and can be equally damaging, e.g., biracial grandchildren are treated negatively compared to the rest of the grandchildren. This type of discrimination can be very subtle such as loving treatment of biracial child combined with a simultaneous refusal to acknowledge biracial features. Cutoffs can also occur by non-White families and communities. For example, more traditional Japanese grandparents may refuse to accept grandchildren who are any other race *and* ethnic background (e.g., Chinese). Rigid, impermeable physical, emotional, and psychological boundaries communicate hatred and judgment; they mirror to a greater or lesser extent community feelings.

The estrangement and isolation described above encourage denial and rejection of the part of the self that has been unaccepted by the extended family; it is very difficult not to internalize this oppression and rejection. As in the case of people who are emotionally deprived of acceptance, some mixed race persons will subsequently try to obtain the approval or acceptance of those persons who are least willing to give it. In the case of biracial children, they may place extra importance on the opinions of persons whose race is the same as their grandparents who initiated the cutoff. Alternately, they may displace anger towards the extended family onto strangers of the same race.

Summary

The process of identity development so far mirrors what Atkinson, Morten, and Sue (1979) describe in their first two stages of minority identity development. In the first stage (Conformity Stage), there is a preference for the dominant culture's values (which in the case of the biracial person may be part of their heritage). In the second stage (Dissonance Stage), information and experiences are likely to create confusion and challenge the individual's idealization of the dominant culture. It is at this point that the individual is usually reaching the end of elementary school and entering junior high school.

Due both to the adolescent's motivation to belong to a community or group and to the adolescent's reaction to a sense of injustice, the biracial individual may seek refuge and acceptance with the group that represents the other half of their heritage. The Minority Identity Development Model predicts that in the third stage (Resistance and Immersion) there will be a simultaneous rejection of the other part of their racial heritage, e.g., being angry and distrustful towards Whites (Atkinson et al., 1979) or the racial-social group with greater status. However, this is where models for identity development are not adequate for the biracial individual's unique situation.

For the biracial individual to reject either part of their racial heritage continues an internalized oppression. In reality, it appears that some biracial persons attempt to do this, but the attempts are likely to be very short-lived due to powerful reminders of both sides of their racial heritage. To reject the dominant culture is to reject one parent and subsequently, an integral part of themselves that is unchangeable, particularly if it is the same-sex parent. And because racial groups other than White have their prejudices and fears, the biracial individual may feel neither fully accepted nor fully privileged by their other reference group. The individual is harshly reminded of their ambiguous ethnic/racial status; they are an *other*. They are *marginal* until they achieve a unique resolution for themselves that accepts both parts of their racial heritage. In order to move out of marginal status they need to place less importance on seeking social approval and even move beyond the dichotomy of thinking about the world and self as White versus non-White, good versus bad, and inferior versus superior. This strategy towards resolution requires the child to do something that in all likelihood they have few models to emulate.

FACING RACISM: THE END OF CHILDHOOD

In retrospective reports, biracial adults report differing degrees of awareness of the extent to which their biracial heritage increased the stress of adolescence (Hall, 1980; Murphy-Shigematsu, 1986; Seattle Times, April 1988). This awareness seems to be effected by the communities in which they have lived, parental support, acceptance by the extended family, racial features, and friends.

Junior high and high school are difficult developmental years as teenagers seek a balance between establishing a unique identity while pursuing conformity to peer values. For many biracial individuals, the teenage years appear to be encumbered by a more painful process than the monoracial person. Racial identity conflict is forced to the surface through increased peer dependence, cliques, dating, and movement away from the family.

Turmoil is generated when acceptance at home is not mirrored in the community. At an age that one depends on peers' reactions as the "truth," the teenager may be angry at their parents for failing to prepare them, or for leading them to believe that they are wonderful, lovable, and likable. This inconsistency results in confusion, grief, and anger. Subsequently, conflicts of vague origin increase between children and parents; the adolescent sentiment, "You don't understand; no one understands!" takes on added meaning. Teenagers feel increasingly isolated when they do not know who to trust and as a result may become vulnerable to interpreting environmental cues. For those biracial individuals who feel a tremendous amount of alienation, they may dismiss the positive feedback about self and become extra sensitive to negative feedback. They may overcompensate academically and or in social relationships in order to prove their worth.

A dual existence may be reported by the biracial person; they may appear to be accepted and even popular, but may simultaneously continue to feel different and isolated. Morishima (1980) suggests there may be more identity conflicts for Asian/White children because of their ambiguous appearance. Many White-Asians reflect feeling different regardless of growing up in predominantly White or Asian neighborhoods (Murphy-Shigematsu, 1986). In contrast, Black-White and Black-Asian persons' racial identities appear to be more influenced by their neighbors' color (Hall, 1980), though this difference may simply reflect the continuing, strong oppression of Blacks leading to less freedom of choice for persons who are part Black. However, the biracial adolescent may not relate their feelings of alienation to their biracial status, particularly in the case of those persons who have appeared to move well between and among racial groups. For therapists working with biracial persons, this source of alienation should always be kept in mind, especially with vague complaints of dissatisfaction, unhappiness, and feelings of isolation.

Dating brings many of the subtle forms of racism to the surface. For mixed race persons, all dating is interracial and can be fraught with all the tensions that have historically accompanied it (Petroni, 1973). For the teenager who has seemingly been accepted by different racial groups and has friends of different races they may be confronted with the "It's okay to have friends who are Black (Asian, White, etc.), but it's not okay to date one, and definitely not okay to marry one." A more subtle form of this racism occurs with parental encouragement of interracial friendships and even dating. However, more covert communication imparts the message, "you can date one, but don't marry one." For those biracial persons who can "pass" as White on the exterior, but do not identify as such, their attraction to non-Whites may be met with statements such as, "You can do better than that." This statement is interpreted as a prejudicial comment towards their internal perception and identification of themselves. For some biracial persons this will be the first time that they experience barriers because of color or their socially perceived ambiguous race. For the child who has grown up in an extended White family and has been encouraged to act White and identify as White, dating is painful. The teenager or young adult may avoid much dating and or continue in their activities in which these conflicts are absent.

A form of racism which surfaces during adolescence and may continue throughout life is "tokenism," which occurs both personally and vocationally. The biracial person's racial ambiguity and partial similarity by values or appearance may be used by a dominant group as a way of satisfying a quota for a person of color who is less threatening than a mono-racial person of color (despite how the biracial person identifies). What makes this type of recruiting oppressive is that the group is using this person to avoid dealing with their racism; furthermore, they are assigning racial identity for the person and not informing her or him of their purpose. The group or organization subsequently uses their association with this person as evidence of their affirmative action or antiracist efforts. As a result, they have actually made this person marginal to the group.

Gender Issues

Like women, non-White persons have had to work harder to prove themselves equal by White, male standards. This observation is true for mixed race persons who may have to fight misperceptions that mixed race persons may be abnormal. The arenas in which biracial men and women have particular difficulties are different. Non-White men, because they have more social, economic, and political power than most women, are particularly threatening to White America. It is hypothesized that mixed race men will have a more difficult time overcoming social barriers than mixed race women; they will have to work harder to prove themselves and experience an oppression, which while shared by other minority group men, may exist also within their minority reference groups toward them.

On the other hand, because women in general are less threatening to the mainstream culture than men, mixed race women may not experience as much direct oppression as mixed race men. Biracial women may, in fact, be perceived as less threatening than mono-racial women of color. They are likely to have difficulty comprehending, and then subsequently coping with pervasive myths that mixed race women are "exotic" and sexually freer than other women (Petroni, 1973; Wagatsuma, 1973). These myths appear to stem from myths that interracial relationships are based upon sex (cf. Petroni, 1973). Coupled with a lack of acceptance, some biracial women become sexually promiscuous in a search for acceptance (Gibbs, 1987). Mixed race women may also have more difficulty in relationships because of intersections of myths, lower status as women, and their search for an identity.

Summary

Racism challenges adolescent optimism. The young person's sensitivity to social approval and the human need for belonging make the resolution of biracial identity a long, uncharted journey. The path is determined by family, community, and peer values and environments. Racial features including skin color of self and family members also shape one's sense of racial identity.

To assume that the biracial person will racially identify with how they look is presumptive, but pervasive. Besides, the biracial person is perceived differently by different people. *Many persons make the mistake of thinking that the biracial person is fortunate to have a choice; however, the reality is that the biracial person has to fight very hard to exercise choices that are not congruent with how they may be visually and emotionally perceived.* She or he should have options to go beyond identifying with one or the other racial group of their heritage; the limitations of this dichotomy of options is oppressive and generates marginal status. To be able to have an expanded slate of options may shorten the journey and reduce the pain involved in resolution of biracial identity.

STRATEGIES FOR RESOLUTION OF "OTHER" STATUS

Several models for identity development exist both in the psychological and sociological bodies of literature. Minority models for identity development share in common the rejection of White values in order to appreciate minority values. However, as pointed out in the Atkinson et al.'s (1979) model, there is an inherent difficulty in rejecting "Whiteness" if one is part White. In fact, the author proposes that for those individuals who are part White to manifest hatred towards Whiteness probably reflects oppression within the nuclear and extended family system. For biracial persons who are a minority-minority racial mix, it is not clear how to apply this model.

A Beginning Schematic for Identity Development

I am proposing a schematic metamodel that might be used to understand the process of identity development for persons with different types of "other" status. This model is schematically a spiral where the linear force is internal conflict over a core sense of definition of self, the importance of which is largely determined by socialization (e.g., race, gender). Different sources of conflict may move the individual forward. It is proposed, however, that in each person's life there are at least one or two significant conflicts during critical developmental periods that move them forward. The circular or system forces encompass the political, social, and familial environments.

I suggest that in the identity development of the biracial person, the strongest recurring conflict at critical periods of development will be the tension between racial components within oneself. Social, familial, and political systems are the environments within which the biracial person appears to seek a sense of self in a circular process repeatedly throughout a lifetime. Themes of marginality, discrimination, and ambiguity are produced by these systems.

At all times, biracial persons contend with both parts of their racial heritage. Early in the process of identity development, after the child has become aware of race, she or he is likely to compartmentalize and separate the racial components of their heritage. The attention they give to aspects of their heritage may alternate (though not necessarily equally) over time. This alternating represents conflict and lack of experience and strategies for integrating components of self. Resolution reflects the lack of need for compartmentalizing the parts of their ethnic heritage.

The rest of this paper is dedicated to outlining four general resolutions of biracial identity. That there is more than one acceptable outcome confronts the limitations of traditional psychological theory which allow for only a single healthy endpoint. If there is another step in the contribution that feminist theory can make to personality development, it might be to provide flexibility and tolerance for more than a single definition of mental health.

The factors and criteria that determine each resolution are outlined. All resolutions are driven by the assumption that an individual recognizes both sides of their heritage. The resolutions that are proposed are an articulation of what appears on the surface: acceptance of the identity society assigns; identification with a single racial group; identification with both racial groups; and identification as a new racial group.

Acceptance of the Identity Society Assigns

Biracial people growing up in more racially oppressive parts of the country are less likely to have freedom to choose their racial identity. They are likely to be identified and identify as a person of color which will be equated with subordinate status. This strategy reflects the case of a passive resolution that is positive but may stem from an oppressive process. However, it is possible for it to be a positive resolution if the individual feels they belong to the racial group to which they are assigned. Affiliation, support, and acceptance by the extended family is important to this resolution being positive.

Individuals who have largely been socialized within an extended family, depending on them for friendship as well as nurturance, are likely to racially identify with this group regardless of their visual similarity or dissimilarity to the extended family. One will tend to identify with the ethnic identity with which society views the family. The advantage of this identification is that the extended (well-functioning) family is a stable, secure reference group whose bonds go beyond visual, racial similarity.

This resolution is the most tenuous of the strategies outlined in that the individual may be perceived differently and assigned a different racial identity in a different part of the country. Because one's self-image in the mind's eye is stable across significant changes, the conflict and subsequent accumulated life experience would need to be tremendous to compel the individual to change their internally perceived racial identity. In the event of this challenge, the biracial person may work towards a more active resolution process. However, it is likely that she or he will still racially identify the same way but based on a different process such as identification with the extended family. Evidence of a positive resolution is that the individual would educate those persons with whom they interact of their chosen identity.

Identification with Both Racial Groups

Some biracial persons identify with both racial groups they have inherited. When asked about their ethnic background, they may respond, "I'm part Black and part Japanese," or "I'm mixed." This resolution is positive if the individual's personality remains similar across groups and they feel privileged in both groups. They may simultaneously be aware that they are both similar and different compared to those persons around them. However, they view their otherness as a unique characteristic of self that contributes to a sense of individuality.

This may be the most idealistic resolution of biracial status, and available in only certain parts of the country where biracial children exist in larger numbers and mixed marriages are accepted with greater tolerance by the community such as on the West coast. This strategy does not change other people's behavior; thus, the biracial person must have constructive strategies for coping with social resistance to their comfort with both groups of their heritage and their claim to privileges of both group.

Identification with a Single Racial Group

The result of this strategy sometimes looks identical to the strategy of assuming the racial identity that society assigns. It is different, however, by the process being active rather than passive and not the result of oppression. In this strategy, the individual *chooses* to identify with a particular racial/ethnic group regardless if this is the identity assumed by siblings, assigned by society, or matching their racial features. This is a positive strategy if the individual does not feel marginal to their proclaimed racial reference group and does not deny the other part of their racial heritage. This is a more difficult resolution to achieve in parts of the country which have the strongest prohibitions against crossing color lines (e.g., the South).

A major difficulty may be faced with this strategy when there is an incongruous match between how an individual is perceived by others and how they perceive themselves. With this strategy, the biracial person needs to be aware and accept the incongruity and have coping strategies for dealing with questions and suspicion by the reference group. Some individuals will need to make a geographic move to be able to live this resolution more peacefully.

Identification as a New Racial Group

This person most likely feels a strong kinship to other biracial persons in a way that they may not feel to any racial group because of the struggle with marginal status. Identification as a new race is a positive resolution if the person is not trying to hide or reject any aspect of their racial heritage. This individual may move fluidly between racial groups but view themselves apart from these reference groups without feeling marginal because they have generated a new reference group. There are few examples of biracial groups being recognized in a positive way. Hawaii perhaps sets one of the best examples with the Hapa Haole (White-Asian) (Yamamoto, 1973).

A clear problem with this resolution is that society's classification system does not recognize persons of mixed race. Thus, this individual would continually experience being assigned to a racial identity and would need to inform people of the inaccuracy when it felt important to them.

Summary

I suggest that these strategies are not mutually exclusive and may coexist simultaneously, or an individual may move among them. Such movement is consistent with a stable, positive sense of identity if the individual does not engage in denial of any part of their heritage (internalized oppression). Two themes are common to the resolutions listed above. First, it is important that the biracial person accept both sides of her or his racial heritage. Second, the biracial person has the right to declare how they wish to identify themselves racially—even if this identity is discrepant with how they look or how society tends to perceive them. Third, the biracial person develops strategies for coping with social resistance or questions about their racial identity so that they no longer internalize questions as inferring that there is something wrong with them. Rather, they attribute questions and insensitivities to ignorance and racism.

Resolution of biracial identity is often propelled forward by the internal conflict generated by exposure to new people, new ideas, and new environments. Subsequently, it is not uncommon that many individuals emerge out of college years with a different resolution to their racial identity than when they graduated high school. Furthermore, geography plays a large part in the options the individual has. Living in more liberal parts of the country may be necessary to exercise a wider range of options with less social resistance.

CONCLUSION

The multiple strategies for resolution of "other" status in this paper constitutes a proposal, challenge, and appeal to theorists of human personality development to be more flexible in considering the range of positive psychological functioning. Psychological theories have been oppressive by their narrow range of tolerance and allowance for positive mental health. As a result, many different types of people can relate to the search for a resolution of other status, though not necessarily based on racial/ethnic ambiguity. If theories of identity development allowed for a slate of equally valid resolutions of conflict around basic components of identity, fewer people may struggle with "identity crises." Because of the role that feminist theory has played in attempting to validate the experience of persons with "other" status by sexual orientation, religious/ethnic identity, etc., *it seems that feminist theorists and therapists may be the persons most able to develop flexible models of mental health that truly allow for diversity.* But first, more feminist theorists and therapists will have to reach out beyond their boundaries of cultural safety to understand issues of race.

Although it appears that the biracial person may have the best of both worlds, this is a naive assumption which presumes that she or he has unopposed freedom to choose how she or he wishes to be perceived. In reality all racial groups have their prejudices which when projected onto the biracial person are the creators of marginal status. The biracial person does not have a guaranteed ethnic reference group if they leave it to the group to determine if they can belong.

The key to resolving other status derived from ethnic ambiguity requires an individual to move beyond the dichotomous, irrational categorization of race by White versus non-White, which in turn has been equated with degrees of worth and privilege in our culture. Toward this goal, three significant assumptions can be made about the experience of the biracial person which subsequently affects their process of identity resolution.

First, the biracial person does not necessarily racially identify with the way she or he looks (Hall, 1980). Because self-image is an emotionally mediated picture of the self, one's perception of self is governed by more than racial features. One's image of self is shaped by the presence or absence of other people similar to them, the racial features of siblings, exposure to people of both races which they inherit, identification with one parent over another, peer reactions, and how the extended family has perceived them as children.

Second, unlike monoracial people of color, the biracial person does not have guaranteed acceptance by any racial reference group. Thus, minority models of identity development do not reflect the resolution of this situation which is the crux of the biracial person's marginal status. *Looking for acceptance from others keeps the biracial person trying to live by "irrational" racial classification rules which may keep her or him marginal to any group.*

The third assumption is that there is more than one possible, positive resolution of racial identity for biracial persons. This assumption reflects a departure from traditional European, male originated identity models which have a single, static, positive outcome. Furthermore, the *resolution strategies for biracial identity can change during a lifetime.* It is this ability to be flexible that may indeed determine both self-acceptance and constructive, flexible coping strategies.

Marginality is a state created by society and not inherent in one's racial heritage. *As long as the biracial person bases self-acceptance on complete social acceptance by any racial reference group, they will be marginal.* Freire (1970) clearly articulates the origin and subsequently difficult resolution of marginality,

> ... marginality is not by choice, (the) marginal (person) has been expelled from and kept outside of the social system ... *Therefore, the solution to their problem is not to become "beings inside of," but ... (people) ... freeing themselves; for, in reality, they are not marginal to the structure, but oppressed ... (persons) ... within it* (author's emphasis). (pp. 10–11)

BIBLIOGRAPHY

Author note: The author wishes to acknowledge feedback from Carla Bradshaw, Ph.D., Laura Brown, Ph.D., Christine C. Iijima Hall, Ph.D., and Christine Ho, Ph.D. which helped shape revisions of this paper.

Allport, Gordon W. (1958). *The nature of prejudice.* Reading, MA: Addison-Wesley.

Atkinson, D., Morten, G., and Sue, Derald W. (1979). *Counseling American minorities: A cross-cultural perspective.* Dubuque, IA: Brown Company.

Dien, D. S., and Vinacke, W. E. (1964). Self-concept and parental identification of young adults with mixed Caucasian-Japanese parentage. *Journal of Abnormal Psychology*, 69 (4), 463–466.

Freire, Paolo (1970). *Cultural action for freedom.* Cambridge: Harvard Educational Review Press.

Gibbs, Jewelle Taylor (1987). Identity and marginality: Issues in the treatment of biracial adolescents. *American Journal of Orthopsychiatry*, 57(2), 265–278.

Goodman, M. E. (1968). *Race awareness in young children.* New York: Collier Press.

Hall, Christine C. Iijima (1980). *The ethnic identity of racially mixed people: A study of Black-Japanese.* Doctoral Dissertation, University of California, Los Angeles.

Henriques, Fernando (1975). *Children of conflict: A study of interracial sex and marriage.* New York: E. P. Dutton and Co., Inc.

Louise, Vivienne (1988). Of Color: What's In a Name? *Bay Area Women's News*, 1(6), 5, 7.

Morishima, James K. (1980). *Asian American Racial Mixes: Attitudes, Self-Concept, and Academic Performance.* Paper presented at the Western Psychological Association convention, Honolulu.

Moritsugu, John, Foerster, Lynn, and Morishima, James K. (1978). *Eurasians: A Pilot Study.* Paper presented at the Western Psychological Association convention, San Francisco, 1978.

Murphy-Shigematsu, Stephen (1986). *The voices of amerasians: Ethnicity, identity, and empowerment in interracial Japanese Americans.* Doctoral Dissertation, Harvard University.

Petroni, Frank A. (1983). Interracial Dating—The Price is High. In I. R. Stuart and L. Edwin (Eds.), *Interracial marriage: Expectations and Realities.* New York: Grossman Publishers.

Poussaint, Alvin F. (1984). Benefits of Being Interracial. In the Council on Interracial Books for Children, *Children of interracial families*, 15(6).

Sickels, Robert J. (1972). *Race, marriage, and the law.* Albuquerque, NM: University of New Mexico Press.

Stonequist, Everett (1935). The problem of the marginal man. *The American Journal of Sociology*, 41, 1–12.

Sue, Derald W. (1981). *Counseling the culturally different: Theory and practice.* New York: John Wiley and Sons.

Wagatsuma, Hiroshi (1973). Some Problems of Interracial Marriage for the Japanese. In I. R. Stuart and L. Edwin (Eds.), *Interracial Marriage: Expectations and Realities.* New York: Grossman Publishers.

Yamamoto, George (1973). Interracial Marriage in Hawaii. In I. R. Stuart and L. Edwin (Eds.), *Interracial Marriage: Expectations and Realities.* New York: Grossman Publishers.

PART IV.

Acculturation and Biculturalism

The mixture of cultures that we experience on a daily basis in multicultural societies such as the United States produces a number of changes in people's worldviews. Psychologists and other social scientists often define this process of culture exchange and learning as acculturation.

Researchers have proposed a variety of definitions of acculturation. For example, some have considered acculturation as a process of culture change at the individual level while others have considered acculturation as the different ways in which culture and personal change can occur (e.g., through cultural transmission, or ecological or demographic changes). Unfortunately, most earlier definitions tended to consider acculturation as a simple continuum of change with a monocultural unacculturated individual at one end and a monocultural acculturated (assimilated) individual at the other end of the continuum. A second and more recent general model of acculturation considers two possible orthogonal dimensions each being related to a given culture (the culture of origin and the host culture). In this model, individuals are able to move within each cultural continuum changing and adapting and learning. This bidimensional model of acculturation allows for the identification of individuals who tend to become bicultural as well as of those who become or remain primarily monocultural. The current understanding of acculturation as at least a bidimensional process is based on the pioneering work of John Berry, a Canadian psychologist who has contributed significantly to the field. The first selection in this section presents a summary of his views.

Inherent in many of the models of acculturation is the notion that biculturalism is indeed possible and frequent among individuals exposed to two or more cultures. As a matter of fact, a number of recent studies have shown that not only is biculturalism frequent but also quite beneficial to individuals. The selection by Teresa LaFromboise, Hardin Coleman and Jennifer

Gerton provides a comprehensive overview of the psychological impact of biculturalism as based on a large body of psychological research.

MEASUREMENT OF ACCULTURATION

There are a large number of instruments that measure acculturation among members of the four major ethnic groups in the United States. Most of them consider acculturation as an unidirectional process or produce acculturation scores that are unidirectional in nature. For example, a number of scales assume that the acculturating individual is moving from a Latino pole (e.g., high proficiency in Spanish) to a nonHispanic pole (e.g., high proficiency in English) implicitly indicating that as gains are made in one cultural domain equivalent, losses must take place in the other cultural domain. Nevertheless, the following are some scales that future researchers may wish to consider in planning their work:

Anderson, J., Moeschberger, M., Chen, M. S., Kunn, P., Wewers, M. E., and Guthrie, R. (1993). An acculturation scale for Southeast Asians. *Social Psychiatry and Psychiatric Epidemiology, 28*, 134–141.

Cuellar, I., Arnold, B., and Maldonado, R. (1995). Acculturation Rating Scale for Mexican Americans-II: A revision of the original ARSMA scale. *Hispanic Journal of Behavioral Sciences, 17*, 275–304.

Landrine, H., and Klonoff, E. A. (1994). The African American Acculturation Scale: Development, reliability, validity. *Journal of Black Psychology, 20*, 104–127.

Landrine, H., and Klonoff, E. A. (1995). The African American Acculturation Scale II: Cross-validation and short form. *Journal of Black Psychology, 21*, 124–152.

Marín, G., and Gamba, R. J. (1996). A new measurement of acculturation for Hispanics: The Bidimensional Acculturation Scale for Hispanics (BAS). *Hispanic Journal of Behavioral Sciences, 18*, 297–316.

Suinn, R. M., Ahuna, C., and Khoo, G. (1992). The Suinn-Lew Asian Self-Identity Acculturation Scale: Concurrent and factorial validation. *Educational and Psychological Measurement, 52*, 1041–1046.

FURTHER READINGS

Aponte, J. F., and Barnes, J. M. (1995). Impact of acculturation and moderator variables on the intervention and treatment of ethnic groups. In J. F. Aponte, R. Y. Rivers, and J. Wohl (Eds.), *Psychological interventions and cultural diversity* (pp. 19–39). Boston: Allyn and Bacon.

Berry, J. W., and Sam, D. L. (1997). Acculturation and adaptation. In J. W. Berry, M. H. Segall, and C. Kagitcibasi (Eds.), *Handbook of Cross-Cultural Psychology* (2nd ed., pp. 291–326). Boston: Allyn and Bacon.

Choney, S. K., Berryhill-Paapke, E., and Robbins, R. R. (1995). The acculturation of American Indians: Developing frameworks for research and practice. In J. G. Ponterotto, J. M. Casas, L. A. Suzuki, and C. M. Alexander (Eds.), *Handbook of multicultural counseling* (pp. 73–92). Thousand Oaks, CA: Sage Publications.

Gordon, M. M. (1964). *Assimilation in American life.* New York: Oxford University Press.

Landrine, H., and Klonoff, E. A. (1996). *African American acculturation: Deconstructing race and reviving culture.* Thousand Oaks, CA: Sage.

Marín, G. (1992). Issues in the measurement of acculturation among Hispanics. In K. F. Geisinger (Ed.), *Psychological testing of Hispanics* (pp. 235–251). Washington, DC: American Psychological Association.

Padilla, A. M. (Ed.). (1980). *Acculturation: Theory, models and some new findings.* Boulder: Westview Press.

Redfield, R., Linton, R., and Herskovitz, M. J. (1936). Memorandum on the study of acculturation. *American Anthropologist, 38*, 149–152.

Rogler, L. H., Cortes, D. E., and Malgady, R. G. (1991). Acculturation and mental health status among Hispanics. *American Psychologist, 46,* 585–597.

Root, M. P. P. (Ed.). (1992). *Racially mixed people in America.* Newbury Park, CA: Sage.

Root, M. P. P. (Ed.). (1996). *The multiracial experience: Racial borders as the new frontier.* Thousand Oaks, CA: Sage.

Tamura, E. H. (1994). *Americanization, acculturation, and ethnic identity: The Nisei generation in Hawaii.* Urbana, IL: University of Illinois Press.

Zack, N. (Ed.). (1995). *American mixed race: The culture of microdiversity.* Lanham, MD: Rowman and Littlefield Publishers.

7.
Acculturative Stress

John W. Berry

One of the central lessons to be learned from the study of cross-cultural psychology is that there are close links between the cultural context in which individuals grow up and the psychological characteristics that they develop. The question naturally arises: What happens to individuals when they come into contact with another culture, either by moving to another one (for example, by becoming immigrants or refugees), or by becoming colonized by a dominant culture (for example, by being an indigenous person in North America)? The answer is that people change, both culturally and psychologically, in numerous and various ways. To help describe these changes, anthropologists and psychologists have coined the term *acculturation*, literally meaning "to move toward a culture." One of the more common features of acculturation is the experience of being stressed by such changes; and for this, cross-cultural psychologists have coined the term *acculturative stress*. In this chapter, we begin with an outline of what is known about acculturation itself; we then use this background as a basis for a discussion of acculturative stress.

ACCULTURATION

Acculturation was first identified as a cultural level phenomenon by anthropologists (e.g., Redfield et al., 1936) who defined it as culture change resulting from contact between two autonomous and independent cultural groups. In principle, change occurs in both groups. In practice, however, more change occurs in the nondominant than in the dominant group. For example, nondominant groups often accept (or may be forced to accept) the language, laws, religion, and educational institutions of the dominant group. However, dominant groups are often influenced in return, for example, in adopting modes of dress and eating habits. These cultural changes are highly variable from one contact situation to another, and the actual outcomes are not very easy to predict.

Acculturation is also an individual-level phenomenon, requiring individual members of both the larger society and the various acculturating groups to engage in new behaviors, and to work out new forms of relationships in their daily lives. This idea was introduced by Graves (1967), who proposed the notion of "psychological acculturation" to refer to these new behaviors and strategies. One of the findings of subsequent research in this area is that there are vast individual differences in how people attempt to deal with acculturative change. These strategies (termed *acculturation strategies*) have three aspects: their preferences ("acculturation attitudes"; see Berry et al, 1989); how much change they actually undergo ("behavioral shifts"; see Berry, 1980); and how much of a problem these changes are for them (the phenomenon of "acculturative stress"; see Berry et al., 1987).

Perhaps the most useful way to identify the various orientations individuals may have toward acculturation is to note that two issues predominate in the daily life of most acculturating individuals. One pertains to the maintenance and development of one's ethnic distinctiveness in society, deciding whether or not one's own cultural identity and customs are of value and to be retained. The other issue involves the desirability of inter-ethnic contact, deciding whether relations with other groups in the larger society are of value and are to be sought. These two issues are essentially questions of *values,* and may be responded to on a continuous scale, from positive to negative. For conceptual purposes, however, they can be treated as dichotomous ("yes" and "no") preferences, thus generating a fourfold model (see Figure 1). Each cell in this fourfold classification is considered to be an acculturation strategy or option available to individuals and to groups living together in a society; these are *assimilation, integration, separation,* and *marginalization.*

When the first question is answered "no," and the second is answered "yes" the *assimilation* option is defined, namely, relinquishing one's cultural identity and moving into the larger society. This can take place by way of absorption of a nondominant group into an established dominant group; or it can be by way of the merging of many groups to form a new society, as in the "melting pot." In either case, sooner or later a single relatively uniform culture evolves.

The *integration* option (two "yes" answers) implies the maintenance of the cultural integrity of the group, as well as the movement by the group to become an integral part of a larger societal framework. In this case there are a large number of distinguishable ethnic groups, all cooperating within a larger social system, resulting in the "mosaic" that is frequently promoted as an alternative to the "melting pot." In this case, there is a plural society in which there are some core values and institutions, but also many cultural variations that are accepted and valued characteristics of the society.

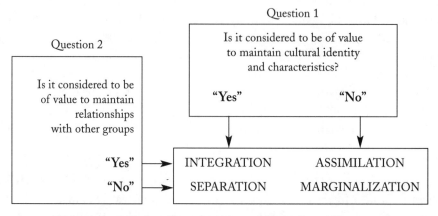

Figure 1. Four Modes of Acculturation as a Function of Two Issues

When there are no relations with the larger society, and this is accompanied by maintenance of a distinct ethnic identity and traditions, another option is defined. Depending upon which group (the dominant or nondominant) controls the situation, this option may take the form either of *segregation* or *separation*. When the pattern is imposed by the dominant group, classic segregation to keep people in "their place" appears. On the other hand, the maintenance of a traditional way of life outside full participation in the larger society may derive from people's desire to lead an independent existence, as in the case of separatist movements. In these terms, segregation and separation differ primarily with respect to which group or groups have the power to determine the outcome.

Finally, there is an option that is difficult to define precisely, possibly because it is accompanied by a good deal of collective and individual confusion and anxiety. It is characterized by striking out against the larger society and by feelings of alienation, and loss of identity. This option is *marginalization,* in which individuals lose cultural and psychological contact with both their traditional culture and the larger society.

It is possible to use this framework to examine acculturation orientations in a number of ways (see Figure 2). If we distinguish between dominant and nondominant groups, and between group and individual orientations, we observe four distinct ways in which to employ this framework in understanding acculturation phenomena. At the group level, we can examine national policies and the stated goals of particular acculturating groups within the plural society. At the individual level, we can measure the general ideology in the dominant population or the attitudes that acculturating individuals hold toward these four modes of acculturation (Berry et al., 1989).

With the use of this framework, comparisons can be made between individuals and their groups (and also between generations within families), and between acculturating peoples and the larger society to which they are acculturating.

Inconsistencies and conflicts between these various acculturation strategies are one of many sources of difficulty for acculturating individuals. Generally, when acculturation experiences cause problems for acculturating individuals, we observe the phenomenon of *acculturative stress.*

ACCULTURATIVE STRESS

In a recent overview of this area of research (Berry et al., 1987), it was argued that stress may arise, but it is not inevitable during acculturation.

	Group	Individual
Dominant Group	National Policies	Acculturation Ideologies
Acculturating Groups	Group Goals	Acculturation Attitudes

Figure 2. Domains of Use of Acculturation Modes

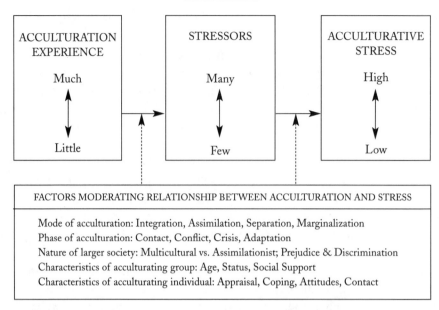

Figure 3. Factors Affecting Acculturative Stress

A framework for understanding acculturative stress is presented in Figure 3. On the left of the figure, *acculturation* occurs in a particular situation (e.g., migrant community or native settlement), and individuals participate in and experience these changes to varying degrees; thus, individual acculturation experience may vary from a great deal to rather little. In the middle, *stressors* may result from this varying experience of acculturation. For some people, acculturative changes may all be in the form of stressors, while for others, they may be benign or even seen as opportunities. On the right, varying levels of *acculturative stress* may become manifest as a result of acculturation experience and stressors.

The first point to note is that relationships among these three concepts (indicated by the solid horizontal arrows) all depend upon a number of moderating factors (indicated in the lower box of Figure 3), including the nature of the larger society, the type of acculturating group, the mode of acculturation being experienced, and a number of demographic, social, and psychological characteristics of the group and individual members. That is, each of these factors can influence the degree and direction of the relationships between the three phenomena at the top of Figure 3. This influence is indicated by the broken vertical arrows drawn between this set of "moderating" factors and the horizontal arrows. These moderating factors may be viewed as sources of variation at both group and individual levels. Each case will have to be considered independently.

Results of studies of acculturative stress have varied widely in the level of difficulties found in acculturating groups. Early views were that culture contact and change inevitably led to stress; however, current views (as depicted in Figure 3) are that stress is linked to acculturation in a probabilistic way, and the level of stress experienced will depend on a number of factors.

The first factor on which acculturative stress depends is one's acculturation strategy: Those who feel marginalized tend to be highly stressed, and those who maintain a separation goal are often almost as stressed; in contrast, those who pursue integration are minimally stressed, with assimilation leading to intermediate levels. The phase of acculturation is also important: Those in first contact, and those who have achieved some long-term adaptation tend to be less stressed than those caught in a conflict or crisis phase, especially, as we have noted, if they also feel marginalized.

Another moderating factor is the way in which the dominant society exerts its acculturative influences. One important distinction is the degree of pluralism present in a society (Murphy, 1965). Culturally plural societies, in contrast to culturally monistic ones, are likely to be characterized by two important factors: One is the availability of a network of social and cultural groups which may provide support for those entering into the experience of acculturation; and the other is a greater tolerance for, or acceptance of, cultural diversity. One might reasonably expect the stress of persons experiencing acculturation in plural societies to be lower than those in monistic societies that pursue assimilation.

In assimilationist societies, there are a number of factors operating that will plausibly lead to greater acculturative stress than in pluralistic societies. If a person regularly receives the message that one's culture, language, and identity are unacceptable, the impact on one's sense of security and self-esteem will clearly be negative. If one is told that the price of admission to full participation in the larger society is to no longer be what one has grown up to be, the psychological conflict is surely heightened. And if, collectively, one's group is offered admission only on terms specified by the dominant society, then the potential for social conflict is also increased. Thus, assimilationist policies and actions on the part of the larger society can be plausibly linked to greater acculturative stress when compared to integrationist policies.

A related factor, paradoxically, is the existence of policies designed to *exclude* acculturating groups from full participation in the larger society through acts of discrimination. To the extent that acculturating people wish to participate in the desirable features of the larger society (such as adequate housing, medical care, political rights), the denial of these may be cause for increased levels of acculturative stress.

A final set of social variables refers to the acceptance or prestige of one's group in the acculturation setting. In most societies, some groups are more acceptable on grounds of ethnicity, race, or religion than others. Those less acceptable run into barriers (prejudices, discrimination, exclusion) which may lead to marginalization of the group and which are likely to induce greater stress.

Beyond these social factors, numerous psychological variables may play a role in the mental health status of persons experiencing acculturation. Here again a distinction is useful between those characteristics which were present prior to contact, and those which developed during the process of acculturation. Certain experiences may predispose one to function more effectively under acculturation pressures. These are: prior knowledge of the new language and culture, prior intercultural encounters of any kind, motives for the contact (voluntary versus involuntary contact), and attitudes toward contact (that can range from positive to negative).

Contact experiences may also account for variations in acculturative stress. Whether they are pleasant (or unpleasant), whether they meet the current needs of the individual (or not), and in particular whether the first encounters are viewed positively (or not) may set the stage for all subsequent ones, and affect a person's mental health.

Among factors that appear during acculturation are the various acculturation strategies:

As noted previously, individuals within a group do vary in their preference for assimilating, integrating, or separating. These variations, along with experiences of marginalization, are known to affect one's mental health (Berry et al., 1987).

The personal and societal outcomes of acculturative stress have been known for decades. At the personal level, reduced health (physical, social, and psychological), lowered levels of motivation, a sense of alienation, and increased social deviance have been documented. At the societal level, there are direct counterparts in increased health costs, lower educational and work attainment (with related higher welfare costs), increased social conflict (intrafamilial and intergroup), substance abuse, criminal activity, and a general societal malaise. Clearly, with these outcomes likely, policies that seek to avoid, or at least control high levels of acculturative stress are to be preferred over those that may increase it.

CONCLUSION

It should be clear that a desire to participate in the larger society, or a desire for cultural maintenance, if thwarted, can lead to a serious decline in the mental health status of acculturating individuals. Policies or attitudes in the larger society that are discriminatory (not permitting participation, and leading to marginalization or segregation) or assimilationist (leading to enforced cultural loss) are all predictors of psychological problems. Acculturative stress is always a possible consequence of acculturation, but its probability of occurrence can be much reduced if both participation in the larger society and maintenance of one's heritage culture are welcomed by policy and practice of the larger society.

BIBLIOGRAPHY

Berry, J. W. (1980). Social and cultural change. In H. C. Triandis and R. Brislin (Eds.), *Handbook of cross-cultural psychology*, (*Volume 5, Social psychology*). Boston: Allyn and Bacon.

Berry, J. W., Kim, U., Minde, T., and Mok, D. (1987). Comparative studies of acculturative stress. *International Migration Review*, 21, 491–511.

Berry, J. W., Kim, U., Power, S., and Bujaki, M. (1989). Acculturation attitudes in plural societies. *Applied Psychology*, 38, 185–206.

Graves, T. (1967). Psychological acculturation in a tri-ethnic community. *Southwestern Journal of Anthropology*, 23, 337–350.

Murphy, H.B.M. (1965). Migration and the major mental disorders. In M. B. Kantor (Ed.), *Migration and Mental Health*. Springfield: Thomas.

Redfield, R., Linton, R., and Herskovits, M. J. (1936). Memorandum on the study of acculturation. *American Anthropologist*, 38, 149–152.

8.

Psychological Impact of Biculturalism
Evidence and Theory

Teresa LaFromboise, Hardin L. K. Coleman, and Jennifer Gerton

A vital step in the development of an equal partnership for minorities in the academic, social, and economic life of the United States involves moving away from assumptions of the linear model of cultural acquisition. In this article we review the literature on the psychological impact of being bicultural. Assimilation, acculturation, alternation, multicultural, and fusion models that have been used to describe the psychological processes, social experiences, and individual challenges and obstacles of being bicultural are reviewed and summarized for their contributions and implications for investigations of the psychological impact of biculturalism. Emphasis is given to the alternation model which posits that an individual is able to gain competence within two cultures without losing his or her cultural identity or having to choose one culture over the other. Finally, a hypothetical model outlining the dimensions of bicultural competence is presented.

Park (1928) and Stonequist (1935) developed the argument that individuals who live at the juncture between two cultures and can lay a claim to belonging to both cultures, either by being of mixed racial heritage or born in one culture and raised in a second, should be considered marginal people. Park suggested that marginality leads to psychological conflict, a divided self, and a disjointed person. Stonequist contended that marginality has certain social and psychological properties. The social properties include factors of migration and racial (biological) difference and situations in which two or more cultures share the same geographical area, with one culture maintaining a higher status than another. The psychological properties involve a state of what DuBois (1961) labeled *double-consciousness*, or the simultaneous awareness of oneself as being a member and an alien of two or more cultures. This includes a "dual pattern of identification and a divided loyalty ... [leading to] an ambivalent attitude" (Stonequist, 1935, p. 96).

Words derisively used to describe the marginal person, such as "apple," "banana," or "oreo," reflect the negative stereotype often applied to people who have intimate relationships with two or more cultures. The common assumption, exemplified by the positions of Park (1928) and Stonequist (1935), is that living in two cultures is psychologically undesirable because managing the complexity of dual reference points generates ambiguity, identity confusion, and normlessness. Park also suggested, however, that the history and progress of humankind, starting with the Greeks, has depended on the interface of cultures. He claimed that migration and human movement inevitably lead to intermingling. Park described the individual who is the product of this interaction as the "cosmopile," the

cosmophile?

independent and wiser person. In other words, even though marginality is psychologically uncomfortable for the individual, it has long-term benefits for society.

Goldberg (1941) and Green (1947), in their responses to the marginal human theory, suggested that people who live within two cultures do not inevitably suffer. Both authors suggested that being a "marginal person" is disconcerting only if the individual internalizes the conflict between the two cultures in which he or she is living. In fact, Goldberg perceived advantages to living at the border between two cultures. According to him, a marginal person may (a) share his or her condition with others of the same original culture; (b) engage in institutional practices that are shared by other "marginal" people; (c) experience no major blockage or frustrations associated with personal, economic, or social expectations; and (d) perceive himself or herself to be a member of a group. Goldberg argued that a person who is part of a subculture that provides norms and a definition of the individual's situation will not suffer from the negative psychological effects of being a marginal person.

The purpose of this article is to review the literature on the psychological impact of being bicultural. We present a definition of cultural competence and discuss models that have been used to describe the psychological processes, social experiences, and individual challenges associated with being bicultural. We identify the various skills we believe are needed to successfully negotiate bicultural challenges and obstacles. Finally, we present a hypothetical model of bicultural competence.

We examined journal articles, books, technical reports, and dissertations from a two-dimensional, level-of-analysis perspective and a subject-matter perspective. Four levels of analysis from the disciplines of psychology, education, sociology, and ethnology were selected for review to support our position that the psychological impact of biculturalism is influenced by an individual's emotional and behavioral characteristics (psychology), relationship with human social structures (education), groups and diverse socioeconomic systems (sociology), and cultural heritage (ethnology). The subject areas reviewed were ones thought to be associated with second-culture acquisition. This included (a) synonyms associated with cultural interactions (e.g., biculturalism, dualism, pluralism, transactionalism, acculturation), (b) descriptors for ethnic group membership, and (c) psychological symptoms (e.g., depression, anxiety, stress) and outcomes (e.g., competence, achievement, health) associated with the process of bicultural adaptation. The time span of this review was unrestricted and yielded theoretical articles dating back to 1929 and empirical articles from around the mid-1960s. Articles not considered for inclusion were ones that were found to be atheoretical, not associated with the major models of dual cultural adaptation, or of questionable quality in terms of research design.

Unfortunately, little empirical research exists in this area and what there is is spread throughout the social sciences. We found that some aspects of the psychological impact of being bicultural have received a great deal of well-designed and controlled study, whereas others have been addressed only along theoretical lines. The result of these inconsistencies is that some of the ideas presented are speculative, whereas others have significant empirical support. We have used this liberal approach because our goal was not merely to report the findings of current empirical research but to provide a model for examining the psychology of biculturalism. At the least, we hope that this article can be used as a springboard for more controlled research on this topic.

CULTURAL COMPETENCE

There is no single definition of culture on which all scholars can agree (Segall, 1986). Attempts to create a satisfactory definition of culture tend to either omit a salient aspect of it or to generalize beyond any real meaning. Despite these problems, there is an abundance of theories available regarding the meaning of the word *culture*. For the purpose of this article, we use a behaviorally focused definition. Like Levine (1982), we believe that human behavior is not just the product of cultural structure, individual cognitive and affective processes, biology, and social environment. Instead, we believe that behavior is a result of the continuous interaction among all of these components. We also ascribe to Bandura's (1978, 1986) concept of reciprocal determinism, which suggests that behavior is influenced by and influences a person's cognition and social environment.

This behavioral model of culture suggests that in order to be culturally competent, an individual would have to (a) possess a strong personal identity, (b) have knowledge of and facility with the beliefs and values of the culture (c) display sensitivity to the affective processes of the culture (d) communicate clearly in the language of the given cultural group, (e) perform socially sanctioned behavior, (f) maintain active social relations within the cultural group, and (g) negotiate the institutional structures of that culture.

It is important to note that the length of this list reflects the difficulty involved in developing cultural competence, particularly if one is not raised within a given culture. We do not, however, perceive cultural competence to be a dichotomous construct whereby one is either fully competent or not at all competent. We view cultural competence within a multilevel continuum of social skill and personality development. For example, an individual may be able to perform socially sanctioned behavior in two cultures with great ease but have difficulty negotiating diverse institutional structures. We also recognize that members of groups within different social strata may have differential access to social, occupational, and political roles associated with cultural competence (Ogbu, 1979). We do assume, however, that the more levels in which one is competent, the fewer problems an individual will have functioning effectively within two cultures.

MODELS OF SECOND-CULTURE ACQUISITION

Five models that have been used to understand the process of change that occurs in transitions within, between, and among cultures are assimilation, acculturation, alternation, multiculturalism, and fusion. Although each was created to address group phenomena, they can be used to describe the processes by which an individual from one culture, the culture of origin, develops competence in another culture, often the dominant majority culture. Each model has a slightly different emphasis and set of assumptions and focuses on different outcomes for the individual. We describe each one, identify its underlying assumptions, and review a number of hypotheses about the psychological impact of biculturalism that each appears to generate. We present, when available, examples from research literature that clarify the hypotheses implicit within each model.

Assimilation Model

One model for explaining the psychological state of a person living within two cultures assumes an ongoing process of absorption into the culture that is perceived as dominant or more desirable. Gordon (1964, 1978) outlined a number of subprocesses constituting various stages of the assimilation process: (a) cultural or behavioral assimilation, (b) structural assimilation, (c) marital assimilation, (d) identificational assimilation, (e) attitudinal receptional assimilation, (f) behavioral receptional assimilation, and (g) civic assimilation. Ruiz (1981) emphasized that the goal of the assimilation process is to become socially accepted by members of the target culture as a person moves through these stages. The underlying assumption of all assimilation models is that a member of one culture loses his or her original cultural identity as he or she acquires a new identity in a second culture.

This model leads to the hypothesis that an individual will suffer from a sense of alienation and isolation until he or she has been accepted and perceives that acceptance within the new culture (Johnston, 1976; Sung, 1985). This person will experience more stress, be more anxious, and suffer more acutely from social problems such as school failure or substance abuse than someone who is fully assimilated into that culture (Burnam, Telles, Karno, Hough, and Escobar, 1987; Pasquali, 1985). The gradual loss of support derived from the original culture, combined with the initial inability to use the assets of the newly acquired culture, will cause stress and anxiety.

Kerchoff and McCormick (1955) found that the greatest incidence of marginal personality characteristics (e.g., low self-esteem, impoverished social relationships, negative emotional states) among Ojibwa Indians occurred in individuals who were inclined to identify with the dominant group but encountered a relatively impermeable barrier to assimilation with that group. Chance (1965) found an overall lack of serious psychological impairment in most subjects of either sex during a period of rapidly increasing bicultural contact. However, subjects having relatively little contact with Western society, but who strongly identified with that society, showed more symptoms of personality maladjustment. Neither the contact index nor the identification index alone revealed significant differences with respect to emotional disturbance. Only the combination of the lower contact rank and high identification rank produced a situation conducive to emotional difficulties in the individual. Demographic factors such as age or education failed to delineate consistent differences in emotional disturbance.

Chadwick and Strauss (1975) found that American Indians living in Seattle maintained a strong sense of Indian identity during periods of economic and interpersonal rejection by the majority group. Even though they were able to achieve marital assimilation and perceived an absence of prejudice against them, they experienced value and power conflicts with the dominant power structure over public or civic issues. A substantial number of American Indians living their entire life in the city were perceived by the researchers to be as traditional as those who had recently left the reservation.

By contrast, Fordham's (1988) study of academically successful African American students identified many of the problems associated with the process of assimilation. According to her findings, successful students felt that they had to reject the values of the African American community in order to succeed in school. This seemed to be a less psychologically complicated task for women, but both sexes found that they had substantial conflict in their social and academic roles. Those choosing to become "raceless" suffered more stress and personal confusion than did those who maintained their African American identification. On the other hand, those who did not become raceless failed to meet the standards imposed by the majority group. In this case, social success in the

African American community was associated with school failure, followed by economic failure. According to Fordham, as long as the choice is between one's ethnicity and school success, the latter will be a Pyrrhic victory.

Assimilation is the process by which an individual develops a new cultural identity. Acquiring this new identity, however, involves some loss of awareness and loyalty to one's culture of origin. Three major dangers are associated with assimilation. The first is the possibility of being rejected by members of the majority culture. The second is the likelihood of being rejected by members of the culture of origin. The third is the likelihood of experiencing excessive stress as one attempts to learn the new behaviors associated with the assimilative culture and to shed the inoperable behaviors associated with the culture of origin.

Acculturation Model

The acculturation[1] model of bicultural contact is similar to the assimilation model in three ways. They both (a) focus on the acquisition of the majority group's culture by members of the minority group, (b) emphasize a unidirectional relationship between the two cultures, and (c) assume a hierarchical relationship between the two cultures. What differentiates the two models is that the assimilation approach emphasizes that individuals, their offspring, or their cultural group will eventually become full members of the majority group's culture and lose identification with their culture of origin. By contrast, the acculturation model implies that the individual, while becoming a competent participant in the majority culture, will always be identified as a member of the minority culture.

Smither (1982) stated that one of the distinguishing characteristics of the acculturation process is its involuntary nature. Most often, the member of the minority group is forced to learn the new culture in order to survive economically. Smither presented five models for understanding the process of acculturation. The first is the multivariate model, in which a quantitative approach is used to understand the factors that influence successful acculturation. The focus of this method is on measuring the interactions among premigration characteristics; conditions, such as income; class status; and various situational determinants in the majority society; such as length of stay, education, or occupation. Supposedly, an understanding of new social, political, cultural, and economic patterns, as well as of personal experience such as identification, internalization, and satisfaction, will emerge from this interaction (Pierce, Clark, and Kaufman, 1978).

Using the multivariate model, Prigoff's (1984) study of the self-esteem, ethnic identity, job aspirations, and school stress of Mexican American youth in a Midwest urban barrio indicated that subjects' use of the Spanish language and ethnic life-style varied inversely with the length of time spent in the United States. He found a significant relationship between ethnic pride and length of stay. In a multivariate study of ethnic migration and adjustment in Toronto, Goldlust and Richmond (1974) concluded that the influence of ethnicity on acculturation was small compared with length of stay and that level of education had a positive influence on acculturation but was negatively associated with an immigrant's primary cultural identification.

When Richman, Gaviria, Flaherty, Birz, and Wintrob (1987) explored the relationship between acculturation and perceptions of discrimination among migrants in Peru, they found that age at the time of migration was closely associated with both level of acculturation and perceptions of discrimination. The advantage of the multivariate model used in these studies is its flexibility in addressing varying situational and other conditions involved in adapting to a new culture.

The second model of cultural acquisition is the communications theory model developed by Kim (1979), which focuses on four areas of communication: intrapersonal, interpersonal, mass media behavior, and the communication environment. In this model, level of acculturation is determined by the degree of facility one has in these various methods of communication in the language of the majority culture.

The third model, put forth by Szapocznik and his colleagues (Szapocznik and Kurtines, 1980; Szapocznik, Kurtines, and Fernandez, 1980; Szapocznik, Scopetta, Kurtines, and Arandale, 1978; Szapocznik, Santisteban, Kurtines, Perez-Vidal, and Hervis, 1984; Szapocznik et al., 1986), focuses on the behavior and values of the individual to assess his or her level of acculturation. This model suggests that individuals will learn the behaviors needed to survive in a new culture before they acquire the values of the majority group. Like the multivariate model, this one views acculturation as being a function of the time an individual is exposed to the majority culture. Sex and age are other factors. It also assumes that exposure to the majority culture will produce cultural competence.

The fourth model, articulated by Padilla and his colleagues, focuses on the cultural awareness and ethnic loyalty of the individual to determine his or her status of acculturation (Olmedo and Padilla, 1978; Padilla, 1980). This model suggests that an individual's preference for the minority, versus the majority, culture provides a measure of acculturation. It posits that the acculturation process exists in five dimensions: language familiarity, cultural heritage, ethnic pride and identity, interethnic interaction, and interethnic distance. This model argues for a multidimensional understanding of the cultural acquisition process.

Many authors combine these dimensions of the cultural awareness and ethnic loyalty model in their conceptual frameworks for studying acculturation. An example is Thompson's (1948) review of the Dakota Sioux, Northern Ojibwa, Navajo, Tohono O'odham (Papago), and Hopi beliefs in immanent justice. According to this belief, the universe is inherently just and sickness arises in retribution for one's failure to fulfill proper tribal roles or adhere to sacred proscriptions. Notably, regardless of the various kinds of social organization or levels of acculturation, tribal members did not display a significant decrease in the belief in immanent justice. This review did not substantiate the deleterious impact of acculturation on cultural beliefs or values. Spindler's (1952) study of belief in witchcraft among Menomini Indians showed that this belief prevailed among subjects of differing acculturation levels. She described the function of this belief as one supporting a social system invested in retaining traditional culture and providing an adaptive response to the hostilities encountered when interacting with members of the encroaching culture.

In her study of inter-ethnic interaction among American Indians relocated to the San Francisco Bay Area, Ablon (1964) found that most Indian relationships with Anglo-Americans were relatively superficial, consisting of necessary communication with workmates and neighbors. Rather than strive for reciprocal relationships with Anglo-Americans, or positions within Anglo-American organizations, relocated Indians continuously strove to reaffirm their tribal orientation and maintain their identification with other Indians through Pan-Indian organizations. The control these subjects exerted in selecting Anglo-Americans with whom to associate offset the tension surrounding the need to interact with them.

Barger's (1977) comparative study of Inuit (Eskimo) and Cree Indians in Great Whale River, Quebec, Canada, demonstrates the need to consider case-specific factors in the statistical approach to studying the acculturation process. Inuits and Crees who resided in the same town in which Anglos were in the minority for 14 years were compared on a number of behavioral and material integration indexes. It was found that the Inuit demonstrated greater levels of acculturation and became more fully integrated into the town life than did the Crees, who were more selective in their participation in town activities. The association between culture change and presumed deviancy among Cree subjects occurred with certain individuals or families rather than with the tribe as a whole. There were, however, no differences between the two groups in overall psychosocial adjustment.

Similarly, when Boyce and Boyce (1983) studied the relationship between cultural background and the report of illness among Navajo students during their first year at a reservation boarding school (the primary mechanism for acculturating Indian people until the 1970s), they found a significant positive association between the number of clinic visits, referrals for health or psychosocial problems, and the degree of cultural incongruity (dissonance between family and community cultural identities). This finding suggests that externally imposed acculturation does have a deleterious impact on one's health.

Smither (1982) argued that the four models reviewed earlier provide insight into the processes of acculturation at the group level but cannot explain or predict individual differences in acculturation. He supported yet another multidimensional framework, a socioanalytic approach to the study of "the personality processes of the individual which facilitate or retard acculturation" (Smither, 1982, p. 62) to explain individual variation in acculturation. He asserted that an individual must expand his or her role repertoire to meet the demands of the majority culture. In the socioanalytic model, acculturation "is a function of the size of the difference between those qualities of character structure which affect role structure in the majority culture and the same qualities of character structure in the minority compared to the majority role structure" (Smither, 1982, p. 64).

Burnam et al. (1987), in a study of the prevalence of eight psychiatric disorders among Los Angeles adults of Mexican ethnicity, used socioanalytic assumptions to help explain the finding that immigrant Mexican Americans had a lower risk factor for these disorders than their native-born peers. They hypothesized that one of the reasons for the difference between the groups was that the individual who chooses to migrate may have a stronger sense of self (e.g., be more ambitious or capable) and may therefore be better equipped to cope with acculturative stress (defined by Williams and Berry, 1991, as anxiety, depression, feelings of marginality and alienation, heightened psychosomatic symptoms, and identity confusion).

Berry and Annis (1974) applied the socioanalytic approach in their investigation of psychological adaptation to culture change among individuals from the James Bay, Carrier, and Tsimashin communities. They found that the greater the cultural discontinuities between the Indian community and the Anglo communities surrounding them, the greater the acculturation stress on the individual. Individuals attaining a degree of separateness from their fellow tribal members and acquiring an independent cognitive style in interactions with their environment were less susceptible to the stresses of socio-cultural change. These studies emphasize the importance of examining the role of individual development when studying the process of second-culture acquisition. However, they do not address the stress associated with any sense of isolation or loss of community and approval.

A series of studies by Ekstrand (1978) revealed evidence for the importance of personality factors in the acquisition of bicultural competence. The studies were designed to determine the optimal age for acquisition of a second language. Ekstrand found that personal factors (e.g., motivation, or personal circumstances) were more salient in the acquisition of language than were social factors (e.g., socioeconomic status, immigrant status, teaching method). This supports the assertion that personality factors must be considered in explaining the variation by which individuals develop competence in a new culture.

According to the socioanalytic approach, role structure, character structure, and psychological differentiation need to be understood in relation to constant variables such as age, race, level of education, or degree of cultural discontinuity because they serve to modify expression of personality and role performance. The socioanalytic model of acculturation concentrates on the individual's personality and how it constrains or facilitates learning and the expression of culturally and situationally appropriate behavior.

These studies lend credence to the conclusion that minority individuals attempting to acculturate will often do so antagonistically (Vogt, 1957) or resign themselves to accepting second-class citizenship within the majority group. Most studies of minority groups do seem to indicate that minorities are often relegated to lower status positions within the majority group. This phenomenon seems to hold true for divergent groups such as ethnic minorities in the United States, Finns in Sweden, Turks in Germany, and Koreans in Japan. These studies also suggest that the most active agent in this process may be the discriminatory behavior of the majority culture. However, the role of minority group members' economic resources has been relatively unexplored in acculturation studies, prohibiting conclusions about the role of socioeconomic status in second-culture acquisition.

Collectively, these studies indicate that acculturation can be a stressful experience, reinforcing the second-class citizenship and alienation of the individual acclimating to a new culture. These studies do support the conjecture that the primary feature of the acculturation model rests on the notion that the individual will never be allowed to lose identification with the culture of origin. Furthermore, this can have negative economic and psychological effects on the individual. This observation led Taft (1977) to argue that the detrimental effects of acculturation can be ameliorated by encouraging biculturalism. Taft (1977) suggested that "the mature bicultural individual may rise above both cultures by following superordinate social proscriptions that serve to integrate the individual's behavior relative to each culture" (p.146). Several of the studies cited support the hypothesis that the more control people have over their relationship with the majority culture, the less likely they are to experience the negative effects of acculturation stress.

Alternation Model

The alternation model of second-culture acquisition assumes that it is possible for an individual to know and understand two different cultures. It also supposes that an individual can alter his or her behavior to fit a particular social context. As Ogbu and Matuté-Bianchi

(1986) have argued, "it is possible and acceptable to participate in two different cultures or to use two different languages, perhaps for different purposes, by alternating one's behavior according to the situation" (p. 89). Ramirez (1984) also alluded to the use of different problem-solving, coping, human relational, communication, and incentive motivational styles, depending on the demands of the social context. Furthermore, the alternation model assumes that it is possible for an individual to have a sense of belonging in two cultures without compromising his or her sense of cultural identity.

Rashid (1984) defined this type of biculturalism for African Americans as the ability to function effectively and productively within the context of America's core institutions while retaining a sense of self and African ethnic identity. LaFromboise and Rowe (1983) defined this type of biculturalism for American Indians as involving dual modes of social behavior that are appropriately used in different situations.

The alternation model is an additive model of cultural acquisition parallel to the code-switching theories found in the research on bilingualism. Saville-Troike (1981) called this code switching the "sensitive process of signalling different social and contextual relations through language"(p.3). This hypothesis implies that individuals who can alternate their behavior appropriate to two targeted cultures will be less anxious than a person who is assimilating or undergoing the process of acculturation. Furthermore, some authors (Garcia, 1983; Rashid, 1984; Rogler, Cortes, and Malgady, 1991) have speculated that individuals who have the ability to effectively alternate their use of culturally appropriate behavior may well exhibit higher cognitive functioning and mental health status than people who are monocultural, assimilated, or acculturated. This complements other research (Lambert, 1977; McClure, 1977; Peal and Lambert, 1962) on the positive effects of bilingualism. In similar fashion, Martinez (1987) found that bicultural involvement was the best predictor of esteem and well-being when studying the effects of acculturation and racial identity on self-esteem and psychological well-being among Puerto Rican college students living on the mainland. Although this theoretical perspective still needs to be explored systematically, it may point to the affective or cognitive mechanism that facilitates a bicultural individual's ability to manage the process of alternation.

The alternation model differs from the assimilation and acculturation models in two significant ways. First, it posits a bidirectional and orthogonal relationship between the individual's culture of origin and the second culture in which he or she may be living rather than the linear and unidirectional relationship of the other two models. In fact, the alternation model suggests that it is possible to maintain a positive relationship with both cultures without having to choose between them. Second, this model does not assume a hierarchical relationship between two cultures. Within this framework, it is possible for the individual to assign equal status to the two cultures, even if he or she does not value or prefer them equally.

The alternation model postulates that an individual can choose the degree and manner to which he or she will affiliate with either the second culture or his or her culture of origin. Sodowsky and Carey (1988) described certain dual characteristics of first-generation Asian Indians that appear paradoxical yet support this assumption. Although the groups as a whole reported a high level of proficiency in reading and speaking English, they preferred thinking in an Indian language (e.g., Hindi, Tamil). Many preferred Indian food and dress at home but American food and dress outside of the home.

Early attempts to define American Indian biculturalism, although nonempirical, adhered to the suppositions of the alternation model. Polgar (1960) studied the behavior of gangs of Mesquakie boys in Iowa as they interacted within their own community and the surrounding Anglo-American community. Polgar found that biculturation was most prominent in the area of recreational activities, in which there was a persistent dualism conditioned by geographical location. Subjects were more active when they were in town than when within the Mesquakie community. Bilingual by the age of 7, they had alternative modes of expression available to them to be used as the situation demanded. They also exerted choice in the gangs with which they chose to affiliate. Of the three gangs profiled in Polgar's study, one in particular illustrated the alternation model of biculturalism. When in town, members of this gang adapted to Anglo-American norms, but while they were in the Mesquakie community they adapted to roles expected by the traditional, political, and religious leaders of the community. Polgar found it convenient, and effective, when analyzing the results of biculturation to view the gangs formed by the boys as transitional patterns in a multilineal scheme of cultural change.

McFee (1968), in studying the selective use of roles and situations by tribal members on the Blackfeet reservation, presented two prototypes of bicultural individuals. One type was Indian in psychological orientation and often included full-blood members of the tribe. Subjects in this category knew Blackfeet culture well, having learned it in their childhood homes and practiced it as adults. They were also educated in Anglo-American schools, had a wide range of experiences in various aspects of Anglo culture, and displayed many characteristics required for effective interactions with Anglo-Americans. Their ambition was to remain Indian but to do so by combining the best of the Indian way with the best of the Anglo way. The second type included subjects raised in Anglo-American families but knowledgeable of Blackfeet culture through early experience prior to removal from the home. Subjects in this latter category were situationally Indian-oriented, having maintained enough contact with the Blackfeet community to learn and speak the language, know the beliefs and rituals, and appropriately use these skills during Blackfeet events. Even though these individuals retained their involvement with the Anglo-American culture, they also did things with and for the Blackfeet community that gained them respect and acceptance by that community.

As Pertusali (1988) discussed in his study of the Akwasasne Mohawk in both segregated and desegregated schools, the alternation model is nonlinear in its emphasis. The Akwasasne Mohawk reported their attempt to develop bicultural competence in their children through an educational program involving academic segregation in the reservation school up to the fourth grade, then a transfer to a desegregated school that delivered a bicultural academic program. This transition sequence would ideally help Mohawk children to develop a positive sense of cultural identity and build a strong academic foundation prior to attending Anglo-American schools. Data obtained from in-depth interviews with administrators and faculty members at both the segregated and desegregated schools and an analysis of the retention rates indicated that the bicultural curriculum was beneficial for both the Mohawk and non-Indian students. Results revealed that the non-Indian students were differentially and more positively influenced by the bicultural curriculum than the Indian students. Cantrall and Pete (1990) also described a curriculum that was based on the alternation model at Greasewood School entitled "Navajo culture: A bridge to the rest of the world" that emphasized decision-making, problem-solving, reflective and critical thinking, valuing, concept formation, and information-processing skills needed to deal with the social order change occurring on the Navajo reservation and internationally. The focus of both of these programs was not on movement from competence in the minority group to competence in the majority group but on ways students maintain competence in their culture of origin while simultaneously acquiring competence in the majority (or more global) culture.

A study of biculturalism and adjustment of Ramallah-American adolescents by Kazaleh (1986) showed that although identity conflict was indeed present, many of the adolescents had acquired an array of mechanisms for dealing with the dissonance and were adept at alternating between both cultural orientations with minimal anxiety. Those who had more difficulty adjusting were the youth whose parents and clan members reacted with greater anxiety to rapid change and resisted mainstream influences.

The alternation model implies that individuals learning to alternate their behavior to fit into the cultures in which they are involved will be less stressed and less anxious than those who are undergoing the process of acculturation or assimilation. Guzman (1986) emphasized the importance of maintaining a behavior-preference distinction in the assessment of Mexican-American adolescents from a bicultural-model-of-acculturation perspective. Furthermore, Adler (1975) suggested that one outcome of the alternation model may well be an enhanced intuitive, emotional, and cognitive experience. The views are again similar to assertions about the positive effects of bilingualism.

What we see as the essential strength of the alternation model is that it focuses on the cognitive and affective processes that allow an individual to withstand the negative impact of acculturative stress. It also looks at the role the individual has in choosing how he or she will interact with the second culture and the person's culture of origin. This model forces us to consider the bidirectional impact of cultural contact. In other words, it allows us to consider the impact that individuals from both cultures have on each other.

Multicultural Model

The multicultural model promotes a pluralistic approach to understanding the relationship between two or more cultures. This model addresses the feasibility of cultures maintaining distinct identities while individuals from one culture work with those of other cultures to serve common national or economic needs. In this model it is recognized that it may not be geographic or social isolation per se that is the critical factor in sustaining cultural diversity but the manner of multifaceted and multidimensional institutional sharing between cultures. Berry (1986) claimed that a multicultural society encourages all groups to (a) maintain and develop their group identities, (b) develop other-group acceptance and tolerance, (c) engage in intergroup contact and sharing, and (d) learn each other's language.

The multicultural model generates the hypothesis that an individual can maintain a positive identity as a member of his or her culture of origin while simultaneously developing a positive identity by engaging in complex institutional sharing with the larger political entity comprised of other cultural groups. In this model it is assumed that public and private identities need not become fused and that the tension of solving internal conflicts caused by bicultural stress need not have a negative psychological impact but could instead lead to personal and emotional growth. Kelly's (1971) finding, that with little difficulty the Tohono O'odham (Papago) in Tucson could occupy roles in the urban Tohono O'odham community parallel to their status in the wider Tucson social structure, supports the feasibility of this hypothesis.

Berry and his colleagues (Berry, 1984; Berry, Kim, Power, Young, and Bujaki, 1989; Berry, Poortinga, Segall, and Dasen, 1992), in their consideration of the acculturation literature, have developed a model that focuses on the process of group and individual adaptation within plural societies. They argued that there are four choices that the group or individual can make in such a situation: assimilate, integrate, separate, and marginalize. Berry and his colleagues argued that individuals and groups in plural societies have to manage two issues. One involves the decision to maintain one's culture of origin and the other is to engage in intergroup contact. Like Ogbu and Matute-Bianchi (1986), Berry and his colleagues proposed a strategy—the integration approach—that allows the individual or ethnic group to both engage in the activities of one culture while maintaining identity and relationships in another. Where the integration model differs from the alternation model is the former's emphasis on the relationship between the two cultural groups and its implicit assumption that they are tied together within a single social structure. The alternation model addresses this relationship and includes relationships that do not necessarily evolve within a larger multicultural framework.

It is questionable, however, as to whether such a multicultural society can be maintained. As Fishman (1989) suggested, cultural separation of groups demands institutional protection and ethnocultural compartmentalization. He suggested that there is little evidence for such structures surviving more than three generations of cross-cultural contact. Examples of this separation being maintained include groups making that choice for ideological reasons, such as the Old Amish and the Hasidim, or groups actively discriminated against by the majority group, such as American Indians, African Americans, or Australian aborigines. In lieu of active discrimination or self-selected separation, it may be difficult to maintain a truly multicultural society over time (Mallea, 1988). Instead, it is more likely that the various groups will intermingle, leading to the evolution of a new culture.

Fusion Model

The fusion model of second-culture acquisition represents the assumptions behind the melting pot theory. This model suggests that cultures sharing an economic, political, or geographic space will fuse together until they are indistinguishable to form a new culture. The respectful sharing of institutional structures will produce a new common culture. Each culture brings to the melting pot strengths and weaknesses that take on new forms through the interaction of cultures as equal partners. Gleason (1979) argued that cultural pluralism inevitably produces this type of fusion if the various cultures share a common political unit. The fusion model is different from the assimilation or acculturation model in that there is no necessary assumption of cultural superiority. The psychological impact of this model is unclear because there are few successful examples of such a new culture. It seems that minority groups become assimilated into the majority group at the price of their ethnic identity. This would suggest that an individual who is a member of a minority group undergoing fusion would have experiences similar to one undergoing assimilation. Once fused, however, the individual's psychological reality would be indistinguishable from a member of the majority group.

On the other hand, the psychological impact that contact with members of the minority group has on those of the majority group has been rarely discussed. Jung (cited in Hallowell, 1957) alluded to the American Indian influence on the U.S. majority group when he described the American Indian component in the character of some of his American clients. Hallowell also pointed out the need to explore the psychological effects of frontier contacts with American Indians in studying the historical development of the American national character. Weatherford (1988) chronicled how the cultural, social, and political practices of American Indians have influenced the way life is lived throughout the world. The idea that minority groups may have a positive impact on the majority culture also has been discussed in the popular press. For instance, a recent issue of *Ebony* (Bennett, 1991) focused on the African-American contributions to American culture in style, politics, entertainment, sports, gender relations, and religion. This view needs to be explored in greater detail by social scientists.

Summary

Each of these models has its own assumptions concerning what happens to a person as he or she undergoes the process of second-culture acquisition. This does not mean, however, that the models are mutually exclusive. Depending on the situation and person, any one of these models may represent an adequate explanation for a person's experience as he or she acquires competency in a new culture. An example would be of an African-American family that has moved from the rural South to an urban area. One member of the family may assimilate into the dominant Anglo-oriented culture, whereas another's attempt to acquire competence in that culture may better be described using the acculturation model. Yet a third member of the same family may choose to actively alternate between the two cultures, and a fourth may seek to live in an environment in which the two cultures exist side by side as described by the multicultural model or have amalgamated as described in the fusion model.

What separates these models are the aspects of the process that they emphasize in their description of second-culture acquisitions. We assume that there are seven process variables related to second-culture acquisition. We believe that some models more readily facilitate the effective functioning of individuals operating in dual cultures. In Table 1, each of the models described earlier is rated on the emphasis it places on the variables of contact, loyalty, and involvement with one's culture of origin and with the second culture.

Table 1. Extent of Attention on Select Process Variables Associated with Models of Second-Culture Acquisition

Model	1	2	3	4	5	6	7
Assimilation	Low	Low	Low	Low	High	High	High
Acculturation	Low	Low	Low	High	Low	Low	Low
Alternation	High	High	High	High	High	High	High
Multicultural	High	High	High	High	Moderate	Low	Low
Fusion	Low	Low	Low	Low	High	High	High

Note. 1 = Contact with culture of origin; 2 = loyalty to culture of origin; 3 = involvement with culture of origin; 4 = acceptance by members of culture of origin; 5 = contact with second culture; 6 = affiliation with the second culture 7 = acceptance by members of the second culture.

This table demonstrates that most of the models assume that an individual will lose identification with his or her culture of origin, a process that can be stressful and disorienting.
What seems clear from the literature we have reviewed, however, is that the more an individual is able to maintain active and effective relationships through alternation between
both cultures, the less difficulty he or she will have in acquiring and maintaining competency in both cultures.

BICULTURAL COMPETENCE

The construct of bicultural competence as a result of living in two cultures grows out of
the alternation model. Although there are a number of behaviors involved in the acquisition of bicultural competence (e.g., shifts in cognitive and perceptual processes, acquisition of a new language) the literature on biculturalism consistently assumes that an
individual living within two cultures will suffer from various forms of psychological
distress. Although it is clear that ethnic minorities in the United States and elsewhere
experience high levels of economic and social discrimination as well as other disadvantages, it is inappropriate to assume that this sociological reality produces a predictable
negative psychological outcome. Research suggests that individuals living in two cultures
may find the experience to be more beneficial than living a monocultural life-style. The
key to psychological well-being may well be the ability to develop and maintain competence in both cultures.

Like Schlossberg's (1981) model for analyzing human adaptation to transition, we
recognize that there are a number of individual characteristics that may be considered
significant in the development of bicultural competence. These include personal and
cultural identity, age and life stage, gender and gender role identification, and socioeconomic status, among others. Not all of these characteristics have an equal impact on an
individual's ability to develop and refine the necessary skills. The relative influence of each
has yet to be determined.

Sameroff (1982) suggested that personal identity is organized around an individual's
concept of self and his or her estimates of his or her personal impact in a given social role
within particular cultural relationships. He referred to the degree to which an individual
has developed a well-formed sense of his or her own identity as distinct from his or her
social organization. The potential criticism of this position is that it reflects the individualistic ideology of Anglo-American society. Without promoting this ideology, we
suggest that the ability to develop bicultural competence is affected by one's ability to operate with a certain degree of individuation.[2] Furthermore, we suggest that bicultural
competence requires a substantial degree of personal integration for one to avoid the negative consequences of a bicultural living situation (Burnam et al., 1987). Triandis (1980)
suggested that two factors determining one's effective adjustment to the majority culture
are self-awareness and the ability to analyze social behavior. This points to the importance
of individual personality in the development of bicultural competence.

In relation to bicultural competence, it is important to focus on two facets of identity
development. The first involves the evolution of an individual's sense of self-sufficiency
and ego strength. This identity is the subject of concern for developmentalists such as
Erickson (1950, 1968), Spencer, Brookins, and Allen (1985). Except for radical behav-
iorists, most psychologists theorize an internal sense of self that is separate from a person's

environment. This sense develops, in relationship to the individual's psychosocial experience, to the point where a psychologically healthy individual has a secure sense of who he or she is or is not (De La Torre, 1977). This sense of self interacts with the individual's cultural context in a reciprocally deterministic manner to develop an ethnic identity (Mego, 1988). We hypothesize that the strength or weakness of this identity will affect the development of a person's ability to acquire bicultural competence.

The other facet of identity development involves the development of cultural identity. This refers to the evolution of a sense of self in relation to a culture of origin and who one is within and without that cultural context. This type of identity involves the manner in which an individual interprets and internalizes his or her sociological reality. One's cultural identity and the individual's relative commitment to that identity is the focus of the acculturation studies discussed earlier and of those authors (Atkinson, Morten, and Sue, 1989; Cross, 1971; Helms, 1990; Sue and Sue, 1990) who have developed models of ethnic identity development. With some variation, all of these models emphasize a similar process through which a minority individual proceeds in order to develop a coherent and healthy sense of self within a bicultural context.

These models imply that one's stage of ethnic identity development will affect the manner in which the individual will cope with the psychological impact of biculturalism. The more integrated the individual's identity, the better he or she will be able to exhibit healthy coping patterns (Gonzalez, 1986; Murphy, 1977; Rosenthal, 1987). These stage models seem to indicate that the highest level of development includes the ability to be biculturally competent (Gutierrez, 1981). Furthermore, these models generate the hypothesis that a minority individual who is monocultural, either in the minority or majority groups, will experience the negative psychological effects of bicultural contact. However, as that person develops a stronger personal identity, he or she can become biculturally competent, thereby reducing the negative psychological impact of biculturalism (Zuniga, 1988).

Oetting and Beauvais (1990–1991) have recently identified an orthogonal model of cultural identification that includes these four categories: (a) high bicultural identification, (b) high identification with one culture and medium identification with another, (c) low identification with either culture, and (d) monocultural identification. They advocated the independent assessment of identification with multiple cultures (e.g., culture of origin and American Indian, Mexican American, Asian American, African American or Anglo American). A series of studies with American Indian youth (Beauvais, 1992; Oetting, Edwards, and Beauvais, 1989) indicated that most children and adolescents on reservations showed medium identification with both Anglo and Indian cultures. Their research with Mexican-American youth living in Southwestern towns and cities containing substantial Hispanic populations, however showed a different pattern of high Hispanic identification and moderate Anglo identification. This line of research in minority adolescent drug use supports the contention that identification with *any* culture may serve as an individual's source of personal and social strength and that such an identification will correlate with one's general well-being and positive personal adjustment. Oetting and Beauvais concluded that it is not mixed but weak cultural identification that creates problems.

This component of bicultural competence suggests the need to maintain a distinction between social variables, such as class and ethnicity, and psychological variables, such as identity development and affective processes. It is important to remember that individuals, not groups, become biculturally competent. This suggests that each person will proceed in the process of cultural acquisition at his or her own rate. Researchers can, and should, make group predictions concerning the process, but they must be cautious when applying these findings to individuals (Murphy, 1977; Zuniga, 1988). As such, to understand the psychological impact of becoming or being competent in two cultures, researchers must look at both individual psychological development and the context in which that development occurs (Baker, 1987; LaFromboise, Berman, and Sohi, 1993).

From our reading of the literature, we suggest the following dimensions in which an individual may need to develop competence so as to effectively manage the process of living in two cultures: (a) knowledge of cultural beliefs and values, (b) positive attitudes toward both majority and minority groups, (c) bicultural efficacy, (d) communication ability, (e) role repertoire, and (f) a sense of being grounded.

Knowledge of Cultural Beliefs and Values

Cultural awareness and knowledge involves the degree to which an individual is aware of and knowledgeable about the history, institutions, rituals, and everyday practices of a given culture. This would include an understanding of the basic perspectives a culture has on gender roles, religious practices, and political issues, as well as the rules that govern daily interactions among members of the culture.

A culturally competent person is presumed to be one who knows, appreciates, and internalizes the basic beliefs of a given culture. This would require an acceptance of a particular culture's basic worldview and the ability to act within the constraints of that worldview when interacting with members of that culture. For example, a study of elementary-age Sioux children living on reservations and in a neighboring boarding school (Plas and Bellet, 1983) showed that the older the children were, the more they differed culturally from younger respondents.[3] More pointedly, on the Native American Value-Attitude Scale (NAVAS; Trimble, 1981), younger children tended to provide the expected Indian response, whereas the older children both maintained a preference for the Indian values of community importance and deference to an indirect style of relating yet adopted a more Anglicized attitude toward school achievement and interpersonal involvement. This finding suggests that differences in worldview and value conflicts may be primary sources of stress for bicultural individuals. If the values and beliefs of the two cultures are in conflict, the individual may internalize that conflict in an attempt to find an integrated resolution, but the difficulty in finding this resolution may well be what motivates the individual to fuse the two cultures as a stress-reducing solution. Future research on bicultural competence must continue to examine these phenomena as being central to identifying an individual's psychological well-being.

Schiller's (1987) study lends support to considering cultural awareness and knowledge as an important component of cultural competence. In a survey study investigating the impact of biculturalism, she examined the academic, social, psychological, and cultural adjustment of American Indian college students. Schiller found that bicultural Indian students were better adjusted, particularly in the academic and cultural domains, than were their nonbicultural counterparts. They had higher grade point averages (GPAs), more effective study habits, and demonstrated a stronger commitment to using resources for academic success. Participation in cultural activities and enrollment in American-Indian-oriented courses was significantly higher for bicultural students. Finally, these students perceived their Indian heritage to be an advantage, more so than did nonbicultural students. A number of recent studies on the relationship between acculturation and the counseling process (Atkinson and Gim, 1989; Curtis, 1990; Gim, Atkinson, and Whiteley, 1990; Hess and Street, 1991; Hurdle, 1991; Ponce and Atkinson, 1989) support the hypothesis that knowledge of the second culture's values and practices facilitates an ethnic minority's willingness to use available psychological services.

Positive Attitudes Toward Both Groups

This aspect of the construct assumes that the individual recognizes bicultural competence as a desirable goal in its own right, holds each cultural group in positive but not necessarily equal regard, and does not endorse positions that promulgate hierarchical relations between two cultural groups.

The inclusion of this component is based on certain theoretical assumptions. Without positive attitudes toward both groups, an individual will be limited in his or her ability to feel good about interacting with a group that is the target of negative feelings. Arguably, the process of interacting with individuals from a culture one does not respect will result in negative psychological and behavioral outcomes. We hypothesize that one reason for the tremendous rate of conduct disorders among ethnic minority adolescents is a result of the negative attitudes those adolescents have toward the dominant Anglo group. This hypothesis is supported by Palleja's (1987) finding that monocultural-affiliated Hispanic young men exhibited more rebellious behavior than did bicultural or Anglo-affiliated monocultural peers and Golden's (1987) finding that Korean-American high school students practicing biculturalism displayed more positive educational outcomes and self-concepts than monoculturally affiliated Korean-American students. Mullender and Miller (1985) initiated a group for Afro-Caribbean children living in White families who were experiencing discomfort or limited support to help them deal with negative feelings associated with racism from the dominant group. Both the White caregivers and the Afro-Caribbean youth benefited from increased knowledge of Caribbean culture and recognition of the importance of the youth having more involvement with the Black community.

One study of Navajo children from five elementary schools in northeastern Arizona by Beuke (1978) did reveal that students in the high Indian–high Anglo cultural identification category had significantly higher self-esteem scores than did those in the low Indian–low Anglo category, regardless of which school they attended. This study on cultural identification initially supports the hypothesis that positive attitudes toward both groups may be an important component in reducing the stress of bicultural contact.

Contact itself is an essential element in one's ability to develop a positive attitude toward both groups. For example, some American Indians come from tribes that maintained considerable autonomy from the encroaching majority culture but then experienced contact at a later point. Individuals from these tribes were less often faced with the contradictions that can result from ongoing contact between different cultures. Of course, there is considerable variation between and within tribal groups regarding the amount and nature of contact with the U.S. majority and other surrounding cultures. Even today, an individual's proximity to a reservation or city influences the bicultural experiences that person has (Little Soldier, 1985). As Berry, Padilla, and Szapocznik and their colleagues have suggested, the length and type of contact individuals from one culture have with the other cultures have a significant impact on their attitudes toward the majority and their own culture.

Information is also an essential element in developing a positive attitude toward both groups. Cultural translators, individuals from a person's own ethnic or cultural group who have successfully undergone the dual socialization experience, can help others in the personal integration process (Brown, 1990). He or she can interpret the values and perceptions of the majority culture in ways that do not compromise the individual's own ethnic values or norms.

Bicultural Efficacy

Rashid (1984) asserted that "biculturalism is an attribute that all Americans should possess because it creates a sense of efficacy within the institutional structure of society along with a sense of pride and identification with one's ethnic roots" (p. 15). As Bandura (1978) has demonstrated, the belief, or confidence, that an individual can perform an action has a hierarchical relationship to the actual performance of that action. In this article, we posit that bicultural efficacy, or the belief that one can develop and maintain effective interpersonal relationships in two cultures, is directly related to one's ability to develop bicultural competence.

We define *bicultural efficacy* as the belief, or confidence, that one can live effectively, and in a satisfying manner, within two groups without compromising one's sense of cultural identity. This belief will support an individual through the highly difficult tasks of developing and maintaining effective support groups in both the minority and the majority culture. It will also enable the person to persist through periods when he or she may experience rejection from one or both of the cultures in which he or she is working to develop or maintain competence (Rozek, 1980).

A study by Kazaleh (1986) showed that the Ramallah-American youth who were afforded more outlets for social expression, whether in the ethnic community or outside of it, presented the image of being more confident in their abilities and tolerant of the ethnic life-style than did those who were overprotected by their families and restricted in their activities with peer groups. In a study of French Canadian adolescent boys learning English, Clement, Gardner, and Smythe (1977) found two factors that were associated with the motivation to learn English. One involved a positive attitude toward the Anglophone community and the other involved the awareness that learning English had an instrumental function in terms of academic achievement and future job performance. These factors, however, were not as predictive of actual competence in English as a student's confidence in his ability to learn the second language. In a study of Asian-American assertion, Zane, Sue, Hu, and Kwon (1991) found that self-efficacy predicted the ability of Asian Americans to be as assertive, in a situationally appropriate manner, as their Anglo-American peers. These findings support the thesis that efficacy is an important factor in the development of bicultural skills.

We hypothesize that an individual's level of bicultural efficacy will determine his or her ability to (a) develop an effective role repertoire in a second culture, (b) perform effectively within his or her role, (c) acquire adequate communication skills, (d) maintain roles and affiliations within his or her culture of origin, and (e) cope with acculturation stress. Furthermore, encouraging the development of an individual's bicultural efficacy is a vital goal of any program (e.g., therapy or skills training) that is designed to enhance his or her performance in a bicultural or multicultural environment. We believe that this statement is as true for ethnic minority people developing competence in a majority culture institution as it is for the majority person developing competence in a bicultural or multicultural environment.

Communication Ability

Communication ability refers to an individual's effectiveness in communicating ideas and feelings to members of a given culture, both verbally and nonverbally.[4] Language competency, in fact, may be a major building block of bicultural competence. As Northover (1988) suggested, "each of a bilingual's languages is the mediator between differing cultural identities within one and the same person" (p. 207). It is vital, however to distinguish between the language-acquisition processes, which have the goal of transferring competency from the minority group's language to the majority group's language and processes oriented toward an individual maintaining the language of origin as well as the acquisition of a second language. Bilingual programs that encourage the maintenance, rather than the transfer, of language skills promote bicultural competence rather than assimilation or acculturation (Edwards, 1981; Fishman, 1989; Thomas, 1983).

Fisher's (1974) study is a good example of the potentially positive impact of a maintenance-oriented program. He examined the effects of a bilingual–bicultural program on the self-concepts, self-descriptions, and stimulus-seeking activities of first graders. He found a highly positive effect for the Mexican-American girls on all three measures, no effect on the Mexican-American boys, no effect on the Anglo girls, and a negative effect on the Anglo boys. The drop in self-concept scores among Anglo boys during the school year was attributed to anxiety from having to learn new cultural competencies in addition to their school work. Fisher did not attempt to explain the sex difference among Anglo students in the change of their self-concept scores. The results of this study suggest that communication competency may have a direct effect on self-concept and other nonintellectual attributes. In a comparative study of Hispanic public community college students in a bilingual program and those who received only English as a second language, Tormes (1985) found that those in the bilingual program consistently performed better on most of the criterion measures (e.g., number of credits attempted and earned, GPAs, and progress toward a degree). Therefore, if a program is designed to maintain one's cultural competence, as well as one's language, it will most likely have a positive impact. If the program does not serve in this capacity, it may have a negative effect, as it did for the Anglo boys in the Fisher study and most minority children in mainstream schools or transfer language programs.

Young and Gardner (1990) found that ethnic identification and second-language proficiency were closely related. Their study of ethnic identification, perceptions of language competence, and attitudes toward mainstream and minority cultures among Chinese Canadians highlights the role of attitude in the development of communication competence. They found that the greater a participant's fear of losing his or her cultural identification, the weaker was his or her language proficiency. Participants who had that fear also had more negative attitudes toward language study. These attitudes were bi-directional, meaning that those Chinese who were identified with Canadian culture thought their Chinese language skills were weak and that their desire to improve these skills was also weak. Those who were proficient in Chinese and fearful of assimilation in Canadian culture were not eager to improve their English-language skills. Participants who had a positive attitude toward both cultures or identified with both cultures were proficient in both languages or were eager to improve their skills in the second language. These studies suggest that both attitude and ethnic identification have an impact on the development of communication competence.

McKirnan and Hamayan (1984), in a study of the ways speech norms are used to iden-tify in-group and out-group membership, confirmed the importance of communication ability as a factor in bicultural competence. They found that Anglo in-group members in a Spanish bilingual program ascribed negative characteristics to Hispanic students on the basis of variations in their style of speech. Although the amount of intergroup contact also contributed to the in-group members' attitudes, the Anglo in-group often used the speech pattern as a trigger for making judgments about the Hispanic speaker. This suggests that communication skills are a cue for the majority group in accepting a member of the minor-ity group. Dornic (1985) pointed out that the stress of using the second language inhibits the performance, in a wide variety of roles, of individuals who are recent immigrants to a new culture. The work of McKirnan and Hamayan and of Dornic, although reinforcing the notion that communication ability is an essential building block of bicultural compe-tence, underscores the important function of various contact situations during formative years on acquiring that ability.

In a study of bicultural communication, Simard and Taylor (1973) found that cross-cultural dyads were able to communicate as effectively as were homogeneous dyads. If there was a difference in the effectiveness of communication, it was determined by the nature of the task rather than the cultural composition of the dyad. These authors used their findings to suggest that cross-cultural communication is a function of both motiva-tion and capability.

LaFromboise and Rowe (1983) evaluated an assertion training program for bicultural competence with urban Indians in Lincoln, Nebraska. The key instructional focus of this program was on the situation-specific nature of assertiveness and language style differ-ences in the assessment of Indian and non-Indian target people prior to delivery of assertive messages. Feedback during training involved the appropriateness of American Indians being assertive with one another and ways for Indians to be succinct and more forceful when being assertive with Anglo-Americans. Behavioral measures of assertive-ness, rated by both Indian and Anglo peer observers, revealed a positive training effect. The actual language form (e.g., conventional English, Indian-style English, and bilingual English and Omaha) was not evaluated here; instead, the perceptions of communicative competence derived from message content and sociolinguistic cues were examined. The results of this study reinforce the importance of defining communication competency within the context of specific situations. As such, bicultural communication competency involves one's ability to communicate in a situationally appropriate and effective manner as one interacts in each culture.

In a 1985 study of acculturative stress among 397 high school students in an urban and multiethnic school, Schwarzer, Bowler, and Rauch found that the more acculturated students who spoke English at home had higher levels of self-esteem and less experience with racial tension and inter-ethnic conflict. Other variables (i.e., length of stay in the United States and ethnic group membership) were related to the findings, but the families' facility with the majority group's language appeared to be the primary factor that ameliorated the stress of living in a bicultural environment (see also Bettes, Dusenbury, Kerner, James-Ortiz, and Botvin, 1990).

When Robinson (1985) analyzed census data to determine background characteristics associated with language retention among Canadian Indians, she found that educational advancement reduced the probability of native-language retention but increased the probability of participation in the labor force. This suggests that attempts to improve the economic conditions of Indians by increasing their education may have a detrimental effect on the maintenance of their native-language skills. However, economic and linguistic acculturation, as described by Robinson, does not necessarily imply complete acculturation of Canadian Indian people. It does suggest that gaining majority group language competency may increase majority culture competency, but it does not suggest that majority group language competency ameliorates acculturative stress. In other words, as important as communication competency is in developing cultural competency, it is not the only skill that relieves the stress of becoming biculturally competent.

Role Repertoire

Role repertoire refers to the range of culturally or situationally appropriate behaviors or roles an individual has developed. The greater the range of behaviors or roles, the higher the level of cultural competence.

In a study of individuals who were working and living in Kenya for 2 years, Ruben and Kealey (1979) found that particular interpersonal and social behaviors led to greater effectiveness at role performance and ease in adjustment. The authors looked at (a) displays of respect, (b) interaction posture (e.g., judgmental or not), (c) orientation to knowledge or worldview, (d) empathy, and (e) role behavior. Coinciding with Smither's (1982) assertions, they found that individuals who had the personal resources to use their social skills in a situationally appropriate manner suffered less cultural shock and were more effective in their vocational duties and social interactions than were those whose behavioral repertoire within the second culture was more limited.

In McFee's (1968) study of acculturation among the Blackfeet tribe, he found that individuals knowledgeable about both Blackfeet and Anglo-American cultures and able to interact easily with members of each by applying this knowledge in a situationally appropriate manner had an important role in both cultures. McFee suggested that such individuals perform an important and valued role for both communities as cultural translators, or mediators, as long as they are not perceived by the minority group as being overidentified with the majority group.

In a study of the complexity of parental reasoning about child development in mothers who varied in ethnic background and biculturalism, Gutierrez and Sameroff (1990) found that the bicultural Mexican-American mothers were better skilled at developing an objective understanding of their child's behavior than were monocultural Mexican-

American or Anglo-American mothers. Their ability to interpret child development as the result of the dynamic interplay between the child's temperament and his or her environment over time and to see that developmental outcomes could have multiple determinants enhanced their parenting role. Those researchers did not, however, examine how bicultural competence originates or elaborate on the psychological results of this form of biculturalism. Determining the psychological impact of this balancing act is an important area of concern for future research. The processes by which these bicultural skills are developed needs to be delineated, and a close look needs to be taken at the individual psychology of those who have developed these skills.

Cuellar, Harris, and Naron (1981), in a study of Mexican-American psychiatric patients, found that the patient's level of acculturation was highly correlated with diagnosis and treatment outcome. The more acculturated individuals received less severe diagnostic labels than less acculturated individuals. In that study, they were looking at the impact of providing bilingual staff and culturally appropriate decor on treatment outcome. They found that the less acculturated patients in the experimental groups were positively affected by the treatment. The treatment had little effect on more highly acculturated patients. The results of this study support the hypothesis that the minority individual who does not have a sufficient role repertoire in either the majority or minority culture receives differential treatment. It also suggests that treatment keyed to the individual's level of cultural identification is more effective than interventions using a monocultural approach.

Further support for the importance of the role repertoire comes from Szapocznik, Kurtines, et al. (1980) and Szapocznik et al. (1984), who determined that the development of bicultural social skills facilitated the adjustment of Hispanic youth. The intervention used with Hispanic families in conflict—bicultural effectiveness training—consisted of the analysis of Hispanic and Anglo cultural conflicts and the presentation of information concerning biculturalism. They found that those who could develop a bicultural repertoire were less likely to experience family or school conflict or become involved in illegal drug use. This line of work reinforces the importance of focusing on bicultural social skills when delivering services to members of the minority group experiencing problems within the majority culture (see also Comer, 1980, 1985; LaFromboise, 1983).

In a study of the psychocultural characteristics of college-bound and non-college-bound Chicanas, Buriel and Saenz (1980) found that the family income and ability to perform masculine behaviors, as measured by the Bem Sex Role Inventory, were the major distinctions between the two groups. The results of this study suggest that knowing the behaviors that have traditionally led to economic success within the American culture, and the ability to be assertive in the majority culture, are aspects of the role repertoire that determine college attendance among Chicanas. Buriel and Saenz also found that family income and sex role identification were positively correlated with biculturalism, defined in their study as "an integration of the competencies and sensitivities associated with two cultures within a single individual" (p. 246). They did not find a causal relation between biculturalism and college attendance; however, they concluded that biculturalism may be an associated factor, particularly as it relates to behavior that leads to college attendance.

When developing programs to facilitate the introduction of ethnic minorities into institutions that are dominated by the majority culture (e.g., universities or corporations), it is vitally important to take the minority individual's dual focus into account (Akao, 1983). Failure to facilitate the maintenance of the minority person's role within his or her culture of origin will lead to either poor retention within the program or aggravate his or her acculturative stress (Fernandez-Barrillas and Morrison, 1984; Lang, Muñoz, Bernal, and Sorensen, 1982; Mendoza, 1981; Van Den Bergh, 1991; Vasquez and McKinley, 1982).

Groundedness

"Every culture provides the individual some sense of identity, some regulation or belonging and some sense of personal place in the school of things" (Adler, 1975, p.20). The literature indicates that the person most successful at managing a bicultural existence has established some form of stable social networks in both cultures. This suggests that the positive resolution of stress engendered by bicultural living cannot be done on one's own (Hernandez, 1981). One must have the skill to recruit and use external support systems. We have labeled the experience of having a well-developed social support system "a sense of being grounded."

Baker (1987) supported this position when she argued that African Americans are best able to avoid the major problems that affect mental health facing their communities (e.g., Black-on-Black homicide, teenage pregnancy, attempted suicide, substance abuse, postincarceration adjustment) when they can call on the resources of the African-American extended family. Both nuclear and extended family models in American Indian communities facilitate this sense of being grounded (Red Horse, 1980). We argue that it is the sense of being grounded in an extensive social network in both cultures that enhances an individual's ability to cope with the pressures of living in a bicultural environment and that acquiring that sense in the second culture is an important outcome of second-culture acquisition (Lewis and Ford, 1991). Murphy (1977) suggested that the ability to become grounded inoculates against the development of psychopathology among immigrants.

Beiser's (1987) study of depression in Southeast Asian refugees underscores the importance of being grounded within one's culture as a coping mechanism for dealing with the psychological impact of entering a new culture. He found that immigrants who either came with other family members, or entered cities with a sizable population of individuals from their home culture, were less depressed after a year's time than were those who came alone or were not involved with people from the home culture. Fraser and Pecora (1985–1986) echoed this finding, discovering that refugees who coped best with the natural reactions to dislocation were those who had "weak ties" in a community. These weak ties are extended family acquaintants, such as an uncle's best friend, who can play an important role in the fabric of daily living by providing support such as childcare or employment information. These networks serve to increase an individual's sense of being grounded in time and space.

Porte and Torney-Purta (1987) demonstrated the positive impact that maintaining a bicultural environment had on the academic achievement and level of depression among Indochinese refugee children entering the United States as unaccompanied minors. They found that children placed in foster care with Indochinese families performed better in school and were less depressed than children placed in foster care situations with non-Indochinese families. The results of this study highlight the importance of providing a culturally relevant environment for individuals learning a second culture.

In a study of the impact of the Chinese church on the identity and mental health of Chinese immigrants, Palinkas (1982) reinforced the perspective that a solid social network, one that simultaneously grounds an individual in parts of his or her home culture while facilitating the acquisition of a new culture, sharply reduces the negative impact of acculturation. Topper and Johnson's (1980) study of the effects of relocation on members of the Navajo tribe provides a graphic example of the psychological impact of losing one's groundedness. They found that relocated individuals were eight times more likely to seek mental health services than were Navajos who had not been forced to relocate. They also reported that 70% of the relocatees were found to be suffering from depression or related disorders.

Rodriguez (1975), in a study of the subjective factors affecting assimilation among Puerto Ricans in New York City, found that Puerto Ricans living in the ghetto had more positive attitudes about succeeding in the mainstream economic system than did Puerto Ricans living in Anglo-dominated suburbs. Those living in the ghetto also claimed to experience less discrimination. As Rodriguez (1975) suggested, "the ghetto . . . provides a psychologically more supportive environment than does the middle class area" (p. 77). These findings highlight the role that being grounded plays for the individual living in two cultures. We believe that groundedness joins behavioral effectiveness and personal well-being as key characteristics of mental health.

Summary

Research suggests that there is a way of being bicultural without suffering negative psychological outcomes, assimilating, or retreating from contact with the majority culture. We recognize that bicultural competence requires a difficult set of skills to achieve and maintain. We do not doubt that there will be stress involved in the process of acquiring competence in a second culture while maintaining affiliation with one's culture of origin. The question we have for future research is whether these difficulties lead to personal growth and greater psychological well-being, or inevitably lead to the type of psychological problems posited by Stonequist (1935) and Park (1928).

MODEL OF BICULTURAL COMPETENCE

The goal of this article was to develop an understanding, on the basis of social science research, of the psychological impact of biculturalism. We wanted to understand which factors facilitate a bicultural role and which ones impede the development of that role. We were particularly interested in identifying the skills that would make it possible for an individual to become a socially competent person in a second culture without losing that same competence in the culture of origin. To focus our exploration, we organized our search around a behavioral model of culture that would allow us to better identify the skills of bicultural competence. We also felt that it was important to describe the different models of second-culture acquisition so that our use of the alternation model could be understood in relation to other theories of biculturalism.

Our exploration of the psychological impact of biculturalism was seriously constrained by the fact that research in this area is spread across several disciplines and represents a wide range of methodologies. This fact made it difficult to derive a composite statement about the results of different studies that appeared to be examining similar aspects of biculturalism. The lack of controlled or longitudinal research compounded this difficulty. As a result, our discussion of biculturalism is speculative in nature. We have, however, been able to identify skills that we hypothesize are central to being a socially competent person in two cultures.

At this point, we want to emphasize that we do not know whether these are the only skills of biculturalism, or whether a person needs to be equally competent in all or a particular subset, in order to be biculturally competent. We do think, however, that the dimensions outlined in this article provide a much needed focus to the research on this phenomenon. We believe that identifying these acquirable skills will allow researchers to focus on the relationship between these skills and an individual's sense of psychological well-being, as well as his or her effectiveness in his or her social and work environments. We also believe that these dimensions can be used as the framework for developing programs designed to facilitate the involvement of minority people in majority institutions such as colleges and corporations (Van Den Bergh, 1991).

Initially, each of the skills needs to be subjected to empirical examination. Reliable methods of assessment need to be developed, and construct validity needs to be established (Sundberg, Snowden, and Reynolds, 1978). Subsequently, the relationship between possessing each skill and school and work performance will have to be identified. Finally, the question as to which skills, or set of skills, are necessary in order to be functionally biculturally competent will have to be answered. In other words, these dimensions appear to describe the skills of a biculturally competent individual. Further research using this framework needs to be conducted to determine the degree to which they are normative or optimal for a person involved in two cultures.

To facilitate that process, we have developed a hypothetical model of the relationships among these skills of bicultural competence. After lengthy consideration, we have come to speculate that these skills may have a rational relationship to each other. We believe that some may be more important than others or that some may have to be developed before others. Furthermore, we developed the assumption that one or more of these skills may be the linchpin between monocultural and bicultural competence. In response to these speculations, in the model we have developed it is assumed that there are hierarchical relations among these skills, not linear ones. By this we mean that some of these skills may be developed before others but that the process of skill acquisition does not have an invariant order. Only empirical study can resolve this issue.

The primary emphasis of the model is on the reciprocal relationship between a person and his or her environment. The model becomes complex when considering the acquisition of second-culture competence because one must include two environments, both the culture of origin and the second culture. An individual's personal and cultural identities are primarily developed through the early biosocial learning experiences that an individual has within his or her culture of origin. These identities will also be influenced by the nature and amount of contact the person has with the second culture. For example, if a person lived in rural El Salvador and had no contact with American culture until forced to emigrate in early adulthood, that person's sense of personal and cultural identity would be much different from his or her U.S.-born child, who has attended public schools since kindergarten. It is our contention that in addition to having a strong and stable sense of personal identity, another affective element of bicultural competence is the ability to develop and maintain positive attitudes toward one's culture of origin and the second culture in which he or she is attempting to acquire competence. In addition, we speculate that an individual will also need to acquire knowledge of both cultures in order to develop the belief that he or she can be biculturally competent, which we have labeled *bicultural efficacy.*

We speculate that these attitudes and beliefs about self, what we think of as the affective and cognitive dimension of the model, will facilitate the individual's acquisition of both communication skills and role repertoire, which are the two facets that make up the behavioral aspect of the model. We hypothesize that the individual who has acquired the attitudes and beliefs in the affective and cognitive dimension and the skills of the behavioral aspect of this model will also be able to develop the effective support systems in both cultures that will allow him or her to feel grounded. Being grounded in both cultures will allow the individual to both maintain and enhance his or her personal and cultural identities in a manner that will enable him or her to effectively manage the challenges of a bicultural existence.

This model represents a departure from previous models in that it focuses on the skills that a person needs to acquire in order to be successful at both becoming effective in the new culture and remaining competent in his or her culture of origin. This difference is represented in Table 2, which rates the five models of second-culture acquisition discussed earlier, on the degree to which the assumptions of each model facilitate the acquisition of these skills.

Table 2 shows that the alternation model, on which our model of bicultural competence is based, is the one that best facilitates the acquisition of these skills. It appears that the multicultural model would also be useful in this area, but as mentioned before, there is little evidence of a multicultural perspective being maintained over more than three generations.

CONCLUSION

We suggest that the ethnic minority people who develop these skills will have better physical and psychological health than those who do not. We also think that they will outperform their monoculturally competent peers in vocational and academic endeavors.

There is widespread agreement that failure to achieve equal partnership for minorities in the academic, social, and economic life of the United States will have disastrous effects for this society. A vital step in the development of an effective partnership involves moving away from the assumptions of the linear model of cultural acquisition, which has a negative impact on the minority individual, to a clearer understanding of the process of developing cultural competence as a two-way street. This will require that members of both the minority and majority cultures better understand, appreciate, and become skilled in one another's cultures. We hope that the ideas expressed here will serve to facilitate that process.

Table 2. Degree to Which Models of Second-Culture Acquisition Facilitate Acquisition of the Skills Related to Bicultural Competence

Model	1	2	3	4	5	6
Assimilation	Low	Low	Low	Low	Low	Low
Acculturation	Low	Low	Moderate	Moderate	Low	Low
Alternation	High	High	High	High	High	High
Multicultural	Moderate	Moderate	Moderate	Moderate	Moderate	Moderate
Fusion	Moderate	Moderate	Moderate	Low	Low	Moderate

Note 1 = Knowledge of culture beliefs and values;   2 = positive attitude toward both groups;   3 = bicultural efficacy; 4 = communication competency;   5 = role repertoire;   6 = groundedness.

NOTES

This article was prepared at the request of the National Center for American Indian and Alaska Native Mental Health Research and was partially supported by the National Institute of Mental Health Grant 1R01MH42473. We are indebted to the following colleagues: Clifford Barnett, Raphael Diaz, Martin Ford, Amado Padilla, and Wayne Rowe for their constructive feedback on earlier versions of this article.

1. We realize that many individuals will disagree with our use of the term *acculturation*. Many have used the term to refer to the multidimensional phenomena that an individual experiences when he or she lives within or between two or more cultures. This term, when used to describe that phenomena, is not meant to imply a directional relationship. We believe, however, that the term *acculturation* is often used in a manner that does imply a directional relationship. In this work we have labeled the general phenomena of developing competence in another culture *second-culture acquisition* and use the term *acculturation* to identify a particular model of second-culture acquisition.
2. See Sampson (1988) for a discussion of the different forms of individualism. We suggest that an ensembled individual, or one who has strong sense of oneself in relation to others, would be able to become biculturally competent. We are arguing that it is the individual who is enmeshed in his or her social context who will have a difficult time developing his or her bicultural competence.
3. Specific Sioux tribal affiliations and names of reservations were not reported in this study.
4. We are not necessarily referring to an individual's ability to communicate in written form. It is certainly possible to be fluent in a language and not be literate.

BIBLIOGRAPHY

Ablon, G. (1964). Relocated American Indians in the San Francisco Bay Area: Social interaction and Indian identity. *Human Organization*, 23, 296–304.

Adler, P. S. (1975). The transitional experience: An alternative view of cultural shock. *Journal of Humanistic Psychology*, 15, 13–23.

Akao, S. F. (1983). Biculturalism and barriers to learning among Michigan Indian adult students. *Dissertation Abstracts International*, 44, 3572A. (University Microfilms No. DA8470162)

Atkinson, D. R., and Gim, R. H. (1989). Asian-American cultural identity and attitudes toward mental health services. *Journal of Counseling Psychology*, 36, 209–212.

Atkinson, D. R., Morten. G., and Sue, D. W. (1989). Proposed minority identity development model. In D. R. Atkinson. G. Morten, and D. W. Sue (Eds.), *Counseling American minorities: A cross-cultural perspective* (pp. 35–52). Dubuque, IA: William C. Brown.

Baker, F. M. (1987). The Afro-American life cycle: Success, failure, and mental health. *Journal of the National Medical Association*, 79, 625–633.

Bandura, A. (1978). The self system in reciprocal determinism. *American Psychologist*, 33, 344–358.

Bandura, A. (1986). *The foundations of social thought and action*. Englewood Cliffs. NJ: Erlbaum.

Barger, W. K. (1977). Culture change and psychological adjustment. *American Ethnologist*, 4, 471–495.

Beauvais, F. (1992). Characteristics of Indian youth and drug use. *American Indian and Alaskan Native Mental Health Research: The Journal of the National Center*, 5(1), 51–67.

Beiser, M. (1987). Influences of time, ethnicity, and attachment on depression in Southeast Asian refugees. *American Journal of Psychiatry*, 145, 46–51.

Bennet, L (Eds.). (1991). How Black creativity is changing America [Special issue]. *Ebony*, 66 (10).

Berry, J. W. (1984). Cultural relations in plural societies: Alternatives to segregation and their sociopsychological implications. In N. Miller and M. Brewer (Eds.), *Groups in contact*. (pp. 11–27). San Diego, CA: Academic Press.

Berry, J. W. (1986), Multiculturalism and psychology in plural societies. In L. H. Ekstrand (Ed.), *Ethnic minorities and immigrants in a cross-cultural perspective* (pp. 37–51). Lisse, The Netherlands: Swets and Zeitlinger.

Berry, J. W., and Annis, R. C. (1974). Acculturation stress: The role of ecology, culture and differentiation. *Journal of Cross-Cultural Psychology*, 5, 382–406.

Berry, J. W., Kim, U., Power, S., Young, M., and Bujaki, M. (1989). Acculturation attitudes in plural societies. *Applied Psychology: An International Review*, 38, 185–206.

Berry, J. W., Poortinga, Y. P., Segall, M. H., and Dasen, P. R. (1992). *Cross-cultural psychology: Research and applications*. New York: Cambridge University Press.

Bettes, B. A., Dusenbury, L., Kerner, J., James-Ortiz, S., and Botvin, G. J. (1990). Ethnicity and psychosocial factors in alcohol and tobacco use in adolescence. *Child Development*, 61, 557–565.

Beuke, V. L. (1978), The relationship of cultural identification to personal adjustment of American Indian children in segregated and integrated schools. *Dissertation Abstracts International*, 38, 7203A. (University Microfilms No. 7809310).

Boyce, W., and Boyce, T. (1983). Acculturation and changes in health among Navajo boarding school students. *Social Science and Medicine*, 17, 219–226.

Brown, P. M. (1990). Biracial identity and social marginality. *Child and Adolescent Social Work Journal*, 319–337.

Buriel, R., and Saenz, E. (1980). Psychocultural characteristics of college-bound and noncollege-bound Chicanas. *Journal of Social Psychology*, 110, 245–251.

Burnam, M. A., Telles, C. A., Karno, M., Hough, R. L., and Escobar, J. I. (1987). Measurement of acculturation in a community population of Mexican Americans. *Hispanic Journal of Behavioral Sciences*, 9, 105–130.

Cantrall, B., and Pete, L. (1990, April). *Navajo culture: A bridge to the rest of the world*. Paper presented at the annual meeting of the American Educational Research Association. Boston.

Chadwick, B. A., and Strauss, J. H, (1975). The assimilation of American Indians into urban society: The Seattle case. *Human Organization*, 34, 359–369.

Chance, N. A. (1965). Acculturation, self-identification, and personality adjustment. *American Anthropologies*, 57, 372–393.

Clement, R., Gardner, R. C., and Smythe, P. C. (1977). Motivational variables in second language acquisition: A study of francophones learning English. *Canadian Journal of Behavioral Science*, 9, 123–133.

Comer, J. P. (1980). *School power*. New York: Free Press.

Comer, J. P. (1985). Social policy and mental health of Black children. *Journal of the American Academy of Child Psychiatry*, 24, 175–181.

Cross, W. E. (1971). The Negro-to-Black conversion experience: Toward a psychology of Black liberation. *Black World*, 20, 13–27.

Cuellar, I., Harris. L. C., and Naron, N. (1981). Evaluation of a bilingual treatment program for Mexican American psychiatric inpatients. In A. Barron (Ed.), *Explorations in Chicano psychology* (pp. 165–186). New York: Praeger.

Curtis, P. A. (1990). The consequences of acculturation to service delivery and research with Hispanic families. *Child and Adolescent Social Work*, 7, 147–159.

De La Torre, M. (1977). Towards a definition of Chicano mental disorder: An exploration of the acculturation and ethnic identity process of Chicano psychiatric outpatients. *Dissertation Abstracts International*, 39, 4025B. (University Microfilms No. 7901909)

Dornic, S. M. (1985). Immigrants, language and stress. In L. H. Ekstrand (Ed.), *Ethnic minorities and immigrants in a cross-cultural perspective* (pp. 149–157). Lisse, The Netherlands: Swets and Zeitlinger.

DuBois, W.E.B. (1961). *The soul of black folks: Essays and sketches*. New York: Fawcett.

Edwards, J. R. (1981). The context of bilingual education. *Journal of Multilingual and Multicultural Development*, 2, 25–44.

Ekstrand, L. H. (1978). Bilingual and bicultural adaptation. In *Educational and psychological interactions* (pp. 1–72). Malmo, Sweden: School of Education.

Erickson, E. (1950). *Childhood and society*. New York: Norton.

Erickson, E. (1968). *Identity, youth and crisis*. New York: Norton.

Fernandez-Barillas, H. J., and Morrison, T. L. (1984). Cultural affiliation and adjustment among male Mexican-American college students. *Psychological Reports*, 55, 855–860.

Fisher, R. I. (1974). A study of non-intellectual attributes of Chicanos in a first grade bilingual-bicultural program. *Journal of Educational Research*, 67, 323–328.

Fishman, J. A. (1989). Bilingualism and biculturalism as individual and societal phenomena. *Journal of Multilingual and Multicultural Development*, 1, 3–15.

Fordham, S. (1988). Racelessness as a factor in Black students school success: Pragmatic strategy or pyrrhic victory. *Harvard Educational Review*, 58, 54–84.

Fraser, M. W., and Pecora, P. J. (1985–1986). Psychological adaptation among Indochinese refugees. *Journal of Applied Social Sciences*, 10, 20–39.

Garcia, H. S. (1983). Bilingualism, biculturalism and the educational system. *Journal of Non-White Concerns in Personnel and Guidance*, 11, 67–74.

Gim, R. H., Atkinson, D. R., and Whiteley, S. (1990). Asian-American acculturation, severity of concerns, and willingness to see a counselor. *Journal of Counseling Psychology*, 37, 281–285.

Gleason, P. (1979). Confusion compounded: The melting pot in the 1960s and 1970s. *Ethnicity*, 6, 10–20.

Goldberg, M. M. (1941). A qualification of the marginal man theory. *American Sociological Review*, 5, 52–58.

Golden, J. G. (1987). Acculturation, biculturalism and marginality: A study of Korean-American high school students. *Dissertation Abstracts International*, 48, 1135A. (University Microfilms No. DA8716257)

Goldlust, J., and Richmond, A. H. (1974). A multivariate model of immigrant adaptation. *International Migration Review*, 3, 193–225.

Gonzalez, M. (1986). A study of the effects of strength of ethnic identity and amount of contact with the dominant culture on the stress in acculturation. *Dissertation Abstracts International*, 47, 2164B. (University Microfilms No. DA8616648)

Gordon, M. M. (1964). *Assimilation in American life*. New York: Oxford University Press.

Gordon, M. M. (1978). *Human nature, class, and ethnicity*. New York: Oxford University Press.

Green, A. W. (1947). A re-examination of the marginal man concept. *Social Forces*, 26, 167–171.

Gutierrez, F. J. (1981). A process model of bicultural personality development. *Dissertation Abstracts International*, 42, 3871B. (University Microfilms No. DA8203892)

Gutierrez, J., and Sameroff, A. (1990). Determinants of complexity in Mexican-American mother's conceptions of child development. *Child Development*, 61, 384–394.

Guzman, M. E. (1986). Acculturation of Mexican adolescents. *Dissertation Abstracts International* 47, 2166B. (University Microfilms No. DA8617666)

Hallowell, A. I. (1957). The impact of the American Indian on American culture. *American Anthropologist*, 59, 201–217.

Helms, J. E. (1990). *Black and White racial identity theory, research, and practice*. Westport, CT: Greenwood Press.

Hernandez, S. M. (1981). Acculturation and biculturalism among Puerto Ricans in Lamont, California. *Dissertation Abstracts International*, 42, 428B. (University Microfilms No. 8113419)

Hess, R. S., and Street, E. M. (1991). The effect of acculturation on the relationship of counselor ethnicity and client ratings. *Journal of Counseling Psychology*: 38, 71–75.

Hurdle, D. E. (1991). The ethnic group experience. *Social Work With Groups*, 13, 59–68.

Johnston, R. (1976). The concept of the "marginal man": A refinement of the term. *Australian and New Zealand Journal of Science*, 12, 145–147.

Kazaleh, F. A. (1986). Biculturalism and adjustment: A study of Ramallah-American adolescents in Jacksonville, Florida. *Dissertation Abstracts International*, 47, 448A. (University Microfilms No. DA8609672)

Kelly, M. C. (1971). Las fiestas como reflejo del orden social: El caso de San Xavier del Bac. *America Indigena*, 31, 141–161.

Kerchoff, A. C., and McCormick, T. C. (1955). Marginal status and marginal personality. *Social Forces*, 34, 48–55.

Kim, Y. Y. (1979). Toward an interactive theory of communication-acculturation. In D. Nimmo (Ed.), *Communication yearbook* 3 (pp. 435–453). New Brunswick, NJ: Transaction Books.

LaFromboise, T. D. (1983). *Assertion training with American Indians*. Los Cruces, NM: ERIC Clearinghouse on Rural Education.

LaFromboise, T. D., Berman, J. S., and Sohi, B. K. (1993). American Indian women. In L. Comas-Diaz and B. Green (Eds.), *Mental health and women of color*. New York: Guilford Press.

LaFromboise, T. D., and Rowe, W. (1983). Skills training for bicultural competence: Rationale and application. *Journal of Counseling Psychology*, 30, 589–595.

Lambert, W. E. (1977). The effects of bilingualism in the individual. In P. W. Hornby (Ed.), *Bilingualism: Psychological, social and educational implications* (pp. 15–27). San Diego, CA: Academic Press.

Lang, J. G., Muñoz, R. F., Bernal, G., and Sorensen, J. L. (1982). Quality of life and psychological well-being in a bicultural Latino community. *Hispanic Journal of Behavioral Sciences*, 4, 433–450.

Levine, R. A. (1982). *Culture, behavior, and personality* (2nd ed.). Chicago: Aldine.

Lewis, E. A., and Ford, B. (1991). The network utilization project: Incorporating traditional strengths of African-American families into group work practice. *Social Work With Groups*, 13, 7–22.

Little Soldier, L. (1985). To soar with the eagles: Enculturation and acculturation of Indian children. *Childhood Education*, 51, 185–191.

Mallea, J. (1988). Canadian dualism and pluralism: Tensions, contradictions and emerging resolutions. In J. Berry and R. Annis (Eds.), *Ethnic psychology: Research and practice with immigrants, refugees, Native peoples, ethnic groups and sojourners* (pp. 13–37). Berwyn, PA: Swets North America.

Martinez, A. R. (1987). The effects of acculturation and racial identity on self-esteem and psychological well-being among young Puerto Ricans. *Dissertation Abstracts International*, 49, 9163. University Microfilms No. DA8801737)

McClure, E. (1977). Aspects of code-switching in the discourse of bilingual Mexican-American children. In M. Saville-Troike (Ed.), *Linguistics and anthropology* (pp. 93–115). Washington, DC: Georgetown University Press.

McFee, M. (1968). The 150 percent man, a product of Blackfeet acculturation. *American Anthropologist*, 70, 1096–1107.

McKirnan, D. J., and Hamayan, E. V. (1984). Speech norms and attitudes toward outgroup members: A test of a model in a bicultural context. *Journal of Language and Social Psychology*, 3, 21–38.

Mego, D. K. (1988). The acculturation, psychosocial development and Jewish identity of Soviet Jewish emigres. *Dissertation Abstracts International*, 49, 4605B (University Microfilms No. DA.21946)

Mendoza, A. P. (1981). Responding to stress: Ethnic and sex differences in coping behavior. In A. Baron (Ed.), *Explorations in Chicano psychology* (pp. 187–211). New York: Praeger.

Mullender, A., and Miller, D. (1985). The Ebony group: Black children in white foster homes. *Adoption and Fostering*, 9(1), 33–40, 49.

Murphy, H.B.M. (1977). Migration, culture and mental health. *Psychological Medicine*, 7, 677–684.

Northover, M. (1988). Bilingual or "dual linguistic identities"? In J. Berry and R. Annis (Eds.), *Ethnic psychology: Research and practice with immigrants, refugees, Native peoples, ethnic groups and sojourners* (pp. 207–216). Berwyn, PA: Swets North America.

Oetting, E. R., and Beauvais, F. (1990–1991). Orthogonal cultural identification theory: The cultural identification of minority adolescents. *International Journal of the Addictions*, 25, 655–685.

Oetting, E. R., Edwards, R. W., and Beauvais, F. (1989). Drugs and Native American youth. In B. Segal (Ed.), *Perspectives on adolescent drug use* (pp. 1–34). New York: Harworth Press.

Ogbu, J. U. (1979). Social stratification and the socialization of competence. *Anthropology and Education Quarterly*, 10, 3–20.

Ogbu, J. U., and Matute-Bianchi, M. A. (1986). Understanding sociocultural factors: Knowledge, identity, and social adjustment. In California State Department of Education, Bilingual Education Office, *Beyond language: Social and cultural factors in schooling* (pp. 73–142). Sacramento, CA: California State University-Los Angeles, Evaluation, Dissemination and Assessment Center.

Olmedo, E. L., and Padilla, A. M. (1973). Empirical and construct validation of a measure of acculturation for Mexican Americans. *Journal of Social Psychology*, 105, 179–187.

Padilla, A. M. (1980). *Acculturation: Theory, models and some new findings*. Boulder, CO: Westview Press.

Palinkas, L. A. (1982). Ethnicity, identity and mental health: The use of rhetoric in an immigrant Chinese church. *Journal of Psychoanalytic Anthropology*, 5, 235–258.

Palleja, J. (1987). The impact of cultural identification on the behavior of second generation Puerto Rican adolescents. *Dissertation Abstracts International*, 48, 1541A. (University Microfilms No. DA8715043)

Park, R. E. (1928). Human migration and the marginal man. *American Journal of Sociology*, 5, 881–893.

Pasquali, E. A. (1985). The impact of acculturation on the eating habits of elderly immigrants: A Cuban example. *Journal of Nutrition for the Elderly*, 5, 27–36.

Peal, E., and Lambert, W. (1962). The relation of bilingualism to intelligence. *Psychological Monographs*, 76(27).

Pertusali, L. (1988). Beyond segregation or integration: A case study from effective Native American education. *Journal of American Indian Education*, 27, 10–20.

Pierce, R. C., Clark, M., and Kaufman, S. (1978). Generation and ethnic identity: A typological analysis. *International Journal of Aging and Human Development*, 9, 19–29.

Plas, J. M., and Bellet, W. (1983). Assessment of the value-attitude orientations of American Indian children. *Journal of School Psychology*, 21, 57–64.

Polgar, S. (1960). Biculturation of Mesquakie teenage boys. *American Anthropologist*, 62, 217–235.

Ponce, F. Q., and Atkinson, D. R. (1989). Mexican-American acculturation, counselor ethnicity, counseling style, and perceived counselor credibility. *Journal of Counseling Psychology*, 36, 203–208.

Porte, Z., and Torney-Purta, J. (1987). Depression and academic achievement among Indochinese refugee unaccompanied minors in ethnic and nonethnic placements. *American Journal of Orthopsychiatry*, 57, 536–547.

Prigoff, A. W. (1984). Self-esteem, ethnic identity, job aspiration and school stress or Mexican American youth in a Midwest urban barrio. *Dissertation Abstracts International*, 45, 2257A. (University Microfilms No. DA8420403)

Ramirez, M., III. (1984). Assessing and understanding biculturalism-multiculturalism in Mexican-American adults. In J. L. Martinez and R. H. Mendoza (Eds.), *Chicano psychology* (pp. 77–94). San Diego, CA: Academic Press.

Rashid, H. M. (1984). Promoting biculturalism in young African-American children. *Young Children*, 39, 13–23.

Red Horse, J. (1980). Family structure and value orientation in American Indians. *Social Casework*, 61, 462–467.

Richman, J. A., Gaviria, M., Flaherty, J. A., Birz, S., and Wintrob, R. M. (1987). The process of acculturation: Theoretical perspectives and an empirical investigation in Peru. *Social Science and Medicine*, 25, 839–847.

Robinson, P. (1985). Language retention among Canadian Indians: A simultaneous model with dichotomous endogenous variables. *American Sociological Review*, 50, 515–529.

Rodriguez, C. (1975). A cost-benefit analysis of subjective factors affecting assimilation: Puerto Ricans. *Ethnicity*, 2, 66–80.

Rogler, L. H., Cortes, D. E., and Malgady, R. G. (1991). Acculturation and mental health status among Hispanics. *American Psychologist*, 46, 585–597.

Rosenthal, D. A. (1987). Ethnic identity development in adolescents. In J. S. Phinney and M. J. Rotheram (Eds.), *Children's ethnic socialization* (pp. 156–179). Newbury Park, CA: Sage Publications.

Rozek, F. (1980). The role of internal conflict in the successful acculturation of Russian Jewish immigrants. *Dissertation Abstracts International*, 41, 2778B. (University Microfilms No. 8028799)

Ruben, B. D., and Kealey, D. J. (1979). Behavioral assessment of communication competency and the prediction of cross-cultural adaption. *International Journal of Intercultural Relations*, 3, 15–47.

Ruiz, R. (1981). Cultural and historical perspectives in counseling Hispanics. In D. Sue (Ed.), *Counseling the culturally different* (pp. 186–215). New York: Wiley.

Sameroff, A. J. (1982). Development and the dialectic: The need for a systems approach. *Minnesota Symposia on Child Psychology*, 15, 83–103.

Sampson, E. E. (1988). The debate on individualism: Indigenous psychologies of the individual and their role in personal and societal functioning. *American Psychologist*, 43, 15–22.

Saville-Troike, M. (1981). *The development of bilingual and bicultural competence in young children.*

Urbana, IL: Clearinghouse on Elementary and Early Childhood Education. (ERIC Document Reproduction Service No. ED 206–376)

Schiller, P. M. (1987). Biculturalism and psychosocial adjustment among Native American university students. *Dissertation Abstracts International*, 48, 1542A. (University Microfilms No. DA8720632)

Schlossberg, N. K. (1981). A model for analyzing human adaptation to transition. *The Counseling Psychologist*, 9, 2–36.

Schwarzer, R., Bowler, R., and Rauch, S. (1985). Psychological indicators of acculturation: Self-esteem, racial tension and inter-ethnic contact. In L. Ekstrand (Ed.), *Ethnic minorities and immigrants in a cross-cultural perspective* (pp. 211–229). Lisse, The Netherlands: Swets and Zeitlinger.

Segall, M. M. (1986). Culture and behavior: Psychology in global perspective. *Annual Review of Psychology*, 37, 523–564.

Simard, L. M., and Taylor, D. M. (1973). The potential for bicultural communication in a dyadic situation. *Canadian Journal of Behavioral Science*, 5, 211–255.

Smither, R. (1982). Human migration and the acculturation of minorities. *Human Relations*, 35, 57–68.

Sodowsky, G. R., and Carey, J. C. (1988). Relationship between acculturation-related demographics and cultural attitudes of an Asian-Indian immigrant group. *Journal of Multicultural Counseling and Development*, 16, 117–136.

Spencer, M. B., Brookins, G. K., and Allen, W. R. (Eds.). (1985). *Beginnings: The social and affective development of Black children*. Hillsdale. NJ: Erlbaum.

Spindler, L. S. (1952). Witchcraft in Menomoni acculturation. *American Anthropologist*, 54, 593–602.

Stonequist, E. V. (1935). The problem of marginal man. *American Journal of Sociology*, 7, 1–12.

Sue, D. W., and Sue, D. (1990). *Counseling the culturally different* (2nd ed.). New York: Wiley.

Sundberg, N. D., Snowden, L. R., and Reynolds, W. M. (1978). Toward assessment of personal competence and incompetence in life situations. *American Review of Psychology*, 29, 174–221.

Sung, B. L. (1985). Bicultural conflicts in Chinese immigrant children. *Journal of Comparative Family Studies*, 16, 255–269.

Szapocznik, J., and Kurtines, W. (1980). Acculturation, biculturalism and adjustment among Cuban Americans. In A. M. Padilla (Ed.), *Psychological dimensions on the acculturation process: Theory, models, and some new findings* (pp. 139–159). Boulder, CO: Westview Press.

Szapocznik, J., Kurtines, W., and Fernandez, T. (1980). Bicultural involvement and adjustment in Hispanic-American youths. *International Journal of Intercultural Relations*, 4, 353–365.

Szapocznik, J., Rio, A., Perez-Vidal, A., Kurtines, W., Hervis, O., and Santisteban, D. (1986). Bicultural effectiveness training (BET): An experimental test of an intervention modality for families experiencing intergenerational/intercultural conflict. *Hispanic Journal of Behavioral Sciences*, 8, 303–330.

Szapocznik, J., Santisteban, D., Kurtines, W., Perez-Vidal, A., and Hervis, O. (1984). Bicultural effectiveness training. A treatment intervention for enhancing intercultural adjustment in Cuban American families. *Hispanic Journal of Behavioral Sciences*, 6, 317–344.

Szapocznik, J., Scopetta, M. A., Kurtines, W., and Arandale, M. A. (1978). Theory and measurement of acculturation. *Interamerican Journal of Psychology*, 12, 113–120.

Taft, R. (1977). Coping with unfamiliar cultures. In N. Warren (Ed.), *Studies in cross-cultural psychology* (Vol. 1. pp. 121–153). San Diego, CA: Academic Press.

Thomas, G. E. (1983). *The deficit difference, and bicultural theories of Black dialect and nonstandard English*. Urban Review, 15, 107–118.

Thompson, L. (1948). Attitudes and acculturation. *American Anthropologist*, 50, 200–215.

Topper, M. D., and Johnson, L. (1980). Effects of forced relocation on Navajo mental patients from the former Navajo-Hopi joint use area. *White Cloud Journal*, 2(1), 3–7.

Tormes, Y. (1985). Bilingual education. English as a second language and equity in higher education. *Dissertation Abstracts International*, 46, 3314A. (University Microfilms No. DA8601699)

Triandis, H. C. (1980). A theoretical framework for the study of bilingual-bicultural adaption. *Intercultural Review of Applied Psychology*, 29, 7–16.

Trimble, J. (1981). Value differentials and their importance in counseling American Indians. In P. Pedersen (Ed.), *Counseling across cultures* (pp. 203–226). Honolulu: University of Hawaii Press.

Van Den Bergh, N. (1991). Managing biculturalism at the workplace: A group approach. In K. L. Chau (Ed.), *Ethnicity and biculturalism* (pp. 71–84). New York: Haworth Press.

Vasquez, M. J., and McKinley, D. L. (1982). Supervision: A conceptual model-reactions and extension. *The Counseling Psychologist*, 10, 59–63.

Vogt, E. Z. (1957). The acculturation of American Indians. *Annals of the American Academy of Political and Social Science*, 311, 137–146.

Weatherford, J. (1988). *Indian givers: How the Indians of the Americas transformed the world*. New York: Fawcett Columbine.

Williams, C. L., and Berry, J. W. (1991). Primary prevention of acculturative stress among refugees: Application of psychological theory and practice. *American Psychologist*, 46, 632–641.

Young, M. C., and Gardner, R. C. (1990). Modes of acculturation and second language proficiency. *Canadian Journal of Behavioral Science*, 22, 59–71.

Zane, N., Sue, S., Hu, L., and Kwon, J. (1991). Asian-American assertion: A social learning analysis of cultural differences. *Journal of Counseling Psychology*, 38, 63–70.

Zuniga, M. E. (1988). Assessment issues with Chicanas: Practice implications. *Psychotherapy*, 25, 288–293.

PART V.

Risk Behaviors

Risk behaviors are essentially those behaviors that may compromise our physical and mental well-being. As detailed in the following articles, this includes a broad scope of behaviors ranging from substance abuse to high risk sexual practices. Systematic evaluation of these behaviors has shed light on the patterns and rates of these risk behaviors, and their predisposing factors for different ethnic groups. As will be seen in Section VIII, such research is essential in the development of culturally appropriate interventions for underserved ethnic populations.

It may be helpful to view the article by Barbara Yee and her colleagues as a compilation of "mini" articles that address a number of different risk behaviors. In reading this article, you will thus gain a greater appreciation of the nature and extent of risk behaviors across a broad spectrum of ethnic groups. Finally, consider what research questions remain unanswered and the types of cultural issues that make this research particularly challenging with ethnic populations.

The article by William Vega and his colleagues represents current research in risk behaviors for ethnic adolescent populations. A strength of this article lies in its cross-cultural comparisons on the prevalence of drug use and related risk factors. The inter-ethnic differences revealed in this study once again underscore the diverse mental health needs across different ethnic communities.

Raul Caetano's (1994) article makes a significant contribution to risk behavior research by examining the role of gender and sociocultural factors in the use of alcohol. His discussion on the influence of acculturation and generational status on alcohol consumption is particularly interesting. Is greater alcohol use witnessed among more acculturated Hispanic women compared to their less acculturated counterparts? Does this vary by the length of time that they have resided in the United States? Caetano provides some interesting answers to these and related questions along with insightful explanations of the research findings.

Finally, Gerardo Marín's article underscores the importance of cultural expectancies in the evaluation of risk behaviors. Specifically, his study assesses expectancies for alcohol use among two different community samples of Mexican Americans and non-Hispanic Whites. Findings from this study demonstrate that different ethnic groups may hold culturally-embedded beliefs about the perceived effects of alcohol. Moreover, such beliefs vary according to an individual's acculturation status and personal pattern of alcohol consumption. In reading this article, special attention should be given to the implications of Marín's findings for alcohol use prevention strategies with Mexican Americans.

FURTHER READING

Botvin, G. J., Schinke, S., and Orlandi, M. A. (Eds.) (1995). *Drug abuse prevention in multiethnic youth.* Thousand Oaks, CA: Sage Publications.

Catalano, R. F., Morrison, D. M., Wells, E. A., Gillmore, M. R., Iritani, B., and Hawkins, J.D. (1992). Ethnic differences in family factors related to early drug initiation. *Journal of Studies on Alcohol, 53,* 208–217.

Collins R. L. (1993). Sociocultural aspects of alcohol use and abuse: Ethnicity and gender. *Drugs and Society, 8,* 89–116.

Connell, J. P., Halpern-Felsher, B. L., Clifford, E., Crichlow, W., and Usinger, P. (1995). Hanging in there: Behavioral, psychological and contextual factors affecting whether African American adolescents stay in high school. *Journal of Adolescent Research, 10,* 41–63.

Epstein, J. A., Botvin, G. J., Diaz, T., and Schinke, S. P. (1995). The role of social factors and individual characteristics in promoting alcohol use among inner-city minority youths. *Journal of Studies on Alcohol, 56,* 39–46.

Moncher, M.S., Holden, G. W., and Trimble, J. E. (1990). Substance abuse among Native-American youth. *Journal of Consulting and Clinical Psychology, 58,* 408–415.

Novins, D. K., Harman, C. P., Mitchell, C. M., and Manson, S. M. (1996). Factors associated with the receipt of alcohol treatment services among American Indian adolescents. *Journal of the American Academy of Child and Adolescent Psychiatry, 35,* 110–117.

Rhodes, J. E., and Jason, L. A. (1990). A social stress model of substance abuse. *Journal of Consulting and Clinical Psychology, 58,* 395–401.

Smith, C., and Krohn, M. D. (1995). Delinquency and family life among male adolescents: The role of ethnicity. *Journal of Youth and Adolescence, 24,* 69–93.

9.
Risk-Taking and Abusive Behaviors Among Ethnic Minorities

Barbara W. K. Yee, Felipe G. Castro,
W. Rodney Hammond, Robert John,
Gail Elizabeth Wyatt, and Betty R. Yung

The health status and health outcomes of many ethnic minorities have remained poor, or have deteriorated, despite massive health promotion campaigns. Multiple factors that encourage ethnic minorities to engage in high-risk behaviors and those that discourage health promotive behaviors must be closely examined before any health interventions are likely to be successful in decreasing substance abuse, high-risk sex, accidental deaths and injuries, and violence. Cultural and contextual factors may put some ethnic minorities in jeopardy and at higher risk for poorer health than their White counterparts (B. W. K. Yee, 1995, in press). This review article identifies contributing factors in high-risk behaviors and highlights research gaps for Americans of African, Indian, Asian and Pacific Islander, and Hispanic descent.

The causes of poor health among ethnic minorities in the United States have been receiving increased attention. The health status and health outcomes of many ethnic minorities have remained poor, or have deteriorated, despite massive health promotion campaigns. It is now time to stop, reassess, and determine which individual, community, and societal interventions will most effectively improve the health of these high-risk minorities.

Most experts agree on the necessity for implementing multidimensional interventions that target those at highest risk of poor health status. This is a difficult and complex task. The factors that encourage ethnic minorities to engage in high-risk behaviors and those that discourage health promotive behaviors must be taken into account, and the social, physical, and contextual environments that place ethnic minorities in jeopardy must be addressed before any intervention is likely to be successful (Yee, 1995; Yee, in press).

The following article briefly reviews the literature on high-risk behaviors among ethnic minority populations, including those behaviors associated with drugs, sex, injuries, and violence. Examples of successful interventions with groups of ethnic minorities are provided, and gaps in the research are identified.

DRUG ADDICTIVE BEHAVIORS IN ETHNIC POPULATIONS: CRITICAL META FACTORS

High-Risk Life-Style and Drug Use

High-risk behaviors, such as alcohol or drug abuse, "unsafe sex," and violence, promote health-damaging conditions. High-risk behaviors frequently cluster in a syndrome called a high-risk life-style (Budd, 1989; Castro, Newcomb, and Cadish, 1987; Harris and Guten, 1979; Istvan and Matarazzo, 1984; Jessor and Jessor, 1977). For example, sexual acting out, violence, and despair have been reported among crack-abusing youth (Carlson and Siegal, 1991).

A study of the risk factors for drug use by African American youth in the southeastern United States, which examined two samples of more than 1,300 7th grade students (Farrell, Danish, and Howard, 1992), identified eight risk factors associated with the use of gateway and illicit drugs. Four meta factors suggested by these analyses were (a) unconventional relationships with adults (e.g., being home alone after school and knowing adults who use drugs), (b) peer influence to use drugs (e.g., friends who approve of drugs and friends who use drugs), (c) antisocial behaviors (e.g., high involvement in delinquent behavior and low use of demanding activity as a coping strategy), and (d) drug-oriented cognitions (e.g., feeling pressure to use drugs, and expectations of future use of drugs).

The prevalence of use in all drug categories increased as a function of the number of risk factors present (Castro, Maddahian, Newcomb, and Bentler, 1987; Maddahian Newcomb, and Bentler, 1986). As peer cluster theory suggests, helping at-risk youth move away from an antisocial drug involves encouraging them to identify with a prosocial reference group (Oetting and Beauvais, 1987).

Unfortunately, information on the factors that promote or maintain the use of alcohol and other illicit drugs by members of various ethnic minority groups is lacking (Lex, 1987). Available data on special subpopulations of ethnic minorities, such as low-acculturated youth from the various Asian American national groups, Native Americans, and low-acculturated Hispanics, are insufficient. For example, Chicano opiate users, tecatos, are suspected to be at higher risk of HIV infection than are their noninjection drug-using peers (Mata and Jorquez, 1988), but empirical data to support this notion are lacking.

Improved research on drug use by ethnic minorities will require greater specificity in sample definition and in sampling procedures, a specificity that avoids the problem of ethnic gloss, which has compromised prior drug research among ethnic minority groups (Trimble, 1991). Another major deficiency has been the lack of a comprehensive and coordinated model for conceptualizing the data gathered in research on drug use and AIDS prevention among various ethnic minority groups (Coates, 1990). Meaningful theories and models for research on drug use by ethnic minorities would provide useful orienting statements that would improve our understanding of the determinants and consequences of drug abuse and offer guidelines for more effective program planning (Flay and Petraitis, 1991).

In the prevention of drug abuse, interventions that decrease the potency of contributing factors and interventions that increase the potency of buffering or protective factors may well reduce the likelihood of drug addiction. To this aim, models are needed for specific subpopulations. Specific models for the various ethnic minority groups (African Americans, Asian Americans, Hispanics, and Native Americans), which may differ slightly from one another, would indicate the unique antecedents (risk factors) of drug addiction for each ethnic group or subgroup, thereby increasing our understanding of the effect that certain cultural characteristics may have on vulnerability to addiction. The following set of potential meta factors, general higher order factors, should be examined in future research on risk factors for drug abuse in various ethnic minority populations.

Contributing Factors

Compromised central nervous system. Inherited biological processes, as well as the pharmacological properties of a drug, may set the stage for drug addiction. For example, depression, particularly if endogenous, may lead to self-medication by a stimulant such as cocaine (Castro, Newcomb, and Bentler, 1988; Khantzian and Khantzian, 1984).

Traumatic events in childhood. Traumatic events, such as child abuse and neglect, may arrest development, leading to deficits in interpersonal trust and social skills, low self-esteem, and a heightened risk of drug abuse.

Environmental cues and stressors. Ethnic minorities are likely to live in physical environments characterized by poverty and economic deprivation. These conditions, which are conducive to low educational achievement, when coupled with the availability of drugs, increase the likelihood of drug abuse. Advertisements targeted toward ethnic minorities in the ghetto, or barrio, encourage the consumption of alcohol and cigarettes (Maxwell and Jacobson, 1989).

Disrupted family systems. Youth whose families are fragmented by divorce or by the loss of one or both parents are at increased risk of drug addiction (Rhodes and Jason, 1990).

Sociocultural conflicts. Conflicts about one's place in society, particularly when linked to feelings of shame and self-doubt regarding one's ethnic identity, may result in antisocial behavior (Kaplan, 1985). Feelings of discrimination, and perceived racism, are central themes affecting many minority youth and must be addressed in culturally sensitive interventions (Maypole and Anderson, 1987).

Social influence. Social influence factors, including the number of nights per week spent on fun and recreation, religiosity, and plans for college, were observed to be strong predictors of risk-taking behavior among African American adolescents (Benson and Donahue, 1989).

Protective Factors

Culturally relevant health education. Health promotion interventions, when tailored to the unique needs, values, norms, attitudes, and expectations of a targeted ethnic minority population, are successful in changing high-risk behaviors (Jimenez, 1987; Kalichman, Kelly, and St. Lawrence, 1990; Peterson and Marin, 1988).

Cultural identity integration. A positive self-concept may operate as a protective factor against high-risk behaviors. Pride in cultural heritage and in oneself may prevent minority youth from engaging in high-risk behaviors (Castro, Sharp, Barrington, Walton, and Rawson, 1991; Oetting and Beauvais, 1990; Phinney, 1990; Westermeyer, 1984).

Social supports and family resources. As suggested by peer cluster theory (Oetting and Beauvais, 1987), actions that discourage high-risk behavior are often prompted by significant others who have a person's best interests in mind. Social supports, social connectedness, and social responsibility to others are partial safeguards against drug abuse and HIV infection (Brown, Chu, Nemoto, Ajuluchukwu, and Primm, 1989).

Adaptive coping skills. Life skills that aid in prosocial behavior often are associated with successful efforts at avoiding high-risk behaviors. Comfort in social skills with sexual partners and positive attitudes toward condom use were related to the adaptive use of condoms (Schilling, El-Bassel, Gilbert, and Schinke, 1991).

Social role–life mission. A strong, energetic focus on a higher life goal may promote a healthier life trajectory. In New York State, methadone maintenance clients who had a strong sense of social role were successful in avoiding HIV infection (Brown et al., 1989). Many factors that predict vulnerability or resistance to drug abuse may also be involved in high-risk sexual behaviors among ethnic minorities.

Sexual Risk Behaviors

Legitimate sexual behavior was once thought to be a private matter between husband and wife. Americans are now beginning to acknowledge the fact that men and women are sexually active regardless of marital status and that their behavior can have enormous personal and public health consequences.

A realistic appraisal of the current sexual climate has been long in coming. Until the landmark empirical study of Alfred Kinsey and his colleagues (Kinsey, Pomeroy, and Martin, 1948; Kinsey, Pomeroy, Martin, and Gebhard, 1953), research on human sexuality rarely examined its physical or psychological consequences (Turner, Miller, and Moses, 1989). Prior to the 1960s, sexual practices were considered wrong, or risky, when they violated rigid moral standards. For example, folk sexual beliefs supported the moral standards of the community, and people were reminded about the dire health consequences of masturbation.

In the 1960s and 1970s, attitudes toward sexuality began to change. Effective methods of birth control generally became more respectable, and concepts of sexuality were expanded to include the idea that both partners had the ability, and the obligation, to give and receive pleasure. Personal freedom and expression provided a foundation for healthy sexuality. Sexual risk taking became more common as people strove to develop individual expressions of sexuality. However, unintended pregnancies and sexually transmitted diseases (STDs) began to increase in number, resulting in efforts to understand and minimize sexual risk taking. The 1960s brought about a proliferation of programs addressing social concerns. Teenage pregnancies were high among Black youth, as well as pregnancies out of marriage. Consequently, sex-related research focused on describing the sexual practices of Black teens and adults, usually using White, middle-class cohorts as the reference group typifying more acceptable behavior (see Zelnick, Kanter, and Ford, 1981). Findings that Black adolescents were likely to have intercourse for the first time and to be unmarried gave the first glance impression that sexual promiscuity was cultural or acceptable within the ethnic group. Research that identified predictors of these sexual patterns, other than race, was scarce. For example, rarely were environmental factors such as poverty or adult supervision or factors that delayed sexual activity examined. Furthermore, adolescents were not asked if these early incidents were consensual or not (Wyatt, 1989). Consequently, the circumstances of these early experiences were not considered.

It is interesting that among Latinas research has also concentrated on fertility and pregnancy. We know very little about ethnicity and sexual practices of sub-ethnic-group Latina populations (Grachello, 1985).

Beginning with the 1980s to the present, sexuality is being viewed within a disease model. We know what behaviors reduce the probability of pregnancy and disease transmission, but our knowledge about many facets of the relationship of health to sexual expression is limited. Our society has moved from one end of the sexual spectrum to the other: Current intervention programs attempt to change sexual behaviors and reduce the threat of HIV and other STDs by disseminating knowledge about risky behavioral practices. We lack comprehensive current studies of human sexuality and, as a result, do not know how to accurately define and effectively implement sexual health in America. In a country in which sexually transmitted diseases are common, we must ask ourselves whether it is sexually healthy for men and women to remain virgins until marriage. What are the health implications for those who never marry? Those issues were not addressed because AIDS became the primary sex-related health problem, and it remains so today. The shift from behavioral descriptions to behavioral interventions was influenced by the need to find effective methods to prevent the spread of HIV and to change practices related to STD transmission. Researchers from the fields of cancer and smoking prevention primarily developed community-based interventions that were initially effective in White, educated, gay male communities (Becker and Joseph, 1988). These intervention programs were less effective in ethnic minority communities, in which a gay community was less visible, women were also at risk, and a variety of economic and critical issues around sex had to be addressed.

Little is known about the sociocultural factors that influence people's beliefs about sexual health and risk taking. Historically, sex research has examined sexual risk taking, including unintended pregnancies and STD transmission, using racial and ethnic categories as the major grouping variable. The use of race was used to identify high-risk groups for HIV/AIDS. Some ethnic groups, specifically African Americans and Latinos, are at higher risk than others (Centers for Disease Control, 1995). However, as mentioned in the era of research on women's reproduction, available information is insufficient to explain what about the ethnicity or culture of those groups, versus other variables, contributes to their risk status (Wyatt, 1991, 1994).

Our lack of knowledge regarding the relationship between ethnicity, culture, and sexual risk taking may be attributable to the lack of a concise conceptual or theoretical framework from which to derive our understanding of human sexuality. We have adapted a normative approach to sexual behaviors, which is based, in part, on highly stratified samples of middle-class Euro Americans. Although at least 22 million Americans have been identified as illiterate, we have treated our data as though the research participants were knowledgeable about human anatomy and its scientific terminology and competent to respond to self-report measures. Some researchers have assumed that representative samples, including ethnic minorities, were willing to discuss their sex lives in depth with strangers in telephone surveys. However, other research suggested that specific information about sexual practice requires more in-depth questioning and that definitions of terms are best obtained through in-depth interviews. Sexual knowledge is limited overall in the United States (Wyatt, 1989, 1991). Consequently, to move beyond describing behaviors (e.g., Have you ever had anal sex without a condom?) to items that assess the circumstance under which unsafe practices occur (e.g., In what situations would you have intercourse without a condom?), comprehensive structured interviews involving face-to-face interviews (Wyatt, Lawrence, Vodounon, and Mickey, 1992) have been found to be more effective. For the past 50 years, we have used the White, middle-class norm for sexual behavior as a research base. Currently, because of past efforts at behavior change (Becker and Joseph, 1988), we are being asked to use a White, middle-class, gay male norm for studying sexual behavior change. Although these models have some efficacy for behavior change, they do not address issues for ethnic minorities. Although some findings appear to be similar for all ethnic groups, it is quite possible that we are neither including the correct variables in our behavior-change equations nor using the appropriate methodologies for studying discrete ethnic and cultural groups (Wyatt, 1994). This issue—most apparent with the rising number of AIDS cases among women and, particularly, ethnic minorities, specifically Blacks and Latinas—has broadened the focus to concerns about the heterosexual transmission of diseases. It has been never more apparent that models to understand sexual risk taking and behavior change are ineffective when women's issues of socialization, power, economic dependence, and disease prevention, along with childbearing issues, are considered. We were poorly equipped to deal with ethnicity and culture as they influence sex and equally as unprepared to address gender issues in this climate of sex as a disease. Because of STDs and HIV in particular, however, we finally have the opportunity to learn about sexuality in general and about the healthy aspects that are now sometimes overshadowed by needed concerns about prevention. It is ironic that sex was not a societal problem for this society until increases in unintended pregnancies occurred. However, Blacks and Latinas are overrepresented in statistics regarding pregnancies and STDs and now in cases of HIV (Centers for Disease Control, 1995). They are the groups who today remain at most risk. It is obvious that to promote planning for childbirth and to stem the tide of disease transmission, gender, ethnic, and sociocultural issues must at last assume a major priority in our concerns about sexual health in America. We can no longer afford to use one reference group to describe normative sexual practices and label groups that differ from the norm as deviant. The spread of sexually transmitted diseases throughout the population increases risks to groups who once considered themselves to be safe. As priorities for research foci change, so must the use of existing measures to assess psychosocial factors related to risk taking and coping with diseases and the theories we use to understand sexual behavior and risk taking.

The most positive result of the AIDS epidemic is that sexuality has become legitimized as an area of study that can have psychological and health-related sequelae. The challenge is to develop approaches that are inclusive of a variety of healthy and risky practices with diverse populations. Given the possible circumstances, it is risky to do any less.

Research Designs and Methodologies

Current research designs and methodologies for investigating sexual risk taking among ethnic minorities can be improved. Most research involving sexuality involves samples from working class, or low socioeconomic, backgrounds and overgeneralizes findings to suggest that behavioral patterns are normative.

Findings regarding sexual risk taking fail to separate consensual from nonconsensual, or abusive, behaviors (Wyatt, 1985; Wyatt and Riederle, 1994). Consequently, behavior-change intervention programs often do not separate risky behaviors from risky partners or life circumstances that increase one's risk status. If economic dependence is at issue, larger concerns such as vocational skill building and self-reliance need to be incorporated into programs that foster behavioral change. Interventions do not include teaching men and women how to avoid or minimize nonconsensual sexual practices among high-risk populations. Minimizing nonconsensual sex increases personal decision making that can be influenced by behavioral interventions focusing on learning more effective and long-lasting strategies for safer sex.

When questions about lifetime high-risk behaviors are asked ("Have you *ever* had anal sex?"), the context in which the behavior occurred is not always obtained (e.g., in jail, as a result of partner swapping, being high on drugs, or rape; Reinisch, Sanders, Hill, and Ziemba-Davis, 1992). Furthermore, some researchers interpret an affirmative response as homosexual behavior, when research indicates that heterosexuals also practice this behavior (Reinisch et al., 1992). Changes in high-risk behavior are unlikely unless the circumstances in which the behaviors occur also change.

Sex-Related Information

Knowledge of human sexuality and cultural values regarding sexual behaviors vary among ethnic minority groups. For instance, ethnic groups from high context (often agricultural) countries and cultures value families, children, and personal intimacy (Wyatt, 1994). They view sex as necessary for procreation and the passage of body fluids as an essential part of life. Often, however, cultural groups have sanctions against sexual knowledge. They consider it synonymous with sexual experience, which, for women and some men, is not culturally sanctioned (Wyatt, 1994).

Touching one's body, or autoeroticism, sometimes is not culturally condoned and is subject to religious censure. These behaviors are central to using male or female condoms or foams and creams. Suggestions that individuals engage in such low-risk behaviors may meet with resistance, which is misinterpreted or misunderstood by interventionists.

For women, and frequently for men, sexual decision making often is influenced more by economic status than by health concerns of life and death conditions. Survival needs outrank the need to minimize risk taking.

Suggestions for the Future

Significant research gaps limit our knowledge of sexual risk behaviors. National studies of the sexual behavior of representative samples of ethnic groups, by geographic area, are needed to better inform us of sexual health and the prevalence of sexual risk taking. Such studies should be conducted by experts who understand the sociocultural, relationship, and health-related issues regarding those specific groups.

Risk taking needs to be redefined so that intentional pregnancies are not misinterpreted as indicators of a lack of concern about disease transmission. Relationships for women do not always lead to marriage. We need to reexamine what multiple partners means, if most people do not marry their first sexual partner in heterosexual samples (Wyatt, 1994). Unless someone can determine how to become pregnant without risking potential infection, we need to increase our understanding of decision making among men and women who desire children, so that we may counsel them more effectively.

The importance of cultural roots and their implications for both prevention of diseases and promotion of health in minority communities remains relatively unexplored. More attention and systematic research efforts must be carried forth in order to fully understand the impact of these critical but complex cultural variables. For example, in two recent articles, the role of African American culture may provide both innovative and insightful journey into the role of culture in AIDS prevention, turning a barrier into an ally. According to Bower (1992), African American cultural elements, such as oral traditions, multiple naming, collective identity, extended families, and sexuality, coupled with racial myths and reaction to blatant discriminatory and unethical medical research history, help us better understand the African American reactions to AIDS prevention efforts. For instance, culturally specific AIDS prevention may be carried out in the oral tradition, by person-to-person or person-to-group format that allows group discussion about the risks of contracting HIV and efficacy of low-risk behaviors—or, use of the African American collective identity to see HIV and AIDS as real risks to the community, as racial discrimination.

In another recent article, Amaro (1995) suggested that culture and its impact on gender roles may systematically influence sexuality and HIV risk. This call for close attention to health values, beliefs, and practices within cultures may provide key intervention strategies to prevent diseases and promote health among our minority communities. Marín and colleagues (Marín, Gomez, and Tschann, 1993; Marín, Tschann, Gomez, and Kegeles, 1993) found important gender differences in sexual behavior that were differentially influenced by acculturation and varied by Latino groups. Close attention to gender by acculturation and within-Latino-group variation is critical to effective AIDS prevention. Amaro and Gornemann (1992) found that power differentials between the genders as perceived by Latina women were the central barrier to HIV risk reduction. Here critical focus-group explorations uncovered key cultural barriers to HIV risk reduction among Latinas. This research strongly supports the notion that using qualitative research coupled with quantitative research can systematically improve our prevention efforts among minority populations.

Cost-effective education on human sexuality and sexual health risks, including STDs, are needed in the schools and in parent education classes. We must communicate to members of ethnic communities that sexual knowledge and sexual health are central to survival. Sexual behavior change that is long lasting will be most effective when researchers consider the multiplicity of issues including ethnic, sociocultural, and environmental factors influencing sexuality and sexual risk taking. The level of commitment toward prioritizing funding of research to address these issues will impact how effectively interventions reach and influence ethnic and cultural groups, and women. These are larger concepts that do not hinge on condom use alone. As is true of drug abuse and sexual abuse, many contributing and protective factors are significant predictors of injury risk among ethnic minority populations.

INJURY RISK BEHAVIORS AMONG MINORITY POPULATIONS: THE LIMITS OF HUMAN PERFECTIBILITY

We all engage in risky behaviors that could lead to unintentional injury. According to Baker, O'Neil, Ginsburg, and Guohua (1992), each year, one in four Americans experiences an injury serious enough to need medical treatment or restrict activity for at least one day. Injuries result in 114 million physician visits per year and 25% of all emergency medical visits. More than 100,000 deaths per year are caused by unintentional injuries. They are the fourth leading cause of death in the United States and the leading cause of death among people under age 44. In terms of loss in years of productive life, unintentional injuries are the most significant health problem in the United States, more significant than any single disease (U.S. Department of Health and Human Services [USDHHS], 1985, 1991).

Injury risk is influenced by a number of demographic factors. Young children under 5 years of age, young adults ages 15 to 24, and elderly people over age 75 have the highest rates of deaths from unintentional injuries. Men have approximately double the risk of death from an unintentional injury of women. American Indians have the highest injury death rate at all ages. Of all deaths among American Indians under 44 years of age, 63% are from unintentional injuries (USDHHS, 1985). Asians and Pacific Islanders have the lowest injury death rates, and Blacks, Hispanics and Whites are in between. Overall, the unintentional injury death rate among Hispanics is reported for 1988 based on data from 26 states and the District of Columbia (USDHHS, 1991). However, detailed data for Hispanics comparable with the 1980–1986 unintentional injury mortality data reported for Whites, Blacks, American Indians, and Asian and Pacific Islanders (Baker et al., 1992) is not available. With a single exception (death in an air crash), the higher a person's income, the lower the injury death rate. The evidence for this (Baker et al., 1992) is ecological data based on the per capita income of the county in which the decedent lived. Therefore, detailed studies need to be done to make the relationship between income and injury death clear. Among behavioral factors, alcohol and drug use, in particular, are associated with injury risk.

Temporal and geographic factors are also associated with injury risk (Baker et al., 1992). Fatalities, for many unintentional injuries, occur more often on weekends and in the summer than at any other time. Injury fatalities vary by cause from state to state.

Fatalities provide the most accurate measure of the impact of unintentional injuries. Motor vehicle crashes are the leading cause of injury death and the leading cause of death in the United States among people under age 34 (John, 1994). American Indians have the highest death rate among the ethnic groups from motor vehicle crashes—more than double that of Whites—and the highest death rate from motor vehicle crashes at all ages; Asians have the lowest. Alcohol is implicated in approximately one half of all motor vehicle fatalities; high blood alcohol content is implicated in more than 50% of all fatal crashes and in more than 50% of fatalities in single-vehicle crashes.

Falls are the second leading cause of unintentional injury deaths (John, 1994). Because falls often contribute to other health problems listed as the cause of death, this number is an underestimate. Old age is the greatest of all risk factors associated with falls. Death from a fall is also associated with race and sex. Whites and women have substantially higher death rates from falls than do non-Whites and men. Death rates from falls are highest in central cities and in rural areas.

Drowning is the third leading cause of unintentional death, resulting in more than 5,000 deaths annually (John, 1994). Approximately 80% of drownings are the result of swimming, rather than boating accidents. The drowning risk for infants is particularly profound with a very high death rate from falling into a body of water. Between 40%–50% of all adult drownings involve high blood alcohol content. The drowning risk for infants is particularly profound, with a very high death rate from falling into a body of water, often a swimming pool. Another peak in drownings occurs around age 18. Rural areas are risky environments. Men have substantially higher death rates than do women. American Indians and Blacks have substantially higher death rates than Whites and Asians, and drowning is higher in low-income areas.

Fires are the fourth leading cause of injury death, resulting in approximately 5,000 deaths annually (John, 1994). Of these, 73% occur in house fires, 28% are the result of cigarettes, 15% are due to faulty heating equipment, 16% are attributable to arson or suspicious circumstances, and 10% are caused by children playing with incendiary devices. Groups at risk include children under 5 years of age, the elderly, and men over age 20. House-fire death rates are similar among American Indians and Blacks, approximately double the death rate among Whites. The death rate from fires in low-income areas is 5 times that in high-income areas. However, place of residence is not a clear factor. Many fires occur in central cities and in rural areas. Alcohol is also implicated in these deaths; approximately 50% of adult deaths are attributed to high blood alcohol levels.

The data on injury deaths attributable to poisoning, listed as the fifth leading cause of injury death (John, 1994), are far less clear. One half of the 13,000 deaths per year attributed to poisoning are ruled suicidal; 99% of these are among adults. Drugs, barbiturates, tranquilizers, heroin, cocaine, alcohol, and other, account for 78% of the poisoning deaths.

Unintentional Injury Research and Risk Reduction

Given the distribution of injury risk and negative health outcomes for ethnic minorities, the following issues need to be addressed: our priorities for change; the reasons some individuals, or populations, are at greater risk than others (e.g., American Indians have extremely high injury mortality rates, whereas Asians have relatively low rates); and whether public health problems should be approached at the individual community, or population level.

Public policy decisions regarding these issues will determine the types of research that scientific investigators choose to pursue, the ways in which government will intervene to reduce health risks, and whether interventions will involve individual behavior change. Many risk behaviors and the psychological mechanisms that lead individuals to ignore or minimize their perceptions of risk can be identified.

People commonly lack the ability to personalize risk; they see how risks affect others rather than themselves. They are prone to a phenomenon known as optimism bias, an unrealistic sense of well-being and competence (Jeffrey, 1989). People tend to let past experiences affect their expectations of the future (Weinstein, 1987): "I have never fallen down the steps when I did this. Therefore, I can continue to do it without risk."

Adolescents often have a perception of immortality. In some ethnic cultures, machismo, or macho, attitudes and behaviors or, perhaps in the case of American Indians, a warrior attitude, make risk-taking expected and acceptable. Aggressive elements in our culture make confrontational behaviors common. Daredevil behaviors (Gibbs, 1988), one-upmanship in peer relations, especially among adolescents, and interpersonal competition result in unintentional injuries and mortality, as do the developmental pursuits of autonomy, independence, and self-esteem (Millstein and Irwin, 1988). Alcohol and drugs lower inhibitions and alter perceptions of danger. A cultural focus on immediate gratification also is at fault.

Most people who study risk-taking behaviors that result in death or injury question whether altering individual behaviors is as effective in lowering risk as altering environmental factors. Attempts to change individual behaviors have been relatively unsuccessful. Individuals change their behaviors under very limited circumstances. Jeffrey (1989) concluded that individual-level interventions are appropriate only if individuals can change their behaviors at very low cost and receive a high, immediate payoff. If the cost of intervention is high, the benefit distant, and the participant sees no immediate advantage, we must design population-based interventions, such as education. Educational efforts, although successful in changing individual beliefs, have been far less successful in changing individual behaviors (Jeffrey, 1989). Education works best on well-educated, future-oriented individuals. In other words, educational interventions leave large segments of minority populations unaffected. If the goal of our efforts is to change behaviors among the individuals who are most at risk of injury death, education is not a good approach.

Personal decision-making issues need to be investigated. Nevertheless, structural and environmental modifications will reduce injury risks and, consequently, deaths from motor vehicle crashes, falls, fires, and drowning more effectively than will educational interventions. Driver- and passenger-side air bags in cars would do more to reduce motor vehicle injuries and deaths than any other factor. Compulsory motorcycle helmet laws (USDHHS, 1990) are an effective risk-reduction measure. Fatal injuries by fire can be reduced by sprinkler systems, operational smoke detectors, and reductions in the flammability and toxicity of home furnishings. Drownings generally occur where people swim unsupervised. Falls particularly affect elderly people; such environmental modifications as improved lighting, hand rails, and other such devices will reduce the incidence and severity of falls.

Jeffrey (1989) framed the choice between individual-intervention and population-intervention approaches very well. He wrote that "successful public health programs must find a way to translate epidemiologic findings into terms that are salient to individuals, or must adopt strategies in which individual decisions about risk behaviors are not as central" (p. 1196). That is the key issue in our efforts to reduce injury death or disability among all populations.

Common contributory and protective factors predict drug, sexual, and injury risk behaviors. These factors are also important predictors of violent behaviors.

Risk-Taking and Abusive Behaviors: Violent Behaviors

Youth homicide and other assaultive violence have been described as epidemic (Institute of Medicine, 1989). Headlines frequently draw attention to violence-related tragedies and the often perplexing circumstances surrounding them. Public health practitioners and policymakers have called for broad-based community efforts to prevent violence, particularly among at-risk youth (Bell, 1987; Prothrow-Smith, 1991). The demand for community action has created a concurrent need for sophisticated preventive approaches that are (a) well informed by public health epidemiology; (b) clinically well conceptualized, particularly from a psychosocial point of view; and (c) culturally appropriate for the intended consumers.

Overwhelming evidence indicates that certain groups suffer disproportionately from violence. Risk factors that significantly increase the probability of serious injury or premature mortality from violent episodes include youth, poverty, male gender, ethnic minority status, and urban residence (Christofel, 1990; Prothrow-Smith, 1991; Rodriguez, 1990). African Americans are the ethnic group at highest risk for homicide. In fact, homicide is the leading cause of mortality for both male and female African Americans between 15–34 years of age (National Center for Health Statistics, 1990, 1992). According to a 1986 mortality chart produce by the Centers for Disease Control (reprinted in Conciatore, 1989), homicide is among the top 10 causes of death for African Americans of all age groups, excluding deaths of people over 65. Homicide rates for young African American women (15 to 34 years of age) are approximately 4 times higher than those for White women in the same age group, yet African American male adolescents or young adults, between the ages of 15 and 24, have the greatest potential for becoming homicide victims—11 times greater than that for their White male peers (Centers for Disease Control, 1990).

The extent of the violence epidemic, and the characteristics of those most affected by it, are not fully known. Of all forms of violence, only homicide rates for Whites and African Americans are reported in national statistics; rates for other ethnic minorities typically are combined and listed as *other* in health or criminal justice databanks (Rosenberg and Mercy, 1991). Regional, metropolitan, or tribal studies must be investigated for indications of the prevalence of assaultive violence among other ethnic minority groups. Several studies have estimated the homicide rates for young adult Hispanic and Native American men to be approximately 3 to 4 times higher than those for White men of the same age (Becker, Samet, Wiggins, and Key, 1990; Smith, Mercy, and Rosenberg, 1986; Tardiff and Gross, 1986). Such studies suggest that contextual or risk factors may differ among ethnic groups. For example, gang membership increases vulnerability among Hispanic male youth, whereas Asian Americans are at high risk of stranger-to-stranger crimes, such as assaults connected with muggings (Loya et al., 1986). Levels of nonfatal violence in any American population are difficult to determine for a variety of reasons (e.g., see discussion in Hammond and Yung, 1993). However, available evidence indicates that African American youth are more likely than members of other racial, ethnic, or age groups to be injured in violent episodes, and male African American youth are more likely to engage in such risky behaviors as carrying weapons and fighting (Centers for Disease Control, 1991; Christoffel, 1990); Shakoor and Chalmers, 1991; Sheley, McGee, and Wright, 1992).

There is a compelling need for continued study of assaultive violence, particularly its prevalence and causation among diverse subpopulations. Although poverty and related structural conditions are recognized environmental correlates of violence among African Americans, their exact role in the transmission of violence is not fully understood (Rosenberg and Mercy, 1991). Despite deficits in the empirical knowledge base and theories regarding violence, a focus on the contextual factors characterizing violence among African American youth could provide conceptual clarity for the development of preventive modalities. Situational characteristics typical of episodes of adolescent interpersonal violence are known to include an intimate relationship between disputants (friends, family members, or acquaintances); it has been estimated that as many as three fourths of all homicides and assaults, among all age groups, occur between people who know each other (Bell, 1987; Prothrow-Smith, 1991). Violent incidents frequently occur when adolescents lose control and react aggressively to real or perceived provocations or arguments (Agnew, 1990; Graham and Hudley, 1992; Slaby and Guerra, 1988). These behaviors have been labeled *expressive violence* (i.e., violence in an interpersonal context), as opposed to *instrumental* or *predatory violence,* typically associated with the commission of a crime, such as robbery (Griffith and Bell, 1989).

Certain programmatic models, long recognized in behavioral and cognitive behavioral psychology, are especially suited to preventive interventions aimed at expressive violence. Clinical approaches designed to prevent or reduce interpersonal violence may be divided into three broad conceptual categories: social skills training, anger-control training, and peer-conflict mediation. Social skills training focuses on teaching individuals or groups communicative responses (e.g., interpersonal problem solving or negotiation) that will provide them with a sense of self-efficacy, positive social adaptation, and influence in relating to others. Anger control is designed to help youth identify affective stimuli and learn specific techniques to inhibit aggressive responses to anger. Peer conflict mediation programs generally train youth to act as third-party intermediaries, negotiating disputes among their peers. Successful mediation programs depend upon well-developed social skills, such as negotiation, in addition to an anger-control repertoire among participants. The first two paradigms, social skills and anger-control training, may be key prerequisites to the effective application of peer-mediation techniques.

Many notable programs use related psychosocial strategies to help children and adolescents develop skills for avoiding conflict (Feindler and Ecton, 1986; Feindler, Marriott, and Iwata, 1984; Goldstein and Glick, 1987; Guerra and Pannizon, 1986). However, most of these programs have been developed for mainstream populations and do not focus on the special needs, concerns, and cultural environments of African American youth. The Positive Adolescents Choices Training (PACT)[1] program, which was developed in response to this need (Hammond and Yung, 1991b), features the extensive use of "Dealing With Anger: Givin' it, Takin' it, Workin' it Out," a procedural guide and videotape series developed for cultural relevance and appeal to African American youth (Hammond, 1991; Hammond and Yung , 1991a). This videotape program, which has been designed for use in a small-group training format, under the guidance of a skilled facilitator, teaches youth target skills that are essential for coping with anger or frustration without resorting to expressive violence. These skills include giving negative feedback (expressing criticism or displeasure calmly), receiving negative feedback (reacting to the criticism and anger of others appropriately), and negotiation (identifying problems and potential solutions and learning to compromise). Ethnically compatible, familiar stimuli are used in all materials and procedures. Peer role models, as well as strong adult role models who effectively encourage group participation in skills practice, demonstrate the skills to be acquired.

The training model involves the introduction and modeling of the behavioral components of the target skills, providing participants with a rationale for the value of each skill and each of its steps in preventing violence. Opportunities for practicing the skill steps and for receiving feedback to reinforce or correct the participants' performances are provided. The videotapes also demonstrate group sessions in which participants depict "less than perfect" skill practice efforts, which tend to increase the program's credibility with participating adolescents. Controlled evaluations of the PACT program suggest that trained youth exhibit positive outcomes when compared with closely matched nonparticipants. The published findings list reductions in violence-related school suspensions, changes in observable prosocial skills, and improvements in the way participants rate themselves and are rated by teachers (Hammond and Yung, 1991b). Recent additions to the program include developing additional anger management and social skills paradigms as well as a companion training program for parents and families in methods to support adolescents' acquisition and maintenance of violence-reducing skills, attitudes, and behavior.

The failure of American culture to address broad environmental and structural problems, such as poverty, inequality, and the easy availability of guns, almost certainly contributes to the continued epidemic rise of violence, particularly among African American youth. Culturally sensitive, psychosocial approaches represent an extremely important avenue for community-based prevention efforts at the individual level as well as in the public health arena. Future applied and programmatic research should elucidate the pivotal contributions health psychology can make in addressing this problem. The PACT project offers one viable, effective approach to interpersonal violence among African American youth. Ideally, this and other projects will continue to develop a wide range of culturally appropriate violence-prevention techniques.

SUMMARY AND CONCLUSIONS

As evidenced by the current literature on drug, sexual, injury, violent risk-taking and abusive behaviors among ethnic minorities, we have only begun to unravel the complexities of this research domain. Common contributory and protective factors apparently predict whether individuals, and their respective ethnic minority groups, are at high health risk (Yee, 1995). Unique social, cultural, and ethnic antecedents must be incorporated into these models if progress is to be made in closing the health gap between high-risk ethnic minorities and their healthier counterparts. To this end, it is critical that we obtain better national data on health status and risk taking and abusive behaviors among Asian and Pacific Islanders (Gock, 1994; Yee, in press; Zane and Kim, 1994) and Native Americans (John, 1994; Kramer, 1992; Nickens, 1990; Wykle and Kaskel, 1994) and Hispanic Americans (Padilla, 1994; Markides, Lee, Ray, and Black, 1993). The absence of this basic baseline data (Angel and Hogan, 1994) not only precludes a comprehensive evaluation of risk taking and abuse behaviors in these populations, but also makes it more difficult to evaluate the success of proposed interventional and policy strategies.

NOTE

1. Funding to support the Positive Adolescents Choices Training (PACT) program described in this article was provide through grants from the Ohio Governor's Office of Criminal Justice Services and the U.S. Department of Health and Human Services, Maternal and Child Health Bureau.

BIBLIOGRAPHY

Agnew, R. (1990). The origins of delinquent events: An examination of offender accounts. *Journal of Research in Crime and Delinquency*, 27, 267–294.

Amaro, H. (1995). Love, sex, and power: Considering women's realities in HIV prevention. *American Psychologist*, 50, 437–447.

Amaro, H., and Gornemann, I. (1992). *HIV/AIDS knowledge, attitudes, beliefs, and behaviors among Hispanics: Report of findings and recommendations*. Boston: Boston University School of Public Health and Northeast Hispanic AIDS Consortium.

Angel, J. L., and Hogan, D. P. (1994). The demography of minority aging populations. In *Minority elders: Five goals toward building a public policy base* (2nd ed., pp. 9–21). Washington, DC: Gerontological Society of America.

Baker, S. P., O'Neill, B., Ginsburg, M. J., and Guohua, L. (1992). *The injury factbook* (2nd ed.). New York: Oxford University Press.

Becker, M. H. and Joseph, J. A. (1988). AIDS and behavioral change to reduce risk: A review. *American Journal of Public Health*, 78, 394–110.

Becker, T., Samet, J., Wiggins, C., and Key, C. (1990). Violent death in the west: Suicide and homicide in New Mexico, 1958–1987. *Suicide and Life-Threatening Behavior*, 20, 324–334.

Bell, C. (1987). Preventive strategies for dealing with violence among Blacks. *Community Mental Health Journal*, 23, 217–228.

Benson, P. L., and Donahue, M. J. (1989). Ten-year trends in at-risk behaviors: A national study of Black adolescents. *Journal of Adolescent Research*, 4, 125–139.

Bower, B. P. (1992). African-American culture and AIDS prevention: From barrier to ally. In Cross-cultural medicine: A decade later (Special issue). *Western Journal of Medicine*, 157, 286–289.

Braithwaite, R. L., and Taylor, S. E. (Eds.). (1992). *Health issues in the Black community*. San Francisco: Jossey-Bass.

Brown, L. S., Chu, A., Nemoto, T., Ajuiuchukwu, D., and Primm, B. J. (1989). Human immuno-deficiency virus infection in a cohort of intravenous drug users in New York City: Demographic, behavioral, and clinical features. *New York State Journal of Medicine*, 89, 506–510.

Budd, R. D. (1989). Cocaine abuse and violent death. *American Journal of Drug and Alcohol Abuse*, 15, 375–382.

Carlson, R. G., and Siegal, H. A. (1991). The crack life: An ethnographic overview of crack use and sexual behavior among African Americans in a midwest metropolitan city. *Journal of Psychoactive Drugs*, 23, 11–20.

Castro, F. G., Maddahian, E., Newcomb, M. D., and Bentler, P. M. (1987). A multivariate model of the determinants of cigarette smoking among adolescents. *Journal of Health and Social Behavior*, 28, 273–289.

Castro, F. G., Newcomb, M. D., and Bentler, P. M. (1988). Depression and poor health as antecedents and consequences of cocaine use. *Psychology and Health: An International Journal*, 2, 157–186.

Castro, F. G., Newcomb, M. D., and Cadish, K. (1987). Lifestyle differences between young adult co-caine users and their nonuser peers. *Journal of Drug Education*, 17, 89–111.

Castro, F. G., Sharp, E. V., Barrington, E. H., Walton. M., and Rawson, R. A. (1991). Drug abuse and identity in Mexican Americans: Theoretical and empirical considerations. *Hispanic Journal of Behavioral Sciences*, 13, 209–225.

Centers for Disease Control. (1990). Homicide among young Black males United States, 1978–1987. *Morbidity and Mortality Weekly Report*, 39, 369–873.

Centers for Disease Control. (1991). Weapon-carrying among high school students. *Journal of the American Medical Association*, 266, 2342.

Centers for Disease Control. (1995, January). *HIV/AIDS surveillance report*. Atlanta, GA: U.S. Department of Health and Human Services.

Christorfel, K. K. (1990). Violent death and injury in U.S. children and adolescents. *American Journal of Disease of Childhood*, 144, 697–706.

Coates, T. J. (1990). Strategies for modifying sexual behavior for primary and secondary prevention of HIV disease. *Journal of Consulting and Clinical Psychology*, 58, 57–59.

Conciatore, J. (1989). Scholars challenged to develop strategy: Attention to "Black-on-Black" crime misleading. *Black Issues in Higher Education*, 6, 11–13.

Farrell, A. D., Danish, S. J., and Howard, C. W. (1992). Risk factors for drug use in urban adolescents: Identification and cross-validations. *American Journal of Community Psychology*, 20, 263–286.

Feindler, E., and Ecton, R. (1986). *Adolescent anger control*. New York: Pergamon.

Feindler, E. L., Marriott, S. A., and Iwata, M. (1984). Group anger control training for junior high school delinquents. *Cognitive Therapy and Research*, 8, 299–311.

Flay, B. R., and Petraitis, J. (1991). Methodological issues in drug use prevention research: Theoretical foundations. In C. G. Leukefeld and W. B. Bukoski (Eds.), *Drug abuse prevention intervention research: Methodological issues* (pp. 81–109). Rockville, MD: National Institute on Drug Abuse.

Gibbs, J. T. (Ed.). (1988). *Young, Black and male in America: An endangered species*. Dover, MA: Auburn House.

Gock, T. S. (1994). Acquired immunodeficiency syndrome. In N. W. S. Zane, D. T. Takeuchi, and K. N. J. Young (Eds.), *Confronting critical health issues of Asian and Pacific Islander Americans* (pp. 247–265). Thousand Oaks, CA: Sage.

Goldstein, A. P., and Glick, B. (1987). *Aggression replacement training: A comprehensive intervention for aggressive youth*. Champaign. IL: Research Press.

Grachello, A. (1985). Hispanics and health care: Hispanics in the social service system. In P. S. J. Cafferty and W. C. McCready (Eds.), *Hispanics in the United States: A new social agenda* (pp. 195–213). New Brunswick, NJ: Transaction Books.

Graham, S., and Hudley, C. (1992). An attributional approach to aggression in African-American children. In D. Schunk and J. Meece (Eds.), *Student perceptions in the classroom* (pp. 75–94). Hillsdale, NJ: Erlbaum.

Griffith, E., and Bell, C. (1989). Recent trends in suicide and homicide among Blacks. *Journal of the American Medical Association*, 262, 2265–2269.

Guerra, N., and Pannizon, A. (1986). *Viewpoints: Solving problems and making effective decisions for young adults*. Santa Barbara, CA: Center for Law Related Education.

Hammond, R. (Producer). (1991). *Dealing with anger: Givin' it, takin' it, workin' it out* [Videotape]. Champaign, IL: Research Press.

Hammond, R., and Yung, B. (1991a). *Dealing with anger. Givin' it, takin' it, workin' it out*. Champaign, IL: Research Press.

Hammond, R., and Yung, B. (1991b). Preventing violence in at-risk African-American youth. *Journal of Health Care for the Poor and Underserved*, 2, 359–373.

Hammond, R., and Yung, B. (1993). Psychologist's role in public health response to assaultive violence among young African-American males. *American Psychologist*, 48, 142–154.

Harris, D. M., and Guten, S. (1979). Health-protective behavior: An exploratory study. *Journal of Health and Social Behavior*, 20, 17–29.

Institute of Medicine. (1989). *Research on children and adolescents with mental, behavioral, and developmental disorders: Mobilizing a national initiative* (Report of a study by a committee of the Institute of Medicine, Division of Mental Health and Behavioral Science). Washington, DC: National Academy Press.

Istvan, J., and Matarazzo, J. D. (1984). Alcohol and caffeine use: A review of their interrelationships. *Psychological Bulletin*, 95, 301–306.

Jeffrey, R. W. (1989). Risk behaviors and health: Contrasting individual and population perspectives. *American Psychologist*, 44, 1194–1202.

Jessor, R., and Jessor, S. L. (1977). *Problem behavior and psychosocial development: A longitudinal study of youth*. New York: Academic Press.

Jimenez, R. (1987). Educating minorities about AIDS: Challenges and strategies. *Family and Community Health*, 10, 70–73.

John, R. (1994). The state of research on American Indian elders' health, income security, and social support networks. In *Minority elders: Five goals toward building a public policy base* (2nd ed., pp. 46–58). Washington, DC: Gerontological Society of America.

Kalichman, S. C., Kelly, J. A., and St. Lawrence, J. S. (1990). Factors influencing reduction of sexual risk behaviors for human immunodeficiency virus infection: A review. *Annals of Sex Research*, 3, 129–148.

Kaplan, H. B. (1985). Testing a general theory of drug abuse and other deviant adaptations. *Journal of Drug Issues*, 15, 477–492.

Khantzian, E. J., and Khantzian, N. J. (1984). Cocaine addiction: Is there a psychological predisposition? *Psychiatric Annals*, 10, 753–759.

Kinsey, A., Pomeroy, W., and Martin, C. (1948). *Sexual behavior in the human male*. Philadelphia: W. B. Saunders.

Kinsey, A., Pomeroy, W., Martin, C., and Gebhard, P. (1953). *Sexual behavior in the human female.* Philadelphia: W. B. Saunders.

Kramer, B. J. (1992). Health and aging of urban American Indians. *Western Journal of Medicine*, 157, 281–285.

Lex, B. W. (1987). Review of alcohol problems in ethnic minority groups. *Journal of Consulting and Clinical Psychology*, 55, 293–300.

Loya, F., Garcia, P., Sullivan, J., Vargas, L., Mercy, J., and Allen, N. (1986). Conditional risks of homicide among Anglo, Hispanic, Black, and Asian victims in Los Angeles. 1970–1979. In *Report of the Secretary's Task Force on Black and Minority Health* (pp. 117–136). Washington, DC: U.S. Department of Health and Human Services.

Maddahian, E., Newcomb, M. D., and Bentler, P. M. (1986). Adolescents' substance use: Impact of ethnicity, income, and availability. *Advances in Alcohol and Substance Abuse*, 5, 63–78.

Marín, B. V., Gomez, C. A., and Tschann, J. M. (1993). Condom use among Hispanic men with secondary female sexual partners. *Public Health Report*, 108, 742–750.

Marín, B. V., Tschann, J. M., Gomez, C. A., and Kegeles. S. (1993). Acculturation and gender differences in sexual attitudes and behaviors: Hispanic vs. non-Hispanic White unmarried adults. *American Journal of Public Health*, 83, 1759–1761.

Markides, K. S., Lee, D. J., Ray, L. A., and Black, S. A. (1993). Physicians' ratings of health in middle and old age: A cautionary note. *Journal of Gerontology: Social Sciences*, 48, S24–S27.

Mata, A. G., and Jorquez, J. S. (1988). Mexican American intravenous drug users' needle sharing practices: Implications for AIDS prevention. In R. J. Battjes and R. W. Pickins (Eds.), *Needle sharing among intravenous drug abusers: National and international perspectives* (pp. 40–58). Rockville, MD: National Institute on Drug Abuse.

Maxwell, B., and Jacobson, M. (1989). *Marketing disease to Hispanics.* Washington, DC: Center for Science in the Public Interest.

Maypole, D. E., and Anderson, R. B. (1987). Culture-specific substance abuse prevention for Blacks. *Community Mental Health Journal*, 23, 135–139.

Millstein, S. G., and Irwin, C. E. (1988). Accident-related behaviors in adolescents: A biopsychological view. In *Alcohol, drugs, and driving: Abstracts and reviews* (Vol. 4, pp. 21–29). Los Angeles: UCLA Alcohol Research Center.

National Center for Health Statistics. (1990). *Prevention profile: Health, United States, 1989* (DHHS Publication No. PHS 90–1232). Hyattsville, MD: Author.

National Center for Health Statistics. (1992). *Unpublished data tables from the NCHS mortality tapes, FBI-SHR.* Atlanta, GA: Centers for Disease Control.

Nickens, H. (1990). AIDS among Blacks in the 1990s. *Journal of the National Medical Association*, 82, 239–242.

Oetting, E. R., and Beauvais, F. (1987). Peer cluster theory, socialization characteristics, and adolescent drug use: A pain analysis. *Journal of Counseling Psychology*, 34, 205–213.

Oetting, E. R., and Beauvais, F. (1990). Orthogonal cultural identification theory: The cultural identification of minority adolescents. *The International Journal of the Addictions*, 25, 655–685.

Padilla, A. M. (Ed.). (1994). *Hispanic psychology: Critical issues in theory and research.* Thousand Oaks, CA: Sage.

Peterson, J. L., and Marín, G. (1988). Issues in the prevention of AIDS among Black and Hispanic men. *American Psychologist*, 43, 871–877.

Phinney, J. S. (1990). Ethnic identity in adolescents and adults: Review of research. *Psychological Bulletin*, 108, 499–514.

Prothrow-Smith, D. (1991). *Deadly consequences: How violence is destroying our teenage population and a plan to begin solving the problem.* New York: Harper Collins.

Reinisch, J. M., Sanders, S. A., Hill, C., and Ziemba-Davis, M. (1992). High-risk sexual behavior among heterosexual undergraduates at a midwestern university. *Family Planning Perspectives*, 24, 116–121.

Rhodes, J. E., and Jason, L. (1990). A social stress model of substance abuse. *Journal of Consulting and Clinical Psychology*, 58, 395–401.

Rodriguez, J. (1990). Childhood injuries in the United States. *American Journal of Diseases of Childhood*, 144, 627–646.

Rosenberg, M., and Mercy, J. (1991). Assaultive violence. In M. Rosenberg and J. Mercy (Eds.), *Violence in America: A public health approach* (pp. 14–50). New York: Oxford University Press.

Schilling, R. F., El-Bassel, N., Gilbert, L., and Schinke, S. P. (1991). Correlates of drug use, sexual behavior, and attitudes towards safer sex among African American and Hispanic men in methadone maintenance. *Journal of Drug Issues*, 21, 685–698.

Shakoor, B., and Chalmers, D. (1991). Co-victimization of African American children who witness violence: Effects on cognitive, emotional, and behavioral development. *Journal of the National Medical Association*, 83, (3), 233–237.

Sheley, J., McGee, Z., and Wright, J. (1992). Gun-related violence in and around inner-city schools. *American Journal of Diseases of Childhood*, 146, 677–682.

Slaby, R., and Guerra, N. (1988). Cognitive mediators of aggression in adolescent offenders: I. Assessment. *Developmental Psychology*, 24, 580–588.

Smith, J., Mercy, J., and Rosenberg, M. (1986). Suicide and homocide among Hispanics in the Southwest. *Public Health Reports*, 101, 265–270.

Tardiff, K., and Gross, E. (1986). Homicide in New York City. *Bulletin of New York Academy of Medicine*, 62, 413–426.

Trimble, J. E. (1991). Ethnic specification, validational prospects, and the future of drug use research. *International Journal of the Addictions*, 25, 149–170.

Turner, C. F., Miller, H. G., and Moses, L. E. (1989). Sexual behavior and AIDS and intravenous drug use. In *National Research Council, Committee on AIDS Research and the Behavioral, Social and Statistical Sciences* (pp. 73–185). Washington, DC: National Academy Press.

U.S. Department of Health and Human Services. (1985). *Report of the Secretary's Task Force on Black and Minority Health: Vol. V. Homicide, suicide, and unintentional injuries*. Washington, DC: U.S. Government Printing Office.

U.S. Department of Health and Human Services. (1990). *Healthy People 2000: National health promotion and disease prevention objectives*. Washington, DC: U.S. Government Printing Office.

U.S. Department of Health and Human Services. (1991). *Health, United States, 1990*. Washington, DC: U.S. Government Printing Office.

Weinstein, N. D. (1987). Unrealistic optimism about illness susceptibility: Conclusions from a community-wide sample. *Journal of Behavioral Medicine*, 10, 481–500.

Westermeyer, J. (1984). The role of ethnicity in substance abuse. *Advances in Alcohol and Substance Abuse*, 4, 9–18.

Wyatt, G. E. (1985). The sexual abuse of Afro-American and White American women in childhood. *Child Abuse and Neglect: The International Journal*, 10, 231–240.

Wyatt, G. E. (1989). Reexamining factors predicting Afro-American and White American women's age at first coitus. *Archives of Sexual Behavior*, 18, 271–298.

Wyatt, G. E. (1991). Examining ethnicity versus race in AIDS related research. *Social Science and Medicine*, 33(1), 37–15.

Wyatt, G. E. (1994). The sociocultural relevance of sex research: Challenges for the 1990s and beyond. *American Psychologist*, 49, 748–754.

Wyatt, G. E., Lawrence, J., Vodounon, A., and Mickey, M. R. (1992). The Wyatt Sex History Questionnaire: A structured interview for female sexual history taking. *Journal of Child Sexual Abuse*, 1(4), 51–68.

Wyatt, G. E., and Riederle, M. H. (1994). Reconceptualizing issues that affect women's sexual decision-making and sexual functioning. *Psychology of Women Quarterly*, 18, 611–615.

Wykle, M., and Kaskel, B. (1994). Increasing the longevity of minority older adults through improved health status. In *Minority elders: Five goals toward building a public policy base* (2nd ed., pp. 32–39). Washington, DC: Gerontological Society of America.

Yee, B.W.K. (1995). *Variations in aging: Older minorities*. Galveston: The University of Texas Medical Branch. Texas Consortium of Geriatric Education Centers.

Yee, B.W.K. (in press). Impact of gender and age upon evaluation of alcohol and drug abuse prevention with Asian and Pacific Islander communities (working title). In *Cultural competence for evaluators: A guide for alcohol and other drug abuse prevention practitioners working with Asian/Pacific Island communities* (Cultural Competence Series, VI). Rockville. MD: Center for Substance Abuse Prevention.

Zane, N.W.S., and Kim, J. H. (1994). Substance use and abuse. In N.W.S. Zane, D. T. Takeuchi, and K. N. J. Young (Eds.), *Confronting critical health issues of Asian and Pacific Islander Americans* (pp. 316–343). Thousand Oaks, CA: Sage.

Zelnick, M., Kanter, J. F., and Ford, K. (1981). *Sex and pregnancy in adolescence.* Beverly Hills, CA: Sage.

10.

Risk Factors for Early Adolescent Drug Use in Four Ethnic and Racial Groups

William A. Vega, Rick S. Zimmerman, George J. Warheit, Eleni Apospori, and Andres G. Gil

Objectives. It is widely believed that risk factors identified in previous epidemiologic studies accurately predict adolescent drug use. Comparative studies are needed to determine how risk factors vary in prevalence, distribution, sensitivity, and pattern across the major U.S. ethnic/racial groups.

Methods. Baseline questionnaire data from a 3-year epidemiologic study of early adolescent development and drug use were used to conduct bivariate and multivariate risk factor analyses. Respondents (n = 6,760) were sixth- and seventh-grade Cuban, other Hispanic, Black, and White non-Hispanic boys in the 48 middle schools of the greater Miami (Dade County) area.

Results. Findings indicate 5% lifetime illicit drug use, 4% lifetime inhalant use, 37% lifetime alcohol use, and 21% lifetime tobacco use, with important intergroup differences. Monotonic relationships were found between 10 risk factors and alcohol and illicit drug use. Individual risk factors were distributed disproportionately, and sensitivity and patterning of risk factors varied widely by ethnic/racial subsample.

Conclusions. While the cumulative prevalence of risk factors bears a monotonic relationship to drug use, ethnic/racial differences in risk factor profiles, especially for Blacks, suggest differential predictive value based on cultural differences.

Experimentation in early adolescence with alcohol, cigarettes, and illicit drugs is an important marker of future persistent drug use.[1,2] Certain risk factors have predicted early drug use with considerable accuracy in a limited number of regional and national studies.[3-6] However, these studies were limited in their ability to make comparisons across the major U.S. ethnic/racial groups.

Consistent monotonic relationships have been found between cumulative risk factors and the use of illicit drugs.[4,5] It is now widely accepted in the drug research field that multiple risk factor models are required for understanding adolescent drug use.[6] Bry et al. state that drug use is best understood as a general coping mechanism, and, as a result, the quantity of risk factors rather than any unique combination predisposes adolescents to drug use.[5] However, Newcomb et al. note that people are not exposed to the same number of risk factors, and that "the likelihood of manifesting drug use may vary according to various characteristics of the individual and their environment."[2]

Comparative epidemiologic studies about adolescent drug use are rare, especially studies contrasting African Americans, White non-Hispanics, and Hispanics. Furthermore, epidemiologic findings about Hispanics are applicable only to Mexican-American and Puerto Rican youth.[7,8] Logically, ethnic/racial groups may be exposed differentially to risk factors, and the number or pattern of factors required to significantly increase risk may differ by group as well. This study reports early adolescent prevalence and risk factor data in four groups residing in southern Florida: Blacks, non-Hispanic Whites, Cubans, and other Hispanics. Risk profiles include a comparative assessment of risk factor distribution and predictive value for each ethnic/racial subsample.

METHODS

Sample

The sample consisted of 6,760 boys from sixth- and seventh-grade classes in the greater Miami area. Dade County, Florida, is predominantly urban, with a 1991 population of approximately 1,937,000, of whom about one half were Hispanic. The Cuban and other Hispanic groups each constitute about 25% of the population; 20% are Black and the remaining 30% are non-Hispanic White. The other Hispanic and Black groups have the lowest mean age and, as a result, are disproportionately represented in the school system.

These data were taken from the first wave of a longitudinal study, conducted during the fall semester of 1990, of the 48 middle/junior high schools in Dade County. Although the largest Hispanic ethnic group is of Cuban origin, the combined other Hispanic subsample, composed primarily of Nicaraguans, Salvadorans, Colombians, Puerto Ricans, Dominicans, and Venezuelans, is more numerous than the Cuban subsample. Many Central Americans in the other Hispanic subsample are recent refugees, are destitute, and reside in congested, low-income areas within Dade Country.

Students in the sixth and seventh grades were given consent forms for written parental approval. Of the 10,423 eligible male students, 79% returned consent forms. Of those returning consent forms, 6,934 (83%) granted permission; thus, the overall consent rate was 66.5%. Usable data were collected for 6,760 male students. The sample included 899 (13.3%) White non-Hispanics, 1,745 (25.8%) Cubans, 2,551 (37.7%) other Hispanics, 1,330 (19.7%) Blacks, and 188 (2.8%) "others."

Comparisons between sample characteristics and those of the sampling universe were made. The only significant differences found were that African Americans were slightly underrepresented in the sample (24.0%) compared with the population (27.9%), and Whites and Hispanics were slightly overrepresented. Whites constituted 20.6% of the sample and 19.1% of the population, and Hispanics constituted 53.7% of the sample and 51.4% of the population.

Measures

Illicit drug use was measured using a series of scales that tapped lifetime use, frequency of use in previous month and previous year, and grade at first use. Because the respondents were in early adolescence, we anticipated very low prevalence rates for specific types of illicit drugs. This turned out to be the case. As a result for the analyses presented in this paper illicit drug use is assessed as a compound variable that includes lifetime use of any illicit substance, including marijuana, cocaine, crack cocaine, PCP, and nonprescribed barbiturates, amphetamines, and tranquilizers. Alcohol, cigarettes, and inhalants were assessed separately and not included in the illicit drug variable.

The risk factors used were selected from the research literature. Following the lead of Newcomb and colleagues, we used 10 risk factors in order to maximize the predictive value of the profile for alcohol and illicit drugs.[2,4] Phill and Spiers reported that depression and poor self-concept were related to drug use.[9] Other investigators have noted the importance of subjective perceptions about peer attitudes toward and behaviors regarding drugs,[10–15] the role of parent modeling[1,16,17] deviance,[18–20] psychological stress,[21,22] family characteristics and emotional ties[23–26] and early use of cigarettes and alcohol.[27–29] Guided by these findings, we identified 10 statistically significant risk factors using bivariate analyses with drug use as the dependent variable.

Most risk factors were operationalized as scales. Cut points were established to ensure reasonably low prevalence of individual risk factors for the sample. No more than one fifth of the sample met the criteria for a specific risk factor, except for the variable parent smoking. The variables used as risk factors in this study are summarized below.

Low family pride. The Family Pride Scale consists of 7 items derived from the work of Olson and colleagues.[30] Each item has a range of 1 through 4. The threshold was greater than 14 for high risk, with 13.9% of sample having this risk.

Family substance abuse problems. Two items tapped whether any family member had problems due to a family member's use of alcohol or other drugs. The threshold was an affirmative response to either question, with 18.4% having this risk.

Parent smoking. Two items inquired how often the mother or father smokes cigarettes, with answers ranging from 1 through 5. The threshold was endorsement of a "sometimes," "often," or "always" response for mother and/or father, with 32.0% having this risk.

Low self-esteem. The Kaplan Self-Derogation Scale is a 13-item scale; each item has a range of 1 through 4.[22] The threshold was a mean of 2.5 or lower (on average, agreement with negative statements about oneself); 18.2% of the sample met the criteria for being at risk.

Depression symptoms. Four items from the Center for Epidemiologic Studies Depression scale were used. Scores ranged from 1 through 4,[31] with higher scores indicating more symptoms. The threshold was a mean of 1.5 (an average frequency of experiencing the symptoms more often than rarely in the previous week), with 14.7% having this risk.

Suicide attempt. Respondents were asked whether they had attempted suicide. The threshold was an affirmative response, with 6.9% meeting this risk criterion.

Perception of high peer substance use. Respondents were asked how many of their friends use cigarettes, marijuana, cocaine, and alcohol, with responses ranging from none (1) to all (4). The threshold was a mean of 1.5 or higher, with 21.6% having this risk.

Perception of peer approval for substance use. Respondents were asked how they thought their friends feel about people who use cigarettes, marijuana, cocaine, and alcohol, with responses ranging from approve a lot (1) to disapprove a lot (4). The threshold was a mean score of less than 3 (i.e., approval); 9.6% were at high risk.

Willingness to engage in nonnormative behavior. Respondents indicated, on a 4-point scale, their agreement or disagreement with statements supporting delinquent or lawbreaking behavior. Respondents who, on average, agreed with the statement were classified as at risk; 15.1% met the criteria for this risk.

Delinquent behavior. A 7-item scale tapping delinquent behavior was taken from the Kaplan Deviance Scale, which assesses serious predatory or antisocial behaviors. [22] Each question required a yes or no response. The threshold was endorsement of two or more behaviors; 18.9% met this risk criterion.

RESULTS

Table 1 presents the prevalence of risk factors in four areas: family, psychosocial, peer, and deviance. Between-group differences for each risk factor were tested using one-way analyses of variance. White non-Hispanics and Blacks had the highest prevalence of low family pride. Blacks and other Hispanics were most likely to report family substance abuse problems but least likely to report parent smoking. Cubans and White non-Hispanics were most likely to indicate parent smoking. Blacks and other Hispanics were highest on the three psychosocial risk factors.

Among peer risk factors, Cubans and White non-Hispanics were highest on perception of high peer substance use. Blacks were highest on perception of peer approval for substance use but lowest on perception of high peer substance use. Among the deviance risk factors, Cubans were the most likely to indicate a willingness to engage in non-normative behaviors, and Blacks were the most likely to report delinquent behavior.

Table 2 presents the cumulative prevalence of risk factors for the sample and for each racial/ethnic group. Overall, the distribution of risk factors was similar for all groups. However, Blacks were less likely to have no risk factors and more likely to have three to six, while White non-Hispanics were more likely to have seven or more. In addition, Blacks had the highest mean number of risk factors.

Table 1. Prevalence of Risk Factors

Risk Factor	Overall, %	White, Non-Hispanics, %	Hispanics, %		Blacks, %
			Cubans	Other	
Family					
Low family pride	13.9	18.5[a,b]	11.0[c]	12.8[d*]	16.8
Family substance use problems	18.4	18.4[a**]	15.0[c**]	20.2	20.1
Parent smoking	32.0	36.4[b**]	36.4[c**]	28.9	28.8
Psychosocial					
Low self-esteem	18.2	13.8[b**]	15.5[c**]	20.0	20.9
Depression symptoms	14.7	13.8[*]	11.6[c***]	15.1[d]	19.5
Suicide attempt	6.9	5.1[b*,f***]	6.1[e***]	7.8	7.6
Peer					
Perception of high peer substance use	21.6	26.1[bf*]	25.4[c***]	20.0[d**]	17.1
Perception of peer approval for substance use	9.6	8.1[f**]	9.3[c***]	9.2[d*]	12.0
Deviance					
Willingness to engage in nonnormative behavior	15.1	10.4[a,b,f*]	17.0	15.8	15.2
Delinquent behavior	18.9	12.6[a,b,f*]	18.3[c*]	18.3[d*]	25.8

a White non-Hispanics were significantly different from Cubans.
b White non-Hispanics were significantly different from other Hispanics.
c Cubans were significantly different from Blacks.
d Other Hispanics were significantly different from Blacks.
e Cubans were significantly different from other Hispanics.
f White non-Hispanics were significantly different from Blacks
*$P < .001$; **$P < .01$; ***$P < .05$.

Table 2. Cumulative Prevalence of Risk Factors

No. of Risk Factors	Overall, %	White, Non-Hispanics, %	Hispanics, % Cubans	Hispanics, % Other	Blacks, %
0	30.4	32.0	31.9	30.5	27.3
1	27.2	25.8	27.3	27.7	26.1
2	16.0	16.9	14.8	16.5	16.4
3	10.0	9.3	10.0	9.8	10.8
4	6.8	6.3	5.6	6.6	9.5
5–6	7.0	6.1	7.6	6.5	8.1
7+	2.5	3.4	2.8	2.4	1.8
Mean	1.7	1.6	1.6	1.6	1.8[a]

a Blacks were significantly different from Cubans and other Hispanics ($P < .01$) and significantly different from White non-Hispanics (P < .05).

The overall prevalence of substance use are shown in Table 3. The data indicate that about 5% of the respondents had used an illicit drug at least once in their lifetime; however, only about 1.5% did so more than two times. Thus, illicit drug use was a fairly rare event among the sixth- and seventh-grade boys in this sample. On the other hand, over one third of the respondents had used alcohol at least once, and about one fifth of them had used alcohol two or more times. About 1 in 5 respondents had tried smoking, but only 1 in 20 had done so two or more times. The prevalence for inhalants was similar to that for illicit drugs. Table 4 reports lifetime substance use and statistical tests of differences among the various racial/ethnic groups. Blacks consistently had the lowest levels of use for all substances. Their prevalence levels were 20% to 30% lower than those in other racial/ethnic subsamples. White non-Hispanics reported more alcohol, cigarette, and inhalant use, whereas Cubans and other Hispanics reported slightly higher levels of illicit drug use.

Table 3. Lifetime Prevalence of Substance Abuse

Substance	Never Used, % (SE)	Ever Used, %	Used > 2 Times, % (SE)
Alcohol	63.1 (0.6)	36.9	18.7 (0.5)
Cigarettes	79.3 (0.9)	20.7	5.3 (0.3)
Inhalants	96.0 (0.2)	4.0	1.6 (0.2)
Illicit drugs	95.2 (0.3)	4.8	1.5 (0.1)

Table 4. Lifetime Prevalence of Substance Use, by Race/Ethnicity

Substance	White Non-Hispanics, % (SE)	Blacks, % (SE)	Hispanics Cubans, % (SE)	Hispanics Other, % (SE)
Alcohol	48.2[a,b,c*] (1.7)	25.0 (1.3)	41.3[d,e*] (1.2)	31.2[f*] (1.0)
Cigarettes	26.8[a,b,c*] (1.5)	12.4 (1.0)	20.5[e*] (1.0)	20.2[f*] (0.8)
Inhalants	5.0[c**] (0.7)	2.6 (0.5)	4.8[e**] (0.5)	3.6 (0.4)
Illicit drugs	4.8 (0.7)	3.7 (0.5)	5.1 (0.5)	5.2[f***] (0.4)

a White non-Hispanics were significantly different from Cubans.
b White non-Hispanics were significantly different from other Hispanics.
c White non-Hispanics were significantly different from Blacks.
d Cubans were significantly different from Blacks.
e Other Hispanics were significantly different from other Hispanics.
*P < .001; **P < .01; ***P < .05.

Figure 1 illustrates the proportion of lifetime alcohol users as a function of risk factors for each racial/ethnic group. The curves are monotonic for all subsamples. However, White non-Hispanics with no risk factors were almost twice as likely to have tried alcohol as Blacks. Cubans with no risk factors had proportions of lifetime use similar to White non-Hispanics, and other Hispanics were similar to Blacks. Beyond four risk factors, the curves for Cuban Hispanics and other Hispanics were similar. At the seven or above risk-factor level, 86.2% of the White non-Hispanics, 81.4% of the Cubans, 80.3% of the other Hispanics, and 86.4% of Blacks had tried alcohol. The strongest association between risk factors and alcohol use occurred with Blacks; their proportion was almost four times greater for those with seven or more risk factors than for those with no risk factors. In comparison, other Hispanics had the second strongest association.

Figure 2 illustrates the proportion of lifetime illicit drug use as a function of risk factors. The curve is monotonic for all groups, except for a minor nonmonotonic fluctuation among Blacks. Few respondents from any subsample who had no risk factors had used an illicit drug. At 7+ risk factors, all subsamples except Blacks had similar proportions, ranging from 36% to 40%. In contrast, the illicit drug use of Blacks with seven or more risk factors was only 12%. All slopes are markedly linear from five through six to seven or more risk factors except the slope for Blacks, which shows a marginal decline. In order to determine the differential patterning of risk factors for each subsample, we conducted a logistic regression analysis for alcohol (Table 5). The low prevalence for illicit drugs made a similar analysis of those drugs unfeasible. Only statistically significant risk factors are reported for each subsample, and both consistencies and dissimilarities are noted. Five risk factors were identified for Blacks, four for White non-Hispanics, six for Cubans, and nine for other Hispanics. Low family pride and willingness to engage in nonnormative behavior were statistically significant for all subsamples. Depression symptoms were important only for White non-Hispanics. Low self-esteem, suicide attempts, and delinquency were important only for other Hispanics. Respondents correctly classified by statistically significant risk factors ranged from only 34% of Blacks to 64.4% of White non-Hispanics.

DISCUSSION

There are several important findings and implications stemming from this study. Risk factors were found to be consistently related to alcohol and illicit drug use among the sixth- and seventh-grade boys in the sample, affirming the value of risk factors for predicting substance use among adolescents. The comparative design of this study made it possible to detect major ethnic/racial subsample differences in prevalence and in risk profiles.

Individual risk factors were found to be distributed disproportionately across subsamples. For example, Blacks and other Hispanics were more vulnerable to depressive mood and low self-esteem. Cubans and White non-Hispanics were most likely to believe that their friends used drugs, while White non-Hispanics reported the lowest levels of family pride. Nonetheless, the cumulative prevalence of risk factors was similar for all subsamples. Although Blacks reported the highest mean number of risk factors, White non-Hispanics were the most likely to have seven or more.

Overall associations between risk factors and proportions of lifetime alcohol or illicit drugs were monotonic, albeit with significant intergroup variations. Blacks appear to be much less sensitive to the cumulative effects of these risk factors in the instance of illicit

William A. Vega et al.

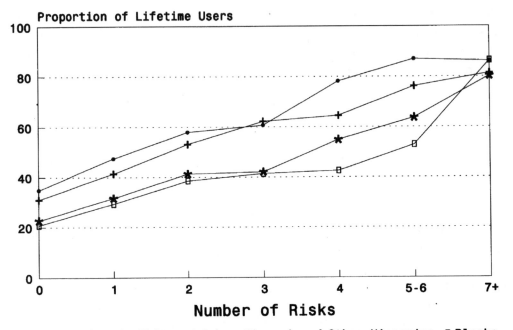

Figure 1. Relationship between risks and lifetime alcohol use.

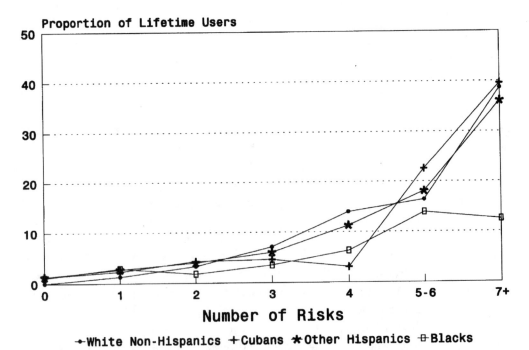

Figure 2. Relationship between risks and lifetime illicit drug use.

Table 5. Logistic Regression of Lifetime Alcohol Use on Risk Factors, by Racial/Ethnic Group

	Other Hispanics (n = 1742)	Cubans (n = 1313)	Blacks (n = 808)	Whites (n = 741)	Total sample (n = 6760)
Perceived peer use	.40***	.40***	.29*	...	.38***
Peer approval	.31***	.28***	...	1.2***	.26***
Low family pride	.37***	.47***	.57***	.39***	.46***
Depression	...	...	...	.42*	...
Delinquency	.88*	...	...	...	.54*
Willingness to engage in nonnormative behavior	.57***	.63***	.49***	.48**	.56***
Family substance use problems	.48***	.30*	.30*	...	.33***
Parent smoking	.18*	.19*	.38**	...	.22***
Low self-esteem	.26**	...	...	...	...
Suicide attempt	.71**	...	...	...	...
Model χ²	262.1	188.0	95.6	146.6	614.2
Users correctly classified %	37.8	53.0	34.0	64.4	42.9

Note. Values shown are standardized coefficients.
*P < .001; **P < .01; ***P < .05.

drug use. Although some investigators have suggested that it is not worthwhile to seek the "best combination" of risk factors, these data suggest the opposite conclusion.[5] The logistic regression analysis indicates subgroup specific patterning of risk factors and differential vulnerability to their combined effects. Whereas two in three White non-Hispanics who used alcohol in their lifetime were correctly classified, only one in three Blacks were correctly classified. These findings could result from greater subcultural resilience among Blacks. [32]

The two Hispanic subsamples were interesting to compare because 35% of the Cuban boys were foreign born and resided in a long-established ethnic enclave in Miami, while nearly 60% of other Hispanic boys were foreign born and more likely to be recent arrivals, often with uncertain residency status.[33] Despite differences in the distribution of risk factors, the two subgroups are similar in having higher levels of family pride than White non-Hispanics and Blacks.[34] The two groups also have (1) similar prevalence levels for lifetime tobacco, inhalant, and illicit drug use; (2) similar risk factor curves for alcohol and illicit drugs ; and (3) similar patterning of specific risk factors for alcohol use. Future analyses of these data for Hispanics will permit finer comparisons in order to determine whether these differences represent cultural/acculturation effects or are conditioned by sociodemographic factors.[35]

NOTES

1. Kandel, D. B., Kessier, R. C., and Margulies, R. Z. (1978). Antecedents of adolescent initiation into stages of drug use: a developmental analysis. *Journal of Youth Adolescence*, 7, 13–40.
2. Newcomb, M. D., Maddahian, E., Sakger, R., and Bentler, P. M. (1987). Substance abuse and psychosocial risk factors among teenagers: Associations with sex, age, ethnicity, and type of school. *American Journal of Drug and Alcohol Abuse*, 13, 413–433.
3. Smith, G. M., and Fogg, C. P. (1978). Psychological predictors of early use, late use, and nonuse of marijuana among teenage students. In A. B. Kandel (Ed.), *Longitudinal Research on Drug Use: Empirical Findings and Methodological Issues* (pp. 101–113). Washington, DC: Hemisphere.

4. Newcomb, M. D., Maddahian, E., and Bentler, P. M. (1986). Risk factors for drug use among adolescents: concurrent and longitudinal analyses. *American Journal of Public Health*, 76, 525–531.

5. Bry, B.H., McKeon, P., and Pandina, R. J. (1982). Extent of drug use as a function of number of risk factors. *Journal of Abnormal Psychology*, 91, 273–279.

6. Gorsuch, R. L., and Bulter M. C. (1976). Initial drug abuse: A review of predisposing social psychological factors. *Psychology Bulletin*, 83, 120–137.

7. Trimble, J. E., Padilla, A. M., and Bell, C. S. (1987). *Drug Abuse among Ethnic Minorities*. Rockville, MD: National Institute on Drug Abuse. DHHS publication no. 87–1474.

8. Chavez, E. L., and Swaim, R.C. (1992). An epidemiologic comparison of Mexican-American and White non-Hispanic 8th- and 12th-grade students' substance use. *American Journal of Public Health*, 82, 445–447.

9. Phil, R. O., and Spiers, P. (1978). The etiology of drug abuse. In B. Maher (Ed.), *Progress in Experimental Personality Research*. New York: Academic Press.

10. Kandel, D. (1973). Adolescent marijuana use: Role of parents and peers. *Science*, 181: 1067–1070.

11. Huba G., Wingard, J., and Bentler, P. (1979). Beginning adolescent drug use and peer and adult interaction patterns. *Journal of Consulting and Clinical Psychology*, 47, 265–276.

12. Braught, G., Brakarsh, D., Follingstad, D., and Berry, K. (1973). Deviant drug use in adolescence: a review of psychosocial correlates. *Psychology Bulletin*, 79, 92–106.

13. Jessor, R., and Jessor, S. L. (1977). *Problem Behavior and Psychosocial Development: A Longitudinal Study of Youth*. New York: Academic Press.

14. Kandel, D., Treiman, D., Faust, R., and Single, E. L. (1976). Adolescent involvement in illicit drug use: a multiple classification analysis. *Sociological Forces*, 55, 438–458.

15. Sadava, S. W. (1973). Patterns of college student drug use: A longitudinal social learning study. *Psychology Reports*, 33, 75–86.

16. Hunt, D. G. (1974). Parental permissiveness as perceived by the offspring and the degree of marijuana usage among offspring. *Human Relations*, 27, 267–285.

17. Smart, R. G., and Fejer D. (1972). Drug use among adolescents and their parents: Closing the generation gap in mood modification. *Journal of Abnormal Psychology*, 79, 153–160.

18. Kaplan, H. (1975). *Self Attitude and Deviant Behavior*. Pacific Palisades, CA: Goodyear.

19. Kaplan, H. (1972). Toward a general theory of psychosocial deviance: The case of aggressive behavior. *Soc Sci Med*. 6, 593–617.

20. Jessor, R., and Jessor, S. L. (1978). Theory testing in longitudinal research on marijuana use. In Kandel, D.P., (Ed.), *Longitudinal Research on Drug Use: Empirical Findings and Methodological Issues*. Washington, DC: Hemisphere.

21. Kaplan, H., Johnson, R., and Bailey, C. (1987). Deviant peers and deviant behavior: Further elaboration of a model. *Social Psychology Quarterly*, 50, 277–284.

22. Kaplan, H., Johnson, R., and Bailey, C. (1986). Self-rejection and the explanation of deviance: Refinement and elaboration of a latent structure. *Social Psychology Quarterly*, 49, 110–128.

23. McCord, W., and McCord, J. (1959). *Origins of Crime*. New York: Columbia University Press.

24. Nye, F. (1958). *Family Relationships and Delinquent Behavior*. New York: Wiley.

25. Padia, R. J., and Scheule, J. (1983). Psychosocial correlates of adolescent alcohol and drug use. *Journal of Studies on Alcohol*, 44, 950–973.

26. Newcomb, M.D., and Bentler, P. M. (1988). *Consequences of Adolescent Drug Use: Impact on the Lives of Young Adults*. Newbury Park, CA: Sage.

27. Teat, F. S., Detels, R., and Clark, V. (1975). Some childhood antecedents of drug and alcohol abuse. *American Journal of Epidemiology*, 102, 377–384.

28. Teat, F. S., and Detels, R. (1976). Relationship of alcohol, cigarettes, and drug abuse in adulthood with alcohol, cigarette, and coffee consumption in childhood. *Preventive Medicine*, 5, 70–77.

29. Kandel, D. B., and Faust, R. (1975). Sequence and stages in patterns of adolescent drug use. *Archives of General Psychiatry*, 32, 923–932.

30. Olson, D. H., McCubbin, H. I., Barnes, H., Larsen, A., Muxen, M., and Wilson, M. (1985). *Family Inventories*. St. Paul, MN: University of Minnesota.

31. Radlof, L. (1977). The CES-D scale: A self-report depression scale for research in the general population. *Applied Psychological Measure*, 1, 385–401.
32. Kessler, R. C. (1979). Stress, social status, and psychological distress. *Journal of Health and Social Behavior*, 20: 259–272.
33. Portes, A. P., and Rumbaut, R. G. (1990). *Immigrant America: A Portrait*. Berkeley, CA: University of California.
34. Vega, W. A. (1990). Hispanic families in the 1980s: a decade of research. *Journal of Marriage and Family*, 52, 1015–1024.
35. Rogler, L. H., Cortes, D. E., Malgady, R.G. (1991). Acculturation and mental health status among Hispanics. *American Psychology*, 46, 585–597.

11.

Drinking and Alcohol-Related Problems Among Minority Women

Raul Caetano

Although drinking by Black and Hispanic women in the United States differs from that of White women in terms of prevalence rates and incidence of alcohol-related problems, factors such as age and employment status have similar effects on drinking in each group. However, influences on drinking among minority women are complex and must be thought of as an interaction of cultural, personal, and historical factors. This interplay is beginning to emerge from ethnic studies.

An issue of *Alcohol Health & Research World* reviews a representative sample of the spectrum of studies found in the current literature that focus on alcohol consumption and drinking problems in women. Although other studies are available (e.g., Wilsnack and Beckman, 1984), few of them assess drinking by ethnic minority women. Leland (1984) reviewed the literature existing for these segments of the population in 1984. At that time no major survey had been conducted with national samples of U.S. ethnic groups. All large surveys had some analysis of data by ethnicity, but because these surveys were designed to focus on the U.S. general population, the number of minority respondents interviewed as part of their samples was small. The consequent analyses were limited in scope and generalizability, and most were not gender specific.

Since Leland's review, several surveys have concentrated on drinking in ethnic minority populations. Among them are those that are part of the Epidemiologic Catchment Area studies (ECA), which focused on Blacks in St. Louis and Mexican Americans in Los Angeles; the 1984 National Alcohol Survey (NAS, 84) and its 1992 followup, which interviewed national samples of Whites, Blacks, and Hispanics; and the Hispanic Health and Nutrition Examination Survey (H–HANES, 1982–1984), which interviewed a large number of Mexican Americans, Cuban Americans, and Puerto Ricans. Studies with a specific focus on women or that reported gender-specific analyses from data collected in these surveys have been published, and some of their findings will be discussed here (e.g., Helzer and Canino, 1992; Burnam, 1989; Caetano, 1991; Herd, 1991; Herd and Caetano, 1987; Markides et al., 1990).

This article examines data on Black and Hispanic women; it also reviews data about White women as a comparison group. These are the 3 groups of women for which national data are available. Because studies of Asian Americans and Native Americans are limited to specific localities, they do not represent drinking by women in these two ethnic groups at a national level. Local analyses were used by researchers studying these groups because the great ethnic variation that exists within each group is reflected in their geographical distribution. Local studies are able to include only the Asian national subgroup or the Native American tribe present in the particular locale in which the study is taking place. Grouping these studies to achieve some broader geographic coverage is not warranted because of the differences in methods across studies.

In this article, findings from NAS–84, conducted by the Alcohol Research Group, will be presented along with new findings from the 8-year followup of this sample conducted in 1992. The first part of the article describes the research methodology used in 1984 and 1992, followed by a discussion of findings on drinking patterns and their sociodemographic correlates. A review of drinking problems among Black, Hispanic, and White women concludes the article.

RESEARCH METHODOLOGY

Sampling and Data Collection in 1984

A total of 1,947 Blacks, 1,453 Hispanics, and 1,777 Whites were interviewed for the NAS–84 survey. Subjects were adults selected at random from among individuals living in households in the 48 coterminous United States. The response rates were 76% for Blacks, 72% for Hispanics, and 73% for Whites.

Data were collected by trained interviewers in face-to-face interviews that lasted an average of one hour. The place of interview was the respondent's home, and the instrument for data collection was a standardized questionnaire. Hispanic respondents were given a choice of being interviewed in English or Spanish—a Spanish version of the questionnaire and bilingual interviewers were assigned when needed. About 43% of these respondents chose to be interviewed in Spanish.

Sampling and Data Collection in 1992

A total of 1,151 Blacks, 1,149 Hispanics, and 1,125 Whites, who had been interviewed in 1984, were selected for reinterview in 1992, using the following criteria. All respondents who in 1984 reported four or more drinking-related problems (i.e., medical, psychological or social problems caused or exacerbated by alcohol use) on a lifetime basis and/or reported currently drinking five or more drinks on one occasion were chosen for followup; this garnered 551 Blacks, 446 Hispanics, and 619 Whites. An additional 600 Black, 703 Hispanic, and 506 White respondents also were selected at random to provide a sample of individuals with a wide range of drinking patterns. Out of the contingent selected for reinterview, followup interviews were successfully completed with 723 Blacks, 703 Hispanics, and 788 Whites, making the overall response rate 70%.[1]

Identifying Participants' Ethnicity

The main ethnic identifier for sample selection and in the analysis of results in both 1984 and 1992 was the ethnicity of the family of origin. The respondent was asked: "Which of these groups describes your family of origin?" Four categories for identifying Blacks, Hispanics, and Whites were provided. Respondents who selected the category "Black, not of Hispanic origin" were identified as Blacks. Respondents who selected "Black of Hispanic origin (e.g., Mexican, Central or South American, or any other Hispanic origin)" and "White of Hispanic origin (e.g., Mexican, Central or South American, or any other

Hispanic origin)" were classified as Hispanics. Respondents who said that their family of origin was "White, not of Hispanic origin" were identified as White.

This ethnic identification methodology groups a variety of White, Black, and Hispanic national groups under all-encompassing ethnic identifying labels. Although cultural diversity exists within each of these larger groups, studies using this general grouping scheme are warranted by the many common social and cultural traits (e.g., language) shared by women in each group.

This article primarily will compare drinking practices and alcohol-related problems among women in the 3 large ethnic groups established using the method described above. However, it also will examine differences between divisions of the Hispanic group made based on individuals' nation of origin (i.e., whether they are of Mexican, Puerto Rican, or Cuban origin). In this way, the article will consider some of the intraethnic variation present in the larger Hispanic ethnic group.

Categorizing Respondents By Alcohol Consumption

Drinkers were placed in categories defining their levels of drinking using a quantity-frequency index. This index is based on the respondent's self-report of frequency and quantity of drinking wine, beer, and spirits during the 12 months prior to the survey. The respondent's frequency of drinking was coded in 1 of 11 categories ranging from "never" to "three or more times a day." Quantity of consumption was assessed by asking for the proportion of drinking occasions on which the respondent drank five or six, three or four, and one or two glasses each of wine, beer, and spirits. This information can be used to classify respondents according to how often they drink five or more drinks of any alcoholic beverage, if they ever do. Cross-tabulating these categories with the frequency of drinking provides the following index categories:

- Frequent heavy drinker: Drinks once a week or more often and has five or more drinks at a sitting, once a week or more often. A drink equals 1 ounce of spirits, a 4-ounce glass of table wine, or a 12-ounce can of beer, each of which contains approximately 12 grams of absolute alcohol.
- Frequent high maximum drinker: Drinks once a week or more often and has five drinks or more drinks at a sitting less than once a week but at least once a year.
- Frequent low maximum drinker: Drinks once a week or more often but never drinks five or more drinks at a sitting.
- Less frequent high maximum drinker: Drinks one to three times a month but has five or more drinks at a sitting.
- Infrequent drinker: Drinks less than once a month but at least once a year and may or may not drink five drinks at a sitting.
- Abstainer: Drinks less than once a year or never has consumed alcoholic beverages.

DRINKING PATTERNS

Comparisons Among Groups in 1984

In 1984 drinking patterns across White, Black, and Hispanic women were different in several ways (Table 1). Abstention was higher among Black women and Hispanic women than among White women. Approximately half of the Black and Hispanic women interviewed reported they had not consumed alcohol in the 12 months previous to the survey. Most women who drank in all three groups were light drinkers (i.e., the majority of them

**Table 1. Drinking Patterns Among White, Black, and Hispanic Women:
1984 and 1992** (in percent)[1]

Drinking Pattern	White (n = 399)		Black (n = 402)		Hispanic (n = 374)	
	1984	1992	1984	1992	1984	1992
Abstention	31	36	46	51	47	48
Infrequent	23	22	18	24	27	34
Less Frequent Low Maximum	6	13	18	15	9	11
Less Frequent High Maximum	6	6	6	4	3	4
Frequent Low Maximum	15	12	9	4	4	3
Frequent High Maximum	8	3	4	4	7	2
Frequent Heavy	4	3	4	5	1	3

[1] Sample sizes are unweighted. Percentages are weighted (i.e., they have been adjusted to allow for differences in sampling techniques).

Note in this table, Chi^2 (χ^2) tests provide an indication of how likely it is that the observed differences between 1984 and 1992 occured by chance alone.

χ^2 = Whites 1984 x 1992 = 18,263; degrees of freedom (df) = 6; $p < 0.01$
χ^2 = Blacks 1984 x 1992 = 18,467; df = 6; $p < 0.01$
χ^2 = Hispanics 1984 x 1992 = 19,560; df = 6; $p < 0.01$

infrequent drinkers and less frequent low maximum drinkers). The proportion of more frequent drinkers,[2] such as those who drank at least once a week, was higher among White than among Black and Hispanic women in 1984.

Another pattern of drinking—drinking five or more drinks at a sitting—also was more common among White than among Black and Hispanic women. This can be seen in Table 1 by adding the less frequent high maximum, frequent high maximum, and frequent heavy drinking categories. The sum of these categories shows that 18% of the White, 14% of the Black, and 11% of the Hispanic women fall into this combined category.

Comparing Changes in Drinking Patterns Over Time

Some of the results of the 1992 followup of the 1984 respondents also are shown in Table 1. Abstention increased among White and Black women but not significantly among Hispanics. Infrequent drinking rose slightly among Blacks and Hispanics but not among Whites. These two categories are constituted by women who either did not drink or who drank less than once a month in the 12 month prior to the survey. Taken together, 75% of the Blacks 82% of the Hispanic, and 58% of the White women are in these two categories, attesting to the low levels of drinking reported by women in survey research.

When all the categories are considered, a decrease in drinking between 1984 and 1992 is revealed. The decrease seem to be slightly more pronounced among White women than among Black and Hispanic women. Given that women in the sample in 1992 are 8 years older than they were in 1984, and given that drinking decreases with age, reductions in drinking from 1984 to 1992 may have been a result of aging of the sample. However results

Table 2. Stability and Incidence of Selected Drinking Patterns Among White, Black, and Hispanic Women: 1984 and 1992 (in percent)1

Drinking Pattern	Stability				Incidence			
	Year	White	Black	Hispanic	Year	White	Black	Hispanic
Abstains	1992	81%	81%	71%	1992	16%	26%	13%
	1984	(93)2	(151)	(188)	1984	[308]3	[257]	[189]
Drinks 1 to 3	1992	49%	21%	19%	1992	18%	10%	10%
times per month	1984	(93)	(81)	(68)	1984	[308]	[327]	[309]
Drinks once a	1992	50%	46%	25%	1992	5%	6%	5%
week or more	1984	(135)	(109)	(52)	1984	[266]	[299]	[325]
Drinks 5 or more	1992	19%	33%	–0–	1992	2%	4%	3%
drinks at least	1984	(31)	(31)	(11)	1984	[371]	[379]	[367]
once per week								
Drinks nearly	1992	32%	31%	–0–	1992	3%	3%	1%
every day or more	1984	(30)	(25)	(5)	1984	[371]	[383]	[372]

1. Sample sizes are unweighted. Percentages are weighted (i.e., they have been adjusted to allow for differences in sampling technique).
2. Under stability, the numbers in parenthesis represent the total number of women who reported the drinking pattern category in 1984. For example, 81% of the 93 white women who were abstainers in 1984 also abstained in 1992.
3. Under incidence, the numbers in brackets represent the total number of women who did not report the drinking pattern category in 1984. For example, of the 308 white women who were not abstainers in 1984, 16% reported abstaining from alcohol in 1992.

from analysis of per capita consumption in the United States (Williams et al., 1992) indicate reductions in alcohol consumption since 1982. Trend analysis on drinking between 1984 and 1990 by Midanik and Clark (in press) indicates that reductions in drinking observed among Whites have not been found among Blacks and Hispanics, confirming the followup finding in the NAS population.

Stability of Certain Drinking Patterns Over Time

Table 2 contains other analyses of longitudinal data (i.e., data from participants studied over time) from 1984 through 1992, showing stability for various types of drinking patterns. Stability indicates the proportion of women who had the same drinking pattern in 1984 and 1992 out of all of those who had that drinking pattern in 1984. In Table 2, for instance, 81% of the 93 White women who were abstainers in 1984 also abstained in 1992.

The results in the table show that abstention is the most stable category in the quantity-frequency index described above, being slightly more constant among White and Black women than among Hispanics. This high rate of stability is not surprising, because abstention commonly occurs in the context of strongly held religious beliefs or social norms that decrease women's access to alcohol and thus decrease their consumption. The other four categories of drinkers in the index show different degrees of stability. White women have a more stable pattern in the categories of drinkers who drink one to three times a month or drink at least once a week; Black women have a more consistent group of frequent heavy drinkers who drink five or more drinks at a sitting at least once a week. Longitudinal data (Caetano and Kaskutas, 1993) from the NAS for 1984 and 1992 on the mean number of drinks consumed per month show that White and Black women who were frequent heavy drinkers had a similar mean consumption in 1984; Whites drank 117.2 drinks per person per month; Blacks drank 120.5 drinks per person per month. However, in 1992, the mean for White women who were frequent heavy drinkers decreased to 104.0 drinks per person per month, whereas the mean for Blacks increased to 148.0 drinks per person per month.

Comparing Incidence Rates

Table 2 also shows results for incidence rates.[3] Incidence is the proportion of women who fit into a drinking category in 1992 out of all those who did not fit into that category in 1984. In Table 2, for example, of the 308 White women who were not abstainers in 1984, 16% reported abstaining from alcohol in 1992. The table indicates that the incidence of abstention is higher among Black women than among White and Hispanic women, and the incidence of drinking one to three times per month is higher among White women. Incidence rates for drinking five or more drinks at a sitting or for drinking nearly every day or more are not very different across the three groups of women. In addition, the across-group comparison from 1984 and the followup from 1992 show once again that compared with men, the majority of women in the United States drink little (Caetano and Kaskutas, 1993).

Comparing Prevalence Rates

Within the higher alcohol consumption categories, prevalence rates for frequent heavy drinking are not very different across ethnic groups, but this pattern of drinking is more stable among Black than among White women. The mean number of drinks per month consumed by Black frequent heavy drinkers is higher than that for Whites. These results contradicted previous survey findings (Clark and Midanik, 1982), which suggested that Black women had both a higher rate of abstention and a higher rate of frequent heavy drinking than did White women. However, the longer career of frequent heavy drinking and higher levels of consumption of Black women put them more at risk for developing alcohol problems than Whites and Hispanics. These findings also were true for differences between frequent heavy drinking among White, Black, and Hispanic men and help explain Blacks' higher rates of medical and other alcohol-related problems when compared with those of Whites (Caetano and Kaskutas, 1993).

Examining Differences Among Age Groups

Results by age for the NAS–84 survey (Herd, 1988; Herd and Caetano, 1987) show that drinking decreases with age among women in all three ethnic groups (Table 3). The variation is such that rates of abstention are two times higher among women who are 60 years of age and older than among women 18 to 29 years of age. However, Black and Hispanic women have higher rates of abstention than do White women in almost all age groups. When compared with Black and Hispanic women in the 18 to 29 and 30 to 39 age groups, White women's higher drinking rates are concentrated in the less frequent high maximum and frequent high maximum drinking categories.

Only in the middle-age group (ages 40 to 59) do Hispanic drinkers consume more than White drinkers consume. This higher rate of frequent high maximum drinking among

Table 3. Drinking Patterns by Age (in years) Among White, Black, and Hispanic Women: 1984 National Alcohol Survey (in percent)[1]

Drinking Pattern	18–29 White (n = 236)	18–29 Black (n = 396)	18–29 Hispanic (n = 280)	30–39 White (n = 217)	30–39 Black (n = 232)	30–39 Hispanic (n = 231)	40–49 White (n = 144)	40–49 Black (n = 141)	40–49 Hispanic (n = 129)
Abstention	22	34	40	30	32	45	35	56	41
Infrequent	20	19	35	16	19	23	21	11	19
Less Frequent Low Maximum	14	22	6	16	18	18	12	11	5
Less Frequent High Maximum	13	4	6	10	6	5	6	5	17
Frequent Low Maximum	11	9	2	7	15	3	13	7	2
Frequent High Maximum	13	6	8	13	5	4	7	4	14
Frequent Heavy	7	6	2	8	5	2	7	6	2

[1] Sample sizes are unweighted. Percentages are weighted (i.e., they have been adjusted to allow for differences in sampling techniques).

middle-age Hispanic women could be explained in terms of an increase in independence among women who are older and have a central role in their family but who also may hold jobs and therefore are able to adopt less traditional roles in the household and in the family.

When analyses compare frequent drinking (drinking once a week or more often) among age groups, results show that such a pattern of consumption is more likely to occur among White women who are younger and who are single. Among Black women, however, it is more likely to happen in younger women regardless of marital status (Herd and Caetano, 1987). These results for Black women contrast with an analysis by Herd (1988), who has reported that Black middle-age women rather than younger women were more likely to drink frequently. (These differences in results are most probably linked to the different analytical methods used to examine these data in the two above-mentioned analyses.) Among Hispanic women, those who are younger (18 to 39) are more likely than other women to drink once a week or more often. Factors such as having an annual family income higher than $30,000 and being single also increase the likelihood of a Hispanic woman drinking frequently (Herd and Caetano, 1987).

Income, Education, and Other Sociodemographic Characteristics

The relationship between sociodemographic characteristics, such as income and marital status mentioned above, and drinking is complex and differs across ethnic groups. Among Black women, for example, sociodemographic factors seem to have a weaker association with drinking than they do among White women (Caetano and Herd, 1984; Herd, 1988). It has been suggested that this may be because minority status or cultural characteristics play a larger role in determining drinking by Black women, thus weakening the role of income, education, marital status, and other sociodemographic characteristics (Caetano and Herd, 1984; Herd, 1988).

Table 3. *(continued)* **Drinking Patterns by Age (in years) Among White, Black, and Hispanic Women: 1984 National Alcohol Survey** (in percent)[1]

Drinking Pattern	50–59			60+		
	White (n = 121)	Black (n = 129)	Hispanic (n = 87)	White (n = 311)	Black (n = 179)	Hispanic (n = 115)
Abstention	35	60	47	49	69	78
Infrequent	21	14	8	18	12	11
Less Frequent Low Maximum	12	12	11	15	8	5
Less Frequent High Maximum	4	2	3	1	2	0
Frequent Low Maximum	22	7	4	15	8	6
Frequent High Maximum	4	4	20	1	0	0
Frequent Heavy	1	2	8	1	1	0

[1] Sample sizes are unweighted. Percentages are weighted (i.e., they have been adjusted to allow for differences in sampling techniques).

When analyses focus on differentiating women who drink from those who do not, Herd and Caetano (1987) have shown a direct positive relationship between drinking and income and education for women in all three ethnic groups, although the results for income are weaker among Black than among White and Hispanic women. Herd (1988) has added employment status to the analyses, showing that White women are more likely to be drinkers if they are single, have a high income, and are employed; Black women are more likely to be drinkers if they are employed. The difference between the initial analyses by Herd and Caetano (1987) and those by Herd (1988) may stem from the inclusion of employment status in Herd's analyses as well as from differences in statistical methods of analysis.

Further considering these sociodemographic factors, Caetano (1991) found that Hispanic women are more likely to be drinkers if they are acculturated (described below), employed, and educated. Gilbert and colleagues (in press) analyses of employment status and drinking among Hispanic women show that professionals have lower rates of abstention and higher rates of frequent drinking (drinking at least once a week) than do women who are homemakers or have blue-collar occupations. Gilbert and colleagues suggest that professional women's increased use of alcohol may be a way to cope with increasingly complex lives, or it may be a result of their increased exposure to public and private activities in which alcohol is present. An additional factor may be that professionals often have more disposable income that could be spent on alcohol.

The Influence of Acculturation on Drinking

Acculturation is a complex term that can broadly be understood as the process by which immigrants adopt the norms, social values, and overall culture of the host country. Because drinking norms vary greatly for women among different cultures, acculturation is studied to determine how women's drinking habits may change as they adapt to a new culture. Acculturation is measured in surveys using a series of questions. In the NAS–84, the acculturation measure was formed from items assessing such attributes as daily use of and ability to speak, read, and write English and Spanish; preference for media in English and Spanish; ethnicity of the people with whom respondents interacted in their church, parties, and neighborhood both at the time of the survey and when growing up, and questions about values thought to be characteristic of the Hispanic way of life.

The acculturation of Hispanics to U.S. society and its effect on alcohol consumption has been the object of several studies (Caetano, 1989; Gilbert and Cervantes, 1987; Markides et al., 1990; Burnam, 1989; Corbett et al., 1991). Although some view acculturation as a stressful process, it may not necessarily be so. The process of adopting the host country's culture also can be gradual and stress free.

Results of research demonstrate that acculturation is a powerful force shaping women's drinking patterns. The NAS–84 shows that Hispanic women who are highly acculturated are more likely to drink than are those who are less acculturated. The abstention rate among less acculturated women was 70%, whereas in the highly acculturated group, it was 32%. In contrast, the proportion of women drinking at least once a week was 22% among the highly acculturated but only 3% among the less acculturated. The effect of acculturation on drinking and heavier drinking among Hispanic women is independent of the effect of other attributes, such as age, income, education, and being born in the United States.

Acculturation to U.S. society leads to a lower rate of abstention and more light drinking among Hispanic women through several mechanisms. It is associated with more opportunities to drink (Caetano, 1987). Hispanic women in the highly acculturated group report a higher frequency of attendance in settings in which alcohol is consumed (e.g., bars and restaurants) than other Hispanic women. Acculturation also may lead to drinking by altering norms and attitudes that regulate alcohol consumption by women. Highly acculturated women have more liberal norms and attitudes toward alcohol consumption than do less acculturated women. For example, U.S.-born Mexican American women are more likely to see positive effects of alcohol use (e.g., they find it helps them to relax in social situations) (Gilbert, 1993) and have more liberal norms and attitudes toward alcohol consumption than do immigrant women (Caetano and Medina Mora, 1988). Together, these changes in opportunities to drink, attitudes, and norms regulating alcohol consumption may create an environment that is much more accepting of women's drinking and thus lead to an increased rate of alcohol consumption among Hispanic women who are acculturated.

The Influence of Generational Status

Generational status (i.e., whether a woman is U.S.-born or has immigrated to the United States) interacts with acculturation and other sociodemographic factors in shaping Hispanic women's drinking practices. To understand the way in which drinking is affected by these factors, it is important to separate the effect of acculturation from generational status, because they commonly have identical influences on drinking. Because these two factors produce the same effects and often co-occur in a single person, women who are highly acculturated to U.S. society are more likely to have been born in the United States. However, it is possible that a U.S.-born woman living in a Hispanic community in the

United States could be less acculturated than a woman born in a Hispanic country but raised and living in the United States in a multiethnic community.

U.S.-born Hispanic women are more likely to drink alcohol than are immigrant women (Caetano, 1987, 1989; Gilbert 1993). Among the U.S.-born women, those of the first generation born in the United States drink more than do second and third generation women. First generation women have a rate of abstention of 22%, compared with 30% among other Hispanic women (Caetano, 1989). Some researchers have interpreted this difference as stemming from conflict between these women and their parents, who bring views on behavior and drinking habits from their country of origin. Likewise, this is thought to be the cause of another pattern of differences in which first generation women have more alcohol-related problems than women in subsequent generations. These characteristics, together with the fact that first generation women have spent their lives in a cultural environment more permissive toward drinking by women, provide some of the reasons for their more widespread use of alcohol when compared with immigrant women.

Hispanic Drinking: Influences of Specific National Origin

Most U.S. Hispanics identify their cultural heritage as connected with Mexico, Cuba, or Puerto Rico. Data from the 1984 survey showed that Mexican American women had an abstention rate similar to that of Cuban Americans (46% and 42%, respectively) and higher than that of Puerto Ricans (33%) (Caetano, 1989). However, Mexican American women had a rate of drinking five or more drinks at least once a week (12%) that was higher than that of women in the other two groups (Puerto Ricans, 3%; Cuban Americans, 7%).

An analysis by Black and Markides (1993) provided somewhat different findings. They reported that any drinking at all was more common among Puerto Rican and Mexican American women than among Cuban Americans. However, national origin did not change the effect of acculturation on drinking described previously. Black and Markides (1993) showed that Mexican American, Cuban American, and Puerto Rican women who were more highly acculturated were more likely to be drinkers and also more likely to have a higher frequency of alcohol consumption than were women at lower acculturation levels.

ALCOHOL-RELATED PROBLEMS

Because they drink less, women have a lower prevalence of alcohol-related problems than do men. This fact has led to more detailed research and analysis of women's drinking and heavy drinking than of their alcohol problems, especially for minority women. The only survey with national data on problems among Black and Hispanic women is the NAS–84, which collected prevalence data on 14 alcohol-related problems from White, Black, and Hispanic women (Herd and Caetano, 1987; Table 4). In general, the proportion of White women who reported alcohol-related problems was higher than the proportion of Blacks and Hispanics reporting them. However, the differences were not greater than 3 percentage points in magnitude. When these data were examined for drinkers only (results not shown), the rates in Table 4 became slightly higher, but White women still reported more problems than did Blacks and Hispanics. This demonstrates that the difference in problem rates across the 3 ethnic groups was not caused by an increased rate of drinking among White women.

Table 4. Alcohol-Related Problems Among White, Black, and Hispanic Women: 1984 National Alcohol Survey (in percent)[1]

Problem	White (n = 1,029)	Black (n = 1,204)	Hispanic (n = 842)
Belligerence	5.7	2.5	3.3
Health Problems	4.8	4.3	3.0
Salience of Drinking	4.6	3.8	3.1
Impaired Control	3.7	2.8	2.5
People Problems	3.5	2.0	3.3
Spouse Problems	3.4	2.4	1.1
Withdrawal Problems	2.9	1.8	0.9
Tolerance	1.8	0.7	0.3
Financial Problems	1.7	0.6	0.2
Job Problems	1.0	0.7	0.2
Police Problems	0.7	0.5	0.9
Binge Drinking	0.6	0.5	0
Craving	0.5	0.5	0.3
Accident	0.4	0.3	0

[1] Sample sizes are unweighted. Percentages are weighted (i.e., they have been adjusted to allow for differences in sampling techniques).

The most frequently reported problems across women in the three groups were salience of drinking (i.e., when other aspects of life take a secondary place to drinking); belligerence; health problems; and other drinking-related problems, such as arguments with people other than the spouse. When these problems were counted and a summary was constructed, the proportion of White, Black, and Hispanic women reporting one or more alcohol-related problems was 12%, 7%, and 6%, respectively (Herd and Caetano, 1987).

Examining Predictors of Alcohol-Related Problems

Comparing factors that predict alcohol-related problems among White, Black, and Hispanic women revealed that White and Black women with less education; who were single, separated, or divorced; and who were younger were more likely to report problems than were other women (Herd and Caetano, 1987).

Among Hispanic women, the factors associated with greater likelihood of reporting alcohol-related problems included being married, being young, and being highly acculturated. An additional factor associated with reporting problems among Hispanic women was being born in the United States and having at least one parent who also was U.S. born. This may be explained by these women having the highest rate among Hispanic women of drinking at least once a week and also drinking five or more drinks per occasion at least once a week.

Among Mexican American women, those who were high in acculturation and those who were single, separated, or divorced were more likely to have alcohol-related problems than were other women. However, when drinking patterns were included in these analyses with Mexican American women, being a more frequent drinker (drinking at least once a week and drinking five or more drinks per occasion at least once a year) was the only characteristic associated with problems.

Prevalence of Alcohol Dependence Among Ethnic Groups

Rather than examining problems per se, other studies have assessed the prevalence of alcohol abuse and dependence as defined in the *Diagnostic and Statistical Manual of Mental Disorders, Third Edition* (American Psychiatric Association, 1980). These definitions require the presence of alcohol-related problems (e.g., withdrawal, impairment of control over alcohol consumption, social or occupational impairment because of use of alcohol) for a positive diagnosis.

Reports based on the Baltimore, St. Louis, and North Carolina general population samples from the ECA study indicated that the 12-month prevalence rate for alcohol abuse and dependence among White and Black women was 1% and 2%, respectively (Robins, 1989).

Data by age from the 5 samples in the ECA study revealed a different pattern in the prevalence of alcohol abuse and dependence across the 2 groups of women. Among White women, prevalence was higher in the 18 to 29 age group, decreasing continuously in older age groups. Among Black women, prevalence rose from the 18 to 29 to the 30 to 44 age groups, remained high in the 45 to 64 age group, and decreased among women 65 years of age and older (Helzer and Canino, 1992). These results reproduce the pattern found among men in the same groups for both alcohol abuse and dependence and for all alcohol-related problems.

Several factors could be behind these differences. Cultural differences could be related to access to alcohol by different sets of ages across the two ethnic groups. Also, drinking by women in each group could reflect men's drinking patterns (i.e., the drinking done by women's male companions, husbands, or boyfriends).

Burnam (1989) and Canino and colleagues (1992) have reported rates of alcohol abuse and dependence for a subpopulation of Hispanics consisting of Mexican American women in the Los Angeles sample of the ECA study. Comparison of Mexican American women with White women showed that White women had higher rates of lifetime alcohol abuse and dependence (9% versus 4.5%), but when the effect of education was controlled in the analysis, the difference disappeared. When data on each dependence problem per se were considered, White women had higher rates than did Mexican American women for 16 of the 24 alcohol-related problems in the survey. Data by generational status showed that the rate for lifetime prevalence of alcohol abuse and dependence was 2% among immigrant Mexican American women and 10% among U.S.-born Mexican American women. All the Mexican American immigrant women with a positive diagnosis of abuse and dependence were in the 18 to 24 age group. Among U.S.-born women, the prevalence was higher for younger women (12% among those 18 to 44 years of age), but older women also qualified for a diagnosis.

DISCUSSION

Explaining the Trends

The results discussed above, especially those that emerged from analyses of the 1984 survey, show drinking by Black and Hispanic women in a new light. Previous studies had put forward explanations of drinking by Black and Hispanic women, most of which relied too heavily on a central assumption about the groups' cultures. Drinking by Black women was thought to be an effect of "matriarchy"—that it was related to the role of head-of-household and breadwinner forced on Black women by the disintegration of the Black family. Abstention and drinking by Hispanic women was explained by "marianismo," which sees women as the center of family life, a vision that demands chastity, purity, and abstention from alcohol.

More recently, explanations of minority drinking have placed considerable emphasis on use of alcohol to minimize stress related to immigration, acculturation, poverty, racial discrimination, and powerlessness. These indeed are powerful constants in the life of minorities in the United States. However, many of these explanations do not actually assess levels of stress among minorities but assume that processes such as acculturation or discrimination increase stress, which then leads to drinking.

Drinking Associated With Normal Life Changes

Drinking also occurs because of ordinary adaptations to changes in norms, attitudes toward drinking, and an increase in disposable income. These changes may come about because of acculturation, immigration, or changes in job status. Also, it is important to acknowledge the existence of some resolutions to stressful situations associated with acculturation or racial discrimination that are healthy and that do not involve the adoption of deviant or pathological behavior. Emphasis on unhealthy solutions limits understanding of the range of coping mechanisms minorities have. Theories based on a single concept are too simplistic to provide an accurate explanation for the drinking behavior of Black and Hispanic women.

Drinking in the Real World

The reality of minority women's lives is not necessarily one dominated by a series of stressful changes or by overriding definitions of their role in their cultures. It is more complex and thus requires more complex explanations. The literature reviewed in this article suggests that to understand drinking by Black and Hispanic women, one must take into account an interplay of cultural, historical, and socioeconomic factors that is just beginning to emerge from ethnic studies.

Herd (1985) has demonstrated how historical factors, such as the migration of Blacks from the rural areas of the South to the industrial cities of the Northeast, influenced Black drinking. Findings from studies examining the effects of generational status and acculturation among Hispanic women have shown that these are powerful forces shaping drinking in this group. Sociocultural and historical influences such as these interact with personal factors, such as age and employment status, and larger environmental characteristics, such as the time and place where drinking occurs, to determine the type of alcohol consumption that takes place and its consequences. Analysis by Wilsnack and colleagues (1987) provides a good example of the complexity of factors that influence women's drinking and problems.

On a more individual scale, women now have diverse societal roles that help determine their opportunities to drink, the amount of money they have to spend on alcohol, and whether those close to them will accept their drinking. Some of these factors have been reviewed by Wilsnack and Wilsnack (in press). Women also are influenced through their recognized role as caretakers or by men's drinking (i.e., drinking by male partners or companions). Often the alcohol-related problems affecting women's lives are those associated with the drinking habits of their fathers, brothers, husbands, and boyfriends.

Environmental factors affecting the availability of alcohol in the community also have to be considered when trying to understand drinking by minority women. Some of these factors include alcoholic beverage prices, advertisements, production, and marketing. The minority-directed advertisement of alcoholic beverages as well as the production of special brands of alcoholic beverages targeting minority drinkers have been the subject of much controversy. Several critics argue that minority neighborhoods have an excessive number of outdoor advertisements and liquor stores, some of which are the focus of crime and drinking by minors. By increasing alcohol availability and the acceptability of drinking in minority communities, these factors could lead to increased drinking and increased incidence of alcohol problems among minority women.

Future research on drinking and alcohol problems among minority women should take this complex web of factors into consideration. The possibility that different types of drinking have different determinants also must be taken into account. It is possible that abstention and light drinking are more determined by cultural, social, and historical characteristics than are heavier patterns of drinking, which lead to alcohol abuse and dependence. Personality characteristics and women's personal and family histories may be of importance in the development of these pathological forms of drinking.

Updated survey research focusing on minority women is needed. The NAS–84 is now old, and more recent data are necessary to provide a current view of drinking by ethnic minority women. Beginning in 1995 the Alcohol Research Group will conduct a survey updating the information from 1984 and allowing for trends analyses between 1984 and 1995.

Unfortunately, this survey will not focus on Asian American and Native American women. National studies with a focus on these two groups of women are particularly scarce and should be conducted in the near future. Clinical studies of the effectiveness of alcoholism treatment and access to treatment with representative samples of minority women also must be executed. Until such research has been completed, highly productive alcoholism treatment programs are unlikely to be developed for these populations.

NOTES

Work on this article was supported by National Alcohol Research Center Grant AA-05595 from the National Institute on Alcohol Abuse and Alcoholism to the Alcohol Research Group, California Pacific Medical Center Research Institute.

1. The response rate varied from 75% among Whites to 68% among Blacks and 63% among Hispanics. Analyses in this article have been performed on weighted data, which correct the figures for the oversampling of heavier drinkers as well as for nonresponse and differences in the probability of selection into the sample. Comparative analysis of 1984 data between the sample reinterviewed and the sample selected for interview (respondents and nonrespondents) yielded no significant differences in the distribution of drinking problems (the mean number of drinks consumed per month or the number of alcohol problems present in the past 12 month).

2. This type of drinking is represented in the quantity frequency category index by the categories "frequent low maximum" and "frequent high maximum" drinking.

3. Incidence is defined as the number of new cases of specific condition, in the case of a drinking category, that occur during a certain period. Prevalence is the number of cases of a condition that are present in population at one point in time.

BIBLIOGRAPHY

American Psychiatric Association. (1980). *Diagnostic and Statistical Manual of Mental Disorders, Third Edition.* Washington, DC: the Association.

Black, S. A., and Markides, K. S. (1993). Acculturation and alcohol consumption in Puerto Rican, Cuban-American, and Mexican-American women in the United States. *American Journal of Public Health* 83(6): 890–893.

Burnam, M. A. (1989). Prevalence of alcohol abuse and dependence among Mexican Americans and non-Hispanic whites in the community. In D. Spiegler, D. Tate, S. Aitken, and C. Christian, (Eds.), *Alcohol Use Among U.S. Ethnic Minorities.* National Institute on Alcohol Abuse and Alcoholism Research Monograph No. 18. DHHS Pub. No. (ADM) 89–1435. Washington. DC: Supt. of Docs. U.S. Govt. Print, Off., pp. 163–177.

Caetano, R. (1987). Acculturation and drinking in social settings among U.S. Hispanics. *Drug and Alcohol Dependence* 19(3): 215–226.

Caetano, R. (1989). Drinking patterns and alcohol problems in a national sample of U.S. Hispanics. In D. Spiegler, D. Tate, S. Aitken, and C. Christian, (Eds.), *Alcohol Use Among U.S. Ethnic Minorities.* National Institute on Alcohol Abuse and Alcoholism Monograph No. 18. DHHS Pub. No. (ADM) 89–1435. Washington, DC: Supt. of Docs., U.S. Govt. Print. Off., pp. 147–162.

Caetano, R. (1991). Findings from the 1984 national survey of alcohol use among U.S. Hispanics. In W. B. Clark and M. E. Hilton (Eds.), *Alcohol in America: Drinking Practices and Problems.* Albany, NY: State University of New York Press, pp. 293–307.

Caetano, R., and Kaskutas, L. (1993). *Longitudinal changes in drinking patterns among Whites, Blacks, and Hispanics.* Paper presented at the Annual Meeting of the Research Society on Alcoholism. San Antonio, TX.

Caetano, R., and Herd, D. (1984). Black drinking practices in Northern California. *American Journal of Drug and Alcohol Abuse,* 20(4): 571–587.

Caetano, R., and Medina Mora, M. E. (1988). Acculturation and drinking among people of Mexican descent in Mexico and the U.S. *Journal of Studies on Alcohol,* 49(5): 462–171.

Canino, G. J., Burnam, A., and Caetano, R. (1992). The prevalence of alcohol abuse and/or dependence in two Hispanic communities. In J. E. Helzer and G. J. Canino, (Eds.), *Alcoholism in North America Europe and Asia.* New York: Oxford University Press, pp. 131–155.

Clark, W., and Midanik, L. (1982). Alcohol use and alcohol problems among U.S. adults: Results of the 1979 national survey. *Alcohol Consumption and Related Problems.* National Institute on Alcohol Abuse and Alcoholism Alcohol and Health Monograph No. 1. DHHS Pub No. (ADM) 82–1190. Washington, DC: Supt. of Docs., U.S. Govt Print. Off., pp. 3–52.

Corbett, K., Mora, J., and Ames, G. (1991). Drinking patterns and drinking-related problems of Mexican-American husbands and wives. *Journal of Studies on Alcohol,* 52(3): 215–223.

Gilbert, M. J. (1993). Intracultural variation in alcohol-related cognitions among Mexican Americans. In R. S. Mayers, B. L. Kail and T. D. Watts (Eds.), *Hispanic Substance Abuse.* Springfield, IL: Charles C. Thomas, pp. 51–64.

Gilbert, M. J, and Cervantes, R. C. (1987). Alcohol services for Mexican Americans: A review of utilization patterns, treatment considerations and prevention activities. In M. J. Gilbert and R. C. Cervantes (Eds.), *Mexican Americans and Alcohol.* Spanish Speaking Mental Health Research Center Monograph No. 11. Los Angeles: University of California, pp. 61–93.

Gilbert, M. J., Mora, J., and Ferguson, L. R. (in press). Alcohol-related expectations among Mexican American women. *International Journal of the Addictions.*

Helzer, J. E., and Canino, G. J., (Eds.). (1992). *Alcoholism in North America, Europe, and Asia.* New York: Oxford University Press.

Herd, D. (1985). Migration, cultural transformation and the rise of black liver cirrhosis mortality. *British Journal of Addiction,* 80(4): 397–410.

Herd, D. (1988). Drinking by black and white women: Results from a national survey. *Social Problems,* 35(5), 493–505.

Herd, D. (1991). Drinking patterns in the black population. In W. B. Clark and M. E. Hilton (Eds.),

Alcohol in America: Drinking Practices and Problems. Albany, NY: State University of New York Press, pp. 308–329.

Herd, D., and Caetano, R. (1987, May). *Drinking patterns and problems among White, Black and Hispanic Women in the U.S.: Results from a national survey*. Paper presented at the Alcohol and Drug Problems Association of North America Conference on Women's Issues. Denver, CO, 3–6.

Leland, J. (1984). Alcohol use and abuse in ethnic minority women. In S. C. Wilsnack and L. J. Beckman (Eds.), *Alcohol Problems in Women: Antecedents, Consequences and Intervention*. New York: Guilford Press, pp. 66–96.

Markides, K., Ray, L. A., Stroup-Benham, C. A., and Trevino, F. (1990). Acculturation and alcohol consumption in the Mexican American population of the southwestern United States: Findings from H-HANES 1982–1984. *American Journal of Public Health*, 80(Suppl), 42–46.

Midanik, L., and Clark, W. B. (in press). The demographic distribution of U.S. drinking patterns in 1990: Descriptions and trends from 1984. *Journal of the American Public Health Association*.

Robins, L. N. (1989). Alcohol abuse in blacks and whites as indicated in the Epidemiological Catchment Area Program. In D. Spiegler, D. Tate, S. Aitken and C. Christian (Eds.), *Alcohol Use Among U.S. Ethnic Minorities*. National Institute on Alcohol Abuse and Alcoholism Research Monograph No. 18. DHHS Pub. No. (ADM) 89–1435. Washington. DC: Supt. of Docs., U.S. Govt. Print. Off., pp. 63–73.

Williams, G. D., Stinson, F. S., Clem, D., and Noble, J. (1992). Surveillance Report No. 23. *Apparent per capita alcohol consumption: National, State and regional trends: 1977–1990*. Rockville, MD: National Institute on Alcohol Abuse and Alcoholism. Division of Biometry and Epidemiology.

Wilsnack, S. C., and Beckman, L. J. (Eds.). (1984). *Alcohol Problems in Women: Antecedents. Consequences and Intervention*. New York: Guilford Press.

Wilsnack, R. W., Wilsnack, S. C., and Klassen, A. D. (1987). Antecedents and consequences of drinking and drinking problems in women: Patterns from a U.S. national survey. In P. C. Rivers (Ed.). *Alcohol and Addictive Behavior*. Lincoln, NE: University of Nebraska Press, pp. 85–158.

Wilsnack, S. C., and Wilsnack, R. W. (in press). Drinking and problem drinking in U.S. women: Patterns and recent trends. In M. Galanter (Ed.), *Recent Developments in Alcoholism. Volume XII. Alcoholism and Women: The Effect of Gender*. New York: Plenum Press.

12.

Expectancies for Drinking and Excessive Drinking Among Mexican Americans and Non-Hispanic Whites

Gerardo Marín

This study was designed to identify the expectancies held by Mexican Americans toward the drinking of alcoholic beverages as well as toward excessive drinking. Random samples of 534 Mexican American and 616 non-Hispanic White residents of San José, California and of San Antonio, Texas were interviewed over the telephone. Mexican Americans were found to have unique expectancies toward drinking of alcoholic beverages and toward excessive drinking that differed from those held by non-Hispanic Whites. In addition, Mexican Americans expected the various outcomes in greater proportion than non-Hispanic Whites and the Mexican American respondents classified as high in acculturation tended to respond in a manner similar to that of non-Hispanic White respondents. Multivariate analyses of variance with common (across ethnic groups) factor scales with ethnicity, gender, and drinking status as independent variables showed main effects for drinking status and for ethnicity. The group differences in expectancies identified here support the need for culturally appropriate interventions that target group-specific beliefs.

A substantial number of studies have researched alcohol-related expectancies under the assumption that the beliefs people have (expectancies) can predict not only behavioral intentions (Fishbein, 1980), but also actual rates of alcoholic beverage intake (Baldwin, Oei, and Young, 1993; Brown, Goldman, and Christiansen, 1985; Oei and Young, 1987; Stacy, Widaman, and Marlatt, 1990; Thombs, 1991) and the behavioral effects of alcohol consumption (Fromme and Dunn, 1992; Hull and Bond, 1986; Nagoshi, Noll, and Wood, 1992). In the various studies, expectancies for the consumption of alcoholic beverages have been found to differ in terms of the respondents' gender (Dermen and Cooper, 1994b; Leigh, 1990: Sutker, Allain, Brantley, and Randall, 1982; Thombs, 1993); their "race" (Connors, Maisto, and Watson, 1988; Dermen and Cooper, 1994a); and their culture (Christiansen and Teahan, 1987; Glassner and Berg, 1984; Teahan, 1987; Teahan, 1988). This study was designed to identify the expectancies held by Mexican Americans toward the drinking of alcoholic beverages as well as toward excessive drinking and to compare them with those held by a group of non-Hispanic Whites.

An analysis of the alcohol expectancies held by Hispanics in general and Mexican Americans in particular is important because the literature shows that Hispanics have some of the highest rates of consumption of alcoholic beverages in the United States and that Hispanic communities are suffering the effects of high rates of alcohol consumption and of alcoholism. For example, results of the 1992 National Household Survey on Drug Abuse showed a lifetime prevalence of alcohol consumption of 75.3% for Hispanics compared with 85.5% for Whites and 75.2% for African Americans (Substance Abuse and Mental Health Services Administration, 1993). At the same time, the 1984 National Alcohol Survey (Caetano, 1989) showed that, as is true in the general population, Hispanic men drank more than Hispanic women. That same study found that Mexican American men were more likely to abstain from alcoholic beverages than men of other Hispanic subgroups but those Mexican Americans who reported drinking drank more heavily and tended to report more alcohol-related problems.

Several additional studies have shown that the rates of heavier drinking are higher among Hispanics than among non-Hispanic Whites (Clark and Midanik, 1982). The Epidemiological Catchment Area Study (Robins and Regier, 1991) conducted in the early 1980s found higher rates of alcohol abuse and dependence (using the *DSM-III* criteria) among Hispanic males 18 years of age and older (15.97%) than among non-Hispanic White males (11.69%). Also of concern is the fact that rates of consumption among Hispanic adolescents are similar or higher than those found among non-Hispanics (Welte and Barnes, 1987). For example, the 1976 through 1989 Monitoring the Future Project surveys of high school seniors (Bachman et al., 1991) showed that Mexican American males (82.4%) reported the second highest prevalence of alcohol use in the 12 months prior to the survey, second only to non-Hispanic Whites males (88.3%). In those same surveys of high school seniors, Mexican American males reported the second highest proportion of daily use of alcohol (8.3%) after American Indian males (10.1%).

Despite the worrisome patterns of alcohol consumption among Hispanics, few studies have analyzed the alcohol-related expectancies held by Hispanics (Cervantes, Gilbert, Snyder, and Padilla, 1990–1991; Marín, Posner, and Kinyon, 1993; Posner and Marín, 1996). The Cervantes et al. (1990–1991) study showed that Hispanic women born in the United States were more likely to consider alcohol as a disinhibiting drink than foreign-born women. Marín et al. (1993) sampled a large random sample of Hispanics in San Francisco, California and found that Hispanics were more likely to expect that drinking of alcoholic beverages would produce emotional and behavioral impairments and ease social interactions. Drinking status and acculturation level of the Hispanic respondents moderated the type of expectancies held by the respondents. Posner and Marín (1996) found that Hispanics held expectancies for driving under the influence of alcohol (DUI) that were different from those held by non-Hispanic Whites. Hispanics tended to report expecting that when DUI an individual would drive carelessly, become angry with other drivers, feel nervous, lose the respect of friends and their self-respect, and would feel guilty. At the same time, non-Hispanic Whites reported in greater proportions than Hispanics that they would not be stopped by the police when DUI, and respondents from both groups did not differ in the proportion indicating that they would have problems controlling the car when DUI. These expectancies differed in terms of the drinking patterns of the respondents so that abstainers reported the likelihood of the various behavioral outcomes to be higher than drinkers.

This study sampled only Mexican Americans and non-Hispanic Whites in California and Texas in order to better identify the alcohol-related expectancies of the largest Hispanic subgroup in the country. Mexican Americans currently account for approximately 64% of the total Hispanic population. Differences in basic cultural beliefs, norms, and values between Mexican Americans and non-Hispanic Whites were expected to have produced different expectancies for the consumption of alcoholic beverages among respondents from each group. In addition, as mentioned above, research has shown that Mexican Americans differ in their consumption patterns from other Hispanic subgroups (Bachman et al., 1991; Caetano, 1989) and could therefore be assumed to hold different expectancies from those held by members of other Hispanic subgroups. The data reported here differ from those of the Marín et al. (1993) study in a number of ways. First, the respondents were asked to report expectancies for drinking of alcoholic beverages as well as for excessive drinking. The expectancies presented to the respondents were chosen after a lengthy procedure designed to identify the culture-specific expectancies of Mexican Americans (Triandis, 1972), a procedure that has been used in previous studies to identify group-specific beliefs, values, norms, and attitudes (Marín, Marín, Pérez-Stable, Otero-Sabogal and Sabogal, 1990; Marín et al., 1993; Posner and Marín, 1996). In addition, respondents were asked to report their own expectancies rather than those they expected from people in general as was done in the Marín et al. (1993) study. The role of acculturation in the respondents' beliefs will also be explored here. This is because the process of acculturation, with its inherent stress, may influence not only drinking prevalence and the number of alcohol-related problems found among Hispanics in the United States (Caetano, 1987a, 1987b; Caetano and Mora, 1988; Marín and Posner, 1995; Neff, Hoppe, and Perea, 1987) but also their expectations regarding the consumption of alcoholic beverages (Marín et al., 1993; Posner and Marín, 1996).

METHOD
Participants

Random samples of residents in San José, California and in San Antonio, Texas were interviewed over the telephone using the Mitofsky-Waksberg random digit dialing approach (Waksberg, 1978). These two cities were chosen because they have sizable numbers of Mexican Americans and would allow for greater generalizability of the data than if only one city had been surveyed. A total of 277 Mexican Americans and 308 non-Hispanic Whites were interviewed in San José. The San Antonio sample consisted of 257 Mexican Americans and 308 non-Hispanic Whites. Data were collapsed across cities for a given ethnic group since, in general, there were no statistically significant differences among respondents of one same ethnic group across cities.

The total sample included respondents of both genders (53.6% of Mexican Americans and 57.5% of non-Hispanic Whites were women). Both ethnic groups were similar in their demographic characteristics except that non-Hispanic Whites tended to be somewhat older (M = 40.1 yrs) than Mexican American respondents (M = 36.2 yrs). The non-Hispanic White respondents also reported an average of more years of formal eduction (M =14.2 yrs.) than Mexican Americans (M = 10.6 yrs.). Mexican Americans reported having lived in the city of the survey for an average number of years (17.9 years) that was similar to that of non-Hispanic Whites (18.9 years). The two groups did not differ in their reported level of employment, Mexican Americans (70.8%) and non-Hispanic Whites (69.4%) reported having been employed for the two weeks previous to the survey in fairly similar proportions. Finally, relatively similar proportions of respondents in each group reported being married at the time of survey (64.4% of Mexican Americans and 62.5% of non-Hispanic Whites).

The majority of the Mexican American respondents (56.6%) reported being born outside the United States. The foreign-born Mexican Americans reported having lived in the United States for an average of 14.5 years with 25.4% having arrived within the five years prior to the survey. As expected, a large proportion (62.5%) of the Mexican American respondents answered the interview in Spanish and scored low in acculturation (56.9%).

Materials

Respondents answered an interview schedule that included questions on expectancies (consequents) for the consumption of alcoholic beverages as well as for their expectancies for the excessive ("a lot") consumption of alcoholic beverages. In addition, respondents were asked to report their personal patterns of alcoholic beverage consumption and standard sociodemographic questions. Ethnicity was ascertained by self-report and then validated with questions related to birthplace and national origin. The respondents answered the questionnaire in the language of their choice (English or Spanish) and questions were double-translated (Brislin, Lonner, and Thorndike, 1973; Marín and Marín, 1991).

The items included in the questionnaire were chosen through a detailed process of instrument development that agreed with the suggestions made by Leigh (1989b) for the construction of new expectancy scales and adhered to the ideas for the development of culturally appropriate instruments for the study of a groups' subjective culture (Triandis, 1972). In the intial phase of the study, 54 Mexican Americans and 11 non-Hispanic Whites were interviewed over the telephone for approximately 60 minutes using open-ended questions dealing with a large variety of topics including their perceptions of why people drink alcoholic beverages, of the positive and negative effects of drinking alcoholic beverages, and typical reactions to drinking. The responses to these questions were content-analyzed in order to identify themes that were common or unique to respondents from each of the two ethnic groups. The results of this content analysis were used in the development of close-ended question stems and response categories utilized in the structured interview schedule.

The structured questionnaire included 36 items dealing with consequent expectations of drinking of alcoholic beverages (e.g., feeling less nervous, become friendlier) and 35 items dealing with expectancies of excessive drinking (e.g., forgetting things, becoming nervous, spending a lot of money). The final set of items included positive as well as negative outcomes and included as a subsample most of the consequent expectancies previously studied among Hispanics in San Francisco (Marín et al., 1993). The items were answered on a four-point Likert-type scale in terms of the possibility that each expectancy would be related to the respondent's drinking of alcoholic beverages (*Yes* = 4; *Maybe yes* = 3; *Maybe no* = 2; and *No* = 1). Following the suggestions made by some authors (e.g., Fishbein, 1980), the respondents were asked to evaluate each item in terms of its personal relevance to their consumption of alcoholic beverages rather than in terms of its importance for people in general as has been done in other studies (e.g., Marín et al., 1993).

Respondents were classified in terms of their drinking patterns using the same categories utilized by the National Institute on Alcohol Abuse and Alcoholism (NIAAA) when reporting the *H-HANES* data: *Abstainers* (66.1% of Mexican Americans and 42.6%

of non-Hispanic Whites) were defined as those individuals who drank less than 12 drinks per year or who had not had a drink in the 12 months prior to the survey. *Light drinkers* (18.5% of Mexican Americans and 31.0% of non-Hispanic Whites) were defined as individuals who drank up to 3 drinks per week while *Moderate drinkers* (11.0% of Mexican Americans and 22.2% of non-Hispanic Whites) were considered to be those respondents who reported drinking between 4 and 13 drinks per week. *Heavier drinkers* (4.3% of Mexican Americans and 4.2% of non-Hispanic Whites) were defined as those respondents who consumed 14 or more drinks per week.

Acculturation by Mexican Americans to the United States culture was measured utilizing a four-point acculturation scale (Marín, Sabogal, Marín, Otero-Sabogal, and Pérez-Stable, 1987) that has been found to be highly valid and reliable. The four items measure language preference and use and are answered on a five-point Likert-format scale. Based on previous research (Marín, 1992; Marín et al., 1987), respondents who averaged 2.99 or less in the acculturation scale were considered to be part of a less acculturated group (56.9%) while those scoring above 2.99 were considered to be highly acculturated.

RESULTS

As mentioned above, in general, the respondents who were members of a given ethnic group did not differ in their responses across cities. As such, their responses were collapsed across cities and the data are reported below in terms of differences across ethnic groups. The proportion of respondents answering each of the items are reported below grouped into two categories (Yes and Maybe yes = Yes; No and Maybe no = No) for ease of presentation. Nevertheless, the data were treated as continuous when conducting factor analyses and parametric inferential statistical tests.

Consequent Expectations for Drinking

Table 1 presents the proportion of Mexican American and non-Hispanic White respondents who agreed with each of the 36 consequent expectations they were asked to consider. Among Mexican Americans, the expectations endorsed by the highest proportion of respondents (more than 65%) were (in order of magnitude) reflexes becoming slower, laughing easily, falling asleep, becoming sleepy, losing coordination, and giving bad example to children while among non-Hispanic Whites the expectations endorsed by the largest proportion of respondents were reflexes becoming slower, becoming more relaxed, laughing easily, enjoying themselves, becoming sleepy, enjoying the taste, and losing coordination.

The non-Hispanic White respondents endorsed in greater proportions than Mexican Americans the expectations that after drinking alcoholic beverages the respondent would enjoy himself or herself, X^2 (1, $N = 1141$) = 111.74, $p < .001$; feel less nervous, X^2 (1, $N = 1140$) = 17.47, $p < .001$; and become more relaxed, X^2 (1, $N = 1135$) = 77.91, $p < .001$. Non-Hispanic Whites also endorsed in greater proportions than Mexican Americans the beliefs that after drinking alcoholic beverages, the respondent would be able to think clearly, X^2 (1, $N = 1142$) = 45.92, $p < .001$ as well as enjoy the taste of alcoholic beverages, X^2 (1, $N = 1148$) = 83.16, $p < .001$. Mexican American respondents on the other hand, endorsed in greater proportion than the non-Hispanic White respondents a larger number of outcome expectations. Mexican Americans expected in greater proportions than non-

Hispanic Whites that after drinking alcoholic beverages they would lose self-control, X^2 (1, N = 1137) = 50.23, p < .001; give a bad example to their children, X^2 (1, N = 1146) = 42.74, p < .001; become violent, X^2 (1, N = 1138) = 125.55, p < .001; have problems at work, X^2 (1, N = 1142) = 145.88, p < .001; become aggressive, X^2 (1, N = 1139) = 79.61, p < .001; have family problems, X^2 (1, N = 1147) = 122.19, p < .001; become depressed, X^2 (1, N = 1135) = 49.51, p < .001; become careless, X^2 (1, N = 1133) = 29.12, p < .001; and become more independent, X^2 (1, N = 1133) = 29.54, p < .001.

Table 2 presents the proportion of Mexican American respondents agreeing with each

Table 1. Respondents (%) Considering Various Events as Outcomes of Alcoholic Beverage Consumption

	All		Men		Women	
	Mexican Americans	Whites	Mexican Americans	Whites	Mexican Americans	Whites
Enjoys self	38.4	69.7*	46.1	75.4*	31.8	65.3*
Feels less nervous	28.5	40.3*	28.9	45.8	28.1	36.0
Enjoys taste	39.7	66.6*	49.0	75.1*	31.6	60.2*
Forgets problems	13.0	16.6	11.3	17.3	14.4	15.8
Becomes more talkative	54.3	56.7	56.1	58.2	52.7	55.4
Becomes friendlier	42.7	52.8	49.0	53.6	37.2	52.0
Feels more liberated	28.9	33.4	26.3	31.9	31.1	34.6
Improves health	3.6	4.9	4.1	7.3	3.2	3.1
Feels more like self	12.4	9.5	12.6	9.2	12.3	9.7
Fights	25.1	16.7	23.6	15.8	26.5	17.5
Becomes sleepy	67.2	66.8	69.5	63.5	65.1	69.1
Loses self-control	44.5	24.5*	42.0	22.7*	46.6	26.0*
Gives bad example to children	65.0	45.7*	59.9	41.5	69.4	48.9*
Becomes violent	31.5	6.0*	29.9	7.3*	32.9	5.1*
Gets slower reflexes	74.8	79.5	77.2	82.4	72.6	77.3
Drinks too much	17.5	21.6	18.0	25.2	17.0	18.9
Gains weight	54.8	52.2	52.0	50.8	57.2	53.1
Has problems at work	62.7	27.2*	59.8	22.6*	65.3	30.7*
Becomes aggressive	38.4	15.2*	33.2	13.5*	43.0	16.5*
Easier to talk with others	41.2	43.3	42.5	46.4	40.1	40.8
Has family problems	60.9	28.5*	58.3	24.8*	63.2	31.3*
Feels at peace	19.5	18.1	22.0	25.4	17.3	12.8
Becomes bolder in actions	36.5	39.0	32.5	40.4	40.0	37.8
Feels strong	22.6	15.2	20.6	14.7	24.4	15.6
Becomes depressed	47.5	27.3*	41.6	23.1*	52.7	30.6*
Falls asleep easily	69.7	61.0	65.2	59.8	73.7	61.8
Thinks clearly	11.2	27.2*	13.0	33.7*	9.6	22.4*
Becomes emotional	41.5	41.8	39.4	31.8	43.3	49.4
Laughs easily	72.0	70.2	68.0	68.5	75.5	71.3
Speaks louder	64.3	54.2	58.3	56.8	69.6	52.1*
Becomes happier	48.1	47.8	48.8	51.2	47.5	45.1
Loses coordination	65.5	65.4	66.3	66.4	64.9	54.6
Becomes more romantic	51.7	40.8	55.5	38.9	48.4	42.3
Becomes careless	62.9	46.9*	61.6	47.3	64.1	46.6*
Becomes more relaxed	50.6	75.8*	50.0	78.4*	51.1	73.8*
Becomes more independent	31.4	17.6*	31.8	17.9	31.1	17.4

* p < .001 with Bonferoni's correction.

Gerardo Marín

of the expected outcomes in terms of their level of acculturation. In general, the Mexican American respondents classified as high in acculturation tended to respond in a manner similar to that of the non-Hispanic White respondents. The less acculturated Mexican Americans chose in greater proportions (65% or higher) the following outcome expectations: having problems at work, having family problems, getting slower reflexes, giving bad example to children, falling asleep easily, laughing easily, becoming careless, becoming sleepy, speaking louder, and losing coordination. The more acculturated Mexican Americans on the other hand, chose more frequently (65% or higher) only two expectancies: laughing easily and getting slower reflexes. As shown in Table 2, chi-square analyses

Table 2. Mexican American Respondents (%) Considering Various Events as Outcomes of Alcoholic Beverage Consumption by Acculturation Level

	Acculturation	
	Low	High
Enjoys self	25.1	56.5*
Feels less nervous	21.7	38.6*
Enjoys taste	27.0	56.9*
Forgets problems	9.3	17.7
Becomes more talkative	59.2	46.5
Becomes friendlier	38.0	48.3
Feels more liberated	25.2	32.2
Improves health	2.3	5.3
Feels more like self	10.0	14.7
Fights	34.0	14.2*
Becomes sleepy	70.7	63.0
Loses self-control	55.4	28.7*
Gives bad example to children	78.6	45.7*
Becomes violent	44.6	14.4*
Gets slower reflexes	79.1	69.5
Drinks too much	18.5	17.0
Gains weight	53.2	56.7
Has problems at work	80.2	38.1*
Becomes aggressive	47.7	26.3*
Easier to talk with others	41.6	40.7
Has family problems	80.0	35.3*
Feels at peace	15.3	25.3
Becomes bolder in actions	38.9	32.6
Feels strong	27.8	16.9
Becomes depressed	61.5	29.4*
Falls asleep easily	73.6	65.5
Thinks clearly	4.7	20.5*
Becomes emotional	40.2	43.0
Laughs easily	71.6	71.2
Speaks louder	69.8	56.9
Becomes happier	46.5	49.4
Loses coordination	68.6	60.3
Becomes more romantic	55.8	46.1
Becomes careless	70.9	51.1*
Becomes more relaxed	40.3	64.6*
Becomes more independent	34.4	26.8

* $p < .001$ with Bonferoni's correction.

showed statistically significant differences for most expectancies between the less acculturated and the more acculturated Mexican Americans.

The responses given by the respondents to each of the 36 consequent (outcome)
expectancy items were submitted to separate (by ethnicity) principal axis factor analyses
with oblique rotations. A comparison of the two factor analyses showed three common
factors across ethnicities. One factor, labeled Social Disinhibition was made up of five
items dealing with drinking of alcoholic beverages making the individual more talkative,
bolder, happier, laugh easily, and more romantic (Cronbach's alpha of .73 among Mexican
Americans and .74 among non-Hispanic Whites). A second common factor was labeled
Friendliness and was made up of three items expecting that by consuming alcoholic beverages the individuals would become more talkative, friendlier, and liberated (Cronbach's
alpha of .71 for Mexican Americans and .74 for non-Hispanic Whites). A third factor,
labeled Belligerence, was made up of five items dealing with having a fight, losing self-
control, becoming violent, becoming aggressive, and drinking too much (Cronbach's alpha
of .79 among Mexican Americans and .72 among non-Hispanic Whites).

A multivariate analysis of variance was conducted with ethnicity, gender, and drinking
status as independent variables and the common factor scales as dependent variables
controlling for nonindependence among the independent variables. This analysis showed
a main effect for drinking status, Hotelling's T (9, 3176) = 9.23, p < .001, and for ethnicity, Hotelling's T (3, 1060) = 6.50, p < .001. There were no statistically significant interactions or a main effect for gender of the respondents.

Separate univariate analyses of variance were conducted within each ethnic group to
identify possible effects of drinking status on the expectancies held by the respondents.
For Mexican Americans, drinking status of the respondents (Table 3) produced a significant main effect, F (3, 512) = 3.77, p < .01 for the Social Disinhibition scale and the same
was true for the Friendliness scale, F (3, 517) = 6.06, p < .001; and, for the Belligerence
scale, F (3, 508) = 3.84, p < .01). Among non-Hispanic Whites, drinking status produced
a significant main effect for the Social Disinhibition scale, F (3, 598) = 11.22, p < .001;
for the Friendliness scale, F (3, 605) = 14.01, p < .001; and, for the Belligerence scale, F
(3, 602) = 4.66, p < .01.

Univariate analyses of variance were also conducted for the various factor scales with
ethnicity as the independent variable. Those analyses showed statistically significant

Table 3. Mean Scores in Drinking Antecedents Factor Scales by Drinking Status

	Drinking Status				
	Abstainers	Light	Moderate	Heavier	All
Social disinhibition					
Mexican Americans	2.24	2.48	2.56	2.54*	2.29
Non-Hispanic Whites	2.04	2.32	2.55	2.38**	2.25
Friendliness					
Mexican Americans	1.98	2.37	2.36	2.39**	2.07
Non-Hispanic Whites	1.99	2.30	2.67	2.45**	2.26
Belligerence					
Mexican Americans	1.92	1.73	1.55	1.69*	1.79
Non-Hispanic Whites	1.51	1.31	1.40	1.59*	1.43

* p < .01; ** p < .001 across drinking status categories

differences in means across ethnic groups (Table 3) for the Friendliness scale, $F(1, 1229)$ = 9.76, $p < .01$ and for the Belligerence scale, $F(1, 1219) = 74.55$, $p < .001$; but not for the Social Disinhibition scale, $F(1, 1217) = .57$, ns.

A multivariate analysis of variance with the common factor scales as dependent variables and acculturation level, drinking status, and gender as independent variables also was carried out controlling for nonindependence for the responses provided by the Mexican American respondents. The analysis showed a main effect for drinking status Hotelling's $T(9, 1403) = 3.50$, $p < .001$. There were no other statistically significant main effects or interactions.

Consequent Expectations for Excessive Drinking

Table 4 presents the proportion of Mexican American and non-Hispanic White respondents who agreed with each of the 35 consequent expectations they were asked to consider for excessive drinking. Among Mexican Americans, the expectations endorsed by the highest proportion of respondents (more than 65%) were (in order of magnitude) becoming sick, having problems speaking, giving bad example to children, making poor decisions, spending lots of money, looking older, forgetting things, having problems at work and with the police, falling asleep, having marital problems, becoming more nervous and insecure, becoming an alcoholic, saying improper things, feeling guilty, doing unusual things, gaining weight, becoming talkative, having less appetite, and becoming depressed. Among non-Hispanic Whites, the expectations endorsed by the highest proportion of respondents were having problems speaking, giving bad example to children, becoming sick, making poor decisions, looking older, spending lots of money, having problems at work, and saying improper things.

The non-Hispanic White respondents endorsed in greater proportions than Mexican Americans the expectations that after excessively drinking alcoholic beverages the respondent would feel more relaxed, $X^2 (1, N = 1145) = 48.52$, $p < .001$. Mexican American respondents on the other hand, endorsed in greater proportion than the non-Hispanic White respondents a large number of outcome expectations for excessive drinking of alcoholic beverages. Mexican Americans expected in greater proportions than non-Hispanic Whites that after drinking "a lot" of alcoholic beverages they would become angry, $X^2 (1, N = 1132) = 59.97$, $p < .001$; feel guilty, $X^2 (1, N = 1140) = 35.25$, $p < .001$; would get into fights, $X^2 (1, N = 1137) = 56.09$, $p < .001$; become more optimistic, $X^2 (1, N = 1136) = 27.31$, $p < .001$; would have marital problems, $X^2 (1, N = 1022) = 38.55$, $p < .001$; spend a lot of money, $X^2 (1, N = 1145) = 17.49$, $p < .001$; become an alcoholic, $X^2 (1, N = 1134) = 36.03$, $p < .001$; have problems with the police, $X^2 (1, N = 1140) = 118.90$, $p < .001$; become moody, $X^2 (1, N = 1137) = 17.79$, $p < .001$; become more nervous, $X^2 (1, N = 1129) = 63.92$, $p < .001$; and become insecure, $X^2 (1, N = 1131) = 60.52$, $p < .001$.

Table 5 presents the proportion of Mexican American respondents agreeing with each of the expected outcomes for excessive drinking in terms of their level of acculturation. As was true for the expectancies for drinking, the Mexican American respondents classified as high in acculturation tended to respond in a manner similar to that of the non-Hispanic White respondents. The less acculturated Mexican Americans chose in greater proportions (65% or greater) the following outcome expectations: becoming sick, giving bad example to children, making poor decisions, having problems with the police, spend-

**Table 4. Respondents (%) Considering Various Events as Outcomes
of Excessive Alcoholic Beverage Consumption**

	All		Men		Women	
	Mexican Americans	Whites	Mexican Americans	Whites	Mexican Americans	Whites
Helps forget problems	8.9	11.2	7.7	10.3	9.9	11.9
Helps enjoy self	25.2	27.6	27.1	30.5	23.5	25.5
Feel more confident	8.8	15.5	8.1	15.8	9.5	15.3
Feel more relaxed	27.5	47.6*	29.3	55.2*	26.0	41.8*
Become sick	88.3	79.4	86.6	71.4*	89.8	85.3
Become depressed	65.8	54.4	59.2	47.1	71.5	60.1
Become angry	53.7	31.0*	53.7	28.1*	53.8	33.2*
Feel guilty	73.6	56.7*	67.9	46.7*	78.5	64.0
Get into fights	43.8	23.0*	41.5	24.2	45.9	22.1*
Become flirtatious	41.8	37.9	34.0	39.8	48.7	36.3
Become talkative	66.7	60.6	64.4	60.7	68.7	60.3
Become more optimistic	27.7	15.0*	26.9	17.7	28.4	13.1*
Helps to sleep better	43.0	39.6	44.5	42.9	41.7	37.0
Become sexually aggressive	33.5	25.9	32.5	26.4	34.3	25.4
Fall asleep	77.5	74.1	74.8	73.2	79.9	74.6
Smoke more	37.2	33.0	41.2	32.3	33.1	33.7
Become more friendly	35.1	42.1	36.0	43.8	34.3	40.7
Say improper things	74.3	69.2	72.8	69.0	75.7	69.2
Become calmer	24.7	22.4	26.8	29.0	22.8	17.7
Do things normally would not do	67.2	62.2	63.7	63.2	70.2	61.3
Gain weight	67.1	65.8	61.8	64.6	71.8	66.9
Have marital problems	76.8	58.4*	76.7	53.4*	76.8	62.0
Give bad example to children	87.4	80.3	84.6	74.3	89.8	84.7
Have problems at work	79.8	71.9	76.8	66.4	82.3	76.0
Spend a lot of money	84.4	74.3*	82.6	76.0	85.9	72.9
Become an alcoholic	74.2	57.1*	72.5	53.7*	75.6	59.6*
Have problems with police	79.3	47.9*	77.7	48.3*	80.6	47.6*
Become moody	72.9	61.1*	69.6	54.1	75.7	66.2
Look older	83.9	76.7	81.7	69.7	85.8	81.9
Become more nervous	74.5	51.4*	68.2	42.4*	80.0	58.4*
Affects speech	84.8	80.4	80.9	78.2	88.3	82.0
Have less appetite	67.1	57.8	62.4	53.9	71.2	61.0
Forget things	82.3	78.0	77.3	72.3	86.7	82.4
Become insecure	74.3	51.8*	68.2	39.5*	79.6	61.2*
Would make poor decisions	87.0	79.1	80.8	72.8	92.3	83.8

* p < .001 with Bonferoni's correction.

ing a lot of money, having problems speaking, having problems at work and with the spouse, forgetting things, feeling guilty, becoming an alcoholic, becoming more nervous, becoming insecure, becoming moody, saying and doing improper things, having less appetite, becoming depressed, talkative, angry, and gaining weight. The more acculturated Mexican Americans on the other hand, chose more frequently (65% or more) the following expectancies: becoming sick, having problems speaking, forgetting things, giving bad example to children, spending lots of money, looking older, falling asleep, having prob-

**Table 5. Mexican-American Respondents (%) Considering Various Events
as Outcomes of Excessive Alcoholic Beverage Consumption
by Acculturation Level**

	Acculturation	
	Low	High
Helps forget problems	5.0	13.7
Helps enjoy self	20.0	30.6
Feel more confident	4.3	14.2
Feel more relaxed	17.4	39.2*
Become sick	94.0	80.2*
Become depressed	74.1	55.2*
Become angry	67.1	35.2*
Feel guilty	83.7	60.0*
Get into fights	53.7	30.3*
Become flirtatious	39.0	45.2
Become talkative	69.7	62.8
Become more optimistic	28.1	26.2
Helps to sleep better	39.9	46.8
Become sexually aggressive	33.1	33.5
Fall asleep	79.5	76.1
Smoke more	41.5	32.2
Become more friendly	27.1	45.9*
Say improper things	80.3	66.2
Become calmer	19.7	31.3
Do things normally would not do	74.8	56.3*
Gain weight	66.2	68.8
Have marital problems	87.6	59.8*
Give bad example to children	93.7	78.7*
Have problems at work	87.6	68.7*
Spend a lot of money	90.0	76.6*
Become an alcoholic	82.6	64.1*
Have problems with police	90.0	65.1*
Become moody	78.0	65.8
Look older	90.3	75.5*
Become more nervous	81.9	63.6*
Affects speech	88.3	79.9
Have less appetite	74.4	57.5
Forget things	84.3	79.3
Become insecure	81.0	65.1*
Would make poor decisions	90.6	82.3

* $p < .001$ with Bonferoni's correction.

lems at work, gaining weight, having problems with the police, saying improper things, and becoming insecure. As shown in Table 5, chi-square analyses showed statistically significant differences for most expectancies between the less acculturated and the more acculturated Mexican Americans.

The responses given by the respondents to each of the 35 consequent (outcome) expectancy items for excessive drinking were submitted to separate (by ethnicity) principal axis factor analyses with oblique rotations. A comparison of the two factor analyses showed five common factors across ethnicities. One factor, labeled Problems was made up of three items dealing with excessive drinking making the individual become an alcoholic, have problems with the police, and spend a lot of money (Cronbach's alpha of .79 among Mexican Americans and .72 among non-Hispanic Whites). A second common factor was labeled Peace of Mind and was made up of three items expecting that by consuming excessive amounts of alcoholic beverages the individuals would forget problems, feel more confident, and enjoy themselves (Cronbach's alpha of .61 for Mexican Americans and .61 for non-Hispanic Whites). A third factor, labeled Social Problems was made up of three items dealing with having marital problems, giving bad example to children, and having problems at work (Cronbach's alpha of .75 among Mexican Americans and .77 among non-Hispanic Whites). The fourth factor labeled Behavioral Deficits included five items dealing with becoming moody, drinking affecting one's speech, forgetting things, becoming insecure, and making poor decisions (Cronbach's alpha of .81 among Mexican Americans and .82 among non-Hispanic Whites). The fifth factor, Peacefulness was composed of three items related to sleeping better, becoming more friendly, and calmer (Cronbach's alpha of .61 among Mexican Americans and .48 among non-Hispanic Whites).

A multivariate analysis of variance was conducted with ethnicity, gender, and drinking status as independent variables and the common factor scales as dependent variables controlling for nonindependence among the independent variables. This analysis showed a main effect for drinking status. Hotelling's $T(15, 3080) = 8.71$, $p < .001$, and for ethnicity, Hotelling's $T(5,1028) = 5.33$, $p < .001$. There were no statistically significant interactions.

Separate univariate analyses of variance were conducted within each ethnic group to identify possible effects of drinking status on the expectancies for excessive drinking held by the respondents. For Mexican Americans, drinking status of the respondents (Table 6) produced a significant main effect; $F(3, 528) = 7.08$, $p < .001$ for the Problems scale and the same was true for the Peace of Mind scale, $F(3, 528) = 19.82$, $p < .001$; for the Social Problems scale, $F(3, 462) = 8.35$; $p < .001$); the Behavioral Deficits scale, $F(3, 518) = 10.54$, $p < .001$; and for the Peacefulness scale, $F(3, 520) = 8.75$, $p < .001$. Among non-

Table 6. Mean Scores in Drinking Antecedents Factor Scales by Drinking Status

	Drinking Status				
	Abstainers	Light	Moderate	Heavier	All
Problems					
Mexican Americans	3.32	3.21	2.85	2.67*	3.20
Non-Hispanic Whites	2.74	2.52	2.50	2.00*	2.58
Peace of mind					
Mexican Americans	1.24	1.41	1.62	2.13*	1.36
Non-Hispanic Whites	1.32	1.45	1.66	1.86*	1.46
Social problems					
Mexican Americans	3.49	3.34	3.06	2.59*	3.38
Non-Hispanic Whites	3.26	2.92	2.72	1.88*	2.98
Behavioral deficits					
Mexican Americans	3.31	3.17	2.77	2.69*	3.17
Non-Hispanic Whites	3.01	2.88	2.74	2.02*	2.87
Peacefulness	1.79	1.96	2.22	2.57	1.90
Mexican Americans					
Non-Hispanic Whites	1.70	1.96	2.18	2.19	1.91

** $p < .001$ across drinking status categories

Hispanic Whites, drinking status produced a significant main effect for the Problems scale, $F(3, 595) = 5.59, p < .001$; for the Peace of Mind scale $F(3, 609) = 10.35, p < .001$; for the Social Problems scale $F(3, 546) = 18.50, p < .001$; the Behavioral Deficits scale, $F(3, 584) = 10.56, p < .001$; and, the Peacefulness scale, $F(3, 600) = 11.53, p < .001$.

Univariate analyses of variance were also conducted with ethnicity as the independent variable and the various factor scales as the dependent variables. Those analyses showed statistically significant differences in means for Mexican Americans (Table 6) and non-Hispanic Whites for the Problems scale, $F(1, 1234) = 118.96, p < .001$; the Peace of Mind scale, $F(1, 1248) = 6.96, p < .01$; the Social Problems scale, $F(1, 1105) = 44.99, p < .001$; and, the Behavioral Deficits scale, $F(1, 1210) = 36.27, p < .001$; but not for the Peacefulness scale, $F(1, 231) = .01, ns$.

A multivariate analysis of variance with the common factor scales as dependent variables and acculturation level, drinking status, and gender as independent variables also was carried out controlling for nonindependence for the responses provided by the Mexican American respondents. The analysis showed a main effect for the level of acculturation of the Mexican American respondents Hotelling's $T(5, 425) = 2.24\ p < .05$, and for drinking status Hotelling's $T(15, 1271) = 2.55, p < .001$; but there were no statistically significant interactions. Univariate analyses among Mexican American respondents showed that there was a significant main effect for acculturation in the Problems scale, $F(1, 528) = 46.41, p < .001$ (less acculturated $M = 3.47$ and more acculturated $M = 2.88$); the Peace of Mind scale, $F(1, 529) = 9.15, p < .001$ ($M = 1.24$ for the less acculturated and $M = 1.50$ for the more acculturated); the Social Problems scale, $F(1, 464) = 48.31, p < .001$ ($M = 3.63$ for the less acculturated and $M = 2.98$ for the more acculturated); the Behavioral Deficits scale, $F(1, 518) = 10.46, p < 001$ ($M = 3.32$ for the less acculturated and $M = 3.03$ for the more acculturated); and the Peacefulness scale, $F(1, 520) = 11.50, p < .001$ ($M = 1.77$ for the less acculturated and $M = 2.07$ for the more acculturated).

DISCUSSION

The data reported here showed that there were important qualitative and quantitative differences in the expectancies held by Mexican Americans and non-Hispanic Whites for the consumption of alcoholic beverages. Differences in the proportion of respondents expecting a given outcome were found across ethnic groups for drinking and for excessive drinking so that Mexican Americans tended to report expecting most of the various possible results of consuming alcoholic beverages in greater proportions than non-Hispanic Whites. Also of interest is the fact that the amount of alcoholic beverages consumed by the respondents tended to influence the type of expectations held where abstainers and light drinkers were more likely to expect negative results whenever alcoholic beverages were consumed. The acculturation level of the Mexican American respondents played an important role in determining the expectations they held so that the highly acculturated held expectancies that closely resembled those of non-Hispanic White respondents.

As mentioned above, a central objective of this study was to identify differences in expectations across ethnic groups. The data reported here showed some similarities in the perceived relevance of various expectancies across ethnic groups as well as fairly consistent differences in the type of expectations held by Mexican Americans and non-Hispanic Whites. In general, Mexican Americans not only expected the various outcomes in greater proportions than non-Hispanic Whites but also were more likely to emphasize a variety of negative outcomes related to personal (e.g., losing self control, having problems at home and at work) and social consequences (such as giving bad example to children).

The findings of culture-specific differences in this study when respondents report their own expectancies resemble the findings of culture-specific expectancies for alcohol consumption when estimating the expectancies held by people in general (Marín et al., 1993) as well as for DUI (Posner and Marín, 1996). These studies confirm therefore the existence of alcohol-related expectancies that are group-specific for Mexican Americans that differ from those held by non-Hispanic Whites. It is difficult at this time to explain the reasons for these patterns in expectations or to identify culture-specific historical circumstances or events that could have produced these expectations among Mexican Americans and not among non-Hispanic Whites. One possibility of course, is the historical differential value assigned to alcoholic beverages in the various cultures represented in the study that in turn may have produced expectancies for the effects of drinking ethanol. Advertising and the presence of alcoholic beverages in the media may also account for some of the differences in expectancies identified in this study. Data on prevalence of alcoholic-beverage consumption has certainly showed differences in quantity and frequency between the United States and Mexico (e.g., Saunders, Aasland, Amundsen and Grant, 1993) which may reflect the subjective value assigned to the consumption of ethanol in those two countries. While the data reported here do not explain the reasons for these differences in expectations, they clearly showed the existence of culture-specific expectancies and support the need to develop culturally appropriate programs for the prevention of alcohol abuse among Mexican Americans that take into consideration these differences in beliefs across ethnic groups (Marín, 1993).

Since alcohol expectancies have been found to predict level of intake in various studies (Brown et al., 1985), the finding that Mexican Americans tended to expect a large proportion of the possible results of drinking alcoholic beverages studied here may serve as a possible explanation for the seemingly disproportionate rates of consumption among Mexican Americans and Hispanics in general (Clark and Midanik, 1982) and of the negative physical (e.g., cirrhosis rates) and behavioral effects (e.g., rates of drunk driving arrests) being experienced by this community.

As reported in previous studies (Fromme, Kivlahan, and Marlatt, 1986; Marín et al., 1993), the amount of alcoholic beverages consumed by the respondents was found to be related to the type of expectations they held. In general, abstainers and light drinkers tended to expect negative emotional and behavioral consequences with the consumption of alcoholic beverages while more frequent drinkers tended to expect more positive outcomes. The positive expectancies held by drinkers can be perceived as reinforcing psychological elements for the consumption of alcoholic beverages that maintain the behavior as has been found for other substances (e.g., Marín et al., 1990; Stacy, Dent, Sussman, and Raynor, 1990). This reinforcing function needs to be addressed in future prevention campaigns by identifying alternatives or emphasizing significant negative outcomes that lower the expected overall utility of drinking alcoholic beverages.

The level of acculturation of the Mexican American respondents showed statistically significant effects in the type of expectancies held by the respondents. Overall, the more acculturated respondents tended to report patterns of expectancies that closely resembled

those of the non-Hispanic White respondents. This modification in beliefs as acculturation proceeds is a phenomenon previously noted in terms of the expectancies held for the
use of cigarettes by Hispanics (Marín, Marín, and Perez-Stable, 1989). These results
demonstrate that as the acculturation process advances, individuals exposed to a new
culture change not only their actions, but also the attitudes and expectancies they have
toward certain behaviors.

The data presented here not only showed the relevance of culture in shaping expectancies but also point to the need for developing culturally appropriate interventions with
Mexican Americans that by targeting the group-specific expectancies identified here must
differ from campaigns directed at the rest of the population (Marín, 1993). A culturally
appropriate prevention campaign will need not only to reflect these differences in
expectancies, but also target the group-specific beliefs that were identified in this study.
In addition, the development of culturally appropriate prevention interventions with
Mexican Americans will need to reflect the differences in expectancies related to the
drinking patterns of the respondents and to their acculturation level. Specifically, the findings reported here imply that prevention campaigns will need not only to differentiate
messages directed at Mexican Americans from those intended for the general population
but that the prevention campaigns will need to target light drinkers differently from heavier drinkers. In addition, the data reported here support the development of culturally
appropriate prevention campaigns that differentially target the less acculturated Mexican
Americans from the more acculturated. This approach at developing culturally appropriate interventions should produce prevention campaigns that are not only more acceptable,
but also more effective (Rogers, 1983; Uba, 1992), an approach that is similar to that
utilized in promotional campaigns that segment targeted recipients of messages in terms
of important psychosocial (e.g., beliefs, values, norms) and relevant sociodemographic
variables.

As with any study, the data reported here have some limitations that need to be considered in future studies. First, our Mexican American sample came from two cities in two
different states. It is conceivable that some differences may have been masked by this
sampling approach and that a truly representative nationwide sample of Mexican
Americans could provide a more comprehensive understanding of the various expectancies. Because of time limitations in the interview schedule, we were unable to obtain an
evaluation of each of the expectancies, a factor that may more appropriately reflect the
personal relevance of expectancies in predicting behavior (Fishbein, 1980; Leigh, 1989a).
Nevertheless, this study provides a fairly comprehensive overview of the expectancies held
by Mexican Americans for the consumption of alcoholic beverages while controlling for
the limitations of previous studies such as using random samples of respondents (Marín
et al., 1993) and asking respondents to report their own personal expectancies (Leigh,
1989a, 1989b). Given the evidence of differences in culture-specific expectancies that has
been reported here, studies need to be developed in the future that look at differences and
similarities between Mexican Americans and members of other major Hispanic subgroups
such as Cuban Americans and Puerto Ricans.

NOTES

The preparation of this paper was supported by grant AA90432 from the National Institute on Alcohol Abuse and Alcoholism (Gerardo Marín, Principal Investigator).

Portions of this article were presented at the XXV Interamerican Congress of Psychology, San Juan, PR, July 1995.

The author acknowledges with thanks the invaluable help provided by Richard Matens, Rosa Marcano, Samuel Posner, and Matthew Hudson in the collection of these data.

BIBLIOGRAPHY

Bachman, J. G., Wallace, J. M., O'Malley, P. M., Johnston, L. D., Kurth, C. L., and Neighbors, H. W. (1991). Racial/ethnic differences in smoking, drinking, and illicit drug use among American high school seniors. 1976–89. *American Journal of Public Health*, 81, 372–377.

Baldwin, A. R., Oei, T.P.S., and Young, R. (1993). To drink or not to drink: The differential role of alcohol expectancies and drinking refusal self-efficacy in quantity and frequency of alcohol consumption. *Cognitive Therapy and Research*, 17, 511–530.

Brislin, R. W., Lonner, W. J., and Thorndike, R. M. (1973). *Cross-cultural research methods*. New York: Wiley.

Brown, S. A., Goldman, M. S., and Christiansen, B. A. (1985). Do alcohol expectancies mediate drinking patterns of adults? *Journal of Consulting and Clinical Psychology*, 53, 512–519.

Caetano, R. (1987a). Acculturation and attitudes toward appropriate drinking among U.S. Hispanics. *Alcohol and Alcoholism*, 22, 427–433.

Caetano, R. (1987b). Acculturation, drinking and social settings among U.S. Hispanics. *British Journal of Addictions*, 19, 215–226.

Caetano, R. (1989). Drinking patterns and alcohol problems in a national sample of U.S. Hispanics. In D. L. Spiegler, D. A. Tate, S. S. Aitken, and C. M. Christian (Eds.), *Epidemiology of Alcohol use and abuse among ethnic minority groups* (pp. 147–162). NIAAA Research Monograph No. 18. DHHS Publication No. (ADM) 89–1435. Washington, DC: DHHS.

Caetano, R., and Mora, M.E.M. (1988). Acculturation and drinking among people of Mexican descent in Mexico and the United States. *Journal of Studies on Alcohol*, 49, 462–471.

Cervantes, R. C., Gilbert, M. J., Snyder, N. S., and Padilla, A. M. (1990–1991). Psychosocial and cognitive correlates of alcohol use in younger adult immigrant and U.S. born Hispanics. *International Journal of the Addictions*, 25, 687–708.

Christiansen, B. A., and Teahan, J. E. (1987). Cross-cultural comparisons of Irish and American adolescent drinking practices and beliefs. *Journal of Studies on Alcohol*, 48. 558–562.

Clark, W. B., and Midanik, L. (1982). Alcohol use and alcohol problems among U.S. adults. In NIAAA (Ed.), *Alcohol consumption and related problems*. (Vol. 1. pp. 3–52). Washington, DC: US Government Printing Office.

Connors, G. J., Maisto, S. A., and Watson, D. W. (1988). Racial factors influencing college students' ratings of alcohol usefulness. *Drug and Alcohol Dependence*, 21, 247–252.

Dermen, K. H., and Cooper, M. L. (1994b). Sex-related alcohol expectancies among adolescents: I. Scale development. *Psychology of Addictive Behaviors*, 8, 152–160.

Dermen, K. H., and Cooper, M. L. (1994b). Sex-related alcohol expectancies among adolescents: II. Prediction of drinking in social and sexual situations. *Psychology of Addictive Behaviors*, 8, 161–168.

Fishbein, M. (1980). A theory of reasoned action: Some applications and implications. In M. M. Page (Ed.), *Nebraska symposium on motivation 1979*. (pp. 65–116). Lincoln, NB: University of Nebraska Press.

Fromme, K., and Dunn, M. E. (1992). Alcohol expectancies, social and environmental cues as determinants of drinking and perceived reinforcement. *Addictive Behaviors*, 17, 167–177.

Fromme, K., Kivlahan, D. R., and Mariatt, G. A. (1986). Alcohol expectancies, risk identification, and secondary prevention with problem drinkers. *Advances in Behaviour Research and Therapy*, 8, 237–51.

Glassner, B., and Berg, B. (1984). Social locations and interpretations: How Jews define alcoholism. *Journal of Studies on Alcohol*, 45, 16–24.

Hull, J. G., and Bond, C. F. (1986). Social and behavioral consequences of alcohol consumption and expectancy: A meta-analysis. *Psychological Bulletin*, 99, 347–360.

Leigh, B. C. (1989a). Confirmatory factor analysis of alcohol expectancy scales. *Journal of Studies on Alcohol*, 105, 268–278.

Leigh, B. C. (1989b). In search of the seven dwarves: Issues of measurement and meaning in alcohol expectancy research. *Psychological Bulletin*, 105, 361–372.

Leigh, B. C. (1990). The relationship of sex-related alcohol expectancies to alcohol consumption and sexual behavior. *British Journal of Addiction*, 85, 919–928.

Madsen, W. (1964). The alcoholic agringado. *American Anthropologist*, 66, 355–361.

Marín, B., Marín, G., Pérez-Stable, E. J., Otero-Sabogal, R., and Sabogal, F. (1990). Cultural differences in attitudes toward smoking: Developing messages using the Theory of Reasoned Action. *Journal of Applied Social Psychology*, 20, 478–493.

Marín, G. (1992). Issues in the measurement of acculturation among Hispanics. In K. F. Geisinger (Ed.), *Psychological testing of Hispanics*. (pp. 235–251). Washington, DC: American Psychological Association.

Marín, G. (1993). Designing culturally-appropriate interventions: Hispanics as a case study. *Journal of Community Psychology*, 21, 149–161.

Marín, G., Marín, B., and Pérez-Stable, E. J. (1989). Cigarette smoking among San Francisco Hispanics: The role of acculturation and gender. *American Journal of Public Health*, 70, 196–199.

Marín, G., and Marín, B. V. (1991). *Research with Hispanic populations*. Newbury Park, CA: Sage.

Marín, G., and Posner, S. F. (1995). Gender and acculturation as determinants of the consumption of alcoholic beverages among Mexican-and Central-Americans. *International Journal of the Addictions*.

Marín, G., Posner, S. F., and Kinyon, L. B. (1993). Alcohol expectancies among Hispanics and non-Hispanic Whites: Roles of respondents drinking status and accumulation. *Hispanic Journal of Behavioral Sciences*, 15, 373–381.

Marín, G., Sabogal, F., Marín, B., Otero-Sabogal, R., and Perez-Stable, E. J. (1987). Development of a short acculturation scale for Hispanics. *Hispanic Journal of Behavioral Sciences*, 9, 183–205.

Nagoshi, C. T., Noil, R. T., and Wood, M. D. (1992). Alcohol expectancies and behavioral and emotional responses to placebo versus alcohol administration. *Alcoholism: Clinical and Experimental Research*, 16, 255–260.

Neff, J. A., Hoppe, S. K., and Perea, P. (1987). Acculturation and alcohol use: Drinking patterns and problems among Anglo and Mexican American male drinkers. *Hispanic Journal of Behavioral Sciences*, 9, 151–181.

Oei, T.P.S., and Young, R. M. (1987). The role of alcohol-related self-statements in social drinking. *International Journal of the Addictions*, 22, 905–915.

Posner, S. F., and Marín, G. (1996). Expectancies for driving under the influence of alcohol among Hispanics and non-Hispanic Whites. *International Journal of the Addictions*, 31, 409–421.

Robins, L. N., and Reigier, D. A. (1991). *Psychiatric disorders in America: The epidemiologic catchment area study*. New York: Free Press.

Rogers, E. M. (1983). *Diffusion of innovations*. New York: Free Press.

Saunders, J. B., Aasland, O. G., Amundsen, A., and Grant, M. (1993). Alcohol consumption and related problems among primary health care patients: WHO Collaborative Project on Early Detection of Persons with Harmful Alcohol Consumption-I. *Addiction*, 88, 349–362.

Stacy, A. W., Dent, C. W., Sussman, S., and Raynor, A. (1990). Expectancy accessibility and the influence of outcome expectancies on adolescent tobacco use. *Journal of Applied Social Psychology*, 20, 802–817.

Stacy, A. W., Widaman, K. F., and Marlett, G. A. (1990). Expectancy models of alcohol use. *Journal of Personality and Social Psychology* 58, 918–928.

Substance Abuse and Mental Health Services Administration. (1993). *National Household Survey on Drug Abuse: Population Estimates 1992*. (DHHS Publication No. [SMA] 93–2053). Substance Abuse and Mental Health Services Administration.

Sutker, P. B., Allain, A. N., Brantley, P. J., and Randall, C. L. (1982). Acute alcohol intoxication, negative affect, and autonomic arousal in women and men. *Addictive Behaviors*, 7, 17–25.

Teahan, J. E. (1987). Alcohol expectancies, values, and drinking of Irish and U.S. collegians. *International Journal of the Addictions*, 22, 621–638.

Teahan, J. E. (1988). Alcohol expectancies of Irish and Canadian alcoholics. *International Journal of the Addictions*, 23, 1057–1070.

Thombs, D. L. (1991). Expectancies versus demographics in discriminating between college drinkers: Implications for alcohol abuse prevention. *Health Education Research*, 6, 491–495.

Thombs, D. L. (1993). The differentially discriminating properties of alcohol expectancies for female and male drinkers. *Journal of Counseling and Development*, 71, 321–325.

Triandis, H. C. (1972). *The analysis of subjective culture*. New York: Wiley.

Uba, L. (1992). Cultural barriers to health care for Southeast Asian refuges. *Public Health Reports*, 107, 544–548.

Waksberg, J. (1978). Sampling methods for random digit dialing. *Journal of the American Statistical Association*, 73, 40–46.

Welte, J. W., and Barnes, G. M. (1987). Alcohol use among adolescent minority groups. *Journal of Studies on Alcohol*, 48, 329–336.

PART VI.

Culture, Behavior, and Health

Our physical health is closely related to our sense of well-being. Even though such an association can seem obvious, psychology's role in studying the complex relation between the psyche and health has been a relatively recent phenomenon. Health psychologists conceptualize "health" as a multifaceted construct comprised of biological, social, cognitive, and behavioral factors rather than the mere absence of disease. This shift has led to greater attention on behaviors and life-styles that prevent illness and improve health. That cultural factors can also play a significant role should come as little surprise. Addressing the interplay of health, ethnicity, and cultural attitudes and norms will lead to greater awareness among ethnic groups on modification of individual responses to life-enhancing or life-threatening conditions. The selection by Shirley Bagley and her colleagues offers a much needed review of what we know about culture and its influence on adaptive health behaviors, that is, positive behaviors or social conditions that serve to protect individuals from certain diseases.

As our knowledge base grows about the influence of culture on health status, we will need to develop culturally appropriate interventions designed to reduce health risks. This call for sensitivity and awareness regarding at-risk ethnic populations is illustrated in the article by Pamela Balls Organista and Kurt Organista. The authors provide insight to an often neglected and underresearched population, Mexican migrant laborers, who are at increasing risk for contracting the HIV virus. Through synthesis of empirical research on cultural norms, attitudes, and beliefs regarding AIDS and sex behaviors, the authors offer recommendations for prevention interventions for both male and female migrants.

FURTHER READINGS

Angel, R., and Thoits, P. (1987). The impact of culture on the cognitive structure of illness. *Culture, Medicine, and Psychiatry, 11*, 465–494.

Cochran, S. D., Mays, V. M., and Leung, L. (1991). Sexual practices of heterosexual Asian-American young adults: Implications for risk of HIV infection. *Archives of Sexual Behavior, 20*, 381–391.

DiClemente, R. J., and Wingood, G. M. (1995). A randomized controlled trial of an HIV sexual risk-reduction intervention for young African-American women. *Journal of the American Medical Association, 274*, 1271–1276.

Flack, J. M., Amaro, H., Jenkins, W., Kunitz, S., Levy, J., Mixon, M., and Yu, E. (1995). Panel I: Epidemiology of minority health. *Health Psychology, 14*, 592–600.

Kato, P. M., and Mann, T. (Eds.). (1996). *Handbook of diversity issues in health psychology.* NY: Plenum.

Molina, C. W., and Aguirre-Molina, M. (Eds.). (1994). *Latino health in the US: A growing challenge.* Washington, DC: American Public Health Association.

Zane, N. W. S., Takeuchi, D. T., and Young, K. N. J. (Eds.). (1994). *Confronting critical health issues of Asian and Pacific Islander Americans.* Thousand Oaks, CA: Sage.

13

Adaptive Health Behaviors Among Ethnic Minorities

Shirley P. Bagley, Ronald Angel,
Peggye Dilworth-Anderson, William Liu,
and Steven Schinke

Race, ethnicity, and cultural attitudes and practices are among the variables that influence health behaviors, including adaptive health behaviors. The following discussions highlight the important role of social conditions in shaping health behaviors and the central role of family in promoting health across the Asian, Hispanic, Native American, and African American ethnic groups. Factors that may lead to health-damaging behaviors are also discussed. The need for additional research that identifies correlations among physiological, social, and behavioral factors and health behaviors, as well as underlying mechanisms, is called for.

Although little is known about the adaptive health behaviors of minority groups, in this article, we nevertheless summarize what is currently known, using both empirical research and theoretical treatises. We address the adaptive health behaviors of four minority groups: Asian Americans, Native Americans, African Americans, and Hispanic Americans. Although there are many similarities, each group presents unique issues related to the study of adaptive health behaviors.

Adaptive health behaviors among Asian Americans are discussed with regard to the usefulness of race and ethnicity as variables in the study of behavior. We suggest that Asian cultural diversity needs to be understood by researchers before they can meaningfully engage in health research with this population. This is especially true because cultural expectations and norms shape the adaptive structures within a culture. We use the cultural characteristics of mainland China and their association with health behaviors as an example.

The discussion on Native Americans emphasizes the influence of social conditions on their health behaviors. We also focus on the health habits and practices of young Native Americans and their potential effects on future health status. We suggest how to intervene in the lives of Native American adolescents to help alter their responses to health-changing conditions.

The last two discussions in this article on African Americans and Hispanics focus on cultural indicators that may help to better understand health behaviors among these two groups. In both discussions, it is clear that the family serves as a major force that helps develop and maintain health-promoting and health-damaging behaviors.

Indeed a common thread among all four discussions is that familial influences must be considered to better understand adaptive health behaviors among minority groups. Thus, future research may benefit from approaches that allow for an examination of individual health behaviors situated in a familial context.

ASIAN AMERICANS
Ethnicity as a Research Variable

There is a conspicuous absence of systematic research on Asian Americans' health status and a corresponding lack of data on adaptive health strategies in this population. There are a number of reasons for this, and they are given elsewhere by Yu and Liu (1992). Briefly, two major reasons for the lack of Asian American health research should be mentioned. First and foremost is the diversity of Asian Americans as cultural groups with respect to major language origins, racial heritage, and religious beliefs and levels of economic development. The sampling of Asian American subgroups poses an enormous problem of sample design accompanied by prohibitive costs associated with sample acquisition. A second and related reason is that there is insufficient political reason to obtain health data from Asian Americans given the myth that Asians are the "model minority" who can take care of their own problems.

Given the lack of information on adaptive health strategies in Asian Americans, our descriptions of the culturally shaped and health-relevant adaptive strategies in this group must be restricted to some carefully collected data on Chinese populations in Shanghai and Hong Kong as examples. Although there are certainly vast differences between Chinese in Shanghai and Hong Kong and those in the United States, these data may nevertheless be used to highlight some of the cultural issues that may be relevant to many Chinese Americans. The Shanghai data come from an on-going and much published database that began in 1987 and deals with the study of the lives of older persons. The sample was selected from one health district consisting of 5,055 households obtained using stratified cluster sampling. The Hong Kong data come from a similar study that took place in 1991 and was based on a random sample of all households that consisted of at least one person 65 years of age and older. Both studies focused on senile dementia and Alzheimer's disease. We selected a number of relevant topics that may shed some light on the adaptive strategies of Chinese families in dealing with old age care.

Social Support

Following current practices, we measured social support using items that accessed social ties; social network; community participation; contacts with friends, relatives, and coworkers; and the presence of confidants. In general, measures of social support were positively related to the degree of life satisfaction and feelings of loneliness and were negatively associated with depressive symptoms as measured by the Center for Epidemiologic Studies Depression scale. These older respondents expressed preference for sharing a residence with their adult children and grandchildren, and these parental and grandparental relationships seemed to be more important than other social ties. With respect to confidants, men most often named their wives as their confidants, whereas women most often named their adult sons. However, widowed husbands, in the absence of a spouse, turned to their children as their confidants. Finally, and overwhelmingly, large proportion of older persons and their children still held on to the traditional values of filial piety and the obligation of adult children to take care of their aging parents. In addition, having confidants was significantly associated with one's general well-being, life satisfaction, and the absence of loneliness. Other forms of social support, formal or informal, that were not related to familial social ties were generally inconsequential with respect to life satisfaction.

It could be argued that urban China, especially Shanghai, has been isolated from outside, non-Socialist societies for so long that the social structure with respect to neighborhoods and *danwai* (one's work unit) might have had an extraordinarily strong impact on the lives of people. Urban China remains very much a *gemeinschaft*, in Tonnies' sense, and social support is determined by the individual's ties to work and social groups. However, we found that much is the same in Hong Kong, which is quite different with respect to social and work roles. Both Hong Kong and Shanghai have a high population density and are generally short of adequate housing. It thus is not surprising to see that household size is small and a household is only available to nuclear family members. Yet, the use of household composition as a measure of the family may mistakenly lead people to believe that nuclear families are the mode in this region. In Shanghai, for example, the necessity of having nuclear units (because of the urban housing shortage) is compensated by what Pan (1991) called the "network of nuclear units" dominated by the parental household. Myron Cohen (1991) cogently pointed out that the change of the Chinese family structure and functions are related to a pragmatic adaptation to preserve the traditional values. It should be remembered that the Chinese strongly value lineal obligations that keep the parents' and children's generations mutually supportive at different times of the family cycle. Children are cared for by their parents when the need for parental care is obvious. Conversely, parents preferred and obtained the care from their children when the former became aged. Here, the need for care requires the nuclear family of the children's generation to make whatever adjustment necessary to ensure the well-being of the older family members. This is an important point often neglected by family sociologists when they discuss the global trends of nuclearization of the family.

Family Structure

The above discussion leads to further explication of the interaction between family and race and care of aged parents. During the past decade, a number of independent studies, including the reports of two successive general censuses of China, have shown that there is a growing trend of what is usually called the "stem family." The first such report came from Fei (1991) on the basis of his successive visits to a village he studied for 40 years. This singular report of such a change challenged many studies of Chinese urban families, which reported that the dominance of the nuclear family was the result of the declining number of multigenerational families under the socialist regime.

In spite of the dominance of the nuclear family, which in many cases is as much the result of the urban housing shortage between 1949 and 1980 as it is the deliberate attempt to discontinue the traditional extended family, there remains a large proportion of nuclear families that includes one or two older grandparents. Whether this is considered a stem family or a nuclear family depends on whether one has the perspective of the older or the younger generation. Instead of saying that there is an increasing number of nuclear families with one or two parents residing in the household of the young couple, Fei (1991) concluded that there is really an increasing number of stem families. This type of residence has made it easier for the middle generation to care for both their parents and their young children. Fei's observations were confirmed by Cohen (1991).

In the context of these recent reports on the changing Chinese family, the Shanghai data demonstrated that there exist both stability and transitions. Family living provides familial support to its members at different stages of the family cycle. When third-generation children need parental care and first-generation grandparents can assist in child rearing, the nuclear unit becomes more flexible and better adapted to the demands of career development and child rearing. This seems to be a collective solution to problems of the young and the old. Unlike the episodic social support given at times of need in the West, the spousal and filial support in Shanghai is much more stable, permanent, and culturally sanctioned. It is an adaptive, though not unique, solution to both the demands of urban living and the need among older persons to have close familial ties during the latter portion of their life cycle.

Family Adaptation to Older Persons' Social Support Functions

When older immigrants from Asia arrive in the United States to live with their adult children, they view social support as deriving primarily from family members. According to a Western value system that values individual freedom and independence, this could induce stress. However, the result could be pathological, neutral, or even positive, depending on the cultural values of the family. In American society, the family adapts to the needs of children by moving to a better school district, making financial sacrifices or even changing jobs, adjusting the time of the family supper, or even postponing holidays. In China, adjusting one's life-style for older parents is no different from providing care and support to one's children. The only difference is that the person being cared for is at a different end of the age spectrum.

Child development experts have argued that children should be cared for by natural parents. Unless parents are unfit for the job, this idea has been considered to be a guiding principle in the United States court system, buttressed by the cannons of social welfare practice. In contrast, the ethos, at least in the West, is that when the roles of caregiving and care-needing are reversed, it is natural for aged parents to be cared for in institutions, rather than by their natural children at home. This prevailing view in America is also gradually influencing health practitioners in many Asian countries. The Shanghai data remind us that the mere presence of adult children is still considered to be the most desirable form of social support by their older parents. It is therefore not surprising that many older Asians in America prefer to be cared for by their natural children. Anecdotal observations suggest that three-generation families are emerging as important institutional adaptive strategies for Vietnamese, Cambodia, and Laotian families. Unfortunately, reports of such strategies have not appeared in professional journals. Such adaptive strategies should be considered to be an important element in understanding health and health care in Asian Americans.

NATIVE AMERICANS

Much evidence suggests that the health of Native Americans is worse than the health of America's general population (Mahoney, Michalek, Cummings, Nasca, and Emrich, 1989; Mao, Morrison, Semencin, and Wigle, 1986; National Cancer Institute, 1986). Health problems of Native Americans are often cited in relation to poverty and substance use. According to the Indian Health Service (IHS) 1990 data, over 28% of the Native American population falls below the poverty line, compared with less than 13% of the general population (Schinke, Botvin, and Orlandi, 1991). The percentage of high school and college graduates among Native Americans is lower than among the general population (55% vs. 66%, and 7% vs. 16%, respectively; Schinke et al., 1990). Native Americans have a rate of alcoholism six times greater than that of all other ethnic groups (Schinke et al., 1988).

Native American people suffer inordinately from cancers linked to behavioral and life-style patterns (Beauvais, Oetting Wolf, and Edwards, 1989; Brown, 1994; Mao et al., 1986; National Cancer Institute, 1986). Cancer is the second leading cause of death among Native American women and the third leading cause of death among Native American men (U.S. Congress, Office of Technology Assessment, 1986). Whereas cancer was a relatively rare problem for Native Americans in the earlier part of this century, deaths from cancer among Alaska Natives and American Indians in the northern United States now exceed average U.S. rates (Stillman, 1992). What is more, the 5-year survival rate for Native American people with cancer is the lowest of any ethnic group in the United States (Stillman, 1992). Lung cancer is the leading cause of mortality due to cancer among Native Americans (U.S. Department of Health and Human Services [USDHHS], 1991). The most dramatic increase in lung cancer mortality has been among Native American women (USDHHS, 1991).

The unhealthy life-style patterns of some Native Americans account for the higher rates of some cancers and other health problems among them. According to the Centers for Disease Control and Prevention (1982), almost half of all factors that influence a person's chance of surviving to age 65 are related to life-style behaviors. Relative to cancer, about 30% of cancer incidence is related to tobacco use, and about 50% of all cancer deaths are related to diet (Cunningham-Sabo and Davis, 1993).

Because young Native Americans are at particularly high risk for later health problems and because these youth have great potential for learning and adopting adaptive health behaviors, we focus our discussion on the health priorities of Native American youth. Data presented here on adolescent adaptive health behaviors and practices are derived from the Adolescent Health Survey, which was conducted between 1988 and 1990 by the University of Minnesota and the IHS (Blum, 1992). Respondents were 14,000 adolescents from 15 states, 50 tribes, and 200 schools. Enrolled in grades 6 through 12, the adolescents surveyed were equally distributed by gender (49% were boys and 51% were girls) and lived in rural areas and on reservations. Almost 50% of the surveyed adolescents lived in a household with two parents, more than 33% lived with a single parent, and the remaining 17% lived in a household with a nonparent relative or with a nonrelative guardian. The adolescents completed a questionnaire concerning their physical and emotional health, substance use, social support, sexual behaviors, antisocial behaviors, and risk-taking behaviors.

Death Rates

The death rate of Native American adolescents is twice as high as that of youths from other ethnic-racial groups, as revealed by comparison data reported in the study. The death rate of Native American boys 10–19 years old is nearly three times higher than that of all other racial and ethnic groups. For older teens, the ethnic disparity only increases. Native American adolescents 15–24 years old have a death rate three times the frequency from unintentional injuries compared with all other ethnic-racial groups. A large percentage of these deaths are associated with substance use. Unintentional injuries and suicide account for nearly three fourths of the total death rate.

Physical Health

One fifth of the adolescents described their health as only fair or poor. Two fifths of the girls and one fifth of the boys believe they are overweight. Some youth may be at risk for health problems due to insufficient exercise, use of tobacco, and diets high in fats and cholesterol and low in vegetables, fruits, and fibers. Poor physical health was found to be related to problems at school, at home, with drug abuse, and from suicide attempts. Possibly, the link between health and these problems suggests maladaptive coping patterns for Native American youths.

About one half of the youths had not had a physical exam in the past 2 years. More than four fifths of the youths had not seen a medicine man in the past 2 years. Half of the boys and three fifths of the girls did not exercise regularly. When assessing their body image, more than one third of the girls said they were not proud of their bodies, whereas less than one fifth of the boys stated the same thing.

Emotional Health

Adolescents rated their emotional well-being during the past month. Poor emotional health was found to be associated with family troubles, lack of supportive adults, various risk-taking behaviors, and suicide attempts. One in five adolescents reported having been a victim of sexual or physical abuse, or both. Adolescents who had attempted suicide, compared with those who had not, invariably reported less favorable emotional well-being, such as feeling bad after sleep, burned out, tense, unhappy, worried, upset, sad, depressed, and lacking in emotional control. Still most of the adolescents surveyed reported high levels of emotional well-being. Nearly 8 of 10 teenagers reported that their family cares about them a great deal; youth who reported that their parents had high expectations of them tended to report doing better in school.

Social Support

When asked about their relations, male and female adolescents rated their families about equally in regards to caring, understanding, fun, and attentiveness. However, female adolescents expressed a greater urge to leave home than male adolescents and got upset at home more often than males. About one fourth of adolescents who were identified as potential problem drinkers stated a lack of caring on behalf of their parents, family, tribal leaders, school, and church. In light of such correlations, some Native American youth may use alcohol as a means of maladaptive coping when they lack positive social supports. Although the use of alcohol may be a maladaptive means of coping with stress, it may permit individuals to live in settings that lack social support.

Nutrition

Nutritional adequacy varies from tribe to tribe because of differing sociocultural and economic factors, food availability, and food preferences. Nutritional factors contribute to at least 4 of the 10 leading causes of death in this population (i.e., heart disease, cancer, cirrhosis, and diabetes). Use of traditional foods has declined, and a dependency on purchased staples has increased. A certain degree of dietary monotony is evident. Intake of high-fat foods is widespread, whereas consumption of grains, fresh vegetables, and fruits is infrequent.

This report on the health of Native American adolescents raises concerns about the use of adaptive and maladaptive coping means by these high-risk youth. In particular, the summarized results suggest potential points of intervention in the following areas: youth involvement in programs to improve their own health, family support, health services, drug and alcohol use, and nutrition education. Other reviews on the health of Native Americans are also available. Especially illuminating are data from the National Institutes of Health on comparative rates of adaptive health behavior for Native American people and for members of other ethnic-racial minority groups and with members of the majority culture (Office of Minority Health, 1989; USDHHS, 1985). Rich data are also accessible on such related health-behavior topics as substance use and preventive health practices, as addressed by other panels presented at conferences and published elsewhere (Beauvais et al., 1989; LaFromboise and Rowe, 1983; Mahoney et al., 1989; Schinke et al., 1986, 1987).

AFRICAN AMERICANS

The literature on adaptive health behaviors among African Americans has been guided, in many respects, by three assumptions: (a) adaptive behaviors among African Americans are cultural in nature; (b) adaptive health behaviors are influenced by macrosocial conditions of the society; and (c) adaptive health behaviors are dynamic to the extent that they are changed and altered by situational factors. These assumptions are not mutually exclusive but instead represent variables that may influence and interact with one another. The idea that adaptive health behaviors are cultural in nature and are influenced by the broader society suggests that they may exist within culturally accepted and appropriate norms and beliefs that are transactionally negotiated within the broader society. The literature also suggests that most adaptive behaviors are linked to shifting priorities and resources among African Americans that are determined by larger systems outside the African American community, such as economic and political institutions (Farley and Allen, 1987). It would follow then that shifting priorities and resources change the nature of adaptive health behaviors and influence appropriate behaviors given available resources. Thus, health behaviors can be dynamic to the extent that resources made available by the broader society and cultural group can change them. Therefore, culturally accepted adaptive behaviors are developed and maintained, for example, by learning to access, translate, and use a health care delivery system in the face of changing health status, income, employment status, and racial climate of the society. The following discussion focuses on the roles African American families play in developing and maintaining adaptive health behaviors that are shaped by culture, society, and changing conditions.

Culture, Family, and Adaptive Health Behaviors

Culture is defined as a total way of life of a group of people and is spiritual, ideological, behavioral, emotional, material, and physical in nature (Keith, 1990). African American families are defined by both blood and relational linkages. Although most kin are related by blood, this is not a requisite. Family membership is not determined by blood only but by the nature of the relationship between individuals who share values, norms, and beliefs. Relational or fictive kin can have the same place, significance, and meaning as blood relatives in the family system. This definition of African American families is exemplified by White-Means and Thornton's (1990) and Lawton, Rajagopal, Brody, and Kleban's (1992) research on caregiving to older persons in Black families. White-Means and Thornton found that taking care of others in the family is not necessarily determined by blood relationships. Their findings showed no difference in incentives to provide care to close relatives and fictive kin in African American families. This was not found among other ethnic groups in their study, with the exception of Whites. Lawton et al. (1992) found that Black caregivers of older persons could just as likely be a close or distant relative, and quality of care did not vary by closeness of blood relationship to the older person.

Given the definition of African American families and the cultural context of family functioning among African Americans, the family serves as a translator, negotiator, gatekeeper, stress absorber, and stress buffer for family members. Furthermore, the family serves as the primary group that gives meaning to, provides interpretation for, and helps create a response repertoire for developing and maintaining certain behaviors. The family also prepares its members to meet and respond to societal conditions that influence their survival and that of the group (Billingsley, 1992). Given the many roles African American families play in assisting and preparing their members for life skills and survival, developing and maintaining adaptive health behaviors are viewed here as a major role of the family. However, not all African American families can provide assistance that fosters adaptive health behaviors. Although the African American community has become more middle class in the past 20 years, a growing underclass, increasing teen and single parent households with poor mothers and children, also appeared in the past 20 years (Horton and Smith, 1990). As a result, for many African American families, such changes in the family may inhibit them from providing assistance to family members to promote adaptive health behaviors.

Although it is beyond the scope of this discussion to address all the specific cultural aspects of the family that influence adaptive behaviors, family expectations and normative behaviors are emphasized here. Family expectations regarding sharing of burdens and problems have served the African American community very well. These expectations have influenced the size and composition of family support networks, proximity to kin, and the kind of support that family members provide one another (Billingsley, 1992; Chatters, Taylor, and Jackson, 1985). For example, research showed that over 50% of low-income African American women who had low birth weight babies had lower perceived family functioning scores than did mothers who had normal weight babies (Reeb et al., 1986). These authors also found that both perceived size and composition of family network correlated highly with family functioning. Women from larger perceived support networks had fewer symptoms of psychological distress such as anxiety, obsession, hostility, and somatization. This research suggests that African Americans often use their families as stress buffers and stress absorbers and that this represents the development of adaptive health behaviors. It is possible that large, viable kin networks in the African American community provide individuals with the resources to develop and maintain certain health behaviors. For example, large kin networks can share goods and services that help promote and maintain health in the form of providing food and self-care information, networking in the health care community on behalf of the family, and helping translate the health care community to the family. Research shows that African Americans are not as likely to share money as a means of support but are much more likely than Whites to share their time with family members (Dilworth-Anderson and Marshall, in press). Sharing or giving time to a sick family member in the African American community can be viewed as a form of health support when one is ill.

Research also suggests that involving the family in the treatment process is congruent with cultural expectations in the African American community. This is especially significant in therapeutic interventions and in encouraging the use of services (Bass, Acosta, and Evans, 1982). Some findings on African American families' social support to children with sickle cell disease showed that support significantly impacted the children's psychological adjustment to the disease (Hurtig, Koepke, and Park , 1989), compliance with treatment and psychosocial functioning (Dilworth-Anderson, 1994). These findings indicated that individual adaptive health behaviors may not exist to the same extent without the support of family among African Americans. For example, if compliance with a particular medical regimen is needed, presenting the expected health behaviors within a sociocultural framework that the family understands may lead sick individuals to practice adaptive health behaviors.

Research also showed that the family serves as a translator of disease and definer of illness behavior according to cultural beliefs. Cultural norms and beliefs about pain and suffering, therefore, influence the type of care that sick family members seek and accept both within and outside the culture. In addition, family cultural norms govern rules regarding appropriate expressions or acceptance of illness (Hernandez, 1991; Kleinman and Kleinman, 1991).

In many African American communities, cultural beliefs about illness are evidenced by the array of self-care regiments older African Americans often use for certain health problems such as diabetes, hypertension, and arthritis (Davis, McGadney, and Perri, 1990). Cultural beliefs are also evident in the meaning, interpretation, and help-seeking behaviors among some African American families as evidenced by responses to relatives who have Alzheimer's disease and other dementias. For a number of African Americans, particularly in the rural south, Alzheimer's disease and other dementias are viewed from the perspective of "folk medicine" (Snow, 1974; Watson, 1984). In many rural African American communities, a greater value is placed on emotional or affective patterns between individuals and role expectations than on intellectual or cognitive abilities (Gaines, 1989). As a result, individuals with dementia can perform roles within the kin system, even when they are disoriented outside this system. Therefore, a person with Alzheimer's disease may be able to function in the family for a long period of time without causing alarm. This person most likely will not receive any clinical intervention for this disease until advanced mental and physical symptoms are apparent (Gaines, 1989).

Given the manner in which many African American families culturally interpret illness and disease, it is possible, for example, that family caregivers of demented patients may not see a need to comply with the medical community's definitions and expected health behaviors. In these situations, the family's beliefs about the illness, which reflect cultural beliefs, serve to govern individual and family health behaviors (Davis and McGadney, 1993). These family and cultural beliefs are viewed as adaptive in that family members continue to play roles and are maintained within the family. In the case of older Alzheimer's disease victims, these beliefs may serve to lessen the possibility of them being institutionalized, which supports other cultural beliefs in the African American community that foster elder care within the family. Such cultural beliefs and attitudes, whether about Alzheimer's patients or about a child with a chronic health problem, can be used by health care providers in helping establish a framework in which to dialogue with families, design interventions for them, and create culturally relevant mechanisms through which families can interpret, translate, and use the health care delivery system within their cultural frame.

Future Outlook

The adaptive health behaviors of African Americans can be developed and maintained within family contexts. These contexts are, in part, shaped by cultural expectations and norms and are influenced by the changing conditions in society. We, therefore, suggest that socially, politically, and economically vulnerable groups, such as many African Americans, will experience difficulty maintaining adaptive health behaviors that have been fostered and developed within the family. Therefore, the strength of the social support system in American families that has addressed health issues may be challenged by changing social and economic conditions that have influenced the health status of the group as a whole. Future research on adaptive health behaviors among African Americans, therefore, need to focus on contextual and societal factors that challenge families' abilities to develop and maintain behaviors that address health needs and concerns.

HISPANICS

A growing body of research clearly demonstrates that the Hispanic population of the United States is not homogeneous. Each of the three major nationality groups—Mexican Americans, Puerto Ricans, and Cubans—differ in terms of educational levels, income, migration history, and health (Angel and Angel, 1993; Bean and Tienda, 1987). These translate into significant differences in aggregate health levels and risk of disease and death (Angel and Angel, 1993; Heckler, 1986). So far we have very little information on the major health risks faced by each Hispanic subgroup, but the data suggest that adaptive health behaviors associated with a traditional cultural orientation have positive effects. Our task as researchers and as developers of public policy is to identify those adaptive aspects of traditional culture and begin to understand how health care reform and public policy more generally might preserve them.

Perhaps the most intriguing finding revealed by research on Hispanics is the potential protective health effect of a traditional cultural orientation among Mexican Americans. Rosenwaike (1987), for example, documented low heart disease and cancer mortality rates among recent Mexican American, Puerto Rican, and Cuban adult immigrants in comparison with native Whites and Blacks. Rosenwaike, as have many others, speculated that recent migrants have retained protective aspects of their culture of origin.

Unfortunately, certain data suggest that this protectiveness is lost in the process of assimilation. For example, Savitz (1986) reported a convergence in rates of cancer for the Spanish-surname population and the general population in Denver, Colorado, during the 1970s. It is highly likely that any protectiveness offered by a traditional cultural orientation is the result of specific behaviors that are lost as the result of incorporation into mainstream U.S. culture. Marcus and Crane (1985), for example, hypothesized that the low incidence of lung cancer among Mexican Americans reported by Samet, Schraag, Howard, Key, and Pathak (1982), therefore, implies increasing male lung cancer rates into the next century. Because smoking and alcohol use among women increase with acculturation and because these behaviors increase the risk of adverse birth outcomes, future generations of Mexican Americans may also suffer poorer health (Amaro, Whitaker, Coffman, and Heeren, 1990; Guendelman, Gould, Hudes, and Eskenazi, 1990; Haynes, Harvey, Montes, Nickens, and Cohen, 1990; Markides, Ray, Stroup-Benham, and Trevino, 1990).

These data for adults are clearly intriguing and suggest that assimilation has complex, and not always positive, health benefits. Unfortunately, so far we do not know how assimilation influences the health of children. However, there are data to suggest that the protectiveness of traditional culture benefits infants as well as adults. For example, Mexican American infant mortality rates compare favorably with those of non-Hispanic Whites (Forbes and Frisbie, 1991). Dodge (1983) reported lower rates of asthma among Mexican American children than among non-Hispanic children.

Although it may be true that assimilation has adverse health consequences for some Hispanics, it is more likely that acculturation (the process of adopting the culture of the host culture) and structural assimilation (through which one enters the economy of the host society) have somewhat independent effects on health. It is likely, in fact, that individuals and groups who are successful in gaining economic success will have health and functional capacity profiles similar to those of middle-class Americans regardless of their cultural orientation, whereas those who remain in poverty will suffer the greatest detriments in health status as a function of less successful structural assimilation. Net of economic success, in fact, it may be the case that the retention of aspects of one's culture of origin may have negative consequences on health in developed societies like that of the United States. The failure to seek timely medical care because of a suspicion of modern medicine, for example, could result in serious threats to health. So far we do not have a clear understanding of the health consequences of the complex association between acculturation and structural assimilation, and it is clear that such an understanding should occupy a prominent place on our future research agenda.

Family structure is clearly an important determinant of children's physical and mental health (Angel and Angel, 1993). Single mothers, including Hispanic mothers, report their children's health to be poorer than do mothers in two-parent families (Angel and Worobey, 1988a). One of the mechanisms of disadvantage associated with the loss of a traditional cultural orientation may be the family disruption and strike accompanying poverty and the disorganized environments of many minority communities (Angel and Angel, 1993).

So far we do not have a good understanding of the specific health risks faced by Mexican Americans, Cuban Americans, and Puerto Ricans. Because each group consists of a different genetic pool, as well as a different cultural group, the identification of the major health risks faced by each requires much more focused research. Puerto Ricans, for example, move freely between Puerto Rico and the mainland where they are exposed to the health risks associated with urban decay and a declining economy. Mexican Americans are concentrated in the Southwest where the health risks they face are different. Cuban Americans have been a very successful immigrant group and face a very different health-risk profile than other Hispanic groups (Angel and Worobey, 1988b).

As is the case with other groups, the data strongly suggest that the family plays a major role in preserving the health of Hispanics. Single Hispanic mothers, like single mothers from other groups, report their children's health to be poorer than do mothers in two-parent families (Angel and Angel, 1993). Although single mothers who have adequate economic and social resources can do an excellent job of raising healthy children, the serious disadvantage that single-parent families often experience clearly undermines the health of both adults and children (Angel and Angel, 1993; Granger, 1982; Hansell, 1991; Horwitz, Morgenstern, and Berkman, 1985; Menken, 1972; Starfield, 1990).

The family operates in many other ways to preserve health. The often documented health benefits of marriage most likely result from the social control that one spouse exerts on the other. It might be a nuisance to be nagged about being overweight or about smoking, but if the result is a loss of weight or cessation of smoking, the health benefits are obvious. As with other groups, then, the role of the Hispanic family and of local support systems in the maintenance of health should be investigated extensively. It is hardly necessary to further document the negative health effects of smoking or drug and alcohol abuse. What researchers need to understand better is how aspects of the community and the family control these behaviors.

At a more global level, researchers must also begin to understand how public policy and the social welfare system of the United States affect family life for Hispanics, as well as for other groups. The United States has no formal family policy and, as most everyone has come to appreciate, the U.S. welfare system is not well designed to enhance family life among those in need. We do not wish to imply that all marriages should be preserved, but a welfare policy that makes it almost impossible for a poor family to stay intact or for a single mother to escape welfare dependency is not adaptive.

Researchers have a long way to go before clearly understanding the protective aspects of specific cultures. For Hispanics, researchers are beginning to understand the complex process that leads from one's cultural orientation, to one's socioeconomic status and family situation, to specific health-risk behaviors. What researchers still lack is an understanding of how to preserve and encourage those aspects of culture and family that promote health. Understanding how to do so should occupy a high place on social and research agendas.

BIBLIOGRAPHY

Amaro, H., Whitaker, R., Coffman, G., and Heeren, T. (1990). Acculturation and marijuana and cocaine use: Findings from H–HANES 1982–84. *American Journal of Public Health*, 80 (Suppl.), 54–60.

Angel, R., and Angel, J. L. (1993). *Painful inheritance: Health and the new generation of fatherless families*. Madison: University of Wisconsin Press.

Angel, R., and Worobey, J. L. (1988a). Single motherhood and children's health. *Journal of Health and Social Behavior*, 29, 38–52.

Angel, R., and Worobey, J. L. (1988b). The health of Mexican American children: Impact of acculturation on maternal reports of children's health. *Social Science Quarterly*, 69, 707–721.

Bass, B. A., Acosta, F. X., and Evans, A. (1982). The Black American patient. In F. X. Acosta, J. Yamamoto, and A. Evans (Eds.), *Effective psychotherapy for low income minority patients* (pp. 83–108). New York: Plenum Press.

Bean, F. D., and Tienda, M. (1987). *The Hispanic population of the United States.* New York: Russel Sage.

Beauvais, F., Oetting, E. R., Wolf, W., and Edwards, R. W. (1989). American Indian youth and drugs, 1976–87: A continuing problem. *American Journal of Public Health,* 79, 634–636.

Billingsley, A. (1992). *Climbing Jacob's ladder. Enduring legacies of African American families.* New York: Simon and Schuster.

Blum, R. (1992). *The state of Native American youth health.* Minneapolis: University of Minnesota Adolescent Health Program.

Brown, A. C. (1994). Dietary survey of Hopi Native American youth. *Journal of the American Dietary Association,* 94, 517–522.

Centers for Disease Control and Prevention. (1982). *Risk factor update: Final report under contract* (USPHS 200–80–0527). Atlanta, GA: Author.

Chatters, L., Taylor, R., and Jackson, J. (1985). Size and composition of the informal helper networks of elderly Blacks. *Journal of Gerontology,* 40, 605–614.

Cohen, M. L. (1991). Modernization of the Chinese family: A pragmatic adaptation to traditional values (in Chinese) In J. Chao (Ed.), *Chinese family and its transition* (pp. 153–22). Hong Kong: Institute of Asia/Pacific Research, the Chinese University of Hong Kong.

Cunningham Sabo, L., and Davis, S. (1993). Pathways to health: A health promotion and cancer prevention project for American Indian youth. *Alaska Medicine,* 35(4), 275–279.

Davis, L., and McGadney, B. (1993). Self-care practices of Black elders. In C. M. Barresi and D. E., Stull (Eds). *Ethnic elderly and long term care* (pp. 73–86). New York: Springer.

Davis, L., McGadney, B, and Perri, P. (1990). Learning to live with diabetes, hypertension and arthritis: *Self care guides for Black elders* (Manuals I, II, and III). Lisle, IL: Tucker.

Dilworth Anderson, P. (1994). The importance of grandparents in extended kin caregiving to Black children with sickle cell disease. *Journal of Health and Social Policy,* 5, 185–202.

Dilworth Anderson, P., and Marshall, S. (in press). Social support in its cultural context. In G. R. Pierce, B. R, Sarson, and I. G. Sarson (Eds.), *The handbook of social support and the family.* New York: Plenum Press.

Dodge, R. (1983). A comparison of the respiratory health of Mexican-American and non Mexican-American White children. *Chest,* 84, 587–593.

Farley, R., and Allen, W. R. (1987). *The color line and the quality of life in America.* New York: Oxford University Press.

Fei, H. (1991). The changing structure of the Chinese family: A rejoinder. In C. Jian (Ed.), *Chinese family and change* (pp. 3–8). Hong Kong: The Chinese University of Hong Kong Press.

Forbes, D., and Frisbie, W. P. (1991). Spanish surname and anglo infant mortality: Differentials over a half century. *Demography,* 28, 639–660.

Gaines, A. (1989). Alzheimer's disease in the context of Black southern culture. *Health Matrix,* 6, 33–38.

Granger, C. (1982). Maternal and infant deficits related to early pregnancy and parenthood. In N. J. Anastasiow (Ed.), *The adolescent parent* (pp. 33–45). Baltimore: Brookes.

Guendelman, S., Gould, J. B., Hudes, M., and Eskenazi, B. (1990). Generational differences in perinatal health among the Mexican American population: Findings from H–HANES, 1982–84. *American Journal of Public Health,* 80, 61–65.

Hansell, M. J. (1991). Sociodemographic factors and the quality of prenatal care. *American Journal of Public Health,* 33, 1135–1140.

Haynes, S. G., Harvey, C., Montes, H., Nickens, H., and Cohen, B. H. (1990). Patterns of cigarette smoking among Hispanics in the United States: Results from H–HANES 1982–84. *American Journal of Public Health,* 80, 47–53.

Heckler, M. (1986). Secretary's foreword and charge to the task force. In *Report of the secretary's task force on Black and minority health* (Vol. 1, p. 9). Washington DC: U.S. Department of Health and Human Services.

Hernandez, G. G.(1991). Not so benign neglect: Researchers ignore ethnicity in defining family caregiver burden and recommending services. *The Gerontologist,* 31, 271–272.

Horton, C. P., and Smith, J. C. (1990). *Statistical record of Black America*. Detroit. MI: Gale Press.

Horwitz, S. M., Morgenstern, H., and Berkman, L. F. (1985). The impact of social stressors and social networks on pediatric medical care use. *Medicial Care*, 23, 946–959.

Hurtig, A., Keopke, D., and Park, K. (1989). Relation between severity of chronic illness and adjustment in children adolescents with sickle cell disease. *Journal of Pediatric Psychology*, 14, 117–132.

Keith, J. (1990). Aging in social and cultural context: Anthropological perspectives. In R. Binstock and L. George (Eds.), *Handbook of aging and the social sciences*. New York: Academic Press.

Kleinman, A., and Kleinman, J. (1991). Suffering and its professional transformation: Toward an ethnography of interpersonal experience. *Culture, Medicine, and Psychiatry*, 15, 275–301.

LaFromboise, T. D., and Rowe, W. (1983). Skills training for bicultural competence: Rationale and application. *Journal of Counseling Psychology*, 30, 589–595.

Lawton, P., Rajagopal, D., Brody, E., and Kleban, M. H. (1992). The dynamics of caregiving for a demented elder among Black and White families. *Journal of Gerontology*, 47, 103–114.

Mahoney, M. C., Michalek, A. M., Cummings, K. M., Nasca, P. C., and Emrich, L. J. (1989). Mortality in a Northeastern Native American cohort, 1955–1984. *American Journal of Epidemiology*, 129, 16–26.

Mao, Y., Morrison, H., Semencin, R., and Wigle, D. (1986). Mortality on a Canadian Indian reserve 1977–1982. *Canadian Journal of Public Health*, 77, 263–268.

Marcus, A. C., and Crane, L. A. (1985). Smoking behavior among U.S. Latinos: An emerging challenge for public health. *American Journal of Public Health*, 75, 169–172.

Markides, K. S., Ray, L. A., Stroup-Benham, C. A., and Trevino, F. (1990). *American Journal of Public Health*, 80 (Suppl.), 42–46.

Menken, J. (1972). The health and social consequences of teenage childbearing. *Family Planning Perspectives*, 4, 54–63.

National Cancer Institute. (1986). *Cancer in minorities: Report of the subcommittee on cancer, part I*. Report of the secretary's task force on Black and minority health. Washington, DC: U.S. Department of Health and Human Services.

Office of Minority Health. (1989). *Cancer and minorities*. Washington, DC: Author.

Pan, Y. K. (1991). The hypothesis of the nuclearization of urban Chinese family. In C. Jian (Ed.), *Chinese family and its transition* (pp. 81–92). Hong Kong: Institute of Asia/Pacific Research, the Chinese University of Hong Kong.

Reeb, K. G., Graham, A. V., Kitson, G., Zyzanski, S., Weber, M. A., and Engle, A. (1986). Defining family in family medicine: Perceived family vs. household structure in an urban Black population. *The Journal of Family Practice*, 23, 351–355.

Rosenwaike, I. (1987). Mortality differential among persons born in Cuba, Mexico, and Puerto Rico residing in the United States, 1979–81. *American Journal of Public Health*, 77, 603–606.

Samet, J. M., Schraag, S. D., Howard, C. A., Key, C. R., and Pathak, D. R. (1982). Respiratory disease in a New Mexico population sample of Hispanic and non-Hispanic Whites. *American Review of Respiratory Diseases*, 125, 152–157.

Savitz, D. A. (1986). Changes in Spanish surname cancer rates relative to other Whites, Denver area, 1969–71 to 1979–81. *American Journal of Public Health*, 76, 1210–1215.

Schinke, S. P., Botvin, G. J., and Orlandi, M. A. (1991). *Substance abuse in childern and adolescents*. Newbury Park, CA: Sage.

Schinke, S. P., Orlandi, M. A., Botvin, G. J., Gilchrist, L. D., Trimble, J. E., and Locklear, V. S. (1988). Preventing substance abuse among American Indian adolescents: A bicultural competence skills approach. *Journal of Counseling Psychology*, 35, 87–90.

Schinke, S. P., Orlandi, M. A., Shilling, R. F., Botvin, G. J., Gilchrist, L. D., and Landers, C. (1990). Tobacco use by American Indian and Alaska Native people: Risks, psychosocial factors, and preventive intervention. *Journal of Alcohol and Drug Education*, 35(2), 1–12.

Snow, L. F. (1974). Folk medicine and older Blacks in southern United States. In W. Watson (Ed.), *Black folk medicine* (pp. 53–66). New Brunswick, NJ: Transaction.

Starfield, B. (1990). Social factors in child health. In M. Green and R. J. Haggerty (Eds.), *Ambulatory pediatrics* (pp. 30–36). Philadelphia: W. B. Saunders.

Stillman, P. (1992, September 23). Racism, poverty contribute to high cancer death rates. *Lakota Times*, p. B4.

U.S. Congress, Office of Technology Assessment. (1986). *Indian health care* (Publication No. OTA-H-290). Washington, DC: U.S. Government Printing Office.

U.S. Department of Health and Human Services. (1985). *Report of the secretary's task force on Black and minority health. Vol. II: Crosscutting issues in minority health*. Washington, DC: Author.

U.S. Department of Health and Human Services. (1991). *Cancer mortality among Native Americans in the United States*. Washington, DC: Author.

Watson, W. (1984). *Black folk medicine: The therapeutic significance of faith and trust*. New Brunswick, NJ: Transaction Books.

White-Means, S., and Thornton, M. (1990). Ethnic differences in the production of informal home health care. *The Gerontologist*, 30, 758–768.

Yu, E.S.H., and Liu, W. T. (1992, December). U.S. national health data on Asian/Pacific islanders: A research agenda for the 1990s. *American Journal of Public Health*, 82, 12.

14.

Culture and Gender Sensitive AIDS Prevention with Mexican Migrant Laborers

A Primer for Counselors

Pamela Balls Organista and Kurt C. Organista

The purpose of this article is to explicate research-informed culture and gender sensitive AIDS prevention strategies aimed at Mexican migrant laborers living and working in the United States for an extended time. This unique and extremely marginalized Latino population is yet another emerging high risk group for contracting the HIV virus. Counselors interested in applying their knowledge of psychology and minority groups to preventing such an AIDS epidemic will be challenged by the complex factors that frame this problem.

This article addresses the following questions based on pertinent literature and original research by the authors and their associates: (a) What is the risk of contracting HIV/AIDS for Mexican migrant laborers living and working in the United States? (b) What are the factors related to culture, gender, and migratory labor that need to be considered by counselors? and (c) How can professional counselors use this information to assist them in providing effective HIV/AIDS prevention strategies with this unique Latino population?

Counselors working with a population at risk for HIV infection are often responsible for the delivery of prevention services in nontraditional settings, including primary health care centers (Kaplan, 1991; Myers, 1992). In particular, Mexican migrant laborers are a new at-risk population that counselors may encounter in federally funded and nonprofit rural health and mental health centers as well as urban county hospitals. In addition, counselors may assume the roles of consultants and case managers as they consult with other health care providers (Dworkin and Pincu, 1993).

It is hard to imagine a Latino group in the United States that is more socially and geographically marginalized than Mexican migrant laborers. The Department of Health and Human Services (DHHS) estimated that there are over 4 million migrant laborers and seasonal farmworkers (including family members) in the United States, and they are predominantly of Mexican origin (DHHS, 1990). Recent reviews of the literature on the threat of AIDS to migrant laborers indicated considerable risk in this unique population (National Commission to Prevent Infant Mortality, 1993; Organista and Balls Organista, 1997).

Certain primary risk factors include significant prostitution use, susceptibility to sexually transmitted diseases (STDs), male homosexual contact, and female migrants having high-risk sexual partners (Carrier and Magaña, 1991; Lafferty, 1991; Lopez and Ruiz,

1995; Magaña, 1991). In addition, problems in actual knowledge regarding HIV transmission and proper condom use have been reported (Organista et al., in press).

Prostitution use. In one survey we conducted in-depth interviews with 501 Mexican migrants that have lived and worked in the United States during the past 15 years (Organista et al., in press). Female as well as male migrants were surveyed in five prototypical "sending communities" in Jalisco, Mexico, with historically high rates of out-migration to the United States. Findings revealed that 43% of the 342 men surveyed reported using prostitutes while in the United States. In fact, compared with single men, married men were as likely to use prostitutes, but were less likely to use condoms.

STDs. Susceptibility to STDs has been documented in a limited number of studies. Lopez and Ruiz (1995) reported a 9% lifetime history of STDs and two active syphilis cases in a sample of 176 Northern California Mexican farmworkers. Carrier and Magaña (1991) found that epidemics of syphilis and chancroid had recently occurred in migrant laborers and the prostitutes they used in Orange County, California. In both of these studies, either no active cases of HIV or a very low number of HIV cases were identified. However, researchers cautioned that because of the high rates of unsafe sex practices and resultant high number of STDs, prevention efforts must be taken with this population to impede a likely HIV epidemic in the near future.

Homosexual behavior. Despite limited research on homosexuality in Mexican migrants, reports have indicated that homosexual/bisexual contact accounts for 65% of AIDS cases in immigrant Latinos born in Mexico, Central America, Cuba, and South America (Díaz, Buehler, Castro, and Ward, 1993). Based on interviews with Mexican migrants, Bronfman and Minello (1992) concluded that homosexual contact is more likely to occur with migration as a result of loneliness, isolation, and fewer sexual restrictions in the United States.

Needle sharing. Another risk factor, needle sharing, is practiced by some Mexican migrants. Although intravenous illicit drug use poses an obvious threat of HIV infection, therapeutic injections of vitamins and antibiotics may present an even greater danger. Lafferty (1991) reported that 2.9% of 411 predominantly Mexican farmworkers reported intravenous illegal drug use, however, 20.3% reported therapeutic self-injection of vitamins and antibiotics. Of these, 3.5% reported sharing needles for therapeutic injections.

Risky sex partners. As stated earlier, our survey (Organista et al., in press) showed no difference in the rate of prostitute use by married men and single men. Yet, married men were less likely to use condoms with prostitutes than were single men. The risk to the wives of these men is obvious and consistent with other studies substantiating other risk factors placing Mexican migrant women at risk. For example, Lopez and Ruiz (1995) found that 9.1% of women in their Mexican farmworkers sample reported having sex with someone who injected drugs during the past year.

AIDS and condom knowledge. Findings from our surveys indicated that AIDS-related knowledge by Mexican migrants show mixed knowledge of AIDS transmission and low and inconsistent condom use (Organista, Balls Organista, Garcia de Alba G., Castillo Moran, and Carrillo, 1996; Organista et al., in press). For example, migrants were very knowledgeable about the major modes of AIDS transmission, but held many misconceptions about contracting AIDS from casual sources (e.g., public bathrooms, kissing on the mouth, taking the AIDS test). Misconceptions about casual modes of transmission could compromise supportive responses to friends or family members within the Mexican migrant population who are infected with HIV. Also, the fact that 50% of the sample believed they could contract HIV from the AIDS test would suggest high inhibition to obtain such screening.

We also found that knowledge of proper condom use is poor, and actual condom use is significantly higher with occasional sex partners than with a regular sex partner. Problematic knowledge about AIDS and condom use is exacerbated by cultural and migratory labor factors that must be considered in prevention strategies, such as limited education; cultural, linguistic, and geographical barriers to health services; and constant mobility.

Wyatt (1994) stated that an ideal AIDS prevention program would be based on an understanding of the normative sex practices for a target group as influenced by variables such as cultural values, gender, socioeconomic status, sexual orientation, and the group's degree of social marginality within society.

ADDRESSING ACCULTURATION, EDUCATION, AND MIGRATORY LABOR ISSUES

As counselors attempt culturally responsive prevention intervention efforts targeting Mexican migrants, they will need to address the following pragmatic needs:

1. Basic AIDS and condom information must be disseminated in Spanish. For example, 81% of our sample spoke only or mostly Spanish (Organista et al., in press).
2. Literature should be geared to appropriate reading levels and should also include nonreading-based (i.e., hands-on) education.
3. To increase the likelihood of health and counseling service use, extensive outreach to where migrants live and work (e.g., labor camps, sending communities) must occur.
4. Because this is a transient group, counselors and other service providers should consider that most contacts will be brief, possibly only a single session. This reality presses the counselor to develop interventions that are accessible, concise, and problem-solving oriented.

ADDRESSING GENDER AND OTHER CULTURAL ISSUES

If attempts are made to provide group psychoeducational interventions or workshops, attention needs to be given toward the tendency for traditional Latino men and women not to talk directly about sexual matters. De la Vega (1990) suggested that sex education for Latinos may necessitate placing men and women in separate rooms with same-sex sex educators, and then reuniting them afterward to begin a dialogue about preventing AIDS. Indeed, we recommend that counselors consider a number of gender-and culture-sensitive intervention issues informed by relevant research and outlined as the following:

Male-focused interventions. Our research has led us to conclude that the highest priority in prevention work is to focus on getting male migrant men to use condoms consistently with occasional sex partners, including prostitutes, in the event that these men pursue extramarital sexual relationships. Although proper and consistent condom use does not give 100% assurance against HIV transmission, it is one of the best preventative behaviors for decreasing the spread of AIDS. Furthermore, married as well as single migrant laborers need to be included in such prevention efforts, especially in view of lower condom use reported by married men.

In a rare intervention study with migrant farmworkers, Connor (1992) evaluated the effectiveness of a program designed to increase condom use with prostitutes, as well as improve AIDS-related knowledge and attitudes, in Mexican male farmworkers ($N = 193$).

Participants in this study were provided AIDS prevention information in the form of Mexican style *fotonovelas* (photo novellas) and *radionovelas* (radio novellas) that were broadcasted daily on a local Spanish language station (participants were given radios and program times). These novellas depicted scenarios in which three male farmworkers used a condom with a prostitute, abstained from sex, and infected his wife and child with HIV, respectively. Also included were instructions on proper condom use and information on the risks of needle sharing.

All participants were given pre- and post-tests. Results showed that these participants made significant gains in AIDS knowledge and related attitudes, and in reported use of condoms with prostitutes. For example, of those men who used prostitutes during the course of the study, 20 of 37 reported condom use after participation in the study, versus 1 of 32 prior to participation.

Because our research reveals poor knowledge of proper condom use (Organista et al., 1996; Organista et al., in press), migrants should be provided with demonstrations and practice with phallic replicas. Furthermore, because carrying condoms has been found to predict condom use with occasional sex partners (Organista, Balls Organista, Garcia de Alba G., and Castillo Moran, in press), migrants should also be given condoms and urged to carry them, given their impoverished and transient lifestyles. In particular, married migrants should be urged to carry condoms because they seem less prepared for safe sex, despite rates of prostitute use comparable to single migrants.

For Latinos, the issue of homosexual contact is complicated by the cultural factor that some Latino men who occasionally have sex with men do not consider themselves homosexual. Research in Mexico has indicated for some time that masculine men who occasionally play the active inserter role with passive, effeminate men may continue to identify themselves as heterosexual and lead predominantly heterosexual lifestyles (Carrier, 1995). In focus groups conducted by the authors, Mexican migrants commonly acknowledged the practice of macho men having sex with men, as previously described, but stopped short of admitting any such personal experience. In fact, only 2% of Mexican migrant men interviewed admitted to homosexual contact (Organista et al., in press).

AIDS prevention interventions with Mexican migrant men must directly address homosexual transmission, via unprotected anal sex, whether or not participants admit to such behavior. In addition, the risk to the females of male sex partners who engage in high risk, unprotected sex with other men needs to be acknowledged. The culture-based responsibility of "protecting one's woman" from contracting a fatal disease should be stressed. One study showed that using condoms to protect one's female partner was a more powerful predictor of condom use than self-protection in Mexican immigrants (Mikawa et al., 1992).

Female-focused interventions. Although Mexican migrants historically have been almost exclusively male, the number of women participating in migratory labor has increased over the last two decades. For example, Massey, Alarcon, Durand, and Gonzalez (1987) found that women comprised 15% to 20% of migrant laborers in four Mexican sending communities surveyed. Within the last two decades, 50% of all Mexican immigrants have been women (Vernez and Ronfeldt, 1991).

We have found that Mexican migrants in general and migrant women in particular believe that women who carry condoms would be seen as promiscuous (Balls Organista and Organista, in press; Organista et al., in press). As such, this strategy, as well as discussing condom use with male partners, runs contrary to culture and gender norms. Although the power differential in traditional Mexican gender roles places women at a disadvantage, female-focused prevention strategies should not be totally abandoned.

Strategies that activate self-protection against AIDS in Mexican migrant women may be consistent with the gender role expansion experienced by these women. Guendelman (1987) has found that seasonal migration to the United States expands the traditional roles of Mexican women to include earning wages, greater purchasing power, more involvement in family decision making, more division of household responsibility with husbands, greater feelings of autonomy, and even lower stress levels than nonworking migrant women. Perhaps the central, culture-based role of being a protective mother can be used to persuade Latinas to think about precautions to prevent the congenital transmission of AIDS to children. Furthermore, an appeal can be made to the woman's role as primary caretaker within the family, and the strong relation between her health and her ability to attend to the family's welfare.

Counselors will need to develop innovative methods of assisting traditional Latinas with the process of verbally negotiating, with their male sex partners, the use of condoms. For example, Comas-Díaz (1985) and Comas-Díaz and Duncan (1985) discussed guidelines for culturally sensitive assertiveness training with Latinas that begins by teaching women to preface their requests to men with qualifiers such as *Con todo respeto* (With all due respect), or *¿Me permite decir algo?* (Will you permit me to say something?). These statements acknowledge the status differential between traditional men and women in a respectful manner and increase the probability of more open communication. In the event that the man does not want to discuss condom use or becomes angry, a counselor can instruct the woman to say something like "I am going to feel very hurt if you do not allow me my say" or "It makes it difficult to feel close to you if you do not consider my view." Women can also remind their male partners of their responsibility to protect them, in this case by using condoms to prevent the possibility of AIDS. Counselors should liberally apply their knowledge of role playing and role reversal to provide practice for such new communication behavior.

These suggestions break new ground in Mexican gender roles, and as such can be challenging interventions. However, in the United States, Latinas represent 21% of all adult female AIDS cases (Amaro, 1988) and Latino children comprise 24% of all pediatric AIDS cases (Centers for Disease Control and Prevention, 1993). These alarming rates warrant serious thinking about the development of gender- and culture-sensitive interventions for Latinas in general, and Mexican migrant women in particular.

CONCLUSION

The counseling profession's mandate to provide culturally responsive mental health services now extends to health care issues, given the increasingly popular subspecialties of behavioral medicine and health psychology (Dworkin and Pincu, 1993; Keeling, 1993). The threat of an imminent AIDS epidemic in the Mexican migrant labor population represents a formidable yet stimulating challenge to counselors interested in applying their knowledge of counseling and ethnic minorities to the complex intersection of AIDS, sexual behavior, culture norms, gender roles, and migratory labor. Although AIDS-related data on Mexican migrant laborers are scarce, we have developed a survey data base with implications for conducting culture and gender sensitive prevention interventions with this unique and extremely marginalized population of Latinos.

BIBLIOGRAPHY

Amaro, H. (1988). Considerations for prevention of HIV infection among Hispanic women. *Psychology of Women Quarterly*, 12, 429–443.

Balls Organista, P., and Organista, K. C. (in press). Exploring AIDS-related knowledge, attitudes, and behaviors in female Mexican migrant laborers. *Health and Social Work*.

Bronfman, M., and Minello, N. (1992). *Habitos sexuales de los migrantes temporales Mexicanos a los Estados Unidos de America, practicas de riesgo, para la infección por VIH* [Sexual habits of seasonal Mexican migrants to the United States of America, risk practices for HIV infection]. Mexico: El Colegio de Mexico.

Carrier, J. (1995). *De los otros: Intimacy and homosexuality among Mexican men*. New York: Columbia University Press.

Carrier, J. M., and Magaña, J. R. (1991). Use of ethnosexual data on men of Mexican origin for HIV/AIDS prevention programs. *The Journal of Sex Research*, 28(2), 189–202.

Centers for Disease Control and Prevention. (1993). National Center for Infectious Diseases. Division of HIV/AIDS. *HIV AIDS Surveillance*. Feb. 1993: Year-end ed., Dec. 1992.

Comas-Díaz, L. (1985). Cognitive and behavioral group therapy with Puerto Rican women: A comparison of content themes. *Hispanic Journal of Behavioral Sciences*, 7(3), 273–283.

Comas-Díaz, L., and Duncan, J. W. (1985). The cultural context: A factor in assertiveness training with mainland Puerto Rican women. *Psychology of Women Quarterly*, 9, 463–476.

Connor, R. (1992). *Preventing AIDS among migrant Latino workers: An intervention and model*. Manuscript prepared for University of California/Healthnet Wellness Lecture Series.

de la Vega, E. (1990). Considerations for reaching the Latino population with sexuality and HIV/AIDS information and education. *Siecus Report*, 18(3), 1–8.

Department of Health and Human Services. (1990). *An atlas of state profiles which estimate number of migrant and seasonal farmworkers and members of their families*. Washington, DC: Office of Migrant Health.

Díaz, T., Buehler, J. W., Castro, K. G., and Ward, J. W. (1993). AIDS trends among Hispanics in the United States. *American Journal of Public Health*, 83(4), 504–509.

Dworkin, S. H., and Pincu, L., (1993). Counseling in the era of AIDS. *Journal of Counseling and Development*, 71, 275–281.

Guendelman, S. (1987). The incorporation of Mexican women in seasonal migration: A study of gender differences. *Hispanic Journal of Behavioral Sciences*, 9, 245–264.

Kaplan, R. M. (1991). Counseling psychology in health settings: Promise and challenge. *The Counseling Psychologist*, 19, 376–381.

Keeling, R. P. (1993). HIV disease: Current concepts. *Journal of Counseling and Development*, 71, 261–274.

Lafferty, J. (1991). Self-injection and needle sharing among migrant farmworkers. *American Journal of Public Health*, 81(2), 221.

Lopez, R., and Ruiz, J. D. (1995). *Seroprevalence of Human Immunodeficiency Virus Type I and Syphilis and assessment of risk behaviors among migrant and seasonal farmworkers in Northern California*. Manuscript prepared for Office of AIDS. California Department of Health Services.

Magaña, J. R. (1991). Sex, drugs and HIV: An ethnographic approach. *Society, Science and Medicine*, 33(1), 5–9.

Massey, D., Alarcon, R., Durand, J., and Gonzalez, H. (1987). *Return to Aztlan: The social process of international migration from Western Mexico*. Berkeley, CA: University of California Press.

Mikawa, J. K., Morones, P. A., Gomez, A., Case, H. L., Olsen, D., and Gonzales-Huss, M. J. (1992).

Cultural practices of Hispanics: Implications for the prevention of AIDS. *Hispanic Journal of Behavioral Sciences*, 14, 421–433.

Myers, J. E. (1992). Wellness, prevention, development: The cornerstone of the professional. *Journal of Counseling and Development*, 71, 136–139.

National Commission to Prevent Infant Mortality. (1993). HIV/AIDS: A growing crisis among migrant and seasonal farmworker families. Washington, DC: Author.

Organista, K. C., and Balls Organista, P. (1997). Migrant laborers and AIDS in the United States: A review of the literature. *AIDS Education and Prevention*, 91(1), 83–93.

Organista, K. C., Balls Organista, P., Garcia de Alba G., J. E., and Castillo Moran, M. A. (in press). Psychological predictors of condom use in Mexican migrant laborers. *Interamerican Journal of Psychiatry*.

Organista, K. C., Balls Organista, P., Garcia de Alba G., J. E., Castillo Moran, M. A., and Carrillo, H. (1996). AIDS and condom-related knowledge, beliefs, and behaviors in Mexican migrant laborers. *Hispanic Journal of Behavioral Sciences*, 18 (3), 392–406.

Organista, K. C., Balls Organista, P., Garcia de Alba G., J. E. Castillo Moran, M. A., and Ureta Carrillo, L. E. (in press). Survey of condom-related beliefs, behaviors, and perceived social norms in Mexican migrant laborers. *Journal of Community Health*.

Vernez, G., and Ronfeldt, D. (1991). The current situation in Mexican immigration. *Science*, 25, 1189–1193.

Wyatt, G. E. (1994). The sociocultural relevance of sex research: Challenges for the 1990s and beyond. *American Psychologist*, 49(8), 748–754.

PART VII.

Psychological Distress

Culture shapes how we construct our social environment and how we experience and describe our internal states. In this context, it is not entirely surprising that the manner in which we experience, express and respond to psychological distress will be largely influenced by our cultural beliefs, attitudes, and values. For instance, past studies show that American Indians and Asian and Hispanic Americans may hold cultural conceptualizations and manifestations of depressive and anxiety symptoms. With the advent of culturally appropriate assessment tools and research methods, psychologists are finally beginning to understand the extent and nature of psychological distress for different ethnic groups in the United States.

The study by Amado Padilla and colleagues was one of the first to investigate the stressors and coping responses of Mexican and Central American immigrants. Although this article is relatively older than the other section selections, the descriptive data remain relevant to the experiences of many recently arrived Hispanic immigrants and refugees. As you read this article, consider how the cultural coping patterns of these groups challenge prevailing stereotypes of Hispanic immigrants entering the United States.

The article by Shelley Adler compels us to extend our current conceptualizations of psychological distress to include culture-bound syndromes. Does our current diagnostic system fully capture the supranormal experiences of the Hmong in this study? Adler attempts to address this question in her examination of Sudden Unexpected Nocturnal Death Syndrome (SUNDS). The phenomenon of SUNDS is a powerful example of how culture and religion influence our experiences and expressions of psychological distress.

The articles by Stanley Sue and his colleagues, and Francis Abueg and Kevin Chun primarily focus on the extent of psychological distress among Asian Americans. As detailed by Sue and his colleagues, the heterogeneity evidenced in the Asian American population presents numerous methodological challenges in determining the prevalence of mental disorders for Asian Americans. Furthermore, as detailed in Abueg and Chun's article, differences in diagnostic criteria and assessment tools across studies lead to further complications in establishing rates of psychological distress. Still, both articles present prevalence data for different Asian American groups which defy the "model minority" stereotype.

Lastly, the article by Robert Roberts, Catherine Roberts, and Richard Chen makes an important contribution to the literature by examining rates of depression among ethnic minority adolescents. Prior to their study, relatively little attention was given to studying rates of mental disorders for this unique population. As you read their article, you will once again discover the importance of making cross-cultural comparisons in determining prevalence and risk status for ethnically diverse samples.

FURTHER READINGS

Hall, C. C. I. (1995). Asian eyes: Body image and eating disorders of Asian and Asian American women. *Eating Disorders: The Journal of Treatment and Prevention, 3,* 8–19.

Kinzie, J. D., Leung, P. K., Boehnlein, J., Matsunaga, D., Johnson, R., Manson, S., Shore, J. H., Heinz, J., and Williams, M. (1992). Psychiatric epidemiology of an Indian village. The *Journal of Nervous and Mental Disease, 180,* 33–39.

Lin, K. M., Lau, J. K. C., Yamamoto, J., Zheng, Y. P., Kim, H. S., Cho, K. H., and Nakasaki, G. (1992). Hwa-Byung: A community study of Korean Americans. *The Journal of Nervous and Mental Disease, 180,* 386–391.

Lorenzo, M. K., Pakiz, B., Reinherz, H. Z., and Frost, A. (1995). Emotional and behavioral problems of Asian American adolescents: A comparative study. *Child and Adolescent Social Work Journal, 12,* 197–212.

Neal, A. M., and Turner, S. M. (1991). Anxiety disorders research with African Americans: Current status. *Psychological Bulletin, 109,* 400–410.

15.
Coping Responses to Psychosocial Stressors Among Mexican and Central American Immigrants

Amado M. Padilla, Richard C. Cervantes, Margarita Maldonado, and Rosa E. Garcia

This study examined the psychosocial stressors experienced by Mexican and Central American immigrants to the United States. Semistructured interviews were conducted with 62 respondents, half of whom were males, who were nearly equally divided between Mexicans and Central Americans. Major identified group stressors were obtaining employment and related financial difficulties, the language barrier of not speaking English, and problems in adapting to the life-style of the United States. Use of a social support network was found effective as a coping response for seeking and obtaining employment, locating a place to live, and overcoming language difficulties. Married respondents with children expressed concern about the availability of drugs and about low moral standards, which they said characterized U.S. society. Men were found to score higher on a measure of depression than were women. This may be due to greater role strain experienced by men who have limited resources to use in the care of their families.

The study of adaptation of recent Latin American immigrants to the United States is an area of investigation that has received little systematic attention in the behavioral sciences. Although adaptation, and more specifically "coping," has progressively become a prominent area of investigation in the general population (Billings and Moos, 1984; Lazarus and Folkman, 1984; Pearlin and Schooler, 1978), little is known about specific coping responses used by immigrants. Information of this type is needed given the large rate of growth of the Hispanic immigrant population. Recent estimates indicate that Hispanics will constitute the largest ethnic minority group in the United States by the year 2000, if not sooner (Congressional Hispanic Caucus, Inc., 1984). The mental health-related needs of this growing community can only be effectively met through a greater understanding of the psychosocial process of immigration. Systematic information is needed with respect to the specific forms of psychosocial stressors experienced by immigrants and to their adaptations to their new environment.

Unlike coping research conducted with other population groups, for example, families of cancer patients (Koocher, 1986), housewives (Kandel, Davies, and Raveis, 1985), and normal community respondents (Pearlin, Menaghan, Lieberman, and Mullan, 1981), event-specific coping research is absent for Latin American immigrants. Although a few coping studies have been conducted with Mexican Americans (California Department of Mental Health, 1982; Mendoza, 1981; Perez, 1983), these studies have examined specific and nongeneralizable samples (e.g., university students, pregnant women). Needless to say, these studies shed little light on the specific stress and coping experiences among recent Latin American immigrants.

Observers have suggested that recent Latin American immigrants are exposed to a variety of stressors associated with language barriers, lowered economic levels, lack of education and work skills, and discrimination (Acosta, 1979; Cervantes and Castro, 1985; Salcido, 1982). In addition, Cervantes and Castro (1985) have presented a framework for conducting systematic research on life domain stressors among Hispanics. The model draws heavily upon the work of Pearlin and associates who attempt to classify stressors along specific life domains including marriage, family, occupation, and economics (Pearlin and Schooler, 1978). Pearlin's approach allows for a much richer description of life stressors and the specific forms of coping that individuals use in confronting these difficulties. Earlier work has assumed general coping styles or types, yet this approach is insufficient since coping is a dynamic process that changes over time (Fleming, Baum, and Singer, 1984). For example, one often confronts problems of living in a trial-and-error way until the most effective coping strategy is hit upon. The definition of coping has expanded to include both cognitive and behavioral efforts to reduce the sources of stress, and these differing forms of coping may often be used together. For instance, language barriers have been identified as a major source of stress for recent Latin American immigrants. What is not known, though, is how these immigrants adapt to the problem of lack of fluency in English to lessen whatever subjective discomfort they may experience from not speaking English. Immigrants also comment on the discriminatory practices of such persons as employers and apartment managers, but little is known about how immigrants circumvent these practices as they adjust to life in the United States.

Drawing upon these concepts, the primary focus of this investigation was to study stress and coping responses qualitatively among immigrants from both Mexico and Central America in general life domains of marriage, family life, occupation, and household finances following the work of Pearlin et al. (1981). Another purpose was to verify the existence of culturally specific stress and coping responses identified by Cervantes and Castro (1985) such as acculturation stress (e.g., language barriers) and perceived discrimination. The addition of these two areas of potential stress to the domains outlined by Pearlin et al. is important since they are consistently mentioned in many impressionistic reports and by those providing clinical services to immigrants. A final objective was to examine the role of gender in the stress-coping process. This was particularly important since recent studies report differing levels of psychological distress among Latin Americans as a function of gender. Although many recent immigrants share common stress and coping experiences, it is also true that gender role demands are different and may shift markedly in making the transition from one culture to another.

METHOD

Respondents

A stratified representative sampling approach was used within three areas of high Hispanic immigrant density. Three bilingual male-female interview teams selected an adult male or female from every third dwelling in the three predesignated areas for interviewing. A total of 244 eligible persons were approached, and 62 consented to be interviewed, resulting in an acceptance rate of 25%. The issue of legal status likely contributed to an acceptance rate that is considerably lower than that realized for similar community studies.

All interviewed respondents were selected on the basis of having resided in the United States for less than 10 years. This ensured relative recency of immigration with accompanying stress-coping experiences characteristic of recent immigrants. In addition, we sought to have equal numbers of males and females and of Mexicans and Central Americans in the sample. Accordingly, 32 respondents were Mexican and 30 respondents represented various Central American subgroups (El Salvador, $n = 17$; Guatemala, $n = 11$; Honduras, $n = 1$; Nicaragua, $n = 1$). All interviews were conducted in Spanish and lasted approximately 1 hour.

The mean age of respondents was 33.8 years. Over half of the respondents were married (56%), and 80% reported having one or more children. The mean monthly household income was $1,189.00, and the average total number of persons living in the home was 5. Respondents averaged 5.5 years of residence in the United States and reported economic reasons as the predominant motivator for migration (56%). Sixteen percent of the sample reported migrating for the purpose of reuniting with family, whereas an additional 15% left their country of origin as a result of political warfare. Mean level of education for all respondents prior to migration was 6.9 years, and 84% of the sample was predominantly Spanish-speaking.

Procedures

Participation was requested following a brief introduction to the study. Special care was taken to assure the immigrants that the study was in no way connected with Immigration and Naturalization Services (INS). Upon consenting to participate, respondents were administered an in-depth open-ended stress and coping interview. In addition to covering issues related to stress in the family, marriage, economic matters, and occupation, respondents were asked about stress related to culture change and discrimination. The open-ended questions asked about general stress and coping experiences of all Latino immigrants (e.g., "In your opinion what are three things that make life difficult for Latinos living in the United States?"), while also asking questions more specific to the individual respondent (e.g., "What were the most difficult experiences *you* had during your first year living in the United States?"). Each set of stress responses was then followed by coping prompts (e.g., "How did you resolve the problem of not having a job when you first came to this country?"; "What did you do if you thought that morals in the United States. were too liberal?"). An attempt was made to obtain up to three specific reports of behaviors of the respondent for each reported stress event. The notion was to collect situation-specific stress-reduction behaviors as opposed to a more general coping style. Each interview was audio recorded.

Following the semistructured interview, respondents were asked to complete the depression and anxiety subscales of the Symptom Checklist–90 Revised (Derogatis, 1978), the Rosenberg Self-Esteem Scale (Rosenberg, 1965), and the Campbell Self-Competence Scale (Campbell, Converse, Miller, and Stokes, 1960). These instruments were previously translated into Spanish by a team of three bilingual researchers and then back-translated. Content discrepancies were discussed until conceptual equivalence of the scales was obtained.

RESULTS

In an effort to review systematically the semistructured interview data, a content analysis of each interview was conducted. Three bilingual judges trained in content analysis by a clinical psychologist proceeded to analyze each interview, selecting out specific stress events and associated coping strategies. Following this, a coding scheme was developed that permitted computer analysis of the data.

Internal consistency reliability coefficients were conducted for each of the four scales used in the study. SCL-90R symptom scales were found to be reliable for this sample. The alpha coefficient for the depression subscale was $\alpha = .85$. The coefficient for the anxiety subscale was $\alpha = .86$. The self-esteem scale was found to be relatively reliable for this sample, $\alpha = .66$, whereas the personal competence scale was found to be unstable, $\alpha = .51$. Given the relatively low estimate of internal consistency for the personal competence scale, it was excluded from this report.

Adaptation/Acculturation Stress

In response to the question, "In your opinion what three things make life difficult for Latinos in this country?" 64% of the males and 83% of the females indicated that not knowing English was the most difficult thing. Not having a job was reported as the second most difficult issue for 51% of the males and 48% of the females. Undocumented status was the next most frequently mentioned response (30% of the total sample) followed by adaptation problems such as transportation and life-style (24%), discrimination (22%), and not having enough money (13%).

In making the question more specific by asking "What were *your* most difficult experiences during your first year here?" respondents reported not having a job (48% males; 42% females) as the most common stressor. This was followed by not knowing English (32% males; 32% females); difficulty in adapting to this country (22% males; 13% females); and not knowing anyone who could help find a job, help with English, or help with children (16% males; 9% females).

Because problems related to language were often referred to in reply to these two questions, coping strategies associated with language were important. In reply to the general assessment "difficult for Latinos," 59% of the subjects indicated that going to school to learn English or some other method of learning English was the preferred way to overcome the language problem. However, surprisingly, in reply to the more specific question regarding themselves, only 4 respondents indicated that studying English was their chosen solution. The most common response was "listening to others speak English" (30%). Other behaviors used by a smaller percentage of respondents included depending on others to interpret, speaking with only those fluent in Spanish, and looking for work in places where there are other Spanish speakers.

Next, responses to not having a job were examined. Of the 31 respondents who reported employment as a stressor in response to the general question, 74% were able to provide some coping response. However, there was no commonly agreed upon response for finding employment. Twenty-two percent said looking for a job, whatever or wherever it might be, was the best solution. This was followed by such things as depending on family or friends (9%), going to school to learn a new skill (6%), working in the fields (3%), or going to factories (3%).

When asked how they dealt with the problem of finding a job, 42% said they sought the assistance of family and friends. Another 28% stated that they would go out looking for work, whatever and wherever it might be. This was followed by responses such as working for less money or trying to be friendly in order to persuade someone to hire them.

We also sought information about stressors associated with leaving their country of origin. In reply to this question, 77% of the males and 93% of the females said the most difficult thing was leaving behind (and now missing) family members and friends. This was followed by less frequent replies such as "leaving my neighborhood" (19% males; 16% females) and "leaving customs of my country" (6% males; 9% females).

Coping with the absences of loved ones resulted in a variety of direct action responses such as maintaining frequent contact by writing letters (20%), telephoning (17%), helping economically by sending money (11%), and visiting family by returning home for a period of time (4%). A few respondents (7%) said that they had solved this problem by bringing (or intending to bring) their children to live with them. One in 6 respondents indicated that there was nothing they could do but resign themselves to the fact that they were separated from their family.

Economic Stress

We were also interested in knowing what economic stressors were associated with recent immigration to the United States. To this question, 74% of the men and 87% of the women said that not having sufficient money for necessities such as rent, food, clothing, and transportation was the major stressor. Understandably, 54% of the males and 45% of the females next indicated that the absence of work was a problem. This was then followed by not being able to find an affordable place to live (35% males; 16% females).

Assistance from family and friends, including having several persons or even families pool together money in order to rent an apartment or house was the most common coping action (28%) given in reply to the problem of housing. Following this, respondents indicated finding a job as rapidly as possible (18%), regardless of what or where it might be, as the next best form of coping. It is important to note that of all respondents identifying financial problems as a primary source of psychosocial stress, only one respondent indicated that returning to Mexico would be a viable solution.

Regarding those specific problems associated with securing employment during their first year in the United States, 40% of the respondents indicated that not knowing English was the primary barrier (51% males; 29% females). Ways of overcoming language barriers were identical to those noted earlier.

Family Stress

Because of the importance given to family cohesion by Latino immigrants, we asked "What major changes do Latino families make in becoming accustomed to American culture?" Thirty-five percent of the respondents stated that adapting to the different food, transportation, and life-style constituted the major changes that the Latino family had to make. Another 25% of the respondents mentioned that having to learn English altered the family; however, it was not clear what this implied. Education was identified by 12% as different from the system to which they were accustomed and as requiring adjustment on their part. Interestingly, a few respondents (8%) mentioned that a stressor for them had to do with the fact that their children could not speak Spanish and did not know the country from which their parents had immigrated. Another 5% felt too dependent on their children and were troubled by this dependency.

Some of our respondents also expressed concern for differences in morality between themselves and Americans. For instance, 16% felt that Americans were much more liberal and that divorce was a problem among Americans.

A follow-up question was asked with regard to current family concerns, worries, and stressors. Forty percent of respondents indicated that ensuring their children received a good education was a primary preoccupation. Thirty-three percent were concerned that their children not develop drug, alcohol, or tobacco addictions, and 18% hoped that their children would develop healthy friendships with "good" children. The need to improve family living conditions was mentioned as a major concern for 11% of the respondents, while an additional 11% were concerned about the general health and well-being of other family members.

We also asked questions related to marital stress and found few stressors in this life area. Forty of our 62 respondents were married, and few indicated any problems. For instance, only 20% of the married respondents expressed any concern because both husband and wife had to work. Similarly only 2 of our 20 married male respondents felt that Latina women had become "too liberal" in the United States.

Finally, we asked our respondents whether they were satisfied with their decision to immigrate to the United States. Eighty-eight percent said yes.

Depression and Anxiety

A final set of analyses was conducted to examine the extent to which the respondents suffered from detectable levels of depression and anxiety. T scores were computed for the SCL-90R anxiety and depression subscales. These T scores are based on nonpatient majority group norms, and therefore caution should be noted for interpreting the definition of "caseness" for this immigrant sample. Overall, the sample obtained a mean T score for depression of 58.5. The mean anxiety T score was 55.7 Central Americans scored slightly higher on the depression scale (M = 59.9) than the Mexican subsample (M = 57.1). A similar pattern was observed for anxiety, with Central Americans scoring somewhat higher (M = 58.3) than Mexicans (M = 52.9). These differences were, however, not statistically significant. When comparing our male and female subsamples, a highly significant difference emerged, with males scoring much higher on the depression scale (M = 62.6) compared to female respondents (M = 54.9, p < .05). No gender difference was found for the measure of anxiety, although there was a trend with males again scoring higher (M = 58.5) as compared to their female counterparts (M = 53.1, p < .09).

Self-Esteem

The relationship between the personal mediating variable of self-esteem and the mental health indicators (e.g., depression and anxiety) was also examined. No group differences in self-esteem scores either for gender or for country of origin were found.

A series of correlations was then computed to examine the relationship between self-esteem and mental health status. Correlations were run for the entire sample, as well as for gender and country of origin subsamples. For the group as a whole, self-esteem was found to correlate significantly and in a negative direction with both depression scores ($r = -.31$; $p < .05$) and anxiety scores ($r = -.35$; $p < .05$).

A similar set of correlations was calculated for gender. No significant correlations for the male subsample were found. In contrast, for females self-esteem was found to correlate significantly with both depression scores ($r = -.44$; $p < .05$) and anxiety scores ($r = -.51$; $p < .05$).

When examining the role of ethnicity, Central American scores on the depression and anxiety scales did not correlate in any significant manner with self-esteem. In contrast, self-esteem scores were found to correlate significantly and negatively with scores on anxiety ($r = -.44$; $p < .05$) for the Mexican subsample.

Given the importance of language as a principle area of psychosocial stress for our respondents, we decided to examine the relationship between self-esteem and symptom dimensions for those who reported some English proficiency ($n = 35$) versus those with no proficiency in English ($n = 27$). Although no differences between these two groups were noted for the symptom dimensions, a significant difference was obtained on self-esteem with those having some English proficiency scoring higher than non-English speakers ($t = -2.92$; $df = 61$; $p < .05$).

A final set of analyses was conducted to examine the relative strength of key demographic variables and self-esteem in predicting symptom scores. Two stepwise multiple regressions were conducted for the pooled sample. In the first regression equation, the variables of education, income, age, years of living in the United States, and self-esteem were entered as predictors of anxiety. The strongest predictor of anxiety scores was self-esteem, which accounted for 13% ($B = -.358$; $p < .05$) of the variance. None of the demographic variables proved to be significant predictors of anxiety scores.

An identical procedure was conducted using depression scores as the dependent variable. Again, self-esteem was the best predictor, accounting for 15% ($B = -.311$; $p < .05$) of the variance in depression scores. Age explained another 6% ($B = -.247$; $p < .05$) of the total variance in depression scores.

DISCUSSION

Immigration is known to be a stressful event in the life of an individual. The purpose of this study was to obtain information concerning the specific stressors experienced by Mexican and Central American immigrants to the United States and to document behaviors in which they engaged to reduce the stress associated with these events. The three major stressors reported by our immigrants were (a) not being able to communicate in English, (b) difficulties in finding employment, and (c) being in the United States illegally. These three stressors were in turn associated with numerous other economic and familial stressors. For instance, our respondents frequently mentioned such stressors as not having enough money to pay bills, difficulty in finding suitable housing, and having to work at whatever types of jobs were available and at whatever wage the employer offered.

Methods for resolving these stressors were interesting, since respondents expressed well-considered responses for overcoming a particular barrier; but, when specifically asked what they had done about lessening the tension created by a personal stress event, it was not unusual to learn that the respondents had not followed their own advice. For instance, our only university-educated respondent, when asked about problems encountered by Latinos, stated, "Well, it's difficult to adapt, the system of work here is a little harder, and the language difference is hard to overcome." In replying to the question of how to resolve these problems our respondent elaborated,

> Well, many make use of other people who can help them, like other Latinos who know English; knowing the language opens the door to jobs and moreover knowing English is indispensible, but if you only speak Spanish you will never learn English.

Still later our respondent said,

> The most difficult experience was not being able to communicate with other people. I felt impotent. . . . The only thing to do is to learn it as fast as possible.

At the same time, although our respondent seemed to be aware that not speaking English was a problem, and aware of what he could do about it, he admitted later in the interview that he had not found the time to study English and still did not speak much English. As a matter of fact, he was now working successfully as a cabinetmaker, but had studied to be a psychologist in Guatemala.

Repeatedly, the problem of language surfaced as a major stressor in association with other problems in adapting to and carving out a livelihood in this country. However, the language barrier for our respondents appeared almost insurmountable for at least two reasons. First, most of our respondents had little formal education and were intimidated by formal methods for learning English such as adult education. Second, because our respondents had little in the way of financial resources with which to sustain themselves, they had no alternative but to find employment as quickly as possible, which left no time to acquire some survival English skills first.

Most of our respondents provided information about the importance of family and friends as a support system that made the path of immigration somewhat smoother. It was not unusual, for example, to learn that friends or family members had assisted with housing in the days and months after immigration. Also, employment was frequently secured through contacts that a person was able to make because of family or acquaintances in the United States. More than anything else, it appeared that the immigrants' social network is the single most important factor in assisting the transition to a new way of life for the recent Latin American arrival. Our research did not attempt to assess the extent of the social network (e.g., number of family and friends) nor the quality of support offered. Prior research (e.g., Keefe and Padilla, 1987) has shown that immigrants have limited social networks in comparison to later generation Mexican-Americans. Further, it would be important to learn how effective, useful, or accurate the support is that immigrants receive from other immigrants who themselves have limited exposure to the English language and U.S. culture and who may also be experiencing a similar level of acculturative stress.

Respondents often indicated that part of the stress they experienced was due to discrimination against Latinos. For example, many indicated that Americans treated them unfairly and had negative stereotypes of them. Respondents stated that generally they believed that Americans thought them to be dirty, welfare recipients, and drunkards. In contrast, they believed that employers thought they were hard workers, but still treated their American co-workers better. Respondents offered few strategies for coping with prejudice and discrimination. They felt that all they could do was to ignore this problem since they would otherwise lose their job or place of residence. Resignation to discrimination directed against them, often because of their illegal status, was commonly mentioned by our respondents. Many also felt that because of their inability to speak English they could do little about how job supervisors or co-workers treated them.

Another important finding was the significantly higher depression scores for males in the study. Studies have shown that Hispanic women score significantly higher than Anglo women on depression (Roberts and Roberts, 1982). However, this is the first reported finding of immigrant males scoring higher on depression than their female counterparts. This difference may be due, in part, to the fact that our male respondents were more likely to be employed and therefore were subjected to more stressors. Because of the few coping strategies available to them, they may experience a greater sense of helplessness and depression. Role strain caused by loss of social status and having few economic or personal resources available to use in the care of family members may also be responsible for the higher depression scores of males. Respondents acknowledged that in many cases, their wives had to work in order for them to survive economically.

When examining the role of personal resources in buffering the effects of psychosocial stress we were able to identify some rather interesting patterns. For example, low self-esteem was found to be related to increased anxiety for our Mexican subsample and was related to increased anxiety and depression in the female subsamples. Self-esteem also appeared to be more important than demographic characteristics, including years lived in the United States, in accounting for increases in both anxiety and depression. Future research should investigate the extent to which self-esteem serves to buffer the effects of exposure to the kinds of stressors this research had identified. It is unfortunate that the measure of personal competence could not be used because of the unreliability of the scale, but in the future, perhaps, a reliable scale can be found in order to use multiple measures of personality characteristics.

Of particular interest here is the role of English-language proficiency in the maintenance or enhancement of self-esteem. Our data suggest that higher levels of English proficiency are associated with greater self-esteem scores. Language proficiency obviously is a key, as many of our respondents mentioned, to creating a more successful life in the United States. With greater English-language skills come increased opportunities, economic enhancement, and associated feelings (i.e., self-esteem) about one's ability to function in society.

Surprisingly, with very few exceptions our respondents expressed satisfaction with their decision to immigrate, and few expressed an interest in returning to their native country. As with other groups of immigrants before them, they believe that ultimately, their life circumstances will improve. They expressed hope for their children through education, even though they worried about the abundance of drugs in their new environment and the apparent lack of values and respect for the family found in American society. Fears about drugs availability and bad peer influences on their children were also seen as stressors by respondents. Their primary response to this was to try to instill a sense of respect in their children and to instruct them about the harmful consequences of drug use. No respondent mentioned that his or her children were actually involved in such drug use.

In sum, we have identified several themes that play a role in the psychological adjustment of recent Latin American immigrants. These stress themes are important for social
service provision to the growing Hispanic population, as well as for directing future
research. For those who work in direct service settings, it would be useful to explore the
deleterious effects of adaptive demands (e.g., language barriers, economic constraints,
separation from family members), and to be able to aid the immigrant in formulating
responses that are effective in alleviating the various sources of psychosocial stress. For
researchers, culturally specific processes of stress and coping need greater elaboration especially among immigrant populations. We need information about what immigrants say and
do about their life situation after immigration. Only then can we understand better their
adjustment to life in the adopted country.

NOTE

This research was supported by the National Institute of Mental Health, Division of Biometry
and Applied Sciences, Minority Research Branch, Grant No. MH 24854 to the senior author,
and by the UCLA Program on Mexico.

BIBLIOGRAPHY

Acosta, F. X. (1979). Barriers between mental health services and Mexican-Americans: An exami-
    nation of a paradox. *American Journal of Community Psychology*, 7, 503–520.
Billings, A. G., and Moos, R. H. (1984). Coping, stress, and social resources among adults with
    unipolar depression. *Journal of Personality and Social Psychology*, 46, 877–891.
California Department of Mental Health, Mental Health Promotion Branch. (1982). *Social support:
    A cross-cultural investigation*. Sacaramento, CA: Author.
Campbell, A., Converse, P. E., Miller, W. E., and Stokes, D. E. (1960). *The American voter*. New York:
    Wiley.
Cervantes, R. C., and Castro, F. G. (1985). Stress, coping and Mexican-American mental health:
    A systematic review. *Hispanic Journal of Behavioral Sciences*, 7, 1–73.
Congressional Hispanic Caucus, Inc. (1984). *National directory of Hispanic elected officials*. Washington,
    DC: Author.
Derogatis, L. R. (1978). *SCL-90-R (Revised) version Manual-I*. Baltimore: John Hopkins University
    School of Medicine.
Fleming, R., Baum, A., and Singer, J. E. (1984). Toward an integrative approach to the study of stress.
    Journal of Personality and Social Psychology, 46, 939–949.
Kandel, D. B., Davies, M., and Raveis, V. H. (1985). The stressfulness of daily social roles for women:
    Marital, occupational and household roles. *Journal of Health and Social Behavior*, 26, 64–78.
Keefe, S. E., and Padilla, A. M. (1987). *Chicano ethnicity*. Albuquerque, NM: University of New
    Mexico Press.
Koocher, G. P. (1986). Coping with a death from cancer. *Journal of Consulting and Clinical Psychology*,
    54, 623–631.
Lazarus, R., and Folkman, S. (1984). *Stress, appraisal, and coping*. New York: Springer.
Mendoza, P. (1981). Stress and coping behavior of Anglo and Mexican-American university students.
    In T. H. Escobedo (Ed.), *Education and Chicanos: Issues and research* (Monograph No. 8) (pp. 89–111).
    Los Angeles: Spanish Speaking Mental Health Research Center.
Pearlin, L. T., Menaghan, E. G., Lieberman, M. A., and Mullan, J. T. (1981). The stress process. *Jour-
    nal of Health and Social Behavior*, 22, 337–356.
Pearlin, L. I., and Schooler, C. (1978). The structure of coping. *Journal of Health and Social Behavior*,
    19, 2–21.

Pérez, R. (1983). Effects of stress, social support and style in the adjustment to pregnancy among Hispanic women. *Hispanic Journal of Behavioral Sciences*, 5, 141–161.

Roberts, R. E., and Roberts, C. R. (1982). Marriage, work, and depressive symptoms among Mexican Americans. *Hispanic Journal of Behavioral Sciences*, 4, 199–221.

Rosenberg, M. (1965). *Society and the adolescent self-image*. Princeton, NJ: Princeton University Press.

Salcido, R. M. (1982). Use of services in Los Angeles County by undocumented families: Their perceptions of stress and source of support. *California Sociologist*, 5, 119–131.

Warheit, G. J., Vega, W. A., Auth, J., and Meinhardt, K. (1985). Mexican-American immigration and mental health: A comparative analysis of psychosocial stress and dysfunction. In N. A. Vega and M. R. Miranda (Eds.), *Stress and Hispanic mental health: Relating research to service delivery* (pp. 76–109). Rockville, MD: National Institute of Mental Health.

16.
Refugee Stress and Folk Belief
Hmong Sudden Deaths

Shelley R. Adler

Since the first reported death in 1977, scores of seemingly healthy Hmong refugees have died mysteriously and without warning from what has come to be known as Sudden Unexpected Nocturnal Death Syndrome (SUNDS). To date medical research has provided no adequate explanation for these sudden deaths. This study is an investigation into the changing impact of traditional beliefs as they manifest during the stress of traumatic relocation. In Stockton, California, 118 Hmong men and women were interviewed regarding their awareness of and personal experience with a traditional nocturnal spirit encounter. An analysis of this data reveals that the supranormal attack acts as a trigger for Hmong SUNDS.

With the fall of the capital city of Vientiane in 1975, thousands of Hmong fled their native Laos and—often after extended delays in Thai refugee camps—began arriving in the United States. The Hmong are more widely known in the West than other Laotian ethnic groups because of their efforts on behalf of the United States during the war in Viet Nam, particularly after it spread to Laos and Cambodia. Thousands of Hmong were funded directly and secretly by the Central Intelligence Agency to combat the Communist Pathet Lao. Hmong men served as soldiers, pilots, and navigators, and their familiarity with the mountain terrain helped make them remarkable scouts and guerrilla fighters.[1] By the end of the civil war, the Hmong had suffered casualty rates proportionally ten times higher than those of Americans who fought in Viet Nam;[2] it is estimated that nearly one-third of the Laotian Hmong population lost their lives.[1] When the Laotian government changed hands after the departure of American troops, large groups of Hmong were forced to flee Laos rather than chance "re-education" camps or possible death under the new Communist regime.

There are currently over 110,000 Hmong living in the United States, with 70,000 in California's Central Valley alone.[3] The city of Fresno is now home to the largest single community of Hmong in existence. The relocation of this large number of refugees from Laos to the United States has been characterized by extraordinary difficulties.

These displaced and resettled Hmong, while finding welcome freedom from persecution and physical annihilation, are nevertheless going through a grave cultural crisis, immersed as they are, an infinitesimal minority, in overwhelmingly dominant majority modes of living, norms of behavior, beliefs and values. Everywhere they face the possibility of cultural annihilation, and struggle to maintain, for themselves and their children, a clear idea of who they are, of their identity as Hmong, of their place in history and in the cosmic realm of spirits, ancestors' souls and human societies.[4]

The Hmong who have fled Laos leave behind them a homeland ravaged by war, but in their transition to the West they are met with new and unique problems. Those Hmong who have come to the United States find themselves suspended between worlds, in a place where their religion, language and skills are de-contextualized and where their previous social support system is greatly weakened.[5] In particular, for many Hmong the relocation marks the end of the prevalent form of their traditional religious beliefs and practices.

In the traditional Hmong worldview, the natural world is alive with spirits. Trees, mountains, rivers, rocks and lightning are all animated by distinctive spirits. Ancestor spirits not only remain around the living, but play an essential role in complex rituals of reciprocity with their living descendants.

> The Hmong celebrate their humanity not as a discrete and impenetrable part of the natural order, but as part of the circle of life of all creation caught up in the rotation of the seasons, and deeply connected with the configuration of the mountains, and the reincarnation of life from generation to generation, even from species to species. Life, in its myriad forms, is intimately articulated through souls and spirits.[6]

In interviews with refugees, it became clear that many Hmong feared that the ancestor spirits who protected them from harm in Laos would be unable to travel across the ocean to the United States and thus could not shield them from spiritual dangers. Solace was taken, however, in the conviction that the myriad evil spirits who challenged Hmong well-being in Laos would also be prevented from following the Hmong to their new home. Among these evil spirits assumed to have been left behind was the nocturnal pressing spirit *dab tsog* (pronounced "da cho").[7] It soon became frighteningly apparent, however, that this notorious evil spirit had made the journey to America as well.

HMONG SUDDEN UNEXPECTED NOCTURNAL DEATH SYNDROME

Since the first reported case, which occurred in 1977, more than 100 Southeast Asians in the United States have died from the mysterious disorder that is now known as SUNDS, the Sudden Unexpected Nocturnal Death Syndrome.[8] The sudden deaths have an unusually high incidence among Laotians, particularly male Hmong refugees. All but one of the victims have been men, the median age is 33, the median length of time living in the United States before death is 17 months,[9] all were apparently healthy, and all died during sleep. The rate of death from SUNDS has reached alarming proportions: At its peak in 1981–1982, the rate of death among 25–44 year-old Hmong men (92/100,000)[10] was equivalent to the sum of the rates of the five leading causes of natural death among United States males in the same age group.[11]

Despite numerous studies of SUNDS, medical scientists have not been able to determine exactly what is causing the deaths of these seemingly healthy people in their sleep.[12] Biomedical studies have taken into account such varied factors as toxicology,[13–17] heart disease,[12,18,19] genetics,[14,15,20,21] metabolism,[15] and nutrition (particularly thiamine deficiency,[22]) but are no nearer to a comprehensive answer. Current medical opinion appears to favor the role of abnormalities of the cardiac conduction system, although a 1988 report from the Centers for Disease Control indicates the incompleteness of this solution: "Only at night, in times of unusual stress, and possibly in conjunction with other, as yet undefined, factors are these people at risk of developing abnormal electrical impulses in the heart that result in ventricular fibrillation and sudden death."[9]

THE NIGHTMARE SPIRIT

Biomedicine thus provides no adequate answer to the question of what causes SUNDS; from my vantage point in the social sciences, however, I propose that an investigation of Hmong traditional belief can reveal the event that triggers the fatal syndrome. The focus of this research is a supranormal nocturnal experience that I refer to as the "nightmare" and that is familiar to the Hmong. I use the word "nightmare" not in the modern sense of a bad dream, but rather in its original denotation as the nocturnal visit of an evil being that threatens to press the very life out of its terrified victim.[23–25]

According to descriptions of the Nightmare spirit,[26] the sleeper suddenly becomes aware of a presence close at hand. Upon attempting to investigate further, the victim is met with the horrifying realization that he or she is completely paralyzed. The presence is usually felt to be an evil one, and often this impression is confirmed by a visual perception of the being, which places itself on the sleeper's chest and exerts a pressure great enough to interfere with respiration. The classic nightmare experience, then, is characterized by the following symptoms: the impression of wakefulness, immobility, sensation of pressure on the chest, realistic perception of the environment, and intense fear. (To avoid confusion, I use *Nightmare* [upper case] to refer to the spirit or demonic figure to which these nocturnal assaults are attributed and *nightmare* [lower case] to refer to the basic experience; that is, the impression of wakefulness, immobility, realistic perception of the environment, and intense fear[27]).

The case definition presented in the *Final Report of the SUNDS Planning Project*[15] emphasizes the need to observe closely people "who fit the demographic characteristics of SUNDS" and who have transient nocturnal events that include

"(1)   a sense of panic or extreme fear,
(2)   paralysis (partial or complete);
(3)   a sense of pressure on the chest;
(4)   a sense that there is an alien being (animal, human, or spirit) in the room; [and]
(5)   a disturbance in sensation (auditory, visual or tactile)."

This list of five symptoms of SUNDS-related events is identical to the characteristics of the nightmare experience as it is known in countless folk traditions, including those of the Hmong. Since the conditions described by Holtan et al. as "SUNDS-related" are consistent with the symptoms of a Nightmare attack, I decided to investigate the possibility that SUNDS is initiated by such a confrontation.

Based on preliminary fieldwork and a review of previous research, I developed the hypothesis that the supranormal nocturnal experience traditionally known as the nightmare and familiar to the Hmong acts as a trigger for the sudden nocturnal deaths.[28] In order to study the prevalence of the nightmare phenomenon and the role of the nightmare in traditional Hmong culture, I interviewed a representative sample of 118 Hmong in Stockton, California. In the course of research it was necessary to establish the veracity of a series of facts: first, that the Hmong supranormal experience that I had isolated was in fact a culture-specific manifestation of the universal nightmare phenomenon; second, that Hmong belief regarding the experience forms a collective tradition; third, that the Hmong nightmare in specific contexts, causes cataclysmic psychological stress; and fourth, by drawing on the growing medical and anthropological literature on ethnomedical pathogenesis, that intense psychological stress can cause sudden death.

The nightmare syndrome appears to be universal in its occurrence. There are innumerable instances of the nightmare throughout history and in a multitude of cultures; from the ancient Greek *ephialtes* (=leap upon) and Roman *incubus* (= lie upon) to contemporary examples such as French *cauchemar* (from La. *calcare* = to trample upon, squeeze), German *Alpdruck* (= elf pressure), Newfoundland "Old Hag,"[23,24,29] Polish *zmora*, and Mexican *pesadilla*.[30] The nightmare's significance and impact vary considerably in different culture cultural settings, but the core nightmare phenomenology appears to be stable cross-culturally.[31]

THE NIGHTMARE AND SLEEP RESEARCH

The consistent features of the nightmare are better understood with the assistance of concepts from laboratory sleep research. Somnologists distinguish between two major divisions of sleep: active sleep (or REM) and quiet sleep. REM sleep is characterized by brain waves resembling those of wakefulness. Unlike the waking state, however, the body is paralyzed, apparently to keep the sleeper from acting out his or her dreams.[32] In rare instances, this normal muscle inhibition or atonia occurs during partial wakefulness. This condition is known as "sleep paralysis," a stage in which the body is asleep, but the mind is not. Often sleep paralysis is accompanied by hypnagogic hallucinations, which consist of complex visual, auditory, and somatosensory perceptions occurring in the period of falling asleep and resembling dreams.[33]

Sleep paralysis and hypnagogic hallucinations are products of "sleep-onset REM," a REM stage that occurs earlier than usual, when the individual is still partially conscious.[24,30,34] Researchers have shown convincingly that sleep-onset REM accounts for the subjective impression of wakefulness, the feeling of paralysis, and, as a result, the tremendous anxiety that mark the nightmare experience.[23,24,27] I extend these explanations of nightmare symptoms to include the fact that the sense of oppression or weight on the chest and the attendant feature of lying in a supine position are a result of the fact that when the sleeper is lying on his or her back, the atonic muscles of the tongue and esophagus collapse the airway. The relaxed muscles not only hinder breathing, but actually create a sensation of suffocation, strangulation or pressure on the chest of the terrified sleeper.[35] The connection between Nightmare attacks and sleep paralysis is highlighted by the fact that Hmong women report that some men, fearing that deep sleep might bring about their deaths, set their alarm clocks to awaken them every 20 or 30 minutes.[15] Ironically, this type of sleep disruption may actually cause sleep-onset REM and nightmares through the mechanism of "REM pressure."[36–38]

THE HMONG NIGHTMARE

In the Hmong language, the Nightmare spirit is referred to as *dab tsog* ("da cho"). *Dab* is the Hmong word for spirit, and is often used in the sense of an evil spirit. Tsog is the specific name of the Nightmare spirit, and also appears in the phrase used to denote a Nightmare attack, *tsog tsuam* ("cho chua"). *Tsuam* means "to crush, to press, or to smother."[39]

In the sample of Stockton Hmong, a total of 58% (36 men, 33 women) had experienced at least one nightmare. The interviews and the personal narratives they elicited clarified that the Hmong supranormal experience that I had isolated was in fact a cultural manifestation of the Nightmare phenomenon. The following is a portion of a narrative from a 33-year-old Hmong man who had a nightmare experience shortly after his arrival in the United States:

> First, I was surprised, but right away, I got real scared. I was lying in bed. I was so tired, because I was working very hard then. I wanted to go to school, but I had no money. I kept waking up, because I was thinking so much about my problems. I heard a noise, but when I turned—tried—I could not move. My bedroom looked the same, but I could see—in the corner—a dark shape was coming to me. It came to the bed, over my feet, my legs. It was very heavy, like a heavy weight over my whole body, my legs, my chest. My chest was frozen—like I was drowning, I had no air. I tried to yell so someone sleeping very close to me will hear. I tried to move—using a force that I can—a strength that I can have. I thought, "What if I die?" After a long time, it went away; it just left. I got up and turned all the lights on, I was afraid to sleep again.

With regard to the emic term for the nightmare experience, 97% of the informants used either *dab tsog* or *tsog tsuam*. All of those who were able to provide a name for the nocturnal encounter could also define it. This widespread awareness of the Nightmare tradition clearly established that Hmong belief regarding the nightmare forms a collective tradition.

DAB TSOG AND HMONG RELOCATION

Since Hmong who maintain their traditional religious beliefs and practices and those who have converted to Christianity both die of SUNDS, the testing of the hypothesis of a belief-triggered disorder necessitated an exploration of the influence of the Nightmare on Hmong of both religions. In the sample, 54% of traditional Hmong and 72% of Christian Hmong had experienced at least one nightmare. The interview data reveals that psychological stress regarding religious practice is present among both traditional and Christian Hmong refugees in the United States and also that this stress is exacerbated in both groups by the supranormal nocturnal assaults. Traditional Hmong face great difficulty in practicing their religion as they had done in Laos. The inability to obtain animals for slaughter, disruption of clan ties and the scarcity of shamans all contribute to the problem of performing expected religious duties. Many Christian Hmong also retain traditional beliefs and have anxieties about not fulfilling their religious requirements. Some Christian Hmong converted out of a sense of obligation to church sponsors and many experience peer disapproval and clan ostracization. Although the more devout Christians I spoke with denied any ambivalence, many of the Christian Hmong informants described ways in which they combined the two religions in order to prevent incurring the Hmong spirits' wrath. It is striking that of the informants who offered an explanation for the cause of SUNDS, 74% suggested an etiology that was directly spirit-related or involved the absence of traditional religion and ritual from their lives.

I have noted an increased incidence of nightmares during informants' times of stress. (Emotional stress, physical exhaustion and sleep deprivation have been shown to be predisposing factors for sleep-onset REM, see [27, 40–42].) According to the traditional belief informants described, *tsog tsuam* assaults are rarely, if ever, fatal on the first encounter.

> It is believed that once you have one of those nightmares—you are visited by one of the *dab tsog* evil spirits—once you are seen by one of those evil spirits, often they will come back to you, until you have the worst nightmare and probably die.

Usually the lethal potential manifests only after an individual has been given time to rectify a situation, but chooses not to, or is unable to, appease the intruding spirit. As one informant explains, because of traditional countermeasures undertaken in Laos, SUNDS deaths did not occur prior to the Hmong exodus: "There were nightmares, but the sudden death was unheard of. It might have happened, but I never heard of it". None of the informants I interviewed recalled incidents of SUNDS deaths in Laos.[43]

DAB TSOG AND HMONG SUNDS

Aside from the conflict between Hmong traditional religion and Christianity, Hmong refugees have experienced a host of hardships including language and employment problems, changing generational and gender roles,[44] survivor guilt[45] and trauma-induced emotional and psychological disorders.[46–48] These changes can affect all Hmong immigrants in varying degrees, but Hmong men, in particular, have had their roles dramatically altered. This gender dichotomy is mirrored by the vast discrepancy in the ratio of male to female SUND deaths.

Since both Hmong men and women suffer from Nightmare attacks, however, why are SUNDS deaths almost exclusively male? The answer lies in the meaning of Nightmare attacks in traditional Hmong culture. Hmong informants explained that among other religious requirements, one's ancestor spirit must be fed annually. If the ancestor spirits are neglected, they become angry, deserting the individual, the head-of-household, and leaving him vulnerable to evil spirit attacks. Most of the Hmong informants perceived a direct casual relationship between failure to perform traditional Hmong ritual and Nightmare attacks. (Etiologies related to either traditional spirits or to the lack of traditional religious practice constituted 81% of all the nightmare causes suggested.) One Hmong man summarized the widely held belief as follows:

> At least once a year those evil spirits must be fed. If someone forgets to feed them, then they will come back and disturb you. If you have *tsog tsuam,* the ancestor spirit is supposed to protect you. If you feed the ancestor regularly, then whenever you have *tsog tsuam,* the ancestor spirits will protect you. Usually the father, the head-of-household, is responsible for feeding the evil spirits. Women have nightmares, too, but not as often as men. The evil spirit would first attack the head-of-household. Coming to this country, people tend to forget to do the rituals. A lot of people either ignore or forget to practice their religious belief ... .Men are the ones who are responsible for feeding both the evil spirits and the ancestor spirits. Since they are not doing their part, it is logical that their soul should be taken away.

This explanation clearly has great significance for the investigation of SUNDS etiology in that it contains a matter-of-fact description of the precise manner in which a man's failure to fulfil traditional religious obligations can result in his death. The inability to fulfil roles and responsibilities with regard to religion (as well as in their lives generally) has a calamitous impact on the psyche of many Hmong males.

Although Hmong women do experience Nightmare attacks and are aware of the roles of both spirits and the absence of traditional religious practices in SUNDS deaths, they also know that *dab tsog* will seek out their husbands, fathers or brothers and the individuals held accountable. As one Hmong informant recalled of her own nightmare experience, "Even though I was very, very scared, I thought was good my husband wasn't there, so the spirit wouldn't hurt him." Several informants suggested that the one woman who died of SUNDS must have been unmarried or widowed and therefore, as the head of her household, the individual who was held accountable by the spirits.

If the nightmare is usually a transient, non-pathological phenomenon, how can it trigger a fatal disorder among Hmong refugees? Nightmare assaults occurred in Laos, but none of the informants I interviewed recalled incidents of SUNDS death in their homeland. I propose that the differences between the Hmong way of life in pre-war Laos and their current situation in the United States are responsible for this phenomenon. The various resettlement stresses I have discussed manifest most strongly during the initial arrival period, thus explaining the overwhelming preponderance of deaths in the two-year period following resettlement in the United States.[49]

The subject of intense emotional stress as the cause of sudden death is a motif well-represented in world folklore throughout history and has also been a topic of serious biomedical investigation. A number of anthropological and biomedical studies suggest a link between psychological stress and sudden death, see for example.[50–55] In the medical anthropological and ethnomedical literature, the notion of beliefs playing a significant role in illness causation (nocebo effect) or its remedy (placebo effect) is widely held.[56] Robert A. Hahn and Arthur Kleinman's notion of the pathogenic effects of belief or "ethnomedical pathogenesis", is a particularly useful concept for the study of the role of traditional belief in SUNDS. Significantly, the concept of ethnomedicogenic illness and healing, with its emphasis on the relationship between the mind/spirit and body, is compatible with the holistic traditional Hmong worldview regarding health.

Since Nightmare assaults and other spirit-related problems did occur in Laos, it is significant that Hmong refugees in the United States attribute SUNDS to traditional spirits. I believe that the differences between the Hmong way of life in pre-war Laos and their current situation in the United States are responsible for this phenomenon. Traditional Hmong culture has sustained a severe disruption. The Hmong have undergone a seemingly endless series of traumatic experiences: the war in Laos, the Pathet Lao takeover and subsequent Hmong persecution (including the threat of genocide), the harrowing nightmare escapes through jungles and across the Mekong River, the hardships of refugee camps in Thailand, and finally resettlement in the United States, with not only housing, income, language and employment concerns, but the separation of families and clans, inability to practice traditional religion, and hasty conversions to Christianity, among many others. These recent changes appear to account for the fact that, while SUNDS deaths occur in the United States, no informant I interviewed was aware of any SUNDS deaths in pre-migration Laos.

When *dab tsog* tormented sleepers in Laos, it did so in a sociocultural context that sustained a fundamental structure of support. Hmong shamans conducted prescribed rituals designed to ascertain the nature of the individual's transgression and sought to appease the angry spirits in order to prevent the possibility of the sleeper's death during a subsequent nocturnal encounter. In the United States, while the majority of Hmong retain many of their traditional beliefs in many instances they have lost their religious leaders and ritual responses. The insular communities that characterized Hmong life in Laos appear to have fostered traditional cultural practices whose presence alleviated, but whose subsequent loss provokes, feelings of terror and impending death associated with negative supranormal encounters. Therefore, although the *dab tsog* attack in Laos was akin to the worldwide Nightmare tradition, the peculiar stresses of the recent Hmong refugee experience have transformed its outcome. In conclusion, the power of traditional belief in the nightmare compounded with such factors as the trauma of war, migration, rapid acculturation, and the inability to practice traditional healing and ritual causes cataclysmic psychological stress that can result in the deaths of male Hmong refugees from SUNDS.[57]

NOTES

The author wishes to express her gratitude to Judith Barker, Carole Browner, Michael Owen Jones, Linda Mitteness and Don Ward for thoughtful discussion on various aspects of this research. A special note of thanks to the Hmong men and women who shared their personal beliefs and experiences with me.

1. Quincy, K. (1988). *Hmong: History of a people*. Cheney: East Washington University Press.
2. Cerquone, J. (1986). *Refugees from Laos: In harm's way*. Washington, DC: U.S. Committee for Refugees.
3. Profiles of the Highland Lao Communities in the United States. (1988). Washington, DC: United States Department of Health and Human Services.
4. Johnson, C. (1985). *Dab neeg hmooh: Myths, legends, and folktales from the Hmong of Laos*. St. Paul, MN: Macalester College.
5. Muecke, M. A. (1983). In search of healers: Southeast Asian refugees in the American health care system. *Western Journal of Medicine*, 139, 335–840.
6. Conquergood, D. (1989). *I am a Shaman: A Hmong life story with ethnographic commentary*, pp. 45–46. Minneapolis: University of Minnesota.
7. Hmong was an exclusively oral language until the 1950s when Christian missionaries in Laos developed a written form using the Roman alphabet. In this essay, underlined Hmong terms represent words in the Hmong language written in the Roman Popular Alphabet (RPA). For ease of pronunciation I provide an English transliteration in quotation marks.
8. The disorder is also known by the acronym SUDS: Sudden Unexplained Death Syndrome. I think that both the unpredictable nature of the syndrome and the fact that 98 percent of the deaths occurred between 10:00 P. M. and 8:00 A.M. [9] warrant the inclusion of both the words "unexpected" and "nocturnal" in the label. Thus, Sudden Unexpected Nocturnal Death Syndrome is a more accurate description of the disorder. My use of the term SUNDS is consistent with that of The SUNDS Planning Project at Saint Paul-Ramsey Medical Center.
9. Parrish, R. G. (1988). Death in the Night: Mysterious Syndrome in Asian Refugees. In E. Berstein and L. Tomchuck (Eds.), *1989 Medical and Health Annual* (pp. 286–290). Chicago: Encyclopedia Britannica.
10. Baron, R. C., and Kirschner, R. H. (1983). Sudden night-time death among southeast Asians too. *The Lancet*, 8327, 764.
11. Munger, R. G. (1987). Sudden death in sleep of Laotian-Hmong refugees in Thailand: A case-control study. *American Journal of Public Health*, 77, 1137.
12. Beginning in 1981, a number of researchers began to note similarities between SUNDS and the sudden deaths of Filipino and Japanese men from disorders known respectively as *bangungut* and *pokkuri*, e.g., Refs [10, 18, 19, 49]. These findings are significant in illustrating that despite peculiar cultural manifestations and elaborations, the phenomenon of SUNDS (like the nightmare itself [31]), appears to be consistent across unrelated cultures.
13. Baron, R. C., Thacker, S. B., Gorelkin, L., Vernon, A. A., Taylor, W. R., and Choi, K. (1983). Sudden deaths among southeast Asian refugees: An unexplained nocturnal phenomenon. *Journal of the American Medical Association*, 250, 2947.
14. Bissinger, H. G. (1981). More cities report death syndrome. *St. Paul Pioneer Press* 6 February, F1, 4.
15. Bliatout, B. T. (1982). *Hmong Sudden Unexpected Nocturnal Death Syndrome: A cultural study*. Oregon: Sparkle Publishing.
16. Holtan, N., Carlson, D., Egbert, J., Mielke, R., and Thao, T. C. (1984). *Final report of the SUNDS planning project*. St. Paul, MN: St Paul-Ramsey Medical Center.
17. Pyle, A. (1981). Death stalking refugees. *The News Tribune* (Tacoma, Washington). 16 April: C1.
18. Kirschner, R. H., Eckner, F.A.O., and Baron R. C. (1986). The cardiac pathology of sudden,

unexplained, nocturnal death in southeast Asian refugees. *Journal of the American Medical Association*, 256, 2780.

19. Otto, C. M., Tauxe, R. V., Cobb, L. A., Greene, H. L., Gross, B. W., Werner, J. A., Burroughs, R. W., Samson, W. E., Weaver, D., and Trobaugh, G. B. (1984). Ventricular fibrillation causes sudden death in southeast Asian immigrants. *Annuals of Internal Medicine*, 100, 45.

20. Marshall, E. (1981). The Hmong: dying of culture shock? *Science*, 212, 1008.

21. Munger, R. G., and Hurlich, M. G. (1981). Hmong deaths. *Science*, 213, 952.

22. *Refugee Health Issues Quarterly*. (1989). Update: sudden unexplained death syndrome among southeast Asian refugees, 4, 1.

23. Hufford, D. J. (1976). A new approach to the "Old Hag": The nightmare tradition reexamined. In W. Hand (Ed.), *American Folk Medicine: A Symposium* (pp. 73–35). Berkeley: University of California Press.

24. Hufford, D. J. (1982). *The terror that comes in the night*. Philadelphia: University of Pennsylvania Press.

25. Ward, D. (1977). The little man who wasn't there: Encounters with the supranormal. *Fabulas J. Folklore Study*, 18, 213.

26. The word mara, from which "nightmare" is derived, can be traced to a proto-Indo-European root that most likely referred to a nocturnal pressing spirit. (Kluge, F. *Etymologisches Wörterbuch der Deutschen Sprache*. Berlin: Walter de ruyter, 1960.)

27. I am indebted to David J. Hufford for his characterization of the nightmare in *The Terror That Comes in the Night* (1992). Although I have altered his configuration slightly [based on the results of my own fieldwork in Jerusalem (1987–88) and Los Angeles (1986–87)] Hufford's criteria, which are unique in the literature on the subject, remain the foundation of the minimal requirements for the nightmare experience as I present them.

28. Adler, S. R. (1991). Sudden unexpected nocturnal death syndrome among Hmong immigrants: Examining the role of the "nightmare." *Journal of American Folklore*, 104, 54.

29. Ness, R. C. (1978). The old hag phenomenon as sleep paralysis: a biocultural, interpretation. *Culture, Medicine and Psychiatry*, 2, 15.

30. Foster, G. M. (1973). Dreams, character, and cognitive orientation in Tzintzuntzan. *Ethos* 1, 106.

31. Hufford, D. J. (1988). Inclusionism verses reductionism the study of culture-bound syndromes. *Culture, Medicine Psychiatry*. 12, 503.

32. Dement, W. C., Frazier, S. H., and Weizman, E.D.T. (1984). *American Medical Association Guide to Better Sleep*. New York: Random House.

33. Hartmann, E. (1984). *The nightmare: The psychology and biology of terrifying dreams*. New York: Basic Books, 1984.

34. Parkes, J. D. (1985). *Sleep and its disorders*. London: W. B. Saunder.

35. Kellerman H. (1981). *Sleep disorders: Insomnia and narcolepsy*. New York: Brunner/Mazel.

36. Rechtschaffen, A., and Dement, W. C. (1969). Narcolepsy and hypersomnia. In A. Kales (Ed.), *Sleep: Physiology and Pathology* (pp. 119–130). J. B. Lippincott, PA.

37. Riley, T. C. (1985). *Clinical aspects of sleep and sleep disturbances*. Boston: Butterworth Publishers.

38. Takeuchi, T., Miyasita, A., Sasaki, Y., Inugami, M., and Fukuda, K. (1992). Isolated sleep paralysis elicited by sleep interruption. *Sleep*, 15, 217.

39. Heimbach, E. H. (1979). *White Hmong-English Dictionary*. Ithaca, NY: Cornell University Press.

40. Hishikawa, Y. (1976). Sleep Paralysis. In C. Guilleminault, W. C. Dement and P. Passouant (Eds.), *Narcolepsy: Proceedings of the First International Symposium on Narcolepsy, Advances in Sleep Research, Vol. 3* (pp. 97–124). New York: Spectrum Publications.

41. Rechtschaffen, A. and Dement, W. C. (1969). Narcolepsy and hypersomnia. In A. Kales (Ed.), *Sleep: Physiology and Pathology* (pp. 119–130). J. B. Lippincott, PA.

42. Riley, T. C. (1985). *Clinical Aspects of Sleep and Sleep Disturbances*. Boston: Butterworth Publishers.

43. Despite the uniformity of opinion among informants regarding the absence of SUNDS deaths in premigration Laos. It is important to note that the forensic diligence to account for unusual death in Laos is not comparable to that of the United States, particularly in the isolated rural villages in which the Hmong lived. Although it is therefore impossible to know with certainty whether SUNDS deaths occurred in Laos, the conviction on the part of Hmong immigrants that the deaths were absent is a

significant element in their dichotomization of experience between premigration Laos and post-resettlement America.

44. Donnelly, N. D. (1989). *The changing lives of refugee Hmong women*. University of Washington doctoral dissertation. University Microfilms International, Michigan.

45. Tobin, J. J., and Friedman, J. (1983). Spirits, shamans, and nightmare death: Survivor stress in a Hmong refugee. *American Journal of Orthopsychiatry*, 53, 439.

46. Westermeyer, J. (1981). Hmong deaths. *Science*, 213, 957.

47. Westermeyer, J. (1987). Prevention of mental disorder among Hmong refugees in the U.S.: Lessons from the period 1976–1986. *Social Science Medicine*, 25, 941.

48. Westermeyer, J. A (1988). A matched pairs study of depression among Hmong refugees with particular reference to predisposing factors and treatment outcome. *Social Psychiatry, Psychiatry, and Epidemiology*, 23, 64.

49. Parrish, R. G., Tucker, M., Ing, R., Encamacion, C., and Eberhardt, M. (1987). Sudden unexplained death syndrome in southeast Asian refugees: A review of CDC surveillance. *Morbidity and Mortality Weekly Report*, 36, 43.

50. Brodsky, M. A., Soto, D. A., Iseri, L. T., Wolff, L. J. and Allen, B. J. (1987). Ventricular tachyarrhythmia associated with psychological stress: The role of the sympathetic nervous system. *Journal of the American Medical Association*, 257, 2064.

51. Cannon, W. (1942). Voodoo death. *American Anthropologist*, 44, 169.

52. Engei, G. L. (1971). Sudden and rapid death during psychological stress: folklore or folk wisdom? *Annals of Internal Medicine*, 74, 771.

53. Greene, W. A., Goldstein, S., and Moss, A. J. (1972). Psychosocial aspects of sudden death: A preliminary report. *Archives of Internal Medicine*, 129, 725.

54. Lown, B., Verrier, R., and Corbalan, R. (1973). Psychologic stress and threshold for repetitive ventricular response. *Science*, 182, 834.

55. Rahe, R. H., Romo, M., Bennett, L., and Siltanen, P. (1974). Recent life changes, myocardial infarction, and abrupt coronary death. *Archives of Internal Medicine*, 133, 221.

56. Hahn, R. A., and Kleinman, A. (1983). Belief as pathogen, belief as medicine: "voodoo death" and the "placebo phenomenon" in anthropological perspective. *Medical Anthropology. Quarterly*, 14, 6.

57. Given that myriad cultures possess traditions of evil Nightmare spirits, do nightmare experiences precipitate similar disorders among other peoples? Although those affected by SUNDS are overwhelmingly Laotian Hmong men, individuals belonging to other groups, notably Filipinos, Thai, Khmu and Cambodians, have died of what appears to be SUNDS. A detailed discussion of these potentially parallel phenomena is beyond the aim of the present paper, but it is important to note that my preliminary investigation of Khmu and Thai sudden deaths indicates that individuals of both groups perceive a connection between Nightmare spirit attacks and sudden deaths in situations of extreme psychological stress. Any definitive statement regarding a correlation between these Nightmare spirits and SUNDS, however, requires an in-depth study of the type presented in this paper that focuses on the beliefs and experiences of the non-Hmong groups affected.

17.

Psychopathology Among Asian Americans

A Model Minority?

Stanley Sue, Derald W. Sue, Leslie Sue, David T. Takeuchi

The prevalence of psychopathology among Asian Americans has been a source of debate. Some investigators believe that the prevalence rate is quite low, whereas others argue that it is fairly high. A review of the literature suggests that at this time, it is not possible to determine the specific rates of psychopathology. However, evidence does suggest that their rates of mental disorders are not extraordinarily low. Thus, public portrayals of Asian Americans as a well-adjusted group do not reflect reality. Attempts to determine the exact prevalence rates have been hindered by characteristics of the Asian American population, particularly its relatively small size, heterogeneity, and rapid changes in demographics. It is suggested that aggregate research, in which different Asian American groups are combined, is important for policy considerations, broad cultural comparisons, and establishing baseline information. To advance scientific contributions and understanding, studies that examine the correlates and course of disorders within specific Asian American groups are necessary as well.

For over three decades, considerable controversy has existed over the mental health of Asian Americans. To some individuals, Asian Americans are seen as being extraordinarily well adjusted, as demonstrated by achievements in occupational, educational, and economic spheres. This view is supported by references to low rates of criminal activity, juvenile delinquency, and divorce. Asian Americans also tend to be physically healthier than other Americans and have longer life expectancies. On the other hand, some investigators argue that mental health and adjustment problems do exist. These problems are often masked by cultural or familial practices, as well as a stereotypic view of Asian Americans. In addition, particular segments of the Asian American population are at particular risk for mental distress (S. Sue and Morishima, 1982).

In this article, we do not intend to settle the debate about the prevalence of mental disorders among Asian Americans, nor do we want to reiterate the various methodological and conceptual problems encountered when conducting valid cross-cultural assessments (e.g., difficulties in achieving translation, stimulus, conceptual, and scalar equivalence on assessment instruments for culturally different populations). Rather, our intent is to apply the research on psychopathology to broader issues involving policy and science. Several arguments are made:

1. Much variability exists in research findings regarding the prevalence of psychopathology
2. It is not possible at this time to specify the prevalence of disorders among Asian Americans, but public stereotypes concerning their extraordinary adjustment are inaccurate
3. The variability and indeterminant nature of the research findings are a function of the heterogeneity of the population, its relative small number, and changing demographics

4. We must distinguish between contributions to policy and to science
5. Research on the aggregate group, that is, combining Asian American groups, is useful and should not be abolished because it can yield policy implications, baseline information, and broad cultural comparisons
6. Science will be more enhanced by specific research than by aggregate research.

Let us begin by reviewing research on the mental health of Asian Americans.

TREATED CASES

Early research on Asian Americans examined their use of treatment services. Investigators consistently found that Asian Americans failed to use mental health services in the same proportion to their population, as did Whites (Leong, 1986). This comparative failure to use services was called *underutilization*. The implications is that Asian Americans were not using services when they needed to. Is it possible that this population is relatively better adjusted than other populations, so that greater utilization of services is unnecessary? In general, every population underutilizes in the sense that not all individuals with psychological disturbance seek help from the mental health system. For example, the Epidemiologic Catchment Area (ECA) study, which compared the prevalence rate of mental disorders with the use of mental health care services, revealed that the vast majority of afflicted individuals did not seek treatment (Shapiro et al., 1984). The real question, therefore, is whether or not Asian Americans with psychiatric disorders have a greater propensity than other populations to avoid using services. In the absence of information on prevalence rates, considerable indirect evidence suggests that Asian Americans are less likely than the general population to use services. Research findings have revealed that few Asian Americans seek mental health treatment and those who do use services exhibit a greater level of disturbance within the client population (S. Sue and Morishima, 1982). A reasonable explanation is that only the most disturbed Asian Americans tend to seek services. Asian Americans who show a moderate degree of disturbance are thus more likely than are comparable White Americans to avoid using services.

The phenomenon of low utilization coupled with severe disturbance among users suggests that moderately disturbed Asian Americans, who may be in need of services, are not seeking treatment. Therefore, attempts to ascertain the actual prevalence rates of psychopathology should not be based solely on clinical samples. Rather, community-based prevalence studies are necessary to provide a clearer picture of the rates of mental illness among Asian Americans.

EPIDEMIOLOGICAL SURVEYS

Within the past decade, results from rigorous, large-scale epidemiological studies have suggested that the prevalence of mental disorders in the United States is quite high. The ECA study indicated that nearly 20% of the American population experienced a mental disorder currently or within the past six months (Myers et al., 1984; Robins and Regier, 1991). Findings from the National Comorbidity Survey (NCS) by Kessler et al. (1994) revealed that nearly 50% of the interviewed respondents, aged 15 to 54 years, reported at least one lifetime disorder, and close to 30% reported at least one disorder within twelve months of the interview.

In a review of the literature on the mental health of various ethnic minority groups,

Vega and Rumbaut (1991) noted that knowledge pertaining to Asian Americans is much less developed than that for African Americans and Latinos. In addition, no national level epidemiological surveys have been conducted. However, epidemiological surveys of the prevalence of psychopathology are available concerning Asians in other parts of the world. These findings may be instructive by helping us to place data on Asian Americans in perspective. Furthermore, the overseas studies have been conducted using relatively large samples of respondents in contrast to the small sample sizes of Asians in the United States.

PSYCHOPATHOLOGY IN ASIAN COUNTRIES

In general, research on Asians in different parts of the world also reveals significant mental health problems. For example, a major survey was conducted of nonpsychotic disorders in Singapore sponsored by the Singapore Association for Mental Health (1989). The survey was based on 1,153 adults between the ages of 21 to 55 years. The General Health Questionnaire (GHQ) was used to ascertain mental health because the instrument had been used in previous studies to establish the prevalence of minor psychiatric morbidity. Results revealed an 18% point prevalence rate for these disorders, indicating a fairly high rate of disturbance.

Several epidemiological studies have been conducted in Taiwan. Using the GHQ Cheng (1985) found a prevalence rate of 26% for mental disorders. In a more recent study, Hwu, Yeh, and Chang (1989) used the Diagnostic Interview Schedule (DIS) to assess prevalence rates among 11,000 respondents, aged 18 years and over. Results revealed rates that were slightly lower than those found in the United States. These cross-national differences in rates may be real. On the other hand, they noted that cross-national comparisons are difficult to make. The types of disorders that are assessed may differ from study to study. In the Hwu et al. study, generalized anxiety disorders were included but were not assessed in the ECA project in the United States, and the study used different exclusion criteria from those employed in the U.S. project.

A major epidemiological study of mental disorders was also conducted in Korea (Lee et al., 1990a, 1990b). The DIS was administered to over 5,000 respondents. Findings revealed that the overall lifetime prevalence rates were lower than those found in the United States, except for alcohol abuse dependence, which was much higher among Koreans than Americans (primarily attributable to heavy drinking among men).

In mainland China, the results of a large-scale epidemiological survey were reported in the *Chinese Journal of Neurology and Psychiatry* (1986). Twelve regions of China and about 38,000 respondents were included in the survey. Interestingly, the overall rates of mental disorder (e.g., schizophrenia, substance abuse, "neuroses," and personality disorders) were fairly low compared to those found in the United States. Nevertheless, every type of mental disorder was found in all segments of the population. In a representative sample of Hong Kong residents, Lau and Mak (1992) estimated the prevalence of psychological ill health to be 18–26% using the GHQ.

Based on these studies, it is apparent that prevalence rates for Asians outside the United States vary. Some investigations have found the rates to be similar to those in the United States, whereas other studies show lower rates. Obviously, cross-national comparisons are fraught with potential problems and confounds. Various groups or populations may manifest different symptoms for the same disorders, exhibit culture-bound syndromes, have different distributions of disorders, and so on. For example, neurasthenia or chronic fatigue syndrome is more commonly found among Asians than Americans; and some culture-bound syndromes, such as *amok* and *koro*, are fairly unique to some Asian cultures (Cheung, 1986). In addition, the differences in the nature and rates of disorders may be attributable to cultural variations, presence of stressors and resources, or gene pools that are associated with a particular society. However, the different prevalence rates may also be caused by investigations that vary in their conceptual assumptions, methodologies, and measures. Furthermore, the cross-cultural validity of diagnostic and assessment procedures is a central issue in studying the rate and distribution of mental disorders among Asians. If case-finding strategies or assessment procedures are inappropriate or culturally biased, then it is difficult, if not impossible, to estimate accurately the prevalence of disorders.

From these studies of overseas Asians, what implications can be drawn for Asians in the United States? First, there is no reason to believe that being Asian is associated with significantly low rates of mental disorders and, therefore, that Asians coming to the United States are less prone to developing these disorders. Second, Asian Americans are likely to be different from their overseas counterparts. Those who emigrate to the United States are not representative of those who remain (some come from educated, upper classes, whereas others have led impoverished lives in their homelands and fled to the United States for better opportunities). Immigrants and refugees encounter unique experiences in the United States, such as exposure to different cultural values, English proficiency problems, minority status including racial/ethnic stereotypes, prejudice, discrimination, and a reduction in available social supports. In turn, these experiences can alter the stress-coping formulas for immigrants to the United States.

Indeed, one might speculate that Asian Americans might be under considerable stress because of these experiences. What do the empirical findings reveal? Again, large-scale and rigorous epidemiological studies have not been conducted on Asian Americans. Under such circumstances, one must form conclusions based on the preponderance of evidence. Until recently, the findings seemed to converge. They revealed that the prevalence of disorders among Asian Americans was as high as, or even higher than, those of other Americans: findings that were inconsistent with the general stereotypes concerning Asian well-being. The studies of Asian American cover broad periods of time, starting from the 1970s to the present.

Many of the available surveys appear to indicate that significant numbers of Asian Americans are experiencing mental and emotional problems. From their interviews of adult residents in a large Chinatown community, Loo, Tong, and True (1989) found that over 33% of their sample reported symptoms of emotional tension. Feelings of depression were also common among the residents, with 40% complaining of a "sinking feeling like being depressed." Additionally, 25% of the residents admitted to having "periods of days, weeks, months when [they] couldn't take care of things because [they] couldn't get going." Finally, Loo et al. reported that 35% of the respondents endorsed four or more items on the Langner Scale, whereas 20% acknowledged seven or more items. Such endorsement rates on the Langner Scale have traditionally been considered as indications of psychiatric impairment. The two most frequently endorsed Langner items included "a memory that's not alright" (40%) and "worrying a lot" (42%). Self-reported impairment among the

Chinese was generally as high as, or higher than, that found in the Midtown Manhattan study, which used the same scale (Srole). Although the sample is not representative of general Chinese American populations, the study points to the levels of distress in the ethnic Chinese enclave.

Several studies have examined the rates of depression among Asian Americans using the Center for Epidemiology Studies of Depression (CES-D). Interviewing Asian Americans located through directories, organizations, and snowballing techniques in Seattle, Kuo (1984) found that Chinese, Japanese, Filipino, and Korean Americans on average reported slightly more depressive symptoms than did Caucasian respondents in other studies. Kuo and Tsai (1986) presented several interesting findings in their study of Asian immigrants who resettled in Seattle. These researchers found that the Koreans, the most recently arrived immigrants, exhibited twice the rate of depression found among the Chinese, Japanese, and Filipino groups under investigation. Immigrants who moved to the United States at an earlier age experienced fewer adjustment difficulties. With respect to social support, immigrants who reported having friends available for frank discussions, or available relatives in one's residential area, exhibited less depressive symptoms than those who lacked such a wide social network. Finally, Kuo and Tsai asserted that immigrants with "hardy" personalities reported less stressful life events, financial worries, adjustment difficulties, and symptoms of depression than those who lacked hardy traits. Essentially, hardy Asian immigrants, or those who felt a sense of control over their life events, maintained a strong commitment to their life activities, perceived change as an exciting opportunity for personal development, and were more likely to display positive adjustment to their new American life-styles.

Using the CES-D, similar findings of prevalence rates were reported by Hurh and Kim (1988). Korean immigrants residing in Chicago (from a Korean directory) had higher scores for depression than did the Chinese, Japanese, and Filipinos in Kuo's (1984) study. High rates of depression were also revealed in a telephone survey of Chinese Americans located in the telephone survey of Chinese Americans located in the telephone directory in San Francisco. Using the CES-D, Ying (1988) found the Chinese Americans to be significantly more depressed than the Chinese Americans in Kuo's (1984) study.

SPECIAL POPULATIONS: REFUGEES

Certain groups such as Southeast Asian refugees and immigrants have extremely high levels of depression and other disorders (Westermeyer, 1988). Studies have also consistently shown that Southeast Asian refugees constitute a high-risk group for mental disorders. Kinzie et al. (1990) reported that 70% of their overall Southeast Asian refugee patient sample met *Diagnostic and statistical manual for mental disorders* (*DSM-III-R;* American Psychiatric Association, 1987) criteria for a current diagnosis of posttraumatic stress disorder (PTSD) and 5% met criteria for a past diagnosis. This elevated incidence of PTSD was even more alarming when group differences were analyzed. In this case, PTSD was diagnosed in 95% of the Mien sample (a highland tribe from Laos) and 92% of the Cambodian sample. The clinical significance of these findings is striking because most of these PTSD sufferers had experienced their traumatic events 10 to 15 years prior to assessment. Last, Kinzie et al. (1990) found that 82% of their overall sample suffered from depression, the most common non-PTSD diagnosis, whereas approximately 16% had schizophrenia.

Similar results were obtained by Mollica, Wyshak, and Lavelle (1987). About 50% of their Southeast Asian refugee patients fulfilled *DSM-III* (American Psychiatric Association, 1980) criteria for PTSD and 71% suffered from major affective disorder. Certain groups had even higher prevalence rates. The Hmong/Laotian group exhibited the highest rates at 92% for PTSD and 85% for major affective disorder, whereas 57% and 81% of the Cambodians suffered from PTSD and major affective disorder, respectively.

Westermeyer (1988) conducted a point prevalence study of adult Hmong refugees, a rural and agrarian people from Laos, and found that 43% met *DSM III* criteria for various Axis I diagnoses such as adjustment disorder, major depression, and paranoia. Westermeyer emphasized that despite the relatively small sample ($N = 97$), the high rate of Axis I diagnoses exhibited by these refugees—twice the expected rate for the general U.S. population points—to the high degree of psychopathology that is likely to occur in Southeast Asian refugee groups.

The elevated prevalence rates of psychopathology in the Southeast Asian refugee community have been linked to repeated exposure to catastrophic environmental stressors such as torture, combat, witnessing the death of family members and friends, and forcible detainment in harsh refugee camp conditions. For example, Mollica et al., (1987) noted that patients in their refugee sample reported an average of 10 traumatic episodes. It also appears that the negative effects of premigration trauma on adjustment may persist over time. In a study of Cambodian adolescents who survived Pol Pot's concentration camps, Kinzie, Sack, Angell, Clarke, and Ben (1989) found that 48% suffered from PTSD, and 41% experienced depression approximately 10 years since their traumatization.

STUDENTS

As noted by Leong (1986), studies of college students also suggest that Asian Americans experience major adjustment problems. The first studies on the adjustment of Asian American students were conducted by D. Sue and Frank (1973), and D. Sue and Kirk (1973, 1975) at the University of California, Berkeley. Results based on the Omnibus Personality Inventory (OPI) suggested that Asian Americans were more likely than were White students to experience loneliness, isolation, and anxiety.

S. Sue and Zane (1985), who also used the OPI, reported similar adjustment difficulties for a sample of recently immigrated Chinese students who spent 6 or fewer years in the United States. These researchers found that the immigrant Chinese students were less autonomous and extroverted, and more anxious than Chinese students who had lived longer in the United States. Interestingly, however, the academic achievement levels of the foreign-born students exceeded those of the general student body. S. Sue and Zane thus cautioned that academic performance should not be used as an indicator of psychological well-being or adjustment for newly arrived Chinese college students. Although the study did not use a comparison non-Asian group, the scores from the Chinese American students were highly similar to those found among Asian American students in the Berkeley study, which did reveal greater disturbance among Asians than non-Asians.

Recently, Okazaki (1994) compared the responses of Asian and White American college students on various measures of depression and anxiety. Results revealed that the Asian American students reported higher levels of depression and social anxiety.

In another investigation, Abe and Zane (1990) found significant differences between

Whites and foreign-born Asian American college students on a measure of psychological maladjustment. Results demonstrated that foreign-born Asian Americans reported greater levels of interpersonal distress than their White counterparts, even after controlling for demographic differences as well as the influences of social desirability, self-consciousness, extraversion, and other-directedness (i.e., being attuned to the desires and needs of others). These results are especially interesting given that the foreign-born Asian Americans in the sample had resided in the United State for an average of 10 years. Abe and Zane proposed that the various stressors faced by many foreign-born Asian Americans, such as language barriers and the loss of social support networks, may have long-term negative effects on psychological adjustment.

Keefe, Sue, Enomoto, Chao, and Durvasula (in press) completed a study of ethnic differences on the MMPI–2 in relation to acculturation. In general, less acculturated Asian American students showed greater elevation on the clinical scales of the MMPI–2 profile than did highly acculturated Asian American students or White students. Highly acculturated Asian American students had greater clinical elevations than their White counterparts. Significant group differences emerged on the Hypochondriasis, Depression, Psychopathic Deviate, Paranoia, Psychasthenia, Schizophrenia, and Social Introversion subscales: Less acculturated Asian American and White students generally fell at the extremes, with the more acculturated Asian American students positioned in the middle of the scale scores.

The results also demonstrated that Asian American students—regardless of their acculturation level—had more somatic complaints, were more depressed and anxious, and felt more often isolated than Whites. Moreover, less acculturated Asian Americans most often perceived their environment as unsupportive. These findings may reflect a cultural response bias among Asian Americans. However, the possibility cannot be ruled out that the results may simply reflect that Asian Americans as a minority group experience greater difficulties in their daily lives, which results in greater disturbance than found among Whites. It is precisely this inability to distinguish between a strict cultural response set interpretation and a minority group-stress interpretation that makes it imperative to conduct further studies into the validity of assessment measures with Asian Americans.

All of these various studies (on students, refugees and immigrants, Chinatown, and community residents) go beyond suggesting that Asian Americans are not a model minority in terms of mental health. They support a more drastic conclusion, namely, that Asian Americans have poorer mental health than do Whites. Before considering this statement, it should be noted that some more recent studies suggest that Asian Americans may indeed be better adjusted.

CHINESE AMERICAN PSYCHIATRIC EPIDEMIOLOGICAL STUDY

The Chinese American Psychiatric Epidemiological Study (CAPES) is undoubtedly the most rigorous and large-scale investigation of any Asian group in the United States to date. The project is a 5-year community epidemiological study investigating the mental health problems and needs for mental health services among Chinese Americans. The study has two specific aims: (a) to estimate the prevalence rates of selected mental disorders among Chinese Americans; and (b) to identify the factors associated with mental health problems among Chinese Americans. This study obtained 1,700 completed household interviews with Chinese Americans residing in Los Angeles county. Follow-up interviews with the same respondents will be conducted 1 year later, which will allow the unprecedented opportunity to note changes in mental health and the factors associated with changes. The target population for the study includes Chinese immigrants and native-born residents of the United States. The study is limited to adults (> 18 years old) who speak Cantonese, Mandarin, or English. Cantonese and Mandarin are the most common Chinese dialects. The research used a multistage sampling procedure to select respondents. The respondents were presented with an interview instrument that included the following components: (a) sociodemographic information including age, gender, educational level, household income, number of household members, year of immigration, country of origin, marital status, education, and English proficiency; (b) Composite International Diagnostic Interview (CIDI) questions related to mood, anxiety, somatic disorders, alcohol use, PSTD, neurasthenia, and chronic fatigue; (c) SCL 90; (d) questions related to stressors including major life events and daily hassles; (e) information on social support, personality, and hardiness; (f) queries concerning help-seeking behaviors and utilization of mental health services; and (g) acculturation questions.

PRELIMINARY RESULTS REGARDING LIFETIME PREVALENCE

Table 1 shows the lifetime prevalence rates found in the CAPES project compared to the ECA (Robins and Regier, 1991) and NCS (Kessler et al., 1994) findings. The comparison involves only mood and anxiety disorders, which are among the most common disorders in the United States. It should be mentioned that the studies used different sample weightings and procedures.

The preliminary results are contrary to the findings of the studies reviewed earlier. Chinese Americans in the CAPES project did not have higher rates of mental disorders than Whites. Although it can be argued that the rates of mood disorders among Chinese Americans are within the bounds of other Americans, the rates for anxiety are surprisingly low. These preliminary findings thus reveal somewhat low rates of psychopathology. Initially, one is tempted to dismiss the findings because many other studies have demonstrated high rates of mood and anxiety problems. However, the CAPES project is the most rigorous, carefully conducted, and comprehensive epidemiological survey, employing the

Table 1. Lifetime Prevalence Rates in Different Studies (%)

	ECA	NCS	CAPES
Manic	0.8	1.6	0.1
Major depression	4.9	17.1	6.9
Dysthymia	3.2	6.4	5.9
General anxiety disorder	—	5.1	1.7
Agoraphobia	5.6	5.3	1.6
Simple phobia	11.3	11.3	1.1
Social phobia	2.7	13.3	1.2
Panic disorder	1.6	3.5	0.4
Panic attack	1.5	—	0.7

Note: ECA = Epidemiological Catchment Area; NCS = National Comorbidity Survey; CAPES=Chinese American Psychiatric Epidemiological Survey.

largest number of respondents ever found in a mental health survey of any Asian American group. Its findings must be taken seriously. Before discussing the implications of the CAPES project, let us cite other recent studies that point to low rates of psychopathology among Asian Americans.

Sasao (1992) examined the use of alcohol, tobacco, marijuana, and cocaine among different Asian groups. In order to decrease problems involving estimation error when only one data source is used, he employed multiple methods, which included telephone surveys, community forums, archival data analysis, and service utilization statistics. The telephone survey involved 1,783 community residents of Chinese, Japanese, Korean, Filipino, and Vietnamese descent in California. Substance use (including alcohol, cigarettes, marijuana, and cocaine) revealed in the telephone survey was generally below that of other groups in the United States. The low rates of substance use were also supported by other indicators. For example, in the archival study of California state records, Asian Americans exhibited low mortality rates due to alcohol- and drug-related causes (the 2% rate was far lower than those of other groups). Asian Americans also had extremely low arrest rates for felony and misdemeanor drug offenses (0.3%). Few individuals used services for drug or alcohol problems.

Sasao also conducted a survey of about 1,000 high school students in the San Gabriel valley of California, which has a high proportion of Asians. Asian Americans had the lowest drug use compared to Latinos, non-Hispanic Whites, and other students. The results from the CAPES and the substance use projects, which are quite advanced and sophisticated, dramatically differ from the findings of the other studies reviewed. Can we make sense of this? Is the model minority image being revived? On the one hand, it is difficult to compare the studies due to their contrasting research methods. For example, one might argue that the studies using self-report measures reveal more psychopathology than do interview procedures. Another possible explanation is that Western-derived measures may have questionable cross-cultural validity. The conflicting results are therefore difficult to interpret. The concern over the validity of measures used with Asian Americans is obviously important. Yet, the epidemiological studies from Asian countries that were cited earlier have all used Western-derived instruments, and the findings appear to be generally satisfactory. We believe, therefore, that the most fundamental problem in Asian American research is not the construction of valid measures, rather, it is the nature of the population.

THE FUNDAMENTAL PROBLEM

What is the nature of the Asian American population? It is small, diverse, and ever changing. Asian Americans represent only about 3% of the U.S. population (in contrast to the world's population, which is about 60% Asian). Consequently, researchers have had a difficult time finding adequate sample sizes and representative samples of Asian Americans. In many studies, convenience samples are used, often from quite different sources. For example, they may be drawn from lists of Asian ethnic organizations, names suggested by other respondents (the snowballing technique), universities rather than communities at large, and so on. Our estimates of the prevalence of psychopathology may conflict because they are based on different kinds of samples. It truly is similar to the situation of trying to imagine what an elephant looks like based on isolated and limited views of its legs, tail, trunk, and ears.

is also extremely diverse and heterogeneous. More
...ding Pacific Islander Americans), speaking more than
...in the Asian American category. Even if we focus on
...eity is problematic and not encountered to the same
...For example, the Chinese American population is far
...ulation in overseas parts of the world. Chinese in the
...native-born and foreign-born individuals who come
...ong Kong, Singapore, Vietnam, and so on. Chinese
...languages, are exposed to American values, and are
...of these factors produce a very heterogenous popula-
...hinese in mainland China lack diversity; rather, it is
...much greater in the Unites States. The same is true of
...: Greater heterogeneity exists for their group in the
...nd. This is an important point to understand. It means
...2) that have been validated with Chinese in China may
...e in the United States. Furthermore, if great diversity
..., by combining all Asian American groups we must
...cal and conceptual headaches. We often feel obligated
...d heterogeneity exist because we want to avoid stereo-
...ually important consideration is that this same hetero-
...ability to draw conclusions or make generalizations.
...rong about trying to study a diverse population. In fact,
heterogeneity is often essential for definitive research. Triandis and Brislin (1984) argued
that having diverse or heterogenous groups can yield significant benefits in terms of
increasing the range of variables to study. For example, suppose we wanted to see how
achievement test scores are related to academic grades, but only had students who had
higher scores on the test. We cannot adequately test the relationship because we do not
also have students who scored poorly, a range-restriction limitation. A full range of scores
is necessary. Thus, heterogeneity can be beneficial and even critical to address fully the
proposed question. The problem confronting Asian American researchers is that the
heterogeneity exists within a relatively small population. Outcomes from research investigations are then highly dependent on the particular samples drawn, and findings may
fluctuate widely.

Finally, the Asian American population is undergoing rapid change relative to other
populations. The Asian American population has doubled in size each decade for about
the last three decades. The composition has changed, too. Whereas Japanese Americans
were the largest group of Asian Americans a couple of decades ago, they are now outnum-
bered by Chinese and Philipino Americans. Today, the Asian American population is
predominantly overseas born, in contrast to the situation three decades ago. These demographic changes are likely to produce different prevalence rates. Because of the traumas
faced by Southeast Asian refugees and their relatively recent entry into the United States,
prevalence rates for mental disorders among Asian Americans have dramatically changed.

In sum, there are some very good reasons why researchers have a difficult time ascertaining the prevalence of mental disorders among Asian Americans and why findings may
be inconsistent. The relatively small size, heterogeneity, and changing demographic char-

acteristics of the population pose more basic difficulties in research than do problems of measurement.

IMPLICATIONS OF THE PROBLEMS

Criticisms over the heterogeneity of Asian Americans often lead to the conclusion that one should never combine Asian American groups or compare the aggregate group with Whites. Such a conclusion is mistaken and premature. After all, social scientists often make broad statements about "human" behavior and devise theories that are intended to cover all human beings. If we make an error in overgeneralizing by discussing Asian Americans, the magnitude of error is certainly not as great as the case of scientists who talk about human nature. The main issue is drawing the right conclusions from aggregate research. Aggregate research is important and meaningful but fraught with potential dangers, if overgeneralized. It is meaningful for policy considerations, for illustrating broad cultural influences, and for establishing baseline data. Traditionally, public policies have largely been directed to Asian Americans rather than to specific Asian groups. Mental health policies and programs are often directed to the aggregate rather than to particular Asian American ethnicities. Research can be used to argue for Asian Americans as a collective. Furthermore, Asian American communities do share some cultural characteristics that may be important to contrast with non-Asian populations, such as their emphasis on collectivism rather than individualism, importance of loss of face, and so forth. Aggregate research is appropriate under such circumstances. The last point is that aggregate research is helpful in providing baseline information and in offering a starting point for more refined, specific group research. Much of the work comparing Asian and White Americans is important because it provides the basic information necessary to compare different Asian groups.

Nevertheless, we believe that the field will advance in a scientific sense by engaging in studies that examine variations within the Asian American group. These differences can serve as variables for the investigation of many issues such as experiences of refugees versus immigrants, acculturation effects, or value differences, factors that distinguish healthy from pathological functioning in a subgroup of Asian Americans. Because of the tremendous heterogeneity among Asian Americans, the effects associated with this heterogeneity should be examined further.

In summary, the specific prevalence rates of mental disorders among Asian Americans have been difficult to determine. Sufficient evidence does exist to show that Asian American are not significantly less prone to mental disorders than other ethnic groups. The relatively small population, heterogeneity, and changing demographic characteristics have hindered a more precise determination of prevalence rates within the Asian American population. Research concerning mental health issues should continue to be based on both the aggregate group (all Asian Americans) and particular Asian ethnicities.

NOTE

This article was supported by NIMH Grants ROI MH44331 and MH 47460. Portions were presented by Stanley Sue at the American Psychological Association Convention, August, 1994, Los Angeles.

ical maladjustment among Asian and Caucasian American
1ds. *Journal of Counseling Psychology*, 37, 437–444.
Diagnostic and statistical manual of mental disorders (2nd

Diagnostic and statistical manual of mental disorders (3rd ed.,

ication: A pilot study of mental disorders in Taiwan.

hong Chinese people. In M. H. Bond (Ed.), *The psychology*
on: Oxford University Press.
:ry. (1986). Methodology and data analysis of epidemi-
s in twelve regions of China [special issue]. *Chinese*

ooting and adjustment: A sociological study of Korean
the National Institute of Mental Health). Macomb, IL:
of Sociology and Anthropology.
1989). Prevalence of psychiatric disorders in Taiwan
riew Schedule. *Ada Psychiatrica Scandinavica*, 79, 136–147.
, R., and Chao, R. (in press). Asian American and White
1PI-2. In J. N. Butcher (Ed.), *Handbook of International*
iiversity. Press.
, Nelson, C. B., Hughes, M., Eshleman, S., Wittchen, H.,
2-month prevalence of DSM-III-R psychiatric disorders
in the United States. *Archives of General Psychiatry*, 51, 8–19.

Kinzie, J., Boehnlein, J. K., Leung, P. K., Moore, L. J., Riley, C., and Smith, D. (1990). The prevalence of posttraumatic stress disorder and its clinical significance among Southeast Asian refugees. *American Journal of Psychiatry*, 147, 913–917.

Kinzie, J., Sack, W., Angell, R., Clarke, G., and Ben, R. (1989). A three-year follow-up of Cambodian young people traumatized as children. *Journal of the American Academy of Child and Adolescent Psychiatry*, 28, 501–504.

Kuo, W. H. (1984). Prevalence of depression among Asian-Americans. *Journal of Nervous and Mental Disease*, 172, 449–457.

Kuo, W. H., and Tsai, Y. M. (1986). Social networking, hardiness, and immigrant's mental health. *Journal of Health and Social Behavior*, 27, 133–149.

Lee, C. K., Kwak, Y. S., Yamamoto, J., Rhee, H., Kim, Y. S., Han, J. H., Choi, J. O., and Lee, Y. H. (1990a). Psychiatric epidemiology in Korea. Part I: Gender and age differences in Seoul. *Journal of Nervous and Mental Disease*, 178, 242–246.

Lee, C. K., Kwak, Y. S., Yamamoto, J., Rhee, H., Kim, Y. S., Han, J. H., Choi, J. O., and Lee, Y. H. (1990b). Psychiatric epidemiology in Korea. Part II: Urban and rural differences. *Journal of Nervous and Mental Disease*, 178, 247–252.

Leong, F.T.I. (1986). Counseling and psychotherapy with Asian-Americans: Review of the literature. *Journal of Counseling Psychology*, 33, 196–206.

Loo, C., Tong, B., and True, R. (1989). A bitter bean: Mental health status and attitudes in Chinatown. *Journal of Community Psychology*, 17, 283–296.

Mollica, R. F., Wyshak. G., and Lavelle, J. (1987). The psychosocial impact of war trauma and torture on Southeast Asian refugees. *American Journal of Psychiatry*, 144, 1567–1572.

Myers, J. K., Weissman, M. M., Tischler, G. L., Holzer, C. E., Leaf. P. J., Orvaschel, H., Anthony, J. C., Boyd, J. H., Burke, J. D., Kramer, M., and Stoltzman, R. (1984). Six-month prevalence of psychiatric disorder in three communities: 1980 to 1982. *Archives of General Psychiatry*, 41, 959–967.

Okazaki, S. (1994). *Cultural variations in the self and emotional distress.* Unpublished doctoral dissertation. University of California. Los Angeles.

Robins, L., and Regier, D. A. (1991) *Psychiatric disorders in America: The Epidemological Catchment Area Study.* New York: Free Press.

Sasao, T. (1992). Substance abuse among Asian/Pacific Islander Americans. In R. C. Cervantes (Ed.), *Substance abuse and gang violence.* Newbury Park, CA: Sage Publications.

Sasao, T. (in press). Identifying "at-risk" Asian American adolescents in multiethnic schools: Implications for substance abuse prevention interventions and program evaluation. In M. Orlandi (Ed.), *Cultural competence for Asian American drug abuse prevention evaluation.* Rockville, MD: Center for Substance Abuse Prevention.

Shapiro, S., Skinner, E. A., Kessler, L. G., VonKorff, M., German, P. S., Tischler, G. L., Leaf, P. J., Benham, L., Cottler, L., and Regier, D. A. (1984). Utilization of health and mental health services: Three Epidemiologic Catchment Area sites. *Archives of General Psychiatry,* 41, 702–709.

Singapore Association for Mental Health. (1989). *SAMH survey of the general health of the Singapore population.* Singapore: Singapore Association of Mental Health.

Sue, D. W., and Frank, A. (1973). A typological approach to the psychological study of Chinese and Japanese American college males. *Journal of Social Issues,* 29, 129–148.

Sue, D. W., and Kirk, B. A. (1973). Differential characteristics of Japanese-American and Chinese-American college students. *Journal of Counseling Psychology,* 20, 142–148.

Sue, D. W., and Kirk, B. A. (1975). Asian Americans: Uses of counseling and psychiatric services on a college campus. *Journal of Counseling Psychology,* 22, 84–86.

Sue, S., and Morishima, J. (1982). *The mental health of Asian Americans.* San Francisco: Jossey-Bass.

Sue, S., and Zane, N. (1985). Academic achievement and socioemotional adjustment among Chinese university students. *Journal of Counseling Psychology,* 32, 570–579.

Triandis, H. C., and Brislin, R. W. (1984). Cross-cultural psychology. *American Psychologist,* 39, 1006–1016.

Vega, W. A., and Rumbaut, R. G. (1991). Ethnic minorities and mental health. *Annual Review of Sociology,* 17, 351–383.

Westermeyer, J. (1988) DSM-III psychiatric disorders among Hmong refugees in the United States: A point prevalence study. *American Journal of Psychiatry,* 145, 197–202.

Ying, Y. (1988). Depressive symptomatology among Chinese-Americans as measured by the CES-D. *Journal of Clinical Psychology,* 44, 739–746.

18.
Traumatization Stress Among Asians and Asian Americans

Francis R. Abueg and Kevin M. Chun

The study of traumatic exprinces among Asians and Asian Americans is characterized by a comparatively small body of literature. The subset of studies devoted specifically to the examination of posttraumatic stress disorder (PTSD) is very limited.
Even the discussion of the application of the construct of PTSD has only recently
been broached for such topics as Asian refugees (e.g., Friedman and Jaranson, 1994;
Kinzie and Boehlein, 1989; Marsella, Friedman, and Spain, 1993; Mollica, 1994) and
Asian war veterans (e.g., Kiang, 1991; Marsella, Chemtob, and Hamada, 1992). Nevertheless, this nascent research literature strongly demonstrates the vast suffering endured by members of various Asian ethnic minority groups. The aim of this chapter
is to draw a clear link between ethnic-specific traumatization, psychopathology, and
the fledgling literature concerned with PTSD, especially that concerning Southeast
Asian refugees settled in North America and Asian American Vietnam veterans.

SOUTHEAST ASIAN REFUGEES

Southeast Asian refugees represent a high-risk population for mental illness because of
their extensive exposure to traumatic events and stressors that typically span four time
periods in the refugee experience: (a) premigration, (b) migration, (c) encampment, and
(d) postmigration.

Premigration stressors include brutalization and death of family and friends, and loss of
property and personal belongings associated with extensive and sustained warfare.
Additionally, many Southeast Asians were subjected to government-sponsored intimida-
tion and threats to their livelihood once the Communists gained power in their homelands in Vietnam, Cambodia, and Laos. *Migration stressors* encompass the separation from
or deaths of family and relatives while fleeing one's home country under life-threatening
conditions. Assaults by border guards while entering neighboring countries were also
common occurrences for many refugees.

Encampment stressors are characterized by prolonged detainment in unsafe, overcrowded, and poorly sanitized refugee camps. Many detained refugees also faced uncer-
tainty surrounding their future and the fate of separated family and friends. Finally,
postmigration stressors involve building a new life in a foreign country, which necessitates
the learning of new skills and cultural norms while dealing with the profound loss of loved
ones, personal belongings, and even a familiar way of life. Because there is wide variability in the experiences and adjustment levels of Southeast Asians, the traumatic experiences, prevalence rates and high-risk correlates of psychopathology, and special treatment
considerations will be presented for each refugee group.

The Vietnamese

The Vietnamese were one of the first Southeast Asian groups to flee their war-torn homelands and journey to the United States (see Mollica, 1994). Premigration stressors for the Vietnamese center around loss of and separation from family and friends, and destruction of personal property during the Vietnam War. Beginning in 1975, first-wave Vietnamese refugees migrated to the United States primarily in family units and represented the educated and professional classes of Vietnam. In contrast, second-wave Vietnamese refugees who fled Vietnam between 1977 and 1980 were mostly of rural and less educated backgrounds (Takaki, 1989). These refugees, most visibly known as the *boat people,* endured severe migration traumas. It is estimated that more than 200,000 of these refugees died at sea as they fled Vietnam on overcrowded and outdated vessels (Lee and Lu, 1989). Furthermore, over 80% of the boats were boarded by pirates who robbed, raped, assaulted, and killed its passengers (e.g., Lee and Lu, 1987; Mollica, 1994).

Those who succeeded in fleeing Vietnam often landed into refugee camps in Thailand, Hong Kong, Indonesia, Malaysia, and the Philippines. In Thailand, Vietnamese refugees faced what was considered the worst camp conditions and many were detained at Sikhiu, a former jail (Beiser, Turner, and Ganesan, 1989). The life situation of those who remained behind in Vietnam was also precarious at best as many faced the constant threat of indefinite imprisonment in reeducation camps where forced labor, starvation, and torture were commonplace. Past studies indicate that Vietnamese refugees exhibit high levels of psychological and physical distress resulting from their past traumas.

In a recent study (Felsman, Leong, Johnson, and Felsman, 1990), the baseline functioning of Vietnamese youths was examined prior to their exposure to postmigration stressors. Psychological distress among Vietnamese adolescents (13–17 yrs.), unaccompanied minors (13–18 yrs, without adult family members or relatives), and young adults (17.5–20 yrs.) was assessed using the General Health Questionnaire (GHQ), Hopkins Symptom Checklist-25 (HSCL), and the Vietnamese Depression Scale (VDS). Results from this study showed that although high anxiety levels and poor general health were clinically significant across all three groups, the young adult group was especially vulnerable to depression, anxiety, and poor general health.

One of the first studies on the general physical and mental health of first-wave Vietnamese refugees also reported high levels of psychological and physical distress using the Cornell Medical Index (CMI) (Lin, Tazuma, and Masuda, 1979). These researchers noted that 53% of their Phase I participants (data collection in 1975) and 55% of their Phase II sample (data collection in 1976, including both Phase I and new participants) manifested psychological problems. Overall dysfunction, which assessed both physical and psychological problems, was seen in 48% of the Phase I and 56% of the Phase II participants.

Lin, Tazuma, and Masuda (1979) concluded that the similarity of the CMI profiles seen in both phases demonstrates that the mental and physical problems exhibited by these Vietnamese refugees were consistent over time for a one-year period. Furthermore, they noted that certain segments of the Vietnamese refugee population were significantly at risk for psychological and physical dysfunction. In particular, divorced-widowed female heads of households, individuals over 46 years old, individuals younger than 21 years old, and women between 21 and 45 years exhibited significant levels of dysfunction.

Demographic, premigration, and postmigration predictors of psychological distress were also established in a state-wide community sample of Vietnamese people living in California (Chung and Kagawa-Singer, 1993). In this study, both anxiety and depressive symptoms were associated with demographic variables that included being female, older age, and little or no formal education in one's homeland. Premigration factors predicting high levels of both anxiety and depression included multiple traumas and fewer years spent in a refugee camp.

The premigration variable—numerous deaths of family members—only predicted anxiety. Postmigration factors predicting both anxiety and depression included a low family income, whereas large family size only predicted depression. Protective factors of psychological well-being among Vietnamese refugees have also been investigated. For example, Tran (1989) found that greater memberships in ethnic social organizations, numerous ethnic confidants, high self-esteem, and high income all significantly contributed to positive psychological well-being for Vietnamese immigrants.

Chun (1991) examined the same statewide sample of Southeast Asians in Chung and Kagawa-Singer's study to investigate correlates of psychosocial dysfunction or impairment in daily living. This variable provides important information beyond knowledge of symptoms alone. In this study, experiential correlates of psychosocial dysfunction included multiple premigration traumas and experiencing few reunions with separated family and relatives. Also, status variables such as being female or unemployed, having poor English-speaking skills, and relocating to a United States residence that is demographically different from one's native residence were correlated with dysfunction among Vietnamese refugees.

Prevalence rates of PTSD among Vietnamese refugees vary across studies. In a study of Southeast Asian patients seen at a specialized refugee clinic, 11% of the Vietnamese sample reportedly suffered from PTSD, a diagnosis that was established using the Diagnostic Interview Schedule (DIS) based on *DSM–III* criteria (Mollica, Wyshak, and Lavelle, 1987). Furthermore, results from this study indicated that multiple traumas was associated with greater susceptibility for PTSD. Kroll et al. (1989) reported that 8.1% of Vietnamese patients in a Southeast Asian psychiatric out-patient population exhibited PTSD. These findings were based on clinical interviews and a 19-item checklist comprising culturally relevant signs of depressive and anxiety symptoms based on *DSM-III* criteria.

This instrument was not cross-validated with other instruments. Women who were widows and increased age until 60 years were associated with increased risk for mental disorders among the general Southeast Asian population in this study. Kinzie et al. (1990) reported that 54% of a sample of Vietnamese psychiatric patients were diagnosed with PTSD using a *DSM–III–R* checklist. Moreover, PTSD was associated with advanced age, female gender, and a diagnosis of depression among this population.

Despite the high levels of psychological and physical distress manifested among the Vietnamese, they are generally better adjusted than other Southeast Asian refugee groups. Across the majority of studies, Vietnamese refugees have exhibited the lowest prevalence rate of PTSD compared with other Southeast Asian refugees. Chung and Kagawa-Singer (1993) also noted that a Vietnamese sample population was relatively well-adjusted compared with Cambodians and Laotians because community supports were already established upon their arrival to the United States by earlier well-educated and professional first-wave Vietnamese refugees. Along similar lines, past community-based studies have shown that Vietnamese refugees report greater happiness and less depression than Cambodian and Hmong refugees (Rumbaut, 1985) and less alienation than Cambodians, Hmong, and Laotians (Nicassio, 1983).

Cambodians (Khmer)

The Cambodians (Khmer) endured particularly severe premigration traumas beginning in 1975 with the rise of the Pol Pot regime. During this time, Pol Pot lead the Khmer Rouge on a bloody campaign of genocide to establish a Marxist agrarian society and rid the country of any Western influence. Mass executions, forced separations of family members, and confinement to work camps especially targeted at the professional and working classes were subsequently introduced on a national scale. Life in the work camps consisted of hard labor, torture, beatings, starvation, disease, and killings. Upon the Vietnamese invasion of Cambodia in 1979, a quarter of Cambodia's population was decimated and thousands fled to neighboring Thailand, where they were placed in refugee camps.

Cambodian refugees represent a special at-risk group for mental and physical illness because of their far-reaching history of premigration traumas. For instance, significantly higher levels of anxiety and depression have been seen in a nonpatient sample of Cambodians compared with Vietnamese and Vietnamese-Chinese refugees (Foulks, Merkel, Boehlin, 1992). Cambodian refugees also appear to have poorer self-perceptions and see themselves as more different from Americans to a greater extent than do Vietnamese, Laotian, and Hmong refugees (Mollica, 1994; Nicassio, 1983). Similarly, Rumbaut (1985) found that in a Cambodian community sample participants reported more depressive symptoms compared with any other Southeast Asian refugee group.

Chung and Kagawa-Singer (1993) likewise reported that participants from a community sample of Cambodian refugees exhibited the greatest psychological distress, as manifested by depressive and anxiety symptoms, than the Vietnamese and Laotians. In this study, less education and small family size in the United States predicted depression, whereas older age, multiple traumas, increased years spent in a refugee camp, and attendance in English as a Second Language (ESL) classes predicted both anxiety and depressive symptoms. Chung and Kagawa-Singer (1993) stated that this latter contradictory finding may reflect the ineffectiveness of ESL classes for Cambodians (These authors posit that the Cambodians may be suffering from trauma-related cognitive impairments that may contribute to their experience of psychological distress while attending ESL classes). Correlates of psychosocial dysfunction among Cambodian refugees include older age, multiple traumas, numerous separations from family and relatives, frequent reunions with family and relatives (which may place added strain on limited household resources), and a prolonged stay in refugee camps (Chun, 1991).

The high rates of traumatization reported among Cambodian refugees also appear to be associated with elevated rates of PTSD. Mollica, Wyshak, and Lavelle (1987) reported that 57% of respondents in a Cambodian psychiatric patient sample suffered from PTSD according to *DSM-III* criteria. Moreover, Cambodians experienced more traumas (M = 16.1 traumas) than the Vietnamese and Hmong/Laotian groups in this study. Of particular concern, Cambodian women who were separated, divorced, or widowed suffered the most traumas and displayed the most serious psychiatric and social impairments of all the patients. Kroll et al. (1989) likewise reported that 22% of Cambodians in a clinic population met *DSM-III* criteria for PTSD, which was the highest percentage of PTSD cases compared to those observed for Vietnamese, Hmong, and Lao refugees. Kinzie et al. (1990) also observed a high rate of PTSD (92%) among their clinic sample of Cambodians using DSM-III-R diagnostic criteria.

In a nonpatient sample of Cambodian refugees, a moderate correlation was found between trauma and psychiatric symptoms (Carlson and Rosser-Hogan, 1991). Nonetheless, 86% met modified *DSM-III-R* criteria for PTSD and emotional distress, whereas 96% experienced high levels of dissociation. The authors of this study concluded that the high rate of dissociation in this Cambodian population supports the universality of dissociation as a response to trauma. Kinzie and Boehnlein (1989) also noted that chronic psychotic symptoms may appear following massive psychological trauma among Cambodian refugees.

Past studies have examined Cambodian adolescents and young adults who were traumatized as children, to establish prevalence rates and correlates of PTSD in this population and examine the natural course of PTSD. Realmuto et al. (1992) reported high rates of traumatization among their nonpatient sample of Cambodian adolescents, especially among older youths. The authors stated that older youths may have reported more traumas for several reasons, namely because they were exposed to more traumas that were not applicable to the very young (e.g. forced labor), or simply because they were able to better comprehend or remember traumatic events than their younger counterparts. In any case, 87% of the Cambodian adolescents in this study met DSM-III criteria for PTSD, and 37% met the *DSM-III-R* PTSD criteria.

Realmuto et al. (1992) reasoned that the disparity between these prevalence rates can be attributed to fewer hyperarousal symptoms, which are required in the *DSM-III-R* classification of PTSD, among this population. Clarke, Sack, and Goff (1993) also found that a strong relationship exists between war trauma experienced in childhood and PTSD symptoms experienced in adolescence or young adulthood. Moreover, Cambodian adolescents and young adults reporting PTSD symptoms also reported greater amounts of resettlement stress than those without PTSD symptoms.

In a follow-up study of Cambodian adolescents who were traumatized as children, Kinzie, Sack, Angell, Clarke, and Ben (1989) found that 48% of their sample satisfied *DSM-III-R* criteria for PTSD. This finding was remarkable considering that over 10 years had elapsed since most of the children were traumatized. Kinzie et al., (1989) concluded that this demonstrated that PTSD was relatively stable and persistent over time. Nevertheless, they also mentioned that the Cambodian adolescents seemed to be functioning well in social, work, and family environments despite their high rates of PTSD.

Sack et al. (1993) examined the same population in Kinzie et al's (1989) study to chart the natural course of PTSD from adolescence to young adulthood. Results from this study indicated that 38% of the overall population exhibited a *DSM-III-R* diagnosis of PTSD. The authors stated that although PTSD persists, its symptoms become less intense and frequent over time. Furthermore, the overall functioning of these Cambodian young adults continued to be impressive; they were free of conduct problems, drug and alcohol abuse, and psychological breakdowns.

It is interesting to note that many Cambodians, with the exception of Cambodian women without spouses, are able to function in their social and occupational milieus despite their high rates of psychological and physical distress (Mollica, Wyshak, and Lavelle, 1987). This may be partly attributed to their general outlook on life and Buddhist beliefs. For example, Rumbaut (1985) noted that the Cambodians in a community sample of Southeast Asian refugees reported the most life satisfaction despite their significantly high levels of depressive symptoms and low self-reports of happiness.

Rumbaut (1985) credits this finding to an interaction between the extensive history of premigration traumas among many Cambodians and cultural appraisals of their life situation that are embedded in Buddhist values. In this case, postmigration stressors may be viewed as minor strains when compared with the severe traumas incurred in Cambodia. Furthermore, as will be discussed later in this chapter, many Cambodians frame their traumatic experiences within their Buddhist beliefs. For many Cambodians, life experiences are thus regarded as meaningful occurrences of fate or *kharma* which, from this spiritual perspective, may then contribute to positive adjustment to past traumas.

Laotians

Beginning with the Geneva Accords in 1954, civil discord erupted in Laos as the North Vietnamese-backed Pathet Lao fought the American-supported Royal Lao government for control of Laos, which had then gained independence from France (Takaki, 1989). As the Pathet Lao seized control of Laos in 1979 with the withdrawal of American troops from Southeast Asia, they embarked upon a massive campaign of retribution against former supporters of the Royal Lao government. During this time, thousands of Laotians of diverse social, educational, and economic backgrounds escaped to the adjacent country of Thailand where almost all were detained in refugee camps.

In general, the psychological and physical functioning of the overall Laotian refugee population was somewhat better than or equal to the functioning of other Southeast Asian refugee groups. Nicassio (1983) found that Laotians maintained the best self-perceptions compared with Vietnamese, Cambodian, and Hmong refugees. Furthermore, Laotians did not view themselves as highly different from Americans. Still, many Laotians have endured traumas that have contributed to mental and physical distress.

Chung and Kagawa-Singer (1993) established demographic, premigration, and postmigration predictors of psychological distress among a community sample of Laotian refugees. These researchers found that Laotian women were at higher risk for depression and anxiety than their male counterparts. Additionally, individuals who resided in the United States for a lengthy period were at risk for depression. The premigration variable—numerous traumatic events—predicted both depression and anxiety. Postmigration predictors of depression and anxiety include unemployment and receipt of public assistance. Finally, high family income predicted depression.

Chun (1991) found that the experiential factors—multiple premigration traumas, and few reunions with family and relatives—were correlates of psychosocial dysfunction among Laotian refugees. Status correlates of dysfunction among this group included being female, unemployment, poor English-speaking proficiency, and relocating to a United States residence demographically different from one's native residence.

Kroll et al. (1989) reported that 19.7% of their Laotian patients suffered from PTSD based on DSM-III criteria. Kinzie et al. (1990) reported a much higher prevalence rate of PTSD (68%) for a clinic sample of Laotian refugees. These researchers also stated that female and older Laotians were most susceptible for developing PTSD. Finally, Mollica et al. (1987) reported the highest prevalence rate of PTSD at 92% for a patient sample of Hmong/Laotian refugees. This latter finding, however, may be artificially inflated by combining traditionally highly traumatized Hmong refugees with the Laotian refugee sample (see also Mollica, 1994).

Hmong and Mien

Both the Hmong and Mien cultures are rooted in tribal, agrarian, and preliterate societies located in the mountainous regions of Laos and other Southeast Asian countries. The Hmong culture did not possess a written language until American and French missionaries developed one in the mid-1950s (Sherman, 1988). The majority of Hmong withstood premigration warfare during their tenure as CIA-sponsored soldiers whose mission was to combat Pathet Lao Communist guerrillas in the early 1960s (Cerhan, 1990). However, the Hmong became targets of deadly recriminations as the Royal Lao government fell to the Pathet Lao in 1979. Many Hmong were then forced to flee their highland homes and cross into Thailand under perilous circumstances and constant pursuit by Pathet Lao militia men.

Similar to the Hmong, the Mien's education and sociocultural tradition were transmitted orally until they formed a written language in 1982 (Moore and Boehnlein, 1991). The geographical location of the Mien's homeland also placed them in the middle of constant but "unofficial" warfare during the Vietnam War until their mass exodus into Thailand. Relatively little research has been conducted with the Mien in comparison with other Southeast Asian refugees. However, the few studies that exist show marked psychological impairment resulting from extensive premigration trauma and significant postmigration stressors.

Both the Hmong and Mien exhibit severe levels of psychological distress and impaired psychosocial functioning. Rumbaut (1985) found that the Hmong reported the least happiness and life satisfaction and the second most depression in his Southeast Asian community sample. Nicassio (1983) similarly reported that the Hmong exhibited much more alienation than other Southeast Asian refugees. Postmigration stressors may be particularly burdensome for the Hmong and Mien given their sociocultural backgrounds and lack of contact with Western technology and cultural norms. Westermeyer (1989) found that failure to acculturate may exacerbate and contribute to paranoid symptoms among Hmong refugees. Specifically, those who had more intense contacts within the Hmong community and more affiliation with Hmong culture exhibited more paranoid symptoms compared with their more Western-acculturated peers.

Westermeyer (1988) conducted a prevalence study to establish the rates and types of *DSM-III* diagnosis among a community sample of Hmong refugees. Results from this study showed that the majority of Hmong refugees (31%) suffered from adjustment disorder. However, none of the refugees were seeking treatment and half were able to function in their families and occupations despite the chronic nature of their symptoms. Westermeyer thus proposed that these refugees were not suffering from a psychological disorder per se, but rather from "refugee adjustment syndrome" or "refugee acculturation phenomenon."

Still, it appears that certain symptoms may subside over time. For instance, Wester-meyer, Neider, and Callies (1989) found that depression, somatization, phobic anxiety, and self-esteem improved over time and with acculturation. However, anxiety, hostility, and paranoid ideations improved the least. Additionally, strong traditional ties, marital prob-lems, and self-reported medical problems were associated with greater psychological distress, whereas older age was related to higher levels of depression. Chun (1991) also found that multiple premigration traumas and poor English proficiency placed Hmong refugees at risk for psychosocial dysfunction.

Both Hmong and Mien refugees traditionally exhibit some of the highest levels of PTSD. For instance, Mollica et al. (1987) reported that 92% of a sample of Hmong and Laotian patients suffered from a DSM-III diagnosis of PTSD. Similarly, Kinzie et al. (1990) found that 93% of a clinic population of Hmong refugees manifested PTSD, the highest rate of PTSD among all Southeast Asian groups. Lastly, Kroll et al. (1989) showed that 11.8% of the Hmong refugees seen in their clinic were PTSD sufferers.

General Conclusions for Southeast Asian Refugee Populations

In sum, there are only a few studies that have actually looked at the prevalence rate of PTSD among Southeast Asian refugees using valid instruments and diagnostic criteria. Also, past findings are often quite variable across studies partly because of differences in sample composition (e.g. patient vs. nonpatient samples) and diagnostic criteria (e.g. *DSM-III* vs. *DSM-III-R* PTSD criteria). Nonetheless, the reported prevalence rates of PTSD for Southeast Asian refugees are remarkably elevated because of the nature and extent of their traumatization. Furthermore, these traumatized Asians manifest clinically significant levels of general anxiety and depressive symptoms.

Generally speaking, the Cambodians (Khmer), Hmong, and Mien refugees represent the three most traumatized groups, with the majority arriving within the last decade. Therefore, the immediate concerns of these refugees may center around their premigra-tion traumas. In contrast, Vietnamese refugees have generally been here the longest, so postmigration stressors such as English speaking difficulties and unemployment may be their primary concern. Unfortunately, research on Lao refugees is lacking. Nonetheless, it appears that Lao refugees fall somewhere in the middle of Southeast Asian groups in regards to trauma exposure and overall adjustment levels. According to Gong-Guy (1987), 17% of the Lao sample population reported one or more premigration traumatic events. The percentage of traumatization among other groups is as follows: Cambodians (43%), Hmong (17%), and Vietnamese (14%).

ASIAN AMERICAN VIETNAM VETERANS

A handful of single-case studies and small-sample diagnostic investigations have directly examined the psychological effects of the Vietnam war on veterans of Asian American descent. Initial observations pointed toward some important consistencies among these ethnic minority veterans. Fighting an unpopular war in Southeast Asia during a period of great racial conflict provided the context for unique stressors and psychological conse-quences for these soldiers.

For example, it has been repeatedly observed that these American soldiers were subjected to racism typically reserved for the enemy, such as being called names such as "gook" and "dink" (e.g., Hamada, Chemtob, Sautner, and Sato, 1988; Marsella, Chemtob, and Hamada, 1990). Loo (in press) identified a number of other race-related stressors and cited numerous anecdotal accounts: being mistaken for the Vietnamese on the battlefield, race-related physical assault or injury, unintended death or grief, near-death experiences, and non-verbal communications of prejudice.

The bicultural identification of many Asian American Vietnam veterans posed another set of stressors before, during, and after the war. One Japanese American patient described this problem to us as the "banana syndrome: being White on the inside and yellow on the outside" (Abueg and Gusman, 1991). To reaffirm his allegiance with his unit, his fellow soldiers, and his country, this patient would exaggerate his American identity. His Southern drawl would become more pronounced, and he became louder and more aggressive and would use racial epithets for the Vietnamese. These behaviors caused great internal conflict: guilt, shame, and a sense of betrayal of people who reminded him so much of his own family.

Chun and Abueg (1989) conceptualized similar conflicts of a Filipino American Vietnam veteran in a triadic fashion: the intersection among peer norms, parental norms, and cultural norms. Depending on the context (being in war or stateside) and salience of social influences (being close to family, friends; practicing traditions of Filipino culture), the axis of this veteran's identity was in a constant state of flux. Most disruptive to establishing some sense of a "centered self" was the fact that profound traumatic conditioning and PTSD had inhibited successful adaptation regardless of ethnic identity. It was hypothesized that the bicultural identity of this Filipino American exacerbated his sense of instability.

Matsuoka and Hamada (1991) made an important contribution to this literature in studying the variation in the expression of PTSD in Asian American Vietnam veterans across three subgroups: Japanese American, Chinese American, and Native Hawaiian. A fourth group comprised Koreans, Filipinos, and Samoans, each of which had a sample size too small to independently study. The first set of findings confirmed a high degree of ethnic identification with the enemy across a sizable proportion of the 44 veterans in the sample. Feelings of estrangement from fellow American soldiers were also commonly reported.

With regard to rates of PTSD, wide variation across subgroups was found (Matsuoka and Hamada, 1991): no Japanese Americans, 13% of Chinese Americans, 29% of Native Hawaiians, and 40% of the other "mixed" group cited earlier had PTSD diagnoses. Although the authors acknowledged the sampling limitations of their study, they speculated that these findings at least point toward more careful study of predisposing economic and social factors that may place certain groups at psychological risk for traumatization.

It is noteworthy that a major study of prevalence rates among Native Hawaiian and Japanese American Vietnam War veterans is currently in progress in Hawaii under the auspices of the National Center for PTSD of the Department of Veterans Affairs. This study is using methodologies similar to those used in the National Vietnam Veterans Research Study (NVVRS) (see chapter 16 by Schlenger and Fairbank in this volume). The results of the Hawaii Study will provide substantive research data on PTSD rates and expressive patterns for these two groups.

CULTURE-SPECIFIC CONCEPTUALIZATIONS OF TRAUMA TREATMENT

The power of the mental health's professional's conceptualization of PTSD (e.g., Friedman and Jaranson, 1994; Friedman and Marsella, this volume) is that the trauma becomes a centerpiece or touchstone upon which treatment can be based. The findings we have summarized in the chapter suggest that the traumatic experience is not homogeneous even within a specific region like Southeast Asia. Instead of simply paying lip service to the notion of cultural sensitivity (Sue and Sue, 1990), we suggest that the clinician must have a fine-grained understanding of the base rates of traumatization, by specific ethnic subgroups.

For those clinicians experienced with trauma, this may appear at face to be a superfluous or redundant recommendation. However, we believe this point needs particular attention because of the typically unavoidable cultural rifts between patient and therapist, subject and scientist. Hence, specific knowledge must include, for example, how premigration traumas varied between Cambodians and Vietnamese. Understanding these finer variations will undoubtedly have an impact on the empathic quality of interviewer questions; moreover, this knowledge may lead to creative interventions yet to be discussed in this literature. For example, Western therapists can begin to actively incorporate Buddhist principles into their practice for ethnic subgroups who adhere to such beliefs (Canda and Phaobtong, 1992). Creative integration of knowledge about subtle variations across and within these various cultures and subcultures will likely have direct impact upon patient disclosure and help-seeking, especially about experiences often so horrific and unspeakable. Many developmental (Loo, 1993) and constructivist (Gusman et al., this volume) approaches have begun to articulate such an integration for clinical work.

BIBLIOGRAPHY

Abueg, F. R., and Gusman, F. D. (1991). *Variability in the treatment of Asian Americans with Post-Traumatic Stress Disorder (PTSD): Four case histories.* Unpublished Manuscript. National Center for PTSD, VAMC (323 A8-MP), Palo Alto, CA.

Beiser, M., Turner, R., and Ganesan, S. (1989). Catastrophic stress and factors affecting its consequences among Southeast Asian Refugees. *Social Science Medicine*, 28, 183–195.

Canda, E. R., and Phaobtong, T. (1992). Buddhism as a support system for Southeast Asian refugees. *Social Work*, 37, 61–67.

Carlson, E. B., and Rosser-Hogan, R. (1991). Trauma experiences, posttraumatic stress, dissociation, and depression in Cambodian refugees. *American Journal of Psychiatry*, 148, 1548–1551.

Cerhan, J. U. (1990). The Hmong in the United States: An overview for mental health professionals. *Journal of Counseling and Development*, 69, 88–92.

Chun, K. M. (1991, August). *Correlates of psychosocial dysfunction among traumatized Southeast Asian refugees.* Paper presented at the Asian American Psychological Association convention, San Francisco, CA.

Chun, K. M., and Abueg, F. R. (1989). *An Ericksonian conceptualization of cultural factors in the adjustment of an Asian American Vietnam veteran.* Paper presented at the 18th Annual Western Psychology Conference for Undergraduate Research, Santa Clara University, Santa Clara, CA.

Chun, K. M., Chung, R., and Sue, S. (1994). *Correlates of psychosocial dysfunction among traumatized Southeast Asian refugees.* Unpublished manuscript. Department of Psychology, UCLA, Los Angeles, CA.

Chung, R., and Kagawa-Singer, M. (1993). Predictors of psychological distress among Southeast Asian refugees. *Social Science Medicine*, 36, 631–639.

Clarke, G., Sack, W. H., and Goff, B. (1993). Three forms of stress in Cambodian adolescent refugees. *Journal of Abnormal Child Psychology*, 21, 65–77.

Felsman, J. K., Leong, F.T.L., Johnson, M. C., and Felsman, L. C. (1990). Estimates of psychological distress among Vietnamese refugees: Adolescents, unaccompanied minors, and young adults. *Social Science Medicine*, 31, 1251–1256.

Foulks, E. F., Merkel, L., and Boehlin, J. K. (1992). Symptoms in nonpatient Southeast Asian refugees. *Journal of Nervous and Mental Disease*, 180, 466–468.

Friedman, M., and Jaranson, J. (1993). The applicability of the PTSD concept to refugees. In A. J. Marsella, T. Bornemann, S. Ekblad, and J. Orley (Eds.), *Amidst peril and pain: The mental health and wellbeing of the world's refugees* (pp. 207–227). Washington, DC: American Psychological Association.

Gong-Guy, E. (1987). *The California Southeast Asian mental health needs assessment* (Contract No. 85–76282A 2). Sacramento, CA: California State Department of Mental Health.

Hamada, R. S., Chemtob, C. M., Sautner, B., and Sato, R. (1988). Ethnic identity and Vietnam: A Japanese-American Vietnam veteran with PTSD. *Hawaii Medical Journal*, 47, 100–109.

Kiang, P. N. (1991). About face: Recognizing Asian and Pacific American Vietnam veterans in Asian-American studies. *Amerasia*, 17, 22–40.

Kinzie, J., and Boehnlein, J. J. (1989). Post -traumatic psychosis among Cambodian refugees. *Journal of Traumatic Stress*, 2, 185–198.

Kinzie, J., Boehnlein, J. K., Leung, P. K., Moore, L. J., Riley, C., and Smith, D. (1990). The prevalence of posttraumatic stress disorder and its clinical significance among Southeast Asian refugees. *American Journal of Psychiatry*, 147, 913–917.

Kinzie, J., Sack, W., Angell, R., Clarke, G., and Ben, R. (1989). A three-year follow-up of Cambodian young people traumatized as children. *Journal of the American Academy of Child and Adolescent Psychiatry*, 28, 501–504.

Kroll, J., Habenicht, M., Mackenzie, T., Yang, M., Chan, S., Vang, T., Nguyen, T., Ly, M., Phommasouvanh, B., Nguyen, H., Vang, Y., Souvannasoth, L., and Cabugao, R. (1989). Depression and posttraumatic stress disorder in Southeast Asian refugees. *American Journal of Psychiatry*, 146, 1592–1597.

Lee, E., and Lu, F. (1989). Assessment and treatment of Asian-American survivors of mass violence. *Journal of Traumatic Stress*, 2, 93–120.

Lin, K. M., Tazuma, L., and Masuda, M. (1979). Adaptational problems of Vietnamese refugees: I. Health and mental health status. *Archives of General Psychiatry*, 36, 955–961.

Loo, C. (1993). An integrative-sequential treatment model for posttraumatic stress disorder: A case study of the Japanese American internment and redress. *Clinical Psychology Review*, 13, 89–117.

Loo, C. (1994). The Asian American Vietnam veteran: Race-related trauma and PTSD. *Journal of Traumatic Stress*, 7, 637–656.

Marsella, A. J., Chemtob, C., and Hamada, R. (1992). (1990). Ethnocultural aspects of PTSD in Asian Vietnam war veterans. *National Center for PTSD Clinical Newsletter*, 1(1), 3–4.

Marsella, A. J., Friedman, M., and Spain, H. (1993). Ethnocultural aspects of PTSD. In J. Oldham, M. Riba, and A. Tasman (Eds.), *Review of psychiatry* (pp. 29–62). Washington, DC: American Psychiatric Press.

Matsuoka, J., and Hamada, R. (1991). The wartime and postwar experiences of Asian-Pacific American Vietnam veterans. *Journal of Applied Social Sciences*, 16, 23–36.

Mollica, R. (1994). Southeast Asian refugees: Migration history and mental health issues. In A. J. Marsella, T. Bornemann, S. Ekblad, and J. Orley (Eds.), *Amidst peril and pain: The mental health and wellbeing of the world's refugees* (pp. 83–100). Washington, DC: American Psychological Association.

Mollica, R., Wyshak, G., and Lavelle, J. (1987). The psychosocial impact of war trauma and torture on Southeast Asian refugees. *American Journal of Psychiatry*, 144, 1567–1572.

Moore, L. J., and Boehnlein, J. K. (1991). Treating psychiatric disorders among Mien refugees from highland Laos. *Social Science Medicine*, 32, 1029–1036.

Nicassio, P. M. (1983). Psychosocial correlates of alienation. *Journal of Cross-Cultural Psychology*, 14, 337–351.

Realmuto, G. M., Masten, A., Carole, L. F., Hubbard, J., Groteluschen, A., and Chhun, B. (1992). Adolescent survivors of massive childhood trauma in Cambodia: Life events and current symptoms. *Journal of Traumatic Stress*, 5, 589–599.

Rumbaut, R. (1985). Mental health and the refugee experience: A comparative study of Southeast Asian refugees. In T. C. Owan (Ed.), *Southeast Asian mental health: Treatment, prevention, services, training, and research* (pp. 433–486). Rockville, MD: National Institute of Mental Health.

Sack, W. H., Clarke, G., Him, C., Dickason, D., Goff. B., Lanham, K., and Kinzie, J. D. (1993). A 6-year follow-up study of Cambodian refugee adolescents traumatized as children. *Journal of the American Academy of Child and Adolescent Psychiatry*, 32, 431–437.

Sherman, S. (1988, October). The Hmong in America: Laotian refugees in the "land of the giants." *National Geographic*, 587–610.

Sue, S., and Sue, D. (1990). *Counseling the culturally different: Theory and practice*. New York: John Wiley and Sons.

Takaki, R. (1989). *Strangers from a different shore: A history of Asian Americans*. New York: Penguin.

Tran, T. V. (1989). Ethnic community supports and psychological well-being of Vietnamese refugees. *International Migration Review*, 21, 833–845.

Westermeyer, J. (1988). DSM-III psychiatric disorders among Hmong refugees in the United States: A point prevalence study. *American Journal of Psychiatry*, 145, 197–202.

Westermeyer, J. (1989). Psychological adjustment of Hmong refugees during their first decade in the United States: A longitudinal study. *Journal of Nervous and Mental Disease*, 177, 132–139.

Westermeyer, J., Neider, J., and Callies, A. (1989). Psychosocial adjustment of Hmong refugees during their first decade in the United States: A longitudinal study. *Journal of Nervous and Mental Disease*, 177, 132–139.

19.
Ethnocultural Differences in Prevalence of Adolescent Depression

Robert E. Roberts, Catherine R. Roberts, and Y. Richard Chen

Data from an ethnically diverse sample of middle school (Grades 6–8) students (n = 5,423) are analyzed for ethnic differences in major depression. The point prevalence of major depression was 8.4% without and 4.3% with impairment. Data were sufficient to calculate prevalences for nine ethnic groups. Prevalences adjusted for impairment ranged from 1.9% for youths of Chinese descent to 6.6% for those of Mexican descent. African and Mexican American youths had significantly higher crude rates of depression without impairment, but only the latter had significantly higher rates of depression with impairment. Multivariate (logistic regression) analyses, adjusting for the effects of age, gender, and socioeconomic status (SES), yielded significant odds ratios for only one group. Mexican American youths were at elevated risk for both depression without (OR = 1.74, p < .05) and depression with impairment (OR = 1.71, p <.05). There was no significant interaction of ethnicity and SES in relation to depression. Females had higher prevalences of depression with and without impairment, as did youths who reported that their SES was somewhat or much worse off than their peers. The data add to growing evidence that Mexican American youths are at increased risk of depression, and that community intervention efforts should specifically target this high-risk group.

There are virtually no data on depression among minority children and adolescents. The dearth of data on minority adolescents is not surprising, given the lack of data on adolescent depression in general. For example, there have been few community-based epidemiologic studies of adolescent depression. Perusing the studies that have been done, it is difficult to identify a coherent empirical pattern due to the great diversity in research designs, study populations, and methods of case ascertainment.

For example, Fleming and Offord (1990) identified nine epidemiologic studies of clinical depression and report that prevalence of current depression ranged from 0.4–5.7% in the five studies reporting such data. The mean prevalence of current major depression was 3.6%. Subsequent to that review, several other articles have appeared. Lewinsohn, Hops, Roberts, Seeley, and Andrews (1993) reported data from a large sample of high school students indicating a point prevalence for DSM-III-R major depression of 2.6%. Garrison, Addy, Jackson, McKeown, and Waller (1992) reported one-year prevalence rates of about 9% for DSM-III major depressive disorder in a large sample of middle-school students.

There is equal diversity in studies that focus on depressive symptoms. Five school-based studies using the Beck Depression Inventory (BDI) reported mean scores ranging from 6.0 to 10.3; the average was 8.6 (Baron and Parron, 1986; Doerfler, Felner, Rowlison,

Raley, and Evans, 1988; Gibbs, 1985; Kaplan, Hong, and Weinhold, 1984; Teri, 1982). At least eight studies, all school-based, have used the Center for Epidemiologic Studies Depression Scale (CES-D; Doerfler et al., 1988; Garrison, Jackson, Marsteller, McKeown, and Addy, 1990; Manson, Ackerman, Dick, Baron, and Fleming, 1990; Roberts, Andrews, Lewinsohn, and Hops, 1990; Roberts and Chen, 1995; Schoenbach, Kaplan, Grimson, and Wagner, 1982; Swanson, Linskey, Quintero-Salinas, Pumariega, and Holzer, 1992; Tolor and Murphy, 1985). These studies reported mean scores for the CES-D in the range of 16–20, with an overall mean of about 17. Prevalence of depressive symptoms using a CES-D caseness criterion of 16 or greater is in the range of 45–55%.

Given the limited number of epidemiologic studies of adolescent depression in general, it is not surprising that there have been few studies published focusing on race or ethnic status. Again, even among this small subset of studies the findings are not cohesive. Although some studies find no evidence of ethnic differences in adolescent depression (Doerfler et al., 1988; Garrison et al., 1990; Kandel and Davies, 1982; Manson et al., 1990), others report that minority adolescents report greater levels of depressive symptoms (Emslie, Weinberg, Rush, Adams, and Rintelmann, 1990; Schoenbach et al., 1982), and others that minority youth have lower levels of depression (Doerfler et al., 1988). But again, it is difficult to draw any firm conclusions concerning ethnic status and risk of depression from these studies, because they employ different measures of depression and they also focus on different ethnic minority adolescents (African American, Hispanic American, Native American, etc.).

Four published studies have included Mexican origin adolescents. Weinberg and Emslie (1987) reported that in their sample of high school students, Anglos had the lowest rates of depression on both the BDI and the Weinberg Screening Affective Scale (WSAS), African Americans were intermediate, and Mexican Americans had the highest rates.

Roberts and Sobhan (1992) analyzed data from a national survey of persons 12–17 years of age, comparing symptom levels of Anglo, African, Mexican origin, and other Hispanic Americans using a 12-item version of the CES-D. Mexican origin males reported more depressive symptoms than other males and the same was true for Mexican origin females, although to a lesser extent. Roberts (1994) examined depression rates among Mexican Origin and Anglo adolescents sampled from middle schools in Las Cruces, New Mexico. The minority youth had significantly higher rates of depressive symptoms on both the 20-item CES-D and the Weinberg Screening Affective Scale. In a second analyses of these data, Roberts and Chen (1995) examined depressive symptoms and suicidal ideation among Anglo and Mexican origin adolescents. The minority adolescents reported significantly more symptoms of depression and thoughts of suicide than their Anglo counterparts. Prevalences were highest for Mexican origin females. There was a strong association between depressive symptoms and suicidal ideation in both groups. Swanson et al. (1992) conducted a school-based survey in three cities in Texas and three in Mexico along the U.S.-Mexico border. The U.S. sample, comprising over 95% Mexican origin adolescents, had a prevalence of 48% using the score of 16 or more on the CES-D.

Other than the Anglo, African, or Mexican American groups, there are basically no data on the mental health of adolescents from the myriad minorities in the United States, many of whom also are economically disadvantaged.

Studies of the relation between ethnic status and psychological distress implicitly or explicitly examine two competing hypotheses, one of which argues that ethnic differences are due primarily to social class effects and the other that there are ethnic effects (both positive and negative) on mental health over and above social class effects. Mirowsky and Ross (1980) have labeled these two arguments, respectively, the minority status perspective and the ethnic culture perspective. The former argument asserts that to the extent an ethnic group is both a minority group and disadvantaged, there are chronic social stressors associated with disadvantaged position that produce greater distress. The latter argument, the ethnic culture perspective, assumes that psychological well-being varies with different cultural patterns in terms of beliefs, values, and life-styles. Thus, disadvantaged social class does not necessarily place members of an ethnic collectivity at greater risk for psychological disorder. Essentially these two arguments turn on a single question of fact: Are the rates of psychological disorder in ethnic minority populations different than the rates in the dominant ethnic population, when social class is controlled? If so, then the ethnic culture hypothesis is supported; if not, the minority status hypothesis is sustained. (Roberts and Vernon, 1984).

More recently, attempts to examine this question have extended the analytic strategy to examine both main and interactive effects of ethnic status and socioeconomic status. For example, Kessler and Neighbors (1986) and Ulbrich, Warheit, and Zimmerman (1989) reported that the effects of social class and the effect of minority status on psychological distress are interactive. That is, the effect of minority status on distress is more pronounced at lower income levels than at higher income levels. The explanations for this relation is that lower status minorities are exposed to more environmental stressors than others and/or they are more emotionally responsive to such stressors, hence higher prevalence of psychological dysfunction (see Kessler, 1979; Ulbrich et al., 1989). However, Somervell, Leaf, Weissman, Blazer, and Bruce (1989) found no evidence of significant or consistent interaction of race (White/Black) with household income or age for depression using data on adults from the five-site ECA study. Roberts and Sobhan (1992) also failed to find interaction effects in a sample of European, African, and Mexican American adolescents. Given that the evidence on interaction effects from studies of adults is mixed, and the only study of adolescents to examine this question did not find evidence for such an effect, additional inquiry clearly is needed. Is this effect a general effect, or conditioned by place, population, or procedures?.

Given the paucity of data on ethnocultural differences in adolescent depression, particularly Hispanic adolescents, our purpose here is to present data on symptoms of major depression in an ethnically diverse sample of middle-school students. We examine the relation between ethnic status, age, gender, and socioeconomic status (SES) on prevalence of major depressive episodes, examining both main and interaction effects.

PROCEDURES

Data presented are from a survey conducted in a school district in the Houston metropolitan area in March 1994. The survey included five middle schools enrolling about 6,400 students in Grades 6–8. Questionnaires were obtained from 5,496 subjects, ranging from 10–17 years of age (see Table 2).

The response rate was 85.3%. Nonparticipants (14.7%) included students absent during the first class period of the day, when the survey was conducted (9.3%), students whose parents declined for them to participate (4.0%), and students who themselves declined to participate (1.4%). Another 73 questionnaires were eliminated due to large numbers of missing data, resulting in 5,423 usable questionnaires. Students who were absent (9.3%) were not followed up either at home or at school.

The questionnaires were administered in classroom settings, monitored by project field staff. Completion took about an hour. Questionnaires were in English. Passive parental and active student consent procedures were used. That is, letters describing the survey were sent to parents requesting permission for their children to participate. Parents who declined returned a postcard. When the questionnaires were distributed, students could decline to participate and designate that on the front of the questionnaire.

Depression is measured using the DSM Scale for Depression (DSD), a self-administered checklist developed from the Diagnostic Interview Schedule for Children (DISC) questions on major depression. There are 31 items (Table 1) covering DSM-IV diagnostic

Table 1. DSM Scale for Depression (DSD)

In the past 2 weeks* . . .

1. Have you been very sad?
2. Have you been grouchy or irritable, or in a bad mood, so that even little things would make you mad?
3. Were there times when nothing was fun for you, even things you used to like?
4. Were there times when you just weren't interested in anything and felt bored or just sat around most of the time?
5. Have you felt like not eating?
6. Have you wanted to eat more than usual?
7. Have you had more trouble sleeping than usual (falling asleep or staying asleep or waking up too early)?
8. Have you slept a lot more than usual?
9. Have you talked or moved around a lot less than usual?
10. Have you been very restless, when you just had to keep walking around?
11. Have you been so down that it was hard for you to do your schoolwork or work?
12. Have you had trouble looking after yourself or your things, like keeping yourself clean or picking up after yourself?
13. Have you felt more tired than usual, so that you sat around and didn't do much of anything?
14. Have you felt like you had much less energy than usual, so that it was a big effort to do anything?
15. Have you felt less good about yourself than usual and blamed yourself a lot for things that happened in the past?
16. Have you been more down on yourself than usual, when you felt that you couldn't do anything right?
17. Have you felt bad about the way you look?
18. Have you felt like you were about to cry or were in tears?
19. Have you had more trouble than usual paying attention to your schoolwork or work, or keeping your mind on other things you were doing?
20. Have you been unable to concentrate or to think as clearly or as quickly as usual?
21. Have you felt that things never seem to work out all right for you?
22. Were there times it was harder for you to make up your mind about things or to make decisions?
23. Have you felt that life was hopeless and that there was nothing good for you in the future?
24. Have you thought more than usual about suicide or dying?
25. Did you wish you were dead?
26. Have you thought about suicide or killing yourself?
27. Have you ever made a plan to kill yourself? (Lifetime)
28. Have you made a plan to kill yourself in the past 2 weeks?
29. Have you ever tried to kill yourself? (Lifetime)
30. Have you tried to kill yourself in the past 2 weeks.
31. Have you
   lost a lot of weight
   lost a little weight
   stayed the same
   gained a little weight
   gained a lot of weight

* Except 27 and 29.

criteria. The time frame is the past 2 weeks. Two items (27 and 29) on suicide plans and attempts also inquire about lifetime experience. The DSD can be scored as a summated scale or can be used to estimate caseness using DSM-IV criteria. Cronbach's alpha in this sample is .93, overall and in most subgroups. There were no demonstrable ethnic differences in reliability on the DSD. The DSD also exhibits good construct validity, correlating inversely with SES, self-esteem, social support, active coping, happiness and optimism, and positively with loneliness and life stress (Roberts, Roberts, and Chen, 1995). Virtually

Table 2. Characteristics of the Study Subjects
(N = 5,423)

Characteristics	n	%
Age		
11 or younger	550	10.2
12	1,528	28.3
13	1,688	31.3
14	1,240	23.0
15 or older	389	7.2
Gender		
Male	2,719	51.2
Female	2,589	48.8
Grade		
6	1,833	34.1
7	1,809	33.6
8	1,737	32.2
Socioeconomic status		
Much worse off	92	1.9
Worse off	328	6.7
About the same	2,494	51.1
Better off	1,218	25.0
Much better off	712	14.6
N/A	32	0.7
Ethnicity		
African American	1,237	26.3
Anglo American	775	16.5
Asian	21	0.4
Cambodian American	22	0.5
Caribbean	19	0.4
Central American	253	5.4
Chinese American	177	3.8
Cuban American	12	0.3
European	64	1.4
Indian American	188	4.0
Korean American	26	0.6
Mexican American	755	16.0
Middle Eastern	49	1.0
Mixed Ancestry	342	7.3
Native American	41	0.9
Other	29	0.6
Pacific Islander	101	2.1
Pakistani American	155	3.3
Puerto Rican	46	1.1
South American	89	1.9
Vietnamese American	304	6.5

all epidemiologic data on depression among adolescents from different ethnic groups is from symptom scales that do not operationalize DSM criteria (see Roberts, Lewinsohn, and Seeley, 1991). Our use of the DSD was designated to correct this, and provide data using contemporary diagnostic nomenclature.

Respondents were scored as meeting diagnostic criteria for DSM-IV major depressive episode (MDE) if they reported (a) that they experienced five or more criterion symptoms, including depressed (or irritable) mood, or anhedonia, in the past 2 weeks, and (b) that they had not experienced death of a significant other in the recent past. DSM-IV specifies that to meet criteria for a major depressive episode, symptoms of depression are not better accounted for by bereavement (American Psychiatric Association [APA], 1994, p. 327).

Two point prevalence rates are presented: (a) For those who met criteria for MDE and (b) for those who met criteria and who also had experienced significant impairment in functioning at home, at school, and with peers. These items also were derived from the DISC. Again, DSM-IV specifies that to meet criteria for MDE, the symptoms of depression must cause significant impairment (APA 1994, p. 327).

Table 3. Prevalence of DSM–IV Major Depression, With and Without Adjustment for Impairment

	Without impairment		With impairment	
	n	%	n	%
Overall	3,959	8.4	3,549	4.3
Gender				
Male[a]	1,889	7.6	1,637	3.5
Female	1,992	8.9	1,844	5.0[b]
Ethnic group				
Anglo American[a]	741	6.3	702	3.9
African American	1,091	9.0[b]	933	3.9
Mexican American	700	12.0[c]	618	6.6[b]
Central American	304	7.9	260	5.0
Indian American	184	7.6	175	2.9
Pakistani American	146	6.9	129	2.3
Vietnamese American	288	6.3	270	3.0
Chinese American	174	2.9	160	1.9
Mixed Ancestry	331	9.4	302	5.6
Age				
12[a]	1,080	7.6	955	3.7
11 or younger	398	9.6	351	3.7
13	1,248	7.9	1,129	4.1
14	931	8.5	843	5.0
15 or older	279	11.1	251	6.4
Socioeconomic status				
About the same[a]	1,870	7.7	1,685	3.9
Much worse off	71	23.9[c]	62	17.7[c]
Somewhat worse off	239	17.6[c]	213	11.7[c]
Better off	920	6.6	849	2.9
Much better off	541	9.6	486	3.7

[a] Indicates reference group.
[b] Significant at .05.
[c] Significant at .001.

Ethnic status is self-designated, using these seven categories: Anglo or White; African or Black; Native American; specific Hispanic groups, including Cuban, Puerto Rican, Mexican, or Central American; specific Asian groups, including Cambodian, Vietnamese, Indian, Pakistani, Chinese, Korean, and Pacific Islander; Other; and Mixed Ancestry.

Characteristics of the sample are presented in Table 2. There was almost equal representation by gender and grade level. About half of the students reported that their SES was about the same as others at their school. More youths reported their SES was better or much better rather than worse or much worse than their peers. The ethnic composition was diverse; with over 20 distinct groups identified. Since some of the groups have small numbers, subsequent analyses focus on the nine largest groups.

RESULTS

Point prevalence rates of MDE, with and without adjustment for role impairment, are presented in Table 3. The point prevalences for the total sample were 8.4% without and 4.3% with impairment.

Table 4. Odd Ratios of DSM-IV Major Depression in Different Ethnic Groups, Adjusted for Age, Gender, and Socioeconomic Status

	Crude			Adjusted		
	OR	SE	p	OR	SE	p
Ethnic group						
Anglo American[b]	1.00	—	—	1.00	—	—
African American	1.00	.25	.989	1.03	.27	.900
Mexican American	1.77	.25	.023[c]	1.71	.26	.042[c]
Central American	1.31	.34	.427	1.22	.37	.596
Indian American	0.73	.49	.533	0.94	.50	.917
Pakistani American	0.59	.61	.399	0.76	.62	.673
Vietnamese American	0.76	.40	.509	0.59	.46	.268
Chinese American	0.47	.61	.229	0.47	.62	.233
Mixed Ancestry	1.49	.31	.208	1.27	.33	.467
Age						
12[b]	1.00	—	—	1.00	—	—
11 or younger	1.01	.33	.973	0.74	.36	.434
13	1.11	.22	.630	1.06	.23	.792
14	1.37	.23	.170	1.23	.24	.394
15 or older	1.78	.31	.060	1.52	.34	.217
Gender						
Male[b]	1.00	—	—	1.00	—	—
Female	1.45	.17	.029[c]	1.55	.18	.014[c]
Socioeconomic status						
About the same[a]	1.00	—	—	1.00	—	—
Much worse off	5.37	.35	.000[d]	5.17	.36	.000[d]
Somewhat worse off	3.31	.24	.000[d]	3.27	.25	.000[d]
Better off	0.75	.23	.242	0.78	.24	.330
Much better off	0.95	.27	.876	1.04	.27	.881

[a] Adjusted for impairment and bereavement.
[b] Reference group.
[c] Significant at .05.
[d] Significant at .001.

Data were sufficient to calculate prevalences of MDE for nine ethnic groups, as indicated in Table 3. Prevalences adjusted for impairment ranged from a low of 1.9% for students of Chinese descent to a high of 6.6% for those of Mexican ancestry. The rate for majority (Anglo) youths was mid-range (3.9%). African Americans and Mexican Americans have significantly higher crude rates without impairment compared to Anglos (the reference group), but only the latter have significantly higher rates with impairment. Females had higher rates than males, and those who are somewhat to much worse off economically had higher rates.

Table 4 presents odds ratios (OR) for crude prevalences as well as odds ratios adjusted for the effects of age, gender, and SES. As can be seen, adjusted odds ratios indicate that only one group has elevated risk: Mexican American students. The OR values are 1.77 (crude OR) and 1.71 (adjusted OR) ($p < .05$). The adjusted OR values also indicated that girls (OR = 1.45–1.55, $p < .05$), and students who reported that their economic circumstances were either somewhat (OR = 3.3, $p < .001$) or much worse off then others (OR = 5.2–5.4, $p < .001$) all had significantly higher prevalences of depression.

To examine the interaction between ethnicity and SES on prevalence of major depressive, we calculated the prevalence for each of 15 subgroups (3 ethnic by 5 SES), with and without adjustment for impairment. Analysis included Anglo, African and Mexican American youths. The chi-square test showed that the interaction effect was nonsignificant both with and without adjustment for impairment. We also used logistic regression analysis to examine the significance of the interaction of ethnicity and SES. The analysis included only three ethnic groups, Anglo, Black, and Hispanic groups, and we adjusted for gender and age. The results showed that the interaction effect was not significant, which is consistent with the calculation of prevalence for each subgroup.

DISCUSSION

There have been few community-based epidemiologic studies of DSM depression among adolescents, and almost none comparing diverse ethnocultural groups. How do our rates compare with other studies?

Fleming and Offord (1990) in their review article reported that prevalences of current depression ranged from 0.4–5.7% in the five studies reporting such data. The mean prevalence of current major depression was 3.6%. Our rates were 8.8% and 4.3% (adjusting for impairment).

Lewinsohn et al. (1993) reported data from a large sample of high school students indicating a point prevalence for DSM-III-R major depression of 2.6%. Garrison et al. (1992) reported 1-year prevalence rates of about 9% for DSM-III major depressive disorder in a large sample of middle-school students. Cooper and Goodyer (1993) reported data from a British sample of 11- to 16-year-old girls indicating a current (past month) prevalence of 3.6% and a 1 year prevalence of 6.0%. Kessler, McGonagle, Swartz, Blazer, and Nelson (1993), based on data from the National Comorbidity Survey, reported 12 month prevalence of DSM-III-R MDE for adults of 10.3% overall, and 12.8% for those 15–24 years of age. Current prevalence data have not been reported.

Our prevalence rates are well within the range reported from recent studies of youths and adults. The relations between prevalence of depression and other factors in our study also are consistent with the literature. Prevalences are higher for those reporting lower economic status. In the case of gender, our data indicate a significant trend toward higher rates for girls. For this sample of middle-school students, the female:male ratio was 1.4, based on prevalence of depression with functional impairment, and 1.2 without impairment. In terms of ethnic status, only the Mexican American adolescents reported significantly higher rates of major depression with impairment, independent of the effects of age, gender, and SES.

Contrary to the findings on adults reported by Kessler and Neighbors (1986) and replicated in part by Ulbrich et al. (1989), we found no evidence of an interaction between ethnic status and SES. Our findings on adolescents replicate our findings in two other studies of adolescent depression (Roberts and Chen, 1995; Roberts and Sobhan, 1992). Thus, we do not find that lower status minority youth are at disproportionate risk of depression compared to lower status majority youth.

The findings that adolescents of Mexican origin have elevated rates of depression corroborate those from other studies. In analyses of data from the 1985 national survey by the National Institute on Drug Abuse (Roberts and Sobhan, 1992), crude prevalence rates were higher for Mexican Americans who were at least 1.5 times more likely to report depressive symptoms than Anglos, adjusting for the effects of age, gender, perceived health, and SES. In analyses of survey data from Las Cruces, New Mexico, Mexican American adolescents reported more symptoms of depression than their Anglo counterparts (Roberts and Chen, 1995). The crude OR was 1.7. However, in that study adjustment for relevant covariates eliminated the differential. In the only other published study comparing Anglo, African, and Mexican American adolescents on depression, Emslie et al. (1990) found females and Mexican Americans to be at greater risk in terms of crude rates.

Why do Mexican American youths have elevated risks for major depressive episodes? One possible explanation appeals to the role of Mexican culture in the epidemiology of depression. For example, Ross, Mirowsky, and Cockerham (1983) reported that persons of Mexican origin are more fatalistic, and fatalism, in turn, increases psychological distress. In a second paper, Mirowsky and Ross (1984) reported that Mexican culture has contradictory effects on mental health, increasing symptoms of depression and decreasing symptoms of anxiety. Increased risk for depression is attributable to a higher prevalence of belief in external control among persons of Mexican heritage. A more recent paper by Neff and Hoppe (1993) suggested that ethnic differences in depression are the result of the complex interaction of acculturation, fatalism, and religiosity. Fatalism, or feelings of a lack of control, may lead to impaired coping effort, which in turn leads to psychological distress because fatalistic beliefs destroy both the will and the ability to cope with life's problems (Kohn, 1972; Pearlin and Schooler, 1978; Wheaton, 1980). Although fatalism appears to be one possible explanation for the higher prevalence of major depressive episodes we observed for Mexican American youths, no studies have yet examined this issue in adolescent samples.

There are other possibilities, of course. One possible explanation appeals to the response style theory of depression formulated by Nolen-Hoeksema (1991). She argued that ruminative response styles are more deleterious to the course and severity of depression than are distractive responses. Since prevalence rates are a function of incidence plus duration, any process that prolongs depression would increase prevalence, all other things equal. Since

Mexican American youths report higher prevalence of depression, particularly Mexican American girls, and women are more likely to use ruminative coping (see Nolen-Hoeksema and Girgis, 1994; Schwartz and Koenig, 1996), such coping styles may be operant. Again, however, no studies of minority adolescents have addressed this question.

Our results, which are generally consistent with other findings, are limited in some respects because of the nature of our measure of psychopathology. Our measure of depression operationalizes DSM criteria and is derived from a structured psychiatric interview, but it still is a self-report instrument. The resulting prevalence rates are not derived from clinical psychiatric assessments. Essentially all studies of ethnic status and psychological disorder among adolescents have relied on nonclinical or nondiagnostic measures of dysfunction, to the exclusion of clinical disorder (for an exception, see Bird et al., 1988). Symptoms of depression are highly prevalent among adolescents in general, and they are the source of considerable suffering. A better understanding of their etiology and consequences is needed. However, absence of a measure of clinical depression omits the more serious forms of depressive illness. From an epidemiological perspective, the differences in prevalence are substantial. For example, studies indicate the prevalence of clinical depression among adolescents is perhaps 3–4% (Fleming and Offord, 1990; Roberts et al., 1991). In the only study of clinical depression among Hispanic youth, Bird et al. (1988) reported the 6-month prevalence of depression/dysthymia in Puerto Rico was 2.8%. By contrast, prevalence rates based on data from depression scales are 4–10 times greater than those derived from clinical interviews. For example, in our Las Cruces study rates of depression using a score of 24 or greater on the CES-D were 20% for Anglo and 30% for Mexican American adolescents. Prevalence based on our measure in this study, the DSD, are congruent with those derived from clinical interviews, and much lower than from studies using most depression scales. Whether nonclinical and clinical depression differ in etiology and consequences is an important epidemiological question, and one for which as yet we have no empirical data.

Another caveat concerns examination of ethnic differentials in mental health. Reliance on ethnic status as the sole measure of the ethnic experience has yielded limited explanatory power (see Trimble, 1990–1991; Roberts and Chen, 1995). Ethnicity is a complex biopsychosocial construct that is only partially operationalized by demographic categories of race or ethnic status. Trimble (1990–1991) has argued that ethnicity can (should) be examined using measures that assess three domains: natal, behavioral, and subjective. There have been few epidemiological studies that have incorporated such a strategy, examining the question of what it is about ethnicity that increases or decreases risk for psychiatric disorder. Several recent studies of adolescents (Roberts and Chen, 1995; Vega, Gil, Zimmerman, and Warheit, 1993) have gone beyond ethnic status and report that language and acculturation, particularly acculturative stress, affect the risk of depression and suicidal behaviors independent of ethnic status. Our own research is following Trimble's strategy to examine this question, and future reports will focus on this expanded assessment of the ethnic experience of adolescents, in particular the role of factors such as fatalism and response styles on risk of depression among Mexican origin youths.

Thus far, there is a paucity of data on the mental health of minority group adolescents. Given the results presented here, and those reported in the limited literature on this issue, more research is in order if we want to better understand whether and how ethnicity constitutes a risk factor for adolescent psychopathology. Such efforts, if they are to succeed, must focus on what factors constitute generalized risk for depression and what factors constitute risks specific or unique to a particular group's ethnic experience. Do Mexican American adolescents, for example, experience unique stress exposure or unique stress vulnerability? More specifically, can we partition the variance in prevalence or incidence of depression into unique and shared components of exposure and vulnerability unique to the experience of Mexican American adolescents and those shared in common with all adolescents? Doing so will permit us to design and implement interventions that target shared risk components (universal interventions) or unique risk components (selective or indicated interventions) (Mrazek and Haggerty, 1994, pp. 19–29). Without such epidemiologic evidence to support our attempts to design community-based interventions, our successes will be few in number and modest in scope.

NOTE

Revision of a paper presented at the 123rd annual meeting of the American Public Health Association, October 29-November 2, 1995 San Diego, California. This research was supported in part by Research Grant No. MH51687 from the National Institute of Mental Health to the first author.

BIBLIOGRAPHY

American Psychiatric Association. (1994). *Diagnostic and statistical manual of mental disorders* (4th ed.), Washington, DC: Author.

Baron, P., and Parron, L. M. (1986). Sex differences in the Beck Depression Inventory scores of adolescents. *Journal of Youth and Adolescence*, 15, 165–171.

Bird, H. R., Canino, G., Rubio-Stipec, M., et al. (1988). Estimates of the prevalence of childhood maladjustment in a community survey in Puerto Rico. The use of combined measures. *Archives of General Psychiatry*, 45, 1120–1126.

Cooper, P. J., and Goodyer, I. (1993). A Community study of depression in adolescent girls I: Estimates of symptom and syndrome prevalence. *British Journal of Psychiatry*, 163, 369–374.

Doerfler, L. A., Felner, R. A., Rowlison, R. T., Raley, P. A., and Evans, E. (1988). Depression in children and adolescents: A comparative analysis of the utility and construct validity of two assessment measures. *Journal of Consulting and Clinical Psychology*, 56, 769–772.

Emslie, G. J., Weinberg, W. A., Rush, A. J., Adams, R. M., and Rintelmann, J. W. (1990). Depressive symptoms by self-report in adolescence: Phase I of the development of a questionnaire for depression by self-report. *Journal of Child Neurology*, 5, 114–121.

Fleming, J. E., and Offord, D. R. (1990). Epidemiology of childhood depressive disorders: A critical review. *Journal of the American Academy of Child and Adolescent Psychiatry*, 29(4), 571–580.

Garrison, C. Z., Jackson, K. L., Marsteller, F., McKeown, R. E., and Addy, C. L. (1990). A longitudinal study of depressive symptomatology in young adolescents. *Journal of the American Academy Child and Adolescent Psychiatry*, 29, 581–585.

Garrison, C. Z., Addy, C. L., Jackson, K. L., McKeown, R. E., and Waller, J. L. (1992). Major depressive disorder and dysthymia in young adolescents. *American Journal of Epidemiology*, 135, 792–802.

Gibbs, J. T. (1985). Psychological factors associated with depression in urban adolescent females: Implications for assessment. *Journal of Youth and Adolescence*, 14, 47–60.

Kandel, D. B., and Davies, M. (1982). Epidemiology of depressive mood in adolescents. *Archives of General Psychiatry*, 39, 1205–1212.

Kaplan, G. A., Hong, G. K., and Weinhold, C. (1984). Epidemiology of depressive symptomatology in adolescents. *Journal of the American Academy Child Psychiatry*, 23, 91–98.

Kessler, R. C. (1979). Stress, social status, and psychological distress. *Journal of Health and Social Behavior*, 20, 259–273.

Kessler, R. C., and Neighbors, H. W. (1986). A new perspective on the relationship among race, social class, and psychological distress. *Journal of Health and Social Behavior*, 27, 107–115.

Kessler, R. C., McGonagle, K. A., Swartz, M., Blazer, D. G., and Nelson, C. B. (1993). Sex and depression in the National Comorbidity Survey I: Lifetime prevalence, chronicity, and recurrence. *Journal of Affective Disorders*, 29, 85–96.

Kohn, M. (1972). Class, family and schizophrenia. *Social Forces*, 50, 295–304.

Lewinsohn, P. M., Hops, H., Roberts, R. E., Seeley, J. R., and Andrews, J. A. (1993). Adolescent psychopathology I: Prevalence and incidence of depression and other DSM-III-R disorders in high school students. *Journal of Abnormal Psychology*, 102, 133–144.

Manson, S. M., Ackerman, L. M., Dick, R. W., Baron, A. E., and Fleming, C. M. (1990). Depressive symptoms among American Indian Adolescents: Psychometric characteristics of the CES-D psychological assessment. *Journal of Consulting and Clinical Psychology*, 2, 231–237.

Mirowsky, J., and Ross, C. E. (1980). Minority status, ethnic culture, and distress: A comparison of Blacks, Whites, Mexicans, and Mexican Americans. *American Journal of Sociology*, 86, 479–495.

Mirowsky, J., and Ross, C. E. (1984). Mexican culture and its emotional contradictions. *Journal of Health and Social Behavior*, 25, 2–13.

Mrazek, P. J., and Haggerty, R. J. (Eds.). (1994). *Reducing risks for mental disorders*. Washington, DC, National Academy Press.

Neff, J. A., and Hoppe, S. K. (1993). Race/ethnicity, acculturation, and psychological distress: Fatalism and religiosity as cultural resources. *Journal of Community Psychology*, 21, 3–20.

Nolen-Hoeksema, S. (1991). Responses to depression and their effects on the duration of depressive episodes. *Journal of Abnormal Psychology*, 100, 569–582.

Nolen-Hoeksema, S., and Girgis, J. S. (1994). The emergence of gender differences in depression during adolescence. *Psychological Bulletin*, 115, 424–443.

Pearlin, L. I., and Schooler, C. (1978). The structure of coping. *Journal of Health and Social Behavior*, 19, 2–21.

Roberts, R. E. (1994). An exploration of depression among Mexican origin and Anglo adolescents, to appear in R. Malgady and O. Rodriguez (Eds.), *Theoretical and Conceptual Issues in Hispanic Mental Health Research*, Krieger Publishing Company.

Roberts, R. E., Andrews, J. A., Lewinsohn, P. M., and Hops, H. (1990). Assessment of depression in adolescents using the Center for Epidemiologic Studies Depression Scale. *Psychological Assessment*, 2, 122–128.

Roberts, R. E., and Chen, Y. C. (1995). Depressive symptoms and suicidal ideation among Mexican Origin and Anglo adolescents. *Journal of American Academy of Child and Adolescent Psychiatry*, 34, 81–90.

Roberts, R. E., Lewinsohn P. M., and Seeley, J. R. (1991). Screening for adolescent depression: A comparison of the CES-D and BDI. *Journal of American Academy of Child and Adolescent Psychiatry*, 30, 58–66.

Roberts, R. E., Roberts, C. R., and Chen, Y. C. (1995). *Ethnicity as a risk factor for adolescent depression*. Presented at the World Psychiatric Association meeting, Search for the Causes of Psychiatric Disorders: Epidemiological Approaches, May 14–17, 1995, New York, NY.

Robert, R. E., and Sobhan, M. (1992). Symptoms of depression in adolescence: A comparison of Anglo, African, and Hispanic Americans. *Journal of Youth Adolescence*, 21, 639–651.

Roberts, R. E., and Vernon, S. W. (1984) Minority status and psychological distress reexamined: The case of Mexican Americans. *Research in Community and Mental Health*, 4, 131–164.

Ross, C. E., Mirowsky, J., and Cockerham, W. C. (1983) Social class, Mexican culture, and fatalism: Their effects on psychological distress. *American Journal of Community Psychology*, 11, 383–399.

Schoenbach, V. J., Kaplan, B. H., Grimson, R. C., and Wagner, E. H. (1982). Use of a symptom scale to study the prevalence of a depressive syndrome in young adolescents. *American Journal of Epidemiology*, 116, 791–800.

Schwartz, J. A., and Koenig, L. J. (1996). Response styles and negative affect among adolescents. *Cognitive Therapy and Research*, 20, 13–36.

Somervell, P. D., Leaf, P. J., Weissman, M. M., Blazer, D. G., and Bruce, M. L. (1989). The prevalence of major depression in Black and White adults in five United States communities. *American Journal of Epidemiology*, 130, 725–735.

Swanson, J. W., and Linskey, A. O., Quintero-Salinas. R., Pumariega, A. J., and Holzer, C. E. (1992). A binational school survey of depressive symptoms, drug use, and suicidal ideation. *Journal of the American Academy Child and Adolescent Psychiatry*, 31, 669–678.

Teri, L. (1982). The use of the Beck Depression Inventory with adolescents. *Journal of Abnormal Child Psychology*, 10, 277–284.

Tolor, A., and Murphy, V. M. (1985). Stress and depression in high school students. *Psychological Reports*, 57, 535–541.

Trimble, J. E. (1990–1991). Ethnic specification, validation prospects, and the future of drug use research. *International Journal of the Addictions*, 25, 149–170.

Ulbrich, P. A., Warheit, G. J., and Zimmerman, R. S. (1989). Race, socioeconomic status, and psychological distress: An examination of differential vulnerability. *Journal of Health and Social Behavior*, 30, 131–146.

Vega, W. A., Gil, A. G., Zimmerman R. S., and Warheit W. J. (1993). Risk factors for suicical behavior among Hispanic, African American, and non-Hispanic white boys in early adolescence. *Ethnicity and Disease*, 3, 229–241.

Weinberg, W. A., and Emslie, G. J. (1987). Depression and suicide in adolescents. *International Pediatrics*, 2, 154–159.

Wheaton, B. (1980). The sociogenesis of psychological disorder: An attributional theory. *Journal of Health and Social Behavior*, 21, 100–124.

The translation of research findings into acceptable and effective interventions is a goal shared by psychologists and other mental health professionals. Unfortunately, what constitutes culturally appropriate treatment is not fully agreed upon by experts. Most research evidence suggests that therapeutic interventions will require more than simple application of traditional modes of therapy to ethnic groups. Experimental studies testing treatment effectiveness have revealed a number of limitations that are generally experienced by ethnic clients. These primary treatment problems include underutilization of services, premature termination, misdiagnosis, and difficulties developing treatments that are sensitive to the cultural values and norms of clients.

The first two selections in this section further explicate common obstacles to treatment and critical components to increasing treatment effectiveness. Lloyd Rogler discusses empirical findings on roadblocks to treatment with Hispanics as a case in point. Next, David Takeuchi, Stanley Sue, and May Yeh study the effects of ethnicity-specific mental health programs versus mainstream programs. Ethnicity-specific programs are designed to exemplify cultural appropriateness through their accessibility, increased likelihood of ethnic-match between client and therapist, and integration of the cultural norms of clients into treatment. The next set of readings by George Renfry on Native Americans, and Kurt Organista and Ricardo Muñoz on Latinos, illustrate how to develop a culturally sensitive treatment that incorporates the cultural beliefs, attitudes, and social realities of ethnic individuals into a mainstream model of therapy (cognitive-behavioral therapy). The two final selections offer treatment recommendations on often neglected ethnic groups. Jewelle Gibbs and Diana Fuery critique the literature on Black women's mental health needs. In particular, they propose suggestions for community-based interventions that are oriented toward promoting the identified strengths of these women. Finally, Davis Ja and Bart Aoki challenge the stereotypes that surround Asian Americans and substance abuse. They offer evidence that suggest that many of the empirical studies have been methodologically flawed and have led to a general underestimation of the levels of drug abuse and dependency among specific Asian American ethnic groups. In addition, they describe effective interventions with attention to the complex interaction of general and cultural-specific issues of substance-abuse treatment.

FURTHER READINGS

Huang, L. N. (1994). An integrative approach to clinical assessment and intervention with Asian-American adolescents. *Journal of Clinical Child Psychology, 23,* 21–31.

Lee, E. (1989). Assessment and treatment of Chinese-American immigrant families. *Journal of Psychotherapy and the Family, 6,* 99–122.

Marín, G. (1993). Defining culturally appropriate community interventions: Hispanics as a case study. *Journal of Community Psychology, 21,* 149–161.

Nagata, D. K. (1991). Transgenerational impact of the Japanese-American internment: Clinical issues in working with children of former internees. *Psychotherapy, 28,* 121–128.

Neighbors, H. W., and Jackson, J. S. (1996). *Mental health in Black America.* Thousand Oaks, CA: Sage.

Ponterotto, J. G., Casas, J. M., Suzuki, L. A., and Alexander, C. M. (Eds.). (1995). *Handbook of multicultural counseling.** Thousand Oaks, CA: Sage Publications, Inc. Emphasis on Chapter 19 (Atkinson, D. R., and Lowe, S. M. The role of ethnicity, cultural knowledge, and conventional techniques in counseling and psychotherapy) and Chapter 20 (Leong, F. T. L., Wagner, N. S., and Tata S. P. Racial and ethnic variations in help-seeking attitudes.)

Rogler, L. H., Malgady, R. G., and Rodriguez, O. (1989). *Hispanics and mental health: A framework for research.* Malabar, FL: Robert E. Krieger.

Sue, D. W., and Sue, D. (1990). *Counseling the culturally different* (2nd ed.). New York: John Wiley.

Sue, S., and Zane, N. (1987). The role of culture and cultural techniques in psychotherapy: A critique and reformulation. *American Psychologist, 42,* 37–45.

Yeh, M., Takeuchi, D. T., and Sue, S. (1994). Asian American children treated in the mental health system: A comparison of parallel and mainstream outpatient service centers. *Journal of Clinical Child Psychology, 23,* 5–12.

20.
Research on Mental Health Services for Hispanics
Targets of Convergence
Lloyd H. Rogler

In reaching to serve the mental health needs of new catchment neighborhoods, the 1963 federally funded Community Mental Health Center (CMHC) program stimulated culturally oriented research on the effectiveness of mental health services for Hispanics. The research, at first scattered and diffuse, has converged on a number of targets. This article examines four of the targets of research and how they can be brought into a unified perspective if they are viewed in temporal order as sequenced disadvantages Hispanics confront in using mental health services. The targets can be arrayed longitudinally: reasons for Hispanics' underutilization of professional mental health services, difficulties in retaining Hispanics in such services, errors in evaluating their mental health, and the problems of adapting treatment modalities to their needs.

Within a few years after President Kennedy's 1963 promise of a "bold new approach" to mental health care (Naierman, Haskins, Robinson, Zook, and Wilson, 1978, p. 3) many previously underserved or unserved Americans began to benefit from the congressionally established Community Mental Health Center (CMHC) program (Tischler, Henisz, Myers, and Garrison, 1972). The program's clinics, designed to help move the focus of mental health care away from human "warehouses" in state and county facilities (Naierman et al., 1978. p. 3) often were located in racially and ethnically diverse neighborhood catchment areas: Their services were used predominantly by economically disadvantaged persons (Naierman et al., 1978). An important but unplanned result of the program was that it stimulated culturally oriented research on the effectiveness of mental health services for cultural minorities, including Hispanics.

Thus, 15 years later, a Report to the President's Commission on Mental Health (Special Populations Sub-Task Panel on Mental Health of Hispanic Americans, 1978) noted the rapid growth of publications on Hispanics' mental health: A computer-based bibliographic system offered about 2,000 citations on this topic, almost all of them published after the enactment of the CMHC program. The Report deplored the quality of the steadily increasing research and emphasized that "Hispanic mental health has yet to attain the status of an integrated body of scientific knowledge" (p. 21). Lack of integration had caused research to grow helter-skelter, with little or no convergence on stable targets. Since then, published research on Hispanics' mental health has continued to grow so vigorously as to defy any attempt to provide a current, article-length review of the literature.

I believe that the convergence in research on the delivery of mental health services, which was not evident at the time of the 1978 report, has now begun to emerge. My first purpose here is to examine four targets in this convergence briefly. They involve the reasons for the Hispanic's underutilization of professional mental health services, difficulties in retaining Hispanics in such services, errors in evaluating their mental health, and problems in adapting treatment modalities to their needs.

My second purpose is to show that each of the four targets address issues in delivering mental health services and in developing further research. The targets can be brought into a unified perspective if they are viewed as sequenced disadvantages that Hispanics encounter in using the mental health delivery system.

The rapid growth of the Hispanic population forms a major part of the increase in American cultural pluralism. Since the 1963 enactment of the CMHC program, the Hispanic population has more than tripled to its current level of over 22 million (U.S. Bureau of the Census, 1990): Among minorities, they are now second in number only to African Americans. When the CMHC program began, Hispanics accounted for less than 4% of the U.S. population: now they are almost 9% and show increasing rates of intercensal increases. Hispanics are markedly diverse in education, occupation, earnings, patterns of intermarriage, regional location, and cultural background: however, the percentage of them living below the poverty level is significantly higher than for non-Hispanic Whites (Rogler, Malgady, and Rodriguez, 1989).

TARGETS OF CONVERGENCE IN RESEARCH
Reasons for Underutilization
This target of convergence contains two core assumptions. The first, that Hispanics suffer disproportionately from mental disorders, is based largely on indirect lines of reasoning, primarily on inferences made from their low education, unemployment, modest occupations, and linguistic and acculturation problems (U.S. Bureau of the Census, 1990). Alternatively, studies with mental health relevant scales indicating that Hispanics have higher symptom levels than other groups (Moscicki, Rae, Regier, and Locke, 1987) are used to infer higher rates of disorders. Even though few epidemiological studies have focused on Hispanics (Karno, Burnam, Hough, Escobar, and Golding, 1987; Moscicki et al., 1987), direct evidence is provided by one of the most recent studies in psychiatric epidemiology, the National Comorbidity Survey (Kessler et al., 1994). This study, based on nationwide sampling and state-of-the-art procedures for measuring mental disorder, shows that Hispanics have higher prevalence of current affective disorders and active comorbidity than non-Hispanic Whites.

This assumption of higher rates of mental disorders is linked to the second assumption, namely, that Hispanics underutilize mental health facilities. It also relies on direct and indirect evidence (Sue, Fujino, Hu, Takeuchi, and Zane, 1991) similar to that adduced for the first assumption. Affirmations of underutilization, however, are consistent with studies indicating that Hispanics suffer from diminished access to general health care (Robert Wood Johnson Foundation, 1987) and by more recent evidence that underutilization of mental health facilities in the general population is greater than estimated previously (Kessler et al., 1994).

The gap between these two assumptions—high levels of mental illness and low levels of utilization—is the main stimulus for research converging on the reasons for underutilization: Despite high needs, Hispanics underutilize because they have indigenous social organizations (Abad, Ramos, and Boyce, 1974; Rosado, 1980) that provide help that is sufficient to keep them from the official mental health system and because of cultural and organizational barriers to mental health care (Padilla and Keefe, 1984; Rosado, 1980).

The social organizations most commonly cited are the family and the network of friends and godparent relationships, religious denominations, spiritualist and folk-healing institutions, and compatriot groups (Abad et al., 1974; Bird and Canino, 1982; Rosado, 1980). Because such organizations are indigenous and function to provide therapy, they are hypothesized to confine emotionally distressed Hispanics within their own group or to delay them in reaching the professional health system (Lefley and Bestman, 1984).

Cultural values (such as familism, respect, and personalism) transported by first-generation Hispanics into the host society are also viewed as impediments to professional mental health care (Abad et al., 1974; Rosado, 1980). Adherence to these values is believed to make Hispanics uncomfortable and even suspicious of the bureaucratic interactions required by mental health facilities. A failure to acculturate, to learn the host society's language, values, and codes of comportment, also impedes utilization (Miranda, Andujo, Caballero, Guerrero, and Ramos, 1976).

However, the dominant reason cited for underutilization is that the mental health system is inadequate to the needs of Hispanics. Models illustrating how to adapt mainstream delivery systems to fit Hispanic clients' needs have been developed (Abad et al., 1974; Fischman, Fraticelli, Newman, and Sampson, 1983; Flaskerud, 1986). At the least, the facility must have practitioners fluent in Spanish and the opportunity of an ethnic match by employing Hispanic mental health practitioners (Flaskerud, 1986; Karno and Morales, 1971). Some settings have attempted to provide ethnic-specific facilities.

Ethnic-specific facilities attempt to fulfill sets of culturally oriented criteria for service delivery (Flaskerud, 1986) in catchment areas with large concentrations of underserved Hispanics (Abad et al., 1974; Fischman et al., 1983; Karno and Morales, 1971; Lefley and Bestman, 1984, 1991). Ideally, the facility is organized comprehensively to attend to the "full range of presenting complaints" (Lefley and Bestman, 1991, p. 477). Clients are to be relieved of the confusing abstractions of classifying their own problems according to unfamiliar professional categories and then seeking help in the bureaucratic labyrinth. The decor should reflect familiar, pride-inducing themes, as in posters of the Puerto Rican Pablo Casals Festival or portraits of the revolutionary Emiliano Zapata. The bilingual, bicultural staff should be culturally sensitive to issues in mental health evaluations, treatment modalities, and aftercare. Help, including job searches and legal assistance (Lefley and Bestman, 1984, 1991), is provided by contacting other service agencies and through educational programs.

In its ideal form, an ethnic-specific facility becomes a *querencia,* a part of the Hispanic neighborhood's territory of comfort and familiarity. The idealized social and clinical functions are seldom, if ever, fully realized, but the model is significant: It embodies standards against which clinics purporting to offer culturally sensitive services are implicitly or explicitly evaluated (Flaskerud, 1986). In research, the features of the model are hypothesized to increase successful mental health outcomes (Takeuchi, Sue, and Yeh, 1995) in retaining clients, improving diagnosis and treatment, and in remedying the problem of underutilization (Abad et al., 1974).

In fact, cross-sectional and longitudinal studies demonstrate that when service facilities incorporate features postulated by this model, Hispanics' utilization of mental health services increases (Fischman et al., 1983; Flores, 1978; Trevino, Bruhn, and Bunce, 1979). Case studies also provide evidence for such increases (Abad et al., 1974; Karno and Morales, 1971; Lefley and Bestman, 1991). Some researchers have concluded that when opportunities for culturally sensitive mental health care are provided, Hispanics will take them (Flores, 1978; Karno and Morales, 1971; Trevino et al., 1979). Culturally sensitized, the facility cuts through layers of impediments to attract the help-seeking pathways of mentally distressed Hispanics. In brief, underutilization is a problem of culturally unadapted facilities.

This conclusion, however, contains many unexamined hypotheses. The convergence of research on this target leaves unexamined the step-by-step progressive effects of culturally sensitive service alterations on indigenous help-seeking pathways (Rogler and Cortes, 1993) and on the subsequent magnitude of client intake from designated catchment areas.

Difficulties in Retaining Clients

Bringing clients to the doorstep of the service facility does not ensure that they will return. Mitchell (1989) estimated that 20–57% of patients in psychotherapy drop out after the first session. Members of cultural minorities appear to drop out disproportionately (Angel and Guarnaccia, 1989; K. Lin, Inui, Kleinman, and Womack, 1982; T. Lin, Tardiff, Donetz, and Goresky, 1978; Sue, 1977). In fact, if the clients replicate the experience of the cultural minorities studied in the greater Seattle area (Sue and Zane, 1987), only one in two will return after the first visit. Hispanics are no exception (Lefley and Bestman, 1984). Attrition instantly eliminates the possibility of professional help, even for clients who have overcome successive barriers in reaching the facility.

Why such tenuous attachments to facilities designed to provide a service? Answers to this question have been sought in the organizational characteristics of the facility, in the ethnic match between client and therapist, and in the client's level of acculturation.

At the level of the facility, research has focused on the impact of ethnic-specific or mainstream services. In one large sample study incorporating 54 mental health centers in Los Angeles County, minority clients in the ethnic-specific facilities were more likely to be retained than those entering mainstream programs (Takeuchi et al., 1995). Mexican American clients were 11 times more likely to return to their own ethnic-specific facilities than to mainstream facilities after one session, even though their ethnic match with the practitioner was not related to retention. This study accentuates the importance of analyzing how organizational components interact in influencing retention and other mental health outcomes.

Among the components, the ethnic match between client and therapist has received the most attention, whether the matching is undertaken in ethnic-specific or mainstream facilities. Ethnic matching, considered to be a means for overcoming underutilization (Flaskerud, 1986; O'Sullivan and Lasso, 1984; Sue, 1992), also has been viewed as a way of retaining clients and improving other mental health outcomes. Several studies indicate that matching improves retention among Hispanics (Flaskerud, 1986; O'Sullivan and Lasso, 1984; Sue, 1992; Sue et al., 1991; Takeuchi et al., 1995).

Matching is implemented by selecting persons with identical nationalities or by selecting therapists and clients who are both "Hispanic" (Flaskerud, 1986). Even clients and therapists with identical nationalities, however, may well have dissimilar cultural orientations because of differences in the length of time spent, and the degree of assimilation, in the host society and (earlier in their lives) because of possible social and cultural differences of their backgrounds in their countries of origin. In turn, the striking demographic and cultural diversity of Hispanic nationalities in the United States affects matching within the broader Hispanic category.

This difficulty gives credence to Sue's (1988) distinction between ethnic matching and cultural matching. In cultural matching, the therapist and the client would share ideas on the nature of the client's problem, the means for solving it, and the goals of treatment. Sue's recommendation is to focus research on cultural matching.

Elaborations of the matching hypothesis become even more complex, however, when attention is given to the client's degree of acculturation. Miranda et al.'s (1976) study of Mexican American female clients found that, for example, clients who terminated therapy prematurely had lower levels of acculturation and were more likely to be in the first generation than clients remaining in therapy.

According to Miranda et al. (1976), the clinical training that Hispanic therapists receive in the United States, which is the customary training, makes it "exceedingly difficult for them to develop appropriate bicultural therapeutic skills" (p. 49). The Hispanic therapists' familiarity with the first-generation culture of their clients may be compartmentalized, or its relevance bypassed in professional life, because the organizing role of cultural concepts in mental health is seldom included in clinical training (Ruiz, 1981; Vargas and Willis, 1994).

Solutions to the retention problem have also focused on the teaching of clients. For example, the research-based slide/cassette program, "Tell It Like It Is," attempted to impart elements of professional mental health culture to working-class White, Black, and Mexican American clients in a Los Angeles clinic (Acosta, Evan, Yamamoto, and Wilcox, 1980). Clients were encouraged to do a number of things, such as to be revelatory in stating their problems, to express feelings openly, even about the therapist, to understand that solutions to problems may take longer than expected, and to keep their appointments.

"Tell It Like It Is" is directed toward clients; therefore, it is related reciprocally to efforts to encourage therapists to learn generic cultural concepts through self-examination (Dillard et al., 1992; Gorrie, 1989) as well as learning about Hispanic cultural groups (Abad et al., 1974; Padilla and Keefe, 1984; Padilla and Salgado de Snyder, 1992; Rosado, 1980). Rosado, for example, illustrated the normative patterns that therapists need to know when working with lower class Puerto Rican clients: an orientation toward the present, beliefs in external supernatural causes, differences in patterns of verbal and non-verbal communication, and beliefs that merge the mind and body. His proposals embed culture in the therapeutic relationship so deeply as to mandate that therapists have the "professional and ethical" responsibility of acquiring sociocultural knowledge of the client (Rosado, 1980, p. 223).

The retention problem means that numerous clients drop out of treatment quickly and prematurely. Solutions for each individual client, therefore, cannot be delayed. One promising approach (Sue and Zane, 1987) focuses on the therapist's credibility from the client's perspective, and on the client's feelings of receiving symbolic gifts. Both aspects can be addressed in various ways during initial clinical contacts. With first-generation Hispanic clients, for example, there can be a nostalgic sharing of memories of the countries of origin (Moll, Rueda, Reza, Herrera, and Vasquez,, 1976), a culturally appropriate use of body language (Rosado, 1980), and a respectful but concerned use of Hispanic pronouns in addressing the client.

The organizational objective is to strengthen clients' tenuous relationship to mental health facilities: the objective of research is to increase our understanding of this process.

Errors in Evaluating Mental Health Problems

The literature is filled with examples of diagnostic errors that occur when the client's culture is disregarded (Mezzich et al., 1993). Concern about such errors is evident in the unprecedented recognition of culture in the fourth edition of the *Diagnostic and Statistical Manual of Mental Disorders* (*DSM-IV*; American Psychiatric Association, 1994). The convergence of research on this topic has focused on diagnostic errors in assessing symptoms, in configuring symptoms into disorders, and in the situation of the diagnostic interview. To explain these points, I shall draw from my own previously published analyses of research (Rogler, 1993, 1996).

To begin with errors in symptom assessment, the diagnosis of Puerto Ricans often confounds manifestations of beliefs in spiritualism with psychotic symptoms (Guarnaccia, 1992). Such manifestations may involve *facultades,* those faculties of the mind that enable mystical communications with the world of spirits (Rogler and Hollingshead, 1985). An understanding of widespread beliefs in a metaphysical universe of good and bad spirits, reincarnation, spiritual callings, and possessions should control culturally unwarranted attributions of psychotic symptoms (Mezzich et al., 1993). Moreover, the comparatively high prevalence of mental health symptoms among Puerto Ricans in epidemiological studies could also be due to the Puerto Ricans' cultural tendency to admit to symptoms more readily (Dohrenwend, 1966) than do members of other ethnic groups. The influence of culture on symptom assessment is documented by other studies (Mezzich et al., 1993).

Beyond symptom assessment, the role of culture is evident in the organization of symptoms in culture-bound syndromes. Of the 25 culture-bound syndromes now described in the *DSM-IV* (1994, pp. 843–849), 7 are Hispanic. Currently the most attention is focused on the Puerto Rican or Spanish Caribbean *ataque de nervios,* which is manifested in sudden seizures that "include uncontrollable shouting, attacks of crying, trembling, heat in the chest rising into the head, and verbal and physical aggression" (p. 845). Ataque de nervios formerly was regarded as a hysterical hyperkinetic seizure (Rogler and Hollingshead, 1985) but now it is conceived as having its own symptomatic integrity; it is not reducible to the more familiar diagnostic categories. This reflects change in taxonomical procedures: the departure from the customary reduction of culture-bound syndromes to the familiar categories of disorders (*DSM-IV,* 1994). Epidemiological studies in Puerto Rico have treated ataque de nervios as a culturally intact symptom configuration and succeeded in documenting its social structural distribution, its psychosocial risk factors, and its comorbid relationship with DSM-specified disorders (Guarnaccia, 1992).

Research on Hispanics also has shown the role of culture in configuring symptoms into the more familiar disorders (Canino et al., 1987). Thus, cultural adaptations by Puerto Rican psychiatrists of those parts of the Diagnostic Interview Schedule (DIS; Robins, Helzer, Croughan, and Ratcliff, 1981) used in assessing obsessive-compulsive disorder, psychosexual dysfunction, dysthymia, and cognitive impairment in Puerto Rico have produced marked changes in prevalence rates. A stateside study of Cuban Americans, Mexican Americans, and Puerto Ricans, also indicates the organizing role of culture. The study has shown that the relationship between scale-measured symptoms of depression, on the one hand, and major depressive episodes, on the other, varies across these three Hispanic groups (Cho et al., 1993). Puerto Ricans who were diagnosed as suffering major depression scored substantially higher on the Center for Epidemiological Studies Depression Scale (Cho et al., 1993) than did Cubans with an identical diagnosis. One interpretation is that Puerto Ricans need more scale-measured symptoms than Cubans to attain the threshold of major depression disorder. Hispanic research has accentuated the cultural complexities of diagnoses.

This complexity returns us to the situation of ethnic matching: this time, to the influence of such matching on the diagnosis of Hispanic clients. According to prevalent belief, ethnic matching reduces diagnostic error because of the shared cultural meanings between diagnostician and client (*DSM–III–R*, American Psychiatric Association, 1987), such as in understanding the metaphysics of spiritualism. The relevant studies, however, have been based largely on clinical observations and inferences, not on experimental designs. Such designs would make it possible to examine how, if at all, variations in diagnostic outcomes result from variations in the structure of the ethnic match, and how the client's dominant language fits into such variations.

One set of clinical observations supports the view that when Spanish-dominant clients report their symptoms in English, they are likely to be regarded as less ill than when they speak their native language (Del Castillo, 1970). The necessity of speaking a less familiar language, it is argued, imposes on the client the discipline of internal translations, which strips away the expression of mental health relevant emotions. Thus, the perception of the client's illness is attenuated. Another set of observations, substantially more controlled than the first, infers more illness when the client speaks the less familiar language (English); having to speak an unfamiliar language creates "disturbances in fluency, organization, and integration" (Marcos, Urcuyo, Kesselman, and Alpert, 1973, p. 658) in the client's presentation of the problem. These differences invite the hypothesis that the cultural distance between diagnostician and client, including the language used during the evaluation, affects diagnostic outcomes.

In summary, research converging on the evaluation of Hispanics' mental health indicates that culture influences psychiatric diagnosis in assessing symptoms, in configuring symptoms into disorders, and in the interpersonal situation of client and diagnostician (Rogler, 1993). Knowledge about cultural influences needs to be integrated into clinical inferences if we are to improve the accuracy of diagnosis.

Treatment Modalities

Convergence of the literature on treatment modalities does not denote agreement about appropriate treatments for emotionally distressed Hispanics. Thus, some advocacy has supported insight-oriented therapeutic modalities: "More self-aware individuals are needed to confront insidious social realities in the outer world, as well as unconscious themes in the inner world" (Maduro and Martinez, 1974, p. 461). Such advocacy does not neglect the insertion of cultural elements into insight-oriented modalities, such as dream analysis, which is congruent with the practices of Mexican folk healers (Maduro and Martinez, 1974). Nor does it neglect the promise of much broader culturally informed adaptations in working with Puerto Rican clients (Bluestone and Vela, 1982).

The balance of advocacy, however, tilts away from the sustained self-examinations of insight-oriented psychoanalytic modalities and toward modalities that are ecologically oriented, active, and directed toward the clients' troublesome interactions with surrounding institutional structures (Ruiz, 1981; Szapocznik, Kurtines, and Fernandez, 1980). Generally, these modalities are thought to be more appropriate to the Hispanics' life circumstances (Ruiz, 1981). The view is that, psychologically, many low-income Hispanics tend not to meet the candidacy requirements of insight-oriented therapies, such as relative freedom from external chaos combined with a persistent motivation to remain in therapy (Bluestone and Vela, 1982). Some of the previously mentioned mental health programs have even attempted to negotiate directly the clients' institutional interests in order to reduce external stresses (Abad et al., 1974; Lefley and Bestman, 1984). The prevalent emphasis is ecological, the imparting of skills, knowledge, and attitudes that helps clients cope with many of the external stresses impinging upon them (Boulette, 1976; Fischman et al., 1983). Whether tacit or explicit, the expectation is that successful coping diminishes inner distress.

Ethnic-specific service facilities and ethnic matching, both previously, discussed, also have been viewed as conducive to effective treatment (O'Sullivan and Lasso, 1984). Both are based on the idea that the therapeutic environment of the facility must be adapted to the clients' cultural characteristics: the former by altering various components of the facility, and the latter by selecting a therapist of the same ethnicity as the client. Applications of these procedures, however, have raised an additional question: Should the social organization and content of the therapy have an isomorphic, mirrorlike relationship to the clients' culture and level of acculturation? For example, if the Hispanic client's culture is governed strongly by the norms of familism, should the choice be family therapy? If the client's culture is strongly authoritarian, should the therapist assume the position of a status superior? Affirmative answers to such questions were based initially on the postulate that the clients' cultural attributes must be replicated isomorphically in therapy.

This postulate has been questioned primarily because of the adaptational requirements imposed on immigrant or second-generation Hispanic clients by the new, host society. Thus Boulette (1976, p. 67), noting that the "poverty and culturally related" subassertiveness pattern of low-income Mexican American women induced chronic and incapacitating symptoms, undertook to provide them with assertiveness training. Boulette believed that assertiveness is required, not only because of the women's troublesome subservient role in traditional paternalistic families, but because of the need to hustle for scarce community resources and to counteract the prejudicial practices and behaviors to which they are subjected. Traditional patterns of feminine compliance are therapeutically modified to meet the demands of the host society. Such modification challenges unqualified applications of the isomorphic postulate and creates the opportunity for studying bicultural techniques in therapy.

Treatment research on Hispanics, in fact, has incorporated bicultural techniques into therapy (Rogler, Malgady, Costantino, and Blumenthal, 1987; Sue and Zane, 1987; Szapocznik et al., 1980). Thus, switching between Spanish and English has been used as a therapeutic technique (Pitta, Marcos, and Alpert, 1978); the language chosen depends on the client's characteristics and on the phase of therapy. Experimental studies testing the therapeutic effectiveness of exposing Puerto Rican children to Puerto Rican folktales (Costantino, Malgady, and Rogler, 1985) have incorporated into their designs departures from the isomorphic postulate: The stories that retained Puerto Rican cultural elements as well as reflecting New York City culture were the most effective in reducing the children's anxieties. If the traditional culture is relevant, so is that of the host society.

DISCUSSION

The convergence of research on the four targets discussed here has occurred recently. Accordingly, each target is surrounded by hypotheses with varying degrees of empirical support in documenting and explaining the disadvantages Hispanics experience in mental health services. Also, because the research has focused mostly on Hispanics experiencing poverty, the independent and interactive effect of socioeconomic status and Hispanic ethnicity on such disadvantages remains largely unexamined. There is a pressing need for future research to consider the role of socioeconomic factors in examining the service delivery disadvantages attributed to Hispanics.

Briefly, the targets of research convergence assert that in comparisons to non-Hispanics:

1. Hispanics are less likely to make contacts with professional mental health facilities.
2. Hispanics are less likely to be retained in the facilities.
3. Hispanics are more likely to be misdiagnosed.
4. Hispanics are less likely to receive adequate therapy.

From the first to the fourth, the targets of convergence represent a sequence of temporally arrayed disadvantages. Thus, the failure to cope with the first disadvantage denies success in coping with the second, and so on through the sequence. The first two disadvantages keep clients from services; the last two deny participating clients the facility's potential clinical expertise. The concept of sequenced disadvantages provides a unified, time-oriented perspective on much of the material that has been discussed. It is also useful at an individual level in examining the experiences of a client traversing through a mental health facility.

Each disadvantage is rooted in the disparity between Hispanic cultural elements and the facility's customary mental health practices. A variety of training and organizational efforts have been implemented to bridge the disparities. With respect to training, therapists have been taught clinically relevant elements of the Hispanic client's culture, and clients have been taught elements of the therapists' professional culture. Organizational changes have involved ethnic matching between client and therapist and the creation of ethnic-specific services. The studies discussed here support the promise of research-based cultural adaptations in the delivery of mental health services; to realize the promise, more definitive research is needed focusing upon the mental health consequences of such adaptations.

The adaptations, however, should be considered in the context of the persistent under-representation of Hispanic health practitioners in general (Ginzburg, 1991) and of cultural minorities in the disciplines of psychiatry, psychology, and social work (Vargas and Willis, 1994). This underrepresentation is likely to increase because Hispanics are rapidly increasing in numbers while increasingly experiencing the high risks of persistent poverty (Massey and Eggers, 1990; McGeary and Lynn, 1988). Thus, recruitment from the small pool of trained Hispanics in the various mental health disciplines provides viable local solutions without improving the Hispanics' overall underrepresentation in mental health disciplines. General solutions based on ethnic matching and on ethnic-specific services will remain difficult to attain. I believe that research-based, cross-cultural training needs to be emphasized if we are to meet the mental health needs of the growing Hispanic population.

NOTE

This invited article formed the basis for the Simón Bolívar Award Lecture given by Lloyd H. Rogler at the 1996 Annual Meeting of the American Psychiatric Association in New York City. The Simón Bolívar Award honored Dr. Rogler as a distinguished statesman in the Hispanic community for making outstanding contributions to education, research, and overall achievement in psychiatry.

This research was supported in part by National Institute of Mental Health Grants 1RO1MH30569 and 1RO1MH45939 from the Services Research Branch. I thank Lori Lattarulo, Kate Monaghan, and Louisa Saratora for their help in reviewing the literature.

BIBLIOGRAPHY

Abad, V., Ramos, J., and Boyce, E. (1974). A model delivery of mental health services to Spanish-speaking minorities. *American Journal of Orthopsychiatry*, 44, 584–595.

Acosta, F. X., Evan, L. A., Yamamoto, J., and Wilcox, S. A. (1980). Helping minority and low-income psychotherapy patients "Tell it like it is." *Journal of Biocommunication*, 7, 13–19.

American Psychiatric Association. (1987). *Diagnostic and statistical manual of mental disorders* (3rd ed.). Washington, DC: Author.

American Psychiatric Association. (1994). *Diagnostic and statistical manual of mental disorders* (4th ed.). Washington, DC: Author.

Angel, R., and Guarnaccia, P. J. (1989). Mind, body, and culture: Somatization among Hispanics. *Social Science and Medicine*, 28, 1229–1238.

Bird, H. R., and Canino, G. (1982). The Puerto Rican family: Cultural factors and family intervention strategies. *Journal of the Academy of Psychoanalysis*, 10, 257–268.

Bluestone, H., and Vela, R. M. (1982). Transcultural aspects in the psychotherapy of the Puerto Rican poor in New York City. *Journal of the American Academy of Psychanalysis*, 10, 269–283.

Boulette, T. R. (1976). Assertive training with low-income Mexican American women. In M. R. Miranda (Ed.), *Psychotherapy with the Spanish speaking: Issues in research and service delivery* (pp. 67–71). Los Angeles: University of California Spanish-Speaking Mental Health Center.

Canino, G. J., Bird, H. R., Shrout, P. E., Rubio-Stipec, M., Bravo, M., Martinez, R., Sesman, M., and Guevara, L. M. (1987). The prevalence of specific psychiatric disorders in Puerto Rico. *Archives of General Psychiatry*, 44, 727–735.

Cho, M. J., Moscicki, E. K., Narrow, W. E., Rae, D. S., Locke, B. Z, and Regier, D. A. (1993). Concordance between two measures of depression in the Hispanic health and nutrition examination survey. *Social Psychiatry and Psychiatric Epidemiology*, 28, 156–163.

Costantino, G., Malgady, R. G., and Rogler, L. H. (1985). *Cuento therapy: Folktales as a culturally sensitive psychotherapy for Puerto Rican children*. Maplewood, NJ: Waterfront Press.

Del Castillo, J. (1970). The influence of language upon symptomatology in foreign born patients. *American Journal of Psychiatry*, 127, 242–244.

Dillard, M., Andonian, L., Flores, O., Lai, L., McRae, A., and Shakir, M. (1992). Culturally competent occupational therapy at a diversely populated mental health setting. *American Journal of Occupational Therapy*, 46, 721–726.

Dohrenwend, B. P. (1966). Social status and psychological disorder: An issue of substance and an issue of method. *American Sociological Review*, 31, 14–34.

Fischman, G., Fraticelli, B., Newman, D., and Sampson, L. (1983). Day treatment programs for the Spanish speaking: A response to underutilization. *International Journal of Social Psychiatry*, 29, 215–219.

Flaskerud, J. H. (1986). The effects of culture-compatible intervention on the utilization of mental health services by minority clients. *Community Mental Health Journal*, 22, 127–141.

Flores, J. L. (1978). The utilization of a community mental health service by Mexican Americans. *International Mental Health Journal*, 24, 271–275.

Ginzberg, E. (1991). Access to health care for Hispanics. *Journal of the American Medical Association*, 265, 238–241.

Gorrie, M. (1989). Reaching clients through cross-cultural education. *Journal of Gerontological Nursing*, 15, 29–31.

Guarnaccia, P. J. (1992). Ataques de nervios in Puerto Rico: Culture-bound syndrome or popular illness? *Medical Anthropology*, 15, 1–14.

Karno, M., Burnam, M. A., Hough, R. L., Escobar, J. I., and Golding, J. M.(1987). Mental disorder among Mexican Americans and non-Hispanic Whites in Los Angeles. In M. Gaviria and J. D. Arana (Eds.), *Health and behavior: Research agenda for Hispanics* (pp. 110–126). Chicago: University of Illinois.

Karno, M., and Morales, A. (1971). A community mental health service for Mexican Americans in a metropolis. *Comprehensive Psychiatry*, 12, 116–121.

Kessler, R. C., McGonagle, K. A., Zhao, S., Nelson, C. B., Hughes, M., Eshleman, S., Wittchen, H. U., and Kendler, K. S. (1994). Lifetime and 12-month prevalence of *DSM-III-R* psychiatric disorders in the United States. *Archives of General Psychiatry*, 51, 8–19.

Lefley, H. P., and Bestman, E. W. (1984). Community mental health and minorities: A multi-ethnic approach. In S. Sue and T. Moore (Eds.), *The pluralistic society: A community mental health perspective* (pp. 116–148). New York: Human Services Press.

Lefley, H. P., and Bestman, E. W. (1991). Public–academic linkages for culturally sensitive community mental health. *Community Mental Health Journal*, 27, 473–488.

Lin, K. M., Inui, T. S., Kleinman, A. M., and Womack, W. M. (1982). Sociocultural determinants of the help-seeking behavior of patients with mental illness. *Journal of Nervous and Mental Disease*, 170, 78–85.

Lin, T. Y., Tardiff, K., Donetz, G., and Goresky, W. (1978). Ethnicity and patterns of help-seeking. *Culture, Medicine and Psychiatry*, 2, 3–14.

Maduro, R., and Martinez, C. (1974). Latino dream analysis: Opportunity for confrontation. *Social Casework*, 55, 461–469.

Marcos, L. R., Urcuyo, L., Kesselman, M., and Alpert, M. (1973). The language barrier in evaluating Spanish-American patients. *Archives of General Psychiatry*, 29, 655–659.

Massey, D. S., and Eggers, M. L., (1990). The ecology of inequality: Minorities and the concentration of poverty, 1970–1980. *American Journal of Sociology*, 95, 1153–1188.

McGeary, M.G.H., and Lynn, L. E., Jr. (1988). *Urban change and poverty*. Washington, DC: National Academy Press.

Mezzich, J. E., Kleinman, A., Fabrega, H., Good, B., Johnson-Powell, G., Lin, K. M., Manson, S., and Parron, D. (1993). *Cultural proposals and supporting papers for DSM-IV*. Submitted to the DSM-IV task force by the Steering Committee, NIMH-sponsored group on culture and diagnosis (unpublished).

Miranda, M. R., Andujo, E., Caballero, I. L., Guerrero, C. C., and Ramos, R. A. (1976). Mexican American dropouts in psychological therapy as related to level of acculturation. In M. R. Miranda (Ed.), *Psychotherapy with the Spanish-speaking: Issues in research and service delivery* (Monograph No. 3, pp. 35–50). Los Angeles: University of California, Spanish-Speaking Mental Health Research Center.

Mitchell, M. E. (1989). The relationship between social network variables and the utilization of mental health services. *American Journal of Community Psychology*, 17, 258–266.

Moll, L. C., Rueda, R. S., Reza, R., Herrera, J., and Vasquez, L. P. (1976). Mental health services in East Los Angeles: An urban community case study. In M. R. Miranda (Ed.), *Psychotherapy with the Spanish-speaking: Issues in research and service delivery* (Monograph No. 3, pp. 21–34). Los Angeles: University of California, Spanish-Speaking Mental Health Research Center.

Moscicki, E. K., Rae, D. S., Regier, D. A, and Locke, B. Z. (1987). The Hispanic health and nutrition examination survey: Depression among Mexican Americans, Cuban Americans, and Puerto Ricans. In M. Gaviria and J. D. Arana (Eds.), *Health and behavior: Research agenda for Hispanics* (pp. 145–159). Chicago: University of Illinois.

Naierman, N., Haskins, B., Robinson., G., Zook, C., and Wilson, D. (1978). *Community mental health centers: A decade later*. Cambridge, MA: Abt Books.

O'Sullivan, M. J., and Lasso, B. (1984). The role of culture and cultural techniques in psychotherapy: A critique and reformulation. *American Psychologist*, 42, 37–45.

Padilla, A. M., and Keefe, S. E. (1984). The search for help: Mental health resources for Mexican Americans and Anglo Americans in a plural society. In S. Sue and T. Moore (Eds.), *The pluralistic society: A community mental health perspective* (pp. 77–115). New York: Human Services Press.

Padilla, A. M., and Salgado de Snyder, N. (1992). Hispanics: What the culturally informed evaluator needs to know. In M. Orlandi, R. Weston, and L. Epstein (Eds.), *Cultural competence for evaluators* (pp. 117–146). Washington, DC: U.S. Department of Health and Human Services, Alcohol, Drug Abuse and Mental Health Administration.

Pitta, P., Marcos, L. R., and Alpert, M. (1978). Language switching as a treatment strategy with bilingual patients. *American Journal of Psychoanalysis*, 38, 255–258.

Robert Wood Johnson Foundation. (1987*). Access to health care in the United States: Results of a 1986 survey* (Vol. 2). Princeton, NJ: Author.

Robins, L. N., Helzer, J. E., Croughan, J., and Ratcliff, K. S. (1981). National Institute of Mental Health Diagnostic Interview Schedule. *Archives of General Psychiatry*, 38, 381–389.

Rogler, L. H. (1993). Culturally sensitizing psychiatric diagnosis: A framework for research. *Journal of Nervous and Mental Disease*, 181, 401–408.

Rogler, L. H. (1996). Framing research on culture in psychiatric diagnosis: The case of the DSM-IV. *Psychiatry*, 59, 145–155.

Rogler, L. H., and Cortes, D. E. (1993). Help-seeking pathways: A unifying concept in mental health care. *American Journal of Psychiatry*, 150, 554–561.

Rogler, L. H., and Hollingshead, A. B. (1985). *Trapped: Puerto Rican families and schizophrenia* (3rd ed.). Maplewood, NJ: Waterfront Press.

Rogler, L. H., Malgady, R. G., Costantino, G., and Blumenthal, R. (1987). What do culturally sensitive mental health services mean? The case of Hispanics. *American Psychologist*, 42, 565–570.

Rogler, L. H., Malgady, R. G., and Rodriguez,O. (1989). *Hispanics and mental health: A framework for research*. Malabar, FL: Krieger.

Rosado, J. W. (1980). Important psychocultural factors in the delivery of mental health services to lower class Puerto Rican clients: A review of recent studies. *Journal of Community Psychology*, 8, 215–226.

Ruiz, R. (1981). Cultural and historical perspectives in counseling Hispanics. In D. W. Sue (Ed.), *Counseling the culturally different*. New York: John Wiley and Sons.

Special Populations Sub-Task Panel on Mental Health of Hispanic Americans. (1978). *Report to the President's commission on mental health*. Los Angeles: University of California, Spanish-Speaking Mental Health Research Center.

Sue, S. (1977). Community mental health services to minority groups: Some optimism, some pessimism. *American Psychologist*, 32, 616–624.

Sue, S. (1988). Psychotherapeutic services for ethnic minorities. *American Psychologist*, 43, 301–308.

Sue, S. (1992). Ethnicity and mental health: Research and policy issues. *Journal of Social Issues*, 48, 187–205.

Sue, S., Fujino, D.C., Hu, L., Takeuchi, D. T., and Zane, N.W.S. (1991). Community mental health services for ethnic minority groups. A test of the cultural responsiveness hypothesis. *Journal of Consulting and Clinical Psychology*, 59, 533–540.

Sue, S., and Zane, N.W.S. (1987). The role of culture and cultural techniques in psychotherapy: A critique and reformulation. *American Psychologist*, 42, 37–45.

Szapocznik, J., Kurtines, W., and Fernandez, T. (1980). Bicultural involvement and adjustment in Hispanic American youths. *International Journal of Intercultural Relations*, 4, 353–365.

Takeuchi, D. T., Sue, S., and Yeh, M. (1995). Ethnic specific programs. Do they work? *American Journal of Public Health*, 85, 638–643.

Tischler, G. L., Henisz, J., Myers, J. K. and Garrison, V. (1972). Catchmenting and the use of mental health services. *Archives of General Psychiatry*, 27, 389–392.

Treviño, F. M., Bruhn, J. G., and Bunce, H., III. (1979). Utilization of community mental health services in a Texas-Mexico border city. *Social Science and Medicine*, 13, 331–334.

U.S. Bureau of the Census. (1990). *Current population survey* (March supplement). Washington, DC: U.S. Government Printing Office.

Vargas, L. A., and Willis, D. J. (1994). New directions in the treatment and assessment of ethnic minority children and adolescents. *Journal of Clinical Child Psychology*, 23, 2–4.

21.

Return Rates and Outcomes from Ethnicity-Specific Mental Health Programs in Los Angeles

David T. Takeuchi, Stanley Sue, and May Yeh

The present study compared the return rate, length of treatment, and treatment outcome of ethnic minority adults who received services from ethnicity-specific or mainstream programs. The sample consisted of 1,516 African Americans, 1,888 Asian Americans, and 1,306 Mexican Americans who used 1 of 36 predominantly White (mainstream) or 18 ethnicity-specific mental health centers in Los Angeles County over a 6-year period. Predictor variables included type of program (ethnicity specific vs mainstream), disorder, ethnic match (whether or not clients had a therapist of the same ethnicity), gender, age, and Medi-Cal eligibility. The criterion variables were return after one session, total number of sessions, and treatment outcome. The study indicated that ethnic clients who attended ethnicity-specific programs had a higher return rate and stayed in the treatment longer than those using mainstream services. The data analyses were less clear cut when treatment outcome was examined. The findings support the notion that ethnicity-specific programs seem to increase the continued use of mental health services among ethnic minority groups.

INTRODUCTION

Intense debate has ensued over whether race-specific policies and programs are appropriate in facilitating social, political, and economic reforms in the United States.[1] Frequently heard are arguments about the value of having programs or policies that are unique to an ethnic minority group rather than applicable to all groups, including Whites. In the mental health field, some investigators have advocated for ethnicity-specific mental health programs and services,[2,3] particularly because of the many problems that have been identified in the proper assessment of psychopathology and the delivery of psychotherapeutic services to ethnic minority populations.[4-13] These programs are specifically designed to serve certain ethnic minority populations and are based in hospitals, clinics, or mental health centers.

Conceptually, ethnicity-specific mental health programs are thought to provide a better match or fit between interventions and the cultural backgrounds and life-styles of ethnic minority clients.[14,15] They typically involve the recruitment of ethnic personnel, modifications in treatment practices that are presumably more culturally appropriate, and development of an atmosphere in which services are provided in a culturally familiar context. Most are located in communities with relatively large ethnic populations and serve a predominantly ethnic clientele.[3] Over the years, many ethnicity-specific programs have been created, particularly in communities with large ethnic populations. Despite the enthusiasm for these programs, the basic questions of whether ethnicity-specific mental health programs are beneficial to ethnic minority clients or society in general and, even more fundamentally, what happens in these programs have been virtually unexplored.[16] No large-scale empirical investigations have examined these questions or the issue of what program features are related to service use and treatment outcomes. Such studies are needed, not only to shed light on directions for public policies and programs but also to eventually identify components of ethnicity-specific services that are associated with therapeutic effectiveness. The present study compared the effects of ethnicity-specific programs with those of mainstream mental health services for three different ethnic groups: African Americans, Asian Americans, and Mexican Americans. The study was based on an extremely large data set from the largest local community mental health system in the nation. Our major purpose was to compare ethnic minority adults who enter ethnicity-specific programs with their counterparts who enter mainstream programs in terms of return rate, length of treatment, and treatment outcome.

METHODS

Data

Data for the study were supplied by the Automated Information System, maintained by the Los Angeles County Department of Mental Health. The county uniformly verifies information related to financial matters. In order to ensure that other data were comparable in quality, we spent 6 months cleaning the data set. Data cleaning required cross checking the data to ensure consistency of information (e.g., correspondence of age and birth date), range checking to ensure that codes were within the field of responses for a particular item, and checking for omission of duplicate cases. The data were eventually placed into a Statistical Analysis System format for use in data analyses. Although reliability and validity are difficult to assess with secondary data drawn from treatment records, these types of data have proven useful in the past in exploring minority mental health issues in geographic settings other than Los Angeles.[17–21]

Sample

This study was limited to minority adults 18 years of age and older who used services at a mental health facility in Los Angeles County between September 1, 1982, and December 31, 1988. The original data set was restricted to this period because of inconsistent data definitions, and diagnostic criteria for disorders in earlier years. Because the total population of adults entering the mental health system during the study time period was quite large (more than 100,000 cases or episodes), sampling was initiated to make the data set more manageable. All Asian Americans were included in the initial sampling plan because they constituted only a fraction of the total client population. For the other three ethnic groups, a random quota sample stratified by age was selected. The total number of African American, White, and Mexican American adults sampled each roughly matched the total for Asian Americans. A similar number of episodes (adults) from each ethnic group was randomly drawn from the original data set.

We selected only adults who entered an outpatient setting that served a predominantly ethnic population or a program that served a predominantly White clientele. Programs meeting two criteria were used in defining an ethnicity-specific or mainstream organization. First, only programs that admitted an average of 75 or more new patients with unduplicated cases per year during the study time period were selected. Since the data set also included individual mental health professionals who provided services in Los Angeles County and who were not affiliated with an agency, the size criterion allowed us to focus on organizations. The inclusion of individual professionals or group practices could reduce the odds that the effects uncovered in the following analyses were due to the talents of a few therapists. Indeed, a check of the final list of providers indicates that this criterion did eliminate individual therapists or small group practices. The criterion of 75 episodes also represented a convenient cutoff. Of the 172 providers examined during this time period, only 4 averaged between 50 and 74 cases (most averaged either 75 or more episodes a year or less than 50 episodes a year). None of these 4 met the second definition of an ethnicity-specific or mainstream organization.

Second, an ethnicity-specific or mainstream program was operationally defined on the basis of its ethnic composition. A program with a majority (more than 50%) of clients from a specific minority group (e.g., Asian, Black, Mexican) was classified as ethnic specific or ethnic. If a majority of a program's clients were White, then the program was considered mainstream. Programs that did not have a majority of either Whites or a specific minority group (n = 20) were eliminated from the present analysis. A total of 54 programs—36 mainstream and 18 ethnicity specific (8 African American, 5 Mexican American, and 5 Asian American)—met both criteria. Ethnicity-specific programs did not differ markedly from mainstream programs in terms of the average number of clients served during the period of the study.

The following groups were also excluded from the data set: (1) adults who used only inpatient services, continuous care, day treatment, or emergency services; (2) American Indians and non-Mexican Hispanics (e.g., mainland Puerto Ricans), because of their relatively small client populations; (3) clients who came into clinics for assessment purposes only; and (4) clients with cases still considered open. Adults who used only inpatient services were excluded because there were too few ethnicity-specific units to compare across ethnic minority groups. The unit of analysis for this study was confined to the first episode during the study time period. Episodes beyond the first entry were excluded to reduce the possibility of having clients who could possibly be biased by repeated experiences in the mental health system over the period of the study. Of course, taking the first entry does not entirely eliminate adults who may have entered prior to the cutoff for our study time period. Nonetheless, the data set was limited to unduplicated cases during this time. After all of the exclusions had been made, the final sample sizes for minority clients who had complete data were as follows: African Americans, 1,516; Asian Americans, 1,888; and Mexican Americans, 1,306.

Measures

The effects of ethnicity-specific programs were assessed on three dependent measures: continuation in services, total number of treatment sessions, and rating on the Global Assessment Scale. Continuation was defined as a return for treatment after 1 session. Although continuation or return (the opposite term is premature termination) can be defined in many ways and clients may improve even if they drop out of treatment, this definition makes intuitive sense since the first session represents the adult's initial contact with the mental health program. Only client-initiated dropouts were included in this study; thus, failure to return after 1 session may have reflected a dissatisfaction with services or the client's (and family's) perception that the goals for treatment were met despite the mental health professional's sense that treatment should have continued. Furthermore, the use of 1 session allowed us to directly compare our results with those obtained by O'Sullivan et al.,[21] Sue,[3] and Sue et al.,[22] who also used 1 session as the criterion. Total number of sessions was calculated for those clients who either terminated or completed treatment. Log transformations were performed on the actual numbers of sessions, since some clients attended well over 100, creating positively skewed distributions. Clients who dropped out of treatment after 1 session (from 11% to 19% of clients, depending on ethnicity) were excluded from the treatment outcome analysis.

The Global Assessment Scale provides a rating of clients' overall psychological, social, and occupational functioning. Therapists perform the ratings on a 100-point scale, with 1 indicating the most severe impairment and 100 referring to good functioning in all areas of life. The instrument is highly similar to the Global Assessment of Functioning scale used on Axis V of the *Diagnostic and Statistical Manual of Mental Disorders* (revised third edition).[23] Reliability of the Global Assessment Scale has been found to be high.[24] Holcomb and Otto[25] have questioned its validity, while Sohlberg found it to have good concurrent and predictive validity.[26]

The following client characteristics were entered as control variables in the multivariate analyses: gender, age, Medi-Cal eligibility, and diagnosis. Age was a continuous variable representing the client's age at the time of admission to the outpatient clinic. Medi-Cal eligibility was determined by the amount of gross family income adjusted for the number of dependents in the household. Among those eligible for Medi-Cal, the state of California helps to pay for their use of health and mental health services. Finally, as a gross means of controlling for disorders, clients were divided into those who were diagnosed with a disorder with psychotic features (serious mental illness) and those who were diagnosed as not having such a disorder (nonserious mental illness).

It is plausible that the impact of ethnicity-specific programs is due entirely to the ethnic match between client and therapist. That is, programs that serve a large number of minorities are more likely to hire ethnic therapists. Thus, the likelihood of the client seeing an ethnic therapist is greater than in a mainstream program. Sue et al. have previously shown that when clients and therapists are matched on ethnicity, the results are generally more favorable than when clients see therapists from a different ethnic group.[22] Ethnic match referred to whether or not the therapist was of the same ethnicity as the client. A Black therapist–Black client dyad or Chinese therapist–Chinese client dyad was considered a match. However, among Asian Americans, a Chinese therapist–Japanese client was not a match. We recognize that ethnic match may be confounded with the issue of language preferences or the ability of a therapist to communicate with the client. Because of the limitations of the data, we could not fully explore this issue. However, a previous study did document that both types of matches (ethnic and language) were highly associated with use of services for Asian Americans and Mexican Americans, especially non-English speakers.[22] Accordingly, we included ethnic match as a control variable to examine the effect of ethnicity-specific programs over and above the effects of ethnic match.

RESULTS

Characteristics of Clients

Table 1 displays some characteristics available of adults who entered each type of program. Generally, those eligible for Medi- Cal were more likely to use community mental health services. A substantial majority of the adults who used either ethnicity-specific or mainstream programs were eligible for Medi-Cal. The proportion of those eligible for Medi-Cal did not vary between mainstream and ethnicity-specific programs among African Americans and Asian Americans. Among Mexican Americans, however, a greater proportion of those eligible for Medi-Cal were likely to enter mainstream programs (75%) than ethnicity-specific programs (69%). In all three minority groups, mainstream programs served a larger proportion of more severely disturbed clients than ethnicity-specific programs. The most striking difference occurred among Mexican Americans, where the proportion of seriously mentally ill patients in mainstream programs was nearly three times the proportion in ethnicity-specific programs (41% vs 14%; $p < .001$). The data on psychiatric diagnoses must be interpreted with caution since the data set did not permit us to evaluate the comparability of assessments conducted in ethnicity-specific and mainstream programs. It is equally plausible that therapists in ethnicity-specific programs may be less inclined to diagnose ethnic consumers with a psychotic disorder. The data also suggested the importance of controlling for these factors in comparing program effects in subsequent analyses.

Table 1 also shows the overlap between ethnicity-specific programs and the matching of clients and therapists on the basis of ethnicity. Ethnicity-specific programs for each group were associated with significantly more client-therapist matches in ethnicity than were mainstream programs. Matching occurred substantially more in African American and Asian American ethnicity-specific programs than in Mexican American programs.

Table 1. Characteristics of Mainstream and Ethnicity-Specific Mental Health Clinics

	African Americans		Asian Americans		Mexican Americans	
	Mainstream	Ethnicity Specific	Mainstream	Ethnicity Specific	Mainstream	Ethnicity Specific
Total sample	664	852	1260	628	965	341
Male, %	50	45*	43	40	43	36*
Eligible for Medi-Cal,%	81	84	72	72	75	69*
Client age, y, mean (SD)	34 (12)	35* (13)	33 (12)	38** (14)	34 (14)	35 (14)
Seriously mentally ill %	54	44**	53	43**	41	14**
Ethnic match, %	17	70**	11	72**	30	58**
Admission Global Assessment Scale rating, mean (SD)	35 (16)	47** (13)	37 (16)	44** (10)	39 (15)	49** (10)
Log of total sessions, mean (SD)	1.1 (1.1)	1.4** (1.2)	1.2 (1.2)	2.4** (1.1)	1.2 (1.1)	2.1** (1.1)
Discharge Global Assessment Scale rating, mean (SD)	46 (16)	50** (13)	46 (16)	49** (14)	50 (14)	54** (11)
Return rate, %	60	77**	64	98**	68	97**

Note: Mainstream programs represent those in which 50% or more of the clients are White; ethnicity-specific programs represent those in which 50% or more of the clients are from the specified minority group. Statistical comparisons were made between mainstream and ethnicity-specific programs within each minority group.

*$P \le .05$; **$P \le .001$.

African Americans in ethnic programs were four times more likely than African Americans in mainstream programs to see an African American therapist (70% vs 17%). The likelihood of match was even greater among Asian American programs, in which matching occurred 6.6 times more often than in mainstream programs. While matching was significantly higher in ethnicity-specific than in mainstream facilities for Mexican Americans, the difference was less pronounced than in the case of the other two ethnic minority groups.

Continuation was defined as return for treatment after one session. Sixty percent of African Americans in mainstream programs and 77% in ethnicity-specific programs returned after one session (X^2 = 52.71. df = 1). Among Asian Americans, 64% in mainstream programs and 98% in ethnicity-specific programs returned after one session (X^2 = 261.11, df = 1). Finally, among Mexican Americans 68% in mainstream programs and 97% in ethnicity-specific programs returned after one session (X^2 = 112.93, df =1). The difference in return rate between mainstream and ethnicity-specific programs within each minority group was statistically significant ($P < .001$). Since adults who entered mainstream and ethnicity-specific programs differed in some demographic and clinical characteristics, we conducted multiple logistic regression analyses to determine whether these initial differences remained after selected factors had been controlled.

Table 2 displays the effects of ethnicity-specific programs for each ethnic minority group (expressed as odds ratios). Each model controlled for the client's gender, age, psychiatric disorder, Medi-Cal eligibility, and ethnic match. Adults who entered ethnicity-specific programs were more likely to return after one session than adults in mainstream programs when other factors were controlled. The most substantive differences between programs occurred among Asian Americans and Mexican Americans. Asian Americans who entered ethnic programs were nearly 15 times (95% confidence interval [CI] = 7.8, 27.4) more likely than Asian Americans in mainstream programs to return after the first session. Mexican Americans were 11 times (95% CI = 6.1, 21.3) more likely to return if they were in ethnicity-specific programs rather than mainstream programs.

We should note that the effects for continuation in treatment were independent of the year in which data were collected. Since our study data span several years, the results may be an artifact of changes in the mental health system over time. We controlled for time and did not find any substantive changes in the results. Similarly, we examined the effect of time on the remainder of our dependent measures and found no major changes in our conclusions.

Table 2. Odds Ratios Derived from Multiple Logistic Regression Assessing the Effects of Ethnicity-Specific Programs on Return after One Session

Type of Program	Odds Ratio (95% Confidence Interval)		
	African Americans	Asian Americans	Mexican Americans
Ethnicity specific	2.88 (2.2, 3.8)	14.63 (7.8, 27.4)	11.32 (6.1, 21.3)
Mainstream (comparison)	1.00 ...	1.00 ...	1.00 ...

Note: All models controlled for gender, age, disorder, ethnic match, and Medi-Cal eligibility.

Length of Treatment

Longer amounts of time spent in mental health treatment settings have typically been associated with better outcomes.[27, 28] Thus, the longer the client stays in the program, the greater the probability that treatment will be successful. Length of treatment was measured by the total number of sessions that the client attended. Since the raw means for the different programs were quite unstable as a result of the wide range in number of client sessions in the different programs, the log of the total number of sessions was used in the remainder of the analyses. Table 3 reveals the standardized multiple regression coefficients estimating the effects of program type on length of stay for each minority group. Ethnic programs for the three minority groups were associated with a significantly greater number of treatment sessions after other variables had been controlled.

Global Assessment Scale Scores

The Global Assessment Scale score at discharge was the only available treatment outcome measure. Since minority clients in ethnic programs had an initially higher social functioning level than minority clients in mainstream programs, the admission score was added as a control variable in the remaining analyses of the discharge score. The effect of ethnicity-specific programs was evident only for African Americans. African Americans who entered ethnicity-specific programs had lower mean scores than African Americans in mainstream programs when other factors were controlled (data not presented).

Ethnic Programs and Ethnic Match

Since program type and ethnic match were highly correlated, there is the possibility that the relationships between these variables and the dependent measures were not additive. To understand these issues more clearly, we examined the interaction between program and ethnic match after controlling for other sociodemographic and clinical factors. The intent of the subsequent analyses was to ascertain whether there was a synergistic effect of ethnic match and program on our dependent measures. In this section, we present the results for continuation after one session and length of treatment (see Table 4). The results for discharge Global Assessment Scale score did not show a consistent pattern for any of the ethnic groups.

The baseline or comparison group in these analyses consisted of minorities who entered mainstream programs and were not matched with their therapists. In Table 4, the results for return rates are presented as odds ratios. Ethnicity-specific programs were associated with higher return rates for all three minority groups, whether or not clients were

Table 3. Standardized Multiple Regression Coefficients Estimating the Effects of Ethnicity-Specific Programs on the Log of Total Number of Sessions

Type of Program	African Americans (n = 1516)	Asian Americans (n = 1888)	Mexican Americans (n = 1306)
Ethnicity-specific program	.14*	.29*	.28*
Adjusted R^2	.08	.22	.15

Note: All models controlled for gender, age, disorder, ethnic match, and Medi-Cal eligibility.
*$P \leq .001$.

Table 4. Estimated Effects of Ethnicity-Specific Programs and Ethnic Match on Return Rate and Total Number of Sessions

	African Americans	Asian Americans	Mexican Americans
Premature Termination, OR (95% CI)			
Ethnic program, client-therapist match	1.94 (1.5, 2.5)	43.62 (19.3, 99.5)	9.47 (4.62, 19.5)
Ethnic, no match	2.16 (1.5, 3.2)	22.34 (9.1, 55.2)	16.85 (5.3, 53.5)
Mainstream, client–therapist match	.45 (0.29, 0.69)	6.32 (3.35, 11.82)	1.04 (0.76, 1.42)
Mainstream, no match (comparison)	1.00 ...	1.00 ...	1.00 ...
Treatment Sessions, Standardized Beta			
Ethnic program, client-therapist match	.12**	.41**	.24**
Ethnic, no match	.06*	.28**	.22**
Mainstream, client–therapist match	−.08	.21**	.04
Mainstream, no match (comparison)	...	...	...

Note: All models controlled for gender, age, disorder, ethnic match, and Medi-Cal eligibility. OR = odds ratio; CI = confidence interval.
$*P \le .05$; $**P \le .001$.

ethnically matched with their therapists. When minority clients entered mainstream programs but were matched with their therapists, the results were mixed. Only Asian Americans who were matched with an Asian therapist returned more often than their counterparts in mainstream programs who were not matched.

Table 4 also displays the interactive effect of program and match on the log of the total number of treatment sessions (values are standardized regression coefficients). The results were quite striking in that ethnicity-specific programs alone, match alone, or a combination of both were significantly associated with a higher number of treatment sessions for Asian Americans. African Americans and Mexican Americans who entered ethnicity-specific programs, regardless of match, were likely to stay longer than African Americans and Mexican Americans in mainstream programs.

DISCUSSION

This study used data supplied by a large management information system derived from naturalistic settings. Since these data were not part of an experimental design, it was not possible to control for a number of factors that could have influenced the results. For example, it is plausible that therapists in ethnicity-specific clinics diagnose patients differently than therapists in predominantly White clinics. Also, clients who enter ethnicity-specific centers may differ from clients who enter predominantly White clinics on a number of dimensions that we were unable to measure in the present study. Despite this general limitation, we believe that the data set provided a propitious opportunity to address how well programs serve ethnic minority consumers and to point to future directions for examination of this issue in more rigorous research designs.

Previous findings have documented that ethnic minorities often lack access to appropriate mental health services.[15,18] The present study provides initial documentation on ethnic minority clients who enter ethnicity-specific programs. In general, the results indicate that ethnic clients involved in such programs return more often and stay for more sessions than those involved in mainstream programs. The effect of program on length of treatment persisted even after differences in client variables and ethnic matching of clients and therapists in the two types of programs had been controlled. The advantage of ethnicity-specific programs over mainstream programs was not maintained when the Global Assessment Scale termination score, the measure of outcome, was used as the criterion and other factors were controlled. It is possible that the Global Assessment Scale, which requires a numerical rating of overall functioning, is a poor or insensitive measure of treatment outcome and that the ratings resulting from this scale, which were determined by the therapist, may have been affected by his or her own involvement in the case and the presence or absence of client-therapist ethnic match. Certainly one limitation of the present study was not having several different outcome measures, and there is a clear need to develop better outcome measures for cultural interventions.

In the present study, it was not possible to identify the precise aspects of ethnicity-specific programs that may explain the findings. Policymakers and social scientists have a critical stake in identifying such elements. First, in light of the growing efforts to change the health care system, there is little empirical basis with which to guide modifications and policies for the delivery of mental health care to ethnic minority groups. Despite conceptual notions about the components of ethnicity-specific services, it is unclear, at this point, what actually constitutes these services. Second, it is highly unlikely that all characteristics of ethnicity-specific services influence use. Anecdotal and observational evidence has suggested that some of the characteristics include having bilingual and bicultural staff, providing an ethnic atmosphere at the agency, having announcements written in ethnic languages, conducting treatment in a more "culturally sensitive" manner, changing hours of operation of the agency, and using culturally appropriate interpersonal styles. Third, it is likely that ethnicity-specific programs are more attractive to certain segments of ethnic minority communities. For example, recent immigrants may find ethnicity-specific programs appealing because these programs have a high number of staff who can communicate with them. Without more systematic investigations of these and other characteristics associated with ethnictiy-specific programs, contributions to theory cannot emerge. What components of ethnicity-specific services result in higher use rates reduced premature termination, more favorable attitudes toward treatment, and ultimately, better client outcomes? By investigating ethnicity-specific services, we can gain insight into the means for improving not only these services but mainstream ones. Given the increasingly multiethnic nature of our society, mainstream services will need to become more responsive to the cultural needs of ethnic clients. Moreover, it is likely that certain components of effective services for ethnic communities will translate to mainstream populations. From our perspective, analysis of ethnicity-specific services is an essential and exciting area of investigation that has been almost completely ignored, despite much discussion about the need for such services.

NOTES

This research was supported by National Institute of Mental Health grant R01 MH44331. We are indebted to the Los Angeles County Department of Mental Health for its assistance in the research.

1. Wilson, W. J. (1991). Studying inner-city social dislocations: The challenge of public agenda research. *American Sociological Review*, 56, 1–14.
2. Snowden, L. R., Collinge, W. B., and Runkle, M. C. (1982). Help seeking and underservice. In L. R. Snowden, (Ed.), *Reaching the Underserved: Mental Health Needs of Neglected Populations* (pp. 298–299). Beverly Hills, CA: Sage.
3. Sue, S. (1977). Community mental health services to minority groups: Some optimism, some pessimism. *American Psychologist*, 32, 616–624.
4. Neighbors, H. W., Bashshur, R., Price, R., Selig, S., Donabedian, A., and Shannon, G. (1992). Ethnic minority mental health service delivery: A review of the literature. In J. Greenley and P. Leaf (Eds.), *Research in Community and Mental Health: A Research Annual* (pp. 55–71). Greenwich, CT: JAI Press.
5. Jones, E. E., and Thorne A. (1987). Rediscovery of the subject: Intercultural approaches to clinical assessment. *Journal of Consulting and Clinical Psychology*, 55, 488–496.
6. Jackson, J. S., Neighbors, H. W., and Gurin, G. (1986). Findings from a national survey of Black mental health: Implications for practice and training. In M. R. Miranda and H.H.L. Kitano (Eds.), *Mental Health Research and Practice in Minority Communities: Development of Culturally Sensitive Training Programs* (pp. 91–116). Washington, DC: US Government Printing Office.
7. Muñoz, R. F. (1982). The Spanish-speaking consumer and the community mental health center. In E. E. Jones and S. J. Korchin (Eds.), *Minority Mental Health* (pp. 362–398). New York: Praeger.
8. Padilla, A. M., and Salgado De Snyder, N. (1985). Counseling Hispanics: Strategies for effective intervention. In P. Pedersen (Ed.), *Handbook of Cross-Cultural Counseling and Therapy* (pp. 157–164). Westport, CT: Greenwood Press.
9. Rogler, L. H., Malgady, R. G., and Rodriguez, O. (1989). *Hispanics and Mental Health: A Framework for Research*. Malabar, FL: Robert E Krieger Publishing.
10. Sue, D. W., and Sue, D. (1990). *Counseling the Culturally Different: Theory and Practice*. New York: John Wiley and Sons.
11. Suinn, R. M., Richard-Figuerod, K., Lew, S., and Vigil, P. (1985). Career decisions and an Asian acculturation scale. *Journal of the Asian American Psychological Association*, 10, 20–28.
12. Szapocznik, J., Rio, A., Murray, E., et al. (1989). Structural family versus psychodynamic child therapy for problematic Hispanic boys. *Journal of Consulting and Clinical Psychology*, 57, 571–578.
13. Trimble, J. E., and LaFromboise, T., (1985). American Indians and the counseling process: Culture, adaptation, and style. In P. Pedersen (Ed.), *Handbook of Cross-Cultural Counseling and Therapy* (pp. 127–134). Westport, CT: Greenwood Press.
14. Brislin, R. (1993). *Understanding Culture's Influence on Behavior*. New York: Harcourt Brace Jovanovich College Publishers.
15. Lefley, H. P., and Bestman, E. W. (1984). Community mental health and minority populations: A multi-ethnic approach. In S. Sue and T. Moore (Eds.), *The Pluralistic Society: A Community Mental Health Perspective* (pp. 116–148). New York: Human Sciences Press.
16. Kramer, B. M. (1984). Community mental health in a dual society. In Sue, S., and Moore, T., (Eds.) *The Pluralistic Society: A Community Mental Health Perspective* (pp. 254–262). New York: Human Sciences Press.
17. Cheung, F., Snowden, L. (1990). Community mental health and ethnic minority populations. *Community Mental Health Journal*, 26, 277–291.
18. Hu, T., Snowden, L., Jerrell, J., and Nguyen, T. (1991). Ethnic populations in public mental health: Services and level of use. *American Journal of Public Health*, 81, 1429–1434.
19. Snowden, L., and Cheung, F. (1990). Use of inpatient mental health services by members of ethnic minority groups. *American Psychologist*, 45, 347–355.
20. Sue, S., McKinney, H. (1975). Asian-Americans in the community mental health care system. *American Journal of Orthopsychiatry*, 45, 11–18.

21. O'Sullivan, M. J., Peterson, P. D., Cox, G. B., and Kirkeby, J. (1989). Ethnic populations: Community mental health services ten years later. *American Journal of Community Psychology*, 17, 17–30.

22. Sue, S., Fujino, D. C., Hu, L. T., Takeuchi, D. T., and Zane N.W.S. (1991). Community mental health services for ethnic minority groups: A test of the cultural responsiveness hypothesis. *Journal of Consulting and Clinical Psychology*, 59, 533–540.

23. *Diagnostic and Statistical Manual of Mental Disorders* (Rev. 3rd ed.). (1987). Washington, DC: American Psychiatric Association.

24. Endicott, J., Spitzer, R. L., Fleiss, J. L., and Cohen J. (1976). The Global Assessment Scale: A procedure for measuring overall severity of psychiatric disturbance. *Archives of General Psychiatry*, 33, 766–771.

25. Holcomb, W. R., Otto, R. L. (1988). Concurrent validity of the Global Assessment Scale: What's in a number? *Psychological Rep.*, 62, 279–282.

26. Sohlberg, S. (1989). There's more in a number than you think: New validity data for the Global Assessment Scale. *Psychological Reports*, 64, 455–461.

27. Baekelund, F., and Lundwall, L. (1975). Dropping out of treatment: A critical review. *Psychological Bulletin*, 82, 738–783.

28. Luborsky, L., Chandler, M., Auerbach, A. H., Cohen, J., and Bachrach, H. M. (1971). Factors influencing the outcome of psychotherapy: A review of quantitative research. *Psychological Bulletin*, 75, 145–148.

22.
Cognitive-Behavior Therapy and the Native American Client

George S. Renfrey

This article discusses therapy and the Native American client. A brief review of the mental health needs of Native Americans and the response of the psychological community to date is provided. It is argued that a culturally sensitive approach to working with this special population is a professional and ethical necessity, and it is suggested that a congruence exists between the cognitive-behavioral approach to therapy and the needs and preferences of Native Americans. Key therapeutic issues and problems presented by working with this population are discussed, and guidelines for dealing with them are suggested. Suggestions for future directions that can be taken toward better serving Native Americans are provided.

Native American worldviews and cultural matrices can be very different from those common to the dominant culture, lending bias to interpretations by non-natives, and retarding authentic understandings. This presents special challenges for mental health professionals who serve them.

These special challenges are a function of both the ubiquitous effects of cultural differences and the special history of the Native American people. They include the need to consider the impact that cultural factors may have on the expression of accepted principles of behavior, the need to analyze behavioral problems that arise within an unfamiliar cultural context, and the effects that cultural differences may have on rapport, therapist credibility, and communication. The therapist may also find that conventional explanations of presenting problems conflict with notions held by their Native American clients and that conventional interventions may be ineffective or produce unexpected iatrogenic effects.

This article discusses each of these problems and argues that cultural sensitivity is an essential part of the solution. A congruence between the cognitive-behavioral approach to therapy and the needs and preferences of Native Americans is suggested. A therapeutic approach calling for an assessment of client acculturation/deculturation and bicultural competence, and the integration of conventional with traditional interventions aimed at biculturally appropriate treatment goals is recommended. Therapeutic style is discussed as is the need for tribal-specific therapist acculturation. Finally, a number of actions are suggested that may lead to improved services to this special population.

CURRENT MENTAL HEALTH NEEDS OF NATIVE AMERICANS

Of this country's ethnic minorities, Native Americans are perhaps the most in need of effective social, health, and mental health services (LaFromboise, 1988; Manson, 1982).

They are among the poorest and hardest hit by unemployment (e.g., Barter and Barter, 1974; Prieto, 1989; Ho, 1987; LaFromboise, 1988), and have a disproportionately high incidence of tuberculosis (e.g., Ho, 1987), cirrhosis of the liver (e.g., May and Dizmang, 1974; Westermeyer, 1974), alcohol and tobacco abuse (e.g., Dozier, 1966; Lewis, 1982; Schinke et al., 1990; Shore, 1974; Weibel, 1982), depression (e.g., Shore, 1974; Tafoya, 1989a), infant mortality (Ho, 1987), and childhood developmental disabilities (see Skidmore and Roberts, 1991). They are at greater than average risk of death by homicide, (e.g., Westermeyer, 1974), suicide, (e.g., Ho, 1987; LaFromboise, 1988; May, 1987; May and Dizmang, 1974; Shore, 1974; Tower, 1989), and, preventable accidents (Barter and Barter, 1974; May and Dizmang, 1974; Westermeyer, 1974), and their delinquency and arrest rates are among the highest of all ethnic groups (LaFromboise, 1988). Citing three epidemiological studies, Trimble (1990) states that the lifetime prevalence of psychiatric problems of Native Americans may exceed 50% in some tribes, although methodological problems limit the generalizability of these findings.

Some authors have argued that epidemiological data on Native Americans can be misleading because large differences in incidence rates between tribal groups are common, with some yielding lower than national averages, and others higher (Barter and Barter, 1974; May and Dizmang, 1974; Shore, 1974; Westermeyer, 1974). Additionally, some have cautioned that journalistic reports of Native American mental health problems are often based on culturally insensitive data collection and interpretation, distorting the magnitude of those problems (e.g., Dinges, Trimble, Manson, and Pasquale, 1981). Caution must be used when applying Western standards of psychosocial well-being to the culturally different. Nevertheless, the most liberal interpretation of available evidence suggests that Native Americans, as a group, have significant mental health care needs.

The causes of the problems are a debated issue. However, core reasons often cited relate to the acculturation and deculturation stressors wrought by the dominant European-American culture (e.g., Christie and Halpern, 1990; Dozier, 1966; French, 1989; Jilek, 1974; Mail, 1989; May and Dizmang, 1974). According to this position, the destruction of traditional cultural values, practices, and means of material support (deculturation), and the failure of the dominant culture to force full assimilation/acculturation have left most Native Americans caught between conflicting cultures. As a result, many find themselves in a socially and economically untenable position. The resulting personal and interpersonal stressors then precipitate diverse health and mental health problems.

The Treatment of Native Americans by the Mental Health Professions to Date

Despite the significance of their mental health needs, Native Americans are seriously under-serviced by the mental health professions in general, and by psychology in particular (e.g., Trimble, 1990). Indeed, Manson (1982) has asserted that they are the most neglected ethnic group by the mental health field, and LaFromboise (1988) has noted that the number of Native American psychologists in proportion to the native population is about one fourth that available to the general population.

A review of the literature on Native American mental health supports Trimble's (1990) contention that until the 1970s, it was common for psychologists to assume that the study of Native Americans was the purview of anthropology (see Kelso and Attneave, 1981, for a complete bibliography). Although this is changing, Trimble and LaFromboise (1985) have pointed out that relatively little of the accumulating literature addresses the counseling process, and research-based reports are minimal. Thus, articles of direct relevance to Native Americans in therapy remain scarce. Indeed, the results of a recent computer search reported by Saks-Berman (1989) show that only 38 articles have been published on psychotherapy with Native Americans within the past 20 years.

This inattention to therapy with Native Americans is even more pronounced within cognitive-behavioral psychology. A review by the present author of the contents of 11 major behavioral and cognitive-behavioral publications (*Behavioral Assessment, Behavioral Counseling Quarterly, Behavior Modification, Behavior Therapy, Behavior Therapy and Experimental Psychiatry, Behaviour Research and Therapy, Journal of Applied Behavior Analysis, Journal of Behavioral Assessment, Journal of Behavior Therapy and Experimental Therapeutics, The Behavior Analyst, The Behavior Therapist*) from their start to the end of 1990 yielded no articles addressing Native American treatment issues, and only one case study with a native client (Conrad, Delk, and Williams, 1974).

In summary, the mental health needs of Native Americans are at least as great as that of any other ethnic group, and yet they are among the most underserved by the professions. That Native Americans are this country's fastest growing ethnic group (Trimble, 1990) suggests that this need-service gap will only worsen unless corrective actions are taken. Since so few Native American psychologists exist, and since the number of Native Americans successfully pursuing higher education is declining in relation to non-natives (Kidwell, 1991), it follows that this task will largely fall on non-natives in the foreseeable future.

The Under-Utilization of Mental Health Services by Native Americans

Native Americans often under-use those services that are available to them (Sue, 1990; Sue, 1977; Sue, Allen, and Conaway, 1978), compounding the problem of deficient service availability. LaFromboise (1988), in a review of American Indian mental health policy, cited several reasons why Native Americans often fail to use available mental health services, and have higher than average dropout rates when they do. These included the common perceptions by Native Americans that Western psychological services: (1) are insensitive and unresponsive to their needs; (2) are to be feared and mistrusted; and (3) tend to impose a Western cultural bias onto Native American problems, resulting in efforts to shape client behavior in ways that conflict with traditional values and lifestyle preferences. Other cited reasons for under-use and early dropout are a preference for more traditional forms of healing (Hippler, 1975; LaFromboise, Trimble, and Mohatt, 1990), perceived conflicts in values held by non-native counselors (Trimble, 1981), and disagreements with non-native counselors about the etiology and treatment of problems (Manson and Trimble, 1982).

The above suggests that cultural ignorance or insensitivity of non-native therapists is largely responsible for this under-use of mental health services. Further, even if Native Americans do seek services, cultural biases may render therapy ineffective or even harmful. French (1981, 1989) has asserted that conventional, ethnocentric counseling is more likely to exacerbate than ameliorate the presenting problems of many Native Americans. If so, then the current pattern of under-use may represent more function than folly. Similarly, Dinges et al. (1981) have suggested that the under-use of conventional mental health services may help prevent further erosion of traditional values and cultural identity. These authors advise that attempts to increase the use of these services should be balanced with concern about increasing the acculturation and deculturation stresses on Native American clients that may result.

For these and other reasons discussed below, psychologist aiming to provide services to this population should do so with cultural sensitivity. Szapocznik, Scopetta, and King (1978) have defined cultural sensitivity as, "a treatment mode built on a set of therapeutic assumptions that complement the patient's basic value structure." This definition will suffice for our present purpose. The issues discussed below relate to general group norms, and their applicability to a given Native American will be affected by factors such as degree of assimilation and individual differences. This should be kept in mind throughout, less ethnic stereotypes be perpetuated in the name of cultural sensitivity.

A Rationale for Cultural Sensitivity with Native Americans

Several other considerations argue for cultural sensitivity in working with Native Americans. First, too little is known about the impact that cultural factors might have on the expression of accepted principles of behavior. Trimble (1990) questions the assumption that empirical findings in psychology are universal, arguing that too few investigations have been conducted to assess the influences of cultural variations. Although basic behavioral principles do appear to have good generalizability between species, we should not assume that higher-level, cognitive-behavioral principles are universal, that they are relatively independent of cultural variations. Only through research and practice that carefully assesses cultural variables can their generality be established.

Second, cultural familiarity may be necessary for accurate and effective analyses of the problems of Native Americans. Problems of behavior arise within a cultural context and useful functional analyses of such are likely to depend upon a working knowledge of that context. This may not present a problem for the clinician when dealing with culturally similar clients, but when working with the culturally different, serious difficulties can arise. Culturally based differences in conditioning histories are likely to create behavioral contexts and motivational variables unfamiliar to the uninformed clinician. Because the learning histories of Native Americans may be radically different from that of non-native therapists, contextual illiteracy and invalid functional analyses of presenting problems may result.

Similarly, since diagnostic classifications were developed and validated largely with members of the dominant culture, they may not be appropriate for some Native Americans with some presenting problems. For example, symptoms of depression in Native Americans may not coincide with middle-class expectations (Goldwasser and Badger, 1989; Trimble, 1990). Conversely, what may appear to be symptoms of depression may, in fact, be an unrelated culture-specific role that has diverse social functions (O'Neil, 1989; Trimble, Manson, Dinges, and Medicine, 1984). This suggests that cultural familiarity is basic to an accurate understanding and analysis of the problems of the Native American client.

A third argument for cultural awareness and sensitivity is that both may be essential to therapeutic rapport and therapist credibility (e.g., LaFromboise, Trimble, and Mohatt, 1990; Lefley, 1984; Trimble and Hayes, 1984), as well as effective communication (e.g., Herring, 1990; LaFromboise, Trimble, and Mohatt, 1990; Skidmore and Roberts, 1991; Spang, 1971; Sue and Sue, 1977; Sue, 1990; Trimble and LaFromboise, 1985). Rapport with many Native Americans may be very hard for non-native therapists to develop because of the extensive history of exploitative and often inhumane treatment by the dominant culture. With such clients, familiarity with and respect for the client's cultural differences should be presumed essential to establishing trust (LaFromboise, Trimble, and Mohatt, 1990).

Although some findings suggest that, all else being equal, Native Americans may perceive other Native Americans as more desirable and/or effective as counselors (e.g., Bennet and BigFoot-Sipes, 1991; Dauphinais, Dauphinais, and Rowe, 1981; Johnson and Lashley, 1989), the literature also suggests that ethnicity may not be as important if the non-native counselor is perceived as trustworthy (LaFromboise and Dixon, 1981), and has shared attitudes and values (Bennet and BigFoot-Sipes, 1991). Similarly, the effects of counselor ethnicity may be at least partially attenuated if s/he employs culturally appropriate communication skills (Dauphinais, Dauphinais, and Rowe, 1981).

Cultural differences in subtle verbal and non-verbal components of communication may also impede communication between Native Americans and the uninformed therapist (Sue and Sue, 1977; Sue, 1990). For example, the expected "pause time" between alternating speakers may be longer for many Native Americans than for non-natives (as much as 4–5 seconds for some tribes versus about 1 second for native English speakers) (Tafoya, 1989a; Trimble and Hayes, 1984). Long pauses during speech are common with some tribes, and silence itself may have communicative functions. This may cause an uninformed therapist to interrupt the native client during speech and to give too little time to respond to questions. Further, many Native Americans expect to take a passive role in treatment and to have the therapist do most of the talking (Dinges et al., 1981; Tafoya, 1989a; Jilek-Aall, 1976). This may be in accordance with traditional healer roles, but it is incongruent with most conventional therapies.

Similarly, non-verbal components of communication, such as handshakes, eye-contact, posture, facial expressions, and proxemics or physical distancing (see Hall, 1969) may differ significantly between the native client and the non-native therapist (see Attneave, 1985; Tafoya, 1989a; Trimble and Hayes, 1984; Sue and Sue, 1977; Sue, 1990). As well, minority cultures (including Native American) have been characterized as favoring high-context communication (see Hall, 1976) which relies heavily on non-verbals and shared meanings (Sue, 1990). Accordingly, a lack of therapist familiarity with these would be expected to seriously impede communication.

Fourth, cultural differences may impede discussions about the etiology of behavioral or medical problems. Schacht, Tafoya, and Mirabla (1989) and others (e.g., Sue and Sue, 1977; Szapocznik et al., 1978; Tafoya, 1989a) have cautioned that Native Americans and the ethnically different in general are more likely to accept causal explanations if they are congruent with the basic beliefs of the culture. Tafoya (1988a) asserts that Western concepts of linear causality may not coincide with the non-linear concepts held by many traditional Native Americans. Such clients are unlikely to accept Western explications if such are presented in opposition to customary explanatory schemes, and therapist credibility and treatment adherence may suffer in the process.

Fifth, cultural sensitivity would enable the therapist to develop and employ interventions that are congruent with the client's worldview and cultural practices. Educators and mental health providers who work with Native Americans widely believe that congruence between their methodologies and the client's worldview and cultural practices is a key to effective services (e.g., Cooley, 1977; Jilek-Aall, 1976; Lafromboise, 1988; Tafoya, 1989b; Schacht et al., 1989; Szapocznik et al., 1978). Culturally congruent interventions would likely enhance therapist and treatment credibility.

Western ethnocentric interventions, even if successful in relieving presenting problems, could alter the Native American's behavior and belief structure as to reduce congruence with traditional cultural norms (Goldstein, 1974). Were this to happen, the client's level of deculturation stress and the erosion of the indigenous culture would increase (Dinges et al., 1981; Jilek-Aall, 1976). Relevant to this, Tyler, Sussewell, and Williams-McCoy (1985) have urged therapists to assess the destructive effects that their activities can have on the ethnically different. Culturally congruent interventions would help therapists avoid increasing the serious acculturation and deculturation pressures already experienced by most Native Americans.

Finally, cultural familiarity would assist the integration of conventional and traditional interventions, the latter still favored by many indigenous people. This final point may prove controversial with those deeply ingrained in the Aristotelian worldview. However, a substantial body of evidence has accrued suggesting that the traditional healing practices of many cultures can prove very effective in dealing with diverse medical and behavioral problems of their members (e.g., Bergman, 1973; Frank, 1973; Jilek, 1971, 1974; Jilek and Todd, 1974; Kleinman and Gale, 1982; Murphy, 1964; Pascarosa and Futterman, 1976; Prince, 1973; Torrey, 1972, 1986). In most tribes, traditional healers hold central and respected positions, and some authors have suggested that working collaboratively with them may be the most effective approach that conventional therapists can take in working with some groups for some presenting problems (e.g., Attneave, 1974; Bergman, 1973; Dinges et al., 1981; LaFromboise, Trimble, and Mohatt, 1990; Lefley, 1984; Leighton and Leighton, 1941; Jilek, 1971, 1974; Rappaport, 1977; Rappaport and Rappaport, 1981; Ruiz and Langrod, 1976; Trimble and Hayes, 1984).

The Congruence Between the Cognitive-Behavioral Approach to Therapy, and the Needs and Preferences of Native Americans

At present, due to a scarcity of controlled investigations, too little is known about Native Americans in therapy to identify treatments of choice or to make definitive comparisons of the efficacy of therapeutic approaches. However, there is good reason to believe that cognitive-behavior therapists are well suited to providing culturally sensitive services to this population. The present time, action orientation of cognitive-behavior therapy and, to some extent, its directiveness seems to be congruent with the needs, values, and expectations of many Native Americans.

Although parallels have been drawn between psychoanalytic therapy and some traditional Native American healing practices (e.g., Pfister, 1932; Wallace, 1958), others have argued that insight oriented therapies are inappropriate for more traditional Native Americans (e.g., Sue and Sue, 1977; Tafoya, 1989a; Trimble et al. 1984). Trimble et al. (1984) link the ineffectiveness of insight-therapies with Native Americans to the ingrained custom of many to avoid self-revelation. Accordingly, to ask such individuals to speak about private thoughts and feelings would be inappropriate. Similarly, French (1981) has asserted that ego and existential psychology have little relevance to many traditionals because their identities and self-concepts are bound to their tribal groups and to nature as a whole.

The ineffectiveness of insight therapies with this population may parallel their impotence with inner-city economically disadvantaged Hispanics. Rogler, Malagdy, Costantino, and Blumenthal (1987) assert that insight-based therapies are irrelevant to the economic and acculturation problems faced by the latter population. That many Native Americans face similar economic disadvantages and acculturation stresses suggests that this might be true for this population as well.

As to what approach may be effective, Tafoya (1989a) has asserted that treatments that are: (a) specific in their directives to alter behavior; (b) involve homework assignments; and (c) concentrate on "altering present actions which then impact emotional states, rather than expecting a therapist to alter the emotional state and then achieve behavior change" (Tafoya, 1989a, p. 76), are more congruent with many traditional Native American healing traditions. Accordingly, they should maximize client adherence. This description closely resembles what has become a hallmark of cognitive-behavior therapy, and suggests that this approach to behavior change may be more culturally congruent than many conventional alternatives. In support of this, French (1989) reports that cognitive-behavioral therapy is a "convenient vehicle" for the didactic and problem solving techniques that he uses with Native American clients.

The foregoing suggests that cognitive-behavior therapy aimed at problem resolution is a promising approach to take with this special population. However, therapists are cautioned against implementing interventions in a conventional manner. Although the general approach of the cognitive-behavior therapist may look promising, clinical assessments, treatment goals, and therapeutic styles require cultural adjustment, as discussed below.

Finally, the functional analytic approach favored by many cognitive-behavior therapists, when employed with adequate knowledge of the contingencies inherent in the indigenous culture, may permit behavioral analyses with minimal Western bias. Such analyses would be more accurate and useful to the therapist, and will be more relevant and acceptable to the Native American client.

Issues and Problems in Conducting Cognitive-Behavior Therapy with Native Americans and Some Suggested Solutions

Cultural heterogeneity. Native Americans are not members of a common culture, but represent a diverse cultural collage. As LaFromboise (1988) points out, there are 511 federally recognized native groups and 365 state-recognized tribes in this country, and more than 200 distinct Native American languages (not dialects) are still spoken. Further, traditional Native Americans can differ from one another in their cultures as widely as their Eurasian counterparts (Attneave, 1985; Tefft, 1967). To add complexity to this, more than 60% of the individuals with Native American status in this country are of mixed ethnic heritage and, regardless of blood quantum, can range from very traditional in alliance and custom to full acculturation to the dominant culture (Trimble, 1990). Stereotypes of Native Americans simply do not apply, and making generalizations across tribal groups should be attempted with extreme caution. Nevertheless, several general issues are germane to clients from all indigenous groups.

Assessment of Acculturation/Deculturation

Many of the issues discussed in this article will be relevant to a given Native American in proportion to his/her level of acculturation and deculturation. Those who are fully acculturated to the dominant culture may not differ greatly from most non-native clients, and cultural sensitivity may be less critical. The issues will be highly relevant for those who remain traditional, and cultural sensitivity will be crucial to effective treatment. Accordingly, an assessment of acculturation status is a necessary first step to providing effective therapy to this population. No simple means exists to do this, but efforts to develop acculturation scales for other minority groups may function as good models for what can be done. For example, Cuellar, Harris, and Jasso (1980) developed a 20-item, bilingual questionnaire that enables the relative acculturation of Hispanics to be rated. Such scales could be developed and validated for clinical use with Native Americans.

French (1981, 1989) has subdivided the continuum of acculturation/deculturation that exists for Native Americans into three categories that he reports to be clinically useful: (1) Traditional Indians, are the least acculturated to the dominant culture and have retained a viable level of their traditional culture (about 20–25% of the population); (2) Middle-Class Indians, have effectively acculturated to the dominant culture (about 15% of the population); and (3) Marginal Indians, caught between cultures, too deculturated to maintain traditional ways and yet not acculturated enough to adapt effectively to the dominant culture (about 65% of the population). Ho (1987) outlines a similar three-level classification scheme for family lifestyle patterns that is reportedly useful in family therapy. Such schemes may prove to be more clinically useful than a continuum of variation, but effective assessment tools must be developed to enable categorization. Such devices would ideally assess both acculturation and deculturation levels.

Assessment of presenting problems—the case for assessment of bicultural competence. Given an assessment of a client's acculturation status, it remains for assessments of presenting problems to be made. These assessments must consider the cultural context within which problems emerge and maintain themselves. Since most Native Americans functions within two cultures, assessments will require a careful consideration of the contexts presented by both. The notion of "cultural competence" may be useful to this end.

Dinges and Duffy (1979) have defined cultural competence as, " . . . that array of internal and external human activities [read behaviors] that constitute a core of culturally valued behaviors denoting effective adaptation by a given culture's terms" (p. 210). Thus, cultural competence is a function of operationally definable skills and knowledge that enable the individual to flourish within a given culture. Conceptualizing mental health problems of Native Americans as direct or indirect functions of deficits in such skills may prove useful.

A skills deficit approach to assessment and therapy with Native Americans was first suggested by LaFromboise and Rowe (1983). According to these authors, Native Americans often seek mental health services because of poor adaptation to the dominant culture. Adaptation is enhanced through analyses of specific skills deficits using purely utilitarian (hence less culturally biased) criteria for social competence, and appropriate training programs. LaFromboise and Rowe (1983) state that such skills training for bicultural competence has several advantages: It is less culturally biased than modes of treatment based on Western notions of healthy psychological functioning; it holds promise for preventive applications; and it is applicable to a wide range of problems that Native

Americans face. An additional benefit is the practical and action-based address of problems brought into therapy, an approach congruent with many traditional healing practices and expectations (Tafoya, 1989a).

LaFromboise and Rowe (1983) have identified several possible problems with this approach; however, its linear concept of causality which may be resisted by many traditionals, and a bicultural lifestyle may be untenable. Individuals seeking a bicultural lifestyle may be stranded between the two cultures, left ineffective in either. Alternatively, one lifestyle may inevitably predominate (e.g., Leon, 1968). However, bicultural adaptation is a preference if not a necessity for many, and its viability is an empirical issue that remains open to direct investigation.

Of greater concern to the present author is that LaFromboise and Rowe's approach does not address several key considerations. To begin with, it does not appear to address problems that reflect poor adaptation to the traditional culture. As noted, French (1989) reports that about 65% of Native Americans are compelled to live within two cultures but are inadequately prepared to live within either. He reports that many of these "marginals" want to become more acculturated to traditional ways but lack the knowledge of how to do so appropriately. Further, he asserts that effective trans-cultural counseling with this group best begins with enhancement of the Native American's traditional identity, followed by training for problem-solving within both cultures. LaFromboise, Trimble, and Mohatt (1990) have affirmed the therapeutic benefits of strengthening the troubled Native American's traditional cultural values and family/community networks.

The clinician should also be aware that some native "mental health problems" may have culturally specific functions and not involve skills deficits or pathology per se. These are best understood from the perspective of the indigenous culture (see O'Nell, 1989; Trimble et al., 1984). For example, *Wacinko*, a "disorder" seen among the Lakota, has a range of symptoms that may suggest a reactive depressive illness; however, it does not appear to be related to depression as it is conventionally conceived. It may best be thought of as a "role" with diverse social functions (see Trimble et al., 1984). At the same time, some problems arguably transcend their cultural contexts altogether (e.g., schizophrenia). This suggests that skills training for bicultural competence, as a therapeutic approach, requires expansion to address these issues if it is to be maximally useful to the cognitive-behavior therapist.

What the preceding discussion argues for is an assessment of specific skills deficits that: (1) prevent the Native American from meeting the demands of the dominant culture (e.g., communications skills); (2) prevent the client from meeting the demands of the indigenous culture (e.g., communications skills or unfamiliarity with traditional ways); and (3) prevent the client from meeting trans-cultural or bicultural demands (e.g., basic child care skills). It also argues for: (4) determining the extent to which the presenting problem has a traditional function within the traditional culture; and (5) determining the extent to which biological factors may be contributing to the presenting problem.

Treatment—a case for the integration of scientific and traditional interventions. Given this multi-dimensional analysis, the therapist can arrange interventions that address each dimension of concern, adjusting for the acculturation status of the client. This might involve fairly standard skills training for a type one or three deficit; referral to or consultation with tribal elders and/or traditional healers for a type two or three deficit; culturally sensitive family therapy and/or traditional interventions for a type four problem (see

Ho, 1987; Schacht et al., 1989; Tafoya, 1989a), some combination of the above and/or appropriate referral to other service providers for a type five problem.

This approach to therapy with Native Americans advocates serving the individual client's needs. It also advocates preserving indigenous cultures through minimizing further client deculturation via the therapy process and promoting retraditionalization when appropriate to client needs. Rogler et al. (1987) identified a conflict that can arise between advocating for the protection of minority group cultures, and providing optimal treatments to members of those minorities. They state that concerned therapists may find themselves conflicted over wishing to provide minority clients with treatments isomorphic to the minority cultures on the one hand, and wishing to provide treatments that will help clients adapt to the dominant culture on the other. This conflict is especially relevant to Native Americans given the impact of acculturation and deculturation stressors. By promoting the identification and separation of the needs of the client in adapting to the demands of both cultures, the expanded bicultural competence model should permit the clinician to minimize this conflict.

The use of traditional healers and interventions will present logistical and conceptual difficulties for many. Non-natives are urged, however, to challenge ethnocentric assumptions about folkhealing, and to consider collaboration with traditional healers. The available evidence would suggest that such is in the best interests of the Native American client. The use of traditional healing methods is arguably appropriate when the client is traditional, the presenting problems are specific to the indigenous culture, or when they would otherwise be effective. Even when a conventional intervention is the treatment of choice, supplementation by a traditional counterpart would likely improve therapist and treatment credibility, treatment compliance and outcome, and/or enhance prevention efforts (Ho, 1987; Jilek and Todd, 1974; LaFromboise, Trimble, and Mohatt, 1990; Lefley, 1984; Manson and Trimble, 1982; Pascarosa and Futterman, 1976; Rappaport and Rappaport, 1981; Trimble and Hayes, 1984). Additionally, some (e.g., LaFromboise, Trimble, and Mohatt, 1990) have argued that traditional healing ceremonies may have broad-acting therapeutic effects. Such ceremonies often include participation by members of the family and community, resulting in enhanced social networks. Given the group (versus individualistic) orientation of many Native Americans, this can be expected to reduce some of the psychosocial stressors that the client may be experiencing. By reaffirming traditional beliefs and values, the ceremonies may also promote culturally adaptive behaviors.

Direct service to clients by indigenous healers is not the only role that they may play in mental health service delivery. Delgado (1979) has identified other roles that could prove helpful, including: (1) acculturation/training of the mental health care professional; (2) consultation; (3) reciprocal referral agent; and (4) cotherapist. Though consultation and referrals have been the most frequently sought collaborations, the unacculturated therapist would do well to approach the Native American healer for instruction in tribal norms and customs. In doing so, the therapist must be able to effect a "student" role when appropriate, and to show a sincere respect for the culture. The present author has found no references in the literature to either failed or successful attempts to conventional/traditional cotherapy.

Attempts to establish a mutually satisfying professional relationship with a traditional healer will likely present many pitfalls and challenges for the conventional therapist. A small body of literature exists that deals with the problems that the therapist can expect to face when trying to coordinate contemporary and traditional mental health services, and interested readers are encouraged to familiarize themselves with it (e.g., Attneave, 1974; Dinges et al., 1981).

For the therapist who is not well integrated with the Native American community served (a process that can take many years), the problems involved may appear insurmountable. In such cases, the Indian Health Service mental health paraprofessional may function as a bridge between the conventional and the traditional (Attneave, 1974; Bergman, 1974).

Therapeutic Style

Studies of therapeutic style and the Native American client are minimal, and the literature sometimes appears to be inconsistent. For example, Dauphinais et al. (1981) reported that Native American students preferred a counseling style that emphasized direct guidance and approval/reassurance, with minimal use of open-ended questions and restatement. Tafoya (1989a) and others (e.g., Herring, 1990; Spang, 1965) have affirmed that a (culturally congruent) directive therapeutic style is appropriate for many Native Americans. At the same time, a directive style has also been identified as potentially problematic. French (1989), for example, has cautioned against a highly directive style that may cause Native Americans to view the non-native therapist as a controlling agent for the dominant culture. The key to this apparent contradiction may lie in the degree of directiveness and the style with which injunctions are offered.

Many native clients are likely to prefer indirect communication and to take exception to the frankness typical of Western conversation (Sue, 1990). Tafoya suggests that Ericksonian-like open-ended injunctions, rather than detailed prescriptive directions should be used. It has also been suggested that the use of traditional and non-traditional myths, and brief case histories of clients who successfully coped with similar problems may be useful. The use of such stories matches many traditional teaching methods and may provide effective behavioral solutions to client problems nonintrusively. They may also help bridge the cultural gap and open lines of communication between the non-native therapist and native client (Jilek-Aall, 1976; Tafoya, 1989a). It follows from above that behavioral contracting may not be appropriate for many Native American clients.

The need for tribal specific therapist acculturation. The preceding suggests that therapists require a fair degree of knowledge of traditional tribal ways to be maximally effective with more traditional Native Americans. At the same time, acculturation to one tribal group may not prepare therapists adequately to deal with traditional members of another tribe, even one that is geographically contiguous. However, this should not prove too troublesome for therapists working in or near a reservation, where most traditionals tend to live, and where they are likely to encounter culturally similar clients.

By contrast, therapists practicing in large urban centers, where more than 50% of Native Americans live, may encounter clients from any number of tribes. However, most such clients will tend to be less traditional than their reservation counterparts and this should lessen the depth of cultural familiarity required of therapists. Nevertheless, it does complicate the work of urban therapists wishing to provide culturally sensitive services to native clients.

Rural therapists who work with the more traditional native client will require in-depth knowledge of tribal norms and customs. Therapists in large urban centers may require greater knowledge of the variations in tribal norms and customs. In either case, considerable acculturation work may be required and the professional demands experienced by most practicing therapists would seem to mitigate against this. Several factors argue for undertaking this work, however. First, providing services to an underserved population can be gratifying in itself.

Second, and of greatest relevance to the urban therapist, there are commonalities in values and worldviews among different tribes (see Attneave 1982; Cooley, 1977; French, 1989; Herring, 1990; Ho, 1987; Spang, 1965; Tafoya, 1981, 1989a) that once attuned to will aid the development of tribal specific sensitivity. These values include: (1) present time orientation, (2) harmony with nature, (3) cooperative relationships with others, (4) sharing, (5) respect for elders, (6) non-interference with others, (7) resentment of authority, (8) strong sense of autonomy, and (9) holism, wherein mind, body, community, and environment are interrelated and inseparable. The Pan-Indian movement, a grassroots effort to provide deculturated Native Americans of all tribes with a universal "Indian" identity and value system, has largely adopted these values. This movement may provide the non-native with a good starting point for acculturation.

Third, and again most relevant to the urban therapist, developing an intimate knowledge of one tribal group will, to some extent, develop those conceptual skills needed for acculturation in general. Accordingly, a considerable savings would be expected in subsequent acculturation work. Finally, the preparation for and process of conducting cross-cultural therapy may prove to be a personally enriching experience. Tyler et al. (1985) have argued that all worldviews are necessarily limited, and that the cross-cultural interchanges of therapy with the culturally different can supplement the therapist's worldview. Such supplementation can help the therapist to transcend cultural limitations and biases, and to enjoy the riches of cultural diversity.

Interested therapists might begin their own acculturation process by exposing themselves to the literature available on Native Americans. This body of literature offers a means to at least a superficial familiarity with the Native American cultures of the past and present. Of particular interest might be the descriptions of traditional Native American healing practices. Such readings cannot, however, eliminate the need to gain cultural familiarity by immersion in that culture first hand. Living in or near Native American communities and participating in the cultures would be a preferred method of acculturation. Fostering mutually respectful working relationships with tribal elders and traditional healers may be the most effective way of gaining both knowledge of and acceptance by the people (see Trimble and Hayes, 1984). Therapist acculturation may prove to be the most challenging professional task faced, but it might also be one of the most personally rewarding.

FUTURE DIRECTIONS

The preceding discussion does not exhaust the issues pertinent to working with Native Americans in therapy. It leaves many questions unanswered, questions for which there are little or no empirical data from which to draw. There are many areas of inquiry and service that might prove fruitful and some have been discussed elsewhere (LaFromboise, 1988;

LaFromboise, Trimble, and Mohatt, 1990; Manson and Trimble, 1982; Trimble, 1990). The following are directions that the present author believes will be fruitful.

Professional organizations in the field, such as AABT, should establish special interest groups focused on Native American issues. These could function to promote and direct relevant research and increase awareness of critical issues.

The development of clinically useful ways to determine the acculturation status of Native American clients would help clinicians to provide services at an appropriate level of cultural adjustment. Variables that may be examined initially for their discriminative potential include language competency and preference, traditional versus non-traditional religious affiliation, the extent and recency of participation in ceremonials, sociographic location, extent of formal education, peer group preferences, and self-identified cultural commitment.

The issue of client-therapist matching would appear to be a particularly critical one with this special population. The few published studies available employed opinion surveys or had Native American subjects rate the effectiveness and/or desirability of therapists in simulated sessions. As important as such studies may be, controlled outcome investigations would provide more dependable and conclusive data. The available literature suggests a number of matching variables that would be important to consider. These include therapist ethnicity, age, gender, therapeutic and communication styles, value system, level of cultural awareness, and degree of recognition by the Native American community in question. Of particular value would be ascertaining how those variables that are controllable by therapists, such as therapeutic style and cultural knowledge, interact with those that are not, such as gender and ethnicity. Such information might enable therapists to maximize their effectiveness with this population through matching compensation strategies.

Too little is known about the Native American client in therapy to identify treatments of choice. The endorsements of therapeutic approaches in the literature appear to be based upon clinical experience and not upon controlled outcome studies. Clearly, such studies are needed for definitive treatment comparisons and recommendations.

A culturally congruent therapeutic style for Native Americans has not been clearly delineated. Further investigations of the effects that the degree and style of directiveness, pacing, the utility of stories and case examples, and the subject and depth of clinical inquiries have on treatment outcome would help do so.

A rapprochement of traditional and conventional interventions should be renewed. Investigations of the relative effects of traditional, conventional, and combined interventions, though difficult to effect, should result in a better understanding of what constitutes effective therapy with this special population. In such studies, the effects of variables such as client acculturation and deculturation, problem type, tribal affiliation, and previous experience with conventional therapy and traditional healing should be examined.

The mental health care professionals, with other social and health-care professionals and tribal elders and healers, should develop research-based tribal-specific intercultural training techniques. "Intercultural Sensitizers" (i.e., brief training programs designed to teach behavioral attributions common to the target culture) appear to hold promise to this end (Salzman, 1990), as do informed guidelines or cultural primers (e.g., Polacca, 1962). Such resources might enable non-native therapists to efficiently gain a working level of cultural sensitivity.

Some authors have worked to combine behavior analytic with culture analytic systems (e.g., Glenn, 1986, 1988; Lloyd, 1985; Malagodi, 1986; Malott, 1988; Vargas, 1985). Such work should continue toward developing a culture analytic scheme that is congruent with, and complimentary to, the fundamental theoretical underpinnings of cognitive-behavioral psychology. Such a scheme would permit the cognitive-behavior therapist to analyze the cultural contexts within which their native client's problems arise, and lead to a more effective cross-cultural technology in general.

Classification schemes for culture-specific functional disorders would facilitate culturally appropriate assessments. Attempts to develop such diagnostic aids with other ethnic groups (e.g., Bernstein and Gaw, 1990) may function as models.

Studies of the applicability of cognitive-behavioral "principles" and interventions across cultural groups would provide an empirical base from which to determine their generality. At the same time, such studies could lead to a better understanding of how such interventions are best tailored to the culturally different.

CLOSING REMARKS

The issues covered in this article are relevant to providing cognitive-behavior therapy to the culturally, ethnically different in general. The demands for cross-cultural therapy are increasing as we are called upon to provide effective mental health care to this country's growing minority populations, and to aid the implementation of psychological services across national boundaries. As argued here, such services must be culturally sensitive if they are to be maximally effective and if we are to avoid disrupting other cultures in the name of enhancing global mental health.

It is time to overcome what Hsu (1976) has called our "culture bound myopia", and to correct our failure to attend to the needs of the ethnically and culturally different. It is proper that cognitive-behavior therapists begin turning their research and professional activities to the mental health needs of specific ethnic minorities, and to developing a trans-cultural cognitive-behavioral technology. Such a technology would enable us to address the behavioral problems of the ethnically and culturally different in their own terms, based on sound, empirical principles.

NOTE

The author would like to thank Malcolm Robertson of Western Michigan University and Lyn Raible of Kalamazoo College for their comments and support.

BIBLIOGRAPHY

Attneave, C. L. (1974). Medicine men and psychiatrists in the Indian health service. *Psychiatric Annals*, 4(11), 49–55.

Attneave, C. L. (1982). American Indians and Alaska Native families: Emigrants in their own homeland. In M. McGoldrick, J. Pierce, and J. Giordano (Eds.), *Ethnicity and family therapy* (pp. 55–83). New York: Guilford.

Attneave, C. L. (1985). Practical counseling with Native American Indian and Alaska Native clients. In P. Pedersen (Ed.), *Handbook of cross-cultural counseling and therapy*. Westport, CT: Greenwood Press.

Barter, E. R., and Barter, J. T. (1984). Urban Indians and mental health problems. *Psychiatric Annals* 4(9), 37–43.

Bennet, S. K., and BigFoot-Sipes, D. S. (1991). American Indian and White college student preferences for counselor characteristics. *Journal of Counseling Psychology*, 38(4), 440–445.

Bergman, R. (1973). Navajo medicine and psychoanalysis. *Human Behavior*, 2, 8–15.

Bergman, R. (1974). Paraprofessionals in Indian mental health programs. *Psychiatric Annals*, 4, 76–84.

Bernstein. R. L., and Gaw. A. C. (1990). Koro: Proposed classification for DSM-IV. *American Journal of Psychiatry*, 147(12), 1670–1674.

Christie, L., and Halpern, J. M. (1990). Temporal constructs and Inuit mental health. *Social Sciences and Medicine*, 30(6), 739–749.

Conrad, R. D., Delk, J. L., and Williams, C. (1974). Use of stimulus fading procedures in the treatment of situation specific mutism: A case study. *Journal of Behavior Therapy and Experimental Psychiatry*, 5, 99–100.

Cooley, C. R. (1977, October). Cultural effects in Indian education: An application of social learning theory. *Journal of American Indian Education*, 21–27.

Cuellar, I., Harris, L. C., and Jasso, R. (1980). An acculturation scale for Mexican American normal and clinical populations. *Hispanic Journal of Behavioral Sciences*, 2(3), 199–217.

Dauphinais, P., Dauphinais, L., and Rowe, W. (1981). Effects of race and communication style on Indian perceptions of counselor effectiveness. *Counselor Education and Supervision*, 21, 72–80.

Delgado, M. (1979). Therapy Latino style: Implications for psychiatric care. *Perspectives in Psychiatric Care*, 17(3), 107–115.

Dinges, N., and Duffy, L. (1979). Culture and competence. In A. J. Marsella, R. G. Tharp, and T. J. Ciborowski (Eds.), *Perspectives on cross-cultural psychology* (pp. 209–232). New York: Academic Press.

Dinges, N. G., Trimble, J., Manson, S., and Pasquale, I. (1981). Counseling and psychotherapy with American Indians and Alaska Natives. In A. J. Marsella and P. Pedersen (Eds.), *Cultural counseling and psychotherapy* (pp. 243–276). Elmsford, NY: Pergamon.

Dozier, E. P. (1966). Problem drinking among American Indians: The role of sociocultural deprivation. *Quarterly Journal of Studies on Alcohol*, 27(1), 72–87.

Frank, J. D. (1973). *Persuasion and healing: A comparative study of psychotherapy*. Baltimore, MD: Johns Hopkins University Press.

French, L. (1981). Counseling American Indians. *International Journal of Offender Therapy and Comparative Criminology*, 25, 139–155.

French, L. (1989). Native American alcoholism: A transcultural counseling perspective. *Counseling Psychology Quarterly*, 2(2), 153–166.

Glenn, S. S. (1986). Metacontingencies in Walden Two. *Behavior Analysis and Social* Action, 5(1and2), 2–8.

Glenn, S. S. (1988). Contingencies and metacontingencies: Toward a synthesis of behavior analysis and cultural materialism. *The Behavior Analyst*, 11(2), 161–179.

Goldstein, G. S. (1974). Behavior modification: Some cultural factors. *The Psychological Record*, 24, 89–91.

Goldwasser, H. D., and Badger, L. W. (1989). Utility of the psychiatric screen among the Navajo of Chinle: A fourth-year clerkship experience. *American Indian and Alaska Native Mental Health Research*, 3(1), 6–15.

Hall, E. T. (1969). *The hidden dimension*. Garden City, NY: Doubleday.

Hall, E. T. (1976). *Beyond culture*. New York: Anchor Press.

Herring, R. D. (1990). Understanding Native-American values: Process and content concerns for counselors. *Counseling and Values*, 34, 134–137.

Hippler, A. E. (1975). Thawing out some magic. *Mental Hygiene*, 59, 20–24.

Ho, M. K. (1987). *Family therapy with ethnic minorities*. Beverly Hills, CA: Sage.

Hsu, F. L. K. (1976). Rethinking our premises. In J. Westermeyer (Ed.), *Anthropology and mental health* (pp. 153–160). The Hague: Mouton.

Jilek, W. G. (1971). From crazy witchdoctor to auxiliary psychotherapist: The changing image of the medicine man. *Psychiatric Clinica*, 4, 200–220.

Jilek, W. G. (1974). Indian healing power: Indigenous therapeutic practices in the Pacific north-west. *Psychiatric Annals*, 4(9),13–21.

Jilek-Aall, L. (1976). The Western psychiatric and his non-Western clientele. *Canadian Psychiatric Association Journal*, 21(6), 353–359.

Jilek, W., and Todd. N. (1974). Witchdoctors succeed where doctors fail: Psychotherapy among Coast Salish Indians. *Canadian Psychiatric Association Journal*, 19(4), 351–356.

Johnson, M. E., and Lashley, K. H. (1989). Influence of Native Americans' cultural commitment on preferences for counselor ethnicity and expectations about counseling. *Journal of Multicultural Counseling and Development*, 17, 115–122.

Kelso, D. R., and Attneave, C. L. (1981). *Bibliography of North American Indian mental health*. Westport, CT: Greenwood Press.

Kidwell, C. S. (1991). The vanishing native reappears in the college curriculum. *Change*, 23(2), 19–23.

Kleinman, A., and Gale, J. L. (1982). Patients treated by physicians and folk healers: A comparative outcome study in Taiwan. *Culture, Medicine, and Psychiatry*, 6, 405–423.

LaFromboise, T. D. (1988). American Indian mental health policy. *American Psychologist*, 43(5), 388–397.

LaFromboise, T. D., and Dixon, D. N. (1981). American Indian perception of trustworthiness in a counseling interview. *Journal of Counseling Psychology*, 28(2) 135–139.

LaFromboise, T. D., and Rowe, W. (1983). Skills training for bicultural competence: Rationale and application. *Journal of Counseling Psychology*, 30(4), 589–595.

LaFromboise, T. D., Trimble, J. E., and Mohatt, G. V. (1990). Counseling intervention and American Indian tradition: An integrative approach. *The Counseling Psychologist*, 18(4), 628–654.

Lefley, H. P. (1984). Delivering mental health service across cultures. In P. B. Pedersen, N. Sartorius, and A. J. Marsella (Eds.), *Mental health services: The cross-cultural context* (pp. 135–171). Beverly Hills, CA: Sage.

Leighton, A. H., and Leighton, D. C. (1941). Elements of psychotherapy in Navaho religion. *Psychiatry* 4, 515–523.

Leon, R. L. (1968). Some implications for a preventive program for American Indians. *American Journal of Psychiatry*, 125(2), 128–132.

Lewis, R. G. (1982). Alcohol and the Native American: A review of the literature. In National Institute on Alcohol Abuse and Alcoholism (Ed.), *Alcohol and health monograph 4: Special population issues* (pp. 315–328). Washington, DC: U.S. Government Printing Office.

Lloyd, K. E. (1985). Behavioral anthropology: A review of Marvin Harris' cultural materialism. *Journal of the Experimental Analysis of Behavior*, 43(2), 279–287.

Mail, P. D. (1989). American Indians, stress, and alcohol. *American Indian and Alaska Native Mental Health Research*, 3(2),7–26.

Malagodi, E. F. (1986). On radicalizing behavior analysis: A call for cultural analysis. *The Behavior Analyst*, 9(1), 1–17.

Malott, R. W. (1988). Rule-governed behavior and behavioral anthropology. *The Behavior Analyst*, 11(2), 181–203.

Manson, S. M. (Ed.). (1982). *Topics in American Indian mental health prevention*. Portland, OR: Oregon Health Sciences University Press.

Manson, S. M., and Trimble, J. E. (1982). American Indian and Alaska native communities: Past efforts, future inquiries. In L. R. Snowden (Ed.), *Reaching the underserved: Mental health needs of neglected populations*. Beverly Hills, CA: Sage.

May, P. (1987). Suicide and self-destruction among American Indian youth. *American Indian and Alaska Native Mental Health Research*, 1(1), 52–69.

May, P. A., and Dizmang, L. H. (1974). Suicide and the American Indian. *Psychiatric Annals*, 4(9), 22–28.

Murphy, J. M. (1964). Psychotherapeutic aspects of shamanism on St. Lawrence Island, Alaska. In A. Kiev (Ed.), *Magic, faith, and healing: Studies in primitive psychiatry today*. London: The Free Press of Glencoe Collier-MacMillan.

O'Nell, T. D. (1989). Psychiatric investigations among American Indians and Alaska Natives: A critical review. *Culture, Medicine and Psychiatry*, 13, 51–87.

Pascarosa, P., and Futterman, S. (1976). Ethnopsychedelic therapy for alcoholics: Observations in the peyote ritual of the Native American Church. *Journal of Psychedelic Drugs*, 8(3), 215–221.

Pfister, O. (1932). Instinctive psychoanalysis among the Navajos. *Journal of Nervous and Mental Disease*, 76(3), 234–254.

Polacca, K. (19620. Ways of working with the Navahos who have not learned the white man's ways. *Journal of American Indian Education*, 2(1), 6–16.

Prieto, D. O. (1989). Native Americans in medicine: The need for Indian healers. *Academic Medicine*, 64(7), 388–389.

Prince, R. H. (1973). Psychotherapy as the manipulation of endogenous healing mechanisms: A transcultural survey. *Transcultural Psychiatric Research Review*, 13, 115–134.

Rappaport, H. (1977). The tendency of folk psychotherapy: A functional interpretation. *Social Psychiatry*, 12, 127–132.

Rappaport, H., and Rappaport, M. (1981). The integration of scientific and traditional healing. *American Psychologist*, 36(7),774–781.

Rogler, L. H., Malgady, R. G., Costantino, G., and Blumenthal, R. (1987). What do culturally sensitive mental health services mean? *American Psychologist*, 42(6), 565–570.

Ruiz, P., and Langrod, J. (1976). Psychiatrists and spiritual healers: Partners in community mental health. In J. Westermeyer (Ed.), *Anthropology and mental health: Setting a new course*. The Hague: Mouton.

Saks-Berman, J. R. (1989). A view from rainbow bridge: Feminist therapist meets changing woman. *Women and Therapy*, 8(4), 65–78.

Salzman, M. B. (1990). The construction of an intercultural sensitizer training non-Navajo personnel. *Journal of American Indian Education*, 30(1), 25–33.

Schacht, A. J., Tafoya, N., and Mirabla, K. (1989). Home-based therapy with American Indian families. *American Indian and Alaska Native Mental Health Research*, 3(2), 27–42.

Schinke, S. P., Orlandi, M. A., Schilling, R. F., Botvin, G. J., Gilchrist, L. D., and Landers, C. (1990). Tobacco use by Native Indian and Alaska Native people: Risks, psychosocial factors, and preventive intervention. *Journal of Alcohol and Drug Education*, 35(2), 1–11.

Shore, J. H. (1974). Psychiatric epidemiology among American Indians. *Psychiatric Annals*, 4(9), 56–66.

Skidmore, J. R., and Roberts, R. N. (1991). Rural Navajo early intervention health promotion: Community principles and behavioral applications.*The Behavior Therapist*, 14(2), 29–30.

Spang, A. (1965). Counseling the Indian. *Journal of American Indian Education*, 5(1), 10–15.

Spang, A. T. (1971). Understanding the Indian. *Personnel and Guidance Journal*, 50(2), 96–102.

Sue, D. W. (1990). Culture-specific strategies in counseling: A conceptual framework. *Professional Psychology: Review and Practice*, 21(6), 424–433.

Sue, D. W. and Sue, D. (1977). Barriers to effective cross-cultural counseling. *Journal of Counseling Psychology*, 24 (5), 420–429.

Sue, S. (1977). Community mental health services to minority groups: Some optimism, some pessimism. *American Psychologist*, 32, 616–624.

Sue, S., Allen, D. B., and Conaway, L. (1978). The responsiveness and equality of mental health care to Chicanos and Native Americans. *American Journal of Community Psychology*, 6(2), 137–146.

Szapocznik, J., Scopetta, M. A., and King, O. E. (1978). Theory and practice in matching treatment to the special characteristics and problems of Cuban immigrants. *Journal of Community Psychology*, 6, 112–122.

Tafoya, T. (1981). Dancing with Dash-Kayah: The mask of the cannibal woman. *Parabola*, 6(3), 6–11.

Tafoya, T. (1989a). Circles and cedar: Native Americans and family therapy. *Journal of Psychotherapy and the Family*, 6(1–2), 71–98.

Tafoya, T. (1989b). Coyote's eyes: Native cognition styles. [Special issue]. *Journal of American Indian Education*, 29–41.

Tefft, S. K. (Spring, 1967). Anomy, values, and cultural change among teen-age Indians: An exploration. *Sociology of Education*, 145–157.

Torrey, E. F. (1972). What Western psychotherapists can learn from witchdoctors. *American Journal of Orthopsychiatry*, 42(1), 69–76.

Torrey, E. F. (1986). *Witchdoctors and psychiatrists: The common roots of psychotherapy and its future.* Northvale, NJ: Jason Aronson.

Tower, M. (1989). A suicide epidemic in an American Indian community. *American Indian and Alaska Native Mental Health Research*, 3(1), 34–44.

Trimble, J. E. (1981). Value differentials and their importance in counseling American Indians. In P. Pedersen, J. Draguns, W. Lonner, and J. Trimble (Eds.), *Counseling across cultures* (pp. 203–226). Honolulu: University of Hawaii Press.

Trimble, J. E. (1990). Application of psychological knowledge for American Indians and Alaska Natives. *The Journal of Training and Practice in Professional Psychology*, 4(1), 45–63.

Trimble, J. E., and Hayes, S. A. (1984). Mental health intervention in the psychosocial contexts of American Indian communities. In W. A. O'Connor, and B. Lubin (Eds.), *Ecological approaches to clinical and community psychology* (pp. 293–321). New York: Wiley.

Trimble, J. E., and LaFromboise, T. (1985). American Indians and the counseling process: Culture, adaptation, and style. In P. Pedersen (Eds.). *Handbook of cross-cultural counseling and therapy.* Westport, CT: Greenwood Press.

Trimble, J. E., Manson, S. M., Dinges, N. G., and Medicine, B. (1984). American Indian concepts of mental health: Reflections and directions. In P. B. Pedersen, N. Sartorius, and A. J. Marsella (Eds.), *Mental health services: The cross-cultural context* (pp. 199–220). Beverly Hills, CA: Sage.

Tyler, F. B., Sussewell, D. R., and Williams-McCoy, J. (1985). Ethnic validity in psychotherapy. *Psychotherapy*, 22(2), 311–320.

Vargas, E. T. (1985). Cultural contingencies: A review of Marvin Harris' cannibals and kings. *Journal of the Experimental Analysis of Behavior*, 43(3), 419–428.

Wallace, A. F. C. (1958). Dreams and wishes of the soul: A type of psychoanalytic theory among the seventeenth century Iroquois. *American Anthropologist*, 60, 234–248.

Weibel, J. C. (1982). American Indians, urbanization, and alcohol: A developing urban Indian drinking ethos. In National Institute on Alcohol Abuse and Alcoholism (Eds.), *Alcohol and health monograph 4: Special population issues* (pp. 315–328). Washington, DC: U.S. Government Printing Office.

Westermeyer, J. (1974). "The drunken Indian": Myths and realities. *Psychiatric Annals*, 4(9) 29–36.

23.
Cognitive Behavioral Therapy with Latinos

Kurt C. Organista and Ricardo F. Muñoz

The purpose of this article is to explicate culturally responsive applications of cognitive behavioral therapy (CBT) to Latinos in the United States. The article defines Latinos, summarizes Latino sociodemographic and mental health profiles, reviews the literature on CBT with Latinos, and then describes culturally competent applications of CBT techniques to common problem themes. Future directions in clinical work and research are also discussed.

At the dawn of the new millennium, an estimated 31 million Latinos will comprise an ethnic minority group almost as numerous as African Americans and deserving of specialized attention to their unique mental health needs. We fully recognize that each Latino is in some ways like no other Latino, and that there are subgroups of Latinos that are quite different from one another. Nevertheless, there are elements of shared history, of language, customs, religion and moral values, and of self-identity and identity attributed by others, which define, however imperfectly, a recognizable subgroup in society that must be properly served. The more clinicians know about a particular subgroup of Latinos (e.g., Mexican Americans, Puerto Ricans, etc.), the more they can conceptualize and treat the mental health problems of that group in a culturally sensitive manner.

In this article, we define Latinos, provide brief summaries of their sociodemographic characteristics in the United States, including prevalence of mental disorders, review the literature on cognitive behavior therapy (CBT) with Latinos, and then describe culturally competent applications of CBT techniques and common problem themes that surface in work with Latinos.

SOCIODEMOGRAPHIC PROFILE OF LATINOS IN THE UNITED STATES

The U.S. Bureau of the Census (1995) reports that there were over 24 million Latinos in the United States in 1992, up from almost 15 million in 1980. The Bureau projected that there would be approximately 27 million in 1995 (10.2% of the total U.S. population), and approximately 31 million in the year 2000. Latinos are individuals with personal and family roots in the countries of Latin America. Many Latinos speak Spanish, and most partake of the blended cultural traditions of the Spanish colonists and the indigenous peoples of the Americas. Latinos may belong to any racial group, including those with roots in Europe, Africa, Asia, and the Middle East. Mexican Americans comprise the majority of Latinos in the United States (62%), followed by Puerto Ricans (12.7%), Cubans (5.3%), Central and South Americans (11.5%), and other Latinos (i.e., not self-identified with the above groups; Marger, 1991).

In terms of socioeconomic status (SES), the annual median family income is $20,654 for Puerto Ricans, $23,018 for Mexican Americans, and $30,095 for Cuban Americans as compared to $39,239 for non-Latino Whites. Only about 10% of non-Latino Whites live below the poverty level as compared to 39% of Puerto Ricans, 30% of Mexican Americans, and 18% of Cuban Americans (Healey, 1995). With regard to education, the percentage of Latinos over 25 years of age that have completed high school is 62% for Cuban Americans, 61% for Puerto Ricans, and 45% for Mexican Americans as compared to 83% for non-Latino Whites. These figures are important when one considers the very stable inverse relation between SES and psychopathology (Bruce, Takeuchi, and Leaf , 1991; Kessler et al., 1994).

PREVALENCE OF MENTAL DISORDERS IN LATINOS

Only in the last 15 years have we begun to acquire information on the prevalence of psychopathology in Latinos in the United States. Although the results of epidemiological mental health surveys are sometimes contradictory and provide only preliminary estimates at best, the findings reviewed are consistent with our clinical experience. Most recently, results from the National Comorbidity Survey (NCS; Kessler et al., 1994), which are based on a national probability sample (N = 8,098) that included a representative number of Latinos, showed that as compared to non-Latino Whites and African Americans, Latinos had significantly higher prevalence of currently diagnosable affective disorders and active comorbidity, meaning three or more concurrent mental disorders.

The NCS findings are inconsistent with past findings from the Epidemiologic Catchment Area (ECA), study that found no differences between ethnic groups in current affective disorders and higher rates of lifetime affective disorder in non-Latino Whites (Weissman, Bruce, Leaf, and Holzer, 1991). Results of the NCS also showed no differences between Latinos and non-Latino Whites in anxiety disorders, in contrast to ECA findings that showed Latinos to be lower than non-Latino Whites in lifetime rates of panic disorder (Eaton, Dryman, and Wiessman, 1991). Thus, the NCS appears to indicate higher depression and anxiety in Latinos than did the ECA.

Prior to the NCS, epidemiological data on Latino mental health has come from the ECA and the Hispanic Health and Nutrition Examination Survey (H-HANES). Two reports from the ECA revealed that Island Puerto Ricans were higher than U.S.-born and Mexico-born Mexican Americans and non-Latino Whites in the number of somatic symptoms they endorsed (Canino, Rubio-Stipec, Canino, and Escobar, 1992) and in diagnoses of somatization disorder (Shrout et al., 1992). Escobar et al. (1987) used the Los Angeles ECA data to compare somatization disorder in Mexican Americans (N = 1,242) and non-Hispanic Whites (N = 1,309) and found that, while Mexican American and non-Latino White men did not differ, Mexican American women over 40 years of age were higher than their non-Latino White counterparts. Somatization in Mexican American women was also found to be positively correlated with age and negatively correlated with level of acculturation. Further, looking just at women who met criteria for depression or dysthymia, Escobar et al. also found that about 50% of Mexican women also met criteria for somatization disorder as compared to 20% of non-Latino White women.

The above findings are similar to those of Kolody, Vega, Meinhardt, and Bensussen (1986), who found a stronger direct linear correlation between depression symptoms and severity of somatization disorder in Mexican Americans as compared to non-Latino Whites. Angel and Guarnaccia (1989) similarly found an inverse relation between depression symptoms and self-rated health in Puerto Ricans and Mexican Americans, based on the H-HANES database, and Moscicki, Rae, Regier, and Locke (1987), in their comparison of Latino subgroups, found elevated depression symptoms only in Puerto Ricans.

Taken together, the above survey data reviewed suggest that Latinos may be at greater risk than the general population for depression, anxiety, and somatization disorders. To what degree group differences remain after controlling for SES is still unclear from the studies reviewed, but poverty is likely to play a central role. For example, the NCS again replicated the stable inverse relationship between psychopathology and SES for all American Psychiatric Association (1987) *DSM-III-R (Diagnostic and Statistical Manual of Mental Disorders)*, Axis I diagnostic categories. Epidemiological surveys have not yet included Central Americans who are at high risk for psychopathology, given their troublesome pre- and postmigration experiences.

Over a million Central Americans have fled to other countries due to guerrilla warfare, counterinsurgency activities, and the incorporation of civilians into civil war conflict (Ferris, 1987). Although these refugees are grateful to escape *la situación,* as they refer to it, relocating to the United States is often regarded as a mixed blessing. Not only do most Central Americans report fleeing their countries of origin under war-related duress (Cordova, 1979; Leslie and Lietch, 1989), but their acculturation to the United States is hampered by a general denial of refugee status (including entitlements to social services) due to limited ability to prove direct political persecution (Ferris). The denial of political asylum leads to inhibited social and community life, mistrust, and perceptions of the U.S. Government as supporting repressive governments in Latin America (Farias, 1991).

This is an unfortunate predicament for Central Americans because studies of community samples report elevated symptom levels of depression, anxiety, somatization, and interpersonal sensitivity as compared to American norms (Plante, Manuel, Menendez, and Marcotte, 1995). In addition, Central Americans are higher than Mexican immigrants in symptoms of depression and migration-related stress (Salgado de Snyder, Cervantes, and Padilla, 1990) and in posttraumatic stress disorder (PTSD; Cervantes, Salgado de Snyder, and Padilla, 1989).

Epidemiological mental health data on South Americans in the United States are largely unavailable. The main reasons for immigration are similar for South American groups as for other Latinos, namely economic hardships and, at times, internal armed conflicts that place people in danger of torture or death (Gonsalves, 1990). As such, themes of loss and trauma are likely in this population, as well as the stress of acculturation and poverty. An additional stress is the greater geographical distance from their country of origin, which makes periodic contact with their families much less likely than for immigrants from Northern Mexico. In addition, having fewer neighbors from their country of origin results in fewer chances to share meaningful memories and customs, such as national celebrations (for example, Independence Day), sharing of national songs, foods, and folk knowledge.

Two conclusions are apparent from this review of the Latino mental health literature: One, much more research on the prevalence of mental health problems in Latinos is needed, and two, the major problems evident at this time (e.g., depression and anxiety disorders) are quite amenable to CBT.

MENTAL HEALTH SERVICE UTILIZATION PATTERNS IN LATINOS

Despite the evident need for mental health services, it is well known that Latinos in the United States underutilize mental health services (Acosta, 1979; Barrera, 1978; Sue, Fujino, Hu, Takeuchi, and Zane, 1991) for a variety of reasons that include lack of service availability, accessibility, and cultural acceptability (Parron, 1982). It has also become clear that such underutilization is not because Latinos suffer less from mental disorders than other groups. For example, the University of California, Los Angeles, ECA study found that of all respondents suffering from major depression, only 11% of Mexican Americans used mental health services as opposed to 22% of non-Latino Whites (Hough et al., 1987).

Although Latinos underutilize mental health services, it is also well known that they overutilize medical doctors for emotional and psychological problems (Karno, Ross, and Caper, 1969; Padilla, Carlos, and Keefe, 1976). For example, Muñoz and Ying (1993) found rates of current major depression to be as high as 25% in Spanish-speaking primary care patients, which is more than double the rate in the general population (Kessler et al., 1994).

Latino service utilization patterns suggest that in addition to decreasing barriers to mental health services (Muñoz, 1982), medical staff also need to be actively involved in outreach to Latinos in hospital settings suffering from diagnosable mental disorders.

WHY CBT WITH LATINOS?

There appear to be clear cultural and economic reasons for advocating CBT for traditionally oriented Latinos of low SES (i.e., traditional value orientation, low level of acculturation, etc.). According to Miranda (1976), the expectations of traditional Latino patients include immediate symptom relief, guidance and advice, and a problem-centered approach. Short-term, directive, problem-solving therapies are also more consistent with the expectations of low income groups whose pressing life circumstances frequently demand immediate attention and interfere with long-term treatment (Goldstein, 1971; Torres-Matrullo, 1982).

The didactic style of CBT helps to quickly orient patients to treatment by educating them about mental disorders and how CBT is used to conceptualize and treat their problems. Not only does this educational approach "demystify" psychotherapy, but it is also consistent with "role preparation," in which patients unaccustomed to therapy are taught what they can expect and what will be expected of them in the attempt to prevent dropout and enhance treatment (Orlinsky and Howard, 1986).

The common use of therapy manuals, homework assignments, and chalkboards help Latino patients to think of therapy as more of a classroom experience that further alleviates the stigma attached to therapy. Many of our Mexican and Central American immigrant patients have repeatedly told us that such stigma is strong in their countries of origin, where scarce mental health services are reserved almost exclusively for psychotic patients in mental hospitals.

Unfortunately, extremely little outcome research on the efficacy of CBT with Latinos has been conducted. One study by Comas-Díaz (1981) investigated the efficacy of cognitive therapy and behavior therapy in a small sample of depressed, Spanish-speaking, unmarried Puerto Rican mothers from low SES backgrounds ($N = 26$). Results showed significant and comparable reductions in depression for both cognitive and behavioral treatments relative to a waiting list control group.

In a preliminary outcome study of CBT with 175 low-income and minority medical outpatients, nearly half of whom were Spanish-speaking Latinos, Organista, Muñoz, and González (1994) found significant pre- to posttreatment reductions in depression, but not to the same extent as results reported in prototypical outcome studies of non-Hispanic White, middle-class patients. Organista (1995) described a case study in which CBT was moderately successful in treating a severe case of major depression and panic disorder in a Central American woman overwhelmed by divorce, single parenthood, and her recent arrival in the United States.

Common problem themes and cultural variables. Problem themes that emerge in psychotherapy with Latinos most often include interpersonal conflicts in marriage and family (Acosta, Yamamoto, and Evans, 1982; Comas-Díaz, 1985; Delgado and Humm-Delgado, 1984). Because Latino patients are predominantly women, therapists need to be cognizant of traditional gender roles prescribing that Latinas be submissive, self-sacrificing, and enduring of suffering inflicted by men (Comas-Díaz, 1985). As Comas-Díaz (1985) and Torres-Matrullo (1982) noted in their work with depressed Puerto Rican women, the depressed thinking of these women appeared related to unrealistic sex-role expectations with respect to prohibiting the expression of anger, remaining married despite the poor quality of the marriage, and the expectation to give help but not to request it.

Such problem themes and gender issues provide therapists with consistent intervention targets when working with Latinos. While no single article could begin to address the myriad of problems facing Latino patients, below we illustrate culturally sensitive ways of engaging Latinos in treatment and the application of specific cognitive behavioral techniques to a small sample of clinical problems that we have encountered in our clinical work.

CULTURALLY RESPONSIVE APPLICATIONS OF CBT

Engagement via Latino values. Engaging Latino patients in treatment can be facilitated by following a culturally sensitive relationship protocol that includes several salient Latino values. For example, *Respeto* is practiced by formally addressing patients as Señora and Señor along with their last names and by maintaining a humble *para servirle* ("to serve you") attitude. *Personalismo* is practiced by taking time to engage in the kind of self-disclosure and small talk, or *plática*, advocated by cultural competence experts to build *confianza*, or trust, with Latino patients (Falicov, 1982).

It is advisable to begin the first session with *plática*, in which therapist and patient share background information about where they are from, their families, work that they have done, and so on. For example, upon learning that one of his patients was from Guadalajara, the first author shared that he had cousins in Guadalajara, and they went on to discuss some of their favorite activities and restaurants in the city. A therapist from another Latin American country might have discussed his or her immigration history (e.g., age of immigration, learning to speak English, and so on). A non-Latino therapist could share an experience of being "different" or of moving from one city to another. On this note, we have had success training non-Latino therapists (who speak Spanish) in the provision of culturally sensitive psychotherapy as described above. Our patients respond positively to the sincere efforts of these non-Latino trainees.

A culturally sensitive approach to beginning treatment personalizes the professional relationship as a prelude for the tasks of therapy. Although there is no direct empirical support for the superiority of a culturally sensitive approach versus a more conventional form of therapy, Sue et al. (1991) found that ethnic and linguistic matching was related to better treatment outcome and lower dropout in Latino patients low in acculturation. Furthermore, our guidelines are consistent with those advocated by Latino mental health experts in the literature (Acosta et al., 1982; Muñoz, 1982; Padilla and Salgado de Snyder, 1985).

Streamlining cognitive restructuring. Although our Latino patients quickly grasp the basic idea of "positive" and "negative" thoughts (i.e., as in the power of positive thinking), they rarely learn to apply a system such as Ellis's A–B–C–D method in which patients are taught to identify the Activating event, Beliefs about the activating event, the emotional Consequences of beliefs, and finally, how to Dispute irrational beliefs related to negative emotional consequences (Ellis and Grieger, 1977). Although the acronym A–B–C–D is intended to convey the method's seeming simplicity, we have found it to be impractical (besides, the acronym does not translate well into Spanish!).

In view of this problem, we recommend teaching Latino patients the difference between "helpful" thoughts, which help to reduce symptoms and initiate adaptive behaviors, and "unhelpful" thoughts that do the opposite. In addition, we greatly streamline cognitive restructuring by teaching what we refer to as the "Yes, but ... " technique, in which patients are taught that much of problematic thinking amounts to "half-truths" about problems that need to be made into "whole-truths." For example, we treated a bright, middle-aged Mexican woman who survived years of serious spousal abuse and whose depression stemmed from the core belief that, "If only I had not married my ex-husband, I would have reached my educational and career goals." The depression-related self-blame in this conviction, as well as the omission of significant accomplishments, was addressed by asking the patient to complete the following half-truth: "Yes, it is sad that I married an abusive man, and that this interfered with my goals, but ... " to which the patient eventually replied, "... but I did finally leave him and I raised four good children all by myself!"

In another case, a young Central American man felt extremely depressed and guilty about not returning home to attend his mother's funeral for fear he would be killed by soldiers. Prior to his flight to the United States, the patient had been kidnapped and blindfolded by soldiers who took him to the outskirts of town where they interrogated him with a gun held to his temple, which they fired, barely grazing his head. When the patient still could not provide information the soldiers demanded, they tied a noose around his neck and pretended they would hang him by walking him over to a makeshift gallows. Shortly afterward, they drove him back to town, still blindfolded, and dumped him out of the car.

When asked what bothered him most about missing his mother's funeral, the patient said he would never be able to properly grieve his mother's death and that perhaps he was a coward not to have returned home. This cognitive life-sentence to misery was countered by asking the patient to complete the following half-truth: "Yes, it is difficult to properly grieve my mother's death, having missed the funeral, but ... ," to which the patient replied, " ... but my life really was in danger!" The patient was reinforced for recognizing that protecting his life was not an act of cowardice and was redirected to respond directly to the content of the incomplete statement. After some thought, he said, " ... but maybe I can ask a priest to say a special mass for her." Working together, we polished up the following coping statements: "Yes, it is difficult to properly grieve my mother's death, but I can still honor her death from here with a special mass." "Yes, it felt bad not to attend the funeral, but protecting my life was not an act of cowardice." This restructuring of the patient's automatic thoughts decreased depressed mood and guilt.

Religion is another cognitive-related domain in which therapists need to work with traditional or religious Latino patients. We reinforce church going and prayer as behavioral and cognitive activities, respectively, that help patients deal with stress and negative mood states. However, we have learned to explore and challenge forms of prayer that seem to lessen the probability of active problem-solving. For example, when patients report that they "just prayed" instead of doing the week's homework assignment, we ask them to share their prayers. They often reply that they asked God to help them with their problems. In such cases, we help patients to shift prayers in a more active direction with techniques like discussing the saying, *Ayudate, que Dios te ayudará*, which is the Spanish equivalent of "God helps those who help themselves." Following this, we model for patients and ask them to recite prayers in which they ask God for support in trying out new behaviors. For example, one young woman suffering from panic disorder with agoraphobia began to pray for support in her efforts to leave her home, attend therapy, and do things by herself.

Assertiveness training. Latino patients commonly report a tendency to *guardar*, or hold in anger, rather than express it to spouses, family members, and others with whom they are upset. The tendency to *guardar* can be viewed as part of a larger culture-based style known as *controlarse*, which refers to the disciplined control of negative thoughts and feelings leading to either resignation or efforts to overcome hardship (Cohen, 1985). If done sensitively, assertiveness training can help overwhelmed Latino patients do more of the latter.

Encouraging descriptions of assertiveness training with Latinos have been reported (Acosta, 1982; Boulette, 1976; Herrera and Sanchez, 1976; Torres-Matrullo, 1982), as well as culturally sensitive guidelines for conducting assertiveness training with ethnic minorities in general (Wood and Mallinckrodt, 1990) and with Latinas in particular (Comas-Díaz and Duncan, 1985). Such guidelines are extremely important in view of recent acknowledgment by experts that assertiveness is a modern, Western, and particularly North American concept and set of techniques that can often be inappropriate in traditional cultural contexts (e.g., Rakos, 1991).

In traditional Latino culture, communication and behavior are more strongly governed by traditional institutions (e.g., family, community, and the church) and values (e.g., deference to authority based on age, gender, social position, etc.) than in mainstream American society. Assertiveness can run contrary to the Latino culture's emphasis on communication that is polite, nonconfrontational, deferential, and even purposefully indirect (e.g., asking one relative to speak to another on one's behalf). Such communication is especially true for women who are taught to be submissive to men and to subordinate their needs to those of the family (Comas-Díaz, 1985).

Despite this cultural dilemma, the argument to do assertiveness training with Latino patients is compelling. For example, Soto and Shaver (1982) found that sex-role traditionalism was inversely related to assertiveness, and that assertiveness was inversely related to psychological distress in their study of Puerto Rican women *(N = 278)*. The question that remains is how to conduct assertiveness training in a culturally sensitive manner.

Contrary to CBT models of assertiveness training (e.g., Lange and Jakubowski, 1977), we do not spend time convincing traditionally oriented patients of their "personal rights," because such a concept is usually foreign to their nondemocratic, nonegalitarian family and friendship systems. Instead, we strive to "biculturate" patients by describing assertiveness as an effective communication skill in mainstream America in areas such as work, school, agency settings, and interpersonal relationships. The emphasis on biculturation is meant to expand communication skills to the mainstream context without devaluing traditional communication styles that are generally appropriate in their cultural context. Care should be taken to stress culturally compatible aspects of assertiveness such as the emphasis on communication that is not only direct but also honest, respectful, a way of cultivating family relationships, and a good way of teaching one's children how to communicate effectively in mainstream society.

Consistent with Comas-Díaz and Duncan's (1985) recommendations, Latino cultural factors that mitigate against developing assertiveness can be discussed as well as strategies for dealing with negative reactions from spouses and other family members. For example, Comas-Díaz and Duncan taught Puerto Rican women to preface assertive expressions with phrases like *Con todo respeto* ("With all due respect") and *Me permite expresar mis sentimientos?* ("Would you permit me to express my feelings?"). In addition, patients are taught to respond to negative reactions to their assertiveness with explanations such as "Expressing my feelings makes me less upset and better able to manage things."

For example, one woman learned how to respond assertively to an older male supervisor who habitually yelled at her at the factory where she cleaned machinery. With the help of modeling by therapists and role-play, the woman was finally able to say to her boss, "With all due respect, Señor, would you please not yell at me when you want to talk to me about my work?" A bit surprised, the boss quickly responded that he would not have to yell at her if she did not make mistakes. But role-playing had prepared our patient for this type of response, to which she replied, "Would you permit me to say something about that?", to which the boss could hardly say no, and the patient continued, "If you really want to help me with my mistakes, please talk to me in a softer voice and I will listen carefully."

Another way to motivate Latino patients to consider assertiveness is to ask them what happens when they hold in negative feelings. Almost without exception, patients describe the exacerbation of existing physical illness such as high blood pressure, diabetes, heart disease, and gastrointestinal problems. For example, one woman who had survived a stroke became very motivated to become assertive as a way of decreasing the probability of a second stroke by not holding in anger and resentment toward a son who drank excessively and became belligerent when intoxicated.

Activity schedules. Pleasant activity schedules and personal contracts to increase activities can be used to achieve an adequate number of pleasant activities for improving mood in the case of depression and to circumvent agoraphobia in the case of panic disorder (Organista, 1995). Because Latino patients are disproportionately poor, care needs to be taken to generate discussions and lists of local activities that cost little or no money (e.g., free admission to museums and zoos on the first Wednesday of the month, walks in the park or on the beach, having a cup of coffee in a charming cafe, etc.).

One drawback with activity-oriented interventions is that the mainstream American value of "taking time out for one's self" is less emphasized in Latino culture, especially for women. However, Latino patients are usually willing to increase pleasurable activities for the purpose of *distraerse,* or distracting themselves from worry and problems. The perception of pleasant activities as a way of temporarily escaping problems provides practition-ers with an opening for emphasizing this effective intervention strategy.

FUTURE DIRECTIONS

In her recent article on multicultural applications of cognitive behavioral approaches, Hays (1995) listed such potential strengths of this approach for culturally diverse clients as its emphasis on the uniqueness of the individual, its focus on client empowerment (self-control), its attention to conscious processes and specific behaviors (thus reducing the potential for mutual misunderstanding that can come when utilizing more complicated theoretical constructs), and the integration of assessment of client progress from the client's perspective throughout the process of intervention. At the same time, she listed several limitations: Although it purports to be value-neutral, several of its core values (assertiveness, personal independence, verbal ability, and change) are far from universal priorities; its emphasis on self-control can imply placing the blame on the individual for problems that are the result of unjust societal conditions; its focus on the present can result in a lack of attention to the client's history; its emphasis on rational thinking and the scien-tific method may devalue "alternative cognitive styles (e.g., less linear styles), worldviews (e.g., more spiritually oriented views), and ways of interacting (cooperative rather than confrontational)" (p. 311).

It should be clear from the above summary of possible strengths and weaknesses of cognitive behavioral approaches that empirical studies in which these approaches are adapted for Latino populations in a culturally sensitive manner are necessary. Bernal, Bonilla, and Bellido (1995) offer a framework for culturally sensitive interventions designed to promote outcome research with Latinos that is "ecologically valid." Ecological validity refers to the environmental and subjective realities of Latinos within the research context. Three of the eight categories from this framework are relevant to the current discussion.

Content. Cultural knowledge includes "fluency" in terms of values and traditions, as well as a practical understanding of the uniqueness of different groups in terms of their social, economic, historical, and political realities. A bicultural provider not only has knowledge and understanding of the content of the cultural group with which she or he is working, but, in addition, does not consider these perspectives to be "exotic" or "foreign" or primar-ily defined in contrast to the perspectives of the dominant culture. The theoretical basis for CBT provides a general direction for treatment. The specific content of general inter-ventions (such as intervention manuals) can be designed with Latino traditions in mind, and individual applications of interventions are tailor-made to fit the individual's age and sex, country of origin, immigration history, and socioeconomic characteristics.

Goals. Treatment and research goals can best be accomplished when the recipients of the interventions feel clearly valued within the context of their own traditions. It is impor-tant that the intervention does not have or appear to have the underlying assumption that the more patients adopt U.S. values and practices, the "healthier" or "better" human beings they will become. Only when the recipients of the intervention feel a genuine sense of respect and shared assumptions, is it possible to begin to look critically at practices learned in the culture of origin or in the United States, and to categorize both in terms of their potential positive and negative effects.

It is also important to address a second level of goals, namely goals of reaching the intended population, keeping them in treatment or research during the screening process, ensuring that attrition is not any greater for ethnically diverse groups, and documenting the effects of interventions. For example, in the Depression Prevention Research Project (Muñoz, Ying, Armas, Chan, and Gurza, 1987), we documented the proportions of Latinos whom we approached during the recruitment phase, who accepted entry into the study, who completed the screening phase, and who eventually were randomized into the actual trial. The proportions remained approximately the same for each of the ethnic groups involved in the study.

Methods. Intervention methods must be developed and adapted to best fit cultural expectations. For example, the methods developed by our group to focus on depression have been greatly influenced by Latino health care utilization. The reluctance of Latinos to use mental health services, and the great reliance on general medical services when confronted with both emotional and physical dysfunction, led us to collaborate closely with primary care clinics starting in the early 1980s. The Depression Prevention Research Project and the Cognitive-Behavioral Depression Clinic specialize in work with English- and Spanish-speaking primary care patients. We believe that an educational approach is more acceptable to Latino immigrants than is becoming a "mental patient," and that concerted treatment and prevention efforts are required to effectively address the impact of depression in the Latino community (Muñoz, 1995).

Another promising area of inquiry is the influence that traditional Latino values and role prescriptions, as well as characteristic social circumstances, may have in precipitating and exacerbating mental health problems. For example, although machismo may be regarded positively insofar as it prescribes responsibility and protecting the family, it also appears to make it difficult for Latino men to ask for professional help for emotional problems and may also contribute to excessive drinking, spousal abuse, etc. Similarly, although the traditional wife-mother role of Latinas (sometimes called *Marianismo*) prescribes tremendous attention to family well-being, and high respect for husbands, negative aspects may manifest themselves in excessive self-sacrifice and low assertiveness with husbands. Deference to authority is another example (i.e., "It is disrespectful to disagree with or to express anger toward authorities such as elders, professionals, bosses, etc.").

Hence, perhaps potentially negative aspects of Latino values could be explicated in forms analogous to Young's (1994) schema-focused approach to personality disorders in which he delineates 15 early maladaptive schemas (EMS) that drive interpersonal problems and that are amenable to cognitive restructuring. For example, one EMS that Young refers to seems similar to the down side of *Marianismo* mentioned above: "Subjugation/Lack of individuation—The voluntary or involuntary sacrificing of one's own needs to satisfy others' needs, often with an accompanying failure to recognize one's own needs" (p. 13). Such a problem could be explicated and reviewed when working with traditionally oriented Latinas. For example, the belief, "As a woman, my family's needs come first and I must endure mistreatment by my husband," could be challenged and restructured as follows: "My family's needs are extremely important. I am a central part of my family. Therefore, my needs are also extremely important"; "Being respectful to my husband does not mean that I cannot express my thoughts and feelings about matters or that I have to endure his mistreatment of me."

Although these examples of restructured thoughts aim to be acceptable within the culture, Rogler, Malgady, Costantino, and Blumenthal (1987) note that it is sometimes necessary to use clinical interventions that may deviate from Latino culture in the interest of the client's well-being (e.g., expanding the adaptive capacities of Latino clients adjusting to life in the United States). Obviously, this is a challenging level of culturally sensitive therapy with Latinos that requires discussion of such deviations with clients.

Finally, acculturative stress should be studied to clarify its role in triggering unhelpful, culturally based attributions in the areas of personal or interpersonal problems. For example, in Szapocznik's work with Cuban families, he has found that parents frequently blame family problems on their children's over-Americanization, and the children, in turn, blame their parents for being too old-fashioned. In his bicultural effectiveness training (BET), Szapocznik, Santisteban, Kurtines, Perez-Vidal, and Hervis (1984) teach all family members to "blame" the acculturation process and challenge them to assist each other's adaptation to American society (e.g., how can parents help their children adapt to American society while still being responsible to the family?). We look forward to addressing these issues as well as hearing from other cognitive behavioral clinicians and researchers interested in Latino populations.

NOTE

We would like to acknowledge support from SCR 43 funds from the Office of the President of the University of California which helped created the Latino Mental Health Research Program (Muñoz, Director) of the Latino Task Force of the University of California, San Francisco, at San Francisco General Hospital. This support has been most helpful in the preparation of this article and in continuing the work described.

BIBLIOGRAPHY

Acosta, F. X. (1979). Barriers between mental health services and Mexican Americans: An examination of a paradox. *American Journal of Community Psychology*, 7, 503–520.

Acosta, F. X., Yamamoto, J., and Evans, L. A. (1982). *Effective psychotherapy for low income and minority patients*. New York: Plenum Press.

Angel, R., and Guarnaccia, P. J. (1989). Mind, body, and culture: Somatization among Hispanics. *Social Science Medicine*, 28, 1229–1238.

Barrera, M., Jr. (1978). Mexican-American mental health service utilization: A critical examination of some proposed variables. *Community Mental Health Journal*, 14, 35–45.

Bernal, G., Bonilla, J., and Bellido, C. (1995). Ecological validity and cultural sensitivity for outcome research: Issues for the cultural adaptation and development of psychosocial treatment with Hispanics. *Journal of Abnormal Child Psychology*, 23, 67–82.

Boulette, T. R. (1976). Assertion training with low-income Mexican-American women. In M. R. Miranda (Ed.), *Psychotherapy with the Spanish-speaking: Issues in research and service delivery* (Monograph #3) (pp. 16–71). Los Angeles: Spanish-Speaking Mental Health Research Center, University of California.

Bruce, M. L., Takeuchi, D. T., and Leaf, P. J. (1991). Poverty and psychiatric status: Longitudinal evidence from the New Haven Epidemiologic Catchment Area Study. *Archives of General Psychiatry*, 48, 470–474.

Canino, I. A., Rubio-Stipec, M., Canino, G., and Escobar, J. I. (1992). Functional somatic symptoms: A cross-ethnic comparison. *American Journal of Orthopsychiatry*, 62, 605–612.

Cervantes, R. C., Salgado de Snyder, V. N., and Padilla, A. M. (1989). Post traumatic stress disorder among immigrants from Central America and Mexico. *Hospital and Community Psychiatry*, 40, 615–619.

Cohen, L. M. (1985). Controlarse and the problems of life among Latino immigrants. In W. A. Vega and M. R. Miranda (Eds.), *Stress and Hispanic mental health: Relating research to service delivery* (DHHS Pub. No. ADM 85–1410, pp. 202–218). Rockville, MD: U.S. Department of Health and Human Services.

Comas-Díaz, L. (1981). Effects of cognitive and behavioral group treatment on the depressive symptomatology of Puerto Rican women. *Journal of Consulting and Clinical Psychology*, 49(5), 627–632.

Comas-Díaz, L. (1985). Cognitive and behavioral therapy with Puerto Rican women: A comparison of content themes. *Hispanic Journal of Behavioral Sciences*, 7(3) 273–283.

Comas-Díaz, L., and Duncan, J. W. (1985). The cultural context: A factor in assertiveness training with mainland Puerto Rican women. *Psychology of Women Quarterly*, 9, 463–476.

Cordova, R. (1979). Undocumented El Salvadorans in the San Francisco Bay Area: Migration and adaptation dynamic. *Journal of La Raza Studies*, 1, 9–35.

Delgado, M., and Humm-Delgado, D. (1984). Hispanics and group work: A review of the literature. *Ethnicity in Group Work Practice*, 85–96.

Eaton, W. W., Dryman, A., and Weissman, M. M. (1991). Panic and phobia. In L. N. Robins and D. A. Regier (Eds.), *Psychiatric disorders in America: The Epidemiologic Catchment Area Study* (pp. 155–179). New York: Free Press.

Ellis, A., and Grieger, R. (1977). *Handbook of rational emotive therapy*. New York: Holt, Rinehart, and Winston.

Escobar, J. I., Golding, J. M., Hough, R. L., Karno, M., Burnam, M. A., and Wells, K. B. (1987). Somatization in the community: Relationship to disability and use of services. *American Journal of Public Health*, 77, 837–840.

Falicov, C. J. (1982). Mexican families. In M. McGoldrick, J. K. Pearce, and J. Giordano (Eds.), *Ethnicity and family therapy* (pp. 134–163). New York: Guilford Press.

Farias, P. J. (1991). Emotional distress and its socio-political correlates in Salvadoran refugees: Analysis of a clinical sample. *Culture, Medicine, and Psychiatry*, 15, 167–192.

Ferris, E. G. (1987). *The Central American refugees*. New York: Praeger.

Goldstein, A. P. (1971). *Psychotherapeutic attraction*. New York: Pergamon.

Gonsalves, C. J. (1990). The psychological effects of political repression on Chilean exiles in the United States. *American Journal of Orthopsychiatry*, 60, 143–153.

Hays, P. A. (1995). Multicultural applications of cognitive-behavior therapy. *Professional Psychology: Research and Practice*, 26, 309–315.

Healey, J. F. (1995). Hispanic Americans: Colonization, immigration, and ethnic enclaves. In J. F. Healey (Ed.), *Race, ethnicity, gender, and class: The sociology of group conflict and change*. (pp. 341–401). Thousand Oaks, CA: Pine Forge Press.

Herrera, A. E., and Sanchez, V. C. (1976). Behaviorally oriented group therapy: A successful application in the treatment of low income Spanish-speaking clients. In M. R. Miranda (Ed.), *Psychotherapy with the Spanish-speaking: Issues in research and service delivery* (Monograph #3) (pp. 73–84). Los Angeles: Spanish-Speaking Mental Health Research Center, University of California.

Hough, R. L., Landsverk, J. A., Karno, M., Burnam, M. A., Timbers, D. M., Escobar, J. I., and Regier, D. A. (1987). Utilization of health and mental health services by Los Angeles Mexican Americans and non-Hispanic Whites. *Archives of General Psychiatry*, 44, 702–709.

Karno, M., Ross, R. N., and Caper, R. A. (1969). Mental health roles of physicians in a Mexican American community. *Community Mental Health Journal*, 5, 62–69.

Kessler, R. C., McGonagle, K. A., Zhao, S., Nelson, C. B., Hughes, M., Eshleman, S., Wittchen, H., and Kendler, K. S. (1994). Lifetime and 12-month prevalence of DSM-III-R psychiatric disorders in the United States. *Archives of General Psychiatry*, 51, 8–19.

Kolody, B., Vega, W., Meinhardt, K., and Bensussen, G. (1986). The correspondence of health complaints and depressive symptoms among Anglos and Mexican-Americans. The *Journal of Nervous and Mental Disease*, 174, 221–228.

Lange, A. J., and Jakubowski, P. (1977). *Responsible assertive behavior: Cognitive/behavioral procedures for trainers*. Champaign, IL: Research Press.

Leslie, L. A., and Lietch, M. L. (1989). A demographic profile of recent Central American immigrants: Clinical and service implications. *Hispanic Journal of Behavioral Sciences*, 11 (4), 315–329.

Marger, M. N. (1991). Hispanic Americans. In M. N. Marger (Ed.), *Race and ethnic relations: American and global perspectives* (2nd ed., pp. 279–320). Belmont, CA: Wadsworth.

Marín, G., and VanOss Marín, B. (1991). *Research with Hispanic populations*. Newbury Park, CA: Sage.

Miranda, M. R. (Ed.) (1976). *Psychotherapy with the Spanish-speaking: Issues in research and service delivery* (Monograph #3). Los Angeles: Spanish-Speaking Mental Health Research Center, University of California.

Moscicki, E. K, Rae, D. S., Regier, D. A., and Locke, B. Z. (1987). The Hispanic Health and Nutrition Examination Survey: Depression among Mexican Americans, Cuban Americans and Puerto Ricans. In M. Garcia and J. Arana (Eds.), *Research agenda for Hispanics* (pp. 145–159). Chicago: University of Illinois Press.

Muñoz, R. F. (1982). The Spanish-speaking consumer and the community mental health center. In E. Jones and S. Korchin (Eds.), *Minority mental health* (pp. 362–398.) New York: Praeger.

Muñoz, R. F. (1995). Toward combined prevention and treatment services for major depression. In C. Telles and M. Karno (Eds.), *Latino mental health: Current research and policy perspectives* (pp. 183–200). Los Angeles: University of California, Los Angeles, Neuropsychiatric Institute.

Muñoz, R. F., and Ying, Y. W. (1993). *The prevention of depression: Research and practice*. Baltimore: Johns Hopkins University Press.

Muñoz, R. F., Ying, Y. W., Armas, R., Chan, F., and Gurza, R. (1987). The San Francisco Depression Prevention Research Project: A randomized trial with medical outpatients. In R. F. Muñoz (Ed.), *Depression prevention: Research directions* (pp. 199–215). Washington, DC: Hemisphere.

Organista, K. C. (1995). Cognitive-behavioral treatment of depression and panic disorder in a Latina patient: Culturally sensitive case formulation. *In Session: Psychotherapy in Practice*, 1, 53–64.

Organista, K. C., Muñoz, R. F., and González, G. (1994). Cognitive behavioral therapy for depression in low-income and minority medical outpatients: Description of a program and exploratory analyses. *Cognitive Therapy and Research*, 18, 241–259.

Orlinsky, D. E., and Howard, K. I. (1986). Process and outcome in psychotherapy. In S. L. Garfield and A. E. Bergin (Eds.), *Handbook of psychotherapy and behavior change* (3rd ed., pp. 311–381). New York: John Wiley and Sons.

Padilla, A. M., Carlos, M. L., and Keefe, S. E. (1976). Mental health service utilization by Mexican Americans. In M. R. Miranda (Ed.), *Psychotherapy with the Spanish-speaking: Issues in research and service delivery* (Monograph #3). Los Angeles: Spanish-Speaking Mental Health Research Center, University of California.

Padilla, A. M., and Salgado de Snyder, N. S. (1985). Counseling Hispanics: Strategies for effective intervention. In P. B. Pedersen (Ed.), *Handbook of cross-cultural counseling and therapy* (pp. 157–164). Westport, CT: Greenwood Press.

Parron, D. L. (1982). An overview of minority group mental health needs and issues as presented to the President's Commission on Mental Health. In F. V. Muñoz and R. Endo (Eds.), *Perspectives on minority group and mental health* (pp. 3–22). Washington, DC: University Press of America.

Plante, T. G., Manuel, G. M., Menendez, A. V., and Marcotte, D. (1995). Coping with stress among Salvadoran immigrants. *Hispanic Journal of Behavioral Sciences*, 17(4), 471–479.

Rakos, R. F. (1991). *Assertive behavior: Theory, research, and training*. New York: Routledge.

Rogler, L. H., Malgady, R. G., Costantino, G., and Blementhal, R. (1987). What do culturally sensitive mental health services mean? *American Psychologist*, 42(6), 565–570.

Salgado de Snyder, Cervantes, R. C., and Padilla, A. M. (1990). Gender and ethnic differences in psychosocial stress and generalized distress among Hispanics. *Sex Roles*, 22(7/8), 441–453.

Shrout, P. E., Canino, G. J., Bird, H. R., Rubio-Stipec, M., Bravos, M., and Burnam, M. A. (1992). Mental health status among Puerto Ricans, Mexican Americans, and non-Hispanic whites. *American Journal of Community Psychology*, 20 (6), 729–752.

Soto, E., and Shaver, P. (1982). Sex role traditionalism, assertiveness, and symptoms of Puerto Rican women living in the United States. *Hispanic Journal of Behavioral Sciences*, 4, 1–19.

Sue, S., Fujino, D. C., Hu, L., Takeuchi, D. T., and Zane, N. W. S. (1991). Community mental health services for ethnic minority groups: A test of the cultural responsiveness hypothesis. *Journal of Consulting and Clinical Psychology*, 59, 533–540.

Szapocznik, J., Santisteban, D., Kurtines, W., Perez-Vidal, A., and Hervis, O. (1984). Bicultural effectiveness training: A treatment intervention for enhancing intercultural adjustment in Cuban American Families. *Hispanic Journal of Behavioral Sciences*, 6, 317–344.

Torres-Matrullo, C. (1982). Cognitive therapy of depressive disorders in the Puerto Rican female. In R. M. Becerra, M. Karno, and J. I. Escobar (Eds.), *Mental health and Hispanic Americans* (pp. 101–113). New York: Grune and Stratton.

U.S. Bureau of the Census. (1995). *Statistical abstracts of the United States*, 1994 (11th ed.). (GPO Pub. #95–0130-P). Washington, DC: U.S. Government Printing Office.

Weissman, M. M., Bruce, M. L., Leaf, P. J., and Holzer, C., III. (1991). Affective disorders. In L. N. Robins and D. A. Regier (Eds.), *Psychiatric disorders in America: The Epidemiologic Catchment Area Study* (pp. 53–80). New York: Free Press.

Wood, P. S., and Mallinckrodt, B. (1990). Culturally sensitive assertiveness training for ethnic minority clients. *Professional Psychology: Research and Practice*, 21, 5–11.

Young, J. (1994). *Cognitive therapy for personality disorders: A schema focused approach* (2nd ed.). Sarasota, FL: Professional Resource Press.

24.
Mental Health and Well-Being of Black Women
Toward Strategies of Empowerment
Jewelle Taylor Gibbs and Diana Fuery

This review of the literature on Black women's mental health has three goals: 1) to describe the mental health issues, needs, and adaptive behaviors of Black women; 2) to discuss the research, intervention, and public policy efforts of mental health professionals and Black women's groups to address the multiple needs of this population; and 3) to identify effective strategies by which community psychologists can improve the mental health status of Black women through efforts to reduce their environmental stressors, to increase their resources and access to services, and to facilitate their empowerment in American society. The authors propose a number of recommendations to improve Black women's mental health, including changes in research paradigms, changes in education and training programs, and the development of culturally competent service delivery systems.

A common aphorism about Black women is that they are triply disadvantaged due to their gender, their ethnicity, and their poverty. According to this view, Black women, as members of three low-status groups, represent the epitome of powerlessness in American society as compared to White middle-class males (Allen, 1981; Ladner, 1986; Pinderhughes, 1989). Presumably, this least favorable combination of low-status positions should predict negative social and psychological consequences for Black women (Belle, 1990; Bennett, 1987; Copeland, 1982).

An alternative perspective on Black women portrays them as strong, resilient, and adaptive in their ability to cope with adversity, support their families, and develop avenues of self-esteem and self-actualization (Giddings, 1984; Hull, Scott and Smith, 1982; Stack, 1974). Ironically, both views reflect the realities of Black women's experience in America. On the one hand, they have been victims of discrimination, economic exploitation, and social rejection for over 370 years. On the other hand, they have overcome many of these barriers through developing a set of cultural attitudes, a pattern of coping strategies, and a series of help-seeking behaviors which have enabled them to survive and sometimes thrive in a frequently hostile, exploitive, and unsupportive environment.

This paper has three major goals: 1) to describe the mental health issues, needs, and adaptive behaviors of Black women; 2) to discuss the research, intervention and public policy efforts undertaken by mental health professionals and by indigenous women's groups to address the multiple-needs of this population; and 3) to identify effective strategies by which community psychologists can improve the mental health status of Black women through efforts to reduce social stressors in their environment, to increase resources and access to services, and to facilitate the empowerment of Black women in American society.

This review will focus primarily on what is known about the current mental health status of Black women who are predominantly urban, low-income and working-class; how they view their own mental health; how they are viewed by mental health professionals; how the concept of empowerment can undergird strategies of prevention and early intervention in the field of community psychology; and how Black women are developing innovative approaches to empower themselves and to promote positive personal, family and community well-being.

DEMOGRAPHIC PROFILE OF BLACK WOMEN

To understand the mental health issues and problems of urban Black women in America, it is necessary to view them in the context of the demographic characteristics and the diversity of the overall Black female population. In 1989, there were over 10 million Black women between 15–65 in the population, constituting 34% of all Blacks and 10.29% of all females in that age range (U.S. Bureau of the Census, 1989). In 1989, the median family income for all Blacks was $20,210 compared to the median White family income of $35,980. Black female-headed households, 43.8% of all Black families, had a median income of $11,630, compared to a median income of $18,950 for White female-headed households, who constitute 12.9% of all White families (U.S. Bureau of the Census, 1990c).

In 1989, 29.8% of all Black families lived below the poverty line compared to 8.6% of all White families. While 49.4% of Black female headed households had below-poverty line incomes, only 28.1% of White female headed households fell below the poverty line. Black women were nearly twice as likely as White women to be welfare-dependent (U.S. Bureau of the Census, 1990c).

Compared to Black men, Black women have a higher average level of education, and a higher proportion are employed in professional and white collar occupations. In 1980, Black women were distributed occupationally as follows: 14.8% in professional and managerial fields, 31.1% in clerical, sales and technical fields, 15% in blue collar skilled occupations, 26% in service occupations, and 13.2% in domestic and unskilled occupations. Professional Black women have essentially reached income parity with White women. However, unemployment rates for Black women are still higher than for White women (11.7% vs. 4.7% in 1988), and the same as Black men (11.7%) (U.S. Bureau of the Census, 1989). Despite the fact that Black women have made greater relative educational and occupational progress in comparison to White women than Black men have made relative to White men, Black women still lag behind Black men in wages and income, as they tend to be concentrated in the lower average paying female-dominated occupations.

Black women are also less likely than White women to be married, to own their own homes, to have health insurance, and to live outside of central cities (U.S. Bureau of the Census, 1989). Moreover, Black women have higher mortality rates than White women due to a greater number of chronic diseases, and the life span of Black women is greater than Black males but less than White males or females (Farley and Allen, 1989). Finally, Black women have fewer males available for marriage than White women, limiting the ability of heterosexual women to have the financial and emotional support of a spouse throughout their adult lives (Wilson, 1987). Despite these factors, many women in the Black community have successfully reared families in multigenerational households or as single parents without consistent support from a spouse or partner.

These demographic descriptors present a rather superficial portrait of Black women who represent a very diverse group with significant intragroup variation in education, income, occupation, household composition, residential and regional location, religion, political affiliation and life-style (Farley and Allen, 1989; Ladner, 1986). The diversity of Black women is a reflection of the post World War II social and economic progress of the Black community, the legislative and judicial challenges to segregation and discrimination, and the post-1960s political initiatives to empower low-income minority groups through community action, educational opportunity, and affirmative action programs (Farley and Allen, 1989). However, Black women's expanded opportunities and life options have been accompanied by a new set of stresses related to mobility: increased competition with Black males and White females in the labor market, "the glass ceiling" in professional and business organizations, two-career families, and sexual harassment in the workplace (Dill, 1979; Ladner, 1986; Smith and Stewart, 1983).

Despite their diversity, a large number of Black women experience some type of chronic stress in their lives ranging from poverty, discrimination, *and* unemployment, to serious health or family problems. As Belle (1990) graphically pointed out in her recent review of the impact of poverty on women's mental health, poor Black women are also more likely to experience more frequent threatening and uncontrollable life events than the general population and, as single parents, more likely to suffer from chronic depressive symptoms and feelings of powerlessness in relation to their multiple social roles. Other researchers have also noted that single-parenthood is a chronic source of stress for low-income Black women (Thompson and Ensminger, 1989; Weissman, Leaf, and Bruce, 1987). Thus, low-income Black women are vulnerable to a number of major social stressors in American society, placing them squarely at risk for the development of psychological problems. However, the effort to document the mental health status of these Black women is hampered by the limitations of the research results, which have often been drawn from methodologically flawed studies which failed to control for socioeconomic, gender, or racial differences within the samples.

PERSPECTIVES ON BLACK WOMEN'S MENTAL HEALTH

Black women have been consistently ignored, mythologized or demeaned in traditional social and behavioral science theories (Dill, 1979; Giddings, 1984; Ladner, 1986). Black feminist scholars have recently challenged the traditional pathological perspectives on Black women and have formulated alternative conceptualizations which focus on their adaptive strengths and resilience (Allen and Britt, 1983; Hull, Scott and Smith, 1982; Smith and Stewart, 1983).

In her discussion of "self-in-relation" theory, Turner (1987) noted how this theory validates the experience of the minority woman's maturation process. She points out that Black women often define themselves in terms of significant relationships, rather than defining themselves through separation, beginning with the mother-daughter dyad, extending to the family, then to the minority community, and finally to the majority community. Throughout this process, the Black woman develops a healthy sense of an autonomous "self," while simultaneously maintaining mutually interconnected relations with close family, friends and significant role models in the community.

While Turner emphasizes the development of self through mutuality in supportive relationships, other authors have proposed that Black women are socialized to be more independent, assertive, and less conforming to female sex-role stereotypes (Cottingham, 1989; Dill, 1979). During their childhood and adolescent years, Black females of all socio-economic groups exhibit levels of self-esteem and positive self-concept which are equal to or higher than Black males and White females (Gibbs, 1985b; Powell, 1985). In their college years, Black females exhibit traits of autonomy, goal-directedness, high achievement motivation, and less fear of success than White women or Black men (Murray and Mednick, 1977; Smith and Stewart, 1983). For these Black women, mutuality in relationships does not seem to preclude individuality in educational and occupational contexts.

In their marital relationships, low and middle-income Black women view themselves as equal partners, sharing decision-making, alternating instrumental and expressive roles, and sharing family responsibilities (Staples and Mirande, 1980). In contrast to White women of comparable backgrounds, older, poor and working-class Black women are more likely to spend a significant part of their lives in extended families, where they assume important child-rearing and household responsibilities (Beck and Beck, 1989). Consequently, the aging process for these Black women may not be as lonely or as traumatic as it is for comparable White women who are more likely to live in non-family situations and less likely to be involved in meaningful social roles in their older years.

Dill (1979) and Cottingham (1989) have emphasized the historical role of work in the lives of Black women. Since most Black women have traditionally been in the labor force, they have developed a more assertive role in their families, demanded more equality in their sexual relationships, taken greater advantage of educational and occupational opportunities, and achieved more economic and social parity with White women as compared to the social and economic position of Black males relative to White males. In fact, some analysts have commented on the apparent irony of the "multiple negative" effect for Black women professionals (Epstein, 1973) and the "positive marginality" effect for Black female community leaders (Smith, 1986), whose dual status facilitates their mobility and their advocacy in situations where they are able to transcend the limitations of stereotyped female or Black expectations, attitudes and behaviors (Smith and Stewart, 1983).

The following section summarizes some of the work about Black women, conducted from a community psychology perspective. Topics covered include psychological well-being, risk and protective factors for mental distress. A critical analysis of this literature indicates that some of the researchers approached the topic of mental health from either a "needs-prevention" point of view or from a "rights-advocacy" point of view (Rappaport, 1981, 1985). This dialectic about mental health issues alternates between perceiving Black women as needing support they are unable to provide for themselves and perceiving them as having rights to services, without considering their available resources and program accessibility. Both of these perspectives are limited, and generally fail to examine the ways in which Black women develop and sustain competencies to face problems of living in this society. An alternative view proposed by several authors suggests that the construct of "empowerment" replaces both the notions of prevention and advocacy which are one-sided and maintain the professional in an expert role as either the "teacher of competencies" or as the "provider of treatment" (Gutierrez, 1990; Rappaport, 1981; Zimmerman, 1990).

An Empowerment Perspective

Rappaport (1985) suggests empowerment has both political and psychological components but is difficult to define in outcome terms. Zimmerman (1990) defines empowerment psychologically as "beliefs about one's competence and efficacy as well as one's involvement in activities for exerting control in the social and political environment" (p.18). Gutierrez (1990) defines empowerment as a process of increasing personal, interpersonal or political power which allows people to take action to improve their life situations. She points to both macro level definitions of empowerment and micro level ones, but joins Gould (1987) and Morell (1987) in the need for empowerment theory to concentrate on the interface between the macro and micro levels. Such a theory would define how individual empowerment can contribute to group empowerment, and how the increase of a group's power can enhance the functioning of its individual members. Zimmerman (1990) suggests concentrating on "psychological empowerment" as an avenue toward understanding this interface. His concept of "psychological empowerment" refers to the individual level of analysis without ignoring the ecological and cultural influences. Most authors agree that research on the concept of empowerment must focus not only on individual psychological concepts nor only on organizational processes, but must also include the interface between the two. Zimmerman (1990), Rappaport (1985) and Pinderhughes (1983) recommend the study of self-help and voluntary organizations as the arena which might clarify this interface. Although this has been presented as a mandate for community psychologists since the early 1980s, much of the literature on Black women continues to present either a needs/prevention or rights/advocacy paradigm for the understanding of this population. The literature on psychological well-being, however, does include some studies which attempt to identify sources of empowerment for Black women. These works will be discussed below.

Psychological Well-Being

In her analysis of data about Black and White women and men from the first National Health and Nutrition Examination Survey from 1971–75, Redmond (1988) found that Black women compared to a Black men, White women and White men, had the lowest scores of all four race-sex groups on the 18-item General Well Being Schedule. However, among Black women, higher levels of well-being were significantly related to education, income, and currently being married. Somewhat contradictory results were found in a study by Reskin and Coverman (1985) who found that Black women reported fewer symptoms than White women on a ten-item physical and psychological distress scale of a national survey by the National Center for Health Statistics in 1959–1962. In their study, marital status, paid employment, and a high household income were similarly related to higher levels of psychological well-being for Black and White women. Differences in results from these two studies may be attributed to several factors, including different time periods, different samples and different measures.

Social Networks

In their National Survey of Black Americans, Neighbors and his colleagues (1983) found that informal social networks provided Black women with a very important source for coping with stress. Other studies of Black adults have also found that family closeness and availability of support from kin networks are positively related to subjective feelings of psychological well-being (Dressler, 1985). There are conflicting results regarding the effects of the proximity, size, and intensity of kin social support networks on Black women; some studies find that large, extended kin networks have positive effects on their mental health (Brown and Gary, 1985), while others find that these networks are ineffective in reducing the risk for depression, especially among younger Black women (Camino, 1989; Dressler, 1985). In their study of childrearing women in Chicago, Thompson and Ensminger (1989) found that emotional support and social integration were significantly related to an increased feeling of psychological well-being. Black women with high levels of social integration in a Texas community also reported fewer symptoms of psychological distress than those with low levels of social integration (Holahan, Betak, Spearly and Chance, 1983). The implications of these findings for low-income urban Black women are not entirely clear, since the effect of social networks appears to be moderated both by characteristics of the networks (proximity, size, and intensity) and by women's characteristics (age, marital status, symptomatology, child-rearing status, etc.).

Protective Factors

Demographic factors found in other studies to be related to psychological well-being for Black women include higher socioeconomic status (Neighbors, Jackson, Bowman, and Gurin, 1983; Redmond, 1988; Reskin and Coverman, 1985), marriage (Redmond 1988; Reskin and Coverman, 1985; Thompson and Ensminger, 1989), employment (Coleman, Antonucci, Adelman, and Crohan, 1987; Thompson and Ensminger, 1989), higher educational level (Comstock and Helsing, 1976; Redmond, 1988); church attendance or religiosity (Edwards, 1987; Thompson and Ensminger, 1989); and residential mobility (Thompson and Ensminger, 1989). These factors can be considered "protective" in that they reduce the risk for psychological distress and symptomatology, although residential mobility may be counterbalanced by the stress associated with moving and the possible stress of social mobility (Myers, 1982). These findings suggest that middle and upper-income Black women, who are both married and employed are likely to experience higher levels of psychological well-being than lower-income women who are both single and unemployed.

Ethnographic studies of urban Black women and their social networks provide a broader perspective delineating Black women's roles as strong leaders in their families, churches, and community organizations (Aschenbrenner, 1983; Hull, Scott, and Smith, 1982; Stack, 1974). In response to segregation and discrimination, Black women have developed a set of implicit attitudes and explicit behaviors which have enabled them to identify internal sources of self-esteem, to maintain their dignity in the face of persistent prejudice and blocked opportunities, to surmount barriers to their aspirations and goals, to support families with meager resources, to rear competent children in a hostile society, and to provide leadership to community organizations despite limited education and training (Giddings, 1984; McAdoo, 1981).

Despite the publicity accorded to a few prominent middle-class Black women leaders, there have been hundreds of unsung poor and working-class Black women who have been crusaders in their own communities for voting rights, better schools, low-rent housing, health clinics, and crime prevention (Giddings, 1984). As Rappaport (1981, 1985) has suggested, these women empowered themselves to obtain rights to which they were entitled.

Most of the studies of psychological well-being for Black women focus on individual or environmental factors which appear to provide some "protective" function. None of the studies reviewed focused on the interface between intrapsychic and environmental phenomena. For these studies to further community psychologists' understanding of how Black women feel empowered, researchers must further analyze the process by which intrapsychic feelings of well-being, self-esteem, and power are impacted by the presence or absence or these protective elements. Such research could further the promotion of social policies and programs which would support and enhance these beneficial elements in communities.

Risk Factors

Demographic factors associated with increased risk for mental distress or disorder in Black women are poverty or low socioeconomic status (Belle, 1990; Bennett, 1987), single parenthood (Belle, 1990; Ladner, 1986; Thompson and Ensminger, 1989), unemployment (Belle, 1990; Thompson and Ensminger, 1989), and neighborhood crime and environmental stress (Parker and Ray, 1990; Riger and Gordon, 1983; Ulbricht, Warheit, and Zimmerman, 1989; Watts-Jones, 1990). These factors also increase the risk for psychological distress in all adults. However, Black women are significantly more likely than members of other sex-race groups to experience a cluster of these risk-multiplying factors, in particular the combination of poverty, single-parenthood and neighborhood crime (Wilson, 1987).

In their National Survey of Black Americans, Neighbors and his colleagues (1983) found that Black women reported higher levels of psychological stress than Black men, a finding that has been replicated in several other studies (Brown and Gray, 1987; Redmond, 1988).

Results of this survey show an important relationship between psychiatric morbidity and health problems among Blacks. High psychiatric morbidity is correlated with the greatest number of health problems including: ulcers, hypertension, diabetes, kidney problems, emotional problems and circulatory problems. Further, Blacks with high levels of psychiatric symptomatology were also more likely to have lower socioeconomic status. These combined results suggest that low-income Black women in poor health are particularly at risk for psychological problems. Recent research by Watts-Jones (1990) further suggests a reciprocal relationship between stress and various psychological and physical impairments among Black women.

Neighborhood crime, both in terms of its actual and its perceived threat, has been identified in several studies as a major source of environmental stress for poor urban Black women, damaging their sense of security and psychological well-being, and causing them to experience high levels of fear and anxiety over the threat of being victimized (Riger and Gordon, 1983; White, Kasl, Zahner, and Will, 1987). Riger and Gordon point out that Black women are twice as likely as White women to experience rape, robbery and other serious crimes (except theft), and they reported feeling twice as unsafe in their neighbor-hood as compared to White women. White and his colleagues (1987) found that both Black and Hispanic women who reported more neighborhood crime also complained of higher rates of agitated depression, phobic anxiety, somatization and hostility even when demographic and actual neighborhood conditions are accounted for.

Similarly, Kasl and Harburg (1975) found that Black women living in "high-stress" census tracts in Detroit were more likely than women in "low-stress" tracts to perceive danger from crime and to express feelings of nervous tension, unhappiness, and marital dissatisfaction. In addition to the threat of crime, low-income Black women often must confront the daily stresses of inadequate housing, deteriorating urban neighborhoods, inferior schools for their children, inaccessible health care, and inefficient transportation systems (Wilson, 1987).

In summary, a balanced perspective on the problems and the strengths of urban Black women provides several contrasting though not incompatible views. One view highlights a group of women who are particularly vulnerable to a number of negative social indica-tors which are associated with decreased levels of psychological well-being and increased risk for mental distress or disorder. An alternative view focuses on the individual, social and cultural factors which have enabled these women to adapt, survive, and even triumph over the triple challenge of being female, Black, and poor. That so many Black women have been able to overcome these socially-imposed limitations suggests that they have developed individual and group strategies to modify their environments and to promote their collective well-being.

ASSESSMENT OF MENTAL HEALTH PROBLEMS

Data from epidemiological surveys, community studies, and utilization studies of outpa-tient psychiatric services have provided several different perspectives on the incidence and prevalence of psychological disorders among Black women. When demographic factors are controlled, the majority of these studies conclude that there are no significant differ-ences between Black women and White women in the prevalence of psychiatric disorders. However, gross rates of disorders, especially depression and phobias, may appear to be higher in studies where socioeconomic status, age, marital status and other factors are not controlled. These rates may also vary depending on the measures used, which raises the critical issue of the validity and reliability of a number of standardized psychodiagnostic instruments currently used to assess psychiatric symptomatology in Black and other minority populations.

How an ethnic group defines psychological stress is also an important factor in inter-preting research on their rates of stress, their patterns of symptomatology and their utiliza-tion of mental health services (Neighbors, Jackson, Campbell, and Williams, 1989).

Since 1980 there have been a number of excellent comprehensive review articles and books dealing with the controversial issues of potential bias in the psychodiagnostic assess-ment of Blacks and other ethnic minority clients in mental health settings (e.g., Adebimpe, 1981; Neighbors, Jackson, Campbell, and Williams, 1989; Snowden Todman, 1982). These issues are too complex to summarize adequately in this paper, but psychologists in clinical and community settings should be aware of the potential ethnic differences in the following areas: patterns of presenting complaints (deFigueiredo and Boerstler, 1988), patterns of expressing symptomatology (Fabrega, Mezzich and Ulrich, 1988; Sussman, Robins and Earls, 1987), the validity of responses to standardized diagnostic instruments and symptom check-lists (Bass, Wyatt, and Powell, 1982; Vernon and Roberts, 1981), interviewer bias in evaluating the severity of responses (Atkinson, 1985; Baskin, Bluestone, and Nelson, 1981; Sue, 1988), differential coping mechanisms to mediate psychological distress (Baskin, Bluestone, and Nelson, 1981; Fabrega, Mezzich, and Ulrich, 1988; Sussman, Robins, and Earls, 1987), and patterns of culturally normative behaviors and personality traits (Adebimpe, 1981; Atkinson, 1985; Mukherjee, et al., 1983). Finally, Neighbors and his colleagues (1989) offer a critique of the current research on mental disorders in Blacks and describe some of the problems involved in comparing results from cross-racial studies which are different in their research design, samples, instruments, and techniques of data analysis.

The bias in assessment and diagnosis actually reflects biased conceptions, negative stereotypes, and popular myths about Black women in the broader society. These stereotypes and misconceptions have been disseminated in generations of literature, promoted through the mass media, and reinforced through social policies which encourage dependency rather than autonomy and empowerment (Giddings, 1984; Ladner, 1986). Concepts such as the "Black matriarch" and the "sexually promiscuous woman" have been linked to images of female heads of household and unwed teenage mothers to foster contradictory images of the Black woman as both the strong, assertive family leader and the immature, impulsive welfare mother. These uni-dimensional stereotypes obviate the need to view the Black woman as a complex human being with all of the motivations, needs, and aspirations of all women, in addition to their shared sense of identity, problems and common goals with Black men (Smith and Stewart, 1983). Further, these stereotypes may affect psychologists' ability to conduct unbiased assessments of Black women, to recognize their strengths as well as their symptoms, and to evaluate the influence of ethnicity and social class on their psychological functioning.

HELP SEEKING PATTERNS

To understand the behaviors of Black women seeking help for psychological distress requires an examination of their use of both formal and informal mental health services. Utilization studies of community mental health and outpatient-psychiatric hospital clinics provide some data on how low-income Black women deal with their psychological problems, particularly since these reported rates reflect a disproportionate number of low-income minority clients (Mollica, Blum, and Redlich, 1980; Neighbors, 1984). As Neighbors and his colleagues (1983, 1987) have pointed out, Black women were more likely than Black men to seek help for psychological problems, but initially turned to hospital emergency rooms, physicians and ministers before contacting a mental health professional. Black women were also more likely than Black men to remain in treatment longer and more likely to receive range of mental health services (Bass, Wyatt, and Powell, 1982).

During the 1970s, regional studies noted a rise in the number of Black women seeking professional mental health services. This increase occurred in Black women 35 to 39 years old but younger Black women, 13 to 19 years old, were making fewer contacts with mental health professionals than in the sixties (Gordon et al., 1976–1977). In the 1975 National

Institute of Mental Health survey of outpatient psychiatric services, Russo and Olmeda (1983) found that 60% of the adult patients 18–64, were female, with Black females having the highest admission rate. Like their White counterparts, the majority of the Black female patients were married and were diagnosed as depressed. More recent studies of multiethnic populations in urban outpatient psychiatric clinics have documented utilization rates ranging from 15% to over 30% for Black women, primarily from low-income backgrounds (deFirgueiredo and Boestler, 1988; Fabrega, Mezzich, and Ulrich, 1988).

In evaluating the differential utilization rates of Black women as compared to White women and Black men, one must understand the social forces which influence their use of mental health services. These include inaccessible health care facilities, lack of health insurance, negative or ambivalent attitudes about mental health providers, and differential treatment within the mental health system (Copeland, 1982; Sue, 1988). For example, Russo and Olmedo (1983) found in their survey that minority women were less likely than White women to receive individual psychotherapy and more likely to receive drug therapy for their psychological problems.

The tendency of Black women to employ alternative methods to cope with psychological stress depresses their utilization rates of formal mental health services. These alternative methods include prayer, extended family support, and sharing limited resources (Dressler, 1985; Neighbors, Jackson, Bowman, and Gunn, 1983). Black women in predominantly Black communities benefit from a number of community structures and institutions which are often unavailable to their counterparts who live in predominantly White communities, such as the extended Black family, neighborhood and in social networks, the Black church, Black civic and social organizations, and Black economic and political institutions (Cheatham, 1990, Giddings, 1984).

For example in her study of Black women community workers, Gilkes (1983) found that their motivation to pursue careers in community work and their motivation to sustain these efforts were closely linked to a sense of community both on the local and national level. These findings are important in understanding the contextual environment that promotes individual and community empowerment as documented in recent research on citizen participation and community development (Chavis and Wandersman, 1990).

In examining mental health issues for Black women, it is not always clear how their mental health problems are related to sexism, a shared identity with all women, or to racism, a shared identity with Black men. However, we agree with the position of Smith and Stewart (1983) that racism and sexism, while independent parallel processes, are also dynamically related to each other. These authors present a compelling argument that Black women have *unique issues* due to their "double jeopardy" status as both Black and female, yet there may be some situations in which this status is perceived as positive and beneficial, e.g., the stereotype of the Black women as strong (cf. Epstein, 1973; Gibbs, 1985b; Smith, 1986). It is important to acknowledge the interactive and dynamic nature of sexism and racism impinging daily on the lives of Black women and to evaluate the situational context of their experiences in order to determine the relative contribution of race or sex as variables in their treatment and in their response to it. Notwithstanding this caveat, it is rather clear from this review that Black women are generally more likely than White and other minority women to experience stresses associated with poverty, racial discrimination, marital instability, severe health problems, violent neighborhoods, lack of access to social and economic resources, and barriers to social mobility (Belle, 1990; Farley and Allen, 1989). On the other hand, they may experience less relative discrimination than Black males in education and employment, have access to greater social support networks, and be more likely to seek professional help for psychological problems.

Although these patterns emerge from a variety of studies, much more research is needed to tease out the relative advantages and disadvantages of the dual marginal status of Black women, their differential vulnerability to stress, and their unique defensive strategies and coping mechanisms, and their use of community resources to empower themselves (Ladner, 1986; Smith and Stewart, 1983).

INTERVENTIONS FOR BLACK WOMEN'S MENTAL HEALTH

This section will focus on three major strategies to address the mental health issues of Black women from a community psychology perspective, e.g.: primary prevention, early intervention, and community-based interventions. The discussion will highlight selected approaches which facilitate the development of coping strategies and reinforce a sense of empowerment among Black women.

Primary Prevention and Early Intervention Approaches

Primary prevention approaches to facilitate the development of psychological well-being and positive mental health among Black women must be embedded in the context of local Black community development and empowerment, with the goal of increasing Black women's opportunities for social and economic self-sufficiency (Allen and Britt, 1983; Bennett, 1987; Copeland, 1982).

Critics of the prevention model argue that when "at-risk" populations such as Black women are identified, they are treated as "children" in need of programs which will intercede before these inevitable problems erupt (Rappaport, 1981). An empowerment model implies that many competencies exist which are thwarted due to social structural barriers and a lack of resources, but these competencies can be strengthened through the support of Black women's local community groups, rather than large centralized social agencies and institutions which control resources.

Examples of such community-based programs are: Afrocentric private schools established in several large cities, senior citizens' recreational and social programs, youth programs for at-risk teenagers, and neighborhood security patrols to deter crime, many of which have been initiated and directed by Black women in their local communities.

Research informed by the empowerment model would study the mediating structures in Black communities such as the church, the family, the neighborhood and voluntary organizations within which the process of empowerment takes place. This approach, however, requires that Black women be viewed not just as child-like "at-risk" individuals with needs, nor simply as citizens with rights and responsibilities. Rather, they would be seen as human beings with both rights and needs which can be met through community-based solutions that promote the empowerment of women (Rappaport, 1981, 1985).

Community-Based Interventions

Community-based interventions to reduce the stressors affecting low-income Black women were pioneered in the initial phase of the community mental health movement as community outreach programs (Gary, 1987; Neighbors, 1984). These programs include agency-based, church-based, and voluntary organization-based programs.

Agency-based programs include parenting groups for teenage mothers and single parent support groups for grandmothers raising their grandchildren, self-help groups for stress management and weight control (Boyd-Franklin, 1987; Mays, 1985–1986). Urban Black churches have also developed extensive programs of education and economic development to enable their members to improve their skills and enhance their economic independence (Harding, 1990).

FUTURE DIRECTIONS

This review of Black women's mental health underscores a number of critical issues for community psychologists in planning programs and services to address their needs and to promote empowerment. These issues will require innovative approaches in the areas of research, education and training, and the delivery of services which are culturally sensitive and responsive to the unique issues facing Black women.

Research Issues

In the area of research, the paucity of data on the specific stressors, patterns of symptomatology, coping strategies and help seeking behaviors among Black women is striking. The prevalence of psychiatric disorders for Black women is masked by including them in the totals for all Black subjects, thus making it impossible for researchers to identify any unique patterns which differentiate them from Black or White males or White females.

The study of empowerment for Black women cannot escape the analysis of both the separate and interactive influences of racism and sexism. In order to better understand their impact, Smith and Stewart (1983) propose several changes in research which will promote an interactive contextual model for understanding the unique experience of Black women. These researchers call for the inclusion of "gender-race group" analysis. Pointing out the propensity to focus on either the race effects (Black vs. White) or the gender effects (men vs. women) in research designed to study the process of racism or sexism, Smith and Stewart (1983) recommend focusing on the group (i.e., Black women) to study the separate and joint effects of racism and sexism. They argue that "group analysis" rather than "effects analysis" will better clarify the specific experience of racism and sexism for Black women which is unique to their group. The reality of racism and sexism can interfere with the development of one's potential (Rose, 1990) thus, research as well as clinical work should include this contextual perspective.

Community psychologists, in particular, should focus their research agendas on identifying the coping mechanisms and adaptive strategies of Black women, who have demonstrated their remarkable resiliency in the face of generations of persistent poverty, discrimination, and lack of social and economic resources (Allen, 1981; Copeland, 1982; Farley, 1988).

In conjunction with studies of coping behaviors, researchers should also further investigate the "protective" factors which buffer the effects of stress in Black women (Belle, 1990; Ladner, 1986; Smith and Stewart, 1983). For example, more studies are needed to reconcile the sometimes conflicting findings of presumed protective factors such as social support systems, marriage and parenthood, religiosity, high socioeconomic status, and social mobility. Future studies of Black women should also recruit samples which are more representative of the diversity in this group, including women in White collar, technical and professional occupations, as well as women who live in a variety of urban, suburban, and rural settings.

One of the major issues in research on Black populations is the validity and reliability of psychodiagnostic instruments used to assess their mental health (Snowden and Todman, 1982; Williams, 1986). Instruments must be developed which are culturally appropriate and psychometrically valid for Black women in all areas of psychological functioning, including symptom check-lists, psychiatric interview schedules, and nonclinical measures of personality and adaptive functioning (Neighbors, Jackson, Campbell, and Williams, 1989).

Finally, in analyzing their data from inter-ethnic or intra-ethnic studies, researchers need to use more sophisticated multivariate analytic techniques in order to isolate the effects of race, gender, and socioeconomic status (Neighbors, 1984).

Education and Training

Translating an expanded knowledge base about the mental health of Black women into graduate school curricula and clinical training programs is the next step, since most psychology training programs currently lack sufficient information about cultural diversity and do not adequately prepare graduate students to deliver services to minority and low-income clients (Evans, 1985; Gibbs, 1985a).

Despite increased recruitment efforts since the early 1970s, minority students are still underrepresented in psychology graduate programs, so university faculties must continue to make concerted efforts to recruit and mentor minority students. Increasing the number of Black psychologists will not only provide more practitioners who will serve disadvantaged minority populations, but it will also produce more researchers and educators who will ultimately increase the knowledge base about Black mental health issues.

Curricula of graduate training programs should be revised to incorporate the growing literature about minorities and cross-cultural psychology, so that this content is "mainstreamed" into all courses and not treated as peripheral material by the faculty and students (Casas, 1985; Evans, 1985; Gibbs, 1985a). As the population of the United States becomes increasingly non-White, the goal of producing culturally-competent psychologists, is a realistic need rather than an idealistic fantasy (Gibbs and Huang, 1989; Isaacs, 1986).

Clinical and community training facilities must include Black male and female clients as well as Black supervisors and consultants, so that graduate psychology interns can become familiar with the range of mental health issues of Black women (Gibbs, 1985a; Gray and Jones, 1987). By gaining experience with Blacks at all levels of the mental health delivery systems, community psychologists will learn effective strategies of prevention, intervention, and treatment with Black women and their families. It is especially important for them to learn how to differentiate between behaviors and complaints that reflect cultural norms and those that reflect psychopathology or dysfunctional family structures, as well as to recognize organizational and social forces within communities which create environmental stressors.

Service Delivery Issues

Many recent publications have discussed the issues of developing and delivering cultur-ally competent services to Black and other minority populations (e.g., Gibbs and Huang, 1989; Neighbors, 1987; Sue, 1988). These issues involve financing, staff recruitment, service delivery patterns, community relations, and continuum of care systems (Isaacs, 1986). To serve Black women more effectively, community mental health centers need more outreach programs, more flexible schedules, better relationships with the "gate-keepers" in the Black community to legitimize their services, more Black staff members, more programs to meet the expressed needs of the local community, and more effective linkages with a range of social services and other service systems for better coordinated services to Black women and their families.

Public Policy and Prevention Issues

Community psychologists need to form coalitions with other human service profession-als to advocate public policies which will substantially modify the social and environmental stresses which Black and other low-income women experience. These efforts should include the establishment of a comprehensive family policy with minimum family income supports, universal health care, education and training programs for unskilled women and men, low-income housing, child care benefits for working women, and legislation to promote equal opportunity in hiring, wages, and promotion (cf. Edelman, 1987; Schorr, 1986). Advocacy efforts should also be directed to stronger enforcement of civil rights laws, rehabilitation of inner-city neighborhoods, and expansion of educational and employment opportunities for Black youth (Gibbs, 1988). Programs of family planning, pregnancy prevention, and teenage pregnancy and parenthood classes are particularly important for lower-income Black adolescent females (Edelmen, 1987).

Such policies and programs would gradually alleviate and ultimately eliminate many of the structural and economic barriers to the ability of Black women to achieve their full potential in American society. As Neighbors (1987) points out, community psychologists should become more involved in primary prevention activities, collaborating with practi-tioners and local community leaders in the development, implementation, and evaluation of activities such as early childhood and school-based intervention programs, youth job training programs, and adult workforce programs designed to alter the participants' competence, self-esteem and expectancies for future success.

This collaborative model represents a rational response to the crisis in health and mental health care for inner-city populations and it also utilizes the talents and resources of Black women leaders. Community psychologists must face the challenge of developing a viable framework for effective collaboration with other mental health professionals and commu-nity leaders in the promotion of positive mental health and political empowerment for Black women, their families, and their communities.

SUMMARY AND CONCLUSIONS

The major goals of this paper were to describe the mental health issues of low income urban Black women, to discuss research, intervention and public policy related to these issues, and to identify effective approaches for community psychologists working with

Black women. The task has been complicated by a number of factors, including the lack of empirical and clinical research on this group, the problematic methodological limitations of many of the studies, the conflicting findings, and the tendency to generalize findings from low-income urban samples to the entire population of Black women.

Black women constitute a very diverse group with a range of mental health issues, coping mechanisms, adaptive behaviors, and service needs. Despite their diversity, Black women also share the common background of slavery, discrimination, economic exploitation, poverty and powerlessness. Since the Civil Rights Movement of the 1960s, they have experienced mixed gains, as they have benefitted from the educational and economic advances, yet they have also been exposed to the increased stresses of integration, mobility and marginality.

Research studies from a broad interdisciplinary search were reviewed and summarized to determine the factors correlated with psychological well-being among Black women, their help-seeking patterns and attitudes toward mental health services, their patterns of symptomatology, and the risk and protective factors which moderate their ability to handle stress. As in the community surveys of Black women, higher levels of symptomatology and poorer mental health were often significantly related to being poor, non-married, unemployed, and younger. Protective factors for Black women included higher socioeconomic status, marriage, employment, older age, and some type of social networks. In fact, Black women frequently utilized informal social networks as their first source of support for emotional distress.

Prevention approaches to address some of the macro-environmental issues impacting on the mental health of Black women were briefly discussed. Early intervention approaches as well as community interventions were described, emphasizing the contribution of churches, community agencies, and self-help groups in empowering Black women to confront the stress-producing factors in their lives. An alternative perspective based on an empowerment model views Black women as active change agents with unrecognized competencies to modify their environments and improve their lives.

Finally, a number of suggestions were proposed to address the obvious need for more information and more attention in community psychology to the status of Black women in this society, including improvements in research designs and methods, changes in education and training programs, and the development of culturally competent service delivery systems.

As the twenty-first century dawns, the field of community psychology must respond to the challenges of an increasingly multiethnic population which will require new theoretical paradigms, new assessment measures, new research methodologies, and new ways of interpreting and treating human behavior from a cross-cultural perspective. Black women are clearly a population group in search of this post-modern breed of research-practitioners, who will, like the Phoenix, rise from the ashes of the outmoded and increasingly irrelevant approaches of today.

NOTE

Articles used in this paper were identified through database searches in PsychLit and Sociofile, limited primarily to the years 1975–1991. In addition to community psychology journals, selected journals in psychiatry, social work, and interdisciplinary mental health fields were particularly useful.

BIBLIOGRAPHY

Adebimpe, V. (1981). Overview: White norms and psychiatric diagnosis of Black patients. *American Journal of Psychiatry*, 138, 279–285.

Allen, W. R. (1981). The social and economic status of Black women in the United States. *Phylon*, 42, 26–40.

Allen, L., and Britt, D. (1983). Black women in American society: A resource development perspective. *Issues in Mental Health Nursing*, 5, 61–79.

Aschenbrenner, J. (1983). Lifelines: Black families in Chicago. Prospect Heights, IL: Waveland Press.

Atkinson, D. (1985). A meta-review of research on cross-cultural counseling and psychotherapy. *Journal of Multicultural Counseling and Development*, 10, 138–153.

Baskin, D., Bluestone, H., and Nelson, M. (1981). Mental illness in minority women. *Journal of Clinical Psychology*, 37, 491–498.

Bass, B. A., Wyatt, G. E., and Powell, G. (Eds.). (1982). *The Afro-American family: Assessment, treatment, and research issues*. New York: Grune and Stratton.

Beck, R. W., and Beck, S. H. (1989). The incidence of extended households among middle-aged Black and white women. *Journal of Family Issues*, 10, 147–168.

Belle, D. (1982). *Lives in stress: Women and depression*. Beverly Hills, CA: Sage.

Belle, D. (1990). Poverty and women's mental health. *American Psychologist*, 45, 385–389.

Bennett, M. B. (1987). Afro-American women, poverty and mental health: A social essay. *Women and Health*, 12, 213–228.

Billingsley, A. (1968). *Black families in White America*. Englewood Cliffs, NJ: Prentice-Hall.

Boyd-Franklin, M. (1987). Group therapy for Black women: A therapeutic support model. *American Journal of Orthopsychiatry*, 57, 394–401.

Brown, D. B., and Gary, L. E. (1985). Social support network differentials among married and unmarried Black females. *Psychology of Women Quarterly*, 9, 229–241.

Brown, D. B., and Gary, L. E. (1987). Stressful life events, social support networks and physical and mental health of urban Black adults. *Journal of Human Stress*, 13, 165–174.

Camino, L. (1989). Nerves, worriation, and Black women: A community study in the American south. *Health Care for Women International*, 10, 295–314.

Casas, J. M. (1985). The status of racial and ethnic minority counseling: A training perspective. In P. B. Pedersen (Ed.), *Handbook of cross-cultural counseling and therapy* (pp. 267–274). Westport, CT: Greenwood Press.

Chavis, D., and Wandersman, A. (1990). Sense of community in the urban environment: A catalyst for participation and community development. *American Journal of Community Psychology*, 18, 55–81.

Cheatham, H. E. (1990). Empowering black families. In H. E. Cheatham and J. B. Stewart (Eds.), *Black families: Interdisciplinary perspectives*. New Brunswick, NJ: Transaction Publishers.

Coleman, L., Antonucci, T., Adelman, P., and Crohan, S. (1987). Social roles in the lives of middle aged and older Black women. *Journal of Marriage and the Family*, 49, 761–771.

Comstock, G. W., and Helsing, K. J. (1976). Symptoms of depression in two communities. *Psychological Medicine*, 6, 551–563.

Copeland, E. J. (1982). Oppressed conditions and the mental health needs of low-income Black women: Barriers to services, strategies for change. *Women and Therapy*, 1, 13–26.

Cottingham, C. (1989). Gender shift in Black communities. *Dissent*, 36, 521–525.

deFigueiredo, J., and Boerstler, H. (1988). The relationship of presenting complaints to the use of psychiatric services in a low income group. *American Journal of Psychiatry*, 245, 1145–1148.

Dill, B. T. (1979). The dialectics of Black womanhood. *Signs: Journal of Women in Culture* and Society, 4, 543–555.

Dressler, W. (1985). Extended family relationships, social support, and mental health in a Southern Black community. *Journal of Health and Social Behavior*, 26, 39–48.

Eaton, W., and Kessler, L. (1981). Rates of symptoms of depression in a national sample. *American Journal of Epidemiology*, 114, 528–538.

Edelman, M. W. (1987). *Families in peril: An agenda for social change.* Cambridge, MA: Harvard University Press.

Edwards, K. L. (1987). Exploratory study of Black psychological health. *Journal of Religion and Health,* 26, 73–80.

Epstein, C. (1973). The positive effects of the multiple negative: Explaining the success of Black professional women. In J. Huber (Ed.), *Changing women in a changing society* (pp. 150–173). Chicago, IL: University of Chicago Press.

Evans, D. A. (1985), Psychotherapy and Black patients: Problems of training, trainees, and trainers. *Psychotherapy,* 22, 457–460.

Fabrega, H., Jr., Mezzich, J., and Ulrich, R. F. (1988). Black-white differences in psychopathology in an urban psychiatric population. *Comprehensive Psychiatry,* 29, 285–297.

Farley, R. (1988). After the starting line: Blacks and women in an uphill race. *Demography,* 24(4), 477–495.

Farley, R. and Allen, W. R. (1989). *The color line and the quality of life in America.* New York: Oxford University Press.

Gary, L. E. (1987). Attitudes of Black adults toward community mental health centers. *Hospital and Community Psychiatry,* 38, 1100–1105.

Gibbs, J. T. (1985a). Can we continue to be color blind and class bound? *The Counseling Psychologist,* 13, 426–435.

Gibbs, J. T. (1985b). City girls: Psychosocial adjustment of urban Black adolescent females. *Sage: A scholarly journal of Black women.*

Gibbs, J. T. (Ed.). (1988). *Young, Black, and male in America: An endangered species.* Westport, CT: Greenwood Press.

Gibbs, J. T., and Huang, L. N. and Associates (1989). *Children of color: Psychological interventions with minority youth.* San Francisco, CA: Jossey-Bass Publishers.

Giddings, P. (1984). *When and where I enter: The impact of Black women on race and sex in America.* New York: William Morrow and Company.

Gilkes, C. (1983). Going up for the oppressed: The career mobility of Black women community workers. *Journal of Social Issues,* 39, 115–139.

Gordon, R., Hamilton, S., Webb, S., Gordon, K., and Plutzky, M. (1976–77). Psychiatric problems of the 1970s. *International Journal of Social Psychiatry,* 22, 253–264.

Gould, K. (1987). Feminist principles and minority concerns: Contributions, problems, and solutions. *Affilia: Journal of Women and Social Work,* 3, 6–19.

Gray, B. A. and Jones, B. E. (1987). Psychotherapy and Black women: A survey. *Journal of the National Medical Association,* 79, 177–181.

Gutierrez, L. (1990). Working with women of color: An empowerment perspective. *Social Work,* 35, 149–153.

Harding, V. (1990). The role of the Black church in the Black community.

Holahan, C., Betak, J., Spearly, J., and Chance, B. (1983). Social integration and mental health in a biracial community. *American Journal of Community Psychology,* 11, 301–311.

Hull, G. T., Scott, P. B., and Smith, B. (Eds.). (1982). *All the women are White, all the Blacks are men but some of us are brave.* Old Westbury, NY: The Feminist Press.

Isaacs, M. R. (1986). *Developing Mental Health Programs for Minority Youth and Their Families: A Summary of Conference Proceedings.* Georgetown University Child Development Center, CASSP Technical Assistance Center, Washington, D.C.

Johnson, E. (1989). Psychiatric morbidity and health problems among Black Americans: A national survey. *Journal of the National Medical Association,* 81, 1217–1223.

Kasl, S. V., and Harburg, E. (1975). Mental health and the urban environment: Some doubts and second thoughts. *Journal of Health and Social Behavior,* 16, 268–282.

Kessler, R., and Neighbors, H. (1986). A new perspective on the relationship among race, social class and psychological distress. *Journal of Health and Social Behavior,* 27, 107–115.

Ladner, J. A. (1986). Black women face the twenty-first century: Major issues and problems. *The Black Scholar,* Sept.–Oct., 12–19.

Mays, V. (1985–86). Black women and stress: Utilization of self-help groups for stress reduction. *Women and Therapy*, 4, 67–79.

McAdoo, H. P. (1981). *Black families*. Beverly Hills, CA: Sage.

Mollica, R., Blum, J., and Redlich, F. (1980). Equity and the psychiatric care of the black patient, 1950–1975. *Journal of Nervous and Mental Disease*, 168, 279–286.

Moore, T. (1982). Blacks: Rethinking service. In L. R. Snowden (Ed.), *Reaching the underserved: Mental health needs of neglected populations* (pp. 165–184). Beverly Hills, CA: Sage.

Morell, C. (1987). Cause is function: Toward a feminist model of integration for social work. *Social Science Review*, 61, 144–155.

Mukherjee, S., Skukla, S., Woodle, J., et al. (1983). Misdiagnosis in bipolar patients: A multiethnic comparison. *American Journal of Psychiatry*, 140, 1571–1574.

Murray, S. R., and Mednick, M. T. (1977). Black women's achievement orientation: Motivational and cognitive factors. *Psychology of Women Quarterly*, 1, 247–259.

Myers, H. (1982). Stress, ethnicity and social class: A model for research with Black populations. In E. Jones and S. Korchin (Eds.), *Minority mental health* (pp. 118–148). New York: Praeger.

Neighbors, H. W. (1984). The distribution of psychiatric morbidity in Black Americans: A review and suggestions for research. *Community Mental Health Journal*, 20, 169–181.

Neighbors, H. W. (1987). Improving the mental health of Black Americans: Lessons from the community mental health movement. *The Milbank Quarterly*, 65, 348–380.

Neighbors, H. W., and Howard, C. (1987). Sex differences in professional help seeking among adult Black Americans. *American Journal of Community Psychology*, 15, 403–417.

Neighbors, H. W., and Jackson, J. S. (1984). The use of informal and formal help: Four patterns of illness behavior in the Black community. *American Journal of Community Psychology*, 12, 629–644.

Neighbors, H. W., Jackson, J. S., Campbell, L., and Williams, D. (1989). The influence of racial factors on psychiatric diagnosis: A review and suggestions for research. *Community Mental Health Journal*, 24, 301–311.

Neighbors, H. W., Jackson, J. S., Bowman, P., and Gurin, G. (1983). Stress, coping and Black mental health: Preliminary findings from a national study. *Prevention in Human Services*, 2, 5–29.

Parker, K. D., and Ray, M. C. (1990). Fear of crime: An assessment of related factors. *Sociological Spectrum*, 10, 29–40.

Pinderhughes, E. (1983). Empowerment for our clients and ourselves. *Social Casework*, 64, 331–338.

Pinderhughes, E. P. (1989). *Understanding race, ethnicity and power*. New York: The Free Press.

Powell, G. J. (1985). Self-concepts among Afro-American students in racially isolated schools: Some regional differences. *Journal of the American Academy of Child Psychiatry*, 24, 142–149.

Rappaport, J. (1981). In praise of paradox: A social policy of empowerment over prevention. *American Journal of Community Psychology*, 2, 1–25.

Rappaport, J. (1985). The power of empowerment language. *Social Policy*, 17, 15–21.

Redmond, S. P. (1988). An analysis of the general well-being of Blacks and whites: Results of a national study. *Journal of Sociology and Social Welfare*, 15, 57–71.

Reskin, B. F., and Coverman, S. (1985). Sex and race in the determinants of psychophysical distress: A reappraisal of the sex-role hypothesis. *Social Forces*, 63, 1038–1059.

Riger, S., and Gordon, M. (1983). The impact of crime on urban women. *Issues in Mental Health Nursing*, 5, 139–156.

Rose, S. (1990). Advocacy/empowerment: An approach to clinical practice for social work. *Journal of Sociology and Social Welfare*, 17, 41–51.

Russo, N., and Olmedo, E. (1983). Women's utilization of outpatient psychiatric services: Some emerging priorities for rehabilitation psychologists. *Rehabilitation Psychology*, 28, 141–155.

Schorr, A. (1986). *Common decency: Domestic policies after Reagan*. New Haven: Yale University Press.

Smith, A. (1986). Positive marginality: The experience of Black women leaders. In E. Seidman and J. Rappaport (Eds.), *Redefining social problems* (pp. 101–113). New York: Plenum Press.

Smith, A., and Stewart, A. (1983). Approaches to studying racism and sexism in Black women's lives. *Journal of Social Issues*, 39, 1–15.

Snowden, L. R., and Todman, P. A. (1982). The psychological assessment of Blacks: New and needed developments. In E. E. Jones and E. J. Korchin (Eds.), *Minority mental health* (pp. 193–226). New York: Praeger.

Solomon, B. (1976). *Black empowerment: Social work in oppressed communities.* New York: Columbia University Press.

Stack, C. (1974). *All our kin: Strategies for survival in a Black community.* New York: Harper and Row.

Staples, R., and Mirande, A. (1980). Racial and cultural variations among American families: A decennial review of the literature on minority families. *Journal of Marriage and the Family*, 887–903.

Sue, S. (1988). Psychotherapeutic services for ethnic minorities: Two decades of research findings. *American Psychologist*, 43, 301–308.

Sussman, L. K., Robins, L. N., and Earls, F. (1987). Treatment-seeking for depression by Black and white Americans. *Social Science Medicine*, 24, 187–196.

Thompson, M., and Ensminger, M. (1989). Psychological well-being among mothers with school-aged children: Evolving family structures. *Social Forces*, 67, 715–730.

Tomlinson, S., and Cope, N. (1988). Characteristics of Black students seeking help at a university counseling center. *Journal of College Student Development*, 29, 65–69.

Turner, C. W. (1987). Clinical applications of the Stone Center theoretical approach to minority women. *Work-in-Progress*, 28, 1–17.

Ulbricht, P., Warheit, G., and Zimmerman, R. (1989). Race, socioeconomic status and psychological distress: An examination of differential vulnerability. *Journal of Health and Social Behavior*, 30, 131–146.

U.S. Bureau of the Census (1990a). *Household and family characteristics.* Current Population Reports: Series P-20, No. 447.

U.S. Bureau of the Census (1990c). *Money income and poverty status.* Current Population Reports: Series P-60, No. 168.

U.S. Bureau of the Census (1989). *The Black population in the United States: March 1988.* Current Population Reports: Series P-20, No. 442.

Vernon, S., and Roberts, R. (1981). Measuring nonspecific psychological distress and other dimensions of psychopathology. *Archives of General Psychiatry*, 38, 1239–1247.

Warheit, G., Holzer, C., and Arey, S. (1975). Race and mental illness: An epidemiological update. *Journal of Health and Social Behavior*, 16, 243–256.

Watts-Jones, D. (1990). Toward a stress scale for African-American women. *Psychology of Women Quarterly*, 14, 271–275.

Weissman, M., Leaf, P., and Bruce, M. (1987). Single parent women: A community study. *Social Psychiatry*, 22(1), 29–36.

White, M., Kasl, S., Zahner, G., and Will, J. (1987). Perceived crime in the neighborhood and mental health of women and children. *Environment and Behavior*, 19(5), 588–613.

Williams, D. H. (1986). The epidemiology of mental illness in Afro-Americans. *Hospital and Community Psychiatry*, 37, 42–49.

Wilson, W. J. (1987). *The truly disadvantaged.* Chicago: The University of Chicago Press.

Woody, B. (1989). Black women in the emerging service economy. *Sex Roles*, 21, 45–67.

Zimmerman, M. (1990). Taking aim on empowerment research: On the distinction between individual and psychological conceptions. *American Journal of Community Psychology*, 18, 169–177.

25.

Substance Abuse Treatment

Cultural Barriers
in the Asian American Community

Davis Y. Ja and Bart Aoki

Asians constitute the largest growing minority in the United States. However, inaccurate perceptions and stereotypes continue to mask a full understanding of the state of knowledge regarding their alcohol and other drug abuse. Much of the existing research has continued this trend by categorizing Asians as "others" or persisting in its attempts to explain low incidence rates by investigating metabolic phenomena. More recent community-based studies have shown alarming incidence rates of specific substance abuse among different Asian ethnic groups. Asian heterogeneity and cultural barriers have also contributed to the lack of knowledge regarding substance abuse prevalence rates. Issues related to taboo, denial, and loss of face further mask understanding of the extent of the problem. Institutional barriers and the lack of community infrastructure make treatment efforts difficult in serving a myriad of Asian groups. For most Asians undergoing treatment, cultural factors need to be considered, including the involvement of the family as well as the risk related to its transition under immigration and the following acculturation patterns. An example of a specific treatment program and activity is discussed in relationship to the cultural factors indicated above. Finally, recommendations are specified for future treatment policy, research, and services.

Preliminary statistics from the U.S. Census Bureau for 1990 reveal that the number of Asians in America has increased a total of 107.8% since 1980. This increase is over twice as much as the next largest group, Hispanics, which increased only 53% since 1980. In 1980, Asians and Pacific Islanders constituted 1.9% (3.5 million) of the total population of the United States. In 1990, the number of Asians and Pacific Islanders had grown to 2.9% (7.2 million). Although the Asian population is still small in proportion to the total population of the United States, Asians are the fastest growing ethnic minority group in the United States, with large concentrations in major metropolitan cities, particularly in coastal cities and counties. For example, Asians in New York City number over 500,000 and comprise 7% of the total population. Asians also represent 29% of the population of San Francisco, and 5.3% of the population of Boston.

Asian and Pacific Islanders have suffered from inaccurate stereotypes about their use and abuse of drugs since the first Asians began to emigrate to the continental United States over 150 years ago. Historically, Westerners considered Asians responsible for spawning opium abuse, disregarding the fact that this practice had been fostered in China by Western imperialism. Today, new notions of Asians as "model minorities," depicted in numerous publications and news weeklies, have contributed to beliefs that Asians use alcohol as well as illegal substances at a lower rate than other groups.

Unfortunately, much of the available research reflecting these findings is fraught with methodological weaknesses and questionable assumptions. This article briefly summarizes the issues related to understanding the current state of knowledge regarding substance abuse in the Asian community, describes institutional barriers and cultural factors that impact the development of treatment approaches, and proposes some models that integrate cultural issues within a treatment paradigm. Finally, implications for policy at different levels of government are discussed, with recommendations for implementation.

CURRENT STATE OF KNOWLEDGE

Fundamental research on substance abuse treatment for Asians is simply not available. The lack of information regarding treatment issues is partially due to three factors: (1) little data and statistics are available regarding Asian drug abuse, (2) extant data indicate that Asians have experienced a lower incidence of drug abuse and dependency, and (3) this pattern of lower rates of substance abuse is related to metabolic and/or genetic factors. However, there is evidence to indicate that these assumptions may be erroneous and that the issues related to treatment are not assessed and comprehended. Also, there is evidence to indicate that the incidence level and the subsequent treatment needs of Asians are partially obscured by the ethnic diversities of the Asian population in the United States as well as by linguistic and cultural factors within Asian American populations.

Inadequacy of Prevalence Data

Currently available national database surveys have either continued to ignore Asians or aggregate the Asian and Pacific Islander data under an "other" category. Consequently, information that may exist for Asians is simply made unavailable. For example, while Blacks and Hispanics were heavily represented and targeted in the National Household Survey on Drug Abuse (National Institute on Drug Abuse, 1990c) conducted in 1988–1989, Asians were not reported at all, because they were incorporated into an "other" category and the sample size was too small. Alaska and Hawaii were excluded outright in the sampling population. Also, information from the Drug Abuse Warning Network (DAWN) summarized data on Asians into the "other" category along with Native Americans and Alaskan Eskimos, rendering any data analysis useless (National Institute on Drug Abuse, 1990a).

The Monitoring the Future series conducted by Johnston, O'Malley and Bachman (1984) makes no consideration for the specification of Asian groups. Similarly, the National Household Survey is "representative of high school seniors throughout the 48 coterminous states," but excludes Alaska and Hawaii, and subsequently all Pacific Islanders and many Asians as well. Perhaps the only exception is the point prevalence survey based on utilization of existing alcohol and other drug abuse treatment programs conducted by the National Institute on Drug Abuse (NIDA) and the National Institute on Alcohol Abuse and Alcoholism (NIAAA). The National Drug and Alcoholism Treatment Unit Survey (NDATUS) does provide information on Asians in a separate category, indicating in 1989 that Asians comprise approximately 0.6% of the total population in treatment across both inpatient and out-patient treatment modalities.

The numbers reported by NDATUS are low in contrast to the current total population of Asians in the United States (0.6% versus 2.9%). This may be accounted for by the lack of culturally relevant services, since no treatment units offering specialized programs for Asians were indicated in the report (National Institute on Drug Abuse 1990b). In addition, without information regarding the ethnicities of the specific Asian ethnic groups, the information is rendered less useful.

Accuracy of Available Research

Although no national prevalence or incidence data are available, there does exist a substantial body of research that appears to indicate that Asian populations experience a lower incidence of drug abuse and dependency (Johnson et al., 1987; Kitano, 1982; Sue and Morishima, 1982; Cohen, 1972; Sue, Zane and Ito, 1979). These have been well summarized elsewhere (Trimble, Padilla and Bell, 1987; Alcohol, Drug Abuse and Mental Health Administration, 1985). However, many of these studies have been criticized recently for methodological weaknesses that result in a generalized underestimation of the levels of substance abuse and chemical dependency.

In a summary of the research literature, Zane and Sasao (1992) noted that in many cases student groups were sampled instead of those potentially at greater risk, such as recent immigrants and adolescents. In addition, inadequate sample sizes, lack of controls for demographic and cultural factors, inadequate translations, and lack of consideration of measurement bias in the utilization of self-report procedures have added to the questionable nature of the results.

At least two studies (Morales, 1991; Wong, 1985), which were conducted in community-based settings, have shown that certain Asian groups demonstrate equivalent or higher levels of specific alcohol and other drug abuse compared to other ethnic groups. In addition, Kitano and Chi's (1987) epidemiological efforts in Los Angeles measuring levels of alcohol use revealed strong evidence of the diverse nature of substance abuse among different Asian groups.

These community-based surveys provide a broader glimpse of the patterns of substance abuse and chemical dependency for Asian ethnic groups and contradict earlier findings of lower incidences. In addition, they begin to provide confirmation of observations of the streets of ethnic communities and in the few treatment settings that are Asian ethnic specific. A more concrete illustration of this pattern was found in a newly developed residential program in San Francisco targeting Asian drug abusers. The Asian American Residential Recovery Services (AARRS) opened in San Francisco in 1985. Within a few months it quickly established a six-month waiting list for its 15-bed capacity.

Issues relating to the underutilization of current non-Asian treatment programs are similar to the issues of cultural insensitivity raised by Sue and colleagues (Sue, 1976; Sue and McKinney, 1976) leading to underutilization of mental health treatment programs by Asians. Sue indicated that clients of differing racial and ethnic characteristics were underutilizing mental health treatment services based on failure-to-return rates following a single session. Substantial evidence seemed to indicate that the factors accounting for underutilization of services reflected whether the treatment interventions were culturally and/or linguistically appropriate or responsive to the needs of the ethnic clients. Sue and others (Wu and Windle, 1980) called for a particular emphasis on and increased utilization of ethnic paraprofessionals, the development of ethnic-specific services somewhat reflective of mainstream and traditional agencies as well as new forms of treatment that reflected cultural relevance. Although Sue's efforts focused primarily on Asian Americans, others have confirmed similar findings for Hispanics (Barrera, 1978; Padilla, Ruiz and Alvarez, 1975) and African Americans (Vail, 1978; Sue, 1977).

Genetic and Metabolic Studies

Because of the prevalent assumption of a lower incidence of drug dependence among Asians, numerous studies have focused on uncovering factors contributing to this apparent pattern. For example, since Wolff's initial report in 1973, an extensive body of research has been generated to understand how genetic and metabolic differences between Caucasians and Mongoloids may contribute to a lower rate of alcohol abuse among the latter. These studies (Suddendorf, 1989; Nagoshi et al., 1988; Lee, 1987; Chan, 1986; Suwaki and Ohara, 1985) attributed an apparent lower rate of alcohol abuse to an inability among Mongoloid races to metabolize alcohol due to a missing liver enzyme (ALDH-I isozyme). However, more recent studies (Johnson and Nagoshi, 1990; Newlin, 1989) have concluded that sociocultural factors seem to play a greater role in alcohol use than physiological factors, such as acetaldehyde metabolism.

Unfortunately, the emphasis in investigating genetic and metabolic reasons behind the lower incidence of Asian substance abuse masked the fact that Asians do abuse drugs. The combination of factors including the lack of national survey data and contradictory findings of abuse has led to the "science" of determining factors underlying the lower Asian incidence rates instead of determining accurately the prevalence rates among the different Asian ethnic groups.

Asian Heterogeneity and Cultural Barriers

Other factors add to the paucity of accurate information regarding substance abuse within Asian communities. A substantial difficulty in understanding the full extent of substance abuse in the Asian community lies in the heterogeneity of the population (Cheung, 1989). Asians in the United States are not one monolithic group. There are at least 32 distinct Asian ethnic groups with different languages, customs, and behaviors. The complexity of the different cultural norms, languages, traditions, values, and beliefs of the numerous Asian groups makes it difficult to measure the extent of complicated social problems, such as substance abuse. In some instances, there may in fact exist more differences than similarities among groups on certain dimensions. For substance ab
group may differ not only in the extent of drugs abused but t
drugs are used. Furthermore, other factors, such as generatior
who are American born and those who are native born, may
in use and abuse patterns. Other key factors include geograph
vidual was raised, socioeconomic status, gender, and sexual c

For example, Morales (1991) reported that in a survey of
hol-related driving offenses, alcohol consumption differed
ethnic groups. Japanese respondents reported frequency rate
tion at twice the rate of Koreans, and over three times the
Pacific Islanders reported greater consumption levels at each

level of Japanese and over six times the level of Filipinos. Kitano and Chi's (1987) random-ized survey of 1,103 subjects of male and female Chinese, Japanese, Koreans and Philipinos in Los Angeles showed significant differences in the rates of consumption among all groups, with sizable numbers of heavy drinkers in both the Japanese and Korean samples.

This diversity in ethnicities and in incidence patterns indicates that the heterogeneity of Asian ethnic groups must be a critical factor in any determination of incidence among these groups. Subsequently, Asians cannot be considered a monolithic entity with simple data aggregation to indicate a particular pattern of use. Asian ethnic groups must be measured within each ethnicity to determine actual incidence levels.

Finally, an important factor that adds to the complexity in understanding the extent of substance abuse in the Asian community relates to cultural difficulty in openly acknowl-edging personal problems. Substance abuse is a taboo issue and not easily discussed within the social frameworks of most Asian ethnic communities. Because drug abuse and depen-dency are considered to be a serious breach of behavior within most of these groups, acknowledging this problem often leads to a significant loss of face for both the individ-uals in question and their families.

Consequently, both the family and the community itself may avoid or deny the behav-iors in question at an intensity beyond the levels of denial usually associated with substance abuse. In the California Statewide Alcohol Needs Assessment, as reported by Morales (1991), respondents to a key informant survey overwhelmingly indicated that denial of substance abuse was the primary barrier to seeking treatment for Chinese, Japanese, Korean, Pacific Islanders, Filipinos, and the Southeast Asians. This cultural over-lay may lean toward more hidden levels of substance abuse within certain Asian groups.

In summary, the incidence and patterns of substance abuse within Asian communities are complex, they may differ for each group, they are still misunderstood, and they are most likely underestimated. Preliminary studies in this area are often conflicting and produce findings that suggest an overall lower level of alcohol and other drug abuse, while obser-vations by community members and treatment providers continue to indicate significant levels of abuse.

INSTITUTIONAL AND COMMUNITY BARRIERS TO TREATMENT

For those engaged in providing treatment services in community settings there is some consensus regarding the existence of formidable barriers in the establishment of treatment services for Asian substance abusers, including substantial institutional barriers involving ignorance, denial, and cultural bias as well as barriers within specific Asian communities that impede organizational capability in providing such services.

Institutional Barriers

times of scarce resources, governmental entities charged with providing social and human es may retrench or rigidify systems in ways that effectively prevent meeting the needs nd emerging populations. Specific institutional barriers include underdocument-ck of culturally specific models of treatment, and scarcity of resources.

entation of Need. Much of the available research literature has indicated not ave lower incidence levels of substance abuse but are devoting consid-sources to determining why there are such low incidence rates; this prevents the prerequisite documentation and demonstration of need required for the establishment of services. This is a common bind that most Asian communities encounter in attempting to establish treatment services. The lack of available data only serves to reinforce the notion that Asians do not need treatment services, despite community-reported increases in drug use and sales, particularly among Asian youths. More recently, the growing incidence of violence and crime among Asians has publicized some of the difficulties that communities are attempting to address. Resources necessary to begin documentation are extremely limited and often unavailable to the Asian community. For example, in the past 15 years NIDA has funded only one research project with an emphasis on Asians.

Furthermore, this lack of documentation implies definitions of risk and prevalence that are often inherently biased against emerging and new Asian ethnic groups. Often, dependence on old utilization data continues to indicate low substance abuse rates by Asians, which then perpetuates the cycle of lack of demonstrated need, which justifies the continuing lack of new resources to determine actual incidence. Furthermore, the utilization rates fail to document Asian substance abuse, particularly if it is substantially different from established patterns. In the 1980s, for example, methaqualone was found to be heavily abused by Asian youths (Wong 1985) but this evidence did not emerge in any other database, including utilization studies, simply because the studies relied on data from established heroin, cocaine, and amphetamine treatment programs.

Lack of Culturally Specific Models of Treatment. Similarly, traditional programs providing services to Asians may utilize established and traditional modalities in serving these populations. Programs such as these are often misguided in assuming the generality and universality of approaches in providing treatment for Asians. The 12-Step approach in outpatient treatment, the therapeutic community in residential treatment, and the cognitive behavior models in inpatient treatment all assume a proper "fit" with all clients. For example, the therapeutic milieu was established through an integration of the encounter-group approach based originally on Syanon games (Enright, 1971). As a psychotherapeutic approach, it is based on the premise of "strengthening the patient's motivation to do the right thing." As one of the oldest approaches in counseling (Korchin, 1976), it emphasizes persuasion and social pressure in moving a person along a "right" direction. Yet toward this end there was little emphasis on developing cultural-specific approaches. Substance abusers, in spite of their cultural orientations, were considered to have universal issues that fit the social, peer, and abstention-oriented approaches of Alcoholics Anonymous (AA) and those inspired by Synanon.

Current treatment programs often attempt to establish cultural relevance through translations and assume that this misguided notion will suffice in providing cultural sensitivity. Asian-specific programs within established treatment settings that maintain similar treatment structures and programs, despite an Asian bilingual staff, are also replicating the idea of a universal approach in their basic treatment. Unless treatment programs are developed specifically for an Asian cultural base, the program may fail to retain Asians and the attendant low enrollment may further the evidence of low utilization by Asian communities.

Scarcity of Resources. In the 1990s most governmental institutions experienced substantial budgetary deficits. Most state and local governmental institutions are operating in a deficit mode and have extremely limited resources. Significant problems lie in establishing new services when current services are often underfunded and overextended. Yet changing demographics, particularly in emerging groups such as the Asian and Hispanic communities, have meant increased competition for finite and, more recently, shrinking resources and funding. Given the substantial changes in demographics, different racial and ethnic communities have conflicted at times in competing for available funding to establish programs. For most existing treatment programs, the priority is maintaining current levels of funding, while for new and emerging groups, such as Asians, it means attempting to establish even minimal services. Even within Asian ethnic groups, the differential rates of demographic change may lead to intercommunity conflict and competition. For example, although the Chinese and Japanese communities have numerous established service programs, the Philipino community does not. However, demographic shifts indicate that the Philipino and Chinese communities continue to grow while the Japanese community has reached a plateau.

Lack of Community Infrastructure

With the exception of a few major metropolitan areas, current services do not have a continuum of care available for Asians. The result is that most human and social service providers for Asians, often ill-equipped to deal effectively with substance abuse, are expected to provide the entire range of care.

Given the needs of their populations, most Asian community organizations are willing to provide these services. Moreover, community-based service organizations are often the only source of assistance available to a number of different Asian ethnic groups. More established Asian groups, such as the Chinese and the Japanese, may have a greater range and level of social, health, and human services available in their communities. Other Asian ethnic groups, particularly emerging immigrant groups—such as Philipinos, Vietnamese, Cambodians, Laotians, Thais, and Pacific Islander groups (e.g., Samoans and Tongans)— often find themselves with a single organizational entity attempting to provide social and human services, mental health counseling, job placement and training, housing, case management, recreational services to youths, senior services, and translation, as well as providing free referral and treatment services for the local government programs inadequately addressing these needs. These overburdened organizations are often the only resource for treating substance abuse in the community. Unfortunately, with no or limited resources there is little chance of truly impacting the needs of a substance abusing population.

In communities where substance abuse has become a significant and growing problem, a larger range of services may be established. For example, in major metropolitan areas with large Asian populations, such as San Francisco, Los Angeles and New York, a continuum of services is now available in the areas of social services, mental health or health. However, a significant problem exists in the economic feasibility for local communities to fully develop the entire range of substance abuse treatment services, particularly if they are addressing the needs of three or more specific Asian ethnic groups.

Subsequently, a significant issue in establishing service models is the need to respond to more than one Asian ethnic group. Despite the difficulties of diversity in establishing treatment programs for several Asian groups, economic realities of funding any programs will force this issue given the large number of different Asian groups. Unfortunately, organizational and service models addressing this type of diversity incorporating two or more ethnic groups are lacking. Previous efforts in organizing Asian ethnic groups are more limited to organizations with agendas related to political or advocacy needs.

CULTURAL FACTORS IN TREATMENT OF ASIANS

In reviewing issues related to the etiology of substance abuse, numerous studies have indicated that substance abuse may be caused by a variety of factors. The list of factors that have been studied in relation to substance abuse within the general population is extensive and varied; these etiologic factors and their conceptual bases have been summarized at length (Johnston, O'Malley and Bachman, 1986; Newcomb and Bentler, 1986; Bush and Iannotti, 1985; Hawkins, Lishner and Catalano, 1985; Kandel, 1980; Jessor and Jessor, 1977; O'Leary, O'Leary, and Donovan, 1976).

In brief, factors identified as having a significant relationship to substance abuse include quality of parenting (Shedler and Block, 1990), lack of cognitive and social skills (Hawkins et al., 1989), prior drug use (Newcomb and Bentler, 1987), initial alcohol or cigarette use (Yamaguchi and Kandel, 1984), rebellious and nonconforming personality (Chassin, 1984), peer influences (Brook, Whiteman and Gordon, 1983, 1982), alcohol or other drug abusing parents (Fawzy, Coombs and Gerber, 1983), family disruption or conflicts (Baumrind, 1985), and cultural influences (Zucker and Gomberg, 1986).

A number of longitudinal studies have also determined that the etiologic basis of substance abuse is highly complex and determined by multiple factors, including both interpersonal and intrapersonal influences. Stein, Newcomb and Bentler (1987) found that no one predictor variable accounted for an adequate understanding of the causal basis of substance abuse, but that a number of predictors—such as personal drug use, social conformity, family disruption, adult drug use, and the influence of peers—were all significant contributors.

Cultural factors may play a role in altering the nature or vector of influence as indicated above within the broader non-Asian population. Cheung (1989) distinguished variables related to ethnicity and substance abuse. For many immigrant populations these include cultural beliefs and attitudes toward alcohol and other drugs, levels of cultural retention and assimilation, and the stability and intactness of social organization within an ethnic community. In addition, these cultural and ethnic variables may be unique contributors to substance abuse in that certain cultural values and customs may have a specific bearing on abuse. And finally, certain risk-related factors stemming from family disruptions from immigration, separate from culture and ethnicity per se, also contribute to substance abuse among certain Asian groups.

Cultural Factors and the Asian Family

Cultural factors differ greatly among Asian ethnic groups, particularly when generational, social class, and educational differences occur. Yet, generally with more traditional immigrant Asian families, the topic of substance abuse brings forth the same cultural response to other events, such as mental illness. Within the family and the community, substance abuse is considered a taboo issue when it occurs within their immediate community, particularly if it impacts the functioning of the family. However, if it does not initially affect functioning of the individual, and if the individual fulfills his or her obligation to the family, it may not be considered a problem. Concerns are raised when illegal behavior and/or drug use begin to present evidence of a belief in a defect or weakness in character that influences the individual's functioning in the family. If this functioning is seriously disrupted, then concerns are heightened around the potential shame and loss of face of the family, particularly for the parents.

In traditional Asian cultures the family is the fundamental unit of production (Shon and Ja, 1982). Patrilineal roles and functions vary depending on where the individual is located within the family hierarchy and structure. Communications are often indirect, based on roles, and subsequently are monodirectional within the hierarchy of the family. Emotions are not shared for fear of emphasizing the individual over the mutual and interdependent needs of the family.

Many Asian substance abusers come from intact families, and when substance abuse begins to disrupt functioning within the interdependent Asian family, initial responses from other family members may be to ignore or deny its existence, with some hope that the problem will disappear of its own accord. At the same time, the family will endeavor to isolate and/or insulate the substance abuser from the community. Kept within the family, the family maintains face. Consequently, there is little effort mobilized toward prevention of the problem within the community.

When a family is finally forced to directly confront a serious problem related to substance abuse, the shame and potential loss of face prompt specific cultural responses aimed at reducing the loss of face. The family may attempt traditional methods, such as the act of shaming or castigation or scolding to resolve the issue. At times, in extreme cases, the family may reject the individual, particularly if it is a sibling, and disown him or her. Problem-solving then becomes nearly impossible; to seek outside intervention brings loss of face and shame to the family. When help is sought within the community, the family then implicitly indicates an admission of failure within their family structure to their community and therefore to the world.

The use of intervention most often will be kept within the extended family network system. Relatives, such as uncles, brothers or sisters, may be asked to intervene, again attempting to rationalize or bringing on the sense of obligation that the substance abusing person may have to his or her parents or to the family. Within this process, the family maintains the problems within the confines of a small portion of the community; beginning with the family, later the extended family, and finally to friends, elders, and the extended network. When all else fails and if the deviant behavior becomes unbearable, the family finally moves beyond the boundaries of their traditional problem-solving processes.

When this occurs, social and human service providers within established organizations may be called for assistance. The loss of face, particularly for the father of the family, marks this point as a pivotal one for treatment and assistance. Clients referred by their family often offer the greatest levels of resistance. Because the problem has emerged outside the extended family network (and out of the normal acceptable parameters), the client's personal loss of face and reluctance to receive treatment is particularly difficult to overcome.

Furthermore, most families will request from providers a quick-fix solution, avoiding their personal responsibility when the identified substance abuser is in the treatment program. This is often due to the expectations of the treatment provider as expert in assisting the abuser. Frequently, there is little understanding regarding the role of the family in contributing to the continuation of drug abuse. Experiences in the San Francisco community have indicated that referrals from Asian families have frequently had high expectations and yet the abuser is extremely resistant, angry over the betrayal by the family, and in denial when brought to treatment.

Many Asian families operate with a cultural perspective of family interdependence rather than the more Western value of independence of the individual. Abusers often take advantage of the existing levels of family interdependence. Within this realm, it is not unusual to find a situation where parents have spent what they consider to be all their problem-solving options in dealing with a substance abuser, yet the abuser continues to live at home and receive money from them as well. In this instance, this cultural norm promotes codependency as well as enabling the abuser to continue in his or her life-style.

Immigration and Risk Factors

Numerous studies have documented that Asian immigrants undergo major and significant stressors leading to psychopathology (Lin 1986; Tung 1985), emotional problems (Sue and Morishima 1982), depression (Kuo 1984) family pathology (Shon and Ja 1982), and identity conflicts (Chin 1981).

Due to the difficulties Asians immigrants face—such as inadequate housing and crowdedness, socioeconomic hardships, difficulties with language and development of survival social and vocational skills, and loss of supportive networks (Takaki 1990; Owan 1985)—families often become dysfunctional in the process of migration. However, cultural parameters, such as parental expectations, poor communication, generational differences, and changes in cultural perspectives between parents and children, exacerbate the risk factors for the family and the community. Many youths are latchkey, and yet are expected to fulfill high expectations from parents who are seldom available due to the economic need for all adult members of the family to be employed.

Asian youths are often faced with changing values and customs in the process of assimilation that may culminate in conflict with the traditional customs and values of their parents. When expectations are impossibly high, particularly in regard to success in school when English is a second language, many youths choose to relate to newer and more attractive Western values propagated by the media. As immigrants, attempts at acceptance within their new culture may drive Asian youths away from the traditional ideals of their parents and toward peer groups with markedly different social and moral values. Despite the mixed and inconclusive research findings regarding the rate of Asian substance abuse, Asian (particularly immigrant) youths are highly vulnerable and at risk for significant levels of substance abuse.

When attempting to communicate, parents may utilize traditional methods of discipline, such as shaming, castigating, and exerting their authority. Yet as effective as these methods may be in their native countries, the transition to a new culture has left Asian youths with new alternatives in response to the rigid and structured processes of the family hierarchy. The move to autonomy and independence by youths leads naturally to rebelliousness and greater reliance on peers and youth groups for assistance and guidance.

Asian Treatment Approaches and Models

Several critical variables are necessary in successfully treating the Asian substance abuser. Initially, motivation is a crucial factor. At AARRS, 60% of the clients are court referred. The remainder involve referrals from friends and family, and those who have exhausted financial resources, needing a "safe haven" from debt collectors or facing potential danger from criminal, drug and gang activity, and/or facing possible incarceration. This bottoming-out process often leads the abuser to services with a motivation of getting off the streets and seeking immediate relief, rather than seeking treatment for their substance abuse per se.

Successful treatment may involve a structured treatment paradigm. When the substance abusing individual is initially exposed to the program, concrete or structured program components often mitigate the confusion, the doubts, and the shame associated with being in this environment. A strong focus on orientation, with clear written guidelines and procedures, provides a foundation by which the Asian individual in substance abuse treatment can find stability.

The intake process can provide the initial basis for this through structured questions, clearly written handouts, and requesting that clients participate by completing a portion of the questions themselves. Although structure can be overdone, the initial contact clarity and stability (with rules, regulations, and procedures) need to be established. A particularly important emphasis is to establish precise limit-setting to provide reinforcement to clients regarding the seriousness of the program.

Many clients are initially skeptical regarding drug abuse treatment facilities and programs. There may be considerable fears and anxieties attached to the process. Many of these fears lie in confronting themselves, recognizing their failures, their fears, their lifestyles and being confronted by others on these issues. Embarrassment, shame, and loss of face often bring on an enormous reservoir of resistance.

Individual and group counseling approaches in substance abuse treatment are generally far more confrontational and directive than normal counseling methods. However, an atmosphere of positive support is necessary. In establishing support, peer group processes seem to work well with Asians, particularly if the group is predominantly Asian. In addition, during the group process, new group norms could be developed through an educative process.

Family counseling is an important component for the Asian client. Because most Asians come from intact nuclear families, family support is crucial. Rather than utilizing an expressive or confrontational process, an educative and supportive approach works better to allow family members to begin shifting their behaviors of interdependency and possibly codependency toward better understanding and communication. Family approaches (Shon and Ja, 1982) emphasizing respect and achieving alliances with the parents establishes stronger therapeutic bonds between the counselor and the family.

The I Can Do That Theater: A Cultural Approach to Treatment

Finally, in developing the AARRS residential program and through the use of expressive arts and psychodrama, an example of an important and creative cultural approach was established that helped to break the shame of the individual and the family within the community. At the AARRS program, an award-winning theater project was established—known as the I Can Do That Theater. Residents at AARRS utilize expressive arts and psychodrama techniques to role-play their lives following the development of a personal script. Many of the scripts are based on feelings toward parents of anger, frustration, sadness, and love.

Following months of rehearsal and dealing with the feelings and issues raised during this time with their counselors and fellow residents, a public performance is held in which the community at large is invited. In most instances, the clients' parents attend as well. In the performance, individuals not only act and play out their feelings, but they publicly acknowledge and apologize for their behaviors to the community, to their friends, and to their families. The process is highly charged and emotionally reactive. This public apology and display of remorse is an inherently culturally appropriate procedure. It is essentially a public atonement process that heals the shame and reintegrates the individual and the family back into the community. It reestablishes the individual and the families within the community and provides them with face and pride in overcoming great odds to rid themselves of their addictions.

POLICY, RESEARCH, AND SERVICE IMPLICATIONS

Local communities need to determine the level and range of Asian-specific services predicated on community parameters established by local groups and organizations. These parameters can be based on need, population size, parity, existing levels of organizations and resources, socioeconomic factors, levels of substance abuse, and levels of available staffing or expertise.

A significant first step is to provide planning and research grants that can begin the process of determining what specific steps need to be taken as well as understanding the extent of the problem in the local community. If federal funds are unavailable, then local governments can begin funding for needs assessment through focus groups, gatekeeper surveys, and convenience samples or surveys utilizing chain referral or snowball sampling methods for each specific Asian group. This will help establish a proper perspective regarding need and the extent of the problem. Planning should incorporate multiple Asian groups and organizations and, if necessary, working with non-Asian organizations with substance abuse expertise.

In many Asian communities, established community-based organizations with a "critical mass" of funding, staffing, and experience may need to assume the lead in developing substance abuse treatment services. For most, establishing prevention services for youths and families may later lead to development of treatment services to youths and adults on an outpatient basis. Prevention services—including education, information and outreach, short-term crisis counseling, case management, and information/referral services—are more often within the reach of the organizational framework of most Asian human services agencies. Other treatment services require a specific expertise that cannot be predicated on case management or short-term counseling approaches and may be beyond the scope of many Asian organizations.

The provision of more formidable treatment services to addicts requires sophisticated levels of expertise, including possible detoxification, medical care and possibly pharmacological care through methadone maintenance—a treatment regime that is often unavailable for Asian Americans. For most communities, existing and current levels of care for this population, whether Asian or White, are inadequately meeting the existing needs of substance abusers. Often, waiting lists are established with wait periods as long as six months to a year. Furthermore, few facilities are prepared to provide culturally sensitive or competent services. Most have no linguistic capability to provide services, whether it is outpatient, inpatient or residential.

With these presenting needs, there is a challenge to develop a model that provides adequate language capability and yet culturally competent services. There are no simple answers to resolving these needs. The most significant question is whether a model of treatment can be developed to address specific ethnic and cultural characteristics of multiple Asian ethnic groups with relevance to both immigrant and nonimmigrant populations.

Advocacy and development of community links are related issues that may lead to alternative service models. This may require working closely with existing non-Asian substance abuse treatment organizations, negotiating with limited funding sources, and providing bilingual staff and culturally sensitive programing for Asians referred to these sites.

For some ethnic groups, particularly recent refugees in more rural or less Asian-populated cities, there are other alternatives that may require fewer resources:

1. Develop planning and self-help groups working with community, social, and religious organizations.
2. Build a consortium with other Asian ethnic groups to establish a minimum base of services.
3. If necessary, integrate a service unit into an existing non-Asian organization with expertise in substance abuse treatment.
4. Establish consultation pools of trained community persons who could consult with other Asian or non-Asian organizations in providing services.
5. Build and utilize indigenous and alternative traditional models of services, including acupuncture, traditional healing, and spirituality.
6. Establish networks and links with existing supportive services for vocational, educational and other needs, and insure language and cultural specificity.

Staff Training

Training becomes a central issue in educating existing staff, peer workers, and administrators about prevention strategies, concepts related to addiction theory, curriculum development, individual and group efforts in treatment of substance abuse, issues related to supportive services (such as NA or AA) or perhaps more significantly, established existing groups (such as churches or organized groups) that openly support individuals in recovery.

In addition, substance abuse treatment is not the same as case management or mental health counseling. Although the ends are similar, the means are quite different. Substance abuse training of existing staff is essential. Additionally, concerns need to be raised regarding the abilities of professionals in counseling or mental health to provide these services without adequate training. It is important to integrate—by working together and learning from each other—professionally trained staff with staff who are in recovery; both contribute to the treatment process.

Recommendations

In summary, research findings on Asians and substance abuse are still inconclusive. More recent studies as well as community and clinical observations have seen increasing problems with substance abuse in Asian communities. Some of the data show significant differences between Asian ethnic groups, indicating a complex and varied picture. In addition, there is evidence of multiple causality for substance abuse in the Asian community from the process of immigration and acculturation as well as from cultural differences.

With the exception of a few programs on the West Coast, substance abuse treatment programs for Asians have only been established recently, and treatment program development for Asian substance abuse is still in its infancy. Treatment programs have yet to establish comprehensive programs providing all levels of services. At the present time, resources are limited and tend to ignore—or at best provide global and at times inaccurate or stereotypical views—the issues related to Asians and substance abuse.

Within this paradigm, specific policy guidelines need to be established, including the following critical areas:

1. Epidemiological studies funded by NIDA and NIAAA that specifically target different Asian ethnic groups on a regional and national level.
2. Current national drug abuse database surveys continue to exclude Asians from their studies. Asians need to be included, utilizing (at minimum) standards based on the U.S. Census.
3. Small planning grants need to be available to assist local Asian communities in developing coalitions in combating substance abuse.
4. Technical assistance from national organizations, such as the National Asian Pacific American Families Against Substance Abuse (NAPA-FASA), for local communities to develop treatment services that are specific to their needs and capabilities.
5. Establish regional (or a national) training and resource center that could help provide training curriculum and program development models and an exchange of information.
6. Develop Asian-specific monographs from the Center for Substance Abuse Treatment (CSAT), the Office for Substance Abuse Prevention (OSAP), NIDA, NIAAA and ADAMHA as a resource for substance abuse treatment programing.
7. Earmark funds and resources from NIDA, NIAAA and ADAMHA for research and demonstration projects and technical assistance specific to Asian communities.
8. Develop and fund demonstration service and treatment models utilizing different approaches to providing multi-Asian ethnic services to both immigrant and American-born Asians.
9. Reprioritize funding as currently allocated on local, state, and federal levels. Until this occurs, funding streams will continue to flow toward services established decades earlier with little relevance toward Asian communities.

BIBLIOGRAPHY

Alcohol, Drug Abuse and Mental Health Administration. (1985). *Alcohol Use Among U.S. Ethnic Minorities*. Research Monograph 18. Washington, D.C.: U.S. GPO.

Barrera, M. (1978). Mexican-American mental health service utilization. *Community Mental Health Journal*. 14, 35–45.

Baumrind, D. (1985). Familial antecendents of adolescent drug use: A developmental perspective. In C. L. Jones and R. J. Battjes (Ed.), *The Etiology of Drug Abuse: Implications for Prevention*. Research Monograph 56. Washington, D.C: National Institute of Drug Abuse.

Brook, J. S., Whiteman, M., and Gordon, A. S. (1983). Stages of drug use in adolescence: Personality, peer, and family correlates. *Developmental Psychology*, 19, 269–277.

Brook, J. S., Whiteman, M., and Gordon, A. S. (1982). Qualitative and quantitative aspects of adolescent drug use: Interplay of personality, family, and peer correlates. *Psychological Reports*, 51, 1151–1163.

Bush, and Ionnatti, L. (1985). The development of children's health orientation and behaviors: Lessons for substance use prevention. In C. L. Jones and R. J. Battjes (Ed.), *The Etiology of Drug Abuse: Implications for prevention*. Research Monograph 56. Washington, D.C.; National Institute of Drug Abuse.

Chan, A. (1986). Racial differences in alcohol sensitivity. *Alcohol and Alcoholism*, 21, 93–104.

Chassin, L. (1984). Adolescent substance abuse. *Advances in Child Behavior Analysis and Therapy*, 3, 99–152.

Cheung, Y. (1989). Making sense of ethnicity and drug use: A review and suggestions for future research. *Social Pharmacology*, 3(1–2), 55–68.

Chin, J. (1981). Institutional racism and mental health: An Asian American perspective. In O. A. Barbarin, P. A. Good, M. Pharr, and J. A. Siskind (Eds.), *Institutional Racism and Community Competence*. Washington, D.C.: National Institute of Mental Health.

Cohen, S. (1979). The oriental syndrome. *Drug Abuse and Alcoholism Newsletter*, 8(10), 1–3.

Enright, J. B. (1971). On the playing fields of Synanon. In L. Blank, G. B. Gottsegen, and M. G. Gottsegen (Eds.), *Confrontation: Encounters in self and interpersonal awareness*. New York: Macmillan.

Fawzy, F. I., Coombs, R. H., and Gerber, B. (1983). Generational continuity in the use of substances: The impact of parental substance use on adolescent substance use. *Addictive Behaviors*, 8, 109–114.

Hawkins, J. D., Catalano, R. F., Jr, Gillmore, M. R., and Wells, E. A. (1989). Skills training for drug abusers: Generalization, maintenance, and effects on drug use. *Journal of Consulting and Clinical Psychology*, 57(4), 559–563.

Hawkins, J. D., Lishner, D. M., and Catalano, R. F., Jr. (1985). Childhood predictors and the prevention of adolescent substance abuse. In C. L. Jones and R. J. Battjes (Eds.), *The Etiology of Drug Abuse: Implications for Prevention*. Reasearch Monograph 56. Washington, D.C.: National Institute of Drug Abuse.

Jessor, R. and Jessor, S. L. (1977). *Problem behavior and psychosocial development: A longitudinal study of youth*. New York: Academic Press.

Johnson, R. C. and Nagoshi, C. T. (1990). Asians, Asian-Americans, and alcohol. *Journal of Psychoactive Drugs*, 22(1), 45–52.

Johnson, R. C., Nagoshi, C. T., Ahern, F. M., Wilson, J. R. and Yuen, S.H.L. (1987). Cultural factors as explanations for ethnic group differences in alcohol use in Hawaii. *Journal of Psychoactive Drugs*, 19(1), 67–75.

Johnston, L. D., O'Malley, P. M., and Bachman, J. G. (1986). *Use of licit and illicit drugs by America's high school students*. Rockville, MD: National Institute on Drug Abuse.

Johnston, L. D., O'Malley, P.M., and Bachman, J. G. (1984). *Drugs and American high school students*. Rockville, MD: National Institute on Drug Abuse.

Kandel, D. B. (1980). Drug and drinking behavior among youth. *Annual Review of Sociology*, 6, 235–285.

Kitano, H.L.L. (1982). Alcohol drinking patterns: The Asian Americans. In *Special Population Issues, Alcohol and Health Monograph* 4. Washington, D.C.: National Institute on Alcohol Abuse and Alcoholism.

Kitano, H.L.L. and Chi, L. (1987). Asian Americans and alcohol abuse: Exploring cultural differences in Los Angeles. *Alcohol Health and Research World* 11(2), 41–53.

Korchin, S. J. (1976). *Modern Clinical Psychology*. New York: Basic Books.

Kuo, W.H. 1984. Prevalence of depression among Asian Americans. *Journal of Nervous and Mental Disease* 172(8), 449–457.

Lee, J. A. (1987). Chinese, alcohol and flushing: Sociohistorical and biobehavioral considerations. *Journal of Psychoactive Drugs* 19(4), 319–327.

Lin, K. M. (1986). Psychopathology and social disruption in refugees. In C. Williams and J. Westemeyer (Eds.), *Refugee Mental Health in Resettlement Countries*. New York: Hemisphere.

Morales, R. (1991). *Alcohol abuse and Asian Americans*. Paper presented at National Institute on Drug Abuse National Conference on Drug Abuse Research and Practice, Washington, D.C., January 21.

Nagoshi, C. T., Dixon, L. K., Johnson, R. C., and Yuen, S.H.L. (1988). Familial transmission of alcohol consumption and the flushing response to alcohol in three Oriental groups. *Journal of Studies on Alcohol*, 49(3), 261–267.

National Institute on Drug Abuse. (1990a). *Data from the Drug Abuse Warning Network (DAWN)*. Rockville, MD: National Institute on Drug Abuse.

National Institute on Drug Abuse. (1990b). *National Drug and Alcoholism Treatment Unit Survey (NDATUS)*. Rockville, MD: National Institute on Drug Abuse.

National Institute on Drug Abuse. (1990c). *National Household Survey on Drug Abuse*. Rockville, MD: National Institute on Drug Abuse.

Newcomb, M. D. and Bentler, P. M. (1987). Changes in drug use from high school to young adulthood: Effects of living arrangement and current life pursuit. *Journal of Applied Developmental Psychology*, 8, 221–246.

Newcomb, M. D. and Bentler, P. M. (1986). Frequency and sequence of drug use: A longitudinal study from early adolescence to young adulthood. *Journal of Drug Education*, 16, 101–120.

Newlin, D. B. (1989). The skin-flushing response: Autonomic, self-report, and conditioned responses to repeated administrations of alcohol in Asian men. *Journal of Abnormal Psychology*, 98, 421–425.

O'Leary, D. E., O'Leary, M. R., and Donovan, D. M. (1976). Social skills acquistion and psychosocial development of alcoholics: A review. *Addictive Behaviors*, 1, 111–120.

Owan, T. (Ed.). (1985). *Southeast Asian Mental Health: Treatment, Prevention Services, Training, and Research*. Washington, D.C: Department of Health and Human Services.

Padilla, A. M., Ruiz, R. A., and Alvarez, R. (1975). Community mental health services for the Spanish-speaking surnamed population. *American Psychologist*, 30, 892–904.

Shedler, J., and Block, J. (1990). Adolescent drug use and psychological health: A longimdinal inquiry. *American Psychologist*, 45(5), 612–630.

Shon, S., and Ja, D. (1982). Asian families. In M. McGoldrick, J. K. Pearce, and J. Giordano (Eds.), *Ethnicity and Family Therapy*. New York: Guilford.

Stein, J., Newcomb, M.D., and Bentler, P. M. (1987). An 8-year study of multiple influences on drug use and drug use consequences. *Journal of Personality and Social Psychology*, 53(6), 1094–1105.

Suddendorf, R. F. (1989). Research on alcohol metabolism among Asians and its implications for understanding causes of alcoholism. *Public Health Reports*, 104(6), 615–620.

Sue, S. (1977). Community mental health services to minority groups. *American Psychologist*, 32, 616–624.

Sue, S. (1976). Clients' demographic and therapeutic treatment: Differences that make a difference. *Journal of Consulting and Clinical Psychology*, 44, 864.

Sue, S., and McKinney, H. (1975). Asian Americans in the community mental health care system. *American Journal of Orthopsychiatry*, 45, 111–118.

Sue, S. and Morishima, J. K. (1982). *The Mental Health of Asian Americans*. San Francisco: Jossey-Bass.

Sue, S., Zane, N., and Ito, J. (1979). Alcohol drinking patterns among Asian and Caucasian Americans. *Journal of Cross-Cultural Psychology*, 10(1), 41–56.

Suwaki, H., and Ohara, H. (1985). Alcohol-induced facial flushing and drinking behavior in Japanese men. *Journal of Studies on Alcohol*, 46(3), 196–198.

Takaki, R. (1989). *Strangers From A Different Shore*. New York: Penguin.

Trimble, J. E., Padilla, A. M., and Bell, C. S. (Eds.). (1987). *Drug Abuse Among Ethnic Minorities*. Washington, D.C.: United States Government Printing Office.

Tung, T. M. (1985). Psychiatric care for southeast Asians: How different is different? In T. Owan (Ed.), *Southeast Asian Mental Health: Treatment, Prevention Services, Training, and Research*. Washington, D.C.: National Institute on Mental Health.

Vail, A. (1978). Factors influencing lower-class Black patients' remaining in treatment. *Journal of Consulting and Clinical Psychology*, 46, 341.

Wolff, P. (1973). Vasomotor sensitivity to ethanol in diverse Mongoloid populations. *American Journal of Human Genetics*, 25, 193–199.

Wong, H. Z. (1985). *Substance Use and Chinese American Youths: Preliminary Findings on an Interview Survey of 123 Youths and Implications for Services and Programs*. San Francisco: Youth Environment Services.

Wu, L., and Windle, C. (1980). Ethnic specificity in the relative minority use and staffing of community mental health centers. *Community Mental Health Journal*, 16, 156–168.

Yamaguchi, K., and Kandel, D. B. (1984). Patterns of drug use from adolescence to young adulthood: III. Predictors of progression. *American Journal of Public Health*, 74, 673–681.

Zane, N. and Sasso, T. (1992). Research on drug abuse among Asian Pacific Americans. *Drugs and Society*, 6(3–4), 181–209.

Zucker, R. A., and Gomberg, E.S.I. (1986). Etiology of alcoholism reconsidered: The case for a biopsychosocial process. *American Psychologist*, 41, 783–793.

Name Index

Subject Index